Kant's *Metaphysics of Morals*
Interpretative Essays

EDITED BY
MARK TIMMONS

OXFORD
UNIVERSITY PRESS

*This book has been printed digitally and produced in a standard specification
in order to ensure its continuing availability*

OXFORD
UNIVERSITY PRESS

Great Clarendon Street, Oxford OX2 6DP

Oxford University Press is a department of the University of Oxford.
It furthers the University's objective of excellence in research, scholarship,
and education by publishing worldwide in

Oxford New York

Auckland Bangkok Buenos Aires Cape Town Chennai
Dar es Salaam Delhi Hong Kong Istanbul Karachi Kolkata
Kuala Lumpur Madrid Melbourne Mexico City Mumbai Nairobi
São Paulo Shanghai Taipei Tokyo Toronto

Oxford is a registered trade mark of Oxford University Press
in the UK and in certain other countries

Published in the United States
by Oxford University Press Inc., New York

ISBN 0-19-825010-X

Kant's *Metaphysics of Morals*

PREFACE

Immanuel Kant's *The Metaphysics of Morals*, originally published in 1797, is his last major work on topics in practical philosophy. It represents Kant's mature thinking about a range of issues in moral and political philosophy, filling out and sometimes refining many issues and doctrines contained in the *Groundwork of the Metaphysics of Morals* (1785) and the *Critique of Practical Reason* (1789). However, until recently, *The Metaphysics of Morals* had received far less scholarly attention than the two earlier works. The seventeen essays that compose this collection are focused primarily on topics and themes from *The Metaphysics of Morals* and continue the recent efforts by scholars to understand and evaluate Kant's practical philosophy in the light of this work.

Seven of this volume's essays were originally presented at the 1997 Spindel Conference commemorating the bicentennial of the publication of *The Metaphysics of Morals*. They are reprinted here (in some cases with revisions) from *The Southern Journal of Philosophy*, 36 (1998), Spindel Conference Supplement. The remaining essays were written for this volume. They are organized roughly according to the order of topics in *The Metaphysics of Morals*.

Following the contents is a list of abbreviations for the writings of Kant that are frequently cited in this volume. Included also is a select bibliography of secondary literature, culled mainly from the past thirty years and organized according to major topics relating to *The Metaphysics of Morals*.

I am grateful to *The Southern Journal of Philosophy* for permission to reprint the papers that originally appeared there. I wish to thank my colleagues, Tom Nenon and Hoke Robinson, for their advice. From Oxford University Press, I wish to thank Peter Momtchiloff, Charlotte Jenkins, and Hilary Walford for their help and encouragement with this anthology. Finally, I owe a special debt of gratitude to Linda Sadler, production editor for *The Southern Journal of Philosophy*, for her many hours of help with every phase of this project.

M.T.

CONTENTS

ABBREVIATIONS

The following abbreviations for Kant's works are used throughout this book and (except as noted below) will be followed by the volume and page number from *Kant's gesammelte Schriften*, edited by the Royal Prussian Academy of Sciences (Berlin: Georg Reimer, later Walter de Gruyter & Co., 1990–). Unless otherwise indicated, all other citations to Kant's writings not included in the list below will be abbreviated Ak. References to the *Critique of Pure Reason* will follow the A (first edition), B (second edition) convention.

A.	*Anthropologie in pragmatischer Hinsicht abgefasst* (*Anthropology from a Pragmatic Point of View*)
Col.	Lecture notes, Collins. From *Eine Vorlesung Kants über Ethik* (*Lectures on Ethics*)
EF	'Zum ewigen Frieden' ('Perpetual Peace')
I.	'Idee zu einer allgemeinen Geschichte in weltbürgerlicher Absicht' ('Idea for a Universal History with a Cosmopolitan Purpose')
G.	*Grundlegung zur Metaphysik der Sitten* (*Groundwork of the Metaphysics of Morals*)
GTP	'Über den Gemeinspruch: Das Mag in der Theorie richtig sein, taugt aber nicht für die Praxis' ('On the Common Saying: That May Be Correct in Theory, but It Is of No Use in Practice')
KpV	*Kritik der praktischen Vernunft* (*Critique of Practical Reason*)
KrV	*Kritik der reinen Vernunft* (*Critique of Pure Reason*)
KU	*Kritik der Urtheilskraft* (*Critique of Judgment*)
MA	'Mutmasslicher Anfang der Menschengeschichte' ('Speculative Beginnings of Human History')
MAN	*Die metaphysischen Anfangsgründe der Naturwissenschaft* (*The Metaphysical Foundations of Natural Science*)
Mro.	Lecture notes, Mrongovius. From *Eine Vorlesung Kants über Ethik* (*Lectures on Ethics*)
MS	*Die Metaphysik der Sitten* (*The Metaphysics of Morals*)

R.   *Die Religion innerhalb der Grenzen der blossen Vernunft* (*Religion within the Boundaries of Mere Reason*)

Ref.   *Reflexionen* (*Reflections*)

Vig.   Lecture notes, Vigilantius. From *Eine Vorlesung Kants über Ethik* (*Lectures on Ethics*)

VRM   'Über ein vermeintesrecht, aus Menschenliebe, zu lügen' ('On a Supposed Right to Lie from Philanthropy')

WA   'Beantworten der Frage: Was ist Aufklärung?' ('An Answer to the Question: What is Enlightenment?')

NOTES ON CONTRIBUTORS

MARCIA W. BARON is Professor of Philosophy at Indiana University. She is author of *Kantian Ethics Almost without Apology* (Cornell University Press, 1995) and co-author (with Philip Pettit and Michael Slote) of *Three Methods of Ethics: A Debate* (Blackwell, 1997).

SHARON BYRD is Professor of Anglo-American Law and Jurisprudence and Director of the Law & Language Center at the Friedrich-Schiller-Universität in Jena, Germany. She is co-editor of *Jahrbuch für Recht und Ethik* and author of articles on Kant's *Doctrine of Right*.

STEPHEN ENGSTROM is Associate Professor of Philosophy at the University of Pittsburgh. He has published articles on Kant's ethics and is co-editor (with Jennifer Whiting) of *Aristotle, Kant, and the Stoics: Rethinking Happiness and Duty* (Cambridge University Press, 1996).

KATRIN FLIKSCHUH teaches philosophy at the University of Essex. She is author of *Kant and Modern Political Philosophy* (Cambridge University Press, 2000) and is currently working on a book on the concept of freedom.

JOSHUA GLASGOW is a Lecturer at California State University–Bakersfield. He specializes in Kant's ethics and ethical theory.

PAUL GUYER is the Florence R. C. Murray Professor in the Humanities at the University of Pennsylvania. His books include *Kant and the Claims of Taste* (2nd edn., Cambridge University Press, 1997), *Kant and the Claims of Knowledge* (Cambridge University Press, 1993), *Kant and the Experience of Freedom* (Cambridge University Press, 1993), and *Kant on Freedom, Law, and Happiness* (Cambridge University Press, 2000). He is the editor of the *Cambridge Companion to Kant* (Cambridge University Press, 1992). He is general co-editor (with Allen Wood) of the Cambridge Edition of the Works of Immanuel Kant, for which (with Allen Wood) he has co-edited and co-translated the *Critique of Pure Reason* (Cambridge University Press, 1998) and edited and co-translated (with Eric Matthews) the *Critique of the Power of Judgment* (Cambridge University Press, 2000).

ROBERT N. JOHNSON is Associate Professor of Philosophy at the University of Missouri, Columbia. His articles on practical reason and Kant's ethics have appeared in journals such as the *Philosophical Quarterly*, *Philosophy and Phenomenological Research*, and the *History of Philosophy Quarterly*.

THOMAS E. HILL, JR. is Kenan Professor at the University of North Carolina at Chapel Hill. He previously taught at UCLA, Pomona College, and was a visitor at Stanford University and the University of Minnesota. He has written numerous articles on Kant's ethics and various moral problems. Many of these are reprinted in his collections of essays, *Autonomy and Self-Respect* (Cambridge University Press, 1991), *Dignity and Practical Reason in Kant's Moral Theory* (Cornell University Press, 1992), and *Respect, Pluralism, and Justice: Kantian Perspectives* (Oxford University Press, 2000).

SARAH WILLIAMS HOLTMAN is Assistant Professor at the University of Minnesota, Twin Cities. She specializes in Kant's practical philosophy as well as moral, political, and legal philosophy more generally. She is author of various articles on Kant's theory of justice.

BERND LUDWIG teaches philosophy at the Universities of Münster and Essen. He is Hochschuldozent at the Universität des Saarlandes. He is author of *Kants Rechtslehre* (Meiner, 1986) and *Die Wiederentdeckung des epikureischen Naturrechts Zu Thomas Hobbes' philosophischer Entwicklung &c* (Klostermann, 1998), editor of *Kant's Metaphysics of Morals* (Meiner, 1998/1990), co-editor (with H. Klemme, M. Pauen, and W. Stark) of *Aufklärung und Interpretation* (Könighausen, 1999), and co-editor (with George Mohr) of a cooperative commentary on the first critique, *Kant: Kritik der reinen Vernunft* (Akademie Verlag, 1998).

ONORA O'NEILL is Principal of Newnham College, Cambridge. She has written widely in ethics and political philosophy, particularly on Kant's practical philosophy and contemporary Kantian work.

THOMAS W. POGGE teaches moral and political philosophy at Columbia University. His recent publications include 'What We Can Reasonably Reject' (*Noûs*, 2001), 'How Should Human Rights be Conceived?' (in Patrick Hayden (ed.), *The Philosophy of Human Rights*, 2001), 'Human Flourishing and Universal Justice' (*Social Philosophy and Policy*, 1999), and 'Kant on Ends and the Meaning of Life' (in Andrews Reath, Barbara Herman, and Christine Koorsgaard (eds.), *Reclaiming the History of Ethics*, 1997).

NELSON POTTER is Professor of Philosophy at the University of Nebraska-Lincoln. He is the author of numerous articles on Kant's ethical theory and is president of the North American Kant Society.

ANDREWS REATH is Professor of Philosophy at the University of California, Riverside. He has written several articles on Kant's ethics and, with Barbara Herman and Christine Koorsgaard, co-edited *Reclaiming the History of Ethics: Essays for John Rawls* (Cambridge University Press, 1997).

MARK TIMMONS is Professor of Philosophy at the University of Memphis. He is author of *Morality without Foundations: A Defense of Ethical Contextualism* (Oxford University Press, 1999) and co-editor (with Walter Sinnott-Armstrong) of *Moral Knowledge?: New Readings in Moral Epistemology* (Oxford University Press, 1996).

KENNETH R. WESTPHAL is Professor of Philosophy at the University of East Anglia (Norwich). He has published many articles on Kant's and on Hegel's political and legal philosophies. His essay, 'Kant on the State, Law, and Obedience to Authority in the Alleged "Anti-Revolutionary" Writings' (*Journal of Philosophical Research*, 1992) received the 1994 George Armstrong Kelly Prize.

MARCUS WILLASCHEK teaches philosophy at the Westfälische Wilhelms-Universität in Münster, Germany. He is author of *Praktische Vernunft. Handlungstheorie und Moralbegründung bei Kant* (Metzler, 1992), and co-editor (with Georg Mohr) of *Kant: Kritik der reinen Vernunft*, vols. 17–18, (Akademie Verlag, 1998).

ALLEN WOOD is Professor of Philosophy at Stanford University. He has also taught at Cornell University (1968–96) and Yale University (1996–2000). He is author of *Kant's Moral Religion* (Cornell University Press, 1970), *Kant's Rational Theology* (Cornell University Press, 1978), *Karl Marx* (Routledge, 1981), *Hegel's Ethical Thought* (Cambridge University Press, 1991), and *Kant's Ethical Thought* (Cambridge University Press, 1999). He is also editor and/or translator of writings of Kant, Hegel, and Marx, including several volumes that have appeared in the Cambridge Edition of the Works of Immanuel Kant, of which he is a general editor.

1

The Final Form of Kant's Practical Philosophy

Allen Wood

By the year 1768, Kant claimed to be at work on a system of ethics, under the title 'metaphysics of morals' (Ak. 10:74).[1] During the so-called silent decade of the 1770s, when Kant was working on the *Critique of Pure Reason*, he promised repeatedly not only that he would soon finish that work but also that he would soon publish a metaphysics of morals (Ak. 10:97, 132, 144).[2] Yet it was not until four years after the first *Critique* that Kant finally wrote a work on ethics, and even then he merely *laid the ground* for a metaphysics of morals by identifying and establishing the supreme principle on which a system of duties would be based (G. 4:392). Three years later, in the *Critique of Practical Reason*, Kant once again dealt entirely with foundational questions in moral philosophy. Kantian ethics is primarily known, especially among English-speaking philosophers, through these two ethical works of the 1780s, neither of which contains anything like a 'metaphysics of morals'.

Many of Kant's chief works in the early 1790s are devoted to practical philosophy. The *Critique of Judgment*'s treatment of taste and teleology is concerned both with moral psychology and with the view of the world that a morally disposed person should take. Other works even deal with the application of Kantian principles to political and religious questions. Yet there is still

---

[1] Translations of Kant's writings are my own. Kant had clearly been thinking already about such a work for several years before 1768. By 1765 Kant had written a short manuscript entitled 'Metaphysische Anfangsgründe der praktischen Weltweisheit' ('Metaphysical First Principles of Practical Philosophy') (Ak. 20:54–7). In a letter of 16 February 1767, Hamann reported to Herder that 'Mr Kant is working on a metaphysics of morals [*Metaphysik der Sitten*], which in contrast to the ones up to now will investigate more what the human being is than what he ought to be' (Karl Vorländer, 'Einleitung', in Kant, *Grundlegung zur Metaphysik der Sitten* (Hamburg: Felix Meiner, 1906), p. vi). From this account, however, it would seem either that Hamann badly garbled Kant's intentions at that time or else that these intentions were very much at odds with what he later understood by a 'metaphysics of morals'.

[2] See Lewis White Beck, *A Commentary on Kant's 'Critique of Practical Reason'* (Chicago: University of Chicago Press, 1960), 7–9.

no *systematic* presentation of the practical philosophy that Kant had been promising for nearly three decades. It is not until 1797 that Kant published the first part of such a system, under the title 'Doctrine of Right', and it is only later in the year that the entire system, the long-promised *Metaphysics of Morals*, finally appears in print, among the very last of Kant's published works.

I. What is a 'Metaphysics of Morals'?

For thirty years Kant intended to entitle his system of ethics 'Metaphysics of Morals'. But, owing to his changing conception of ethical theory, and especially of the role of the empirical in a system of ethics, he did not always mean the same thing by this title. His first use of the term, in about 1768, probably expressed his rejection of the moral sense theory of Shaftesbury and Hutcheson, with which we find Kant toying in his lectures of the early 1760s and in the prize essay *Inquiry Concerning the Distinctness of the Principles of Natural Theology and Morals* (1762–4). But it is not clear that at this time his use of the term 'metaphysics' means anything beyond the idea that morality must be grounded in the analysis of *concepts* rather than in the immediacy of *feelings*.

By the time of the *Critique of Pure Reason*, 'metaphysics' (when applied to either nature or morals) refers to a body of synthetic a priori principles, and this sense governs Kant's use of the term in the *Groundwork* (1785). At this point, Kant conceives of a 'metaphysics of morals' as a system of moral principles, or even of moral *duties*, which would be entirely a priori, and hence could be spelled out entirely independently of any empirical knowledge of human nature. Thus, within the domain of moral philosophy, Kant ordains a strict separation between a 'metaphysics of morals' and a doctrine of 'practical anthropology' to which the principles of such a metaphysics would be applied.[3] In the *Groundwork*, as in the *Critique of Practical Reason*, the term 'metaphysics' again underlines Kant's insistence on the apriority of the supreme principle of morality and the purity of the moral motive. He is worried that to permit these to be adulterated by anything empirical may be to open moral theory to our human tendency to falsify moral principles by accommodating them to the self-love that biases all human inclinations. Kant requires so sharp

---

[3] In the Mrongovius transcription of his lectures on moral philosophy, which is probably contemporaneous with the *Groundwork*, he remarks that the second part of moral philosophy may be called '*Philosophia moralis applicata*, moral anthropology. . . . Moral anthropology is morals that are applied to men. *Moralia pura* is built on necessary laws, and hence it cannot base itself on the particular constitution of a rational being, of the human being. The particular constitution of the human being, as well as the laws which are based on it, appear in moral anthropology under the name of "ethics"' (Mro. 29:599).

a separation of the empirical part of moral philosophy from the moral part that he even suggests they be carried out by entirely different researchers, in order to reap the benefits of a division of intellectual labour (*G.* 4:388–9).

Yet in the *Groundwork* and the second *Critique*, it remains quite unclear what Kant intends a purely a priori system of principles to contain. If he intends anything like the system of duties that eventually emerged in *The Metaphysics of Morals*, he never hints at what a purely *metaphysical* system of duties might be like. Obviously the illustrations he gives in both works, and in particular the four famous examples he twice discusses in the *Groundwork*, involve the application of the pure moral law to the empirical nature of human beings, since they involve conceiving of our maxims as laws belonging to that nature, and they make use of empirical information about the natural purpose of self-love and about the usefulness of human talents, as well as about the fact that human beings need sympathetic help from others if they are to have a rational expectation of achieving the contingent ends they actually set.

In *The Metaphysics of Morals*, Kant does once again contrast the referent of that title with 'practical anthropology'. But the sameness of the terminology may cause us to overlook the major change that has occurred in the way the two parts of moral philosophy are conceived. In the Preface to the *Groundwork*, a 'metaphysics of morals' contains *only* a priori principles; *everything* empirical is consigned to 'practical anthropology'.

A metaphysics of morals is, namely, a 'pure moral philosophy, completely cleansed of everything that might be only empirical and that belongs to anthropology' (*G.* 4:389). In *The Metaphysics of Morals*, however, Kant concedes that the system of duties falling under that title consists of pure moral principles *in so far as they are applied to human nature*: a metaphysics of morals itself, he says, 'cannot dispense with principles of application, and we shall often have to take as our object the particular nature of human beings, which is known only by experience' (*MS* 6:217).[4] A metaphysics of morals is bounded, on the empirical end, only by the fact that it limits itself to duties that can be derived from the pure principle as applied to *human nature in general*, leaving to a more broadly empirical moral philosophy all duties that involve reference to particular conditions of people and special human relationships (*MS* 6:468–9).[5] As the scope of a metaphysics of morals expands in the direction of the empirical, that of practical anthropology seems correspondingly to con-

[4] See Ludwig Siep, 'Wozu Metaphysik der Sitten?' in *Grundlegung zur Metaphysik der Sitten: Ein kooperativer Kommentar*, ed. O. Höffe (Frankfurt: Klostermann, 1989), 31–44.
[5] It is doubtful that Kant holds consistently even to this restriction, since in *The Metaphysics of Morals* he deals with juridical duties arising out of family relationships, and ethical duties pertaining to friendship, as well as the relationship between benefactors and beneficiaries.

tract; for now it concerns itself with 'the subjective conditions in human nature that hinder human beings or help them in *fulfilling* the metaphysics of morals' (*MS* 6:217) and not, apparently, with the comprehensive treatment of the human nature to which the a priori principle of morality is to be applied.

Perhaps it deserves emphasis that, in *The Metaphysics of Morals*, Kant is asserting as firmly as ever that the *supreme principle of morality* itself is wholly a priori and borrows nothing from the empirical nature of human beings. The earlier claim he is withdrawing is only that a metaphysics of morals concerns solely 'the idea and the principles of a possible pure will and not the actions and conditions of human volition generally' (*G.* 4:391). Or, to put it in other words, Kant now regards a metaphysics of morals as constituted not by a set of wholly pure moral principles, but instead by the system of duties that results when the pure principle is applied to the empirical nature of human beings in general.

II. A System of Duties

In addition to this significant change in the meaning of its title, there are a number of other things in *The Metaphysics of Morals* that ought to surprise anyone whose image of Kantian ethics is based on the earlier, more foundational works. In effect, however, this means that *The Metaphysics of Morals* ought to be both surprising and enlightening to most Anglophone moral philosophers, since their image of Kantian ethics is derived almost exclusively from the *Groundwork* and the second *Critique*. Even those who have dipped into *The Metaphysics of Morals* have seldom let it shape their conception of the basic principles and standpoint of Kantian ethics that they have obtained especially from the first fifty or so pages of the *Groundwork*. They have almost never let it significantly influence their interpretation of what they have already read in those pages. Consequently, the familiar image of Kantian ethics is in serious error on some fairly basic points.

For example, it is almost universally supposed that Kant's conception of ordinary moral reasoning is that, when considering a course of action, we should formulate the appropriate maxim and decide whether it can be universalized. Kant's admirers, in fact, as well as his critics, tend almost by reflex to think of the universalizability test as his most (or even his only) significant contribution to moral reasoning. But a universalizability test is used very seldom in *The Metaphysics of Morals*. In fact, it is used exclusively in connection with a single duty: the ethical duty of beneficence to others (*MS* 6:393, 453). Perhaps this should not have come as a surprise, since *The Metaphysics of Morals* is a system of positive duties and the universalizability test is almost exclusively of negative import, used mainly in deciding whether a given maxim is permissible or impermissible rather than in establishing positive duties. Beneficence to others is in fact the only case where it can be used to ground a positive duty, since in Kant's view there is only one end that all human beings have necessarily—namely, that of their own happiness. Hence, it is only in this one case that we necessarily adopt a maxim (that of self-love) and therefore have a duty to adopt it only in a form that may be universalized—namely, that which includes also having the happiness of others as an end (*MS* 6:453).

In *The Metaphysics of Morals*, Kant conceives of ordinary moral reasoning as the prioritizing, weighing, and balancing of *duties*—and of the obligating reasons (*rationes obligandi*, *Verpflichtungsgründe*) based on them (*MS* 6:224). Some duties, those that are strict or perfect, require specific actions or omissions; others, the wide or imperfect duties, require only the setting of ends. With wide duties, there is consequently considerable latitude for different agents, or for the same agent at different times, to decide how far and by which actions she will promote these ends. It is only in the case of strict duties that the performance or non-performance of an action is wrong or blamable; actions in promotion of the ends grounding our wide duties are meritorious, but the omission of any specific action of this kind is not wrong unless it involves the general abandonment of the required end. Kant's category of wide duties thus encompasses much of what others prefer to categorize as 'supererogation' and regard as falling altogether outside the scope of *duty* properly speaking. Kant, however, thinks that the concept of duty applies to such actions because we can, and sometimes must, rationally constrain ourselves to perform them.[6]

III. Right and Ethics

The *Groundwork*, with its examples of perfect and imperfect duties and duties to oneself and to others, prepares us for the taxonomy of ethical duties found in *The Metaphysics of Morals*—even if it has not prepared most of the *Groundwork*'s readers to think of this taxonomy as central to Kant's conception of moral reasoning. But the *Groundwork* does not prepare us at all for a whole new division of duties separate from all ethical duties, with its own fundamental principle: I mean, the principle of right and the class of juridical (or coercively enforceable) duties.

---

[6] The best treatment of this topic is found in Marcia W. Baron, *Kantian Ethics Almost without Apology* (Ithaca, NY: Cornell, 1995), 21–110.

The principle of right is: 'Any action is right if it can coexist with everyone's freedom in accordance with a universal law, or if on its maxim the freedom of choice of each can coexist with everyone's freedom in accordance with a universal law' (*MS* 6:230). This principle bears a superficial resemblance to the Formula of Universal Law. Like that formula, it provides us with a test only of the permissibility (in this case juridical permissibility) of actions, and it does so with reference to some possible universal law. But Kant presents no deduction of this principle, nor does he explain how it applies to examples. The latter task would seem to be redundant in any case, since it turns out later in the *Doctrine of Right* that which actions accord with right, along with the content of rights of property, is to be determined not by the application of any such procedure but by the external legislation of the general will of a specific civil society, in so far as the legitimacy of this legislation can be derived from a pure theory of right and satisfies its general conditions for rightfulness (*MS* 6:264–6, 311–14).[7]

Discussions of the *Doctrine of Right* usually take it for granted that the principle of right is somehow to be derived from the fundamental principle of morality in one or another of its formulations. There are three points in the text of *The Metaphysics of Morals* that might be read in this way. One is in the Introduction, where Kant seems to present the Formula of Universal Law as an illustration of the general idea of legislation for freedom, and then proceeds to distinguish juridical from ethical legislation as two species of such legislation (*MS* 6:214). This might suggest that he intends to derive the principle of right, on the one hand, and the Formula of Universal Law as a law of ethical duties, on the other hand, from a more general principle grounding both of them. The second is Kant's remark that our innate right to freedom (as specified by this principle) 'belongs to every human being by virtue of his humanity' (*MS* 6:237). This might suggest that the principle of right, governing all rights and hence also the innate right to freedom, could be grounded in the Formula of Humanity as End in Itself. The third is Kant's remark that a doctrine of morals (*Sitten*) is called a doctrine of duties rather than of rights because our awareness of the concept of right as well as that of duty proceeds from the *moral* imperative whose command gives us the concept of duty (*MS* 6:239).

This last passage tells us that we derive the *concept* of right from the moral imperative, but does not assert that the *principle* of right is derived from it. And

---

[7] This last clause is important because Kant is by no means a legal positivist. He shares with the natural-law tradition the idea that laws are not juridically valid unless they are consistent with what is right in itself, and his theory of right includes a derivation of these conditions of rightness from other principles, such as the innate right to freedom (*MS* 6:237), juridical postulate of property (*MS* 6:250), and the idea of an original contract (*MS* 6:340; cf. *MS* 8:297–8, 304–5).

neither of the other two suggestions is ever actually developed in the direction of deriving the principle of right from that of morality. Later in *The Metaphysics of Morals*, in the *Doctrine of Virtue*, Kant very explicitly discredits the whole idea that the principle of right could be derived from the fundamental principle of morality by declaring that the principle of right, unlike the principle of morality, is *analytic* (*MS* 6:396). The analyticity of the principle is clearly the best explanation of Kant's omission of any deduction of it, and also renders redundant any derivation of the principle from the law of morality, since it would be nonsense to think that we need to derive an analytic proposition from a synthetic one.

But how are we to understand the claim that the principle of right is analytic? Kant says it is analytic because we do not need to go beyond the concept of freedom in order to see that external constraint is rightful if it checks the hindering of outer freedom (*MS* 6:396). Even if we grant this point, however, it is hard to see how it shows that, in order to do no one wrong, my action must coexist with the freedom of all according to universal laws. In the *Doctrine of Right*, Kant declares that the concept of right is *not* made up of two elements—namely, an obligation to act in accordance with universal law and also an authorization to coerce others to fulfil this obligation. Instead, the authorization to coerce is supposed to be included in the concept of right itself. This was the main point Kant had made against Gottlieb Hufeland in his review of the latter's *Essay on the Principle of Natural Right* (1785) (Ak. 8:128–9). Hufeland had derived the authorization to coerce those who would violate rights from an alleged natural obligation to increase our own perfection. Kant insisted that this would have the absurd consequence that one may not refrain from enforcing all one's rights to the full. Instead, he argued that the authorization to coerce another who hinders one's rightful action is already contained analytically in the concept of the action as rightful.

As for the principle of right itself, I suggest that Kant intended it merely as an *explication of the concept* of right, telling us what it *means* for an action to be juridically right (or not wrong, not a violation of anyone's right to external freedom). This is plausible if we accept the idea that right is analytically connected with some notion of legislation, and also that the scope of the duties it imposes is restricted to what may be externally coerced in the name of protecting external freedom. The only claim here Kant thinks we might not concede to be analytic is that we have an authorization or warrant (*Befugnis*) to coerce anyone whose action violates the principle (since Hufeland had thought this needed to be derived from an independent obligation to promote one's own perfection).

Even if we do not question Kant's analysis of the concept of right, however, we may still think that his principle has to go beyond that concept if it is to provide us with a *reason* (a moral one) for respecting the external freedom of others. Now there is no question that Kant believes the dignity of humanity provides us with a *moral incentive* for respecting people's rights. It might thereby also provide us with strong moral incentives for setting up a just system of right and for trying to reform existing legal and political systems so that they better protect the rights of persons and do not infringe on them. But to confuse all these (quite correct) points with the idea that this moral incentive grounds the principle of right is to miss entirely Kant's distinction between the juridical and ethical realms and the systems of duty constituting them. That distinction is based on the idea that it is only in the ethical realm that duty must be the ground or incentive for action; juridical duties are precisely those where the incentive need not be duty—it may, for example, be the threat of coercion connected to the law by the legislative authority that promulgates it (*MS* 6:218–19). Thus, although it may make a difference to the *moral worth* of my action of repaying a debt whether I do so from duty or only because I fear that my creditor will sue me, this makes no difference at all to whether my act of repayment is *just* or fulfils a juridical duty. Hence, it would be superfluous, and even contradictory, to the very concept of the juridical, to include the rational incentive of duty as part of its principle.

Juridical duties, in other words, are those whose concept contains no specific incentive for doing them, while ethical duties are those connected in their concept with the objective incentive of duty or rational lawfulness. That is why their principle requires a deduction in order to establish this synthetic connection. Because juridical duties are independent of the incentive for doing them, it is not out of place for Kant to refer at times to the existence of moral incentives for us to respect the right to external freedom that human beings have in virtue of their humanity. But these moral incentives have nothing to do with the *principle* of juridical duties. In other words, a civil society based on right requires no *moral* commitment on the part of its members to respect one another's rightful freedom. It requires only a system of external legislation, backed by coercive sanctions sufficient to guarantee that rights will not be infringed. 'It cannot be required [by right] that this principle of all maxims be itself in turn my maxim, that is, it cannot be required that *I make it the maxim* of my action, even though I am quite indifferent to his freedom or would like in my heart to infringe upon it. That I make it my maxim is a demand that ethics makes on me' (*MS* 6:231).

The principle of right merely tells us which actions do and do not infringe external freedom (and therefore count as 'right'). It does not, however, directly *command* us to perform those actions (as the moral principle does). Through the principle of right, 'reason says only that freedom is limited to those conditions in conformity with the idea of it and it may also be actively limited by others; and it says this as a postulate that is incapable of further proof' (*MS* 6:231). The principle of right therefore differs from the principle of morality in two crucial ways: first, it tells us, as that principle does not, which actions are 'right'—which actions infringe external freedom in general and which do not. But, secondly, the principle of right also lacks one element essential to the principle of morality: its criterion of external rightness, though it refers to what can be consistent with external freedom according to a universal law, makes no mention (as the Formulas of Universal Law and Autonomy do) of what a rational being can or does *will* to be a universal law. This goes along with the fact that it does not itself directly command or enjoin the conduct whose rightness it defines and specifies.

Of course, right (*Recht*) along with ethics (*Ethik*), in the context of *The Metaphysics of Morals*, both belong to practical philosophy or 'morals' (*Sitten*). Both parts involve categorical imperatives, because Kant holds that juridical duties *as such* are also ethical duties (*MS* 6:219). In so far as juridical duties are regarded as ethical duties, they can be brought under the principle of ethics, which can also be used to show that we have good reasons for valuing external freedom (or right) and respecting the institutions that protect right through external coercion. To this extent, it may be correctly said that Kant's theory of right falls under or can be derived from the principle of morality. That is, this may be said *in so far as juridical duties are regarded not merely as juridical but also as ethical duties*. Considered simply as juridical duties, however, they belong to a branch of the metaphysics of morals that is *entirely independent* of ethics and also of its supreme principle.

'Kantian' treatments of individual rights, and of other topics related to natural right, law, and political authority, have often been inspired by the *Groundwork*'s formulations of the principle of morality. Whatever their philosophical merits, such accounts necessarily diverge from Kant's own treatment of such topics, simply because the territory covered by the *Doctrine of Right* necessarily falls entirely outside that surveyed by both the *Groundwork* and the second *Critique*.

Such treatments of external right can also infect the understanding of Kantian ethics proper, because they may involve some deeply un-Kantian assumptions about morality itself. Perhaps the commonest such assumption in Anglophone philosophy is the idea (found in chapter 3 of Mill's *Utilitarianism*) that morality, like right, is a mechanism of social coercion, differing only in the degree of heavy-handedness of the sanctions it employs. Kantian morality, however—though the *content* of its duties may be socially oriented—is never about the *social* regulation of individual conduct. It is entirely about enlightened individuals autonomously directing their own lives. From a Kantian standpoint, any use whatever of social coercion in any form to *enforce* ethical duties (whether through private blame, or public opinion, or the associations of moral education to shape people's feelings) must be regarded as a wrongful violation of individual freedom by corrupt social customs.

Another important philosophical point is contained in the claim that right is independent of ethics. Kant's theory of ethics requires conduct to conform to and be motivated by the considerations cited in Kant's own moral theory if it is to be regarded as virtuous or meritorious. (Conduct that is motivated solely by self-interest, or concern for the greatest aggregate happiness, or obedience to the divine will, and not by respect for rational nature or the universal law of one's own autonomous reason, does not count as meritorious according to Kant's theory.) But conformity to right, and the institution of systems of right, as long as they do in fact protect right or external freedom, may be motivated entirely by non-Kantian considerations—such as rational self-interest, the Hobbesian quest for peace, or obedience to the divine will. This means that Kant's practical philosophy can ground and endorse any set of political institutions that is substantively just, even if others accept and participate in those institutions on the basis of values and motivations that are quite alien to anything in Kant's practical philosophy. This is a large advantage of Kant's theory of right, as applied to a society in which many people are not Kantians (or subscribers to any particular moral philosophy). This advantage would be forfeited by Kantians who want to hold that the principle of right requires the moral law as its foundation.

IV. Applying the Moral Law

The common picture of Kantian moral reasoning is one of agents fastidiously testing their maxims for universalizability and confining themselves to the straight and narrow path allowed them by a strict and demanding set of duties. In contrast to this picture, *The Metaphysics of Morals* is anything but a system of unexceptionable rules dictating a single determinate action on each occasion and forbidding all others. Kant even explicitly condemns any theory of that type, saying that it 'would turn the government of virtue into a tyranny' (*MS* 6:409). It would be equally misleading, however, to think of ethical duties as mere side constraints on our pursuit of a set of private ends and projects with whose content morality has nothing to do. As Kant sees it, morality ought always to have a role in shaping our ends. Ethical duties are based on the principle that human ends ought to include both one's own perfection and the happiness of others. Of course any given agent will specify these moral ends in ways that are suited to her individual situation, talents, resources, and temperament. If you are virtuous, the content of your life, the projects that give it meaning and direction, will prominently include the development of your particular capacities, talents, or virtues and the promotion of the ends of people you know or choose to help. The only limits here are that both these ends and the means chosen towards them should violate neither your perfect duties to yourself nor your duties of respect to others.[8] Within these constraints, Kantian ethics encourages human beings to set their own ends and devise their own plan of life, commanding them only to include among their ends some whose pursuit is morally meritorious.

When we appreciate how broadly the ends of morality are conceived, we should find it highly implausible that a person could decently choose anything as what Bernard Williams calls a 'ground project' that would not fall somewhere within the scope of our ethical duties to promote our own perfection and the happiness of others. Kant's ethical theory thus not only *permits* moral agents to pursue such projects, but it even *underwrites* that pursuit, claiming that it has moral merit. Of course the complexities of human life are such that sometimes our pursuit of ends that are meritorious in the abstract may involve us in a morally impermissible course. Leni Riefenstahl, for example, may have found that in order to pursue her career as a filmmaker she had to put her talents at the service of a monstrous political regime, and even to become complicit in its crimes against humanity. We can agree that there is something tragic in a case where, in order merely to comply with strict duties, an artist would have to abandon a career that constituted the meaning of her life. For there is nothing inherently evil about that career and, in less unlucky circumstances, its pursuit would even constitute a determinate way of fulfilling the wide duties to promote her perfection and benefit others. Yet, in the circumstances we are supposing, it would be far from evident that morality is subversive of personal integrity in any sense that ought to make us worry about the reasonableness of its demands. On the contrary, what should worry us are the theories (or antitheories) that would make it easier to rationalize complicity

---

[8] Kant's objection to considering your own happiness as a duty is that it makes no sense to constrain yourself to promote an end when you have it spontaneously without constraint. Against considering the perfection of others our end, Kant argues that we must not paternalistically impose our concepts of virtue or perfection on them but, rather, assist them in achieving their own ends whenever these are not immoral. Consistent with this, Kant allows that we may ('indirectly') have duties to promote our own happiness when we must constrain ourselves to do so in the course of promoting perfection, and to promote the perfection of others, whenever this so harmonizes with their ends that it can be brought under the heading of promoting their happiness (*MS* 6:386–8). Kant's categorization of duties of virtue should not be seen as excluding our own happiness or the virtue of others from the ends of morality but, rather, as specifying the right headings under which these goods have to be brought if their pursuit is to be morally meritorious.

with evil on the ground that morality's demands are too strict and that suggest that we must sacrifice our integrity unless we are prepared to pursue our projects in defiance of morality.

V. The Primacy of the Formula of Humanity

In the *Groundwork*, Kant proposes to identify and establish—though not to apply—the supreme principle of morality. If asked what formulation of the moral principle Kant does propose in that work, I venture to say that most people would immediately cite the first one Kant provides—the Formula of Universal Law: 'Act only in accordance with that maxim through which you can at the same time will that it become a universal law' (*G*. 4:421; cf. *G*. 4:402). Kant in fact offers a *system* of three formulas: the first identifying the principle by the form of universal law, the second by the motive of the end in itself, and the third by the complete determination of maxims contained in the idea of autonomy or the rational will as universally legislative for a realm of ends (*G*. 4:437). In the *Groundwork* itself it is only the third formulation, which is presented as derived from the first two, that is used to *establish* the principle in the third section. And, since the *Groundwork*'s aim is only to formulate and establish the principle, the question is left open which formulation is most suitable for deriving duties from the law or applying it in particular cases.

The common impression that this role is assigned to the Formula of Universal Law is possibly strengthened by Kant's procedure in the *Critique of Practical Reason*. For although he does not actually engage in applying the law, his favourite examples in that work seem to involve use of the universalizability test for maxims, and the procedure of application he identifies as the 'typic of pure practical judgment' consists in envisioning what would happen if one's maxim were made a universal law of nature (*KpV* 5:67–71). Further, Kant's emphasis in this work on the moral law as an exclusively *formal* principle of the will, abstracting from all ends whatsoever (*KpV* 5:21–3), and his omission of the idea of an objective end as the motive of the will (which was associated in the *Groundwork* with the Formula of Humanity as End in Itself (*G*. 4:427–9)) might even arouse the suspicion that Kant has abandoned the latter formula, or at least sees it as playing no significant role henceforth in the ethical theory he proposes.

Anyone who thinks along these lines ought to find Kant's system of duties in *The Metaphysics of Morals* something of a shock. For there, as we have seen, the Formula of Universal Law is employed in the derivation of only one duty, the duty of beneficence. By contrast, the Formula of Humanity as End in Itself (or the related idea of the dignity of humanity or rational nature) is explicitly mentioned in connection not only with the right to freedom involved in all juridical duties (*MS* 6:237), but also in justifying no fewer than nine of the sixteen ethical duties Kant lists (*MS* 6:423, 425, 427, 429, 436, 444, 454, 456, 459, 462). Four others are based on this formula by implication, since they are derived from the imperfect duty of acting from the motive of duty, which is based on the dignity of humanity (*MS* 6:392, 444). Kant's practice, then, overwhelmingly prefers the Formula of Humanity as the formula in terms of which the moral law is to be applied.

VI. Ends and Virtues

It is probably no accident that Kant makes most frequent use in the *Doctrine of Virtue* of that formulation of the moral law that most stresses the *ends* of actions. For in the *Doctrine of Virtue*, the entire organization of ethical duties, and even the concept of a 'duty of virtue', is teleological: a duty of virtue is an end that it is our duty to have (*MS* 6:394–5). This fact too ought to surprise readers of the *Groundwork* and *Critique of Practical Reason*, who know (if they know nothing else) that Kant is the arch-enemy of all teleological systems of ethics. Of course, the teleology of the *Doctrine of Virtue* is based not on a *material* end—an end the desire for which grounds our choice of actions, which are valued simply as means to it—but is rather derived from a formal principle, which tells us which ends are objectively worth pursuing and hence gives rise to a rational desire for them (*MS* 6:211). But the centrality of ends in the *Doctrine of Virtue* is such that one should not say that Kant is opposed to an ethical theory *oriented* to the pursuit of ends. His position is rather that such theories cannot be *grounded* on any end (such as happiness) that is represented simply as a natural object of desire; the ends of morality must instead be grounded on rational principle, which must in turn be grounded on an *end in itself*, or a value possessing objective worth for reason. In Kant's theory, of course, such a principle is a categorical imperative, and the corresponding end or value is the dignity of humanity. This is not a relative end to be brought about—a not yet existing object to be pursued just because we desire it. It is something already existing that is an end in the sense that we are to act for the sake of its worth, which is to be respected in all our actions. The ends we do desire and pursue according to reason are those whose pursuit expresses our *respect* for the dignity of rational nature. We respect our own worth as rational beings when we perfect our rational powers, and we show respect for the rational nature of others by promoting the ends they have set according to reason (whose sum total is their happiness).

The other great prejudice about Kantian ethical theory is that it is an ethics of rules rather than of virtues—or, as it is sometimes put, of 'moral doing' rather than 'ethical being'. But the very title 'Doctrine of Virtue' ought at least to make us stop and think about this prejudice before accepting it. Kant's ethical theory is explicitly oriented to the promotion of virtue, as the capacity or strength of the will to overcome the obstacles in our nature to doing our duty (*MS* 6:380). Kant also recognizes a plurality of virtues, each corresponding to a duty of virtue, or an end that it is our duty to have (*MS* 6:382). A virtue, in other words, is the strength of our commitment to an end adopted from moral considerations. I can have one virtue and lack another if my commitment to one such end or set of ends (for example, my commitment to respecting the rights of others) is strong (and capable of overcoming inner obstacles to pursuing the end), but my commitment to another end (for example, to the happiness of others, and to voluntarily promoting it through acts of charity) is weak and usually incapable of overcoming the corresponding obstacles.

Because Kant bases all specific ethical duties on our virtuous commitment to ends, within the system of ethical duties he grounds the duty to act in certain ways exclusively on the promotion of ends. In the language of twentieth-century Anglophone ethical theory, this means that, within the system of duties, he holds to the priority of the 'good' over the 'right', and is therefore a 'consequentialist' rather than a 'deontologist' in the main senses those terms now have for moral philosophers. But, of course, the *fundamental principle* on which Kant grounds ethics is not consequentialist. This points to the importance of distinguishing the *fundamental principle* of an ethical theory from the *style of reasoning* it recommends in ordinary deliberation. We may (as Kant does) advocate consequentialist reasoning in much moral deliberation without accepting a consequentialist foundation for morality.

Kant's way of thinking about moral ends also differs in important ways from standard versions of consequentialism. It recognizes no principles of summing, averaging, maximizing, or satisficing as essential to moral reasoning. When Kant says that the happiness of others is an end that is also a duty, he means that it is meritorious for me to promote any permissible part of anyone's happiness, but he does not think it is required (or even meritorious) for me to strive to maximize the happiness of others. He thinks it is more meritorious to promote your happiness if I must make sacrifices to do so than if I do not, but it would not have been more meritorious for me to make two people happy instead of you, or even more meritorious to have made you even happier than I do make you.

It is sufficient for an action to accord with a duty of virtue if it sets the right end and sufficient for it to conflict with a duty of virtue if it sets an end contrary to this. Hence, Kant's consequentialism about moral duties does not entail certain problems and paradoxes of self-defeat that typically plague consequentialist theories that incorporate assumptions about summing and maximizing. I act contrary to duty in setting a bad end (such as the deception or the unhappiness of another), even if setting that bad end turns out ironically to be the best way of maximizing it (if, for example, my trying to deceive people turns out, ironically, to maximize their believing what is true, or my trying to make them unhappy turns out to maximize their happiness).

VII. Duty and Love

When people criticize Kant for not having an ethics of virtue, the thought they probably most often have in mind is that Kant fails to recognize the moral importance of having feelings, emotions, or desires that are *spontaneously* in harmony with morality. Probably nothing in Kant's ethical writings has earned him more hostility than his attempt to appeal to moral common sense on behalf of the claim that the man whose sympathetic feelings have been eclipsed by the weight of his own sorrows displays a good will and performs acts with moral worth when he is beneficent from duty, even though his earlier beneficent acts performed from sympathy had no such worth. Many people's hostility to Kantian ethics seems to resemble an allergic reaction, and for most of them it was probably this passage in the *Groundwork* that occasioned their first sneeze. Even those of us who are sympathetic to Kant's position usually have the sense that he has left out something important at this point. We cannot help thinking that we would always rather be helped by someone who feels something for us than by one who acts charitably merely from the thought of duty. Because sympathy is a mode of perception of others' needs as well as a motive of action, we may reflect that beneficence from cold duty may actually result in worse actions than beneficence from sympathy. We think that help given from mere duty will in any case be grudging help and therefore damaging to the self-esteem of those helped in ways that it would not if the help came from someone who enjoyed helping.

Kant does describe the case as one in which the man of warm temperament, now rendered unsympathetic by his own sorrows, 'tears himself out of this deadly insensibility and does the action without any inclination, simply from duty' (*G.* 4:398). He clearly misjudges the intuitions of ordinary rational morality if he thinks that this description is going to inspire all his readers with esteem for the agent whose motivations for a beneficent action are described in these terms. But Kant's presentation of this case is often mistaken for a general account of what his theory takes the 'motive of duty' to be. From what Kant tells us right in this passage itself, however, we should know that generalizations based on this example are apt to mislead. First, in reading the example there is a temptation to overlook Kant's remark that actions done from duty are *difficult* to distinguish from actions done from an immediate inclination (*G.* 4:397). This presumably means that both are actions we *want to do.* They are not actions done grudgingly (though in the case of duty they may involve a measure of self-constraint, such that the moral reason why we want to do them will often have to overcome other motives we have for not doing them). Kant's example of the man weighed down by sorrows is an attempt to construct a case in which action on the moral motive of duty can (for once) be easily distinguished from immediate inclination. It should not be supposed that such cases will be typical of actions motivated by duty but, on the contrary, that the more typical case is one where this motive is found alongside empirical inclinations from which it is hard to distinguish it. Even in the case Kant describes, there is no *opposing* motive (no desire *not* to help those in need), but only an *absence* of an inclination to act—out of which, however, the agent is moved by the thought of duty, which makes him *want* to help.

What we are told about the motive of duty in section two of the *Groundwork* helps further to correct the impression we may have formed on the basis of Kant's discussion of this example. For there Kant identifies the 'motive' (*Bewegungsgrund*) proper to morality with the dignity of humanity as an end in itself (*G.* 4:427–8). This means that, according to Kant's theory, the sorrowful man who acts from duty is not moved merely by the stony thought 'it is my duty to help'. He acts instead out of a recognition that those in need of his help are ends in themselves. Their *dignity* gives him a reason to care about them and gives them a claim on his help, whether or not he feels like helping them. This will make him more and not less sensitive both to their needs and to the dangers his helping may present to their self-respect than he would be if his motive were sympathy or some other contingent liking.

Like any sympathetic interpretation of this passage from the *Groundwork*, however, the above remarks are necessarily an exercise in damage control. Moreover, they leave untouched one unpleasant and seemingly unbudgeable fact: in the *Groundwork*, the properly moral motive for benefiting others apparently can have nothing to do with any sort of affective or emotional involvement with them or their needs. This makes it all the more significant, however, that we get a very different kind of supplement to Kant's account of moral motivation if we look at what he says in *The Metaphysics of Morals* about what the mind's receptiveness to duty presupposes as regards the feelings of the moral agent. In the *Doctrine of Virtue*, Kant lists four feelings that 'lie at the ground of morality as *subjective* conditions of receptiveness to the concept of duty' (*MS* 6:399). It cannot be a duty to have these feelings, Kant insists, because they are presuppositions of moral agency, since it is only 'by virtue of them that [one] can be put under obligation.—Consciousness of them is not of empirical origin; it can, instead, only follow from consciousness of a moral law, as the effect this has on the mind' (*MS* 6:399). Respect (for the law, and for rational nature in the person of a rational being) is the only one of the four feelings that Kant has discussed in any detail in earlier writings (*G.* 4:401 n.; *KpV* 5:71–89). The other three are 'moral feeling', 'conscience', and 'love of human beings' (*MS* 6:399–403). 'Moral feeling' is 'the susceptibility to feel pleasure or displeasure merely from being aware that our actions are consistent with or contrary to the law of duty' (*MS* 6:399), while 'conscience' is 'not directed to an object but merely to the subject (to affect moral feeling by its act)' (*MS* 6:400). Moral feeling is a feeling of pleasure or displeasure, produced by rational concepts rather than by empirical causes, and directed to *actions*; 'conscience' (regarded here as a capacity for a certain kind of feeling) is moral feeling when it is directed not to actions but to the subject's own self. It is a disposition to feelings of contentment with oneself when one is aware of having done one's duty, but to feelings of displeasure with oneself when one is aware of having transgressed duty.

The feeling on which I want to concentrate our attention is 'love of human beings'. In his discussion of this feeling, Kant again makes the distinction, familiar to readers of the *Groundwork*, between pathological love (a liking for and disposition to benefit another based on pleasure in the other or in her perfections) and practical love, which is a desire to benefit another in response to a command of duty (*G.* 4:399). In *The Metaphysics of Morals*, he makes the same point about the two sorts of love that he made there—namely, that only practical love, not pathological love, can be a duty (*G.* 4:399; *MS* 6:401). When Kant makes this point in the *Groundwork*, we usually tend to think that Kant regards practical love as the only sort of love that is relevant to morality, and infer that he thinks we should ascribe no moral significance at all to *felt* love. This is probably because we combine the idea that pathological love cannot be commanded with the idea that actions done from sympathy are lacking in moral worth, and conclude that Kant regards love (in so far as it involves *feelings*) as part of what is being distinguished from (and thereby *excluded* from) the motive of duty.

The discussion of love of human beings in *The Metaphysics of Morals*, however, shows us that such an understanding of the *Groundwork* must be seriously mistaken. For what we have been told there is that there is a certain kind of *felt* love for other human beings that is not of empirical origin but is an effect that the moral law has on the mind.[9] This love cannot be commanded, and it cannot be a duty to have it; however, this is not because it is irrelevant to moral motivation. On the contrary, it is because a susceptibility to this felt love is *presupposed* by morality in such a way that, if we had no such susceptibility, we would not be moral agents at all. The love of human beings must be a felt love and not a practical love. For he is explicitly discussing *feelings* that *cannot* be commanded or obligatory. Felt love is the only kind of love that cannot be commanded or obligatory, while practical love is not a feeling, and it can be commanded. Kant reinforces the point that it is love as feeling rather than practical love that he is talking about when he notes that practical love is only 'very inappropriately' called 'love' (love, properly speaking, is a *feeling*).

Kant's discussion of love of human beings in *The Metaphysics of Morals* forces us to revise many of the conclusions we are likely to form based on Kant's more famous discussion of beneficence in the first section of the *Groundwork*. Although Kant describes the sorrowful man who acts beneficently from duty as 'tearing himself out of his deadly insensibility' and acting 'without any inclination', in *The Metaphysics of Morals* it cannot be his view that beneficent action done from duty is done in the absence of feelings of love for those to whom one is beneficent. On the contrary, his position now is that the very possibility of our being under a duty to be beneficent to others presupposes that we have a predisposition to feel love for them, a love that is not of empirical origin but an effect of the moral law on our mind.

Of course, there is no reason to think that the love for human beings, which arises from the effect of the moral law on the mind, is the only kind of felt love there is. Kant tells us that love in general is a pleasure taken in another (or in another's perfections), leading to a desire to benefit the other for her own sake (*MS* 6:401–2; Col. 27:417–18). In the case of the love that lies at the ground of morality, this is presumably a pleasure taken in the rational representation of the dignity of the rational nature of the other, which prompts us to treat the other as an end in itself. But, since there are many other perfections in people besides their rational nature that may prompt us to love them, there are clearly

---

[9] Kant never explicitly describes *Menschenliebe* as a species of 'pathological' love, and Daniel Guevara has suggested to me that pathological love in Kant's vocabulary must refer to a feeling which is of *empirical* origin (for textual support of this suggestion, see *KrV* A802/B830). In that case, however, the dichotomy between 'pathological' and 'practical' love, which Kant seems to treat as exhaustive, cannot be so, because then *Menschenliebe* would fall into neither category. From the *Groundwork* onwards, Kant clearly recognizes the feeling of respect as one that is not of empirical origin but is 'self-wrought by a rational concept' (*G.* 4:401 n.). But it is not until *The Metaphysics of Morals* that he explicitly holds that there can be other feelings of non-empirical origin and, in particular, that there are feelings of *love* that originate in pure reason rather than in sensibility or in reason as sensibly affected. *Menschenliebe* is a *felt* love; whether or not we decide to call it a form of 'pathological' love, it is not practical love.

many sorts of love that are grounded on empirical inclinations and have nothing to do with moral conduct or motivation.

Moreover, there is presumably no obvious way to tell, in a given case, which sort of love we are feeling just by feeling it. This is clearly one reason why Kant says that actions done from duty are difficult to distinguish from those done from an immediate (empirical) inclination. It is, in consequence of this, also why he had to devise an *atypical* case—in which sympathy (or other forms of love as empirical inclination) plays a minimal part in motivation—when he wanted us to experience clearly the difference between our intuitive evaluation of beneficent action done from duty and our evaluation of such actions when they are motivated by contingent inclinations deriving from a sympathetic temperament.

Readers of the *Groundwork* miss the point when they conclude from Kant's discussion of these cases that he accords no moral value to beneficence done from love. The point is instead that he wants to distinguish motivations arising from our *temperament* (from what is placed in us contingently by nature) from properly moral motivations arising in us necessarily from moral reason and our awareness of duty. Owing to the difficulty of distinguishing the felt love presupposed by morality from pathological love arising from inclination, it would not have been to Kant's purpose in the *Groundwork* to mention that, at least in the case of beneficent actions, acting from duty as he understands it not only does not exclude a feeling of love for those we benefit, but in fact actually presupposes such a feeling as a condition of our receptiveness to the motive of duty. All the same, by mentioning this Kant could surely have prevented much of the pernicious misunderstanding to which his doctrines have been subject.

According to *The Metaphysics of Morals*, in fact, it is not clear that there *could* be a beneficent action done from duty that was *not* also done from a feeling of love for human beings. For Kant says that our very receptivity to concepts of duty depends on our having certain feelings that follow from our consciousness of the moral law (*MS* 6:399). One of these feelings—the one apparently pertaining to beneficent actions—is love of human beings. If Kant's famous example in the *Groundwork* is to be consistent with this at all, then it *cannot* be read as saying that the sorrowful man feels no love for those he helps. Instead, his 'tearing himself out of dead insensibility' would have to consist in his making himself actively susceptible to the feelings of love for those he helps that lie at the ground of his moral predisposition.[10] His generous acts, though per-

---

[10] *Tearing himself out of* insensibility is, of course, the exact opposite of *remaining in* this unfeeling state. So no reader of the *Groundwork* may be excused from error who thought that the man in Kant's example helps

formed from feelings of love, are performed 'without inclination' only in the sense that the felt love from which they are performed is not an *empirical* inclination, but a feeling (like respect, conscience, or moral feeling) that is a direct effect of the moral law on the mind.[11] The man acts *virtuously* in acting from duty in helping others only if he is strongly committed to their happiness as an end and if this commitment is strong enough to overcome the various obstacles to helping them he might find in himself (his own self-love, for example, or moral lethargy, or simply the deadly insensibility into which his sorrows have plunged him). The man's good will, in the sense of his *virtue*, is expressed through the strength of his love for those he helps.

In this way, I think, it is possible to interpret the *Groundwork*'s description of this example in such a way that it is consistent with the later doctrine of *The Metaphysics of Morals*. This is admittedly an interpretation very different from the one most readers spontaneously give to the *Groundwork*, and I think we must admit it is also one they could not be blamed for not reaching based on that text alone. What this shows, however, is once again that, if the *Groundwork* and the second *Critique* are to be properly understood, then they need to be read in the light of *The Metaphysics of Morals*.

Our conclusion about the common image of Kant's moral psychology, therefore, must be the same as that about the other aspects of Kant's practical philosophy we have been examining. It is a mistake to think that rights and juridical duties for Kant rest on the moral imperative, or that Kant's chief moral principle is the Formula of Universal Law and the associated belief that ordinary moral reasoning for Kant consists in the testing of maxims for universalizability, or that Kantian ethics has no place for ends or virtues. *The Metaphysics of Morals* represents the *final form* of Kant's practical philosophy

others while continuing to feel nothing for them. Such errors might, however, be explained (not excused) by the widespread influence of the empiricist prejudice that all volition must arise from the passive experience of desire, and hence that neither desire nor practical feelings could ever arise from an active volition. It is fundamental to Kant's moral psychology, however, that action done from duty always involves desires and feelings of the latter kind (see *MS* 6:212–13). See next note.

[11] This points to a common misunderstanding of Kant, based on a failure to observe the precise meaning of his terminology. When philosophers read about 'inclination' in Kant, they frequently translate this (perhaps antiquated terminology) into the more common philosophical talk about 'desire'. But for Kant inclination (*Neigung*) is significantly narrower in its meaning than desire (*Begehren, Begierde*). Kant defines inclination as 'habitual sensible desire' (*MS* 6:212; *A.* 7:251, 265). It is crucial for Kant, who holds that pure reason can of itself be practical, that not all desire is empirical or sensible in origin. For Kant, unlike Hume, reason is not practically inert and is not concerned merely as a faculty making theoretical judgements based on perceiving relations of ideas. (Even Hume concedes that what his own theory calls 'calm passions' is called 'reason' in everyday parlance.) The grounds for Kant's broader use of 'reason' raise issues about Hume's psychology that are too complex to discuss here. The main point, however, is that when Kant says that the man acts without inclination, this does not entail that he acts without desire (which Kant, along with the rest of us, would regard as certainly unappealing and perhaps even impossible).

not only in the sense that it was literally his last work on the subject, but also in the far deeper sense that it was the system of duties for which all his earlier ethical writings were always intended as mere groundings, propaedeutics, or preparatory fragments.

2

Kant's Deductions of the Principles of Right

Paul Guyer

I. Are Kant's Principles of Right Derived from the Supreme Principle of Morality?

In the *Doctrine of Right*, Part I of his 1797 *Metaphysics of Morals*, Kant appears to derive his 'universal principle of right'—'Any action is *right* if it can coexist with everyone's freedom in accordance with a universal law, or if on its maxim the freedom of choice of each can coexist with everyone's freedom in accordance with a universal law' (*RL*, Introduction, §C, 6:230)[1]—from the fundamental principle of morality, which presents itself to us in the form of the Categorical Imperative. He appears simply to apply that fundamental principle's requirement that we use our power of free choice and of action upon our choice in accordance with the condition that the maxims upon which we choose to act be universalizable (e.g. *G.* 4:402, 421) to the external use of our freedom—that is, to our physical actions in so far as they can affect other persons, in order to derive the rule that we act only in ways that leave others a freedom of action equal to our own, regardless of our purposes in and our motives for so acting, those being subjects for ethical but not legal rules. He then seems to derive further, more specific principles of right from the universal principle of right by

I would like to thank Bernd Ludwig, Mark Timmons, Kenneth Westphal, and Allen Wood for helpful comments on an earlier draft of this paper.

[1] In addition to the abbreviations established for this volume, I have included *RL* for the *Doctrine of Right* (*Rechtslehre*), Part I of *The Metaphysics of Morals*. Quotations from *The Metaphysics of Morals* as well as the *Groundwork*, *Critique of Practical Reason*, and 'Theory and Practice' follow the translation by Mary Gregor from Immanuel Kant, *Practical Philosophy*, ed. and trans. Mary Gregor (Cambridge: Cambridge University Press, 1996), with a few modifications; I also follow Gregor's rather than the Academy's numbering of sections in *The Metaphysics of Morals*. Translations from Vigilantius are from Immanuel Kant, *Lectures on Ethics*, ed. Peter Heath and J. B. Schneewind (Cambridge: Cambridge University Press, 1997). Translations from the *Critique of Pure Reason* are from Immanuel Kant, *Critique of Pure Reason*, ed. and trans. Paul Guyer and Allen W. Wood (Cambridge: Cambridge University Press, 1998). Translations from Kant's preparatory notes for *The Metaphysics of Morals*, printed in volume 23 of the Academy edition, are my own.

additional arguments. In particular, he seems to derive the principle that violations of right may be prevented or punished by coercion through the supposition that the proposition that a hindrance to a hindrance of an effect itself promotes that effect is true by the law of non-contradiction, or is an analytic truth, in which case it follows that 'Right and authorization to use coercion therefore mean one and the same thing' (*RL*, Introduction, §E, 6:232). And he presents the central principle of 'private right'—that is, the principle that it must be possible for persons to acquire property rights, including rights to land, to movable objects upon the land, to specific performances by others in the fulfilment of promises and contracts, and to the long-term services of others within the family and household—as a 'postulate of practical reason with regard to rights' that, although itself a 'synthetic *a priori* proposition', is also supposed to follow from the universal principle of right, 'in a practical respect, in an analytic way' (*RL*, §6, 6:250). Even more specific rights, such as the right to acquire property in land by 'first appropriation', are said to follow from the more general principles by a 'deduction' (*RL*, §17, 6:268). Kant seems to have promised such a derivation of the principles of right from the supreme principle of morality four years prior to *The Metaphysics of Morals*, in the 1793 essay 'On the Common Saying: That May Be Correct in Theory, but It Is of No Use in Practice', which had stated that 'the concept of an external right as such proceeds [*geht ... hervor*] entirely from the concept of *freedom* in the external relationship of people to one another' (GTP 8:289), and then to have confirmed his delivery on that promise in the *Doctrine of Right*, which states that 'we can know our own freedom (from which all moral laws, and so all rights as well as duties proceed), only through the *moral imperative*, which is a proposition commanding duty, from which the capacity for putting others under obligation, that is, the concept of a right, can afterwards be developed [*entwickelt*]' (*RL*, Introduction, 'Division of the Metaphysics of Morals as a Whole', 6:239).[2] Surely this means that the Categorical Imperative, the form in which the supreme principle of morality presents itself to creatures such as ourselves, whose power of choice can also be tempted by inclination, is both the means by which we know of our freedom and also the principle by means of which we must restrict our freedom in

---

  [2] In his edition of *The Metaphysics of Morals*, Bernd Ludwig has suggested that this 'Division' belongs in the general introduction to *The Metaphysics of Morals*, following 6:221, rather than in the specific Introduction to the *Doctrine of Right*. See Immanuel Kant, *Metaphysische Anfangsgründe der Rechtslehre: Metaphysik der Sitten*, pt. I, ed. Bernd Ludwig (Hamburg: Felix Meiner, 1986), 31–4, also pp. xxxi–xxxii. The word *entwickelt*, which Gregor translated as 'explicated', is one of those words that makes Kant's arguments in this late work so obscure. It is hardly clear from this term whether Kant thinks that rights and duties can be derived from the concept of freedom or from the Categorical Imperative by straightforward analysis or by some other method of argument.

order to determine both our legally enforceable rights against one another as well as our ethical duties to ourselves and to one another.

Several writers have recently challenged this natural interpretation and argued that Kant did not intend to derive the principles of right from the fundamental principle of morality at all but, instead, intended them to stand on their own as rational but not moral principles of human conduct. Allen Wood has argued that 'Kant very explicitly discredits the whole idea that the principle of right could be derived from the fundamental principle of morality',[3] and Marcus Willaschek has argued that Kant supposes, at least part of the time, that 'the fundamental laws of the realm of right are expressions of human autonomy akin to, but independent from, the moral domain'.[4] These authors have based their surprising conclusion precisely on what seems like part of the evidence for the ordinary view that Kant's philosophy of right is derived from his supreme principle of morality—namely, his claims that the connection of coercion to right is *analytic* and his designation of the principles of acquired right as a *postulate* of practical reason. Thus, Wood says that Kant discredits the idea of a derivation of the principles of right from morality simply 'by declaring that the principle of right, unlike the principle of morality, is *analytic*',[5] and Willaschek seconds that claim, while adding that Kant's statement that 'the "universal law of right" is "a postulate that is incapable of further proof [*keines Beweises weiter fähig*]" (6:231) . . . would be astonishing if Kant held that this law was a special instance of a more general principle whose validity Kant, on his own account, had proven in the *Critique of Practical Reason*'.[6] To reach their conclusion, both authors must assume that an analytic proposition, because it is true in virtue of the containment of its predicate in its subject concept and the law of non-contradiction, neither needs nor can receive any sort of justification beyond the analysis of the concepts that comprise it. Willaschek must also assume that anything Kant calls a postulate cannot have a foundation in any more fundamental principle, such as the supreme principle of morality.

Strictly construed, the claim that Kant's universal principle of right is not derived from the Categorical Imperative, understood as the requirement to act only on maxims that can also serve as universal law, is correct because the principle of right concerns only the compatibility of our actions with the freedom of others, and does not concern our maxims at all, a fortiori their universality.

---

3 Wood, this volume, 7.

4 Marcus Willaschek, 'Why the *Doctrine of Right* does not belong in the *Metaphysics of Morals*', *Jahrbuch für Recht und Ethik*, 5 (1997), 205–27, at 208.

5 Wood, this volume, 7.

6 Willaschek, 'Why the *Doctrine of Right* does not belong in the *Metaphysics of Morals*', 220.

However, any broader claim that the principle of right is not derived from the fundamental principle of morality, in the sense of the fundamental concept of morality, is surely implausible. The foundational assumption of Kantian morality is that human freedom has unconditional value, and both the Categorical Imperative and the universal principle of right flow directly from this fundamental normative claim: the Categorical Imperative tells us what form our maxims must take if they are always to be compatible with the fundamental value of freedom, and the universal principle of right tells us what form our actions must take if they are to be compatible with the universal value of freedom, regardless of our maxims and motivations. Thus the universal principle of right may not be derived from the Categorical Imperative, but it certainly is derived from the conception of freedom and its value that is the fundamental principle of Kantian morality.[7]

At the same time, Kant's suggestion that the universal principle of right flows directly from the concept of freedom should not be taken to suggest that this principle, the connection of coercion to right, or the postulate of right regarding property stand in no need of further justification or what Kant sometimes calls deduction. While the characterization of an analytic judgement as one that is true in virtue of its concepts and the laws of logic alone seems like a textbook definition of the analytic (see *KrV* A6–10/B10–14), Kant himself does not assume that the logical character of analytic judgements relieves us from all further obligation to justify them. On the contrary, both in the *Critique of Pure Reason* and in polemical writings from the beginning of the 1790s, closer to the period of *The Metaphysics of Morals*, Kant consistently maintains that even analytic judgements have no cognitive value without a

---

[7] In maintaining that the universal principle of right is not derived from the Categorical Imperative but is derived from the concept of freedom as the fundamental principle of morality, I am differing from the position of Allen D. Rosen, *Kant's Theory of Justice* (Ithaca, NY: Cornell University Press, 1993), 50–5. I am also thereby suggesting that the structure of Kant's argument in the *Doctrine of Right* of *The Metaphysics of Morals* is similar to that of the *Doctrine of Virtue*. As Allen Wood has pointed out, in the latter part of the work Kant almost never derives the duties of virtue from the Categorical Imperative as the Formula of Universal Law, but almost always derives these duties directly from the concept of humanity, or our obligation to preserve and promote humanity as an end and never merely as a means; see Allen W. Wood, 'Humanity as an End in Itself', in Hoke Robinson (ed.), *Proceedings of the Eighth International Kant Congress*, vol. i, pt. 1 (Milwaukee, WI: Marquette University Press, 1995), 301–19, repr. in Paul Guyer (ed.), *Kant's Groundwork of the Metaphysics of Morals: Critical Essays* (Lanham: Rowman & Littlefield, 1998), 165–87, and Allen Wood, *Kant's Ethical Thought* (Cambridge: Cambridge University Press, 1999), Conclusion, especially 325–33. If freedom—the freedom to set and pursue our own ends—is the defining characteristic of humanity (see e.g. the Introduction to the *Doctrine of Virtue*, 6:387), then the duties of right are simply the coercively enforceable subset of our duties to preserve humanity, while the duties of virtue include those duties to preserve humanity that are not coercively enforceable as well as all duties to promote humanity. See also Paul Guyer, 'Moral Worth, Virtue and Merit' in Guyer, *Kant on Freedom, Law, and Happiness* (Cambridge: Cambridge University Press, 2000), ch. 9.

proof of the 'objective reality' of the subject concepts on which they are based—that is, a proof that such concepts describe real objects or real possibilities for objects. And it is by no means obvious that by calling a principle a postulate Kant means to imply that it cannot be derived from a more fundamental principle. It certainly is his view that one synthetic a priori judgement can be derived from another, so by calling the principle of acquired right synthetic a priori Kant cannot mean to imply that it is not derivable from the general principle of right and through that from the supreme principle of morality. Moreover, those propositions that Kant most prominently labels postulates— the postulates of pure practical reason asserting the existence of freedom, God, and the immortality of the soul—are clearly subject to elaborate proofs. So, by calling a principle of right a postulate, Kant may mean to suggest something about *how* such a proposition must be proved, but not that it cannot be proved.

My plan for this chapter is the following. First, I examine some of Kant's general claims about analytic judgements and postulates in order to show that Kant's application of these concepts to principles of right does not by itself imply that those principles are independent from the fundamental concept of morality. Then I examine some of Kant's specific claims about the principles of right in order to show that Kant by no means intends to imply that these principles can stand independently of the fundamental concept of morality, but rather that he intends to deduce them from that concept. I then discuss two of Kant's central claims: the allegedly analytic proposition that right and the authorization to use coercion mean one and the same, and the postulate of practical reason with regard to the right to acquire property, showing that Kant attempts to establish the conditions of both the moral and theoretical possibility of these claims by arguments that can only be considered deductions. Whether Kant's arguments fully satisfy his own expectations for deductions or ours is probably impossible to answer, given how many ways he used the term 'deduction' and the debates that have raged in recent years about the nature of transcendental arguments. So I will not attempt to answer such questions.

II. Analytic Judgements and their Justification

On Kant's conception of analytic judgements, the claim that a principle of right is analytic is hardly incompatible with the assumption that it flows from the concept of freedom as the supreme principle of morality. Further, for Kant the truth of an analytic proposition depends upon the justification of the concept that it analyses; in the case of a principle of right, its truth thus depends upon the objective reality of the fundamental concept upon which the supreme principle of morality depends, the concept of freedom. The present section comments on Kant's general concept of analyticity; more specific observations about just what propositions about right Kant claims to be analytic and what they presuppose will be offered later.

Kant's conception of analyticity is not as simple as it may seem. Kant famously introduces his concept of analytic judgements by claiming that in such judgements 'the predicate *B* belongs to the subject *A* as something that is (covertly) contained in this concept *A*' and thus that they are judgements 'in which the connection of the predicate is thought through identity' (*KrV* A6–7/B10–11).⁸ This is usually interpreted to mean that an analytic judgement, or, as we would say, an analytic proposition, is one that is *true* in virtue of what is contained in its subject concept and the laws of logic alone. But Kant does not say anything about truth in this passage; he only says, vaguely, that in an analytic judgement the 'connection' between subject and predicate is 'thought' through a logical law. Whether this is supposed to be enough to explain or justify the truth of the proposition is far from obvious; it certainly leaves open the possibility that a full justification for belief in the truth of an analytic proposition may require some sort of justification for the subject concept itself. It is certainly not obvious that the subject concept of an analytic judgement cannot itself be derived from some more fundamental source, some more fundamental intuition, concept, or principle that would be part of the basis for the truth of the analytic judgement built upon that subject concept.

Following his introduction of the concept of an analytic judgement, Kant does make it clear that the fact that a proposition may be *proved* by means of an inference or chain of inferences proceeding strictly in accordance with laws of logic is *not* enough to show that the proposition—presumably, the truth of the proposition—is *known* by means of logic alone, or even that the proposition is actually analytic. He says that prior philosophers failed to recognize that 'Mathematical judgements are all synthetic':

For since one found that the inferences of the mathematicians all proceed in accordance with the principle of contradiction (which is required by the nature of any apodictic certainty), one was persuaded that the principles could also be cognized from the

⁸ It has sometimes been thought that Kant offers two different concepts of or criteria for analyticity, one in which a judgement is analytic if the predicate is contained in the subject concept and another in which it is analytic if it depends on the law of identity or some related principle of logic; see e.g. Lewis White Beck, 'Can Kant's Synthetic Judgments Be Made Analytic?', *Kant-Studien*, 67 (1955), 168–81; repr. in Beck, *Studies in the Philosophy of Kant* (Indianapolis: Bobbs-Merrill, 1965), 74–91 (see esp. 74–81). It is clear from Kant's text that he does not intend two different conceptions or criteria, but rather supposes that an analytical judgement can be 'thought' through the law of identity *because* its predicate is contained in its subject concept.

principle of contradiction, in which, however, they erred; for a synthetic proposition can of course be comprehended in accordance with the principle of contradiction, but only insofar as another synthetic proposition is presupposed from which it can be deduced, never in itself.   (*KrV* B 14)

This says that provability in accordance with the law of contradiction, and, presumably, by any other purely logical principle, such as the law of identity,[9] is not enough by itself to establish analyticity. The status of a proposition ultimately depends upon the status of the premisses of its proof: if they are synthetic, then the conclusion is synthetic even though reached by purely logical inferences. If it always takes a synthetic proposition to establish the justifiability of any concept that could be used as a premiss in a logical inference, this would actually imply that all propositions that can be known to be true are really synthetic. Kant does not draw this conclusion in the first *Critique*, although, as we will see momentarily, that may be his ultimate position. But, even apart from that conclusion, the present argument is enough to establish that the mere fact that one proposition can be proven from another in accordance with the law of identity or contradiction is hardly enough to establish that the subject concept of a proposition and with it the truth of the proposition do not depend upon something more fundamental. Thus, even if Kant says that a principle of right is provable in accordance with the principle of identity or of contradiction, that by itself hardly implies that this principle can be known to be true without appeal to some more fundamental concept or principle, and may not even by itself actually imply that the principle is analytic.

Before leaving the first *Critique*, we should also look at Kant's introduction of the concept of a deduction. Kant introduces the concepts of deduction in general and of transcendental deduction in particular in the 'Transcendental Logic' in order to explain our knowledge of synthetic a priori cognitions that go beyond those explained solely by appeal to our a priori intuition of space and time; thus, a transcendental deduction is needed to explain our cognition of the universal principle of causation, for example, as contrasted to a mathematical theorem. But Kant does not say that only synthetic a priori propositions need a deduction; in fact, he says that *any* concept the use of which cannot be justified by an immediate appeal to experience needs a deduction.

---

[9]   In his earliest philosophical work, the *New Elucidation of the First Principles of Metaphysical Cognition* of 1755, Kant had argued that the principle that all identities are true and the principle that all contradictions are false are actually two separate logical principles (1:389; see David Walford (ed.), *Immanuel Kant: Theoretical Philosophy 1755–1770* (Cambridge: Cambridge University Press, 1992), 7). In the *Critique of Pure Reason*, Kant tends to treat the principles of identity and of contradiction interchangeably.

In fact, he introduces the concept of deduction by none other than the example of rights, arguing that claims of right always need a deduction:

Jurists, when they speak of entitlements and claims, distinguish in a legal matter between the question about what is lawful (*quid juris*) and that which concerns the fact (*quid facti*), and since they demand proof of both, they call the first, that which is to establish the entitlement of the legal claim, the **deduction**. We make use of a multitude of empirical concepts without objection from anyone . . . because we always have experience ready to hand to prove their objective reality. But there are also concepts that have been usurped, such as **fortune** and **fate** . . . and then there is not a little embarrassment about their deduction because one can adduce no clear legal ground for an entitlement to their use either from experience or from reason.   (*KrV* A84/B116–17)[10]

This implies that any concept the 'objective reality' of which cannot be established by a straightforward appeal to experience of an object that satisfies it needs a deduction of some kind. And, as Kant's example implies, claims of right, as opposed to mere descriptions of fact, can never establish their objective reality by a direct appeal to experience. While particular claims of right are not the same as principles of right, of course, surely this suggests that, if the principles of right are to be shown to have binding force for us, which can hardly be shown by an appeal to experience, the concepts on which they are based must have their objective reality established by some form of deduction. Thus, even if certain principles of right do have the logical structure of analytic judgements, it seems unlikely that Kant intended that the principles of right can be known to be valid by analysis of their concepts alone.

Kant further expounded his view about analyticity in a polemical exchange with the Halle Wolffian Johann August Eberhard, who in a series of publications from 1788 to 1792 attempted to show that Kant's claim that mathematical propositions are synthetic a priori is false, and that, as he took Leibniz to have already shown, all mathematical results can be proven by purely logical inferences from appropriate definitions, such as definitions of number, and hence are analytic.[11] In response to this charge, Kant insisted upon the point already made in the first *Critique* that a proposition may have a strictly analytical *proof*, which proceeds by unpacking the predicates contained in a concept,

    [10] Dieter Henrich has emphasized the legal origins of Kant's notion of deduction in a number of articles; see 'Kant's Notion of a Deduction and the Methodological Background of the first *Critique*', in Eckart Förster, *Kant's Transcendental Deductions: The Three 'Critiques' and the 'Opus postumum'* (Stanford: Stanford University Press, 1989), 29–46.

    [11] Eberhard's articles were published in the first four volumes of the journal *Philosophisches Magazin*, edited by himself, J. G. Maaß, and J. E. Schwab. For a description of his attack, see Henry E. Allison, *The Kant–Eberhard Controversy* (Baltimore: Johns Hopkins University Press, 1973), 6–45.

but the objective reality of the concept, that is, its application to anything real, and thus the *truth* of everything that follows from it, even in the strictest accordance with the laws of logic, can never be established by analysis alone, but always needs to be established by some other, and thus synthetic method—this is what Kant had meant by his statement that analysis always presupposes synthesis (see *KrV* B130). Indeed, Kant argues, by suitable definitions *any* proposition might be given an analytical proof, but such a proof implies the truth of nothing unless the construction of the definition itself can be justified. Kant had already implied this in the first *Critique* when he stated that 'Prior to all analysis of our representations these must first be given, and no concepts can arise analytically as far as **the content is concerned**. The synthesis of a manifold . . . first brings forth a cognition' (*KrV* A77/B103). But the point is made even more clearly in the debate with Eberhard. In Kant's main publication in the debate, *On a discovery according to which any new* Critique of Pure Reason *has been made superfluous by an earlier one*, Kant focuses on the case of mathematics, basing his argument on the insight that real progress in mathematics was made only when mathematicians realized that 'the objective reality of [a] concept, i.e. the possibility of the existence of a thing with these properties, can be proven in no other way *than by providing the corresponding intuition*';[12] that is, no matter what they could prove from the concept of an object, the mathematicians had first to prove that the object itself could exist in order to assign any truth to the results of their proofs. In a further reply to Eberhard, Kant's disciple Johann Schultz stated the point more generally:

If one wishes to decide about a judgment, one must in each case know previously what should be thought under the subject as well as the predicate. . . . Let one place just so many marks in the concept of the subject that the predicate, which he wishes to prove of the subject, can be derived from its concept through the mere principle of contradiction. This trick does not help him at all. For the *Critique* grants him without dispute this kind of analytic judgment. Then, however, it takes the concept of the subject itself into consideration, and it asks: how did it come about that you have placed so many different marks in this concept that it already contains synthetic propositions? First prove the objective reality of your concept, i.e. first prove that any one of its marks really belongs to a possible object.[13]

---

[12] *On a Discovery*, 8:191; Allison, *Kant–Eberhard*, 110.

[13] Schultz's review of Maaß's discussion of the analytic/synthetic distinction, 20:408–9; Allison, *Kant–Eberhard*, 175. This passage was famously cited by Lewis White Beck in his article showing that Kant had prefigured some of the objections of Willard Quine and Morton White to the logical positivist's use of the analytic/synthetic distinction, in which he argued that the issue important to Kant survived their critique; see Beck, 'Can Kant's Synthetic Judgments Be Made Analytic?'.

No matter what you can prove from a definition, the reality of the object defined and the suitability of the definition to the object must first be proved if genuine knowledge is to result from the logical exercise of analysis.

Given Kant's statement in the first *Critique* that any proposition proved by logical methods is ultimately synthetic if the initial premisses of its proof are, his position in this debate with Eberhard may imply that there are, in the last analysis, no genuinely analytic judgements.[14] But even if that conclusion is not drawn, the application to practical philosophy of the Kantian position in its most fundamental form, summed up in the axiom that analysis always presupposes synthesis, surely means that normative principles can never be established by an analysis of definitions that may turn out to be arbitrary inventions, but must be shown to have a foundation in something justifiable or even inescapable. The justification of practical propositions cannot, of course, take precisely the same form as that of theoretical propositions: practical propositions state what ought to be, not what is, so their concepts may not need objective reality in precisely the same sense as theoretical concepts do.[15] But they clearly need a foundation in something real. For the principles of right, the only non-arbitrary foundation available is the concept of freedom, the proof of the objective reality of which is in turn the fundamental issue for Kant's practical philosophy, ultimately solved by the validation of our assumption of our freedom through our awareness of the binding force of the Categorical Imperative. The task for the philosophy of right must then be to show that principles of right have an indisputable foundation in the reality of freedom, and that the scope of these principles is precisely delimited by what is required for the preservation of freedom. Whatever may be analytically 'developed' out of the concept of right has no force unless the concept of right itself can be shown to be grounded in the nature and reality of freedom.

III. Postulates and Provability

Let us now consider possible implications of Kant's characterization of some or all of the principles of right as 'postulates'. In different passages, Kant suggests,

[14] See Beck, 'Can Kant's Synthetic Judgments Be Made Analytic', 168–81. Essentially, Beck argues that, while Kant has room for purely analytic judgements in uninterpreted formal systems, on his account even those mathematical propositions that may be logically derived from adequate definitions are synthetic if interpreted as knowledge claims about objects.

[15] See *KrV* A633/B661: 'theoretical cognition [is] that through which I cognize **what exists**, and practical cognition [is] that through which I represent what **ought to exist**'.

first, that *all* practical laws are or are like postulates; second, that the *general* principle of right is a postulate; and, third, that the particular principle of right that states that it must be right to acquire property is a postulate. It will be useful to have his statements before us.

First, on practical laws in general, Kant writes:

The simplicity of the [Categorical Imperative] in comparison with the great and various consequences that can be drawn from it must seem astonishing at first, as must also its authority to command without appearing to carry any incentive with it. But in wondering at an ability of our reason to determine choice by the mere idea that a maxim qualifies for the universality of a practical law, one learns that just these practical (moral) laws first make known a property of choice, namely its freedom, which speculative reason would never have arrived at, either on *a priori* grounds or through any experience whatever, and which, once reason has arrived at it, could in no way be shown theoretically to be possible, although these practical laws show incontestably that our choice has this property. It then seems less strange to find that these laws, like mathematical postulates, are *incapable of being proved* and yet *apodictic*, but at the same time to see a whole field of practical cognition open up before one, where reason in its theoretical use, with the same idea of freedom . . . must find everything closed tight against it. (*MS*, Introduction, III, 6:225)

Even without detailed analysis, two points are obvious in this passage. First, within two sentences Kant can say that practical laws are like mathematical postulates and yet are also consequences drawn from the Categorical Imperative, which Kant is here equating with the fundamental principle of morality; evidently, the way in which practical laws are like mathematical postulates does not preclude their being derived from a more fundamental principle of morality. Second, Kant's analogy between practical laws and mathematical postulates does not seem to mean that they are incapable of proof altogether, but rather that there is some sense in which these laws, or the fact of our freedom on which they depend and which they reveal, is a matter for *practical* rather than *theoretical* cognition. In other words, by calling practical principles postulates Kant apparently does not intend to imply that such laws admit of no proof at all, but rather to say something about the kind of proof of which they do admit.

Next, Kant calls the universal principle of right a postulate. This comes in the course of his comment that right requires only legality, not morality—that is, for purposes of right it is sufficient that we act in accordance with the universal principle of right even if we are not actually motivated by it as our maxim:

Thus the universal law of right, so act externally that the free use of your choice can coexist with the freedom of everyone in accordance with a universal law, is indeed a law that lays an obligation on me, but it does not at all expect, far less demand, that I *myself should* limit my freedom in these conditions just for the sake of this obligation; instead, reason says only that freedom *is* limited to these conditions in conformity with the idea of it and that it may also be actively limited by others: and it says this as a postulate that is incapable of further proof.   (*RL*, Introduction, §C, 6:231)[16]

Here Kant states that the universal principle of right is a postulate incapable of further proof *while* stating that the principle expresses the restriction of the use of freedom to the condition of its consistency with a like use by others, and indeed perhaps he means that the principle of right is a postulate just *because* it expresses the restriction of the use of freedom to the condition of its consistency with a like use by others. Thus, Kant apparently does not mean that the principle of right is not derived from a more fundamental principle of the supreme moral value of freedom; rather, he seems to mean that the principle of right needs no *further* proof just *because* it is derived directly from the application of the most fundamental concept of morality to the case of external action—that is, the case in which one person's use of his freedom to act has the potential to limit or interfere with other persons' use of their freedom to act.

Finally, Kant calls the principle that 'It is possible for me to have any external object of choice as mine' a 'postulate of practical reason with regard to rights', or also, in the next paragraph, a 'presupposition of practical reason' (*RL*, §6, 6:250). Yet Kant immediately proceeds to supply an argument for this 'postulate', and this argument, in the form of a *reductio*, begins by asking what would follow 'If it were nevertheless not within my *rightful* power to make use of it, that is, if the use of it could not coexist with the freedom of everyone in accordance with a universal law.' In other words, the postulate of practical reason with regard to rights is to be *derived* from the universal principle of right by a proof that the acquisition of property is consistent with and indeed required by the general principle that each person's external use of freedom be consistent with everyone else's. So whatever Kant means by calling the principle of property a postulate, it *cannot* be that this principle is not derivable from

---

[16]   In correspondence, Allen Wood has objected that my account of the derivation of the principle of right from the fundamental concept of morality runs the risk of making individual motivation a fit subject for juridical legislation, a result that Kant surely and rightly wished to avoid. But this objectionable result certainly does not follow from my approach. As he does in section one of the *Groundwork*, Kant can use his account of the pure character of morally praiseworthy moral motivation to identify the necessarily formal character of the fundamental principle of morality (see esp. *G.* 4:402), yet that principle, once identified, can still require certain actions or omissions of us as obligations that must be fulfilled regardless of our motivation for doing so. The duties of right are precisely obligations that flow from the fundamental concept of morality that we must fulfil even if our motivation for so doing is not our respect for the fundamental principle of morality itself; that is just why there is typically nothing praiseworthy about fulfilling the obligations of right. Again, see Guyer, 'Moral Worth, Virtue and Merit'.

a more general principle of right, and thereby from the even more fundamental supreme principle of morality.

So what can Kant mean by calling moral laws in general, the universal principle of right, and the particular principle of right that licenses the acquisition of property—the 'permissive law of practical reason' (*RL*, §6, 6:257)—postulates? Here it may be helpful to recall that there are three other kinds of propositions that Kant calls postulates: the 'postulates of empirical thinking in general' in the 'System of the Principles of Pure Understanding'; mathematical postulates, which he discusses in order to elucidate the postulates of empirical thinking in general; and the postulates of pure practical reason.

We can consider the first two sorts of postulates together, since Kant explains what he means by mathematical postulates in order to explain the 'postulates of empirical thinking in general'. The latter are the principles governing the application of the modal categories of possibility, actuality, and necessity, which are derived from analysis of the logical functions of judgement, to the objects of human experience: thus, calling an object possible implies that its concept is consistent with the pure forms of human intuition and conceptualization; calling an object actual means that sensation, as the matter of intuition, provides evidence of the objective reality of its concept; and calling an object necessary means that it is subsumed under causal laws (see *KrV* A217–18/B265–6). Kant does not explain why he calls these principles or as he also says 'definitions' of the modal concepts 'in their empirical use' (*KrV* A219/B266) 'postulates' until the end of the section expounding them; but then what he says is that he calls them 'postulates' *not* because they are 'propositions put forth as immediately certain without justification or proof' (*KrV* A232/B285), but rather because, like postulates in mathematics, they do not add to the content of a concept but rather 'assert . . . the action of the cognitive faculty through which [the concept] is generated'. 'In mathematics a postulate is the practical proposition that contains nothing other than the synthesis through which we first give ourselves an object and generate its concept' (*KrV* A234/B287). The postulate for a mathematical concept is thus the principle telling us how to construct an object that instantiates the concept in intuition, like the rule that a circle can be drawn by keeping a single curved line on a plane equidistant from a single centre point; a postulate for a modal concept is a principle telling us how to use such a concept, such as the rule that a concept may be called actual if the predicates included in its concept are not only consistent with our forms of intuition but are also instantiated in our sensation.

By calling such a principle a postulate Kant does not mean that it cannot be proved; on the contrary, he says explicitly that, if postulates 'could claim unconditional acceptance without any deduction, merely on their own claim, then all critique of understanding would be lost'. Thus for any postulate 'if not a proof then at least a deduction of the legitimacy of its assertion must unfailingly be supplied' (*KrV* A233/B285–6). Rather, what may not be subject to further proof, at least in the case of a mathematical postulate, is the possibility of the action *through which* the concept is provided with its construction, for it is the construction itself that is the proof of the possibility of the concept of a given figure. Kant's view thus seems to be that a postulate is the assertion of the possibility, actuality, or necessity of a concept, and that it *needs* to be proved, but that the proof can be given only through a construction, as in the case of a mathematical postulate, or something more like the description of the general conditions for a construction or verification, as in the case of the postulates of empirical thinking in general. But, whatever the details, Kant makes it plain that by calling a principle a postulate he hardly means to imply that it needs no proof or deduction; rather, by so doing he means to say something about the kind of proof that it permits.

The third and most prominent context in which Kant ordinarily uses the term 'postulate' is, of course, that of the postulates of pure practical reason. In his most extensive treatment of the postulates of pure practical reason, Kant introduces two such postulates—namely, those of the immortality of the soul and of the existence of God (*KpV* 5:122–3, 124–32) (although often he also speaks of the existence of freedom as a postulate of pure practical reason, and thus proceeds as if there are three such postulates). In introducing the postulates of immortality and the existence of God, Kant states that a postulate of pure practical reason is 'a *theoretical* proposition, though one not demonstrable as such, insofar as it is attached inseparably to an *a priori* unconditionally valid *practical* law' (*KpV* 5:122). On this definition, a postulate of practical reason is not a moral law or command itself, but an existential proposition, thus a proposition with the form of a theoretical proposition although not demonstrable as such, that is connected with a moral law or command. Kant does not make clear in this definition what sort of 'connection' he has in mind. But his very first mention of the doctrine of the postulates of pure practical reason, which was in fact already introduced in the first *Critique*, does spell out what connection he has in mind:

Now if it is indubitably certain, but only conditionally, that something either is or that it should happen, then either a certain determinate condition can be absolutely necessary for it, or it can be presupposed as only optional and contingent. In the first case the condition is postulated (*per thesin*), in the second it is supposed (*per hypothesin*). Since there are practical laws that are absolutely necessary (the moral laws), then if these necessarily presuppose any existence as the condition of their **binding** force, this existence has to be **postulated**, because the condition from which the inference to this determinate condition proceeds is itself cognized *a priori* as absolutely necessary. (*KrV* A633–4/B661–2)

This makes clear that a postulate is a theoretical proposition asserting the existence of an object or state of affairs that is a condition of the possibility of the binding force of a moral command. The binding force of a moral command depends upon the possibility of carrying it out; so the theoretical condition of the possibility of the binding force of a moral command is whatever entity or state of affairs must exist in order to explain how what the moral law commands can be carried out.

As is well known, Kant then reaches the postulates of immortality and the existence of God as the conditions of the possibility of the moral law through the concept of the highest good, and this is in fact why Kant does not initially treat the existence of our own freedom as a postulate of pure practical reason, although later he often lumps freedom in with the other two: immortality and the existence of God are necessary not in order to explain the binding force of the moral law as such—for that, the presupposition of our freedom suffices— but in order to explain the possibility of the attainment of the *object* of the moral law—that is, the state of affairs that the moral law commands us to realize. This is what Kant calls the 'highest good', or the attainment of the greatest happiness possible consistent with the conscientious observation of the moral law. There are different interpretations of the meaning of Kant's concept of the highest good: many interpret him to assume that the pursuit of happiness is a natural tendency of human beings that has no foundation in the moral law and simply has to be constrained by it; I believe that Kant's view is not so dualistic, but is rather that the fundamental principle of morality itself, by commanding us always to preserve and promote human freedom, and thereby to treat ourselves and others always as ends and never merely as means, actually requires us to promote the realization of the ends of all humans in so far as they are consistent with each other, and that such a realization would be precisely the realization of the greatest happiness consistent with the observation of the moral law.[17] But the details of how Kant introduces the highest good as the object of morality need not concern us here; what interests us is the connection between the highest good and the postulates of immortality and the existence of God. Briefly, Kant's argument is this: the realization of both virtue and happiness requires the perfection of our moral disposition, or virtue, on the one hand, and the maximal fulfilment of lawful human ends, or happiness, on the other.

---

[17] See Guyer, 'From a Practical Point of View', in Guyer, *Kant on Freedom, Law, and Happiness*, ch. 10.

The perfection of the human moral disposition, Kant supposes, would require an indefinitely long lifespan, or immortality, in order to overcome the propensity to evil that is otherwise natural to human beings. The maximal fulfilment of human ends, however, is something that can happen only in nature (because it is only in nature that the human desires that may be transformed into legitimate ends can be fulfilled), but we can have reason to believe that nature is suitable for the fulfilment of human purposes only if we believe that the laws of nature have been written to be compatible with the moral law—something we cannot ascribe to our own power but only to that of God as the author of nature. As Kant puts it,

Therefore the supreme cause of nature, insofar as it must be presupposed for the highest good, is a being that is the cause of nature by *understanding* and *will* (hence its author), that is, **God**. Consequently, the postulate of the possibility of the *highest derived good* (the best world) is likewise the postulate of the reality of a *highest original good*, namely of the existence of God.   (*KpV* 5:125)[18]

Kant's reasoning is thus as follows. The moral law commands the realization of the highest good (literally, the 'highest derived good'), so, since the binding force of an obligation depends upon the possibility of its realization ('ought implies can'), for the moral law even to have binding force requires that the realization of the highest good be *possible*. But for the highest good to be possible, we must suppose that both immortality and the existence of God (the 'highest original good') are *actual*. The possibility of the binding force of the supreme principle of morality, as a moral command, thus requires us to believe in the truth of certain theoretical propositions, that is, assertions of the existence of some object or state of affairs, even though these theoretical propositions can have no theoretical proof. Purely theoretical consideration can and indeed must be able to show them to be free of inconsistency, thus to possess what Kant calls 'logical possibility'; but only moral considerations can give us reason to believe that the concepts employed in these theoretical propositions have any objective reality, or what Kant also calls 'real possibility'.

Besides containing a clear statement of what Kant means by a postulate of pure practical reason, the first *Critique* also contains a clear statement of what he means by his claim that such a postulate is theoretically indemonstrable but practically certain. Kant says:

Of course, no one will be able to boast that he **knows** that there is a God and a future life; for if he knows that then he is precisely the man I have long sought. . . . No, the

---

[18]   Kant uses the same formula at *KrV* A811/B839.

conviction is not **logical** but **moral** certainty; and, since it depends on subjective grounds (of moral disposition), I must not even say 'It is morally certain that there is a God', etc., but rather 'I am morally certain', etc. That is, the belief in a God and another world is so interwoven with my moral disposition that I am in as little danger of ever surrendering the former as I am worried that the latter can ever be torn away from me. (*KrV* A828–9/B857–8)

There can be no theoretical proof of the existence of such things as immortality and God, Kant has argued throughout the first *Critique*, because such objects could not be presented within the limits of human intuition. But it is nevertheless necessary for us to believe in the existence of these objects because it would be incoherent for us to attempt to fulfil the command of morality to bring about the highest good without also believing in these objects—even the possibility of realizing the highest good depends on their actuality. Thus our belief in the existence of these objects has the same grip upon us as the moral law itself.

One last point should be noted. In the last passage cited from the *Critique of Practical Reason* (5:125) Kant used the word 'postulate' not once but twice: he said that the postulate of the possibility of the highest derived good, the highest good in its ordinary sense, is 'likewise' the postulate of the reality of the highest original good, the existence of God. Both of the postulates referred to here could be understood as theoretical propositions affirmed on practical grounds: the real possibility of the highest good could be understood as the condition of the possibility of the binding force of the moral law, and the actuality of God in turn as the condition of the real possibility of the highest good. Earlier on that page, however, Kant employed a twofold use of the term that might be taken differently. Here he wrote:

There is not the least ground in the moral law for a necessary connection between the morality and the proportionate happiness of a being belonging to the world as part of it. . . . Nevertheless, in the practical task of pure reason, that is, in the necessary pursuit of the highest good, such a connection is postulated as necessary: we *ought* to strive to promote the highest good (which must therefore be postulated). Accordingly, the existence of a cause of all nature, distinct from nature, which contains the ground of this connection, namely of the exact correspondence of happiness with morality, is also *postulated.*   (*KpV* 5:125)

In the last sentence of this quotation, Kant clearly means to use the term 'postulate' to characterize the affirmation on moral grounds of the theoretical proposition asserting the existence of God as the cause of nature. In what precedes, however, he uses the term to characterize the assertion of the *necessity* rather than the *possibility* of the highest (derived) good itself. But since Kant never supposes that the *existence* of the highest good is necessary, but only that it is possible, he must here be suggesting that the postulate of the highest good is necessary as a practical *command* following from the moral law rather than a theoretical *condition* of the possibility of the binding force of that law. In other words, in this instance Kant may be using the term 'postulate' to characterize the status of one moral command, the command that we seek to realize the highest good, as depending upon a more fundamental moral command—namely, the supreme principle of morality itself. In this sense, of course, a practical postulate could not be a practical principle that is independent of the fundamental principle of morality; on the contrary, such a postulate would be so called precisely because of its dependence on the most fundamental moral principle.

Three conclusions follow from this discussion. First, as far as theoretical postulates are concerned, mathematical postulates are so designated simply because the objective validity of their concepts must be established by a construction in pure intuition, or depends upon the possibility of an action of construction. It may seem natural to suppose that mathematical postulates are also fundamental in the sense of not being derivable from any more fundamental propositions—that they are not theorems that are proven, but axioms from which theorems are proven; but Kant does not actually say that. In turn, the more general postulates of empirical thinking are so called solely in virtue of one point of analogy with mathematical postulates: as mathematical postulates depend upon construction in pure intuition for demonstration of the objective reality of their concepts, so the postulates of empirical thought in general describe the kinds of constructions in or relations to pure and empirical intuition that can verify the objective possibility, actuality, or necessity of concepts of objects. Kant never says that these postulates themselves cannot be derived from anything more fundamental; on the contrary, he says they do need a deduction, and they receive that deduction precisely by being derived from the application of certain of the functions of judgement to the forms of human intuition.

Secondly, in its most usual sense a postulate of pure practical reason is not a moral command at all, let alone an underivable or primitive one, but a theoretical proposition asserting the existence of the conditions necessary for the possibility of fulfilling a moral command, our confidence in which, however, is based not on any theoretical proof but solely on our confidence in the binding force of the moral command itself. If there are postulates of pure practical reason with regard to rights in this sense, it would be natural to think of such postulates as concerning the conditions of the possibility of the binding force of those principles of right: a postulate of practical reason regarding a right would then be the assertion that the conditions for the realization of that right obtain. Pursuing the analogy with mathematical postulates further, Kant might even mean that a postulate of practical reason with regard to a right is the construction of the conditions under which the right may be realized. Such a construction might be practical rather than theoretical in virtue of demonstrating that there is a consistent idea of the use of freedom that would realize such a right rather than proving that such a use of freedom ever has been, is currently, or will in the future be realized. But the key idea would be not that the principle of right cannot itself be derived from a more fundamental moral principle, but rather that the conditions of its realizability must be shown to be possible.

Finally, if in the context of principles of right Kant uses the term 'postulate' in the last of the senses we have considered, he might not mean by a postulate of practical reason with regard to a right a proposition asserting the possibility of the realization of the right, but the principle or command of right itself; but, even so, if his usage in this case is to be analogous to that in the *Critique of Practical Reason,* by calling such a principle a postulate he would not mean that it is not derivable from a more fundamental moral law, but precisely that it is, just as the postulate of moral necessity of the highest derived good is derived by the application of the supreme principle of morality to the human pursuit of ends. Such a principle could still be called a postulate because the principle from which it is derived is not provable by theoretical means, but only practically. In this sense, a principle of right might be derivable from the fundamental principle of morality yet still be called a postulate.

I now turn directly to what Kant says about the principles of right themselves in order to argue that, while Kant has certain reasons for calling them analytic and postulates—where he does—he still intends them to 'proceed from' or be deduced from the supreme principle of morality.

IV. Are All Principles of Right Analytic?

To begin, we must be careful in drawing inferences from Kant's statements about the analyticity of principles of right, because Kant in fact applies the analytic/synthetic distinction to principles of right in a number of different ways, and the same principle may be analytic by one criterion but synthetic by another.[19] And, if this is so, then, even apart from Kant's general argument that

---

[19]   This point is noted in passing by Leslie Mulholland; see Mulholland, *Kant's System of Rights* (New York: Columbia University Press, 1990), 243.

the objective reality of the subject concept analysed in an analytic judgement itself needs a deduction, there can still be something about a principle of right that obviously needs a deduction—namely, whatever it is that makes it synthetic on one way of drawing the analytic/synthetic distinction—even if there is something else that may not need proof—namely, what makes it analytic on another way of drawing the distinction.

Specifically, Kant sometimes says that all principles of right are analytic, in contrast to principles of ethics—that is, principles commanding duties of virtue—which are all synthetic; yet he also says that it is only the principle of the innate right to freedom—that is, freedom of the person—which is analytic, while all principles of acquired right—that is, all principles of property rights—are synthetic. And even when he says the former, what Kant means is that principles of right flow directly from the fundamental moral requirement that we use our freedom only in universally acceptable ways, whereas principles of ethics depend upon the additional assumption that we necessarily will certain ends. We find Kant saying this several times in his preparatory notes for *The Metaphysics of Morals*. In one passage, he writes that 'All laws of right (concerning what is mine and yours) are analytic (on account of freedom)—all laws of ends are synthetic. . . . The duties of right follow from external freedom analytically; duties of virtue follow from internal freedom synthetically' (*Loses Blatt Erdmann*, C1, 23:246). In another note, Kant expands upon this cryptic comment:

The doctrine of right is that which contains what is consistent with the freedom of the power of choice in accordance with universal laws [*was mit der Freyheit der Willkühr nach allgemeinen Gesetzen bestehen kann*].

The doctrine of virtue is that which contains what is consistent with the necessary ends of the power of choice in accordance with a universal law of reason.

The former are negative and analytic in their internal and external relationship and contain the internal as well as the external conditions of possible external laws.

The second are affirmative and synthetic in the inner and outer relationship, and no determinate law can be given for them.

The first duties are *officia necessitatis* and the second are *officia charitatis*. (*Loses Blatt Erdmann*, 50, 23:306–7)

On this account, principles of right are analytic because they simply state the conditions under which freedom can be used in accordance with universal law—that is, the conditions under which multiple persons can exercise their individual freedom of choice consistently with each other—while principles of ethics are synthetic because they assume that human beings have necessary ends and state the conditions under which the use of our power of choice is consistent with the realization of those ends. The proof of a principle of ethics must therefore appeal beyond the concept of freedom itself to a necessary end of mankind, while the proof of a principle of right need demonstrate only that a relationship among persons is one that is consistent with the concept of freedom itself. Of course, to say the latter is to say precisely that a principle of right *is* derived from the concept of freedom and expresses the conditions necessary for the instantiation of the concept of freedom in relations among persons. Thus Kant's claim that principles of right are analytic is itself a claim that such principles 'proceed from' and therefore can be proven by appeal to the concept of freedom.

Kant makes the same point in the 1793–4 lectures on the metaphysics of morals transcribed by Johann Friedrich Vigilantius by using his ever-handy distinction between the formal and the material rather than the distinction between the analytic and the synthetic. Here he says that we arrive at duties of right by considering merely the formal consistency of our use of freedom, while we arrive at ethical duties by considering the consistency of the object, purposiveness, or 'matter' of our actions with the formal requirement of freedom. In his words:

If we consider the use of our freedom merely under a formal condition, the action is lacking in a determinate object that might essentially contribute a determination thereto, or we abstract from all objects. The determinate form points to a limitation of freedom, namely to the universal legitimacy of the action. . . . For this formal condition has reference to strict right, or duty of right. . . .

If, on the other hand, we consider duties and their grounds of determination in regard to matter, then the action has need of an object to which it is related. This object, or the matter in this determination of duty, is the end of the action . . . there is an end that we *ought* to have in view when performing our duties, and which must thus be so constituted that the condition of universal rectitude can coexist with it. So in this principle also, right and obligation are present, but if the action is judged solely according to the material principle, the latter stands *in oppositio* to strict right in the purposiveness of the action. Apart from the freedom of the action, there is thus another principle present, which in itself is enlarging [*erweiternd*], in that, while freedom is restricted by the determination according to law, it is here, on the contrary, enlarged by the matter or end thereof, and something is present that has to be acquired.   (Vig. 27:542–3)

Kant's use of the term 'enlarging' (*erweiternd*) indicates that this is another way of saying that the principles of right are analytic and the principles of ethics or duties of virtue synthetic, because a synthetic judgement is one that enlarges or amplifies its subject concept while an analytic judgement merely clarifies its

Paul Guyer

subject concept (see *KrV* A7/B11). Again, Kant's point is that principles of right are derived by the limitation of freedom to the conditions of the universal consistency of its use, whereas principles of ethics state how certain ends may be pursued consistently with the universal realization of freedom. But again, for Kant to make this contrast is also for him to state that the principles of right are derived from the fundamental moral concept of freedom by considering how it must be limited or restricted among any population of interacting persons not in order to pursue any particular ends but simply for the sake of its own universalization. The *formality* of principles of right does not suggest the independence of the principles of right from the fundamental principle of morality, but their direct dependence upon it.[20]

While Kant thus uses the analytic/synthetic distinction to contrast duties of right and ethical duties, he also uses it to draw a contrast *within* the domain of principles of right. This is the contrast between the innate right to freedom of the person and acquired rights to property. Kant makes this contrast in the *Doctrine of Right* by using his contrast between 'empirical possession', or physical detention of an object—holding it in one's hands or sitting on it—and 'intelligible' or 'noumenal possession', a right to control its use and disposition that does not depend upon current physical detention of it, but instead ultimately consists in an agreement among possible users of the object concerning who will have the right to it. Kant's argument is that one (ordinarily) has the right to control one's own body without any special consent from others, thus that forcible removal of an object from one's bodily grasp or of one's body from an object on which it currently sits would be interference with a right to freedom that does not depend upon the concurrence of others; but that the removal of an object from one's intelligible but not physical possession can only be a wrong if there is a prior agreement that one has a right to it. In Kant's words:

All propositions about right are *a priori* propositions. . . . An *a priori* proposition about right with regard to *empirical possession* is *analytic*, for it says nothing more than what follows from empirical possession in accordance with the principle of contradiction,

---

[20] Kant's use of the analytic/synthetic distinction to draw the distinction between duties of right and ethical duties is clearly connected to his contrast between the Categorical Imperative as testing for contradictions in the *conception* of the universalization of maxims and contradictions in *willing* the universalization of maxims in the *Groundwork* (G. 4:424). However, this distinction in the *Groundwork* is equated with the distinction between perfect and imperfect duties, and that then raises the question of why Kant does not include all the perfect duties, the duties that arise from the Contradiction in Conception test, among the duties of right, which include none of the perfect duties to oneself and only some of the perfect duties to others. The substantive reason for this is that only some duties to others are morally appropriate candidates for coercive enforcement; Kant struggles for the right way to say this in the Vigilantius lectures, but explicitly draws a contrast between coercive and non-coercive strict duties at least once (Vig. 27:581–2). For further discussion of this issue, see Guyer, 'Moral Worth, Virtue and Merit'.

namely that if I am holding a thing (and so am physically connected with it), someone who affects it without my consent (e.g., snatches an apple from my hand) affects and diminishes what is internally mine (my freedom). . . .

On the other hand, a proposition about the possibility of possessing a thing *external to myself* . . . goes beyond those limiting conditions; and since it affirms possession of something even without holding it, as necessary for the concept of something external that is mine or yours, *it is synthetic*. Reason then has the task of showing how such a proposition, which goes beyond the concept of empirical possession, is possible *a priori*. (*RL*, §6, 6:250)

On this account, the innate right to freedom of the person is analytic precisely because it flows from the concept of freedom itself, while the possibility of acquired rights needs a deduction—which will presumably consist in showing the compatibility of possession without detention with the concept of freedom, or even the necessitation of the possibility of such a form of possession by the concept of freedom.

What will be involved in the latter deduction is suggested in one of Kant's notes for *The Metaphysics of Morals*, which even bears the contrasting propositions that 'The principle of all propositions of innate right is analytic' and 'The principle of an acquired right is synthetic' as its title. Here Kant argues that to establish the right to freedom of the person—that is, the right to maintain or change one's own body or mind as one pleases as long as so doing does not impinge upon others—one does not have to go beyond the concept of freedom itself, whereas to explain the possibility of a right in something other than one's own body and mind one has to bring in further factors, in particular, the nature of the *other thing* that one proposes to control and the will of *other persons* who might also control that other thing:

For in the case of propositions of the first sort we do not proceed beyond the conditions of freedom (we do not supply the power of choice with any further object), the condition, namely, that the power of choice must be consistent with the freedom of everyone in accordance with a universal law. . . .

In the case of propositions of the second kind I supplement the power of choice with an external *object* which by nature belongs to no one, i.e., which is not innate and therefore cannot be deduced [*gefolgert*] analytically from freedom as the object of the power of choice.

The synthetic *a priori* principle of acquired right . . . is the correspondence of the power of choice with the idea of the united will of those who are restricted by that right. For since all right that is not innate is an obligation (to do or refrain from doing something) on another on whom it is not laid innately, but this cannot be done by another person alone, since that would be opposed to the innate freedom, and thus it can only happen in so far as his will is in agreement with it . . . thus only through the united will can a right be acquired. *(Loses Blatt Erdmann*, 12, 23:219–20)[21]

As Kant also says, 'The synthetic principle of external right cannot be anything other than: all distinction of mine and yours must be able to be derived from the compatibility of the possession with the idea of a communal choice under which the choice of everyone else with regard to the same object stands' (*Loses Blatt Erdmann*, 11, 23:215). Kant's idea is that we do not have to appeal to anything other than the idea of freedom itself in order to justify the innate right to freedom of the person—that is what freedom in the external use of the power of choice *means*. However, to explain the possibility of rights to property that go beyond one's own person we have to explain how the exercise of freedom in control of an external object is consistent both with the nature of the object and with the freedom of the other persons who could, at least as far as their own innate right to freedom would seem to imply, also use or control the object. Providing such an explanation is the task of Kant's theory of acquired right or property. It is certainly a deduction of the possibility of acquired right, in the form of an explanation of the conditions of possibility of acquiring property consistently with the freedom of all who might be able to use the object acquired or who could be affected by the acquisition of it.

Before examining more fully Kant's deduction of the possibility of acquired right, however, we must first pause over the suggestion that the principle of innate right is analytic. We shall see that, while Kant does believe that the universal principle of right flows directly from freedom as the fundamental concept of morality, this by no means frees him from the burden of providing a deduction of a proposition that is at least intimately connected with the universal principle of right.

V. The Universal Principle of Right and the Authorization to Use Coercion

Kant's most basic claim in the general introduction to *The Metaphysics of Morals* is that 'The concept of *freedom* is a pure rational concept', and that 'On this concept of freedom, which is positive (from a practical point of view), are based unconditional practical laws, which are called *moral*' (*MS*, Introduction, III, 6:221). Moral laws, in turn, as Kant has already made plain, include both the principles of right as well as the laws of ethics:

---

[21] For many similar passages, see *Vorarbeiten zur Rechtslehre*, 23:227, 235, 297, 303, 309, and 329.

In contrast to laws of nature, these laws of freedom are called *moral* laws. As directed merely to external actions and their conformity to law they are called *juridical* laws; but if they also require that they (the laws) be the determining grounds of actions, they are ethical laws. . . . The freedom to which the former refer can be only freedom in the *external* use of choice. (*MS*, Introduction, II, 6:214)

Kant argues that the *reality* of freedom is not proven from the concept of freedom itself, but is rather proven through our consciousness of the binding force of the 'moral concepts and laws [that] have their source' in the reality of our freedom (*MS*, Introduction, III, 6:221). But this means that there is one way in which all moral laws, not only the principles of right which do not refer to any particular ends of human beings but also the ethical laws that do, must be synthetic, because they presuppose the reality of freedom.[22] This is so, even though by the criterion of reference to necessary ends, the principles of right are analytic.

In the further introduction to the *Doctrine of Right*, Kant clearly has the dependency of the principles of right upon the *concept* of freedom in mind when he writes that in the case of right 'All that is in question is the *form* in the relation of choice on the part of [multiple persons], in so far as choice is regarded merely as *free*, and whether the action of one can be united with the freedom in accordance with a universal law', and thus when he concludes that 'Right is therefore the sum of the conditions under which the choice of one can be united with the choice of another in accordance with a universal law of freedom' (*RL*, Introduction, §B, 6:230). But in fact Kant does not specifically use the language of analyticity at this point in his exposition, and thus does not explicitly assert that the universal principle of right is analytic. Rather, he explicitly raises the flag of analyticity only at the next step, his assertion that the fulfilment of obligations under the laws of right, unlike those under ethical laws, may be coercively enforced. In fact, it is only in making *this* claim that Kant first explicitly uses the language of postulation as well as that of analyticity. First he says that 'reason says only that freedom *is* limited to those conditions in conformity with the idea of it and that it may also be actively limited by others; and it says this as a postulate that is incapable of further proof' (*RL*, Introduction, §C, 6:231); next he says that 'there is connected with right by the principle of contradiction an authorization to coerce someone who infringes upon it' (*RL*, Introduction, §D, 6:231); and finally he says that 'Right and authorization to use coercion therefore mean one and the same thing' (*RL*, Introduction, §E, 6:232). None of these claims suggests that the content and scope of the princi-

---

[22] This point has been stressed by Mulholland, *Kant's System of Rights*, 171.

ples of right are proven independently of the fundamental moral concept of freedom, nor that the binding force of the principles of right is independent of the binding force of the supreme principle of morality itself; they claim only that 'no further proof' is needed *for the right to enforce legal obligations coercively* because the concept of right and that of coercion are connected 'by the principle of contradiction' or 'mean one and the same thing'. Kant's claim about the analyticity of the principles of right, then, seems to come down to the assertion that the connection between right and coercion is analytic.

Is Kant right to make even this limited claim? His argument for this claim is as short as it is famous:

Resistance that counteracts the hindering of an effect promotes this effect and is consistent with it. Now whatever is wrong is a hindrance to freedom in accordance with universal laws. But coercion is a hindrance or resistance to freedom. Therefore, if a certain use of freedom is itself a hindrance to freedom in accordance with universal laws (i.e., wrong), coercion that is opposed to this (as a *hindering of a hindrance of freedom*) is consistent with freedom in accordance with universal laws, that is, it is right.   (*RL*, Introduction, §D, 6:231)

If one use of coercion would interfere with or destroy an exercise of freedom that is in accordance with universal law, then another use of coercion, designed to prevent the first instance of coercion, will preserve the possibility of the originally intended use of freedom, and in that regard is consistent with it and actually promotes it. Is this an analytic judgement, true by the law of (non-) contradiction? Kant supposes that it is, and most commentators have followed him without questioning his claim. However, the very language of Kant's argument seems to undermine any suggestion that the connection of coercion to right is merely analytic: Kant says not that a hindrance to a hindrance to freedom is simply identical with the lawful use of freedom, but rather that a hindrance to a hindrance of freedom 'promotes this effect' (*ist eine Beförderung dieser Wirkung*), or actually secures or produces freedom. This sounds like the language of *real causality*, not that of *logical identity*; but real causality is a synthetic connection, needing an explanation. In particular, in order to avoid the obvious objection that two wrongs simply *cannot* make a right, Kant seems to need to show that the use of coercion against coercion *can* cause the desired effect—namely, the preservation of freedom in accordance with a universal law; and to prove this would certainly be to prove a synthetic rather than an analytic proposition. For Kant to think otherwise would be for him to commit what he had diagnosed as one of the cardinal sins of philosophy as early as 1763, when he warned against confusing logical and real relations, for instance, confusing the logical relation of contradiction with the real opposition of forces[23] or the logical relation of ground and consequence with the real relation of cause and effect.[24] If he is not to make such a mistake, Kant needs to explain *how* the use of coercion can preserve freedom and *why* only it can do so. Thus, the claim about rights that Kant most explicitly says is analytic, at least within the *Doctrine of Right*, even if it is itself analytic, certainly depends upon a synthetic proposition and needs a deduction.

In fact, a variety of Kant's comments reveal that he at least tacitly recognizes that the deduction of the authorization to use coercion must ultimately contain both a theoretical and a moral element—that is, that it must show that there is a use of coercion that can cause a state of universal freedom in a way that respects the rights of all involved. The first comment about his argument that Kant makes shows that he recognizes that this purportedly analytic proposition needs the kind of proof he ordinarily gives to one kind of synthetic a priori proposition, even if not the kind needed by a causal proposition, and thus that it needs a theoretical deduction. He claims that the *concept* of right must be supplemented by a demonstration of the possibility of a *construction* of a sphere of right, analogous to the kind of construction of a mathematical object that is necessary to demonstrate the objective reality of a mathematical concept:

The law of a reciprocal coercion necessarily in accord with the freedom of everyone under the principle of universal freedom is, as it were, the *construction* of that concept, that is, the presentation of it in pure intuition *a priori*, by analogy with presenting the possibility of bodies moving freely under the law of *equality of action and reaction*. In pure mathematics we cannot derive the properties of its objects immediately from concepts but can discover them only by constructing concepts. Similarly, it is not so much the *concept* of right as rather a fully reciprocal and equal coercion brought under a universal law and consistent with it, that makes the presentation of that concept possible.   (*RL*, Introduction, §E, 6:232–3)

Kant continues with the mathematical analogy by noting that, just as mathematical constructions are carried on by means of straight and curved lines whose relations to each other can be precisely determined, so a condition of right requires the determination of '*what belongs to each* . . . with mathematical exactitude', a determination that indeed is not just analogous to mathematical construction, but that is actually based in one of the most fundamental forms of applied mathematics—namely, surveying. However, this is an antici-

---

[23]   See *Attempt to Introduce the Concept of Negative Magnitudes into Philosophy*, Ak. 2:165–204, at 2:171–2.
[24]   *Negative Magnitudes*, Ak. 2:201–2.

pation of a point that, as we shall see in the next section, should only come into the final stage of Kant's deduction of the acquired right to property. What Kant needs here is rather a more general proof of the real consistency of a legal system of coercion with the preservation of universal freedom: only this would be the construction of a 'law of a reciprocal coercion necessarily in accord with the freedom of everyone', the proof of the objective reality of a concept of freedom that can be coercively enforced.

Such a construction cannot be purely mathematical (any more than the proof of the equality of action and reaction can be purely mathematical), because, by Kant's own account, freedom (just like action and reaction) is a kind of causality: the causality by means of which changes in our intentions can effect changes in our bodies and the world around them, and, in the case of the external use of freedom that is relevant to the concept of right, the causality to effect changes in the circumstances of other persons affected by our actions. As Kant himself had stated in the *Groundwork*, freedom, 'although it is not a property of the will in accordance with natural laws, is not for that reason lawless but must instead be a causality in accordance with immutable laws but of a special kind' (*G.* 4:446). The point is undeniable in the case of right, because the condition of right is defined causally from the outset, in so far as it is defined as a condition in which the actions or external use of the power of choice of each leaves all others an equal freedom; and coercion is equally clearly a causal concept, the concept of an action of one person that can cause a change in the intentions of another through the latter's representation of what has happened or will happen to him because of the action of the former.[25] Thus what Kant must demonstrate in order to prove the objective reality of the concept of right, even if, or more precisely, *just because* the concept of authorized coercion means the same thing as the concept of right, is that it is theoretically possible to use coercion in a way that can actually cause a universal condition of right.

Does Kant ever provide such a proof? Most commentators accept Kant's claim that the connection of right and the authorization to use coercion is analytic without recognizing that even on Kant's own account the objective reality of the subject concept in an analytic judgement needs a deduction. Mary Gregor, for instance, claims that the connection stands by itself because the concept of right requires the restriction of freedom to the condition of its accordance with universal law, and coercion just *is*, as Kant says, the 'active'

---

[25]   This is particularly clear in Hume's famous account of how the 'constancy and fidelity' of a prisoner's executioners constitute just as reliable a natural force as 'the operation of the ax or wheel'; see *A Treatise of Human Nature*, bk.II, pt. III, sect. i.

institution of that restriction.[26] But such a claim still presupposes that it is possible for an action to count as both the coercion of another and yet as a preservation of freedom. Bernd Ludwig, by contrast, holds that Kant recognizes the need to prove the *moral* possibility of coercion, but then argues that this is not much of a challenge for Kant because, since an unprovoked use of coercion would not itself be an instance of the lawful exercise of freedom—that is, of the use of freedom in accordance with a universal law—it is itself outside the protected sphere of right, and another coercive act aimed against it therefore *could not* be incompatible with the lawful use of freedom.[27] But this argument, which in any case fails to address the issue of the theoretical possibility of coercion *promoting*, that is, causing freedom, assumes that the freedom of the *perpetrator* of an act of unprovoked coercion can simply be ignored as unlawful, thus that the freedom of the perpetrator does not have to be preserved at all. However, this is not compatible with Kant's idea that principles of right can preserve a truly *universal* condition of freedom. To show that this is possible, Kant needs to prove that, although an unprovoked and unanswered act of coercion would certainly destroy the freedom of its *victim*, the further use of coercion as a hindrance to such coercion can itself preserve the freedom of *everyone*, including the would-be perpetrator as well as his victim. This requires a proof that coercion can actually be an effective cause of universal freedom.

To be sure, Kant does sometimes try to establish what is clearly the *moral* possibility of coercion for the sake of freedom, although by an argument different from the one that Ludwig suggests. Thus, in the Vigilantius lectures, he states the following:

The right to resist the other's freedom, or to coerce him, can only hold good insofar as my freedom is in conformity with universal freedom. The ground for that is as follows: the universal law of reason can alone be the determining ground of action, but this is the law of universal freedom; everyone has the right to promote this, even though he effects it by resisting the opposing freedom of another, in such a way that he seeks to prevent an obstruction, and thus to further an intent. For in the coercion there is presupposed the rectitude of the action, i.e., the quality that the agent's freedom accords with universal freedom. The other, however, obstructs the action by his freedom; the latter I can curtail and offer resistance to, insofar as this is in accordance with the laws of coercion; so *eo ipso* I must thereby obstruct universal freedom by the use of my own. From this it follows that I have a right to all actions that do not militate against the

---

[26]   See Mary Gregor, *The Laws of Freedom: A Study of Kant's Method of Applying the Categorical Imperative in the* Metaphysik der Sitten (Oxford: Basil Blackwell, 1963), 43.

[27]   Bernd Ludwig, *Kants Rechtslehre, Kant Forschungen*, ii (Hamburg: Felix Meiner, 1988), 97.

other's right, i.e., his moral freedom; for to that extent I can curtail his freedom, and he has no right to coerce me.   (Vig. 27:525–6)

Several pages later, Kant again emphasizes that the 'right of coercion' depends on the condition that 'my action (the freedom of my action, that is) is directed according to universal law, and thus effects no abridgement of universal freedom' (Vig. 27:539). In these passages, Kant directs our attention not to the fact that the *perpetrator* of a crime would use his freedom lawlessly and thus step outside the protection of the law, but rather to the fact that one who would use coercion *against* such a crime must do so in accordance with universal freedom and thereby without militating against the right—that is, the moral freedom—of the other. However, this specification of the proper moral position for the use of coercion still seems to presuppose that in the proper circumstances the use of coercion can bring about the condition of universal freedom. So it looks as if it still needs to be shown that this can actually be done, —that is, that it is theoretically possible for one person to exercise coercion against another without depriving the latter of his right or his part in universal freedom.

In at least one case, Kant clearly does recognize that the possibility of a law depends upon the theoretical possibility of a causally effective use of coercion to achieve its intended end. Kant implies that a proposed use of coercion as a hindrance to coercion must be shown to be causally effective in his discussion of the so-called right of necessity. In the case of a shipwreck, he argues, one person has no right to push another off a floating piece of wreckage in order to save his own life, yet there can be no penal law against such an act because in such circumstances there can be no effective use of coercion as a hindrance to coercion: the threat of possible capture and punishment, no matter how severe, can hardly outweigh the certainty of drowning that faces the person willing to save his own life at the cost of another's, and therefore it cannot modify his behaviour. In this case 'a penal law . . . could not have the effect intended' (*RL*, Introduction, Appendix II, 6:235–6), and so while there is no right to self-preservation in such a case there can also be no right to punish such an attempt. Here Kant recognizes that there is a *factual* question whether an act of coercion against coercion could preserve the freedom it is intended to (in this case, the freedom of the unlucky soul pushed off the wreckage), and thus that here the proposition that the use of coercion *can* be a hindrance to a hindrance to freedom is synthetic, not analytic. Yet it is not clear from this that Kant recognizes that a general proof that a hindrance to a hindrance to freedom can preserve or promote freedom must actually be a proof of a causal and therefore synthetic proposition.

Perhaps in spite of his clear recognition that the objective reality of the concept of right needs a deduction, thus that the analysis of the concept of right must, like any analysis, presuppose a synthesis, Kant was distracted by his focus on the mathematical aspect of the *determination* of claims of right (what is necessary to make them precise) and thereby failed to provide the necessary argument that coercion can ever contribute to a condition of universal freedom. Yet it should not have been hard for him to provide the necessary argument or 'construction'. It could go something like this: while one person who would commit an unprovoked act of coercion against another would certainly deprive the latter of his use of freedom—for a short period, a long period, or permanently, depending upon the nature of the injury he would inflict—the judicial threat and even use of coercion against such a would-be perpetrator does not deprive him of his freedom in the same way that he would deprive his victim of his. When the laws and the sanctions for breaking them are known, it can be argued, anyone who chooses between conforming to them and breaking them can make his own choice freely. If he chooses to conform his behaviour to the law, he may have to give up his particular desire to do violence to another, but at least he does so freely; and, if he chooses to break the law, he does that freely too, and can then even be said to suffer the consequences of his action freely, though undoubtedly not gladly. The point is that while in either case there are ways in which his freedom is limited, he is not simply deprived of it in the way that the victim of a crime is. His freedom is limited—indeed, this is what it means for freedom to be limited to the conditions of its own universality, that is, compatibility with the freedom of others—but unlike his victim's it is not destroyed.[28]

If Kant needs an argument like this, then his connection of right and the authorization to use coercion not only needs but also can have a deduction that establishes the theoretical condition for the rightful use of coercion—namely, that it can actually bring about a condition of universal freedom, as well as specifying the moral constraints on the use of coercion. Perhaps Kant was never completely clear that the argument required for the deduction of the authorization to use coercion for the sake of right must have both a theoretical and a practical component. In the case of the postulate of practical reason

---

[28] This argument seems open to the objection, pressed upon me by Mark Timmons, that even the would-be perpetrator of a crime leaves his victim a choice, and thus freedom: 'Your money or your life!', after all, leaves the victim a choice. But here the criminal places his victim in a situation or forces upon him a choice that is not necessitated as a condition of preserving the universality of freedom, its maximal distribution to all consistent with the equal freedom of each, while the choice offered by a penal code—'Refrain from this crime or suffer the lawful penalties for committing it'—is a restriction of choice justified by the need to preserve the universality of freedom.

regarding the acquired right to property, however, he does seem to recognize clearly that establishing the possibility of the rightful acquisition of property involves both a moral inference from the concept of freedom as well as theoretical and clearly synthetic premisses about the conditions of the possibility of our experience as well. Let us now see how he supplies such a complex deduction while still calling the principle of acquired right a postulate.

VI. The Deduction of the Postulate of Practical Reason with Regard to Acquired Right

I now turn to Kant's theory of acquired right. Although Kant centres his account of property rights around a 'postulate of practical reason', he makes it abundantly clear that such a postulate rests upon synthetic propositions and therefore needs a deduction. He provides such a deduction in the form of an extended demonstration that the conditions for the possibility of a rightful acquisition of property can be satisfied in our relations to physical objects and to each other in space and time. This argument is meant to show that it is possible to acquire property in a way consistent with the universal principle of right or the preservation of universal freedom in the external use of our power of choice and to show that the institution of the state is necessary for rightful property claims actually to be acquired. It seems clearer here than in the case of the authorization of coercion that Kant intends his argument to demonstrate both the moral and the theoretical possibility of rightful property claims, and in this case the two aspects of the deduction can even be associated with particular stages of Kant's exposition: in the first chapter of 'Private Right', 'How to have something external as one's own' (*RL* 6:245), Kant explains the moral condition for the rightful acquisition of property, and in the second chapter, 'How to acquire something external' (*RL* 6:258), Kant establishes the theoretical conditions for the rightful acquisition of property, which must ultimately be realized in the state, before finally arguing that the establishment of the conditions for the rightful acquisition of property is actually a moral necessity.

Kant introduces the postulate of practical reason with regard to acquired rights or property in §6 of the *Doctrine of Right*, immediately following the contrast between the analyticity of the principle of empirical possession and the syntheticity of the principle of intelligible possession that was cited in Section IV. Kant's initial statement of the 'Postulate of practical reason with regard to rights' might initially appear to be simply a statement of a theoretical possibility: 'It is possible for me to have any external object of my choice as mine, that is, a maxim by which, if it were to become a law, an object of choice would *in itself* (objectively) have to *belong to no one* (*res nullius*) is contrary to right' (*RL*, §6, 6:246).[29] However, that the possibility of property is to be established by showing that its denial would be contrary to right suggests that Kant intends to show that its assertion is compatible with right, so what is ultimately to be proved seems to include the moral as well as the theoretical possibility of property. The moral side of the claim seems predominant a page or two later when Kant states that the postulate of practical reason with regard to rights is 'that it is a duty of right to act towards others so that what is external (usable) could also become someone's' (*RL*, §6, 6:252); indeed, the second formulation of the postulate appears to tells us it is a duty of right to establish claims to property, while the first appears to tell us only that such claims are morally permissible. In fact, Kant's complete deduction of the postulate attempts to prove both of these claims as well as to prove the theoretical possibility of the rightful acquisition of property. First, Kant will show under what conditions the acquisition of property can be compatible with the principle of universal freedom—this is the establishment of what Kant calls a 'permissive law of practical reason' (*RL*, §6, 6:247).[30] Then, Kant demonstrates the theoretical possibility of the rightful acquisition of property. Finally, Kant will argue that we actually have a duty to establish determinate property claims, which can only be done by means of the state or civil condition, when the particular empirical circumstances of our existence are such that we cannot otherwise avoid conflict with other people—under these circumstances the establishment of property rights is a moral necessity and not merely a moral and theoretical possibility. Kant's complete account of the application of the universal principle of right to the actual circumstances of human existence thus includes both a permissive law and a duty concerning property. Given this elaborate argument, Kant's designation of the principle of property as a postulate can hardly be meant to obviate the need for a deduction of it from the general principle of right and through that from the supreme principle of morality.

Yet in calling the principle of property a postulate, Kant might seem to imply that the theoretical possibility of property cannot be proved except by inference from its moral necessity. Thus, in introducing the second statement of the postulate just quoted, he writes that 'The possibility of this kind of pos-

---

[29] I translate Kant's term *rechtswidrig* as 'contrary to right' rather than 'contrary to rights', as Gregor does (*Practical Philosophy*, 405); I see no syntactical basis for her use of the plural, and it seems misleading to me, as it suggests that the denial of the possibility of acquiring property would be contradictory to particular and therefore already established rights, which is tautologous, rather than contrary to the principle of right, which is what Kant's ensuing argument clearly intends to establish.

[30] This passage has been moved from §2 to §6 by Ludwig and Gregor, and thus actually succeeds the first formulation of the postulate at 6:250.

session, and so the deduction of the concept of nonempirical possession, is based' upon this postulate (*RL*, §6, 6:252). Here he seems to mean that the theoretical possibility of the acquisition of property is problematic and can be inferred from the moral necessity of acquired right only by means of an 'ought-implies-can' argument: 'There is, however, no way of proving of itself the possibility of nonphysical possession or of having any insight into it (just because it is a rational concept for which no corresponding intuition can be given); its possibility is instead an immediate consequence of the postulate referred to' (*RL*, §6, 6:252). This is clearly an echo of Kant's central argument that the reality of the freedom of the will can be inferred only from our awareness of the binding force of the Categorical Imperative. Kant reiterates the claim several pages later when he states that 'we cannot see how intelligible possession is possible and so how it is possible for something external to be mine or yours, but must infer it from the postulate of practical reason' (*RL*, §7, 6:255). These passages suggest that we need to be precise in how we characterize the second stage of Kant's extended argument: perhaps we should say that in this stage Kant expounds the conditions that make it possible to acquire property consistently with the general principle of right given the fundamental conditions of actual human existence—namely, in the spatiotemporal circumstances of life on the surface of a naturally undivided sphere—without attempting to prove that such conditions can actually be fulfilled otherwise than by means of the practical certainty provided by the moral possibility and indeed necessity of the acquisition of property. It should still seem reasonable to characterize this part of Kant's argument as a deduction of the theoretical rather than the moral possibility of property.

It cost Kant a great deal of effort to sort out the stages of his argument, and perhaps he never signposted them for us as clearly as we would have liked. Yet I believe it is ultimately possible to discern the outlines of the kind of complex deduction that has been described in the first seventeen sections of 'Private Right'. This argument consists of four main steps, the first two focusing on the moral possibility of property, the third on the conditions that are necessary for satisfying the moral constraints on property given the general structure of our physical circumstances, and the fourth showing that it is actually a moral necessity to establish determinate property rights in the particular empirical circumstances of our existence, which include unavoidable contact with other people. At the first stage of this deduction, Kant argues that there can be no objection from the side of *objects* to our acquisition of property rights in them. Second, he argues that it is possible for all who might use any object to agree to the assignment of the right to it to a particular person, via a *general will* or multilateral agreement to assign unilateral rights to the object, and that only the consent of the general will to individual rights to property can make those individual rights compatible with universal freedom. Third, he argues that there is actually a way for an individual to acquire a right to an object in space and time as we experience them, either through first acquisition of a previously unowned object or through voluntary transfer of an already owned object from its previous owner to a new one, consistent with the general terms for individual ownership laid down by the general will. Finally, he argues that, in the actual circumstances of our existence, where contact and potential conflict with others cannot be avoided, the rightful acquisition of property can take place only within a civil condition subject to a rule of law that can both make property claims determinate and enforce them, or at least in anticipation of such a state—only a person willing to submit to the rule of a state can rightfully claim property and forcibly require others to recognize his claim.

I will hardly have room here to analyse convincingly all the details of this argument, let alone consider its normative implications.[31] I will simply try to provide some of the evidence for the key steps in Kant's argument that can be found in the published text as well as in Kant's preparatory notes, which never give a consecutive statement of Kant's whole argument but sometimes illuminate its individual steps.[32]

Following his initial statement of the postulate in §6, Kant takes the first step of his argument by arguing that it would be a contradiction in practical reason itself to deny ourselves the use of objects: 'freedom would be depriving itself of the use of its choice with regard to an object of choice, by putting *usable* objects beyond any possibility of being *used*; in other words, it would annihilate them in a practical respect and make them into *res nullius*' (*RL*, §6, 6:246). This presupposes the canon of rationality that underlies all of Kant's claims about contradictions in willing, the presupposition that if it is rational to will an end then it must also be rational to will the means (see *G*. 4:417). But, just as that principle must always be restricted by the permissibility of using an object in question as a means—the restriction most obviously exemplified in Kant's second formulation of the Categorical Imperative as the requirement that we always be

---

[31]   I have tried to provide some suggestions in that direction in 'Kantian Foundations for Liberalism', *Jahrbuch für Recht und Ethik*, 5 (1997), 121–40, and 'Life, Liberty and Property: Rawls and the Reconstruction of Kant's Political Philosophy', *Recht, Staat und Völkerrecht bei Immanuel Kant*, eds. Dieter Hüning and Burkhard Tuschling (Berlin: Duncker & Humblot, 1998), 273–91, both repr. as chs. 7 and 8, respectively, of my *Kant on Freedom, Law, and Happiness*.

[32]   Among commentators I have read, Leslie Mulholland, I believe, comes closest to appreciating the full complexity of Kant's complete deduction of acquired right; see *Kant's System of Rights*, chs. 8 and 9. But though I have learned more from Mulholland than from any other commentator, I think the reconstruction I will give makes it easier to see the outlines of Kant's argument than Mulholland's does. However, I do not pretend to engage Mulholland here on the many difficulties he finds in the details of Kant's argument.

able to treat humanity as an end and never merely as a means (*G.* 5:429)—so here too the argument that it would be irrational to deny ourselves the use of something that could be useful as a means must be supplemented by the premiss that it is permissible to treat an external object merely as a means. Kant recognizes the need for this additional assumption in one of his notes:

That one person should restrict another in the use of external objects . . . to the limits of their physical possession would contradict the use of freedom in consensus with the freedom of others in accordance with universal laws and hence with the rights of mankind in general, for in that case freedom in accordance with laws of freedom would make itself dependent upon objects, which would presuppose either the representation of an obligation toward objects (just as if they also had rights) or a principle that no external object should be mine or yours, either of which, as a principle robbing freedom of its use, is self-contradictory. Thus the principle of freedom in the idea of a collective and united power of choice of itself (*a priori*) extends rightful possession beyond the limits of physical possession.   (*Loses Blatt Erdmann*, 33, 23:288)

The moral possibility of property rights rests, in the first instance, on the assumptions that it would be irrational to deny ourselves the use of objects that can be used as means to our ends and that, at least in the case of physical objects, the objects themselves have no rights, or we have no obligations to them, that would block this use.[33] Kant assumes this is obvious in the case of non-human physical objects (although contemporary advocates of animals' rights might not take it to be obvious). In the case of rights against other persons in the form of contracts for specific performances and long-term relations of servitude, the point of Kant's further arguments is to show that these rights are limited but not excluded by the humanity of those who are obligated, because they can be instituted in ways that do not reduce the obligees to mere means who are not also ends. Kant's argument also makes the major assumption that the usefulness of objects presupposes long-term individual control or intelligible possession of them, which he never spells out.[34]

The second main step of Kant's argument, already hinted at in the last sentence of the last quote, is that, since any property right restricts the freedom of others who might also have been able to use the object in question, such a right can be rightfully acquired only under conditions in which all could freely and

---

[33] See also Mulholland, *Kant's System of Rights*, 250.

[34] Mulholland argues that Kant may not have been attempting to prove that *individual* possession of property is necessary, since some forms of common possession, such as by nomadic bands, seem to work perfectly well and to be compatible with Kant's general claim that it would be irrational to deny ourselves the use of objects as far as the objects are concerned; see *Kant's System of Rights*, 275. But the whole issue of whether property rights must be private certainly needs more of an airing than Kant gives it.

rationally agree to the individual acquisition of the right. Kant expresses this condition in the *Doctrine of Right* by arguing that, since 'a unilateral will cannot serve as a coercive law for everyone with regard to possession that is external and therefore contingent, since that would infringe upon freedom in accordance with universal laws', it 'is only a will putting everyone under obligation, hence only a collective general (common) and powerful will, that can provide everyone this assurance' (*RL*, §8, 6:256). But this almost immediately conflates the moral condition that others be able to agree to the property right with the theoretical condition that there must be a means to enforce this collective agreement, which is part of the deduction of the empirical conditions of the possibility of property that belongs only later in Kant's argument. The continuation of Kant's note just cited may clarify his statement of the condition for the moral possibility of property, although it too quickly moves on to the theoretical condition as well:

The possibility of such a principle, however, lies in the presupposition that with regard to corporeal things outside us the free power of choice of all must be considered as united and indeed as originally so, without a juridical [*rechtlich*] act, and indeed because it is related to a possession which is original but communal, in which the possession of each . . . cannot be determined except in accordance with the idea of the consensus of all with a possible aggregate choice. The possibility of merely rightful possession is, as given *a priori*, the rightful determination of it, but is not possible through the individual choice of each, but only through external positive laws, thus only in the civil condition.   (*Loses Blatt Erdmann*, 33, 23:288)

This note, however, clearly states the moral condition by itself:

With regard to the possession of a thing external to me I cannot, according to the laws of freedom, exercise any coercion against others unless all others to whom I might stand in this relation can agree with me about it, i.e., through the will of all of them united with my own, for in that case I coerce them through their own wills in accordance with laws of freedom. For all, the concept of a right is a concept of reason which through the idea of a united will grounds all external mine and yours.   (*Loses Blatt Erdmann*, 6, 23:277–8)

This passage also makes the point clearly:

An exclusion of all others through my own power of choice alone, however, is a categorical imperative for others to consider such objects as belonging to me. Thus such an imperative actually exists, as it were an obligation can be laid upon the objects to obey only my will, and freedom in regard to corporeal things is a ground of external coercive laws and indeed without a *factum iniustum* [doing an injustice] to others. . . . But this law is a law of the communal [*gemeinschaftlichen*] power of choice for without this it would rob itself of the use of external things.—Thus it is the communal will together with the communal original possession that makes external things in whose possession I am by nature into my own.   (*Loses Blatt Erdmann*, 32, 23:286–7)

Since any property right is a restriction of the freedom of others, and indeed one that may ultimately be coercively enforced, it cannot be right unless it is one that others could freely agree to. This is the moral condition that property rights must be compatible with the universality of freedom in its external use, or the condition that the so-called postulate of acquired right must itself be derivable from the general principle of right.

   The next stage of Kant's argument is what we may consider the deduction of the theoretical possibility of property, the explanation of 'How to acquire something external' in a way that is consistent not only with the moral requirements of the general principle of right but also with the physical conditions of our existence. Kant begins the second chapter of 'Private Right' with a recapitulation of the two distinct steps in the first part of his deduction:

The principle of external acquisition is as follows: that is mine which I bring under my *control* (in accordance with the law of outer *freedom*); which, as an object of my choice, is something that I have the capacity to use (in accordance with the postulate of practical reason); and which, finally, I *will* to be mine (in conformity with the idea of a possible united *will*).   (*RL*, §10, 6:258)

The first two parenthetical clauses express what I have been calling the first stage of Kant's moral deduction, and the last expresses the second. Kant then embarks upon the theoretical portion of his deduction. This is essentially the following argument, appealing to the most general features of the spatiotemporal conditions of human existence: all rightful possession of property must, given the temporal nature of our experience, originate in a rightful act of acquisition of the property. Such an act could be either a rightful transfer of the property from one owner to another or a rightful first appropriation of the property. There would be an infinite regress if only the former were possible, so the latter must also be possible. But, since the spherical surface of the earth is not naturally divided into lots (this expresses the spatial condition of our experience (see *RL*, §13, 6:262)), any original appropriation of land (the 'substance' which is the basis for all movable property as 'accidents' (see *RL*, §12, 6:261)) must be an individual appropriation from a previously undivided common. Yet if such an appropriation is to confer a rightful title, it must begin from a condition of rightful ownership, so it must be conceived of as a transfer of an original rightful possession of the undivided commons to a rightful possession of a divided portion of the whole. Kant does not conceive of this transfer from the undivided whole as a historical event. 'Original possession in common is, rather, a practical rational concept which contains *a priori* the principle in accordance with which alone people can use a place on the earth in accordance with principles of right' (*RL*, §13, 6:262). That is, to ask whether a people as a whole that possessed the land as a whole could freely and rationally agree to a particular system for the distribution of individual property rights is a test of the rightfulness of such a system, which is required by both the moral condition set by the general principle of right and the theoretical condition set by the physical circumstances of our existence.

In his notes, Kant clearly labels this argument a 'Deduction of the right to an original appropriation of the land'. Here is a compact version of it:

It is grounded on a *factum* which is original, i.e., not derived from any rightful act, namely the original community in the land.

The original appropriation of the land must be independent [*eigenmächtig*], for if it were grounded on the approval [*Einwilligung*] of others it would be derived.

However, the right of the appropriator cannot stand in an immediate relation to things (here, to the land), for to the right there corresponds *immediately* the obligation of others; but things cannot be made to have obligations. Thus the appropriation of a piece of land is possible only through a *rightful act*, i.e., it is possible not through one whereby the appropriator is immediately connected to the land, but only through one whereby the appropriator is *mediately* connected to the land, namely by means of the determination of the will of one person to oblige every other negatively in accordance with universal laws to refrain from the use of a certain piece of land, which restraint is possible only in accordance with universal laws of freedom (i.e., in accordance with laws of right. . . .

In this respect, however, the appropriator can only take possession of a piece of land in order to have it as his own through his private choice, i.e., independently, by means of a rightful act, for otherwise he would place an obligation on everyone through his own merely unilateral will, consequently only as the consequence of a possession in which he finds himself originally (prior to any rightful act), and this also as a common possession by all who could make claim to the same land, i.e., a possession that can unite all possible possession on the land of the earth through one will, which contains an original community (*communio originaria*) of the entire land of the earth, on which alone the act of first taking possession is grounded.   (*Loses Blatt Erdmann*, 56, 23:316)

Kant may seem to contradict himself, saying first that original possession cannot be a rightful act and then that it must be a rightful act of taking a piece of property out of the undivided commons with the consent of all or through the will of all. But the contradiction can be avoided if we interpret him to mean that, although historically the initial appropriation of property may or even must precede the organization of any public entity to license it, morally such an appropriation can create a right only if it is possible to see the individual possession of property as one that could be agreed to through a common or united will by all who could also claim it. It is through such a rational idea that both the theoretical and the moral constraints on the acquisition of property can be satisfied.

That both moral and historical, thus theoretical, constraints must be satisfied in the deduction of the possibility of property is also evident in the final stage of Kant's argument, in which he argues that historically property must be acquired in the state of nature and thus prior to the existence of the civil condition in the form of an organized juridical system, because securing the possession of property is the reason for the creation of a civil entity, yet that, because only the expression of the common will through a juridical entity can make the possession of property legitimate as well as secure, the acquisition of property in the state of nature must be 'provisional' and can only be rendered 'conclusive' through the creation of a civil state (*RL*, §15, 6:264). Kant's argument for this final claim depends on both moral and theoretical considerations, and leads to the final, moral conclusion of 'Private Right', that we actually have a duty to leave the state of nature and enter the civil condition. The moral argument is that, since the '*rational title* of acquisition can lie only in the idea of a will of all united *a priori*', and 'the condition in which the will of all is actually united for giving law is the civil condition', therefore 'something external can be *originally* acquired only in conformity with the idea of a civil condition, that is, with a view to its being brought about' (*RL*, §15, 6:264). The theoretical argument, however, is that the state is what we might think of as both a mathematical and a psychological condition of the possibility of secure property claims. The mathematical argument is that, since property claims extend beyond the body of the individual, yet beyond the body of the individual there are no other naturally defined boundaries, the state is necessary to introduce determinate boundaries between claims; thus the surveying of boundaries and the recording of deeds to property are among the most basic functions of the state. The psychological argument is that, since no one can reasonably expect to enjoy a claim to property unless others are also allowed to do so as well, but also that no one can reasonably be expected to confine his claims to his own property unless others can also be expected to do so, a system for the public enforcement of the boundaries of properties claims is as necessary as a public system for defining them. Thus the office of sheriff is as basic to the state as is that of the recorder of deeds.

Kant tends to stress the second of these two theoretical conditions in the published text of the *Doctrine of Right*, as when he writes that 'it is only a will putting everyone under obligation, hence only a collective general (common) and powerful will, that can provide everyone this assurance' (*RL*, §8, 6:256). Again, however, passages in his notes clearly reveal his fuller argument. A passage like this one expresses the role of the state in creating determinate boundaries between property claims: a person 'rightfully possesses a piece of land that he does not occupy . . . not through his own power of choice . . . only insofar as he can necessitate others to unite with him into a common will in order to draw the boundaries for each' (*Loses Blatt Erdmann*, 32, 23:285). And one like this explicitly refers to both the surveying and the enforcement functions of the state:

Every human being has an innate right to be some place on the earth, for his existence is not a *factum* [deed] and therefore not *iniustum* [unjust]. He also has the right to be in several places at once *incorporealiter* if he has specified them for his use, though not through his own will alone. But since every one else also has this right, the *prior occupans* has the provisory right to coerce each who would hinder him to enter into a contract to determine the boundaries of the permissible possession and to use force against the refusal [to accept them].   (*Loses Blatt Erdmann*, 10, 23:279–80)

This passage also points to the moral aspects of Kant's thesis that conclusive possession of property can exist only in a civil condition. On the one hand, Kant holds that, since it is both morally and theoretically possible to acquire property consistent with the universal principle of right, thus that property can be claimed consistently with universal freedom, everyone has a right to claim property, and therefore has a right to coerce others into joining with him to form a state in order to establish property rights. At the same time, since property rights are coercive, they can be rightful only if they are claimed with an eye to the creation of a civil condition. 'Therefore something external can be *originally* acquired only in conformity with the idea of a civil condition, that is, with a view to it and to its being brought about, but prior to its realization (for otherwise acquisition would be derived)' (*RL*, §15, 6:264). But, since the psychological and physical conditions of our existence are such that we inevitably will attempt to claim property rights in circumstances where that will bring us into conflict with others, we also have a *duty* to claim such rights with an eye to the civil condition and in turn to bring about that civil condition. Thus Kant concludes his exposition of 'Private Right' and makes the transition to 'Public Right', his deduction of the conditions necessary for the rightful existence of the state, by means of a complement to the postulate of acquired right—namely, 'the postulate of public right':

From private right in the state of nature there proceeds the postulate of public right: when you cannot avoid living side by side with all others, you ought to leave the state of nature and proceed with them into a rightful condition, that is, a condition of distributive justice.—The ground of this postulate can be developed analytically from the concept of *right* in external relations, in contrast with *violence*.   (*RL*, §42, 6:307)

This passage can also stand as one last reminder that Kant cannot mean postulates with regard to right to be principles that stand independently of any deduction. On the contrary, the postulate of public right proceeds from the postulate of private right, just as the postulate of private right has proceeded, by what turns out to be a complex deduction involving both moral and theoretical arguments, from the universal principle of right, which itself proceeds from the supreme moral principle of the absolute value of freedom in its external as well as its internal use.

To sum up this long argument, as has recently been emphasized, there are certainly contexts in which Kant calls some principles of right 'analytic' and contexts in which he calls some of them 'postulates'. But we have to be careful about what he means, since he uses each of these terms in a variety of ways. Further, Kant's general philosophy makes it clear that both analytic propositions and postulates ultimately need a deduction of the objective reality of their key concepts. Finally, Kant's philosophy of right, as expounded in both the *Doctrine of Right* in the published *Metaphysics of Morals* as well as in the many preparatory notes for this work that have come down to us, clearly recognizes the need for such deductions and at least in the case of the principles of private right provides an extensive exposition of such a deduction. Kant's deduction of the objective reality of a concept of right that authorizes its coercive enforcement may be sidetracked by his misleading comparison of such a deduction with a mathematical construction, but there can be no mistaking the key steps by which he expounds the conditions of the possibility of the right to acquire property, even though he calls the principle of such a right a 'postulate'. As in the less complete argument that Kant gives in the case of the authorization to use coercion, the deduction of acquired right involves both moral and theoretical components. The fundamental argumentative strategy of Kant's philosophy of right is thus to argue that the key principles of right, even if for various reasons they are called analytic and designated as postulates, are consistent with and required by the most basic moral and theoretical conditions of human existence.

3

Which Imperatives for Right? On the Non-Prescriptive Character of Juridical Laws in Kant's *Metaphysics of Morals*

Marcus Willaschek

I. Introduction

'Right', according to Kant, is 'the sum of the conditions under which the choice of one can be united with the choice of another in accordance with a universal law of freedom' (*MS* 6:230).[1] The realm of Right[2] allows us to 'unite' everyone's spheres of free agency by symmetrically limiting each person's freedom just as much as necessary to guarantee the same degree of freedom to everyone. From this conception of Right, Kant derives a rule he calls the 'universal law of Right': 'so act externally that the free use of your choice can coexist with the freedom of everyone in accordance with a universal law' (*MS* 6:231).

This universal law of Right is formulated as a prescriptive rule, or, in Kantian terms, as an *imperative*, which does not describe what people do, but prescribes what they *ought* to do. Surprisingly, however, Kant continues that the universal law of Right 'is indeed a law that lays an obligation on me, but it does not at all expect, far less demand, that I *myself ought to*[3] limit my freedom to

I would like to thank Katrin Flikschuh, Wilfried Hinsch, Bernd Ludwig, Kenneth R. Westphal, and Mark Timmons for extremely valuable comments on an earlier version of this chapter.

[1] English translations of Kant's works are from *The Metaphysics of Morals*, ed. and trans. Mary Gregor (Cambridge: Cambridge University Press, 1996), and *Perpetual Peace and Other Essays*, trans. Ted Humphrey (Indianapolis: Hackett, 1983), although I sometimes change the translations where necessary to bring out more clearly an aspect of the original on which I rely. Also I have capitalized some occurrences of 'right' in Gregor's translations of *The Metaphysics of Morals*, which does not use the 'Right'/'right' distinction). All other translations from Kant's writings are mine.

[2] I will use 'Right' with capital 'R' to designate the juridical realm, 'right' with small 'r' to refer to subjective rights, both of which translate Kant's term *Recht*.

[3] Gregor translates '*selbst* einschränken *solle*' as 'I *myself should* limit'. But Kant intends 'solle' to contrast with the equally italicized 'sei' ('is') in the last part of the sentence ('sein/sollen', 'is/ought'), which strongly suggests 'ought' instead of 'should'.

those conditions just for the sake of this obligation; instead reason says only that freedom, in its idea, *is* limited to those conditions and that it may also be physically limited by others' (*MS* 6:231; emphasis in original). I find this passage puzzling: How can a prescriptive rule like Kant's universal law of Right *not* 'expect, far less demand' that its addressees ought to act accordingly? The obvious response would be that this is not what Kant says; all he says is that this law does neither expect nor demand that its addressees act accordingly *just for the sake of this obligation*—that is, out of respect for the law itself. This would not exclude that one *ought* to act in accordance with the law for some other reason. But if this is what Kant wants to say, why does he bring in the contrast between 'is' and 'ought', and between 'myself' and 'by others'? Why does Kant apparently deny the prescriptive character of the universal law of Right altogether ('says only that my freedom . . . *is* limited') and invoke external coercion instead ('physically [*tätlich*] limited by others')? In this chapter, I will argue that, in the background of this puzzling passage (and similar ones, which will be discussed below), there lies a paradox about how the realm of law, or Right, according to Kant can be prescriptive at all. Juridical prescriptions would have to be either categorical or hypothetical imperatives; as it turns out, on Kant's conception of Right they can be neither.

In Section II, I will briefly recall Kant's conception of Right. Then (Section III) I will argue that it gives rise to a paradox: The unconditional character of the law, together with its restriction to 'external' actions (as opposed to 'internal' motivation), excludes an understanding of juridical laws as *prescriptive*. Next (Section IV) I will consider, and reject, a possible way out of this paradoxical situation. Then (Section V) I will look at a number of passages where Kant himself seems to draw the conclusion that juridical laws, as such, do not have prescriptive force and that acknowledging a duty of Right does not, in itself, constitute a reason to act accordingly. That Kant is drawn to what might be called a 'non-prescriptive' conception of (strict) Right can also be seen from §E of the 'Introduction to the *Doctrine of Right*', where Kant claims that 'strict Right' can be represented as a system of reciprocal *coercion* in analogy to the law of the equality of action and reaction (Section VI). In closing (Section VII), I will argue that, even if the paradox of the non-prescriptive account of Right cannot be dissolved, the paradox can be 'tamed' by embedding Kant's account of 'strict Right' in his broader conception of 'morals' (*Sitten*). The questions raised in this chapter will be discussed in a Kantian framework, but their relevance is broader: they concern the problem of how to reconcile the right/ethics distinction with the prescriptive character of the law.

I should stress at the outset that Kant's 'non-prescriptive' conception of (strict) Right and his emphasis on coercion do not make him a legal positivist;

after all, Kant argues that legal coercion is *legitimate* only within the limits of non-positive principles of Right. Moreover, Kant seems to see the non-prescriptive conception of Right as a mere abstraction or idealization that in real life is always 'mingled' with ethical considerations—something to which I will return at the end of the chapter.

II. Kant's Conception of Right

Before Kant, in the Introduction to the *Doctrine of Right*, gives the explicit definition of Right quoted above, he implicitly introduces his conception of Right in the general introduction to *The Metaphysics of Morals*. Together with Ethics, Right constitutes the domain of 'Morals'. Right and Ethics thus share certain fundamental features (cf. *MS* 6:222), the most important of which are the notion of obligation, understood as the 'necessity of a free action under a categorical imperative of reason'; the notion of a 'practical law', which specifies the way in which a purely rational being *necessarily* acts; and, finally, the notion of an 'imperative', which prescribes those actions for non-purely rational beings like us, thereby 'necessitating' our wills (*MS* 6:222; cf. *MS* 6:221). Imperatives that prescribe an action without appealing, either explicitly or implicitly, to the material ends and needs of its addressee, Kant calls 'categorical' imperatives; all other imperatives are called 'technical'. Since a law and its corresponding imperative share the same content and differ only in 'force', we may think of imperatives as prescriptive *versions* of practical laws.[4] Kant himself often states what he calls practical 'laws' in imperative form (cf. for example, the 'universal law of Right' (*MS* 6:231)) and even calls imperatives 'laws' (for example, 'A categorical imperative . . . is a practical law' (*MS* 6:222–3)). Further concepts shared by Right and Ethics include, among others, 'duty', 'deed', and 'person'.

Given this common background, Kant then distinguishes between Right and Ethics by drawing three interrelated distinctions: between two kinds of lawgiving, between two kinds of laws, and between two kinds of incentives (see *MS* 6:218, also *MS* 6:214).[5] *Ethical* laws require compliance from a specific incentive—namely, from the idea of duty; they must be obeyed for their own sake and not (merely) for prudential reasons. *Juridical* laws, by contrast, do not

---

[4] See Otfried Höffe, 'Der kategorische Rechtsimperativ. "Einleitung in die Rechtslehre"', in O. Höffe (ed.), *Metaphysische Anfangsgründe der Rechtslehre* (Berlin: Akademie Verlag, 1999), 55.

[5] I follow the reordering of the sections of the 'Introduction' suggested by Bernd Ludwig, *Kants Rechtslehre* (Hamburg: Meiner, 1990) and adopted by Mary Gregor in her translation.

require a specific incentive. Nevertheless, juridical laws have to come with an incentive, too. Even though Kant sometimes seems to suggest that there is no specific incentive connected with juridical laws (which 'admit' other incentives than the idea of duty (*MS* 6:219)), this means only that no specific incentive is normatively *required*. Since in 'all lawgiving . . . there are two elements: first, a law . . . and second, an incentive', juridical laws would not be *laws* if they were not backed by an incentive sufficient to enforce them: 'since it [that is, juridical lawgiving] still needs an incentive suited to the law, it can only connect external incentives with it' (*MS* 6:219)—that is, incentives external to the agent whose choice they are supposed to determine. Thus, the incentive juridical lawgiving connects with its laws is external constraint, or 'coercion' (*MS* 6:220).

Obviously, no one is *required* to obey juridical laws only coercively in the way one is required to obey ethical laws from the idea of duty; but, if someone does not obey juridical laws voluntarily, he or she may legitimately be coerced by others to obey them. Juridical laws can only require external behaviour, but not motivation, since external coercion (as the specific incentive connected with juridical laws) does not (reliably) effect the inner attitude or motive. Hence, when Kant defines Right in the Introduction to the *Doctrine of Right*, he explicitly restricts the realm of juridical rights and obligations to the 'external and indeed practical relation of one person to another, in so far as their actions, as deeds, can have (direct or indirect) influence on each other' (*MS* 6:230).

This does not mean that, as far as Right is concerned, motivation is irrelevant; after all, we often can tell what kind of action has been done only by considering its motivation.[6] Kant acknowledges this by referring, in his universal principle of Right, not only to external actions, but also to their maxims: 'Any action is *right* if it can coexist with everyone's freedom in accordance with a universal law, or if on its maxim the freedom of choice of each can coexist with everyone's freedom in accordance with a universal law' (*MS* 6:230). Thus, juridical laws may specify kinds of required or prohibited behaviour in terms of their maxims. Indeed, they may even require to act 'externally' only on universalizable maxims. But

it cannot be required that this principle of all maxims [namely, the universal principle of Right] be itself in turn my maxim, that is, it cannot be required that I make it the maxim of my action; for anyone can be free so long as I do not impair his freedom by my *external action*, even though I am quite indifferent to his freedom or would like in my heart to infringe upon it. That I make it my maxim to act rightly is a demand that Ethics makes on me.   (*MS* 6:231)

---

[6] Whether something is a successful murder or a mistaken attempt at cooking a nice mushroom dinner depends, among other things, on what the agent wanted to achieve.

And Kant concludes: 'Thus the universal law of right: so act externally that the free use of your choice can coexist with the freedom of everyone in accordance with a universal law' (*MS* 6:231).

Because Right is restricted to external actions, no one is juridically required to obey the law out of respect for the law. Whether one is a law-abiding citizen out of respect for the law, prudence, or fear of punishment does not make any *juridical* difference. The quality of an act's being lawful, independently of its motivation, Kant calls its 'legality', as opposed to its 'morality', which *further* requires that the act be motivated by the idea of duty (*MS* 6:219). This means that, with respect to juridical laws and obligations, it is possible to consider them from an ethical point of view, too: 'It is no duty of virtue [that is, no ethical duty] to keep one's promises, but a duty of Right, to the performance of which one can be coerced. But it is still a virtuous action (a proof of virtue) to do it even when no coercion must be feared' (*MS* 6:220).

In sum, we can say that the primary difference between Right and Ethics concerns the question which incentive is connected in which way with the respective laws: juridical laws require *only* 'external' legality, and therefore *can* be enforced by coercive means; ethical laws *additionally* require 'inner' morality, and therefore *cannot* be externally enforced.[7] The claim that juridical laws require only legality I will call the Externality Thesis.[8]

III. The Paradox of Juridical Imperatives

Even though Kant intends the Externality Thesis to be an analytical truth, in the light of later experiences with totalitarian regimes, it turns out to imply substantial restrictions of legitimate state power. For instance, no one can be held responsible for obeying the laws of their country without proper enthusiasm, as long as they in fact obey them, which in turn means that there is no legitimate reason for state authorities even to *enquire* into people's motivation for obeying the law. Thus the Externality Thesis, together with the distinction between Right and Ethics built on it, is rightly considered as containing a philosophically and politically important insight.[9] But, on the other hand, at

---

[7] For a more detailed account of Kant's distinction between Right and Ethics and the numerous problems connected with it, see Marcus Willaschek, 'Why the *Doctrine of Right* does not belong in the *Metaphysics of Morals*: On some Basic Distinctions in Kant's Moral Philosophy', in *Jahrbuch für Recht und Ethik*, 5 (1997), 205–27.

[8] The Externality Thesis is a special (namely, juridical) case of what Mark Timmons calls the 'Independence Thesis'; see Timmons, this volume.

[9] See e.g. Wolfgang Kersting, *Wohlgeordnete Freiheit. Immanuel Kants Rechts und Staatsphilosophie* (Frankfurt/M.: Suhrkamp, 1984), ch. 3; Otfried Höffe, *Kategorische Rechtsprinzipien—ein Kontrapunkt der*

least in its Kantian framework, the Externality Thesis seems to lead to a paradox. We can see this if we ask what kind of imperatives correspond to juridical laws. On Kant's view, valid juridical laws, both positive and natural, are 'practical' laws (see *MS* 6:222, 224); they hold unconditionally in that their validity does not presuppose, on the side of those subjected to the laws, any 'material' ends or needs, but only (external) freedom (see *MS* 6:230). Thus, only categorical imperatives can give expression to juridical laws, since only they prescribe actions unconditionally, without presupposing an end (*MS* 6:222). All other imperatives, which Kant calls 'technical' (*MS* 6:222) or 'hypothetical' (*G.* 4:414), prescribe an action only as means to an end.

Now we must distinguish between *obeying* an imperative and merely acting *in accordance* with it.[10] Someone acts in accordance with an imperative if she acts as the imperative prescribes. But this may be quite accidental; the person in question may have acted as she did without even considering the imperative in question. *Obeying* an imperative, by contrast, means that one acts as one does *because* this is what the imperative demands. (This does not mean that there may be no other motive present, but that, even if there were no other motive, the imperative alone would suffice to motivate compliance.) By insisting that imperatives are meant to 'necessitate' the will of those who may possibly be tempted to violate the laws (cf. *MS* 6:222; *G.* 4:413–14), Kant makes it clear that the whole *point* of imperatives, as opposed to their corresponding practical laws, is to be *obeyed*. Hence, the point of *categorical* imperatives is to be obeyed unconditionally, not (merely) because of some end one may have, but (also and in any case) because that is what the imperative demands. Put differently: the only way to obey a categorical imperative, as such, is to obey it for its own sake. (At first glance, it may perhaps seem possible to obey a categorical imperative not for its own sake, but for some other reason—for instance, out of fear of punishment. But in fact, this is a conceptual impossibility: since *obeying* a categorical imperative means that one would have followed its prescription anyway, even if no threat of punishment were connected with it, complying with it *exclusively* out of fear of punishment precisely means not to *obey* it.)

But then, it seems, juridical laws cannot find expression in categorical imperatives, after all, because juridical laws do *not* require obedience for their own sake. According to the Externality Thesis, the juridical rightness of an act

---

Moderne (Frankfurt/M.: Suhrkamp, 1990), ch. 3.3; Daniel O. Dahlstrom, 'Ethik, Recht und Billigkeit', in *Jahrbuch für Recht und Ethik*, 5 (1997), 55–72; and Paul Guyer, 'Kant's Foundations for Liberalism', in *Jahrbuch für Recht und Ethik*, 5 (1997), 121–40.

[10]   This distinction is meant to parallel that between 'acting from duty' and 'acting in accordance with duty' (see *G.* 4:397 ff.).

does not depend on whether it has been done out of respect for the law or for some other reason. But neither can juridical laws issue in merely hypothetical imperatives, perhaps of the general form: 'If you want to avoid (the risk of) coercion and punishment, do X', since in this case they would bind only those who in fact want to avoid (the risk of) coercion and punishment.

Thus it seems that, on Kant's view, juridical laws, as such, cannot give rise to imperatives at all, since these would have to be categorical imperatives in order to prescribe unconditionally, but they cannot be categorical imperatives if they respect the externality of Right.[11] If we understand imperatives, quite in keeping with the role Kant attributes to them, as the prescriptive versions of rational principles (and categorical imperatives as prescriptive versions of purely rational principles), we are forced to the paradoxical conclusion that, in a Kantian framework, juridical laws cannot be prescriptive, in the sense that they do not issue prescriptions meant to direct the behaviour of their addressees. This does not mean that juridical laws are *descriptive*; they do not just express empirical generalizations or predict legal consequences of various acts. Juridical laws can still be *normative* in that they define a non factual standard of rightness; but, paradoxically, they cannot *prescribe*, *command*, or *require* that their addressees act in accordance with that standard.[12]

The paradox of juridical imperatives can be stated in more general terms as the problem of how to reconcile three prima facie plausible claims: (1) the Unconditionality Thesis, to the effect that juridical laws hold unconditionally; they do not bind only those who share certain ends, but everyone (or, in the case of positive laws, everyone under a given jurisdiction); (2) the Prescriptivity Thesis, that juridical laws are, or contain, prescriptions that tell people what they

---

[11] Otfried Höffe regards the idea of 'categorical imperatives of right' (*kategorische Rechtsimperative*) as central to Kant's philosophy of Right (cf. Höffe, *Kategorische Rechtsprinzipien—ein Kontrapunkt der Moderne*; see also Höffe, 'Der kategorische Rechtsimperativ. "Einleitung in die Rechtslehre"', 53). If the above argument is correct, this is a misnomer, since there are no 'imperatives of right', precisely because these imperatives cannot be categorical. However, Höffe also speaks of 'categorical principles of right' (*kategorische Rechtsprinzipien*) and in many contexts seems to use 'principle' and 'imperative' interchangeably (see e.g. Höffe, *Kategorische Rechtsprinzipien—ein Kontrapunkt der Moderne*, 17). Therefore, I believe that for Höffe nothing hinges on whether these principles are imperatives or not. Kant himself does not use the expression 'imperative of Right' (*Rechtsimperativ*); in the *Doctrine of Right*, there are only seven occurrences of the term 'imperative' (*MS* 6:239, 252, 273, 280, 318, 331, 336), three of which concern *the* Categorical Imperative of morality (*MS* 6:239, 252, 280). Of the remaining occurrences, one concerns the *ethical* (imperfect) duty to 'strive' for the well-being of the state (*MS* 6:318); the other three do concern juridical questions, but the 'imperatives' mentioned there are best understood as concerning *ethical* duties—duties to obey the respective juridical laws (the principles of promise keeping and of penal justice, respectively) 'even where no coercion must be feared' (cf. *MS* 6:220).

[12] This has been stressed by Allen Wood, 'The Final Form of Kant's Practical Philosophy', this volume, p. 8: 'the principle of right merely tells us which actions do and do not infringe external freedom (and therefore count as "right") without, however, directly commanding us to perform those actions'.

ought and what they *ought not* to do; and (3) the Externality Thesis, according to which juridical laws only require external compliance, not compliance for the sake of the law.

Holding all three of these claims jointly may not lead into formal contradiction. But still, any two of them weigh strongly against the remaining third one.[13] It seems, therefore, that unconditionally valid juridical laws cannot be both prescriptive and respect the Externality Thesis: even though juridical laws do not explicitly *require* to be obeyed for their own sake (that is, from the idea of duty), the only way to *obey* them at all (as opposed to merely acting in accordance with them) is to obey them for their own sake. Since the point of prescriptions is to be obeyed, the unconditionality and prescriptivity of the law seem to exclude its externality.[14]

Now this may seem to tell against the unconditionality, rather than the externality, of the law. Kant himself draws attention to the problem of the very possibility of unconditional (categorical) imperatives in the *Groundwork* (see *G.* 4:419, 453 ff.); his final solution in the second *Critique* invokes his doctrine of the 'fact of reason', which has seemed mysterious even to many sympathetic readers.[15] Whether for good reasons or not, Kant holds on to both the Unconditionality and Externality Theses; consequently, he is under pressure to give up the Prescriptivity Thesis.

I think that it is this pressure that explains the puzzling passage about the 'universal law of Right' from which we started (*MS* 6:231): This law, Kant says, 'lays an obligation [*Verbindlichkeit*] on me'. This calls for a categorical imperative, since, as we have seen, obligation is *defined* as 'the necessity of a free

[13] If, for instance, juridical laws take the form of unconditional (categorical) prescriptions, how can they be restricted to external compliance? The point of a prescription is to motivate (in Kantian terms: to 'necessitate') its addressees to act as prescribed. Now many prescriptions, even though unconditional if taken at face value, are really conditional or hypothetical: the warning 'Do not throw' on a parcel is not overtly conditional, but it derives its prescriptive force entirely from the wish that the parcel's content not be shattered. If juridical laws, too, were to hold only conditionally, this would mean that the corresponding prescriptions derive their force entirely from some empirical motive of their addresses—for instance, from their desire to live peacefully or, perhaps, their fear of punishment. If, by contrast, juridical laws hold unconditionally, then no such motive must, and indeed can, be supplied.

[14] Perhaps one might try to argue that there is an analytical connection between what is (morally or juridically) right and what one ought to do; see e.g. R. M. Hare, *The Language of Morals* (Oxford: Clarendon Press, 1952), ch. 12. But first, Kant himself does not regard this connection as analytic, but as synthetic (through the idea of freedom; see *G.* 4:420, 447). And, secondly, such an analytic connection would make things even worse for Kant: if a law cannot be prescriptive, because no type of imperatives would be adequate to express it, an analytic link between 'right' and 'ought' would mean that the law could not even define what is right. This would obviously be absurd. By contrast, the view that the law, as such, is not prescriptive in the relevant sense may be paradoxical; but, as will emerge below, it is not absurd.

[15] For an attempt to demystify this Kantian doctrine, see Marcus Willaschek, *Praktische Vernunft. Handlungstheorie und Moralbegründung bei Kant* (Stuttgart/Weimar: Metzler, 1992), §10.

action under a categorical imperative of reason' (*MS* 6:222). But then the intended impact of the law could only be to necessitate the will of rational beings 'through the mere representation of this action itself' (Kant's definition of a categorical imperative (*MS* 6:222))—that is, to make them obey the law for its own sake. That, however, would violate the externality of the law. Therefore, Kant is forced to clarify that the universal law of Right 'does not at all expect, far less demand', obedience for its own sake. But since, as an unconditionally binding law of reason, it cannot *demand* compliance only on condition of some motive or other, Kant has no choice but to deny the prescriptive character of the law altogether: 'instead, reason only says that freedom, in its idea, *is* limited . . . and that it may also be physically limited by others' (*MS* 6:222).

Before I turn to other passages in order to confirm this interpretation, I want to consider briefly what seems to be a way out of the paradox under consideration.

IV. Habermas on Factual Coercion and Normative Validity

In his *Faktizität und Geltung*, Habermas calls the Kantian idea that juridical laws, regardless of their moral acceptability, only demand 'objective' compliance, a 'paradox'.[16] Although he does not elaborate on this, the paradox mentioned by Habermas and the one investigated here seem to be essentially the same: as Habermas sees it, the moral acceptability of juridical laws is a necessary condition for their normative validity; but still, they differ from moral norms in that compliance with them does not require a moral stance and thus can, and may, be enforced by coercion. This is paradoxical in that the reason why juridical laws are normatively valid seems to be unconnected to the only motivation for compliance the law itself supplies.

Interestingly, Habermas finds the solution for this Kantian paradox in Kant's own notion of 'legality': juridical norms, under different perspectives, are both coercive laws and laws of freedom. Therefore, they allow their addressees two different stances towards them: we can regard a juridical law and the threat of coercion and punishment connected with it as a merely factual constraint on our behaviour, to be taken into account for prudential reasons; if we obey the law for these reasons, our actions have, in Kantian terms, 'legality' but not 'morality'. However, we can also consider the law as being either legitimate or

---

[16] Jürgen Habermas, *Faktizität und Geltung* (Frankfurt/M: Suhrkamp, 1992), 47.

illegitimate and, if the former, obey it out of 'respect for the law'.[17] Although both perspectives exclude each other,[18] each is available at any given time. The *point* of valid juridical laws, according to Habermas, is that they are supposed to guarantee both: factual compliance, if necessarily enforced by coercion, and a kind of legitimacy that makes it possible to obey them out of respect for the law.[19] Habermas thus sees Kant's notion of legality as a model for the mediation of 'facticity' and 'legitimacy' in modern legal systems.[20]

Applied to the conflict between the three theses mentioned above, Habermas's solution comes to this: the Unconditionality Thesis concerns not motivation, but normative validity. It says that the normative validity of juridical laws does not depend on empirical motivation; according to Kant, it presupposes no material ends, but only freedom of choice (see *MS* 6:222). The Externality Thesis, by contrast, does not concern normative validity, but factual motivation: juridical laws do not require obedience for any specific reason, which does not exclude that their normative validity depends, precisely, on the *possibility* of obeying them out of respect for the law. While the Unconditionality and Prescriptivity Theses express a normative perspective on the law, the Externality Thesis expresses the possibility, and legitimacy, of a purely 'strategic' perspective on the law. By distinguishing between these two perspectives, it is possible to combine the three theses in question.

The problem with this proposal, however, is that the distinction between the two perspectives simply comes down to the distinction between Right and Ethics. Habermas is correct that there is a perspective available from which it is possible to obey juridical laws out of respect for the law. But, according to Kant, this perspective is an ethical one, from which we do not only require that people in fact obey the law, but also require a specific motive. When it comes to law, strictly speaking, however, we must abstract from people's motivation for acting rightly. Therefore, from this perspective, the thought that the legitimacy of a given law might motivate someone to obey it is not available. To be sure, only if the law is legitimate is one obligated to obey it.[21] But, if the law is legitimate, one is obligated to obey it, whatever one's reasons. Since the law can neither require one to obey the law for its own sake (by issuing categorical imperatives) nor require one to obey the law under the condition that

---

¹⁷ Ibid.   ¹⁸ Ibid. 49.   ¹⁹ Ibid.   ²⁰ Cf. ibid. 47, 143 ff.

²¹ According to Kant, a law is legitimate if (*a*) it follows from (is an instance of) the Universal Principle of Right or (*b*) if it is issued by a legitimate legislator (cf. *MS* 6:224, 230). Since legitimate legislators may issue laws that conflict with the Universal Principle of Right, this means that there can be formally legitimate, but materially unjust laws (cf. *MS* 6:318–23). Kant holds that the material injustice of a law neither ethically nor juridically warrants breaking it (unless it conflicts with 'inner morality' (*MS* 6:371), which presumably means that it requires one to act contrary to the Moral Law).

one pursue some material end or other (by issuing a hypothetical imperative), it seems that, according to Kant, the law cannot prescriptively *require* one to obey at all, but can only coerce one into compliance. Put differently, the fact that there is a juridical duty to do something, independently of ethical considerations and apart from coercion, does not give me a *reason* to act accordingly.[22] As has been argued by Mark Timmons, among others, Kant is an 'internalist' about moral obligation in the following sense: to be morally obligated to do something, according to Kant, implies the existence of a corresponding motive (namely, the motive of respect for the moral law).[23] As Kant's account of (both categorical and hypothetical) imperatives makes clear, he is also an internalist about normative requirements (prescriptions) in general: to be normatively required to do something implies the existence of a corresponding motive. Concerning obligations generated by juridical laws, however, Kant cannot be an internalist, since together with the Externality Thesis this would imply that, where external coercion, for contingent reasons, fails to supply a motive, there is no (juridical) obligation to obey the law. Of course, Kant wants to be able to say that one is obligated to obey the law in any case. But since this obligation, as such, does not provide a motive to act accordingly, on Kant's internalist view about normative requirements, it cannot be understood as *prescribing* or *requiring* something, but merely as indicating what, according to the law, would be the right thing to do. Again we end up with the paradoxical result that, once we abstract from motivation in the way the Externality Thesis demands, juridical laws, as such, cannot be prescriptive. I will now turn to various passages where Kant himself seems to acknowledge this consequence.

V. Coercion, Necessitation, and Strict Right

(*a*) Coercion and Necessitation in Kant's Lectures

In §D of the Introduction to the *Doctrine of Right*, Kant argues that it *follows* 'by the principle of contradiction' that Right is 'connected with an authorisation to use coercion' (*MS* 6:231). Since an action is 'right' if it is 'consistent with freedom in accordance with universal laws', any coercion is right that is 'a

---

[22] Again, this consequence of Kant's conception of Right has been noted by Allen Wood; see Wood, this volume.

[23] See Timmons, this volume (sect. II (*a*)), as well as Mark Timmons, 'Kant and the Possibility of Moral Motivation', *Southern Journal of Philosophy*, 23 (1985), 377–98.

hindering of a hindrance to freedom' (*MS* 6:231)—to freedom, that is, within the limits of Right.[24] In *The Metaphysics of Morals*, Kant is not very explicit about what rightful coercion consists in. But, in his lectures on ethics, on moral philosophy, and on the philosophy of right (as documented by extensive students' transcripts), we find detailed reflections on the concept of coercion.[25] There Kant defines 'coercion' (*Zwang*) as the 'necessitation of a reluctant act' (see Mro. 27:1416; similarly *MS* 6:379) and distinguishes between 'objective' and 'subjective' necessitation, on the one hand, and 'pathological' and 'practical' coercion, on the other (see Mro. 27:1407, 1416). (Since coercion is a species of necessitation, Kant also speaks of subjective/objective coercion and of practical/pathological necessitation.)

Subjective necessitation flows from those subjective impulses, which have, at a given time, the greatest causal power on a person's will; objective necessitation consists in there being reasons for an act that derive from its 'goodness' (*Bonitaet*) (Mro. 27:1416). This 'goodness' can be instrumental, prudential, or moral, and it gives rise to imperatives, which can be 'problematical', 'pragmatical', or 'categorical', respectively (Mro. 27:1407). These imperatives are the 'formulae' (*Formeln*) of the respective kinds of objective necessitation (Mro. 27:1407)—that is, they give expression to the impact of the 'objective' reasons on the 'subjective' will. Thus, objective necessitation is *prescriptive*, while subjective necessitation is *factual* (causal).[26]

The distinction between 'pathological' and 'practical' coercion, by contrast, concerns the proximal causes through which coercion proceeds: if an act is made necessary by physiological or psychological factors (*per stimulos*, impulses), the coercion is pathological (from Greek *pathos*, affection); if it is 'necessitated' by rational considerations (*per motiva*), however, the coercion is practical (cf. Col. 27:257, 1416). Although the distinctions between the subjective and the objective, on the one hand, and between the pathological and the practical, on the other, stress different aspects of agency, Kant regards them

[24] The idea of an analytic connection between right and coercion is not peculiar to Kant; it can be found in many writers of the time—for instance, in Baumgarten, on whose *Initia philosophiae practicae* Kant's lectures on ethics were based (see *Initia* §61, repr. in 19:7–91). What Kant, in his lectures, takes credit for is to have *derived* the authorization to coerce from the definition of right (see *Naturrecht Feyerabend*, 27:1335). On this, see Marcus Willaschek, '"Verhinderung eines Hindernisses der Freiheit" und "Zweiter Zwang". Bemerkungen zur Begründung des Zwangsrechts bei Kant und Hegel', in Barbara Merker, George Mohr, and Michael Quante (eds.), *Subjektivität und Anerkennung* (Frankfurt: Suhrkamp, forthcoming).

[25] In what follows, I will mainly draw on the so-called Philosophische Moral Mrongovius (Mro. 27:1397–1581), which dates from the early 1780s. Very similar passages can be found in several other transcripts.

[26] This is the reason why in Kant the distinction between the 'subjective' and 'objective', with respect to the will, parallels the one between 'what in fact does happen' and 'what ought to happen' (see *G*. 4:420–1 n., 427; *KpV* 5:19). This usage is still present in *The Metaphysics of Morals* (see *MS* 6:218, 225).

as coextensional: 'Practical necessitation is an objective necessitation of a free action, pathological is a subjective necessitation' (Mro. 27:1407; cf. Mro. 27:1417). Both 'subjective' necessitation and 'pathological' coercion are defined as proceeding 'per stimulos', while 'objective' necessitation is defined as 'the necessity of an act out of objective motives', and 'practical' coercion as necessitation 'per motiva' or 'motives of reason' (Mro. 27:1416).

Since human choice is free (an *arbitrum liberum*), and pathological coercion is incompatible with freedom, Kant holds that, strictly speaking, all coercion of humans is practical coercion. And practical coercion, it turns out, is not really coercion (necessitation) at all: Man 'is not coerced, but convinced [*bewogen*]' (Mro. 27:1417). Nevertheless, 'man can be coerced pathologically, but only *comparatively*, for example, by torture' (Mro. 27:1417). Even though their freedom, in principle, allows humans to withstand *any* pathological coercion, exercising this freedom becomes increasingly difficult the stronger the 'stimuli' are. In so far as humans *can* be pathologically coerced (namely 'comparatively'), 'the means of pathological coercion regard the representation of the consequences connected with the act and proceed a. *per placentia* . . . b. *per minas* . . . *Placentia* et *minas* are also called *extorsiones*, because by [their] representation one tries to elicit in people that degree of inclination of which one believes that human freedom will not have sufficient power for [overcoming] it' (Vig. 27:521).

As the context makes clear, this is precisely the kind of coercion connected with juridical laws (cf. Vig. 27:522–3, 1419). This is echoed in *The Metaphysics of Morals*, where Kant says that the specifically juridical incentive 'must be drawn from *pathological* determining grounds of choice, inclinations and aversions' (*MS* 6:219).[27] Since pathological coercion, qua 'subjective', is opposed to 'objective' or 'practical' coercion (coercion through imperatives based on reasons of goodness), it becomes apparent that the kind of necessitation connected with the law cannot be prescriptive (*per motiva*, 'through reasons of goodness'), but only factual coercion (*per stimulos*).[28] This is confirmed by a *Reflexion* from the early 1780s, where Kant writes that, as far as external (juridical) laws are concerned, 'the motive is not duty. *The ought here is coercion*. We are not required to do from inner motives what we are coercively

---

[27] Kant does not mention purely physical means of coercion, such as bodily resistance or detention (probably because Baumgarten explicitly sets physical coercion aside; see *Initia* §50). But we may assume that physical coercion is included in the juridical repertoire as final measure. In the late 1770s, Kant notes: 'He who has a right against someone can disturb him in every joy, snatch him from the altar. . . . The capacity to coerce is power [*Gewalt*]' (*Ref.* 7006, 7008, 19:224–5).

[28] However, in the same lecture Kant says: 'All *obligationes* whose motives are subjective or internal, are ethical obligations; all *obligationes*, however, whose motives are objective or external, are juridical in the

ordered to do. The *imperativus iuridicus* is *externe tantum obligans* and not at all moral. It is the imperative of rightful power [*Gewalt*] and its *necessitating force, too*, is only in proportion to this power' (Ref. 7271, 19:299; first and last emphases added).

(*b*) The Two Elements in All Lawgiving

The distinction between 'subjective' and 'objective' necessitation is present in *The Metaphysics of Morals*, too. There, Kant says that in 'all lawgiving . . . there are two elements: first, a law, which represents an action that is to be done as *objectively* necessary, that is, which makes the action a duty; and second, an incentive, which connects a ground for determining choice to this action *sub-jectively* with the representation of the law' (*MS* 6:218). It may seem that here we have a distinction that allows us to dissolve the paradox of juridical imper-atives: while juridical laws 'objectively' require their addressees to obey them, 'subjectively' the laws are enforced by coercion. But Kant immediately blocks this way by continuing: 'By the first [element] the action is represented as a duty, and this is a *merely theoretical cognition* of a possible determination of choice, that is, of practical rules. By the second the obligation so to act is con-nected in the subject with a ground for determining choice generally' (*MS* 6:218; emphasis added). A 'merely theoretical cognition' of a practical rule means: knowing what one would have to do if one were to act on that rule. Thus, the fact that Kant calls this 'representing the action as duty' does not mean that the first of the two 'elements' in all lawgiving is *prescriptive*.[29]

Prescriptive rules of action (imperatives (see *MS* 6:220)), on Kant's view, arise from the possible conflict between what is objectively right and what is subjectively desired (see *G.* 4:413). Where subjective inclinations can conflict with insights of practical reasons, these insights (the theoretical cognition of

---

strict sense' (Mro. 27:1420). Since, immediately before, Kant had defined 'objective motives' as 'reasons for what we ought to do', this seems to contradict the above interpretation. But, on the other hand, Kant says that the 'internal motive' is called 'duty', the 'external motive' is called coercion. This shows that the terms 'subjective' and 'objective' must have a different meaning when applied to motives from the one they have when applied to kinds of necessitation or coercion (since external coercion is subjective necessitation, but an objective motive). In any case, in the lectures, things may not be quite as straightforward as I present them in the text. Moreover, we must be careful in attributing the views expounded in the lectures to Kant, and to the Kant of *The Metaphysics of Morals* in particular. The general distinction between the objective/practi-cal/normative, on the one hand, and the subjective/pathological/factual, however, is clearly still present in the later writings and therefore can be drawn on in interpreting Kant's views in *The Metaphysics of Morals*.

[29] See Leslie A. Mulholland, *Kant's System of Rights* (New York: Columbia University Press, 1990), 145, for a different interpretation according to which the first 'element' falls into two parts, one of which is an imperative. Since imperatives, for Kant, are '*practical* rules' (*MS* 6:222), this interpretation does not seem to fit Kant's claim that the first element contains a merely 'theoretical cognition'.

practical rules) take on a prescriptive character and are supposed to *motivate* the required behaviour, to become an 'incentive'. If in fact they do, the action is said to have been done 'out of respect for the law' or 'from duty'.[30] This incentive is the second element in 'ethical lawgiving'. 'Juridical lawgiving', by contrast, is characterized by the fact that the incentive (which makes what is objectively necessary subjectively efficacious) is not the idea of duty (*MS* 6:219), but 'external coercion' (*MS* 6:220).[31] It is this distinction between juridical and ethical lawgiving on which Kant's distinction between Right and Ethics is based[32] and which excludes that juridical laws are prescriptive: since in the realm of Right we abstract from what 'internally' motivates people to obey, or disobey, the law, and rely exclusively on 'external' coercion, we abstract precisely from the prescriptive, or normative, force of practical laws. It seems, then, that these laws cannot *require* someone to do something, but only *warrant* the use of coercion in order to bring about lawful behaviour.

(c) Strict Right

Consequently, in the Introduction to the *Doctrine of Right*, Kant represents the realm of Right not as a realm of rights *and obligations*, but merely as a realm of rights, conceived of as authorizations to coerce. As Kant announces in the title of §E, 'strict' Right ('that which is not mingled with anything ethical' (*MS* 6:232)),[33] 'can also be presented as the possibility of a complete and reciprocal coercion consistent with everyone's freedom in accordance with universal laws (*MS* 6:232).[34] And he proceeds: 'This proposition says, in effect, that Right should not be conceived as made up of two elements, namely an obligation in accordance with a law and an authorization of him who by his choice puts another under obligation to coerce him to fulfil it. Instead, one can locate the concept of Right directly in the possibility of connecting universal reciprocal

---

[30] For a more detailed account, see Willaschek, *Praktische Vernunft*, §§4, 10.

[31] Therefore, the sentence following the distinction between the two kinds of lawgiving ('Hence the second element is this: that the law makes duty the incentive' (*MS* 6:218)) can apply only to ethical laws, not to juridical laws.

[32] See Kersting, *Wohlgeordnete Freiheit. Immanuel Kants Rechts und Staatsphilosophie*, 175; Willaschek, 'Why the *Doctrine of Right* does not belong in the *Metaphysics of Morals*', 217–18. Contrary to positivist ways of drawing this distinction, Kant draws his Right/Ethics distinction *within* natural law, solely with respect to the motive sufficient to guarantee compliance with the respective laws. (This distinction is prefigured in Kant's lectures from the 1780s (see Mro. 27:1418–19).)

[33] Although 'strict Right' primarily contrasts with 'Right in a wide sense (*ius latum*)' (*MS* 6:233–4), Kant actually explains what strict right is by way of contrast to the 'moral concept of right'.

[34] Gregor translates 'durchgängigen wechselseitigen Zwanges' in the title of §E as 'fully reciprocal coercion', reading 'durchgängigen' as an adverb that qualifies 'wechselseitig', which is grammatically impossible. What Kant speaks of is a 'complete' or 'thoroughgoing' coercion.

coercion with the freedom of everyone' (*MS* 6:232). Here, Kant is not merely saying that an obligation and the corresponding authorization to coerce should be seen as two sides of the same coin. His view is more radical than that: for some person A to be under a juridical obligation to do F *just means* that others are juridically authorized to coerce A into doing F. This radical view follows immediately from the non-prescriptive character of the law: if an obligation is 'the necessity of a free action under a categorical imperative of reason' (*MS* 6:222), and if there can be no juridical imperatives, obligations can play no role in 'strict Right'. All that remain are authorizations to coerce.[35] Kant thus turns the paradox that juridical laws, on his account, cannot be prescriptive, into a positive doctrine: a conception of Right that completely sets aside anything ethical has no need for prescriptions and imperatives.

Kant emphasizes that strict Right, too, is 'based on everyone's consciousness of obligation in accordance with a law' (*MS* 6:232). But this obligation does not have any prescriptive force, and therefore we 'may not and cannot' (*MS* 6:232) appeal to it in order to motivate others to act in accordance with Right. Once we abstract from all ethical considerations, authorizations to coerce others into lawful behaviour are all that remain of the idea of Right. Kant gives the following example: 'Thus when it is said that a creditor has a right to require his debtor to pay his debt, this does not mean that he can remind the debtor that his reason itself puts him under an obligation to perform this' (*MS* 6:232; emphasis added). In his lectures, Kant had used the same example to illustrate the possibility of external 'moral coercion' (practical coercion of others through moral, as opposed to pragmatic, motives): 'for example, when I owe something to someone, and the other person says: if you want to be an honest man, you must pay me; I don't want to sue you, but I cannot release you, because I need it, then this is external moral coercion through someone else's choice' (Mro. 27:1418). In the terminology of *The Metaphysics of Morals*, the other person is 'reminding me' that my own reason puts me under an obligation to pay my debts. So why does Kant, in *The Metaphysics of Morals*, hold that the creditor *cannot* 'remind the debtor that his reason itself puts him under an obligation', as far as Right is concerned? The answer should now be obvious: because this would 'remind' him of a categorical imperative, which requires compliance for its own sake and is therefore inadmissible in law. Hence, the 'right to require his debtor to pay his debt' simply comes down to an authorization to coerce him into paying. In the passage from *The Meta-*

---

[35] It is these authorizations that distinguish rightful uses of coercion from pure violence; of course, someone may thus be authorized (having a right that puts others under an obligation) without being able, or willing, to make use of it.

physics of Morals, Kant continues: 'it [the right to require the debtor to pay] means, instead, that coercion that constrains everyone to pay his debts can coexist with the freedom of everyone, including the debtor's, in accordance with a universal external law: *Right and authorisation to use coercion therefore mean one and the same thing*' (MS 6:232; emphasis added).

Surely people often feel obliged to do what is juridically right, quite independently of any external coercion. And indeed there is such an obligation. But, according to Kant, it cannot be appealed to in a strictly juridical context, since there it is not available as something that might prescribe, and thereby motivate, rightful behaviour.

This view, which excludes obligations corresponding to subjective rights as irrelevant from the realm of Right altogether, can be found not only in *The Metaphysics of Morals*, but (restricted to subjective rights in the state of nature) already in Kant's 1784 review of Hufeland's *Versuch über den Grundsatz des Naturrechts*:

Although he [Hufeland] bases the whole science of natural rights on obligations, he nevertheless warns us not to understand them as the obligation of others to satisfy our right (Hobbes already notes that, where coercion accompanies our demands, no obligation of others to subject to this coercion can still be thought). From this he [Hufeland] infers *that the doctrine of obligations in natural Right is superfluous* and may often mislead. *In this the reviewer readily joins the author.* For here the question is only under which conditions I may exert coercion without contradicting the universal principles of *Right*. Whether the other person, according to the same principles, may remain passive or react is his affair to investigate as long as we consider everything in the state of nature. ('Hufeland–Rezension', 8:128; emphasis added)

What Kant 'readily' agrees to in his Hufeland review and what is implicit in the Introduction to the *Doctrine of Right* is not just the Hobbesian point,[36] mentioned by Kant, that I have an unalienable right to self-preservation and therefore no obligation to 'remain passive' when coerced. Rather, Kant accepts Hufeland's stronger claim that, as far as natural right is concerned, obligations drop out of the picture entirely; all we need are conditions for the rightful use of coercion.[37] Juridical laws as such, independently of ethical considerations,

[36] A 'man cannot lay down the right of resisting them, that assault him by force, to take away his life. . . . The same may be sayd of Wounds, and Chayns, and Imprisonment' (Thomas Hobbes, *Leviathan*, ed. Richard Tuck (Cambridge: Cambridge University Press, 1991), 93; cf. 98, 151).

[37] As the end of the quote from the Hufeland review indicates, the situation is different in a civil state; Kant continues: 'in a civil state, the judge's verdict, which grants the right to one party, always corresponds to an obligation of the opponent' ('Hufeland–Rezension', 8:128). See also Vig. 27:528: 'In *statu naturali*

do not *require* anyone to do something; they only issue *warrants* to coerce those who hinder other people's rightful use of freedom.[38]

Let me repeat that the view I attribute to Kant does not collapse the realm of Right into a system of merely coercive acts. Right consists in authorizations, which are *normative* statuses, and someone may be thus authorized without being willing, or able, to make use of this authorization. Also, I do not deny that there is, according to Kant, an obligation to act lawfully that takes on a prescriptive character quite independent from other people's authorization to coerce—namely, an *ethical* obligation. But juridical laws as such, on this view, are not prescriptive. They do not tell us what to do and what not to do; they merely authorize the use of coercion in accordance with universal laws. As I will argue in the next section, this non-prescriptive conception of (strict) Right is also implicit in Kant's favoured analogy for the realm of Right, the movement of bodies under the law of equality of action and reaction.

VI. Kant's Dynamical Model of Right

In §E of the Introduction to the *Doctrine of Right*, Kant calls the 'law of a reciprocal coercion necessarily in accord with the freedom of everyone under the principle of universal freedom' a 'representation' of the concept of strict Right (*MS* 6:232). Further, Kant claims that there holds an analogy between this representation of Right and the possibility of bodies moving freely under 'the law of the equality of action and reaction' (*MS* 6:232), which Kant in the *Critique of Judgment* even uses as a paradigmatic case of an analogy (*KU* 5:464–5). This idea is present not only in the *Doctrine of Right*, but also in Kant's *Reflexionen* from the 1760s, his lectures from the 1780s, and in several of his published writings.[39] Unfortunately, Kant never spells out in detail what the analogy consists in.

In order to understand the point of the analogy, I suggest looking briefly at Kant's discussion of the 'law of the equality of action and reaction' (Newton's

everyone is in the state of his private right; he determines his and the rights of other men according to his own judgement and seeks to achieve them according to his own power [*nach eigener Gewalt*]. . . . If somebody enters *in statum civilem*, however, he is also obliged to subject to public justice.'

[38]   In the review of Hufeland, Kant continues: 'Further, this remark is very useful in natural law in order not to tangle the proper ground of Right [*den eigentlichen Rechtsgrund*] with an admixture of ethical questions' ('Hufeland–Rezension', 8:128). This, too, is echoed in *The Metaphysics of Morals* in the distinction between the 'moral concept of Right' and the 'strict Right': while (only) the former 'is related to an obligation corresponding to it' (*MS* 6:230), the latter 'is not mingled with anything ethical' (*MS* 6:231).

[39]   Cf. e.g. 'Bemerkungen zu den Beobachtungen über das Gefuehl des Schönen und Erhabenen', 20:165; *Ref.* 6667, 19:128; *Naturrecht Feyerabend*, 27:1335; *KU* 5:464; GTP 8:292.

Third Law) in his *Metaphysical Foundations of Natural Science* (*MAN* 4:544–51).[40] There, he distinguishes a 'mechanical' version of that law (which concerns the *transmission* of motion) from a 'dynamical' version (*MAN* 4:548). Since Kant, in *The Metaphysics of Morals*, calls the concept of Right, represented as 'fully reciprocal and equal coercion brought under a universal law', a 'dynamical concept' (*MS* 6:233), we may assume that it is the dynamical law that Kant has in mind.[41] And, indeed, what Kant has to say about it precisely fits his analogy to Right:

There is yet another, namely a dynamical law of the equality of action and reaction of matters, not in so far as one transmits its motion to the other, but in so far as one originally invests the other with it and, through resistance of the other, at the same time generates motion in itself. . . . when matter A attracts matter B, it forces B to approach, or, which is the same, A resists the force by which B seeks to move away. But, since it is just the same whether B moves away from A or A from B, this resistance at the same time is a resistance that B exerts on A in so far as A seeks to move away from B. Thus, pull and counterpull are equal to each other. Equally, when A pushes back matter B, A resists the approach of B. But, since it is one and the same whether B approaches A or A approaches B, B equally resists the approach of A; thus pressure and counterpressure, too, always equal each other.   (*MAN* 4:548–9)

If we consider two bodies (or 'matters') A and B as analogous to two people C and D under juridical laws, what corresponds to pressure and counterpressure (or to pull and counterpull, respectively) in the juridical sphere? Since Kant talks of 'reciprocal coercion', one might at first think that A's pressure on B corresponds to C's coercing of D, while B's counterpressure corresponds to D's coercing of C. The analogy would then say that it is possible to represent strict Right, with respect to C and D, as a situation in which C's coercion of D is equal to D's coercion of C (and in accordance with their freedom under universal laws).

But that does not make sense: if C owes money to D, but D does not owe money to C, C may rightfully coerce D to pay the debt, but not vice versa. How, then, can there be equality of rightful coercion? The point of the analogy becomes apparent when we consider Kant's derivation of the authorization to

[40]   For a different reference to *The Metaphysical Foundations of Natural Science* in a similar context, see Matthias Kaufmann, 'The Relation between Right and Coercion: Analytic or Synthetic?', *Jahrbuch für Recht und Ethik*, 5 (1997), 77–8. Kaufmann argues that the connection between Right and coercion, according to Kant, is synthetic, in so far as these concepts are applicable to human beings.

[41]   See also *KU* 5:464–5, where Kant, in drawing the analogy in question, refers to the 'law of equality of action and reaction in the reciprocal attraction and repulsion of bodies', which is the dynamical, not the mechanical, version of the law.

coerce in §D of the Introduction to the *Doctrine of Right*: 'Resistance that coun-teracts the hindering of an effect promotes this effect and is consistent with it. Now whatever is wrong is a hindrance to freedom in accordance to universal laws. But coercion is a hindrance or resistance to freedom'; therefore, coercion that acts 'as a hindering of a hindrance of freedom' is right (*MS* 6:231).

Here, too, we have forces and counterforces: free agency in accordance with universal laws, on the one hand, free agency *not* in accordance with universal laws, on the other. The latter is a 'hindrance or resistance' to the former, since the universal laws in question limit the freedom of one only where it conflicts with the rightful freedom of others. (For instance, they allow me to use my money as I please, unless I owe some of it to someone else.) Now, in order to prevent wrongful behaviour, what is necessary (and therefore 'right') is a coercive force precisely as strong as the resistance against rightful uses of freedom: a weaker force would not achieve its end of securing rightful uses of freedom, a stronger force than necessary would itself amount to a hindrance of rightful freedom. (If a creditor coerces a debtor into paying by breaking his bones, he violates the rights of the debtor—that is, his freedom in accordance with universal laws.)

Returning to Kant's analogy, we now can see that what corresponds in the realm of Right to pressure and counterpressure in dynamics is the *resistance* to rightful uses of freedom, on the one hand, and rightful uses of *coercion*, on the other. Coercion must be equal to the hindrance of rightful freedom. As we have seen above, this can be achieved if the coercion connected with the laws is such that it elicits 'in people that degree of inclination of which one believes that human freedom will not have sufficient power for [overcoming] it' (Vig. 27:521). Thus, a legal system of 'complete and reciprocal coercion' (*MS* 6:232) would not leave its subjects any choice as to whether they want to obey the law or not.[42] After all, there is no right to the *possibility* of breaking the law. As long as a system of coercion is consistent with everyone's freedom under universal laws, it does not restrict the *rightful* use of freedom at all. Rather, if effective, it secures everyone's freedom by restricting it to the conditions of its rightful use.

Now under a legal system in which coercion really equals the hindrance of rightful freedom, the idea of prescriptions or imperatives does not apply: just as, according to Kant, the idea of a moral 'ought' is not applicable to a holy will, since such a will necessarily conforms with the moral law (*MS* 6:379, 383; cf.

---

[42] Therefore, no ethical motivation is necessary to establish a legal system. In 'Perpetual Peace', Kant famously claims that the task of devising such a system could be solved even for 'a race of devils', that is, a people of malevolent, but rational egoists: 'it requires only that we know how to apply the mechanism of nature to men so as to organize the conflict of hostile attitudes present in a people in such a way that they must compel one another to submit to coercive laws' (EF 8:366); see also the mechanistic metaphors for the workings of a state in I. 8:25 and WA 8:37.

MS 6:222), the idea of a juridical 'ought' would not be applicable to a people under a perfect legal system, since they are forced to obey its laws anyway. A law that not only adequately describes the actual behaviour of human beings, but even supports predictions and counterfactuals (and therefore cannot possibly be violated), is not a prescriptive law (a norm) at all, but a descriptive law on a par with the laws of nature. This is just what Kant's analogy between Right and dynamics suggests: if 'complete and reciprocal coercion' in analogy with bodies under the law of equality of action and reaction is, as Kant claims, the appropriate intuitive representation of the concept of Right, we end up with a purely non-prescriptive conception of Right. We can still say that, as with God and the holy will of angels, evaluative terms such as 'good' and 'right' are applicable even where a given behaviour necessarily conforms to a (moral or juridical) law. But *prescriptive* expressions such as 'should' and 'ought to' make no sense where those to whom they are addressed cannot but obey the laws in question.

That Kant's conception of strict Right does not leave room for prescriptions is further confirmed by considering how the 'dynamical' model of Right hangs together with Kant's views about subjective rights. On this model, having a right to do something is equivalent to having the right to exercise one's freedom (that is, to act in a particular way). What A's exercising a right consists in depends on whether A meets with 'resistance' or not. If there is no resistance, A just does what she has a right to do. If B 'hinders' A in exercising her right, however, the only way in which A can exercise her right is by coercing B to comply. Thus, on this model, there is as little room for the idea that someone standing under a juridical obligation might anticipate the coercion and comply voluntarily as there is room for the idea that one body anticipates the pressure of another body by initiating the counterpressure on its own. Kant's analogy between Right and dynamics therefore implies that in a case of conflict there is no leeway between someone's making use of her right and her use of coercion: if someone's freedom is unwarrantedly limited by someone else, her rightfully acting as she chooses *consists* in overcoming a 'hindrance to freedom' (that is, in coercion).

Of course, it is humanly impossible to realize a juridical system that works in analogy with a dynamical system. All actual juridical systems leave much room for rational deliberation and free choice as to whether one wants to obey the law or not. But these, according to Kant, are empirical imperfections that do not concern the *concept* of strict Right. The distinction between voluntary and coerced compliance that these imperfections make applicable is juridically irrelevant—that is just what the Externality Thesis says. In closing, I now want to ask whether the fact that actual legal systems only approximate the idea of strict Right allows us to evade the paradox from which we started.

VII. The Paradox Tamed

Obviously, there is no problem for Kant to explain how *ethical* laws can be pre-scriptive, since they explicitly require obedience from the idea of duty and thus can find adequate expression in categorical imperatives. And, as we have seen, Kant allows a perspective on juridical laws that treats them as demands of Ethics: 'all duties, just because they are duties, belong to Ethics' (*MS* 6:219; cf. *MS* 6:394). In the case of the duty of Right to fulfil one's contracts, for instance, ethics teaches that 'if the incentive which juridical lawgiving connects with that duty, namely external constraint, were absent, the idea of duty itself would be sufficient as an incentive' (*MS* 6:220). In this sense, one categorically ought to obey not only the laws of Ethics but also the laws of Right.[43]

In real life, juridical laws and duties are typically not considered in isolation from ethical considerations in the Kantian sense. After all, we *do* demand, and often expect, ourselves and others to obey the law 'even where no coercion must be feared', which, according to Kant, is an ethical duty, not a juridical one (see *MS* 6:220). Could this be the key to a dissolution of our paradox?

Strict Right, conceived as the possibility of a system of reciprocal coercion consistent with everyone's freedom under universal laws, may really allow no place for prescriptive requirements, since it 'requires only external grounds for determining choice;[44] for only then is it pure and not mixed with any precepts of virtue. Only a *completely* external Right can therefore be called *strict* (Right in the narrow sense)' (*MS* 6:232). But it is obvious that no existing system of Right will ever meet this criterion. Kant's conception of strict Right is a mere idealization for purposes of theoretical exposition; it *abstracts* from the ethical consid-erations with which, in real life, Right is always 'mingled'. So I suggest we understand Kant as saying that juridical laws indeed are prescriptive, but *only* when considered from an ethical perspective.[45] In effect, this would be Haber-mas's solution considered above, with the single difference that the law as such, considered as strict Right, would still not be prescriptive. Juridical laws allow a

---

[43] Is Kant referring to this ethical perspective on the realm of Right when he speaks of 'the concept of Right, in so far as it is related to an obligation [*Verbindlichkeit*] corresponding to it (i.e. the moral concept of Right)'? Since Kant terminologically distinguishes between 'moral' and 'ethical' (*MS* 6:214), this seems improbable. On the other hand, an obligation is analytically linked to a categorical imperative, which, as we have seen, can only belong to Ethics, but not to Right. It seems to me to be an open question how the 'moral' concept of Right relates to 'strict Right', on the one hand, and to juridical laws and duties considered as part of Ethics, on the other.

[44] That strict Right *requires* only external determining grounds of choice of course means not 'requires of its subjects that they act only on external determining grounds', but 'requires, in order to function properly, nothing but external determining grounds'.

[45] In the 'Appendix to the Introduction to the *Doctrine of Right*', Kant seems to imply that something deserves the name of 'Right' only if it is strict: both equity and the so-called right of necessity, which accord-ing to Kant people think of as 'Right in a *wider* sense (*ius latum*)', turn out not to belong to the Kantian

perspective under which they turn out to be prescriptive, but this perspective is an ethical one; from this perspective, people ask for normatively binding reasons to obey a given law, and, if the law indeed is unconditonally valid (is binding irrespective of prudential reasons), then there is such a reason to obey the law—which, because of the unconditional validity, is a reason to obey it for its own sake. But we cannot, at the same time and from the same perspective, abstract from motivation in the way required by the Externality Thesis. If we insist on externality, the prescriptive character of the law becomes invisible: all that remain are authorizations—not to prescribe, but to coerce others into rightful behaviour.

Unless we give up either the unconditionality or the externality of the law, the paradox of juridical imperatives will simply not go away. But, if the realm of Right is embedded in the broader perspective of morals (as Kant embeds the *Doctrine of Right* in *The Metaphysics of Morals*), the prescriptivity of juridical laws can be accommodated nonetheless.[46] Even if the paradox does not go away, in this way it can at least be tamed. I believe that it is an important insight on Kant's part, even though he never makes it explicit, that we *can* have both externality and prescriptivity of the law, but that, unless we give up the idea that the law must be valid unconditionally, we cannot have them at once from one and the same perspective.

---

realm of Right at all (see *MS* 6:233–6). But here Kant defines 'a right in the *narrow* sense (*ius strictum*)' as a right connected with an authorization to coerce (*MS* 6:233). First, this is most naturally understood as applying to subjective *rights*, rather than to the realm of *Right*. And, secondly, even when applied to the latter, this is much weaker than the definition of the preceding §E, where a system of Right is said to be strict if it is 'not mingled with anything ethical' and thus is 'completely external'. Strict Right in this latter sense may still be a mere idealization while any right (or Right) deserving its name has to be strict in the former sense (of carrying with it an authorization to coerce).

[46] In Willaschek, 'Why the *Doctrine of Right* does not belong in the *Metaphysics of Morals*', I argue that the *Doctrine of Right* does not really belong in *The Metaphysics of Morals* in the sense that juridical rights and duties do not follow from the Categorical Imperative, which defines the field of morals. When considered from the perspective of Kant's philosophy of Right, however, it now turns out that the *Doctrine of Right* does belong in *The Metaphyisics of Morals*, after all, since only in this broader context is it possible to accommodate the prescriptive character of the law.

4

A Kantian Justification of Possession

Kenneth R. Westphal

The nature and justification of rights to ownership have been both central and vexed in Modern and contemporary philosophy; central, because so many of our individual and joint activities depend on the use and distribution of goods; vexed, because there are competing definitions, justifications, and sets of rights to individual and joint use of goods. Kant believed that his Critical philosophy could both clarify and resolve some of the most basic issues involved in this debate. However, with rare exception, Kant has not been viewed as a major theorist on these topics.[1] This is due, in part, to the difficulty of Kant's philosophy, to the relative neglect of Kant's *Rechtslehre* even among Kant scholars until quite recently, and to the brevity and obscurity of Kant's arguments about the right to possession found therein. I contend, nevertheless, that Kant establishes some very significant points about our rights of possession.[2]

Kant recognized that the most important and controversial rights of possession are not analytic truths, and he followed Hume in holding that no norm can be justified solely on the basis of empirical evidence. Consequently, Kant regarded rights as a proper topic for his Critical philosophy, which aims to provide a priori justification for certain synthetic propositions. As he noted to himself, the central difficulty involved in justifying rights to possession is to show, in this instance, 'how synthetic propositions regarding right are possible a priori, that is, without presupposing another right, that is, possession' (Ak. 23:302.28–30).[3] With this, Kant rejects both the early Modern natural law fic-

I thank Onora O'Neill for helpful suggestions on a previous draft.

  [1] The exception is Jeremy Waldron, *The Right to Private Property* (Oxford: Clarendon Press, 1988).

  [2] Both Kant's discussion and my reconstruction of it raise many exegetical and philosophical issues that cannot be addressed here. I discuss them in 'Do Kant's Principles Justify Property or Usufruct?', *Jahrbuch für Recht und Ethik*, 5 (1997), 141–94. I ask that aficionados and sceptics please kindly consult that essay, which also remarks on the secondary literature. I wish to acknowledge my great debt to the pre-eminent work of Onora O'Neill.

  [3] All translations are mine. Occasionally, paragraph numbers are referred to within particular sections or line numbers are indicated by decimals.

tion of an original common ownership of the earth and the Lockean strategy of basing rights to property on ownership of one's own body. Though Kant's full account incorporates the notion of an original common ownership of the earth,[4] this notion has its home in a theocentric view of the world and began to wane in European political culture when Grotius realized that political philosophy must be made independent of theology, because religious schisms were too deep and too sustained to provide a univocal, uncontroversial basis for politics.[5] Locke's account, of course, directly raises two questions Locke failed to address: how do we have an ownership right at all in our own body, and why should labouring on some unclaimed object constitute its appropriation, rather than our loss of labour power? Kant is right to seek an original, rather than a derivative, justification of possession.

I have been speaking deliberately of 'possession' and 'ownership', rather than 'property'. Kant rightly presents his argument in terms of 'possession' (*Besitz*), not 'property' (*Eigentum*). Individual private property is a complex package of rights containing several distinct 'incidents'—that is, specific rights and liabilities.[6] These include:

1.   The right to *possess*: strictly, the exclusive right to control something physically, and freedom from unpermitted interference by others.

2.   The right to *use*: the owner's personal use and enjoyment of the thing in question.

3.   The right to *manage*: powers to decide how, when, and by whom something shall be used, including licensing, contracting its use or exploitation, permitting others to enter or use it, and defining the limits of such permission.

4.   The right to *income* from a thing: the right to any product of it or a reward for exploiting it or for permitting others to use it.

5.   The right to *capital* in the thing: the power to alienate something and the liberty to consume, waste, or destroy part or all of it.

[4]   See Jeffrey Edwards, 'Disjunktiv- und kollektiv-allegemeiner Besitz: Überlegungen zu Kants Theorie der ursprünglichen Erwerbung', in D. Hüning and B. Tuschling (eds.), *Recht, Staat und Völkerrecht bei Immanuel Kant* (Berlin: Duncker & Humblot, 1998), 121–39. Kant's 'Antinomy' concerning the possibility of possession (§7) also suggests that rights of possession could be generated without relying on the fiction of original common possession of the earth. I omit discussion of this Antinomy because it does not advance Kant's argument.

[5]   See J. B. Schneewind, *The Invention of Autonomy* (Cambridge: Cambridge University Press, 1998), chs. 2–4.

[6]   A. M. Honoré, 'Ownership', rpt. in E. A. Kent (ed.), *Law and Philosophy: Readings in Legal Philosophy* (New York: Appleton-Century-Crofts, 1970), 533–48, 537–8.

6.   The right to *security*: the right to remain something's owner indefinitely at will, provided one remains financially solvent.

7.   *Transmissibility*: the power to transfer something to a successor indefinitely. This absence of term means that a thing never ceases to be one's property.

8.   The *prohibition of harmful use*: the owner's right to use or to manage something is restricted to activities that do not directly harm others.

9.   *Liability to execution*: the liability to have property taken away for serious debt or insolvency.

10.   The right of *residuary*: the thing reverts to a particular party, the owner, whenever others' subsidiary rights to it lapse.

Given the complexity of private property rights, one may well doubt whether they could be justified a priori. One of Kant's lessons is that they cannot. Kant's a priori justification of ownership rights concerns only the rights to possession and to use, not to property. Unfortunately, this crucial distinction too often has been disregarded. If ordinary usage generally fails to distinguish 'property' from 'possession[s]', even the most low-level legal usage does: the criminal charge of 'being in possession of stolen goods' would be nonsense without a distinction between possession and property. Or, to remain within the realm of legitimate norms, even the most incidental rental contract gives one a temporary right to possess and to use someone else's property. Kant appears quite aware that most of the specific rights involved in individual private property can be specified, indeed constituted, only within the legal institutions of a specific society. They are thus topics of political debate and legislation. Kant's case for the legitimacy of the state, and of our obligation to be members of a state, rests on his justification of much more modest rights to possession.[7]

I shall reconstruct Kant's justification for rights to possession and show, briefly, that Kant's justification of rights to possession suffice for his justification of our membership in a (legitimately constituted) state. First, I present the key points of Kant's official justification of possession, largely following his order of discussion. This highlights some important issues, including the need

---

[7]   Sometimes it is suggested that Kant's terminological association of *Mein und Dein* with the Latin terms generally used for property, *meum vel tuum* (*MS* 6:237.24–5), or his association of *das Seine* with *Eigenthum* (property (*MS* 6:270.10–11)) shows that he must be attempting an a priori justification of property, not merely possession. This suggestion disregards the fact that Kant's metaphysical level of analysis and argument (on which, see below) must disregard the legal specifics required to define and to institute full-fledged property rights.

to reconstruct Kant's account because of some crucial oversights in his argument.

Kant opens his discussion (§1) by noting that something distinct from oneself is rightly one's own only if another's unauthorized use of it constitutes an injury. This relation, supposedly, can hold regardless of whether one currently detains the item physically. The intended relation is normative and intelligible, not merely factual and physical.

Kant also asserts that 'the subjective condition of the possibility of use in general is *possession* [*Besitz*]' (§1 ¶1). Kant's statement is an identity. Inverting it shows that his statement serves as a definition of possession: possession is the subjective condition of the possibility of use in general. This accords with Kant's repeated definition in his working notes of 'possession' and 'right' in terms of legitimate *use* of something.[8] As mentioned, Kant is right to focus on possession and use and to disregard the further incidents involved in property rights.

In §2 Kant states the 'Juridical Postulate of Practical Reason'. This Postulate purports to establish that any object of will can coherently be regarded, objectively, as possibly mine or yours (*MS* 6:246.33–5). This is to say, in principle, any thing may be possessed. Kant's Postulate states:

It is possible to have any external object of my will [*Willkür*] as mine; that is, any maxim according to which, if it were a law, an object of will must become *in itself* (objectively) *ownerless* (*res nullius*) is contrary to right.   (*MS* 6:246.5–8)

Kant establishes this Postulate, however, only under the proviso that formally, one's will (that is, one's chosen course of action) regarding the thing is consistent with the outer freedom of all, according to a universal law (*MS* 6:246.17–19). This is a crucial assumption. Kant seeks to ensure that it is automatically fulfilled by abstracting from all characteristics of the thing in question, other than its being an object of will. This is why he insists that pure practical reason can issue only formal laws governing our will (*MS* 6:246.19–22). On this basis, Kant infers, there can be no absolute (that is, unconditional) prohibition on the use of things. If there were, outer freedom, the freedom to act, the sole innate right on which all other acquired rights are based (*MS* 6:237–8), would contradict itself. Presumably, this is because outer freedom would thereby block any prospect of outer action. We shall see that perhaps Kant should have taken more

---

[8] e.g. Ak. 23:277.5–6, 278.23–5, 287.20–2, 301.11–12, 307.18–20, 309.15–18. Kant does not state the complementary 'objective' conditions of use; presumably they are two: that something can be used to some end and especially that one's use is consistent with the free action of others in accord with a universal law.

seriously this prospect of outer freedom being incoherent, as well as the prospect of conditional but nevertheless contingently exceptionless prohibitions on the use of things. The move from pure metaphysical principles of right to establishing actual use rights for human beings is not so simple as Kant's official argument suggests.

The important point for now is that the 'possibility' of having objects of one's will as one's own mentioned in Kant's Postulate must be understood as an extreme abstraction. This level of abstraction accords with the *metaphysical* character of Kant's analysis (*MS* 6:216–17). The relevant possibility must be abstract, in part because of the two assumptions just noted, but also because nothing in Kant's Postulate shows or entails that intelligible possession is possible. It seems fairly clear that Kant means to abstract also from the distinction between physical and intelligible possession. However, at most this abstraction specifies a general concept of ownership—that is, ownership *per se*, with two species: physical and intelligible possession. Kant's abstraction does nothing to show that this general concept, nor one of its still mysterious species, intelligible possession, has a legitimate use, that is, that there can be such a thing as intelligible possession, possession *sans* physical detention. At the end of §1 Kant notes that the possibility of such a species of possession must be proven (*MS* 6:246.1), and in §3 Kant's discussion appears to presume that he has proven that intelligible possession is possible, for there he reiterates (from §1) that someone else's unauthorized use of something could not be an injury unless one owned it. Indeed, in §4 (¶2) Kant avers that the genuine sense of 'owning' something pertains only to intelligible, not to mere physical, possession. Fortunately, the core of Kant's justification of ownership rights is where it belongs (§6), which contains Kant's express 'deduction' (that is, legitimation) of the concept of intelligible or 'merely rightful' possession.

Section 2 contains two other significant points. First, Kant distinguishes between having something in one's power (*Macht*) and having it in one's control (*Gewalt*).[9] Merely to think of something as an object of will requires only being aware of having the power, the physical capacity, to use it. To have an object in one's control requires an act of will (*MS* 6:246.25–32); though Kant does not name it, it is an act of appropriation. Secondly, Kant claims that this Postulate constitutes a permissive law of practical reason. The Postulate permits us to obligate others to refrain from using certain objects of our will, sim-

---

[9] '*Gewalt*' can mean power to compel, to control, or (political or legal) authority. It may appear that Kant intends to use the term here in a normative sense connoting 'authority'. However, his use of the term only slightly later, in a nearly parallel context (*MS*, §4c, 6:248.24), plainly associates *Gewalt* with direct control rather than normative authority.

ply because we have taken them into our possession. Generating such obligations extends the scope of practical reasoning in a way that transcends mere
analysis of concepts (*MS* 6:247.1–8). We shall consider below whether or how
this alleged 'permissive law' to obligate others is consistent with the sole innate
right to freedom, freedom from the determining will of others (*MS* 6:237.
27–9).

Section 5 provides nominal and real definitions of outer possession. The
nominal definition simply recalls the point (from §1) that one can be injured
by someone else's use of something only if one possesses that thing. The real
definition, which Kant claims suffices for its deduction, is this:

Something external is mine, if and only if disturbing my use of it would constitute
injury, *even if I do not possess it* (if I am not holding or occupying it).   (*MS* 6:249.5–7)

Only if somehow I am related to something else can its unauthorized use by
another party injure me. This is not a promising basis for proving that the concept of intelligible possession has a legitimate use, because this real definition
could provide such a ground of proof only if it could be shown, independently, that I could be injured by someone else's use of something. Demonstrating
the possibility of such injury requires first establishing that I have such a normative relation (namely, possession) to the thing in question. Fortunately,
Kant's official deduction (§6), though problematic, does not attempt the
impossible.

There is reason to believe that the text of §6 is corrupt because five paragraphs in it (¶¶4–8) do not contribute to Kant's argument.[10] Kant first indicates (¶1) that understanding how possession is possible requires understanding
how a merely rightful, non-physical, or 'intelligible' possession is possible.
Understanding this, in turn, requires understanding the a priori possibility of
a synthetic principle of right. The relevant principle must be synthetic because
the only principle of right that can be justified analytically, Kant contends
(¶2), is that interfering with someone's physical possession and use of something directly interferes with their innate right to freedom, and as such is
wrong, since any maxim that enjoins such interference directly contradicts 'the
axiom of right' (*MS* 6:250.6). This axiom appears to be his Universal Law of
Right, mentioned in the Introduction to the *Rechtslehre*:

---

[10]   The response of some scholars to this corruption is excessive. Bernd Ludwig replaces §6 ¶¶4–8 with
§2 in his edition of Kant's *Metaphysische Anfangsgründe der Rechtslehre* (Hamburg: Meiner, 1986), which is
followed in the revised edition of Gregor's translation contained in the Cambridge Edition of the Works of
Immanuel Kant. However, in §7 Kant clearly identifies the postulate contained in §2—*as* belonging in §2
(*MS* 6:254.12). I concur with Gregor in resisting such drastic re-editions of Kant's text.

Act outwardly in such a way that the free use of your will can coexist with the freedom of all in accord with a universal law. (*MS* 6:231.10–12)[11]

Because the innate right to freedom inherently involves the right to act outwardly, interfering with anyone's use of something he or she holds (provided that this use is itself rightful because it is compatible with the freedom of all, in accord with a universal law) directly interferes with that person's innate right to freedom and violates the Universal Law of Right: universalizing one's maxim of interference would entail that everyone act on the maxim to interfere with others' use, and this would make some others' use impossible and, indeed, preclude their acting on the maxim of interference.

The important case, Kant notes (¶3), concerns possession without detention. The right to possession without detention is a 'synthetic proposition', because the proscription on interfering with possession *sans* detention does not follow analytically from the innate right to freedom. Because this proposition concerns a right (which is normative, not simply factual), it must be a priori (*MS* 6:249.34). Hence intelligible rights to possession are a central case in point for Kant's Critical a priori justification of key synthetic propositions.

After contrasting his strategies for justifying theoretical and practical propositions (¶9), Kant purports to justify the possibility of rightful, intelligible possession in one short paragraph (¶10). Kant's justification is based on a new 'Juridical Postulate of Practical Reason', namely:

It is a duty of right, so to act towards others that what is external (usable) can also become someone's own. (*MS* 6:252.13–15)

Kant points out that, if indeed this is a duty, then whatever conditions are required to act on this duty must be fulfilled. In this way, Kant's argument here parallels his Postulates of Practical Reason in the second *Critique*. One key condition for acting on this duty, of course, is that things can be possessed. Kant insists that the relevant form of possession is non-physical or intelligible (*MS* 6:252.15–17). If that is correct, then such non-physical possession—possession without detention—must indeed be possible, if we are obligated to respect rightful, intelligible possession, even if we cannot further understand how such possession is possible.

This is not an impressive argument and calls to mind Russell's complaint about Dedekind's postulates—namely, 'The method of "postulating" what we

---

[11] Kant refers to this same principle also as the 'law of external freedom' (*MS*, §§6, 7, 6:251.26, 253.26–7).

want has many advantages; they are the same as the advantages of theft over honest toil.'[12] In the present case, Kant asserts that the relevant kind of possession must be intelligible, and he asserts (as a 'postulate') that we have a duty to behave in ways that allow people to possess things. Surely Kant is right that, if we have this duty, then in principle things can be possessed. Yet why should we believe this is a duty? *Do* we have such a duty? Can Kant offer any insight into the grounds of such a duty?[13]

I shall suggest affirmative answers to these questions, though deriving them requires developing Kant's Critical metaphysics, by enriching somewhat the empirical concept of our finite human form of rational agency used in Kant's a priori analysis. Deriving them also requires shifting somewhat the key question. Asking, in effect, 'How is possession *sans* detention possible?' tends to presume that such possession is possible, and directs attention away from the question, *whether* such possession is possible, and altogether occludes the question, Is such possession required, and if so, why? This question must be answered in order to provide grounds for Kant's 'postulate' of the duty so to act towards others that things may be possessed. Fortunately, Kant's Critical metaphysics provides grounds for answering this key question.

Even in its official version, Kant's justification of rights to possession is not purely a priori; it is in Kant's Critical sense 'metaphysical'. Like *The Metaphysical Foundations of Natural Science*, *The Metaphysics of Morals* takes pure a priori concepts in connection with an empirically given concept of a certain kind of being in order to explicate the basic rational principles governing that kind of being.[14] In *The Metaphysics of Morals*, Kant applies pure universal normative principles to human nature in order to develop the basic principles of rights and duties governing human affairs (*MS* 6:216.37–217.4). The whole of Kant's *Metaphysics of Morals* concerns human beings, as having *Willkür*, a mixed will that is affected but not determined by sensuous inclinations, that can determine what to do on the basis of principles (*MS* 6:213–14). In the *Rechtslehre* Kant expressly appeals to another fact, not about human nature *per se*, but about the human condition, our natural environment, in order to justify our duty to be members of political states: namely, the fact that we live on

[12] Bertrand Russell, *Introduction to Mathematical Philosophy* (London: George Allen & Unwin; New York: Macmillan, 1919), 71.

[13] On Kant's understanding of 'postulate' in this context, see Guyer, this volume. He rightly points out that Kant's juridical postulates are subject to proof; I reconstruct Kant's proof in what follows.

[14] *MAN* 4:470.1–12, 473.5–10; *MS* 6:216.28–217.8. Regarding the Critical metaphysics, see my essay, 'Kant's Dynamic Constructions', *Journal of Philosophical Research*, 20 (1995), 33–81, and Hans-Friedrich Fulda, 'Zur Systematik des Privatrechts in Kants *Metaphysik der Sitten*', in Hüning and Tuschling (eds.), *Recht, Staat und Völkerrecht*, 141–56.

a finite surface (a globe) and we are sufficiently populous that we cannot, in fact, avoid each other (§§9, 13, 42). My reconstruction shall stress two further facts about human nature, closely related to these. First, we are *finite* rational agents because we cannot produce things *ex nihilo* by willing them into existence. The fact that we must act on things around us in order to achieve our ends (including meeting our obligations and securing our basic needs) is a basic fact about human agency directly relevant to Kant's metaphysical analysis of our rights and obligations. (Note that such facts are involved explicitly in Kant derivations of moral duties—for example, relieving distress, truthfulness.) Secondly, I submit that it is similarly a fact—despite Marx's messianic hopes to the contrary—that relative scarcity is endemic to the human condition.

With this background in mind, I now offer a reconstruction of Kant's justification of rights to possession, based on a 'Contradiction in Conception' test using Kant's Universal Law of Right. Because juridical rights are strict rights, the relevant test should not concern a 'Contradiction in the Will'; because the rights at issue are juridical, the test should use Kant's Universal Law of Right. This Law tests maxims in view of their compatibility, when universalized, with like outward behaviour of all (*MS* 6:230–1, 246); it abstracts from ethical considerations of motives or the moral worth of actions. Introducing this test makes explicit several features of Kant's reasoning. Kant's official argument appeals to a 'maxim' that is shown to be prohibited because it directly 'contradicts' the Universal Law of Right (§6 ¶2). Kant recognizes that his justification of possession appeals to the concept of freedom, which is only justified by the Categorical Imperative (§6 ¶10), and in some of his notes Kant describes the obligation to respect rightful claims to ownership as involving a 'categorical imperative' (Ak. 23:286–7). An explicit Contradiction in Conception test provides a sound, distinctly Kantian argument for rights to use things, and these rights match the minimal, provisional ownership rights Kant sought to justify in his analysis of 'Private Right'. Moreover, the main points involved in this test are clearly expressed in some of Kant's working notes (Ak. 23:230.26–231.5, 281.26–32, 309.29–11).

Justifying rights to possession requires what I shall call Kant's Principle of Rational Willing, stated in the *Groundwork*:

Whoever wills the end, also wills (necessarily in accord with reason) the sole means to it which are within his or her control [*Gewalt*].   (*G.* 4:417–18)

Though Kant discusses this principle in connection with hypothetical imperatives, it holds of rational pursuit of ends generally, regardless of their source.

Whether set on the basis of inclination or reason, rational pursuit of ends employs jointly sufficient means to attain them. Note, too, that Kant's *Rechts-lehre* abstracts from the issues about motives that are central to his ethical contrast between hypothetical and categorical imperatives. Finally, invoking this principle does not reduce Kant's tests to prudential or consequentialist considerations.

Three basic facts about the human condition require rights to possession. First, we cannot will our ends into existence *ex nihilo*. Thus we must make use of materials around us in order to obtain our ends. At a minimum, this includes the air, water, and food required for us to act at all (including dutifully) and the clothing, shelter, and tools we need to maintain ourselves. Secondly, our ends, regarding both the basic needs just mentioned and the elective ends we choose to pursue, are complex, temporally extended, and more or less integrated; we cannot simultaneously physically hold or occupy all that living, even at a subsistence level, requires. Consider that we cannot simultaneously occupy shelter and obtain food. (Even a greenhouse must be built with glass and stocked with seeds, both brought from elsewhere.) Were we to produce something at home to trade with others for food, this would require intelligible rights to possess things at least on the part of trading partners. Alternately, portable shelters that could be carried while obtaining food can be made only with equipment that is not simultaneously portable, at least not without using animals or machines, which would require intelligible rights to possess and to use *them*. Human life requires regular and reliable use of things, including sources of food and shelter, which cannot all be physically held or 'empirically possessed' simultaneously. (Kant was clearly aware of this (Ak. 23:230–1).) If we cannot count on the resources of some of our activities remaining available to us regularly and reliably, even when not presently using them, we cannot engage in those activities, and we cannot engage in most of our other activities. For example, it makes no sense to leave home for the day to secure one's livelihood (however one does it) if one's home is either removed or taken over by others when one leaves. Even packs of thieves must honour their principles for distributing loot. Consider instead the simplest mode of life in the most favourable circumstances, a small nomadic group of hunter-gatherers in a temperate and abundant region. Such people need every day certain tools, clothes, and carrying devices that cannot be physically detained while sleeping. Such groups require some form of recognized possession. Hermits, too, cannot avoid reliance on recognized possession, for they require social upbringing before they are able to leave society.

The third important fact is that we are too populous to avoid one another and each other's things and projects. In conditions of superabundance, where a substitute is lying around for anything someone happens to take, rights of possession would not be required. Rights of possession are required only in conditions of relative scarcity. Though Kant does not explicitly mention relative scarcity, he does mention the inevitability of living in close quarters and its attendant mutual interference (§§8, 9, 13, 42). Because mutual interference is a local phenomenon, it is tantamount to relative scarcity, and Kant's argument collapses without reference to relative scarcity. In this connection, Kant adopts Rousseau's point that our mutual interference is a function of population density, and may thus count as a historical development rather than a timeless truth about our unsociability. In this regard, Kant's justification of rights of possession is based on a logical, even a historical, contingency—though one that has long since been a constant and unavoidable feature of the human condition.

These three facts make rights to possession necessary for anyone's free action. In view of these facts, the Principle of Rational Willing commits each of us to willing to possess at least some things *sans* detention. This commitment can be formulated as a maxim, 'I will to possess some things I need, even when I do not physically hold them'. The question remains, under what conditions is this maxim possible and legitimate? The answer to this question can be presented only sequentially, though the parts to the answer mutually require each other, and hold and are justified only as a system.

Possessing things without physically detaining them can be effective, of course, only if one's possessions are recognized and respected by others; the very point of rights of possession is to coordinate our actions and avoid mutual interference. As we saw, Kant claims that the Juridical Postulate of Practical Reason, that things can be possessed, permits us to obligate others to respect our possessions, and that their obligation stems directly from our act of taking something into possession (*MS* 6:247, 255). Is this not a unilateral imposition, incompatible with the innate right to freedom? No, because others act under the same conditions we do. They, too, must will to possess things they cannot simultaneously physically detain. Most importantly, a Contradiction in Conception test shows that willing to have rightful (non-physical) possession of things commits us to respecting each others' rights of possession.

The maxim to be tested is one by which an agent regards others' possessions as available resources. On this maxim, if the sole sufficient means to obtain one's end happened to include items possessed by others, one would, in accord with the Principle of Rational Willing, will to make use of things possessed by others in order to achieve one's ends. (Because the prohibition on interfering with things detained by others follows from the innate right to freedom, the relevant sense of the phrase 'things possessed by others' concerns non-physical, 'merely rightful' or 'intelligible' possession. This is the only kind of possession I shall henceforth discuss.)

The maxim to be tested may be called the Maxim of Arrogant Willing, according to which:

> Whenever the sole sufficient means to achieve my ends happen to include things possessed by others, I will nevertheless regard them as being under my control and will use them to achieve my ends.

It may be suggested that under any of three circumstances this maxim could be universalized:

1. Resources are in fact plentiful enough that among the things *not* possessed by others there were always sufficient means for achieving one's ends.

2. One renounced an end whenever its achievement required using something held by another who denies permission to use it.

3. One allowed others freely to make use of things one possesses whenever those things were among the sole sufficient means to their ends.

The first two prospects can be directly eliminated.

In the first case, one might universalize the Maxim of Arrogant Willing because one would never need to act on it. The permission it sanctions would be established, but not exercised. This strategy appears to rest on consequentialist or prudential considerations and on betting about the course of one's life in the world, all of which is foreign to Kant's central principles. As noted, Kant's justification of rights of possession is based on the historical fact that there are not now, nor have there for eons been, nor will there be, conditions of such abundance as to avoid issues about distributive justice. *Pace* Marx, relative scarcity is endemic to the human condition. Supposed 'prudential' reasoning or betting about prospects of abundance sufficient to meet one's needs without ever finding that crucial means to one's ends are possessed by others is fantasy. It is tantamount to wishing, not to willing, and certainly not to rational willing. Consequently, the first circumstance for universalizing the Maxim of Arrogant Willing is empty.

In the second case, stoic self-reliance may appear to allow one to universalize the Maxim of Arrogant Willing. However, instead of universalizing that maxim, this kind of self-reliance eschews altogether the Maxim of Arrogant Willing by rescinding ends whenever they are beyond one's present means. Hence the second condition for universalizing that maxim is also empty.

The third case is the serious one. Can one allow others free use of one's possessions, with the proviso of making free use of theirs? This may seem to obviate the notion of rights of possession altogether. I do not believe that is quite the case, and the real problem is more revealing. On Kant's view, willing is distinguished from wishing by actual conduct using means to achieve one's end; rational is distinguished from irrational willing by employing effective and jointly sufficient means to achieve one's end. Therefore it is not rational to will to allow others freely to make use of one's possessions if they happen to be among the sole sufficient means to their ends. Such permission undermines one's reliable and effective use of one's own possessions. The very point of having *rights* of possession is to use things reliably and effectively. Undermining reliable and effective use of one's own possessions is instrumentally irrational because it undermines one's own rational agency. Consequently, one cannot rationally will to allow others to act on the Maxim of Arrogant Willing—that is, that others freely make use of those things one possesses in order for them to achieve their ends. Consequently, one cannot universalize the original (first-person) Maxim of Arrogant Willing, according to which one would will to make use of those things possessed by others in order to achieve one's own ends.

Because the only possible human conditions under which the Maxim of Arrogant Willing could be universalized do not obtain in human life, the Maxim of Arrogant Willing is not a permissible maxim for human agents. Consequently, given the three facts mentioned above, our commitment to willing to possess some things *sans* detention likewise commits us to respecting others' rights to possess other things. Consequently, by this Contradiction in Conception test (using the Universal Law of Right), we are obligated to support a system of rights to possession, in particular, by respecting others' particular rights to their possessions.

The next step in Kant's argument is to derive the right to obligate others to respect one's particular rights of possession. The Universal Law of Right expresses a negative constraint on actions—namely, that our external actions are to be compatible with the freedom of everyone in accord with universal law. This Law thus grounds what can be called Kant's Principle of Permission, namely:

An action is *allowed* (*licitum*) if it is not opposed to obligation; and this freedom that is not limited by any opposing imperatives is called an authorization [*Befugnis*] (*facultas moralis*).   (*MS* 6:222.26–9)

Taking an object into possession for use is legitimate, provided that no one else already possesses it. This is the point of Kant's talk about first possession: if no one possesses an object, then no one has a right to it that would be violated if one takes it into possession; hence no one else would be injured by one's so doing. Things are 'things' in so far as they are not free agents; as such they are not morally responsible and cannot obligate us morally.[15] Because no one else would be injured by taking an unclaimed object into possession, doing so is permissible and right.[16]

One's legitimate claim to possess an object for use gives one a right to that object, a right that is not innate, but acquired. The important point here is that, if someone else interferes with one's legitimate possession, this is an invasion or injury of one's freedom and rights. As an infringement of one's freedom and rights, that act is unjust. In this way, then, one's legitimate voluntary act of claiming or using an object generates obligations on the part of others to respect one's acquired right. On Kant's view we are 'authorized' to generate such obligations on the part of others by the first 'Juridical Postulate of Practical Reason' (§2), which states that 'it is possible to have any and every external object of my will as mine' (*MS* 6:246.5–6), where an 'object of one's will' is simply anything that one has the physical power to occupy or use in some way (*MS* 6:246.9–10). Kant calls this a 'permissive law of practical reason' (*MS* 6:247.1–2). He states the point of this permissive law most directly a bit later:

When I declare (by word or deed): 'I will that an external thing shall be mine,' I thereby declare it obligatory for all others to refrain from the object of my will—an obligation that no one would have without this rightful act of mine.   (*MS*, §8, 6:255.26–9)

According to Kant, when one acquires a right to possess something, all others acquire obligations to respect one's right to that thing, and they acquire these obligations through one's very act of acquiring a right to that thing.

Furthermore, Kant argues that acquiring a right of possession also immediately generates the obligation to respect others' rights to use other things. Included in my claim to something, Kant states,

is an acknowledgement of being reciprocally bound to everyone else to an equivalent restraint regarding external things that are their own, since the obligation involved here derives from a universal rule of external rightful relations.   (*MS*, §8, 6:255.29–33)

The relevant 'universal rule', plainly, is the Universal Law of Right. In order rationally to will that one be able to possess external objects, one must will that

---

[15] *MS* 6:223.24–34, 418.27–419.2; cf. Ak. 23:281.17–18. On Kant's views of our obligations to non-rational (hence non-moral) nature, see Allen Wood, 'Kant on Duties Regarding Nonrational Nature' and Onora O'Neill, 'Necessary Anthropocentrism and Contingent Speciesism', both in *Proceedings of the Aristotelian Society*, suppl. vol. 72 (1998), 189–210, 211–28, respectively.

[16] *MS*, §§2, 6, 6:247.1–8, 250.18–27, 251.23–36. This draws Kant's doctrines of possession and of acquisition together. Although he devotes separate chapters to these doctrines, he in fact links them (*MS*, §2, 6:247.1–8). Not harming others through first acquisition requires sufficient resources so that one person's appropriation is not directly someone else's vital loss; see below.

others not interfere with one's possessions. One cannot will that others not interfere with one's possessions consistently with one's (possible) maxim to infringe others' rights of possession. The universalized counterpart of one's maxim would be that others are to act so as to disregard one's own particular rights to possessions, and this is incompatible with one's intention to possess things for use. Kant's postulated 'duty of right' (§6, ¶10) to respect the legitimate claims and detentions of others is thus a strict duty—a duty of *right* rather than virtue—following from an application of a Contradiction in Conception test based on the Universal Law of Right to the case of finite rational human wills and the material conditions of our agency. Kant's justification of rights to possession involves no unjust unilateral obligation of others because, in obligating others to respect our possessions, we also obligate *ourselves* to respect their possessions. This is not *unilateral* obligation because we recognize others to be like ourselves: finite rational agents living in sufficient proximity to interact with us and the things we use on a finite globe with finite resources.[17] Establishing and respecting rights to possession secures a degree and kind of freedom of action not otherwise possible, because our activities are ongoing and require ongoing use of various things. Under the conditions stated above, freedom from unjust interference with our use of things is necessary to act on our obligations, as well as on our basic and our elective ends.

However, does taking an unclaimed object into possession not restrict the freedom of action of others, because one's act prevents them from doing what they might otherwise have done—namely, take that very object into possession at a later date? Is this not a unilateral imposition of an obligation, such as is proscribed by our innate right to freedom, which includes independence from the determining will of others? Kant expressly denies that any of us can unilaterally obligate others (*MS*, §§11, 15, 6:261.8–9, 264.20–2). Fortunately, taking things into possession involves no such unilateral obligation. Kant expressly states that the innate right to freedom extends only to freedom of action that is compatible with the freedom of others in accord with a universal law, and he expressly states that this innate right to freedom involves our innate equality, which is independence from being bound by others—so far as one cannot also mutually bind them (*MS* 6:237.29–34). One key claim in Kant's Critical metaphysics of right is that we recognize that other human beings are finite rational agents like ourselves (cf. *MS*, §42, 6:307.14–26). Consequently, we know that they must act towards their ends by using things around them. Consequently, the same principle of permission to acquire possessions

---

[17] *MS*, §§9, 13, 42, 6:256.33–5, 262.22–6, 307.8–308.2.

and the same correlative principle of obligation to respect others' rights of possession govern them just as they govern us. Consequently, we are permitted to obligate others to respect our claims to use things only because we are obligated, both by our own claims and by others' claims, to respect others' claims to use things, and because others can and must acquire similar rights to possession, along with the correlative obligations to respect others' possessions.

This covers original acquisition. However, most rights to things are derivative and based on transfer (including exchange or gift), at least of the materials used to produce things. Kant's notion of having a right to 'possess' someone else's act grounds the rights of contractual obligation generally (§§4, 7). Kant analyses transfer of title to things on the basis of contractual obligation; this justifies any second possessor's rights by fair receipt of title from previous owners of rights to those things.[18]

Each of us is thus committed to willing that rightful possession be possible, and each of us is thereby committed, via a Contradiction in Conception test, to respecting others' rights of possession. This is to say, given the three facts discussed above, we are rationally committed to establishing and supporting a common system of rights of possession. The minimum sufficient condition of regular and reliable use of things is a system of conventions according to which things will be regularly available to possess for use in attaining ends. Such a system of conventions may be considerably weaker than property rights, in so far as it need not involve sole authority over the disposition of anything, it need not involve the same object being available each time one needs an item of that kind, and it need not involve unlimited term of use. These rights, of course, also do not involve the incidents of the right to the income from the thing, the right to the capital, the incident of transmissibility, the liability to execution, and the incident of residuarity that characterize liberal private ownership of property. Because all of Kant's grounds of proof refer to use and the rightful conditions of use, he has said or shown nothing that justifies stronger rights. Kant was right to formulate his argument in terms of possession, not property, for he realized that most of the incidents characteristic of private property can be neither specified nor justified apart from specific legal institutions. Possession is a proper topic for what Kant calls 'Private Right'; property is a creature of 'Public Right'.

A system of rights to possess objects for use is obligatory for finite rational human beings on the basis of a Contradiction in Conception test. The maxim

---

[18]   Cf. *MS*, §§6, 39, 6:251.18–22, and Kant's aside, 'although according to everyone's concepts of right something external can be acquired by occupation or by contract . . .' (*MS*, §44, 6:312.28–30).

that there be such a system is obviously coherent with its universalized counterpart. The maxim that there be no such system is not compatible with its universalized counterpart. This may be called the Maxim of No Intelligible Rights to Use Things, according to which:

> I will that there be no system of conventions whereby things not physically in my grasp or occupied by me are regularly made available for my claim, detention, and use in obtaining my ends.

Under the three conditions identified above, this maxim is incompatible with anyone's willing of ends not within his or her present means! Given the fact that each of us has such ends, and the fact that we cannot expect not to have such ends over the course of our lives, this maxim is in contradiction of the Principle of Rational Willing.[19] That is a significant defect. However, to proscribe freeloading, the universalized counterpart maxim must be tested. One might will that there be no system whereby things are regularly and reliably made available for individual possession for use; provided that many others willed that there be such a system, one could benefit from that system while repudiating it 'in principle'. The prospect of freeloading is blocked by the universalization test. If the original Maxim of No Intelligible Rights to Use Things is universalized, then no one would will there to be a system whereby things can be possessed for use. Given the three facts noted above, this is incompatible with rationally willing one's own ends because it permits others to make use of one's would-be possessions, which thwarts one's own free actions by making willing unreliable and ineffective. Thus, as finite rational human beings, each of us is obligated by the Universal Principle of Right to will that there be a system of conventions governing rightful possession. In this way, individual rights to possession can be derived from the sole innate right to freedom of action, in conjunction with relevant basic facts about our finite form of rational agency and our finite circumstances of action. This derivation in the main defends Kant's justification of rights to possession *sans* detention.

Reconstructing Kant's justification of possession on the basis of these facts highlights both Kant's debt to and his advance over prior natural-law theories. Before Kant, natural-law theories appealed to basic, salient facts about human nature and the human condition in order to determine basic principles of jus-

---

[19]   Here the maxim of rescinding one's ends whenever they exceed one's own resources is relevant. However, the innate right to freedom combined with the basic needs required by our finite form of rational agency set certain limits below which the elective renunciation of ends cannot go. Cooperation with others and the agreement about principles and practices this requires is, in any event, unavoidable. Barbara Herman points out that in dire conditions one's stoic resolve may waver (and one cannot count on it not wavering), so that the self-sufficient 'stoic' may need the assistance of others to maintain his or her maxim of self-reliance! See *The Practice of Moral Judgment* (Cambridge, MA: Harvard University Press, 1993), ch. 3, esp. 55–67.

tice. Those facts, it was argued, so constrained our choice of principles of conduct as to make some principles 'necessary'.[20] Kant rejected this strategy as inadequate because such empirical factors are insufficient to generate or to justify norms (*G.* 4:389–92). Kant contends that norms can be generated and justified only by a priori principles. Occasionally Kant's rhetoric (especially in §§2–7) suggests that a priori principles alone *suffice* to generate and to justify specific norms for human conduct.[21] However, Kant's considered arguments are in his Critical sense *metaphysical* because, assuming certain very basic facts about human nature and the human condition, they use a priori principles to generate and to justify norms for human conduct. Accordingly, previous natural-law theory provided necessary but insufficient conditions for generating and justifying norms for human conduct. On the basis of the Universal Law of Right, in conjunction with basic facts about human nature and the human condition, Kant argues that we are rationally committed to this obligation, regardless of and prior to any choice, convention, agreement, or calculation of utility. Consider Kant's gloss on natural right: 'by natural law [*Naturrecht*] is understood only the non-statutory, and thus simply the right that can be known a priori by every person's reason …' (*MS*, §36, 6:296). In this important regard, Kant renews and extends the natural-law tradition. However, Kant's approach is constructive. Nothing intrinsic to the world order makes things liable to possession; the link between Kant's two 'Postulates' is that things can in principle be possessed (§2) only if we act towards one another in ways that allow things to be possessed (§10).

The rights to possession justified by this Kantian argument are conditional. They are conditional on the facts mentioned above, and in two further ways. First, they are conditional on the objects we use being in certain ways benign. In a bizarre world in which any object used by one person concurrently and ineluctably produced, say, strong toxins for others, no rights to use could be justified, and rights to possession without use would be pointless. (Then again, in such a world, our species would not long survive—certainly not long enough to develop technology for handling such toxins!) Secondly, they are conditional on scarcity being relative, not abject. In a world of abject scarcity, one person's use or possession of something is directly another person's vital deprivation. In conditions of abject scarcity, one person's freedom of outer

---

[20]   Stephen Buckle, *Natural Law and the Theory of Property: Grotius to Hume* (Oxford: Clarendon Press, 1991).

[21]   On the relations between Kant's moral philosophy and the natural law tradition, see J. B. Schneewind, 'Kant and Natural Law Ethics', *Ethics*, 104 (1993), 53–74, and *The Invention of Autonomy*, 518–22. He notes that natural-law theorists prior to Kant appealed to some supreme authority, whether divine or monarchical, to determine the content and bindingness of obligations. Kant rejected this appeal as heteronomous.

action cannot, or little of it can, coexist with the like freedom of others in accord with a universal law. In such conditions, rights to use or possess things cannot be justified; they would lapse.

It is very important to note, however, that the conditional nature of these rights and their attendant obligations does not make them elective and does not make them heteronomous in the sense rejected by Kant. These rights and their attendant obligations are autonomous in the sense that they are legislated by each of us for ourselves. Neither their content, justification, nor their obligatory force depends on our contingent wants, preferences, or elective ends; nor do they depend on another's will, whether human or divine. Given the basic facts about human nature and the conditions of human life discussed above, we are committed to willing there to be a system of such rights, and we are committed to accepting the attendant obligation to respect others' particular rights to possessions. The Contradiction in Conception test reconstructed here is not consequentialist in nature because it turns on confronting two intentions (one expressed in a maxim, the other expressed in its universalized counterpart), and it turns on the counterfactual case of universal behaviour in accord with the intention in question. No issues about *de facto* degree of general compliance, or counterfactual extent of harm, or the kinds or extent of benefits pertain to Kant's justification of rights to possession. In this regard, though the substance of Hume's account of the conventions governing property accords in many ways with Kant's, their justifications differ fundamentally. Where Hume looks to utility, Kant looks to freedom as the fundamental basis and justification of norms. What justifies these conventions as legitimate is their being necessary enabling conditions for free, legitimate action. What is wrong with non-compliance with these conventions is not disutility to some or failure to maximize overall utility, though both are true. Instead it is that non-compliance involves illegitimate action of one's own and renders impossible legitimate free acts of others. Indeed, non-compliance makes it impossible for at least some others to act on the same maxim of non-compliance. Thus they cannot act on the maxim of those who disregard rights to possession; this maxim cannot be universalized because it cannot be adopted by all. Nevertheless, in the subsidiary moral-pragmatic vein of his grounds for membership within civil society (and for obedience to political authority), Kant offers such prudential considerations for compliance to those who, like the rational race of devils described in 'Perpetual Peace' (EF 8:366), cannot think or act beyond their own self-interest.[22]

---

[22] Though it cannot be developed here, I believe this observation may resolve the debate about whether Kant's principles of justice are justified (only) prudentially; see especially Otfried Höffe, 'Kant's Principle of

In conclusion, it is important to note that taking Kant at his word, that he justifies possession (*Besitz*) not property (*Eigentum*), does not deflate Kant's argument for membership in political society. The rights justified so far are in an important sense provisional (§9). Principles that specify right action are insufficient without adequate incentives to follow them. Kant insists that legislation involves two integrated aspects: a rule of action and an incentive to act (*MS* 6:218.11–23). Kant defines justice in terms of outward behaviour, strict compliance, and external legislation. By 'external legislation', Kant means the possibility of coercive enforcement, of being compelled either to do or to forbear certain outer actions (*MS* 6:232.23–9). (This is distinct from punishment.) Consequently, the juridical incentive to act cannot be good intentions (of whatever kind), but can only be threat of sanctions. Kant further argues that duties of right *per se* are coercively enforceable, because their coercive enforcement counteracts what would otherwise be the illegitimate coercive interference with rightful activity (*MS* 6:230–2). However, it is a fact about human nature, sufficiently known to us in our own case, that people tend to impose themselves on others (§42). Such self-interested imposition is manifest in the facts that human beings tend to infringe on the rightful free acts of others, and that disputants in such cases typically cannot judge such infractions impartially. No unilateral will can be entrusted, and so cannot be permitted, to enforce principles of justice impartially; and 'biased enforcement of justice' is oxymoronic. Would-be unilateral enforcement of rights cannot be universalized because such a maxim, however well-intentioned, is fallible and would involve unjust infringements on legitimate free actions (*MS*, §§8, 9, 6:256.5–8, 257.10) and because no unilateral will can obligate others, in this case, to comply with would-be coercive enforcement.

Rights to possession are merely provisional if they lack legitimate means of enforcement (§9) and if they lack publicly recognized title (§15). Consequently, when social life meets the conditions outlined above, so that rights of possession are necessary, it is likewise necessary to form a civil society—that is, to establish common, official public means for guaranteeing rights of possession (*MS*, §§8, 9, 15, 42, esp. 6:256.27–31). The only way to enforce rights impartially, and so legitimately, is multilateral, via public courts of distributive

Justice as Categorical Imperative of Law', in Y. Yovel (ed.), *Kant's Practical Philosophy Reconsidered* (Dordrecht: Kluwer, 1989), 149–67; Bernd Ludwig, 'Will die Natur unwiderstehlich die Republik?', and Reinhard Brandt, 'Antwort auf Bernd Ludwig: Will die Natur unwiderstehlich die Republik?', both in *Kant-Studien*, 88 (1997), 218–28, 229–37, respectively. On the moral–pragmatic dimensions of Kant's grounds for obedience to political authority, see my essay, 'Kant on the State, Law, and Obedience to Authority in the Alleged "Anti-Revolutionary" Writings', *Journal of Philosophical Research*, 17 (1992), 383–426.

justice. Hence the possibility in principle that things may be possessed, mentioned in Kant's Juridical Postulate of Practical Reason (§2 ¶1), and likewise our obligation to act towards others so that things may be possessed (§6 ¶10, which Kant also calls the 'Juridical Postulate of Practical Reason') require acting so as to establish and follow impartial, bilateral, public legislation and courts of distributive justice. These are basic institutions of civil society; thus only in civil society are rights to possession peremptory and not provisional (*MS* 6:257.4–5). In this regard, Kant treats the social contract merely as an ideal model (*MS* 6:318, 371–2).[23] (In turn, public legislation and courts must themselves be legitimate, which Kant sought solely in a republican constitution.) The principles of possession justified in 'Private Right' are instituted, but not constituted, by convention or social contract. The conditions that obligate us to establish rights to possession also obligate us to establish public legislation and courts. This obligation is not elective and is not based on desires or utility. Only the specific methods and regulations governing possession, and any further rights or incidents that may define property in a society are constituted by convention or social contract—that is, by positive legislation.[24]

[23] I discuss this point in 'Kant on the State, Law, and Obedience to Authority', along with Kant's republicanism.

[24] By introducing government as a guarantor of rights of possession, I have justified neither collective nor state forms of property. Governmental enforcement of rights of possession does not justify a government's having any of the incidents involved either in property or in possession, much less having all of them. Kant's justification of civil society, which I can only sketch here, deserves much closer analysis. Two good starts are made by Karlfried Herb and Bernd Ludwig, 'Naturzustand, Eigentum und Staat', *Kant-Studien*, 83 (1993), 283–316, and Hans-Friedrich Fulda, 'Kants Postulat des öffentlichen Rechts (*RL* §42)', *Jahrbuch für Recht und Ethik*, 5 (1997), 267–90.

5

Kant's Theory of Contract

Sharon Byrd

I. Introduction

For the modern legal mind, one of the oddest constructions in Kant's contract doctrine is his fourfold acts-of-choice requirement for the closing of a contract. For Kant every contract consists of two preparatory and two constitutive acts of choice having legal effect. The first two are the offer and the approval of what has been offered. The second two are the promise and the acceptance of that promise.[1] This approach seems odd today, because modern contract law requires only an offer and an acceptance, but not an additional preceding set of legally effective declarations of will.

Another extremely puzzling feature of Kant's theory of contract is his 'Dogmatic Division of all Rights Acquirable through Contracts' in §31 of the *Doctrine of Right*. This division, Kant claims, establishes a true system, which is complete and exhaustive, as befitting a metaphysical doctrine of Right. The table he gives us is supposed to encompass innumerable empirical instances of acquiring rights through contracts, all of which correspond to one or another of the twelve contracts he lists.

Although not much has been written on Kant's theory of contract, still some authors have tried to explain the rather unusual fourfold acts-of-choice requirement. Some of the explanations focus on traditional conceptions of the contracting process, indicating that the preparatory declarations relate to pre-contractual negotiations,[2] or to the *invitatio ad offerendum*, an invitation to

---

[1] 'In jedem Vertrage sind zwei *vorbereitende* und zwei *constitutirende* rechtliche Acte der Willkür; die beiden ersteren (die des *Tractirens*) sind das *Angebot* (*oblatio*) und die *Billigung* (*approbatio*) desselben; die beiden andern (nämlich des *Abschließens*) sind das *Versprechen* (*promissum*) und die *Annehmung* (*acceptatio*)' (*MS* 6:272). Translations from the German are my own. However, I consulted *Practical Philosophy*, ed. and trans. Mary Gregor (The Cambridge Edition of the Works of Immanuel Kant; Cambridge: Cambridge University Press, 1996).

[2] See e.g. Howard Williams, *Kant's Political Philosophy* (New York: St Martin's Press, 1983), 110–11. This attempt to explain Kant, however, has several disadvantages. First, as an attempt to explain Kant in

others to make offers or submit bids that can either be accepted or not.[3] Another has tried to parallel Kant's thoughts to the Roman law *constitutum*, whereby an unenforceable promise could be converted into an enforceable promise by simply repeating the declarations made when the original but non-binding contract was closed.[4] Bernd Ludwig has tried to explain it in terms of the three moments of acquisition of external objects of choice, claiming that the first act of choice, the offer, places the offeror's choice within the offeree's power to acquire.[5] As for the table of twelve types of contracts, I am aware of no one who has even discussed it, let alone attempted to explain it, in depth as part of Kant's theory of contract.

modern terminology, it ignores the realities of the contracting process. Generally, whether an offer is called an offer or not, it will be viewed as such by courts, at least after it has been accepted by the party to whom it is addressed. It is, therefore, legally irrelevant whether there was any negotiation process or not, and Kant seems to have *legally relevant* declarations of will in mind. Secondly, and perhaps more importantly, there is no reason to suppose that the negotiation process will consist of *exactly two* expressions of will. Negotiations can extend over a considerable period of time and involve a great number of expressions of individual will. Yet Kant seems to have exactly two preparatory declarations in mind. One could argue that what Kant means is the last two declarations in a successful negotiation process, successful in the sense that these last two declarations coincide and thus permit the parties to go forward with the real contract. But as soon as that occurs, we already have an offer and a corresponding acceptance and no longer negotiation. Leslie Mulholland (*Kant's System of Rights* (New York: Columbia University Press, 1990), 261) takes a similar approach, focusing on the need to have the promisee agree to accept the promisor's promise.

  [3] See e.g. Huntington Cairns, *Legal Philosophy from Plato to Hegel* (Baltimore: Johns Hopkins Press, 1967), 426. At least under German law, a shopkeeper who places an article with a price tag in his shop window does not make an offer to sell the article. Instead the customer, by indicating his desire to purchase the article, makes the offer, which the shopkeeper can either accept or reject. This approach seems fairly plausible, except for the fact that it applies only to situations where goods are placed on display or advertised. Furthermore, it involves only three, and not four, declarations: the shopkeeper's offer, the customer's promise, and the shopkeeper's acceptance (in Kant's terminology). The same is true of the tendering process. Another way of looking at what Kant may have had in mind is by focusing on the issue of how long an offer remains open. Must it be accepted immediately, within a reasonable time, or at any time in the future? If the two preparatory declarations lay the groundwork for the constitutive declarations, then one would expect that a promise can be effectively accepted only if accepted immediately, indeed so immediately that it can be seen as occurring simultaneously. Kant does state that before acceptance the promisor is still free, arguably meaning free to revoke his promise. (Mulholland points out, however, that if the promise and acceptance are abstracted from conditions of time, then a revocation of the promise would also occur simultaneously with the promise itself and be self-contradictory (*Kant's System of Rights*, 262).)

  [4] Gertrude Lübbe-Wolff, 'Begründungsmethoden in Kants Rechtslehre untersucht am Beispiel des Vertragsrechts', in Reinhard Brandt (ed.), *Rechtsphilosophie der Aufklärung* (Berlin: de Gruyter Verlag, 1982), 286, 294. Still another has tied Kant's thoughts to Grotius and the natural-law tradition, focusing more on the simultaneity of the two declarations of will needed for the acquisition of the promisor's choice (Wolfgang Kersting, *Wohlgeordnete Freiheit* (Berlin: de Gruyter Verlag, 1984), 175 ff.).

  [5] Under this interpretation, the first two declarations correspond to the second moment of original acquisition, or to the capacity to use a certain object external to myself: 'Im vorbereitenden Akt erweist sich— durch das (empirisch) gegebene Angebot—die Leistung des Promissars als Gegenstand meiner Willkür. Wie der Erweis der Erwerbarkeit im Sachenrecht durch die declaratio an der Sache erbracht wird, so zeigt sich im Angebot die Willkür des anderen als in meiner Macht stehend' (Bernd Ludwig, *Kants Rechtslehre* (Hamburg: Meiner Verlag, 1988), 136).

Any attempt to interpret Kant from the modern law of contract, and particularly from the Anglo-American point of view, is doomed to failure. Placing Kant within his own tradition, be it the Roman law or the natural-law tradition, has its merits. But it can give us only the backdrop for Kant's own thoughts, thoughts that were not simply a repetition of what Kant had received from the Romans or the natural lawyers. Ludwig's attempt at least interprets the fourfold acts-of-choice requirement on the basis of Kant's own ideas within *The Metaphysics of Morals*. This approach seems to me to be the soundest of what has been offered, but it fails to see Kant's work as part of a future development. I think, to do Kant justice, one has to view his work in the light of the ideas of his time, but also in the light of what expired shortly after publication of his own work.

On this note, I will attempt to explain Kant's theory of contract as a contribution to the future. Kant's contribution was a decisive step he took in the chain of development of the so-called principle of abstraction. The future I am thinking of begins around 1815, just eighteen years after *The Metaphysics of Morals* was published, when Friedrich Carl von Savigny in his lectures on *Pandektenrecht* at the University of Berlin, began developing the principle,[6] which he first published in 1840[7] and then again in 1853.[8] Savigny formulated the principle of abstraction in a manner that had decisive influence on the subsequent development of the German law of contract. Kant's contribution to this development must be seen within a framework contemporary for Kant. In the *Doctrine of Right* he focuses primarily on a problem of current relevance during the latter half of the eighteenth century. This problem was how to conceptualize the transfer of ownership of objects from one person to another through a contractual relationship. Kant's focus on this problem helped lay the foundation for Savigny's later influential move.

I shall proceed as follows. First, I shall explain the principle of abstraction as Savigny formulated it and show its relevance for conceptualizing sales contracts. From this discussion, it should become clear that developing a theory of transferring ownership rights was a more pressing problem for Kant than developing a theory of contractual obligation through promising. I shall then examine §§18–21 of the *Doctrine of Right* in an attempt to show that the fourfold acts-of-choice doctrine provides an intellectual basis for Savigny's principle of abstraction. In the second half of the chapter, I shall turn to Kant's 'Dogmatic Division of all Rights Acquirable through Contract'. I shall point

---

[6] Wilhelm Felgentraeger, *Friedrich Carl von Savignys Einfluß auf die Übereignungslehre*, Abhandlungen der Rechts- und Staatswissenschaftlichen Fakultät der Universität Göttingen, 3rd issue (Leipzig: Scholl Verlag, 1927), 32 ff.

[7] Friedrich Carl von Savigny, *System des heutigen römischen Rechts*, iii (Berlin, 1840).

[8] Friedrich Carl von Savigny, *Das Obligationsrecht*, ii (Berlin, 1853), 256 ff.

out why this table cannot be seen as a static list of twelve types of contracts. Instead it must be seen dynamically as various aspects of a contractual relationship in terms of what is being acquired. Each group of three contractual relations forms a progression, and each turns on seeing the contractual relationship from a different perspective.

II. Savigny's Principle of Abstraction

Let us begin by considering the following scenario: A hands over a gold watch to B. From this much we can know very little about what has happened regarding the watch. Is A selling it to B or giving it to her as a birthday present? Is he merely returning it to B after having borrowed it, or perhaps lending it to her to use? All of these alternatives relate either to why A is handing the watch over to B, or to what the status of the watch is after the act. A might be handing it over to B in order to sell it, to donate it, to return it, or to lend it. After the act, the watch is now B's watch, if A is selling it or donating it to B. It is still B's watch if A is returning it to B after borrowing it. It is still A's watch if A is lending it to B. These various possibilities, in other words, all relate to either an agreement between A and B as to their respective roles in the transaction (as a seller, as a buyer, as a donor or donee, etc.) or to the status of the watch as being still or no longer A's or B's watch.

Recognition of the fact that two distinct legal relations are involved in an agreement to transfer an object from one party to another is what can be called the principle of separation. The principle of separation is that the contract of obligation is separate from the contract of transfer. The contract of obligation is the parties' agreement, for example, to sell and buy the watch. Under the contract of obligation, the seller is obligated to transfer ownership of the watch to the buyer, and the buyer is obligated to pay a certain amount of money for the watch to the seller. The contract of obligation provides the answer to the question: why is A handing the watch over to B? The answer is that A agreed to sell it to B.

But the contract of obligation merely relates to duties A and B have with regard to the future. The watch is not yet B's watch simply because A agreed to sell it to her. A may destroy, sell, or give the watch to someone else before the date on which A is obligated to transfer it to B. If A does so, he has not destroyed, sold, or given away B's watch, but his own watch. The watch is not yet B's watch, because B has not accepted any specific watch as *the* watch she contracted to buy. Accordingly, in order for B to be able to say it is her watch, A and B must agree to transfer ownership of the watch from A to B, and B must actually take possession of the watch. The contract of transfer provides the answer to the question: what is the status of the watch after A hands it over to B? The answer is that it is now B's watch.

Savigny's principle of abstraction depends on the principle of separation. The principle of abstraction is that the validity of the contract of transfer is independent from, or must be determined in abstraction from, the validity of the contract of obligation. Accordingly, if the contract of obligation is for one reason or another void, the contract of transfer may still be valid. Savigny makes his argument by positing the following cases:

there are cases of undoubtedly valid transfers [*Tradition*], whereby not the trace of an obligation is present. When a beggar is given a donation, ownership in the coin is unquestionably transferred, and here one perceives an obligation neither before nor afterwards. The same is true when one person requests a loan of money and the other hands the money over to him without having previously obliged himself through a contract.

The argument essentially is that a transfer of ownership in an object may be valid even though the parties had not previously entered into any contractual agreement whatsoever. If that is true, then the same must be true when the parties enter into a prior contractual agreement, but the agreement is void. Savigny, however, continues:

One can undertake a transfer for very different purposes: it can occur when an object is loaned, given in deposit, or as security, and in these cases obviously ownership is not transferred; it can however, also occur in consequence of a sale, an exchange, or in the above mentioned cases of a gift or a loan, and in all of these cases ownership transfers. Where is the true difference between these two classes of cases? Only in the fact that in the latter cases the previous owner *intends* to transfer ownership, in the former, on the other hand, he *does not so intend*. From this it follows that the transfer [*Tradition*] itself transfers ownership through the corresponding *wills of both acting persons*, but without these wills it does not.[9]

---

[9] 'es giebt Fälle unzweifelhaft gültiger Tradition, wobei von einer Obligation keine Spur vorhanden ist. Wenn einem Bettler ein Almosen eingehändigt wird, so geht unstreitig das Eigentum des Geldstücks durch Tradition über, und dabei ist weder vorher noch nachher eine Obligation wahrzunehmen. Eben so, wenn Einer um ein Gelddarlehen bittet, und der Andere ihm das erbetene Geld einhändigt, ohne sich dazu zuvor durch Vertrag verpflichtet zu haben. . . . Man kann eine Tradition vornehmen zu sehr verschiedenen Zwecken: es kann geschehen, indem man eine Sache vermiethet, zur Aufbewahrung hingiebt, oder als Pfand, und in diesen Fällen geht gewiß kein Eigenthum über; es kann aber auch geschehen in Folge eines Verkaufs, eines Tausches, oder in den so eben angeführten Fällen eines Geschenks oder eines Darlehens, und in allen diesen Fällen geht Eigenthum über. Worin liegt nun der wahre Unterschied zwischen diesen beiden Classen von Fällen? Lediglich darin, daß in den letzten Fällen der bisherige Eigenthümer das Eigenthum übertragen *will*, in den ersten dagegen *nicht will*. Daraus folgt, daß die Tradition das Eigenthum überträgt durch den

Savigny was a Romanist, so he drew heavily on Roman legal sources. Indeed he even seems to think that the basis for his principle was to be found in the writings of Gaius, an idea that is generally rejected today. Under Roman law, which of course had an enormous effect on the development of continental European law, simply a contract of obligation accompanied by delivery of the object sold was sufficient.[10] Accordingly, Roman law did not understand the principle of separation, let alone the principle of abstraction. But more important for my thesis here is that Roman law did not have any theory of the nature of a contract of transfer. It located the reason (*iusta causa*) for the actual delivery of the object in the contract of obligation, as does modern French law and the common law. Indeed the German legal system is one of the few, if not the only, legal system that has a principle of abstraction incorporated within its *Civil Code* today.[11]

III. Kant's Theory of Contract

If we return to Kant's *Doctrine of Right*, we will quickly discover that many of the issues we would expect to find raised in a theory of contract are nowhere to be found. Kant wastes not one word on problems that could occur in the formation of a contract, such as mistake, duress, or any of the other typical defences to an action for breach of contract.[12] That is because Kant is not interested in the formation of the contractual obligation nor in elaborating on any reasons why and which promises should be legally binding. He even expresses his impatience with those, such as Moses Mendelssohn, who spend their time trying to show that people should be legally bound to keep their promises. I am

übereinstimmenden *Willen beider handelnden Personen*, ohne diesen Willen aber nicht' von Savigny, *Das Obligationsrecht*, ii, 256–7; my translation.

[10] Reinhard Zimmermann, *The Law of Obligations* (Capetown: Juta, 1990), 239–40.

[11] §433 *Bürgerliches Gesetzbuch* (= Civil Code, hereinafter *BGB*), which is located within the special part of the German *Civil Code* on the law of obligations, provides: 'The contract of sale obliges the seller of an object to deliver the object to the purchaser and to transfer ownership of it to him. . . . The buyer is obliged to pay the seller the agreed sales price and to accept delivery of the object purchased.' §929 *BGB*, which is located within the special part of the German *Civil Code* on the law of property, provides: 'To transfer ownership in a movable object it is necessary that the owner deliver the object to the acquirer and that both owner and acquirer agree that ownership shall transfer.' Through the contract of obligation the buyer acquires a right to coerce the seller to enter into a subsequent agreement—namely, the contract of transfer.

[12] In his discussion of equity, he gives some thought to what we might call today an inferior bargaining position, but he certainly does not admit it as a defence to performance (*MS* 6:234–5). In his chapter on acquisition through the judgement of a court, he also considers the issue of revocation of a promise before performance is due, but here too denies that it can be done effectively for the law (*MS* 6:297–8).

not trying to deny that one could come up with a fairly reasonable theory of contract from Kant's legal philosophy in general, which would include a discussion of most of these issues. But Kant himself does not bother to give it to us in his *Doctrine of Right*.[13] What he does give us is a very detailed description of transferring ownership rights. That is not too surprising considering that the *Doctrine of Private Right* is devoted entirely to Kant's theory of ownership and acquisition. Contract law, as a part of the *Doctrine of Private Right*, is a theory of acquisition derivatively through another person's right to what is acquired.

Accordingly, I would suggest that Kant is concentrating on developing a theory of the contract of transfer, and that he basically takes the contract of obligation for granted. His primary focus is on how the contract of transfer is formed and how ownership of a physical object can be transferred from one owner to another. To put his arguments in the proper framework, I might again point out that, under a principle of separation, we need (1) a contract of obligation, such as a simple sales contract; (2) a contract of transfer in which the seller agrees to transfer ownership of a specific object to the buyer and the buyer agrees to accept ownership rights to that object; and (3) delivery of the object into the buyer's possession. Ownership of the object is *not* transferred until *both* the agreement on the transfer of ownership of a particular object is reached *and* the object is actually delivered into the other person's possession.

In §§18–21 of the *Doctrine of Right*, Kant uses the example of a sales contract, in §21 for the sale of a horse, to illustrate his point. He emphasizes throughout that what I acquire through the contract is 'the causality of another's choice with regard to a performance he has promised me'.[14] In other words, I do not directly acquire the horse but, rather, the right to coerce the seller to bring the horse within my control so I can make it mine. Through the contract Kant is concentrating on, I acquire a right to actual delivery (*traditio* (*Übergabe*)) of a particular horse. Kant states that actual delivery is the performance he has promised me, and it is the act of choice that he has given into my control under the contract.[15]

---

[13] Kant was obviously aware of the issues, because he discussed them in the light of Gottfried Achenwall's *Jus Naturae* in his lectures during the winter semester of 1784. See Gottfried Feyerabend, 'Kants Vorlesungen über Moralphilosophie', in *Kant's gesammelte Schriften*, ed. Royal Prussian Academy of Sciences (Berlin: Walter de Gruyter & Co., 1979), 27.2,2:1348–64, hereinafter cited as Feyerabend.

[14] 'Was ist aber das Äußere, das ich durch den Vertrag erwerbe? Da es nur die Causalität der Willkür des Anderen in Ansehung einer mir versprochenen Leistung ist, so erwerbe ich dadurch unmittelbar nicht eine äußere Sache, sondern eine That desselben, dadurch jene Sache in meine Gewalt gebracht wird, damit ich sie zu der meinen mache' (*MS* 6:273).

[15] 'Denn alles Versprechen geht auf eine *Leistung*, und wenn das Versprochene eine Sache ist, kann jene nicht anders entrichtet werden, als durch einen Act, wodurch der Promissar vom Promittenten in den Besitz derselben gesetzt wird, d.i. durch die Übergabe' (*traditio*) (*MS* 6:274–5).).

There are several reasons why Kant must be thinking of a contract of transfer, and not primarily of a contract of obligation, in §§18–21. First of all, if Kant were discussing a contract of obligation, he would not be so concerned with the simultaneity of the declarations of will. He is concerned with that because, as he points out in §18 and again in §20, one cannot acquire ownership rights contractually through dereliction, meaning that the owner abandons the object and the new owner acquires it, or through the owner's renunciation of his ownership right and the new owner's independent acquisition. Both of these negative acts terminate ownership making the object masterless (*herrenlos*) and providing an opportunity for *original* acquisition of that object. But they cannot provide the basis for contractual acquisition, because contractual acquisition is *derivative*. The ownership right must be derived from what belongs to another. Consequently, that right must move from the seller to the buyer through simultaneous declarations of will, or through one united will with respect to ownership of the object sold. Simultaneity thus avoids having the object ownerless at any point in time. That problem of course does not arise for a contract of obligation, which is the exchange of promises with respect to a future transfer of rights.

Secondly, Kant often uses what he calls the *pactum re initum* to illustrate what he conceives of as occurring through the contract. The *pactum re initum* is a contract that is immediately followed by delivery of the object acquired. The reason why Kant uses the *pactum re initum* is that it makes conceptualization of the transfer of ownership rights simpler. It permits us to visualize the ownership right, which is being transferred through the contract, as moving from the promisor to the promisee with the object itself.[16] That, however, is not to say Kant insists that delivery occur simultaneously with the contract. Indeed in §21 he considers the case in which delivery does not occur until

---

[16] That Kant is thinking of transferring ownership rights to an object through a contract is abundantly supported by various passages in §§18–21 (*MS* 6:271–6), e.g. 'Erwerbung durch die That eines Anderen, zu der ich diesen nach Rechtsgesetzen bestimme, ist also jederzeit von dem Seinen des Anderen abgeleitet, und diese Ableitung als rechtlicher Act kann . . . allein durch *Übertragung* (*translatio*) [*geschehen*], welche nur durch einen gemeinschaftlichen Willen möglich ist, vermittelst dessen der Gegenstand immer in die Gewalt des Einen oder des Anderen kommt, alsdann einer seinem Antheile an dieser Gemeinschaft entsagt, und so das Object durch Annahme desselben (mithin einen positiven Act der Willkür) das Seine wird.—Die Übertragung seines *Eigenthums* an einen Anderen ist die *Veräußerung*. Der Act der vereinigten Willkür zweier Personen, wodurch überhaupt das Seine des Einen auf den Anderen übergeht, ist der *Vertrag*' (*MS* 6:271). Furthermore, according to Feyerabend's lecture notes Kant speaks of *translatio dominii*, meaning transfer of *ownership*, in the same terms as in *MS* §§18–20—namely, that transfer occurs through the *Promißio* and the *Acceptio*, and that both must occur simultaneously so that the object does not become *res nullius* or *jus in re jacente* (Feyerabend, 27.2,2:1350–1). When Kant is speaking of problems that can arise in the contract of obligation, he usually does not use the word *translatio* but rather *pactum*. See also *MS* 6:273–4.

some time after the contract has been closed.[17] Instead the *pactum re initum* is used to divert attention away from delivery and focus attention on the transfer of the ownership right to the object acquired. The transfer of ownership is a contract whereby intelligible possession is transferred through one common will and the object that has been promised is represented as acquired in the sense of noumenal possession, even though the seller does not yet have the object purchased under his physical control (phenomenal possession). Putting it under his physical control is the act of choice the buyer acquires through the contract of transfer, and it is actual delivery of the object that is performance (*Leistung*) under this contract. But, as Kant points out in §4 of the *Doctrine of Right*, I cannot view another's performance as being mine only when it has already passed into my control (as in the *pactum re initum*), but rather only if I can say that it is mine, even though the time for this performance is yet to come, even though I do not yet have the object promised in my physical possession. But to be able to do that I must first reach an agreement as to the transfer of the ownership right to that object, and it is this agreement that is the contract of transfer.[18]

Thirdly, in §19 Kant compares acquisition through the contract to acquisition of external things by taking control of them (*Bemächtigung*). This type of acquisition is original rather than derivative and, without doubt, relates to acquisition of ownership rights and not to anything one could compare to a contract of obligation. Like the contract discussed in §19, which depends on the united will of the two contracting parties, original acquisition depends upon the idea of a universal legislating will through which everyone is bound

---

[17] In §21 (*MS* 6:274–6) Kant also considers the question of whether we need a separate contract to go along with actual delivery of the horse purchased and concludes that we do. One might wonder why I am not claiming that this contract is the contract of transfer in Savigny's terminology. Unfortunately, I do not think that Kant means a contract of transfer here but, rather, a simple agreement on the time at which delivery of the horse is to take place. This agreement, which Kant calls an act of possession (*Besitzakt*), permits the buyer to take the horse from the seller. It appears Kant considered it, because Achenwall thought it was unnecessary: 'To transfer ownership of a thing, from the point of view of natural law, agreement is sufficient' (ad transferendum rei dominium naturaliter . . . sufficit consensus habentis et egentis) (Gottfried Achenwall, *Jus Naturae* (6ᵗʰ edn. Göttingen: Victor Bossiegel, 1767), I, para 166); 'For alienation of a thing, from the standpoint of natural law, delivery of the thing is not required' (Ad rei alienationem sufficit consunsus, nuda nimirum voluntatis utriusque consentientium declaratio; ad alienationem rei naturaliter non requiritur rei traditio) (Achenwall, *Jus Naturae*, I, para. 167). Without it, however, a buyer could simply depossess the seller at any time he pleased after the contract of transfer had been closed, indeed even through the use of force.

[18] 'Nun ist die Frage, wie der acceptant acquirirt? Dadurch daß der andre verspricht oder renuncirt auf seine Rechte? Nein . . . Voluntatis simultaneitas muß seyn, denn anders kann das Recht nicht transferirt werden. . . . Was Voluntas communis festsetzt, ist Recht. Alle beiden waren frei . . . Jeder bestimmt seinen Willen selbst, und schränkt seinen Willen ein. Beide müssen in einem Augenblick wollen, daß *die Sache sollte ihm gehören*' (Feyerabend, 27.2,2:1351; emphasis added).

to agree with the choice of the person making the acquisition. It is only through the agreement with everyone else that the right to own the object can vest in one single person. Under a sales contract, the seller has the ownership right to the object. It is this right that must be transferred through the parties' united will. Such a contract, however, can be characterized only as a contract of transfer and not a contract of obligation.

Section 19, therefore, primarily relates to the contract of transfer of ownership rights and thus the acquisition of the right to coerce the seller actually to deliver the object purchased to the buyer. The agreement constituted through the offer and approval of the offer, or the first two acts of choice having legal effect, is the contract of obligation, with which Kant is not particularly concerned. He is not particularly concerned with it because 'through it alone nothing is acquired'. It is through the contract of transfer of ownership that an object can be acquired, or through the second two acts of choice having legal effect, the promise and its acceptance.

How are these ownership rights (*das Seine*) acquired? Before they are transferred both parties are free (*weil ich vor der Acceptation noch frei bin*). They are free not in the sense that they have not already entered into an agreement, or a contract of obligation in the traditional sense. They are free because they have not yet agreed that ownership of a specific physical object should transfer from the seller to the buyer. The seller has to obligate himself to deliver this particular horse to the buyer, and the buyer has to agree to accept that particular horse as his.

IV. Kant's Theory as the Basis of Savigny's Conceptualization

We can now return to my original hypothesis, namely, that Savigny's theory depended upon a conceptualization of the contract of transfer. Recall that Savigny's argument presumed that no preceding contract of obligation even existed. When I give a beggar on the street a coin, no doubt ownership of the coin passes with putting the coin in the beggar's hand, even though I never closed a donative contract of obligation with him before the actual delivery of the coin. That is because I intend to transfer ownership of the coin to him and he intends to accept it as his. I have concluded a contract of ownership transfer concurrently with the actual delivery, a *pactum re initum*, that does not depend on any previous contract of obligation for its validity. The contract of transfer instead tells us what it is that the transferor is giving up: in the case of the donation, full ownership rights in the coin. Furthermore, when I hand over something in deposit, or as a loan, the reason why the ownership of the object remains mine is because I do not intend to transfer this right. Instead I intend to transfer mere possession of the object in the case of the deposit, or of the right to use the object in the case of a loan. It is the contract of transfer that establishes the right being transferred through physical delivery of the object.

It is no wonder that Savigny uses the *pactum re initum* to prove his point. It is by doing so that one can forget about the contract of obligation—promises and their acceptance and why we should keep them—and come to the discovery that it is a different contract that determines what it is that is being acquired. It is by abstracting from conditions of time for actual performance, and imagining the delivery as being simultaneous with the agreement on the meaning of the act of delivery, that best illustrates the intellectual need for a separate contract of transfer and, for Savigny, that proves that this transfer is valid, even though any prior contract of obligation is void or never even existed.

V. Kant's Table of Contracts

When I first began working on Kant's theory of contract, I did so in an attempt to understand his 'Dogmatic Division of all Rights Acquirable through Contracts' (*MS* 6:285–6). I might emphasize that this table relates directly to *transfers* of rights and not to the creation of obligations. The legally necessary consequence of these various transfers of rights is *acquisition*. Since the table concerns rights acquirable through contracts, these rights include rights to physical objects, to services, and to the person of another.[19] The table therefore encompasses all derivatively acquirable rights to external objects of choice.

A natural way of going about interpreting these twelve types of transfers, of course, would be through using Kant's table of categories in the first and second *Critiques*. But, before trying to force these transfers into categories, let us examine them merely in the light of what we know from *The Metaphysics of Morals*.

The table, Kant claims, is based on principles of logical (rational) division, which indicates that there are only three pure types of contracts, namely, those involving unilateral acquisition (gratuitous contracts: Group A), or bilateral

---

[19] Accordingly, Bernd Ludwig's placement of §31 directly after §21 seems to me to be false (Ludwig, *Kants Rechtslehre*, 74–5). As should be seen from the following text, this table includes transfers of the person of the other—for example, through the *mandatum* and the *praestatio obsidis*. Ludwig is right in saying that the marriage contract does not appear in the table. But the marriage contract is just one example of this type of transfer of a right to the person of another akin to a right to a thing. The table cannot be complete unless it includes the transfer of this sort of right, and thus must come after all three types of rights (*ius reale*, *ius personale*, and *ius realiter personale*) have been discussed.

acquisition (onerous contracts: Group B), or no acquisition but rather security for what is someone's own (Group C). Kant further subdivides the group of contracts involving bilateral acquisition into contracts of alienation (Group B.I) and contracts to let and hire (Group B.II). Under each of these four headings, Kant locates three types of contracts. Kant claims that the table is complete and includes the a priori elements of a true system, dogmatically rather than empirically organized.

It is a serious mistake to approach this table statically, thinking that Kant intends to list twelve types of contracts under which all empirical instances of contracting will nicely fall. The table, instead, is dynamic. Each group relates to aspects of contracting that can be combined with the relevant aspects in the various other groups producing a wealth of different individual contractual relationships.

Let us first examine the contracts in Group A, the group of gratuitous agreements. Here we have (*a*) the deposit (*depositum*), (*b*) the lending agreement (*commodatum*), and (*c*) the donation (*donatio*). The fact that these contracts have been selected as *the three* types of *gratuitous* contracts is purely arbitrary.[20] I may deposit goods with someone for safekeeping and he may keep them for free or charge me for the service. There is nothing inherently gratuitous about a contract of deposit. Nor is there anything inherently gratuitous about lending a specific object to someone else. I may charge him to use it or I may let him use it for free. And, as Kant himself points out, the donation is similar to a sales contract if the transfer is undertaken for payment.[21]

Furthermore, if approached from the perspective of gratuitousness, the list is structurally inconsistent. When I deposit something for safekeeping with another person who does not charge me for keeping it, it is I who receive or acquire a benefit. But when I lend or donate something to another person, it is that other person who acquires a benefit. Calling these contracts gratuitous

[20] In fact they were considered to be gratuitous under Roman law (Zimmermann, *The Law of Obligations*, 188 (*commodatum*), 213 (*depositum*)), but so were the *mutuum* and the *mandatum*, both of which Kant sees as onerous contracts (ibid. 154 (*mutuum*), 415 (*mandatum*)). Indeed under German law, the *mandatum* is still considered to be gratuitous. Achenwall recognizes that a *mandatum* can be either gratuitous or onerous: 'Mandatum gratuitum et onerosum esse potest' (Achenwall, *Jus Naturae*, I, para. 223). See also Feyerabend: 'Mandatum kann seyn Beneficium oder onerosum. Ich kann gratis für einen andern handeln, auch pro patio. Das Letztre ist eine Art von locatio conductio. Man sieht aber ein Mandat doch immer zum Teil als pactum gratuitum an, so daß man das pretium nicht mercis, sondern Honorarium nennt. Beim merces bestimme ich die Arbeit, und kann sie erzwingen. Beim mandat aber kommt viel auf die Geschicklichkeit an, und auf die Gewissenhaftigkeit, die man doch nicht erzwingen kann; daher erweißt ein mandatarius einem andern immer zum Teil ein beneficium. Er kann also nach den Regeln thun, aber er könnte vielleicht noch mehr thun. So bezahlt man dem Professor, Advocaten, Hofmeister etc. Honoraria' (Feyerabend, 27.2,2:1362–3).
[21] 'Pacta onerosa sind: (1) Emtio, venditio. Es ist ähnlich mit der Donation, nur daß jenes pactum beneficium, der Promißor ist emtor, der acceptans, venditor' (Feyerabend, 27.2,2:1360).

does not seem to offer much assistance in interpreting the relationship between the three contractual arrangements within this group. What is it about these three agreements that makes it logical to include them in this order in one group?

If we focus on the right that is being given up through the agreement, we see a progression in the amount of rights transferred to the other person. When I deposit goods with someone, I transfer merely possession of the goods but no right to use them to the other party. When I lend something to someone, I transfer both possession of the object and the right to use it in certain specified ways to the borrower. When I make a gift, I transfer full ownership rights, which include the right to possess the object, the right to use it in any way one may please, and the right to permanently exclude all others from using the object against the owner's will.[22]

Parallel to the relationship between the deposit, the loan, and the donation is Kant's 'Principle of External Acquisition'. To acquire something external to myself, I must first bring the object under my control, or I must have it in my physical *possession*; secondly, it must be something that I have the capacity to *use*; and, finally, I must will it to be *mine* in conformity with the Idea of a possible united will. 'Conformity with the Idea of a possible united will' means that I have to be able to impose an obligation on everyone else not to interfere with what I claim is mine, which is another way of defining a right *in rem* to a physical object. Accordingly, the first group of contracts, the so-called gratuitous contracts, represents the quantity or extent of rights to a physical object that can be transferred through a contract, namely, possession, use, and ownership rights.

The second group (B.I) comprises contracts for the alienation of goods and things. It includes (*a*) the exchange of one good for another good (*permutatio stricte sic dicta*), (*b*) the sale of goods for money (*emtio, venditio*), and (*c*) the loan of things for consumption (*mutuum*). Although the first two contracts, the barter and the sale, look like traditional buying–selling arrangements, the third does not. The third contractual arrangement is a loan of fungibles, like money or grain, that is to be repaid in kind. It is thus a loan for consumption (*mutuum*). Since it is included within contracts involving bilateral acquisition, it is a loan for interest, the debtor acquiring the right to use the money, the

---

[22] This interpretation is supported to some extent by Hegel's *Grundlinien der Philosophie des Rechts*, §80 (Berlin: Nicolaischen Buchhandlung, 1821), 83–6. See also Feyerabend: 'Bei einem Pacto commodando wird der usus concedirt, der Commodus bleibt dem Dominus . . .' (Feyerabend, 27.2,2:1358); 'Bei der Donation wird res gratis alienirt. Beim commodato wird die Sache nicht alienirt, sondern nur usus rei meae erlaubt. Beim Leihen bleibe ich dominus, beim Schenken nicht . . .' (ibid. 1357).

creditor acquiring interest for that use.[23] It seems similar to the lending agreement (*commodatum*) in Group A, but this time it is attached to a fee for the right
to use what is loaned. That impression, however, is misleading, because it makes
one think that the debtor, like the borrower, acquires only use rights and not
ownership rights to the goods or money loaned. When goods or money are
loaned on the condition that they be returned only in kind, however, the debtor
acquires ownership rights over what he has borrowed. He can convert the
money or grain into anything he likes, may sell it, or even burn it. If the object
borrowed is destroyed or stolen through no fault of the debtor, he must still
compensate the creditor, because the debtor, unlike the borrower of a specific
thing, is the owner of the object borrowed for consumption.[24] That leaves us
with three relationships, all of which involve transferring full ownership rights
to the other party. In Group B.I, therefore, we do not have a progression in the
extent or quantity of the rights being transferred, as we do in Group A.

Kant gives us some help in interpreting this group of contracts. Immediately
following his table, he first indicates that the concept 'money' might appear to
be empirical, and would thus have no place in a metaphysical doctrine of Right,
where division must be made in accordance with a priori principles. Still, he
insists that one can consider only its *form*, abstracted from the matter that is
exchanged, and resolve the concept of 'money' into pure intellectual relations.[25]
What Kant means with the 'matter' that is exchanged is the actual silver coin. As
matter, it is a good, which could be acquired for its own intrinsic worth. Its
'form', on the other hand, is its nature as a means of exchange and measure of
human industry. As a means of exchange it is irrelevant whether we are talking
about any particular silver dollar or German mark. And we do not attempt to
acquire it for its own intrinsic value but rather to use it to acquire goods that do
have some particular value for us. Similarly, when we use the term 'goods' we are

---

[23] 'So ists auch beim Gelde und jeder andern Sache, die in genere restituirt werden kann, ich kann es
gratis mutuiren, oder pro certo pretio. Pactum quod pro usu rei mutuae pro aliquo pretio sit ist usura . . . Es
ist Zins, Interesse. Wir nennen Zins, welches für einen Gebrauch einer rei in specie gegeben würde' (Feyerabend, 27.2,2:1362).

[24] 'Wenn ich jemand einen usum rei statuire, doch so, daß er mir die Sache in genere zurückgebe, ist
pactum de mutuando, oder mutuum. Dazu gehören res fungibiles, Sachen, die entweder durch den
Gebrauch verbraucht werden, oder deren Gebrauch bloß in alienando besteht, die also nicht in genere
zurückgegeben werden können . . . Kommt dem Mutuatarius das Geld weg, so ist ers schuldig zu bezahlen,
denn es heißt res interit domino, und mutuatarius ist hier Herr übers Geld, commodatarius aber nicht'
(Feyerabend, 27.2,2:1362). That the borrower of a specific thing is not required by law in a civil social order
to compensate the lender in the case of accidental destruction or loss is clear from Kant's discussion in §38
of the *Doctrine of Right* (*MS* 6:300).

[25] In his excursus on 'What is Money?', Kant, using Adam Smith's definition, states that it 'brings the
empirical concept of money to an intellectual concept by looking only to the *form* of what each party provides in return for the other in onerous contracts (abstracted from their matter) . . .' (*MS* 6:289).

not referring to any specific good, such as a chair, but rather generally to anything we value because of the purpose for which we might be able to use it.

We receive further assistance in interpreting the contracts in Group B.I by consulting Grotius, on whom Achenwall relies in describing the *form* of the exchange in onerous contracts.[26] Under the legal expression *do ut des* Grotius includes six types of exchanges, all of which involve objects, money, or the use of an object. I may give you an object, for example, so that you give me an object in return, or give me money in return, or give me the right to use some object of yours in return, and so forth.[27] Furthermore, he discusses the *mutuum* as giving on the condition that the same in amount will be returned, which can be undertaken with money or any object that is evaluated only in terms of weight, number, or amount. Finally, he discusses *facio ut facias*, indicating that the combinations here are innumerable depending on the nature of the action, but include generally performing some action so that the other person (1) gives me an object, (2) gives me money, or (3) gives me the use of an object.[28]

I would suggest that all of these relationships are captured in Kant's group of contracts of alienation (B.I), if they are seen only from the point of view of the *form* of the exchange taking place. First, it is important to realize that the word 'goods' (*Ware*) as Kant uses it encompasses more than Grotius' things or objects (*res*). The concept of 'goods' includes 'things', 'services', and 'the use of things', but does not include money.[29] Accordingly, when Kant speaks of 'goods for goods' in the first contract in B.I, he means 'things for things', 'things for services', and 'things for the use of things'. When Kant speaks of 'goods for money' in the second contract, he means 'things for money', 'services for money', and

---

[26] 'In pacto oneroso ist praestatio rei oder operae, ersteres ist dare und 2tens facere. Kömmt das do 2mal vor in pacto oneroso, so heißts do ut des, kommt facio 2mal vor, facio vt facias, kommt das do und facio nur einmal vor, so heißts: do vt facias, facio vt des. Diese beiden letzteren sind ganz einerlei, denn der eine sagt do ut facias, und der andere facio vt des. Daher hat der Autor recht, wenn er 3 annimmt' (Feyerabend, 27.2,2:1360).

[27] Grotius calls the exchange of an object for an object *permutatio*, the exchange of an object for money *emptio* and *venditio*, and the exchange of the use of an object for money *locatio conductio*: 'rem pro re, ut in ea quae specialiter, dicitur permutatio . . . pecuniam pro pecunia, quod . . . mercatores hodie [*vocant*] cambium: aut rem pro pecunia, ut in emptione ac venditione: aut usum rei pro re: aut usum rei pro usu rei: aut usum rei pro pecunia; quod postremum locatio conductio dicitur' (Grotius, *De Jure Belli Ac Pacis*, bk. II, ch. XII, para. 3, no. 4 (1st edn. 1625, cited here from B. J. A. de Kanter-Van Hettinga Tromp (ed.) (Lugduni Batavorum: E. J. Brill, 1939)).

[28] 'Facti cum facto permutatio innumeras habere potest species pro factorum diversitate. At facio ut des, aut rem, aut pecuniam; atque id quoque in factis quotidianae utilitatis locatio conductio dicitur . . . aut ut des rem, aut usum rei' (Grotius, ibid., no. 5).

[29] 'Der intellectuelle Begriff, dem der empirische vom Gelde untergelegt ist, ist also der von einer Sache, die, im Umlauf des Besitzes begriffen (*permutatio publica*), den *Preis* aller anderen Dinge (Waaren) bestimmt, unter welche letztere sogar Wissenschaften, so fern sie Anderen nicht umsonst gelehrt werden gehören . . .' (*MS* 6:288).

'the use of things for money'. The final contract, the loan for interest, is distinct, because it is limited to 'things' that can be returned in kind, but includes 'money for money', 'grain for grain', and any other exchange where the things exchanged are themselves interchangeable.

We thus have the following concepts used in Group B.I, seen from the point of view of the *form* of what it is that is exchanged: (1) goods, including services and use rights, which have a specifically defined purpose and thus intrinsic value; (2) money, which has no intrinsic value, but represents all goods as a means of commerce and is thus completely interchangeable; or (3) a thing with a specific intrinsic value, such as grain, that is seen from the perspective of a medium of exchange, or as something, like (and including) money, that is completely interchangeable. If we look at the exchange involved in the three contracts in B.I we then have (*a*) non-fungible goods with intrinsic value in exchange for non-fungible goods with intrinsic value; (*b*) non-fungible goods with intrinsic value in exchange for fungible money with no intrinsic value; and (*c*) fungible goods or money, both of which could be seen as having intrinsic value but which are used as if they did not, in exchange for the same type of fungible goods or money.

We can see again that the heading 'bilateral acquisition' was not particularly useful in deciphering Group B.I. The loan (*mutuum*) is not included in this group of onerous contracts, because of the interest one must pay. Quite like the group of so-called gratuitous contracts, which one cannot explain by referring to their gratuitous nature, one cannot explain this group by focusing on the criterion of bilateral acquisition, or even on the criterion of alienation. Instead, we can explain it by looking at the nature or quality of the thing one receives in terms of the value we assign to it, either as having intrinsic value and thus being non-fungible, as having no intrinsic value and thus being completely fungible, or as possibly having intrinsic value, such as one particular silver dollar or grain when used to feed animals, but being treated as if it had none.

The third group of contracts—contracts to let and hire—comprises (*a*) the rental agreement (*locatio rei*), (*b*) the service contract (*locatio operae*), and (*c*) the agency agreement (*locatio personae*[30]—*mandatum*). Again we find an overlap between the contracts in this group and those in other groups. The rental agreement is the same as the lending agreement (*commodatum*), but this time as an onerous contract for payment of a rental price. Furthermore, it is the

---

[30] That *mandatum* can be called *locatio personae* can be seen from Kant's 'Anhang erläuternder Bemerkungen' (*MS* 6:360–1), where he responds to criticism of the concept 'right to a person akin to a right to a thing': 'Ein solcher Vertrag ist nicht der einer bloßen *Verdingung* (*locatio conductio operae*), sondern der Hingebung seiner Person in den Besitz des Hausherrn, *Vermiethung* (*locatio conductio personae*), welche darin von jener Verdingung unterschieden ist, daß das Gesinde sich *zu allem Erlaubten* versteht, was das

same as the loan for consumption (*mutuum*), 'if the object is to be returned only *in specie*', a possibility Kant expressly refers to.[31] Accordingly, the rental agreement is included in Group B.II not because it is one of twelve unique types of contractual agreement, but rather because of its relation to the other two types of agreements within this particular group.

What is this relationship? All three of these contracts are aimed at acquiring the use of something. None of them relates to ownership rights. The thing that one acquires a right to use is either a physical object (but not 'goods'), or the performance of some service, or the person himself.[32] To take a more modern example, let us imagine a factory for the production of some product. Either I may transfer the use of my machine to the owner of the factory, or the use of my labour in the sense that I come and operate a machine for one day in her production plant, or the use of my full talents in running the factory if I am hired as the owner's agent to act on her behalf. In the third agreement, I transfer rights to the use of my person. The principal who hires me as her agent can

---

Wohl des Hauswesens betrifft und ihm nicht als bestellte und specifisch bestimmte Arbeit aufgetragen wird; anstatt daß der zur bestimmten Arbeit Gedungene (Handwerker oder Tagelöhner) sich nicht zu dem Seinen des Anderen hingiebt und so auch kein Hausgenosse ist.' Domestics in the service of the family (*famulatus domesticus*) are not employed as workers or labourers, but rather in a type of principal-agency agreement (*mandatum*). NB they are not bondsmen (*Leibeigener—servus*), see 'Allgemeine Anmerkung' (*MS* 6:330). Here we see that the right to a person akin to the right to a thing is indeed part of the table of all acquirable rights; cf. n. 19.

[31] Kant also accepted the possibility of generic sales, such as: the next haul of fish or twenty bottles of wine or ten bushels of grain from the next harvest, where the *exact* object of the sale was not specified in the contract of obligation. Roman law did not recognize such sales contracts; see Zimmermann, *The Law of Obligations*, 238–9. This difference points to another reason why it is correct that Kant had two contracts plus delivery (*traditio*) in mind. The Romans, who understood only that there was a contract of obligation and actual delivery, could not account for generic sales. If the specific object was not defined in the contract of obligation, it could not be determined whether delivery actually satisfied the obligation created by the contract. If one realizes that the contract of transfer covers the agreement on the transfer of ownership of the specific object, then generic sales present no theoretical problem. See Feyerabend, 27.2,2:1355: 'Wenn jemand einen Theil eines Stück Tuchs kauft, und der andre hernach das ganze, so acquirirt der in specie, der die Sache sich hat versprechen lassen, jus in re, und der in genere es sich hat versprechen lassen, jus person-ale'. The right *in personam* would follow from the contract of obligation, which until the exact piece of the cloth had been identified in the contract of transfer could not be a right *in rem*.

[32] This three-part division is not particularly uncommon. Höpfner, for example, distinguishes between *locatio conductio rei*, *locatio conductio operarum* (for so-called illiberal services), and *mandatum* (for so-called liberal services). Höpfner was a professor of law in Giessen and friend of Goethe's. The difference between illiberal services and liberal services is the difference between receiving services from someone who has not been educated in the liberal arts and from someone who has: 'Der Miethcontract ist zweyerley. Wenn ich einem den Gebrauch einer Sache vermiethe, so heißt es *locatio conductio rei*. Verdinge ich meine Dienste, so heißt es *locatio conductio operarum* . . . Die Dienste müssen übrigens illiberale seyn. Liberale Dienste sind kein Gegenstand des Miethcontracts, und was man dafür bezahlt, heißt nicht *merces*, Miethgeld, sodern *honorarium* . . . Wenn ich einem also liberale Dienste umsonst leiste, so heißt der Contract *mandatum* . . .' (Ludwig Julius Friedrich Höpfner, *Theoretisch-practischer Commentar über die Heineccischen Institutionen* (1ˢᵗ edn., 1783, cited here from the 8ᵗʰ edn. (Frankfurt/Main: Franz Varrentrapp, 1818), 668 ff.)).

expect more from me than just the performance of certain specified work. She can expect me to act on her behalf to the full extent of my abilities to run her factory. She acts through me and my acts are imputed to her as her own, at least to the extent I act within the limits of the mandate given.[33]

The most obvious comparison to the relationship involved in Group B.II is to Kant's 'Division of Acquisition of the External Mine and Thine' according to the *matter* or the object I acquire as being either a corporeal *thing* (substance (*locatio rei*)), or another's *performance* (causality (*locatio operae*)), or another *person* himself, that is, the status of that person (*locatio personae*), in so far as I acquire a right of disposal over that status (commerce with the person), meaning a right to determine the way in which the person relates to me (*MS* 6:259–60).[34] The third group of contracts (B.II), therefore, can be explained in terms of the three external objects of choice according to the categories of substance, causality, and community.

The final group of contracts includes three types of security arrangement (*cautio*). It comprises (*a*) the giving of a pledge, or the pawning agreement (*pignus*), (*b*) the agreement to assume liability for another person's promise (*fideiussio*), and (*c*) the personal surety agreement, or personally vouching for a person's performance (*praestatio obsidis*). This group is on a metalevel with respect to the other three groups, because it does not really involve acquisition but rather securing what is supposed to be acquired. These three contracts, therefore, can be entered into to secure performance of any of the contracts in the other three groups.[35] Furthermore, security can be given either for free or for some price, and therefore the contracts can involve unilateral or bilateral acquisition.[36]

The first agreement is the giving of a pledge in the form of some object to secure a loan. If the debtor defaults on the loan, the creditor can sell the object pledged to satisfy the debt, but, if the sale does not bring enough money, the creditor can only turn to the debtor for the residue. The object pledged gives the creditor the possibility of satisfying the debt, but no guarantee other than

[33] In Kant's excursus 'What is a Book?', he discusses the agency agreement in more detail, using the example of the publisher of a book who speaks for its author on mandate (*MS* 6:289–91).

[34] See also Feyerabend: 'Ich handle durch einen andern, wenn seine Handlung juridisch als meine angesehen werden kann. Das geschieht, wenn ich ihn an meiner Stelle bevollmächtige. Dem eine Sache aufgetragen wird zu thun, ist mandatarius, der Bevollmächtiger mandans. Die Vollmacht mandatum, und der Bevollmächtigte, Demandatus. Wenn jemand für einen andern was thut auf seinen Willen, und in seinem Nahmen, so wird der mandans als der Sache Urheber angesehen werden. Mandatum repraesentirt die Person eines andern. Er muß nicht übers Mandat herausgehen, sonst ist er von allem übrigen als der Urheber anzusehen' (Feyerabend, 27.2,2:1362).

[35] 'Cautio ist ein pactum, welches mit allen andern kann verbunden werden, indem es die Sicherheit eines Pacti giebt' (Feyerabend, 27.2,2:1363).

[36] '*Sicherheit des Seinen* (der einerseits wohlthätig, andererseits doch auch zugleich belästigend sein kann) . . .' (*MS* 6:285).

the ability to use the object pledged for this purpose. The second agreement, the agreement to assume liability for the debtor, permits the creditor actually to collect on the debt through the performance of another person, the person who guarantees that in the case of default he himself will pay. Finally, what Kant calls the personal surety is an arrangement whereby the surety gives himself up, literally as a hostage (*obses*), to the creditor. This arrangement might seem somewhat strange within the field of private law, but certainly was not totally uncommon in international law at the time Kant wrote *The Metaphysics of Morals*, nor was it uncommon for private-law agreements during the later Middle Ages.[37] Pufendorf also refers to the giving of a hostage as security, within his chapter on additional or accessory contracts,[38] but states: 'The obligation of hostages [*obsidum obligatio*], in view of the fact that it is scarcely ever taken cognizance of apart from treaties and civil government, will be treated more conveniently in a later connection.[39] Accordingly, Pufendorf recognizes that this type of surety agreement belongs within the field of private law, but chooses to discuss it where it is more common—namely, in the field of international law. Finally, Schiller's famous ballad 'Die Bürgschaft', relates the tale of a hero who is caught in the act of attempted assassination of a tyrant king. The king condemns the hero to death, but permits him to leave the kingdom for thirty-six hours on the giving of his friend as a hostage. If the hero does not return on time, the friend will be executed instead. The friend literally gives himself up, or puts himself in the place of the debtor, to secure performance.[40]

Although at first glance this group seems to involve the same progression as that used to explain Group B.II, namely, use of a thing, use of services, and use of another's person, but this time to secure a debt—that interpretation is less

[37] See Grotius, *De Jure Belli Ac Pacis*, bk. III, ch XX, para 52 ff.; de Vattel, *Le Droit des Gens ou Principes de la Loi Naturelle*, bk. II, ch. XVI, para. 245 ff. (1ˢᵗ edn. 1757, cited here from M. S. Pinheiro (ed.), M. P. Royer-Collard (trans.), Paris: J. P. Aillaud, 1835), 486 ff. That Kant was familiar with de Vattel's work is clear from his lectures, see Feyerabend, 27.2,2:1392.

[38] 'After principal contracts, which subsist by themselves, we must now turn to accessory pacts, which are not entered into of themselves and alone, but are only added to others. . . . Others [accessory pacts] contribute some stability and security to contracts already determined and defined' (Samuel Pufendorf, *De Jure Naturae et Gentium*, bk. V, ch. X 'De Pacti Accessoriis', para. 1 (1ˢ edn. 1672, cited here from a photographic reproduction of the 1688 edition: *The Classics of International Law*, ed. James Brown Scott, trans. C. H. Oldfather and W. A. Oldfather (Oxford: Clarendon Press, 1934), 525).

[39] Ibid., para. 12, 531. In paras. 9, 10, and 11, Pufendorf discusses the fiduciary agreement; in para. 12 the giving of hostages; and in paras. 13, 14, 15, and 16 the pledge (*pignus*).

[40] Friedrich Schiller, 'Die Bürgschaft', *Schillers Sämtliche Werke*, i (Stuttgart, n.d.), 193:

> 'Was wolltest du mit dem Dolche, sprich!'
> Entgegnet ihm finster der Wüterich. —
> 'Die Stadt vom Tyrannen befreien!' —
> 'Das sollst du am Kreuze bereuen.'

than satisfying. Why would Kant simply repeat a group of relationships within a table that is supposed to represent a complete, exhaustive logical division and thus a true system within a metaphysics of Right? I would suggest that this group can be explained in terms of the progression of security attained through each of the arrangements. Pledging an object gives the creditor the possibility of satisfying the debt in the case of default, but no real security that the object will bring enough to cover the loan. Having someone assume liability for the debtor gives the creditor security, because the person obliges himself actually to pay back the debt. The creditor is thus not dependent on being able to sell some object that may or may not provide enough through the sale to satisfy the debt. Taking someone as a hostage—however odd it might seem[41]—is at least systematically consistent as constituting the highest degree of security one could receive. Since Kant indicates that this group of contracts is not really a distinct group like the others, but rather on a metalevel in the sense that the three security agreements in Group C can be used in connection with any of the other contracts, a natural way of explaining Group C is in terms of Kant's category of modality.[42]

This brings me back to the original question in interpreting Kant's table of all rights that can be acquired by contract, namely, is the table best interpreted in the light of Kant's twelve categories in the *Critique of Pure Reason*?[43] Since I am not an expert on Kant's theoretical philosophy, I will only venture to proffer for discussion a suggestion as to their appropriate ordering under the categories of quantity (Group A), quality (Group B.I), relation (Group B.II), and

> 'Ich bin,' spricht jener, 'zu sterben bereit
> Und bitte nicht um mein Leben;
> Doch willst du Gnade mir geben,
> Ich flehe dich um drei Tage Zeit,
> Bis ich die Schwester dem Gatten gefreit;
> Ich lasse den Freund dir als Bürgen:
> Ihn magst du, entrinn' ich, erwürgen.'

The last line is a play on the old German legal proverb: 'Bürgen soll man würgen.' For arguments supporting this interpretation and generally on the use of hostages in ancient Greece and under German law of the Middle Ages, see the fascinating discussion in Udo Ebert, 'Friedrich Schillers Ballade "Die Bürgschaft" im Lichte des Strafrechts', *Zeitschrift für die gesamte Strafrechtswissenschaft*, 108 (1996), 467.

[41]   Now that I have benefited from Ebert's article ('Friedrich Schillers Ballade'), it no longer seems as strange to me as it did when I wrote the original draft of this article.

[42]   'Die Kategorien der modalität haben das Besondere an sich: daß sie den Begriff, dem sie als Prädicate beigefügt werden, als Bestimmung des Objects nicht im mindesten vermehren, sondern nur das verhältniß zum Erkenntnißvermögen ausdrücken' (*KrV* A219/B266).

[43]   Ludwig points out that Kant refers to his table of categories explicitly in the *Doctrine of Right* only in §4 regarding external objects of choice and the categories of substance, causality and community (Ludwig, *Kants Rechtslehre*, 126). Kant's failure to refer to them explicitly, however, is not a reason to rule out his having had them in mind when developing the table of contracts.

modality (Group C). Quantity here would then mean the extent or amount of rights transferred through the agreement, namely, either (*a*) possession, (*b*) use, or (*c*) ownership rights. Quality would mean the nature of the exchange in terms of (*a*) something with intrinsic value, (*b*) something with no intrinsic value, and (*c*) something with intrinsic value seen as having no intrinsic value. Relation, perhaps the easiest to defend since Kant himself refers to this category,[44] would mean the relation of (*a*) external objects of my choice to me, namely, physical objects, (*b*) the choice of another to perform an act, and (*c*) the status of another in relation to myself. Finally, modality, which is on a metalevel with respect to the other categories of contracts, would mean (*a*) the possibility of being secured through the pledge of an object, (*b*) the reality of being secured through another person's agreement to satisfy the debt, and (*c*) the necessary security obtained through the taking of a hostage.

---

[44] 'Der äußeren Gegenstände meiner Willkür können nur *drei* sein: (1) eine (körperliche) *Sache* außer mir; (2) die *Willkür* eines anderen zu einer bestimmten That (*praestatio*); (3) der *Zustand* eines Anderen in Verhältniß auf mich; nach den Kategorien der *Substanz, Causalität* und *Gemeinschaft* zwischen mir und äußeren Gegenständen nach Freiheitsgesetzen' (*MS* 6:247). Although the discussion immediately following this passage suggests that acquisition through contract is limited to 'die Willkür eines anderen zu einer bestimmten Tat', that is clearly misleading, because I can acquire physical objects, such as a horse, through contract (*MS* 6:274–6), and, although the right of one spouse to the other is instituted through the law (*lege*), Kant still speaks of the 'Ehevertrag'.

6

Is Kant's *Rechtslehre* a 'Comprehensive Liberalism'?

Thomas W. Pogge

I. Introduction

Beginning in 1985,[1] John Rawls has repeatedly emphasized that modern, pluralistic societies should be structured in accordance with a *political* conception of justice. In doing so, he has insisted that his own liberalism should be understood as political, in contrast to the *comprehensive* liberalisms of Kant and Mill.[2] While this refinement in Rawls's position has been discussed by many, his characterization of Kant's liberalism as comprehensive has not been critically explored in the literature. My interest in beginning such an exploration here is entirely focused on Kant. My guiding thought is that we can gain a better understanding of Kant's *RL* by confronting it with the distinction Rawls developed two centuries later.[3]

By calling a conception of social justice comprehensive, Rawls means that it relies on 'conceptions of what is of value in human life, as well as ideals of per-

In revising this chapter, I have learned a lot from the lively discussions it has evoked in Memphis and Lawrence. Many thanks also to Rüdiger Bittner, Ernesto Garcia, Samuel Kerstein, and Fang-Li Zhang for their detailed and very helpful critical comments and suggestions.

[1] John Rawls, 'Justice as Fairness: Political not Metaphysical', *Philosophy and Public Affairs*, 14 (1985), 223–52.

[2] Rawls criticizes here the way he had described his conception in *A Theory of Justice* (Cambridge, MA: Harvard University Press, 1971), remarking that in this earlier work 'no distinction is drawn between moral and political philosophy' and 'nothing is made of the contrast between comprehensive philosophical and moral doctrines and conceptions limited to the domain of the political. . . . Although the distinction between a political conception of justice and a comprehensive philosophical doctrine is not discussed in *Theory*, once the question is raised, it is clear, I think, that the text regards justice as fairness and utilitarianism as comprehensive, or partially comprehensive, doctrines' (John Rawls, *Political Liberalism* (New York: Columbia University Press, 1993), pp. xv–xvi, hereafter *PL*).

[3] I will cite only the introductory materials (6:203–28) of Kant's *Die Metaphysik der Sitten* as *MS*, materials from the first part *Metaphysische Anfangsgründe der Rechtslehre* (6:229–372) as *RL*, and materials from the second part *Metaphysische Anfangsgründe der Tugendlehre* (6:373–493) as *TL*. In quoting or citing these materials, I also append line numbers when appropriate. All translations from Kant's works are my own.

sonal virtue and character, that are to inform much of our non-political conduct' (*PL* 175; cf. *PL* 13). He contends that 'Kant's doctrine is a comprehensive
moral view in which the ideal of autonomy has a regulative role for all of life'[4]
and also, more cautiously, that 'the basic conceptions of person and society in
Kant's view have, let us assume, a foundation in his transcendental idealism'
(*PL* 100).

Evoking Isaiah Berlin, Rawls mentions as one main drawback of comprehensive conceptions of social justice that they are likely to be socially divisive—
for example, in their approach to public education: 'The liberalisms of Kant
and Mill may lead to requirements designed to foster the values of autonomy
and individuality as ideals to govern much if not all of life' (*PL* 199). But such
requirements lead to a fatal dilemma, given what Rawls calls the 'fact of oppression'—namely, 'that a continuing shared understanding on one comprehensive
religious, philosophical, or moral doctrine can be maintained only by the
oppressive use of state power' (*PL* 37). The comprehensive liberalisms of Kant
and Mill can maintain their own social pre-eminence only by violating their
own principles against the use of state oppression (*PL* 37 n. 39).

Rawls does not define political conceptions of social justice simply as ones
that are non-comprehensive or *freestanding*. Rather, he adds two further elements to his definition—namely, that political conceptions of social justice
apply to, and only to, the basic structure of a closed and self-contained society
(*PL* 11–12) and that they are 'expressed in terms of certain fundamental ideas
seen as implicit in the public political culture of a democratic society'.[5] To
avoid the problems Rawls points to, Kant's liberalism need only be freestanding, not political; and so I ignore these two further elements. Simply put, our
question is then whether Kant's *RL* is freestanding—or beholden to and hence
biased towards other parts of his philosophical corpus, such as his teachings
about good will and autonomy or his transcendental idealism.

Let us begin with some straightforward points. It can hardly be disputed
that Kant did develop and endorse the doctrine of transcendental idealism and
an ideal of autonomy. But this cannot decide our question. For the fact that the
author of a conception of social justice has also held and expressed broader religious, moral, or philosophical views—and surely Rawls himself has held, and
presumably expressed, such views as well—does not show that the conception
of social justice he sets forth depends upon these broader views in any way.

---

[4] *PL* 99. Cf. *PL* 78, where Rawls holds that Kant's comprehensive liberalism expresses the 'ethical value of autonomy'.

[5] *PL* 13. His distinction between *comprehensive* and *political* conceptions of social justice is then not exhaustive, though the two labels are, of course, mutually exclusive.

Nor can our question be settled by pointing to Kant's claim that his *RL* fits into the broader world view of his critical philosophy or by noting that Kant presents his entire philosophy as a system, unified by certain key terms, propositions, and methods. For it does not follow from the fact that a conception of social justice fits into one comprehensive world view that this is the *only* comprehensive world view into which it fits or that it cannot *also* 'be presented without saying, or knowing, or hazarding a conjecture about, what such doctrines it may belong to, or be supported by' (*PL* 12–13). We can see this clearly by considering that Rawls presents his own political conception of social justice as 'a module, an essential constituent part, that fits into and can be supported by various reasonable comprehensive doctrines' (*PL* 12) and even claims, in developing his model case of an overlapping consensus, that his own *justice as fairness* fits into *Kant's* comprehensive world view (*PL* 145, 169).

What must be shown, then, to disqualify Kant's liberalism as comprehensive is not that it is entailed by his broader philosophical system, but, conversely, that Kant's broader philosophical system is presupposed by his liberalism. This liberalism is comprehensive, if it cannot be presented as anything but an integral part of Kant's philosophical world view.

I will here make the case for the hypothesis that the liberalism set forth in Kant's *RL* is *not* comprehensive, does *not* presuppose either Kant's moral philosophy or his transcendental idealism. I do not pretend that this case is fully conclusive. But it is a case that should be answered by those who dismiss Kant's political philosophy as dependent on metaphysical or moral views that we cannot expect to be freely endorsed by the citizens of modern societies.

Before devoting the rest of this chapter to supporting my hypothesis, let me concede that Kant, even if innocent of the charge of comprehensive liberalism, is guilty of the expositional flaw Rawls now believes[6] to be exemplified by his earlier work: Kant sometimes (falsely) suggests that his liberalism is dependent on his philosophical world view and hence comprehensive.[7] That he does so is not surprising. Kant is deeply committed to his moral philosophy and to his transcendental idealism; and these teachings would be more significantly

---

[6]   See Rawls's self-criticism cited in n. 2.

[7]   Let me cite one sample passage, which suggests that juridical possession presupposes (inner) freedom of the will and the Categorical Imperative: 'No one should be surprised that the theoretical principles of external mine and thine trail off into the intelligible and represent no expanded knowledge: for the concept of freedom on which they rest is incapable of a deduction of its possibility and can only be inferred from the practical law of reason (the categorical imperative) as a fact of reason' (*RL* 6:252.24–30; cf. *RL* 6:245.16–21). I should add that my own previous understanding of Kant's political philosophy was hardly clear on this point either. See my 'Kant's Theory of Justice', *Kant-Studien*, 79 (1988), 407–33.

vindicated by his liberalism, if this liberalism were dependent upon rather than merely supported by them.[8]

II. Kant's Definition of *Recht* (§§A–B)

The liberalism Kant develops in the *RL* is constructed from a sparse arsenal of basic elements. Some of these are definitions. Thus Kant declares that, in contrast to a *thing*, a '*person* is a subject whose actions are capable of *imputation*' (*MS* 6:223.24–5). He continues: '*Moral* personality is therefore nothing other than the freedom of a rational being under moral laws . . . from which it follows that a person is subject only to laws that it (either alone or at least jointly with others) gives to itself' (*MS* 6:223.25–31). With much help from Rüdiger Bittner and Joachim Hruschka, but following neither of them, I read this as follows. By italicizing 'moral', Kant flags that this word narrows the meaning of 'personality'. The most plausible specification, which would also vindicate the 'therefore', is this: having *moral* personality means being a subject whose *inner* actions are capable of imputation, a subject with (transcendental) freedom of the will. This is the narrow, strong concept of person at work in Kant's moral writings.[9] Persons in the wider, weaker sense are then subjects whose *external* actions can be imputed to them as expressive of their will, choice, or intentions. Kant makes clear that—while the *TL* has to do with both inner and external actions and freedom and thus must work with the stronger concept of *moral* personality—the *RL* has to do with only the *external* actions and only the *external* freedom of persons and therefore requires only the weaker concept of person *simpliciter* or (what one might call) juridical personality (*MS* 6:214.13–30).[10]

Suppose there are persons—not just one, but a plurality. And suppose they move in the same space in such a way that the actions of one may obstruct those of another. Let us say that a person's external freedom is constrained exactly in so far as others are obstructing actions that she could otherwise perform if she

---

[8]   Mark the sense of triumph Kant expresses when he finds himself compelled to conclude that his moral philosophy presupposes his transcendental idealism: 'Practical reason itself, without any collusion with the speculative, provides reality to a supersensible object of the category of causality, viz. to freedom . . . i.e. it confirms through a fact what there could only be *thought*. This strange but incontrovertible assertion of the speculative Critique, that *the thinking subject is only an appearance to itself in inner intuition*, now finds its full confirmation in the critique of practical reason' (*KpV* 5:6.7–16).

[9]   See e.g. *G.* 4:428.21–9 with *G.* 4:446–8; *KpV* 5:87.3–4, 162.17–20; *R.* 6:27–8; and *TL* 6:434–5. Cf. also *KpV* 5:97.6–7 on imputation pursuant to the moral law (Categorical Imperative).

[10]   On this reading, Kant may still be committed to the claim—synthetic and made outside the *RL*—that all persons have moral personality.

so chose, and that her external freedom is insecure in so far as others *can* obstruct her otherwise possible actions. A person's external freedom is *secure*, then, in so far as possible obstructing actions by others are themselves obstructed. The security of a person's external freedom thus requires that the external freedom of others (to obstruct her external freedom) be constrained. Therefore, a plurality of persons can have security of their external freedom only if and in so far as the external freedom of each is constrained so as to be consistent with the constrained external freedom of all others.

Kant defines *Recht* as 'the whole of the conditions under which the choice of one can coexist [*zusammen vereinigt werden kann*] with the choice of the other according to a universal law of freedom' (*RL* 6:230.24–6).[11] The word 'choice' here is Mary Gregor's rendition of *Willkür*. And this translation seems all right if we attach two clarifications. First, 'someone's choice' must be understood not in the sense of decision (as in 'she came to regret her choice'), but in the sense of domain of her control (as in 'this is her choice; for her to decide, up to her'). Secondly, we must understand someone's choice not locally, as what is up to her on some occasion, but globally, as what is up to her over a lifetime. I read Kant's expression 'external freedom' as synonymous with choice in this sense. As a final clarification one might add that, although Kant speaks of only two persons here, his definition is meant to cover an indefinite plurality. He defines *Recht* then as the whole of the conditions under which the external freedom of any person can coexist with that of all others according to a universal law of freedom.

Domains of external freedom can coexist when there is no action any person might perform within her domain that would render impossible another's action within his. To ensure such mutual consistency of choice, a universal law will need to include a large variety of restrictions and should thus be thought of as a *body* of law—a familiar meaning of the word 'law', exemplified in such locutions as *Grundgesetz* or 'Common Law'. To ensure mutual consistency, such a law must apply to all persons, must specify precisely for each what she may, must, and must not do. But it need not treat all equally by making ultimately the same demands on each. I propose then to read the word 'universal' (*allgemein*) here in the weak sense of 'applying to all', not in the stronger sense that also entails equality of persons under the law.[12] To be sure, Kant's liberalism

---

[11] In an earlier parallel passage, Kant defines *Recht* as 'the restriction of the freedom of each to the condition of its coexistence [*Zusammenstimmung*] with the freedom of everyone in so far as this freedom is possible according to a universal law' (GTP 8:289–90).

[12] But does this not go against how Kant uses the same expression in the first formula of the Categorical Imperative: 'Act only on that maxim through which you can at the same time will that it become a universal law' (*G.* 4:421.7–8)? It is true, of course, that the Categorical Imperative involves the idea of equality

does require equality under the law. But this requirement is not a matter of what *Recht* is, by definition, but a matter of what Kant claims *Recht* ought to be. *Recht* may be instantiated in many different ways, only some of which involve equality under the law.

We have yet to explain what Kant means by 'the whole [*Inbegriff*] of the conditions'. I take this expression to have a twofold significance. First, by referring to conditions in the plural, Kant suggests that *Recht* is more than merely this single condition: that there be a universal law restricting everyone's external freedom so as to ensure mutual consistency. Such a universal law is insufficient for *Recht* because—as the familiar case of human beings illustrates convincingly—persons may not pay attention to it. A universal law makes it possible for persons' choices to coexist only if it is *effective*; and the conditions that render it effective must then be included among 'the whole of the conditions' of Kant's definition. These effectiveness conditions may include institutional mechanisms through which the universal law is authoritatively formulated and announced, authoritatively interpreted and applied, and also enforced.[13] A particular instantiation of *Recht* may then—and among human beings *will*— have two components: a body of law that delimits each person's domain of external freedom and institutional mechanisms that make this law effective.

Secondly, in associating *Recht* with a *complete* set of conditions, Kant is also suggesting the exclusion of any redundant restrictions. The set of conditions must not only be *in*clusive so that conditions it contains are jointly sufficient, but must also be *ex*clusive so that no restriction is dispensable, for the maintenance of mutually secure domains of external freedom. *Recht* excludes any restrictions that make no contribution to such mutual security and thus

under the law. But this idea is not implicit in the concept of a universal law, but arises through how the Categorical Imperative constructs universal laws from one agent's contemplated maxim(s): the very permission one is inclined to give to oneself is made universal—that is, extended to all. Cf. my 'The Categorical Imperative', in O. Höffe (ed.), *Grundlegung zur Metaphysik der Sitten. Ein kooperativer Kommentar* (Frankfurt: Vittorio Klostermann, 1989), 172–93; repr. in P. Guyer (ed.), *Critical Essays on Kant's Groundwork of the Metaphysics of Morals* (Totowa: Rowman & Littlefield, 1998).

[13] Kant suggests that these effectiveness conditions are not affected by empirical information about human beings: 'However good-natured and law-abiding one may imagine human beings, it nevertheless lies a priori in the rational idea of such a (non-juridical) state that, before a public law-governed condition has been established, individual human beings, peoples, and states can never be secure from violence against one another resulting from each one's own right to do *what seems right and good to it* independently of another's opinion' (*RL* 6:312.6–12). I am not so sure that he can exclude a priori the possibility that some species of persons might spontaneously converge upon a single system of rules and then follow these rules correctly without any further incentives. Still, the main point, which I do not contest, is the converse: one cannot exclude a priori the possibility that persons will fail spontaneously to converge upon a single system of rules and then to follow these rules correctly without any further incentives. Kant's 'totality of conditions' thus cannot be reduced to the merely notional existence of a universal body of law that, if correctly followed by all, would ensure mutual consistency.

involves (in modern jargon) a Pareto-efficient distribution of external free-dom.[14] Kant displays this limitation rather clearly in the paragraph preceding his canonical definition of *Recht*, saying that 'the concept *Recht* . . . has to do only with the external and indeed practical relation of one person to another in so far as their actions, as [imputable] deeds, can mutually influence one another' (*RL* 6:230.7–11) and is not concerned with persons' inner states, such as their wishes, needs, or ends (*RL* 6:230.11–19). It may well be desirable that persons' actions should harmonize with their own and others' wishes, needs, and ends. But this, for Kant, is a concern of ethics—not of *Recht*, which deals with, and only with, the preconditions for mutually secure domains of external freedom. *Recht* solves the problem of possible conflicts among actions and leaves aside all other possible conflicts that may arise among actions, wish-es, needs, and ends.[15]

My explication of Kant's canonical definition makes *Recht* essentially equiv-alent to *Rechtszustand*, which should be translated as 'juridical state' or 'juridi-cal condition'.[16] As Kant defines it here, *Recht* is not a system of rules such that, if all persons correctly observed them, no person's action would ever obstruct another's. Rather, *Recht* is a property of a world of persons capable of obstruct-ing one another's actions—or capable of constraining one another's external freedom. It is instantiated in such a world if and only if this world is so struc-tured that the external freedom of persons is, in accordance with a universal law, constrained in such a way that each person's constrained external freedom is secure. *Recht* is instantiated when persons coexist under an effective legal order that delimits and sustains mutually secure domains of external freedom. This explication of *Recht* strongly confirms my above conjecture that 'universal' must be read in the weak sense. A complete and effective legal order, even with-out equality under the law, instantiates *Recht* or a juridical condition. All that is required for such a condition is that there be an effective body of public stand-ing laws that constrains each person's freedom in predictable ways and thereby predictably delimits and secures each person's constrained external freedom.[17]

---

[14] This sentence states merely that such redundant restrictions are not part of *Recht*; and this does not entail that they are inconsistent with *Recht* or *unrecht*—though Kant, as we shall see, has a tendency to slide from one claim to the other.

[15] See Note A.

[16] As Kant suggests through the Latin *status iuridicus* (GTP 8:292.33; EF 8:383.13). He can appropriate-ly use the adjectives *rechtlich* and *gesetzlich* in German, so long as these are understood as 'instantiating *Recht*' and 'governed by laws', respectively. Translations as 'rightful', 'lawful', or 'legal' are mistaken, because a juridi-cal state may well be unjust (in reference to natural law) and, as constitutive of legality, cannot itself be legal, or lawful, in reference to positive law. (Cf. how *rechtlich* contrasts with *rechtmäßig* at EF 8:373 n. 30–1.)

[17] If this explication of Kant's definition is correct, then *Recht* as used in this definition is not equivalent to either 'law' or '(social) justice'. When law is incomplete or ineffective, there is law without *Recht*. And when

If this is what *Recht* is, what then is *Rechtslehre*? This is not a trivial question, because there is a significant ambiguity in the German ending -*lehre*. In one sense, this ending indicates an intellectual discipline or field of study. This use occurs, for instance, in the word *Arzneimittellehre*, which is the study of medical remedies, or pharmacology. Taken in this sense, *Rechtslehre*—or *the Rechtslehre*, with the definite article—would be the intellectual discipline that reflects upon the establishment and maintenance of *Recht*—that is, of mutually secure domains of external freedom among persons. This field of study might be thought of as consisting of two branches: empirical *Rechtslehre*, which reflects upon our historical experience with actual attempts to establish and maintain *Recht*, and philosophical *Rechtslehre*, which reflects more abstractly on whether and how *Recht* can be and should be established and maintained. Kant, of course, would be operating within the latter branch of the philosophical *Rechtslehre*.

In its other sense, the ending -*lehre* indicates a particular theory, doctrine, or approach within some field of study. This use occurs, for instance, in the expression *Mendelsche Vererbungslehre*, which is a biological theory yielding specific predictions about the transmission of traits from plants and animals to their offspring.[18] Taken in this sense, *a Rechtslehre* (now with an *in*definite article) would be a particular theory about *Recht*; and a philosophical—or, as Kant likes to say, metaphysical (*RL* 6:284.9)—*Rechtslehre* would then be a particular theory about whether and how *Recht* can be and should be established and maintained. From here on I will use the word in this latter sense, as a substitute for 'Kant's liberalism' (and as distinct from *RL*, the text).

Kant acknowledges and at once downplays the ambiguity, stressing that there can be only one true doctrine within each field of study (*MS* 6:207.11–29), hence only one philosophical doctrine of *Recht*, so that the study of *Recht* should ideally coincide with the study and refinement of the one true doctrine of *Recht*. Highlighting the distinction is worthwhile nonetheless in that it provides a helpful perspective on Kant's enterprise. We should be able to analyse the *RL* into two main components. The first component consists of Kant's definition of *Recht* and of his analysis thereof, which generates whatever propositions follow from this definition analytically. The second component consists of whatever substantive elements Kant adduces to show the possibility and

---

law is complete and effective, there may be *Recht* without justice, for example, *Recht* that imposes very different constraints on different persons. This is not to deny, of course, that Kant also uses the word *Recht* in its common meaning, as denoting a society's body of law, as well as of course in its even more common meaning of '(a) right (to)'.

[18]   Gregor Johann Mendel (1822–1884) was an Austrian botanist.

desirability of *Recht* and of certain instantiations thereof. It is this second component that might most plausibly be suspected of presupposing other parts of his philosophical world view.

III. Kant's Universal Principle of *Recht* (§C)

After explicating the notions of *Recht* and *Rechtslehre* in §§A–B, Kant goes on, without any transition, to enunciate what he calls the universal principle of *Recht*. He does not make clear what the canonical text of this principle is supposed to be, but two formulations seem pertinent. One has the look of a definition and is given in quotes as the first paragraph of the section; the other has the look of an imperative, is given in the fourth paragraph, and is specifically referred to as the universal law of *Recht*. The first formulation is:

(1)   Any action is *right* [*recht*] if it, or if pursuant to its maxim the freedom of choice of each, can coexist with everyone's freedom according to a universal law   (*RL* 6:230.29–31)

That this sentence is meant to provide a sufficient *and necessary* condition for the rightness of actions is shown by the very next sentence, which infers that certain actions, because they 'cannot coexist with freedom according to universal laws' (*RL* 6:231.1–2), commit a wrong (*Unrecht*).

The second formulation demands:

(2)   So act externally that the free use of your choice can coexist with the freedom of everyone according to a universal law.   (*RL* 6:231.10–12)

Since Kant offers no argument for either formulation, and since at least the second formulation looks like a straightforward variant or application of the Categorical Imperative, one can easily be led to presume that Kant is here presupposing the moral philosophy he had developed in the *Groundwork* and *Critique of Practical Reason*. The end of §C, however, must count strongly against this presumption. Kant writes there that his principle in its second formulation 'does not at all expect, far less demand, that I *myself ought to* restrict my freedom to those conditions just for the sake of this obligation; instead, reason says only that my freedom *is* in its idea restricted to those conditions and also may forcefully [*tätlich*] be so restricted by others' (*RL* 6:231.13–17; cf. *RL* 6:231.3–9). What looks like an imperative addressed to me turns out then to be a permission addressed to my fellows, who may force me to act externally so that the free use of my choice can coexist with the freedom of everyone according to a universal law. And this permission exists of course quite generally, not just with regard to myself: persons may force any person to act externally so that the free use of his or her choice can coexist with the freedom of everyone according to a universal law.

One might think that the second formulation—even if it is really a permission rather than an imperative—is still a *moral* claim whose justification presumably depends on Kant's moral philosophy. There is, however, a far more convincing alternative interpretation, which seeks support for the permission in question not from other parts of Kant's corpus, but from the immediately preceding discussion of *Recht*, and thus understands it not as a moral, but as a *juridical* permission. We saw in the previous section that Kant defines *Recht* as a property of a world of persons capable of obstructing one another's actions. Now Kant is using this definition to define a property of external actions. The relation of these two properties to one another will turn out to be complex, and I will deal with it in a moment. But that there is this connection is strongly suggested by the fact that both the definition of *Recht* as well as the two formulations now before us are dominated by expressions of the form 'can coexist . . . according to a universal law'.[19] My conjecture then is that Kant thinks of actions as either fitting or not fitting with *Recht*, which, as we have seen, is a certain organization of a world of persons. Let us say then that, depending on whether actions satisfy or fail to satisfy the 'can coexist . . . according to a universal law' expression, they either accord or fail to accord with *Recht*. The two formulations of §C can now be put, simply, as follows:

(1*a*)   Any action is right if it accords with *Recht*, and wrong otherwise.

(2*a*)   So act externally that your actions accord with *Recht* (that is, are right).

As we have seen, Kant reads the second formulation as tantamount to a permission:

(2*b*)   Persons may force any person to act rightly, or: Persons may obstruct wrong actions.

Now the idea of reading the 'may' in the sense of a juridical permission is simply to read statements about what persons may do as equivalent to statements about what it is right, in the sense of (1*a*), for them to do. Making this substitution turns (2*b*) into

---

[19]   The formulations of the condition differ, but they do not differ much. I will return to this point.

(2*c*)   It is right to force a person to act rightly (that is, it is never wrong to obstruct wrong actions).

On this reconstruction of the text, (1) then turns out to be a definition of 'right' (and 'wrong') as applied to actions; and (2) turns out to be a theorem about the rightness and wrongness of action-obstructing actions—the theorem proven in §D.[20]

We have yet to unpack the predicate 'accords with *Recht*'. As is to be expected, Kant gives the most elaborate and careful explication in the definition—that is, in (1). This explication involves a disjunction. This may suggest that Kant is here offering persons a choice between two different ways of acting rightly.[21] But I find it more plausible to read him as distinguishing two cases, implying that what it means for an action to accord with *Recht* varies depending on whether the action takes place in a context where *Recht* is instantiated or in one where it is not. So I propose the following rendition of (1):

(1*b*)   When *Recht* is instantiated, an action is right if and only if it can coexist with everyone's freedom according to a universal law (which we must presume to be the universal law that figures in the existing instantiation of *Recht*). When *Recht* is not instantiated, an action is right if and only if pursuant to its maxim the freedom of choice of each can coexist with everyone's freedom according to a universal law.

The basic idea of this definition is then the following. When *Recht* is instantiated (case 1), an action is right if it conforms to the existing law, and wrong otherwise. Here, actions accord with *Recht* if and only if they comply with existing law. When *Recht* is not instantiated (case 2), an action is right if and only if its maxim is consistent with a possible universal law. Here, actions accord with *Recht* if and only if they anticipate a possible instantiation of *Recht*.

Case 2 is problematic in at least two respects. The first problem is that, if we read the word 'universal' in the weak sense I have advocated above, then it would seem that, when *Recht* is not instantiated, any (or almost any) action can be juridically permissible—provided only that the agent's maxim anticipates

---

[20]   It is this theorem that, in the Introduction to *TL*, Kant refers to as the 'supreme principle of the *Rechtslehre*' and as an 'analytic proposition' (*TL* 6:396.2, 10–11).

[21]   Sam Kerstein points out that the 'or' could also be read as explicative. He adds that, though it is quite hard to see how the two phrases it connects could be equivalent, they are too obscure for this possibility to be ruled out. I concede all three points, I but still find the interpretation I provide in the text more convincing than its two alternatives.

some, however ludicrously inegalitarian, instantiation of *Recht*.[22] The second problem with case 2 is that Kant's focus on agent maxims is odd because he insists so strongly—even in this very section (*RL* 6:231.3–5)—on the irrelevance of inner states. He does not seem to want to allow for the possibility that whether some given action is juridically right or wrong depends on the maxim on which it is performed. If we take this insistence seriously,[23] then we seem compelled to say that, when *Recht* is not instantiated, an action is right if and only if it *could* be performed on a maxim pursuant to which the freedom of choice of each can coexist with everyone's freedom according to a universal law.

A common element in both of these problems is that, when *Recht* is not instantiated, the threshold for juridically right conduct may turn out to be implausibly low. This difficulty can be alleviated by strengthening what it means for conduct to anticipate a possible instantiation of *Recht*—along the following lines. When *Recht* is not instantiated, then my conduct is right if and only if there is an instantiation of *Recht* that (A) is practicable and such that my conduct is consistent with (would be legal under) it and (B) is realistically attainable and such that my conduct facilitates (or, at least, does not hamper) its realization. It must be possible, that is, to understand my conduct as proceeding from maxims that are mindful of the *exeundum e statu naturali*. There is good evidence that Kant did indeed hold this view and took the goal-directed element (B) to be contained in (1). In §42, he writes: 'In a situation of unavoidable proximity, you ought, with all others, to leave the state of nature and make the transition into a juridical condition' (*RL* 6:307.9–11).[24] He immediately goes on to say that 'the reason for this can be developed analytically out of the concept of *Recht*' (*RL* 6:307.12–13) and, in explicating this reason, he identifies a person's being obliged to leave the state of nature with others being permitted to coerce him to do so (*RL* 6:307.24; cf. *Ref.* 7735, 19:503.28–30). So Kant clearly considered it juridically impermissible not to cooperate with others towards the establishment of *Recht* (for only those whose conduct is juridically impermissible are targets for juridically permissible coercion).

---

[22]   This problem may seem to be a reason for holding that at least here the word 'universal' should be read in the strong sense, so that the mutually consistent domains of external freedom envisaged in (1*b*) are required to be *equal* domains. I reject this reading for two reasons. First, the word 'universal' occurs in (1) only once, in reference to both cases 1 and 2. For case 1, however, Kant needs 'universal' to have its weak sense because he holds it to be juridically impermissible to disobey *any* existing instantiation of *Recht*— whether it provides equality under the law or not (see n. 46). Secondly, I want to avoid, if at all possible, the conclusion that the equal juridical standing of all persons is smuggled in, that Kant begs rather than answers the question why an action that anticipates an *in*egalitarian instantiation of *Recht* should count as juridically wrong (as not according to *Recht*). I will have much more to say on this issue below.

[23]   We need not take it seriously, if we allow ourselves to correct Kant's 'second mistake', detailed in n. 15.

[24]   Cf. also *RL* 6:343.23–5, 350.6–8; EF 8:349 n. 16–24.

Let us take stock. I have tried to show that Kant conceives of the core of his *Rechtslehre* as independent from the rest of his philosophy. What this means can be made vivid by conceiving of his *Rechtslehre* as a game, though doing so is misleading in so far as games are normally limited, for instance, to a chess-board or soccer field—while this game covers everything persons might do externally. Kant's *Rechtslehre* game is governed by rules, which are binary by exhaustively dividing all possible actions by persons into those that are right (*recht*) and those that are wrong (*unrecht*) or, equivalently, into juridically permissible and juridically impermissible moves. One important theorem about this game is that coercive moves are permissible (right) *if* and *only if* any moves they obstruct are impermissible (wrong).[25] Both conditionals follow from Kant's definition of *Recht*. It cannot be permissible to obstruct a permissible move because, under any instantiation of *Recht*, all permissible choices are compatible ('can coexist'). And it cannot be impermissible to obstruct an impermissible move, because any such restriction would be redundant; *Recht* excludes any conditions that make no contribution to the maintenance of mutually secure domains of external freedom.[26] This is not a trivial theorem—no conception of ethics I know of, Kant's included, makes it permissible to oppose any and all wrong actions—and Kant appears to be rather pleased that so substantial a result can be derived from so slender a basis.

The basic idea behind the metaphor of the *Rechtslehre* game is straightforward. To play this game is to be disposed to prefer juridically permissible over juridically impermissible conduct. Given Kant's theorem, this preference will spread: the fact that we have it will give others, who know that we have it, a reason to develop the same preference, because they know that we are less likely impermissibly to obstruct their permissible conduct than permissibly to

---

[25] This needs to be put more carefully. The fact that a move is impermissible (does not accord with *Recht*) entails that it is permissible to obstruct it—but not necessarily that anyone may do so. For it is possible that, if several try to obstruct an impermissible move, these would-be obstructors will obstruct one another. A legal order may, therefore, have to restrict the permission to use coercion by further rules or to certain officials.

Also, the fact that a move is permissible does not entail that it is impermissible to pre-empt it, thus rendering it impermissible. It may be permissible for any person to occupy some as yet unoccupied piece of land or space with the consequence that moves into it by others become impermissible and obstruction of such moves permissible.

[26] Kant offers a very compressed derivation of this theorem in §D (*RL* 6:231). One might comment that it is indeed relatively straightforward to get from Kant's concept of *Recht* to the permission to use coercion against impermissible conduct if such coercion is a matter of preventing a transgression at the border (blocking someone's path into another's domain) or a matter of terminating a transgression (ejecting someone from another's domain). The connection is harder to make when it is a matter of punishing someone who is well within her own domain for a transgression that is now wholly in the past. One might try to argue here that such punishment is permissible because it is a necessary by-product of a permissible prior (unsuccessful) attempt at deterrence.

obstruct their impermissible conduct. As these players' dispositions strengthen, and as more persons are drawn into the game, mutually secure domains of (constrained) external freedom emerge.

Starting out from §C, I have in this section sketched the rudiments of a game by saying something about its norms and something about how it might tend to go. As indicated, this game is connected to Kant's definition of *Recht* in this way. If the conduct of all persons consisted exclusively of juridically permissible (right) moves, then *Recht*—mutually secure domains of external freedom—would be established and maintained. Still, describing such a game, some principled way of sorting all external actions into juridically permissible and juridically impermissible ones, would seem to be a pointless exercise. Seeking the point of this exercise finally gets us to the second, substantive component of Kant's *Rechtslehre*.[27]

While we can view the universal principle of *Recht* as its core, Kant's *Rechtslehre* goes beyond this core in two related directions. On the one hand, it aims to offer a justification of this principle—seeks to give persons a reason for pursuing the instantiation of *Recht* through playing the *Rechtslehre* game. To be sure, each of us may have reason to play along if we know that the others are; but why should we, all of us as a group, play this game? The mere fact that the norms of the game instruct us to do so by defining certain conduct options as permissible and the remainder as impermissible cannot provide an answer to this question. We still need a reason for paying any attention to these norms. On the other hand, Kant also aims to strengthen the norms by going beyond what can be derived from his universal principle of *Recht*. He aims to specify the *Rechtslehre* game in such a way that it manifests a preference not merely for the instantiation of *Recht* (for a juridical condition over a state of nature) but also for a particular way of instantiating *Recht* over all alternative instantiations. The second of these projects presupposes the first in that at least some of Kant's attempts to strengthen the norms are justified by appeal to the point of the *Rechtslehre* game. I will discuss these two projects in the final two sections.

IV. The Point of *Recht*

Kant holds that persons have reason to take an interest in the *Rechtslehre* game because of their prior interest in securing the external freedom of (at least some) persons against obstructing actions by others. When *Recht* is not instantiated, persons' attempts to act are likely to be obstructed in various and unpredictable

---

[27]   These two components are introduced at the end of Section II.

ways, and they will often fail to complete the actions they want to perform on account of such obstructions and will frequently not even attempt to do what they want to do from fear of being so obstructed. When *Recht* is instantiated, the conduct options of persons are constrained by firm restrictions on their external freedom. These constraints are, however, regular and predictable and give each person a clearly delimited space of options that are secure from the obstructing actions of others. Persons' external freedom is enhanced far more by the security that some of their options gain by being protected through an effective legal order than it is reduced by the added obstacles that legal prohibition imposes on their remaining options. Therefore persons tend to benefit, on balance, from the existence of a juridical condition.[28] Since the *Rechtslehre* game tends towards the establishment and maintenance of a juridical condition, it makes sense for persons interested in securing their own and/or others' external freedom against obstructing actions to play this game.

The text leaves little doubt, I believe, that Kant saw the point of mutually secure domains of external freedom in the enhancement of external freedom it makes possible.[29] He seems to be at some pains, however, to present the superiority (in terms of external freedom) of a juridical condition as knowable a priori.[30] The argument I have loosely sketched in the preceding paragraph, by contrast, sounds rather empirical; and this is so because I am unable to conceive of a plausible a priori argument. We cannot know a priori, for example, how severely persons can obstruct one another's conduct, how insecure their options would be in the absence of an effective legal order, how constraining the rules imposed by such an order would be, and how securely it would protect the options it permits. We also cannot rule out a priori that capacities and vulnerabilities are distributed very unevenly among persons, so that the balance of pros and cons differs from person to person. Without taking such empirical complexities into account, one cannot endorse Kant's conclusion that persons with an interest in external freedom have reason to play the *Rechtslehre* game.

---

[28] This reasoning could be strengthened significantly by detailing how the establishment of *Recht* will also engender many new conduct options—involving new social practices or new technologies, for example—that would never emerge without an effective legal order.

[29] 'Freedom (independence from the coercive choice of another), in so far as it can coexist with the freedom of everyone else according to a universal law of freedom, is this sole original right to which every human being is entitled by virtue of his humanity' (*RL* 6:237.29–32). 'The concept of an external *Recht* derives entirely from the concept of *freedom* in the external relations of human beings to one another and has nothing whatever to do with the end that all human beings have by nature (the goal of happiness)' (GTP 8:289.29–33). Note that asserting the avoidance of interpersonal conflicts as the rationale would not explain Kant's exclusion from *Recht* of what I have called redundant restrictions.

[30] Cf. once more, for example, the quote from *RL* 6:312.6–12, cited in n. 13.

But reaching this conclusion involves still further difficulties. Playing the *Rechtslehre* game is supported in so far as persons have an interest in having a large and stable set of valued options that are secure from obstructing actions by other persons. But then it is hard to see why persons should not also have an interest in having their options expanded and protected against obstacles and threats of other kinds. So Kant must show either that persons do not have this further interest or that this further interest does not furnish a reason that might outweigh their reason—based on their interest in securing their external freedom against obstructing actions by other persons—in favour of playing the *Rechtslehre* game.[31] This difficulty can be generalized to other interests that might be attributed to persons—interests in happiness, knowledge, wisdom, salvation, moral perfection, and so on. With respect to any such purported interest, Kant needs to show either that persons do not have it, or that it should not count as providing a relevant reason, or that the reason it provides does not affect the balance of reasons so as to upset the claim that persons have reason all things considered to play the *Rechtslehre* game.[32]

Kant may not have a fully satisfactory response to these further difficulties, but I think his key idea for such a response would be that *Recht* must be based on, and only on, interests that we necessarily have as (interacting) agents. Only if it is so based can we show that the instantiation of *Recht*, and hence participation in the *Rechtslehre* game, is in the interest of each and every person. Only if it is so based can *Recht* stand above the potentially contested, divisive, and shifting interests that persons may contingently attribute to themselves and to others. But the only interest that persons, whom Kant defines by reference to a capacity to choose their conduct, can be said to have necessarily is the interest in the fullest exercise of this capacity and hence in the availability of a wide range

---

[31] In particular, Kant must exclude the preferability of a legal order that, though it constrains persons' external freedom more than is necessary to establish mutually secure domains, enhances their external freedom on the whole by facilitating (for example, through technology) the removal of natural obstacles and threats or the creation of additional options. This difficulty does not come into view for Kant, because he does not clarify his notion of external freedom and, in particular, does not discuss what obstacles and threats are to count as reducing a person's external freedom. Without explicit defence he thus reasons as if the interest in securing one's external freedom against obstructing actions by other persons were exhaustive of the interest in external freedom. Having highlighted this problem, I will use the latter, briefer label from now on.

[32] We can learn from this paragraph that Kant's position on the point of government and an effective legal order is quite close to that defended by Isaiah Berlin and differs dramatically from what Berlin attributes to Kant: the view that law and government should be concerned to enhance citizens' positive freedom or moral autonomy. Contrast Isaiah Berlin, 'Two Concepts of Liberty', in his *Four Essays on Liberty* (Oxford: Oxford University Press, 1969), and the Rawls passages cited in n. 4 with, for example: 'But woe to the legislator willing through coercion to bring about a constitution directed to ethical ends! For he would thereby not merely attain the opposite of the ethical [ends], but would also undermine and render insecure his political [ends]' (*R.* 6:96.1–4).

of secure options from which to choose. As agents, we want our lives to be determined by our own choices rather than by the choices coercively imposed on us by others.[33]

On this reconstruction, Kant emerges as the freestanding liberal *par excellence*. Rather than presuppose much more than Rawls does—his moral philosophy and transcendental idealism—he in fact presupposes much less. He makes no appeal to fundamental ideas prevalent in the public culture of his society, nor does he insist that persons have certain moral powers and matching higher-order interests in their development and exercise, nor does he seek to identify all-purpose means needed for realizing the conceptions of the good that citizens of a society like his own are likely to have. Rather, he bases the establishment and maintenance of *Recht* exclusively on persons' fundamental a priori interest in external freedom.[34]

This freestanding argument for *Recht* can be embedded in diverse comprehensive views. It can be embedded, for instance, in a Kantian morality that holds each person to be duty bound to afford tangible assurance to every other person: because I owe it to those around me to help secure their external freedom against obstructing actions by myself (and by others?), I morally ought to contribute to the establishment and maintenance of *Recht*. At another extreme, it can also be embedded in a Hobbesian prudential account: because my fundamental interest is to secure my external freedom against obstructing actions by others, I prudentially ought to contribute to the establishment and/or maintenance of *Recht*. Kant himself stresses the availability of this latter embedding in a famous passage from 'Perpetual Peace', where he discusses the best instantiation of *Recht*: 'Now the *republican* constitution is the only one that is fully appropriate to the right of human beings. But it is also the most difficult one to establish and even more so to maintain, so that many claim that it could function only in a state of angels' (EF 8:366.1–4). He goes on to write that, on the contrary, even utterly selfish persons, intelligent devils, would have reason to establish and maintain such a constitution:

The problem of setting up a state . . . is solvable even for a people of devils (if only they have understanding). It is this: A set of rational beings who on the whole need for their preservation universal laws from which each is however secretly inclined to exempt himself is to be organized and their constitution arranged so that their private attitudes, though opposed [to one another], nevertheless check one another in such a way that these beings behave in public as if they had no such evil attitudes.   (EF 8:366.15–23)

---

[33] This is not, of course, meant to be a satisfactory argument, only the sketch of an argument that Kant might reasonably have thought to be available. It is not clear, in particular, how the argument can derive the interest from the capacity and how it can confer special significance upon obstructions *by other persons*.

[34] See Note B.

This passage shows clearly, I believe, that Kant wants his argument for *Recht*, and for a republican instantiation thereof, to be independent from his morality. This morality may well give its adherents moral reasons for supporting *Recht* and a republican constitution in particular. But it does not therefore have a special status with respect to *Recht*, because it is, as the quote shows, just as true that selfishness gives its immoral adherents selfish reasons for supporting *Recht* and a republican constitution in particular.

This conclusion seems to go against the very core of Kant's philosophy: if everyone's participation in the *Rechtslehre* game were prudentially motivated, no one would be playing this game from duty or for the sake of genuine moral principles, and there would then presumably be no value in human beings living on this earth, even if *Recht* prevails.[35] But this is no reason to lament the fact that *Recht*, and a republican constitution, can be achieved without moral motives. To the contrary! This fact makes it much easier to establish and maintain an enlightened juridical condition, which in turn greatly facilitates the development of our moral dispositions.[36]

The conclusion also seems to collide head-on with the basic structure of *The Metaphysics of Morals*, of which the *RL* is, of course, an integral part. In the introductory materials preceding the *RL* (which has its own introduction), and elsewhere as well, Kant stresses the unity of the entire work, claiming that he is providing a systematic account of both *Recht* and ethics—an account that develops both of them out of their common root in human freedom and the Categorical Imperative (see *MS* 6:207, 214, 215.16–23, 221–2, 225–6): 'The supreme principle of the *Sittenlehre* [that is, of both *RL* and *TL*] is therefore: act on a maxim that can also be valid as a universal law' (*MS* 6:226.1–2).

My conclusion is not in fact, however, threatened by these passages. It is true Kant seeks to establish not merely the consistency of his *Rechtslehre* with the rest of his philosophy, but also its unique standing as the one and only *Rechtslehre* firmly grounded in morality. Thus he aims to show that those who accept his moral philosophy must also accept his *Rechtslehre*. But it does not follow from this that he also aims to show that anyone who accepts his *Rechtslehre* must also accept his moral philosophy. We should be careful to avoid this erroneous inference and should therefore take care to distinguish between the two directions of support—a distinction that tends to get lost when the issue is framed in terms simply of 'dependence' or 'independence'.

---

[35] I am here alluding, of course, to Kant's famous saying: 'If justice perishes, then it no longer has any value that human beings are living on the earth' (*RL* 6:332.1–3).

[36] Without this fact, humankind might well have been caught in a Catch-22 situation: needing the security of a juridical state in order to develop effective moral motives and needing effective moral motives to make the transition into a juridical state.

Failure to make this distinction vitiates Wolfgang Kersting's critique of what he calls the independence thesis (*Unabhängigkeitsthese*) and attributes to Julius Ebbinghaus, Klaus Reich, and Georg Geismann.[37] Kersting correctly explicates this thesis as asserting 'a complete independence of the *Rechtslehre* from both the doctrine of transcendental idealism and from the critical moral philosophy'.[38] On the next page, however, he refers to the 'independence between [*sic*] transcendental idealism and critical moral philosophy on the one hand and the *Rechtslehre* on the other'[39] and immediately proceeds to demolish this thesis by pointing out that Kant argues for *Recht* by appeal to moral notions, asking rhetorically: 'What sense does it make to develop *Recht* as part of a metaphysics of morals, if the *Rechtslehre* does not care whether or not natural causality is humanity's fate?'[40] Doing this would indeed make no sense, if Kant were committed to the *mutual* independence of his *Rechtslehre* and morality. But the independence thesis does not assert this. And so we can easily answer Kersting's question: developing his *Rechtslehre* as part of a metaphysics of morals makes sense, because Kant wants to show that it has a basis in morality, is the only doctrine of *Recht* that fits into his moral philosophy. By showing that M entails R, Kant establishes merely a one-sided dependence of M on R; he establishes that R's failure would entail the failure of M, that M cannot stand without R. And this does *not* imply, of course, that R is dependent upon (cannot stand without) M.[41]

Some minor textual obstacles remain even after this clarification. Thus Kersting correctly points out that Kant 'employs elements of his theoretical philosophy' when he uses the terms *sensible* and *intelligible* to distinguish between physical and juridical possession.[42] But I dare say that, in a pinch, this distinction can be drawn without recourse to Kant's theoretical philosophy and has in fact been so drawn long before Kant ever put pen to paper. It does not follow from Kant's eagerness to present his *Rechtslehre* as an integral part of his overall philosophy that he did not *also* want it to be freestanding: presentable on its own. The two modes of presentation are compatible, and Kant thus does not have to choose between them.

---

[37] Wolfgang Kersting, *Wohlgeordnete Freiheit* (Berlin: Walter de Gruyter, 1984), 37–42 (hereafter cited as *WF*). The foremost champion of the 'independence thesis' is Julius Ebbinghaus, who has (rather polemically) argued for it in a number of essays, which are collected in his *Gesammelte Schriften*, ii. *Philosophie der Freiheit* (Bonn: Bouvier, 1988), hereafter cited as *PdF*. Kersting also cites Klaus Reich, *Kant and Rousseau* (Tübingen: Mohr-Siebeck, 1936), 17, and Georg Geismann, *Ethik und Herrschaftsordnung* (Tübingen: Mohr-Siebeck, 1974), 56 (55–88 are pertinent).

[38] *WF* 37.   [39] Ibid. 38.   [40] Ibid.   [41] See Note C.

[42] *WF* 38 n. 57; cf. n. 7.

V. The Fine-Tuning of *Recht*

When *Recht* is not instantiated, persons are juridically obliged to cooperate in its establishment. In the light of the vast range of possible instantiations of *Recht*, such cooperation involves an immense coordination problem. Persons must coordinate on a single set of descriptions in terms of which legal rules are to refer to action-tokens, and they must coordinate on a division of labour between rigid and generative rules[43] and ultimately on one particular complete set of such rigid and generative rules.[44] If the *Rechtslehre* game is to be effective in guiding persons towards the fulfilment of their presumed interest in external freedom, then it must involve not merely a preference for *Recht* as such, but also a preference ordering over the many possible instantiations of *Recht*. This is an important point for my interpretation. For it may well seem that the interest in external freedom is too indeterminate to justify clear-cut rankings of alternative instantiations of *Recht*. But this appearance is deceptive, as the justification may proceed indirectly: our interest in external freedom justifies the master preference for the instantiation of *Recht* over its non-instantiation, and the fulfilment of this master preference *requires* secondary preferences sufficient to solve the coordination problem.

The secondary preferences Kant proposes, which often seem rather arbitrary and *ad hoc*,[45] become far less implausible if we view them as resting on such a two-stage justification. Kant is then not engaged in sorting possible rules into those that are correct and those that are incorrect by the lights of reason. Rather, he evaluates rules as more or less suitable for solving a coordination problem that simply has to be solved. Since he feels compelled by the task of a *Rechtslehre* to offer a salient solution that can guide the establishment of *Recht*, he does not feel that he has the luxury to confine himself to rationally compelling solutions. If no rationally compelling solution can be found, then the most salient one will have to do, even if it looks to Kant just barely more salient than some competitor.

It is clear what the juridical status of these secondary preferences must be. When *Recht* is not instantiated, then these preferences are juridically relevant by

---

[43] By generative rules, I mean rules enabling voluntary rule changes. Examples are rules governing unilateral appropriation, contracting, and political decision making. Kant briefly mentions the distinction at *RL* 6:237.18–23.

[44] A set of rules is complete if and only if it uniquely sorts all possible actions into those that are legal and those that are not. I take for granted that the rules must also satisfy the universal principle of *Recht*—for example, must count as legal any action that it is illegal to obstruct.

[45] His preferred rules for the unilateral appropriation of land are a good example: 'as if the soil were saying: if you cannot protect me, then you cannot command me either' (*RL* 6:265.4–5). States therefore own oceanic fishing grounds and continental shelves as far as their land-based cannons reach (*RL* 6:265.5–10).

determining who is cooperating in the establishment of an effective legal order and who is not. While it is juridically permissible to coerce the latter, it is juridically impermissible to coerce the former. When *Recht* is instantiated, then the secondary preferences are juridically irrelevant. It is juridically permissible for the sovereign to maintain an inferior instantiation and juridically impermissible for citizens to obstruct the sovereign's efforts to do so. And this, of course, is the position Kant in fact defends.[46]

There is space to discuss, at least briefly, the most important secondary preference of Kant's *Rechtslehre*—its general and pervasive preference for equality among persons. This preference for equality may seem to furnish the most powerful challenge that those who read Kant in the spirit of Kersting and Rawls can level at those who—like Ebbinghaus and myself—view Kant as holding that his *Rechtslehre* can stand on its own, independently from his moral philosophy and transcendental idealism. It is surprising that it has not, to my knowledge, been posed.

This is how the challenge might go. In the instructions it gives to the holders of sovereign power when *Recht* is instantiated and to all persons when *Recht* is not instantiated, Kant's *Rechtslehre* favours equal domains of external freedom, ultimately to be secured under a republican constitution, which requires equal access to political participation and thus popular sovereignty on equal terms. It is not hard to sketch how this preference for equality can be supported on the basis of Kant's moral philosophy: it would be morally wrong for some to claim more external freedom and more access to political participation than can possibly be granted to all others as well.[47] Now, if the independence thesis were correct, then Kant would need to offer for his egalitarian preference another defence that appeals solely to persons' interest in their own external freedom and not to any principle of universalizability. However, no such defence appears in the text. One can still insist, of course, that Kant really meant his *Rechtslehre* to be presentable on its own, but one can do so only at the cost of accusing Kant of introducing the egalitarian preference surreptitiously —either by equivocating on the word 'universal'[48] or by illicitly appealing to

---

[46]   For example, when he insists again and again that it is wrong for subjects to disobey the sovereign or its authorized representatives (*RL* 6:320–3, 371–2; GTP 8:299–305; EF 8:382; *Ref.* 7989, 19:574–5, 8051, 19:594). It is worth stressing that Kant does not declare it wrong to disobey a tyrant who rules by whim, who does not specify and maintain mutually secure domains of external freedom (*Rechtssicherheit*). But Kant does not clarify *how* law-governed an exercise of power must be for it to count as establishing a juridical condition. And he does not explain why the distinction between whimsical and law-governed oppression should have such great significance for persons interested in their own external freedom.

[47]   Filling in such a sketch is much harder, as numerous attempts in the secondary literature attest. But let me here just stipulate, for the sake of the argument, that Kant has a promising argument of this sort.

[48]   This sort of 'smuggling operation' was briefly discussed in n. 22.

morality while pretending not to do so. Because the independence thesis requires such a severe accusation, it should be abandoned in favour of the more charitable interpretation defended by Kersting and assumed by Rawls.

I am not sure whether I can adequately meet this challenge, but the following points may make a decent start. To begin with, let me note that I would not view it as a great disaster to have to accuse Kant of the smuggling operation effected by the equivocal use of the word 'universal', because, as far as I can see, Kant is undeniably involved in precisely this smuggling operation in the important §2 (*RL* 6:246–7). He gives there two formulations of a 'juridical postulate of practical reason' without apparently noticing the difference between them. One formulation suggests that it would violate the universal principle of right (would constitute 'a contradiction of external freedom with itself' (*RL* 6:246.24–5)) if the use of a usable object were forbidden to all persons (*RL* 6:246.10–17; cf. *RL* 6:252.13–15, 6:301.9–10).[49] The other formulation asserts that each person is equally permitted, and on the same terms of original appropriation, to acquire unowned objects (*RL* 6:247.1–6). Obviously, the latter claim is stronger than the former by demanding not merely that each usable object must be accessible to some person(s), but that each such object must be accessible to *any* person *on equal* terms (that is, on the basis of temporal priority). In so far as the smuggling accusation is true (at least in regard to this passage), it must count against Kant himself and, if anything, *for* my interpretation.

Still, it would be much nicer if the enterprise I read Kant as engaged in could be reconstructed as successful, or at least promising. And, indeed, I believe that a defence of the egalitarian preference in terms of salience is no less promising than many of Kant's rather weak arguments—especially in 'Part I: Privatrecht' of the *RL*—for more specific solutions ('secondary preferences'). Kant actually presents an argument of this kind:

All actions relating to the right of other human beings whose maxim is incompatible with publicity are wrong (*unrecht*).

This principle should be considered not merely an *ethical* one (belonging to the *Tugendlehre*), but also a *juridical* one (concerning the *Recht* of human beings). For a maxim that I must not *declare openly* without thereby ruining my own intention, that must absolutely be *kept secret* if it is to succeed, and that I cannot *publicly acknowledge* without thereby inevitably provoking the resistance of all against my plans—such a maxim can derive this necessary and universal, hence a priori foreseeable, resistance of

---

[49] Such a universal prohibition would be a paradigm case of a redundant restriction, one that makes no contribution to the maintenance of mutually secure domains of external freedom.

all against me only from the injustice with which it threatens everyone.   (EF 8:381.24–35)

I read this passage as further explicating our juridical obligation to cooperate in the establishment and maintenance of *Recht*. To be juridically permissible, persons' conduct must anticipate a practicable and realistically attainable effective legal order. Conduct that, if fully public, would mobilize widespread resistance fails this test and thus is juridically impermissible. Conduct that anticipates an inegalitarian legal order is a special case: there would be widespread resistance to such conduct, if it were fully public, and the attempt to establish such an inegalitarian legal order, too, would be widely resisted and is thus unrealistic.

This argument works, however, only if persons are roughly equal in strength and competence. If they are not, then it is the attempt to establish equality under the law that is unrealistic, because this bargain offers a much more favourable cost–benefit ratio to the weak and to those who lack the competence to follow the rules reliably than to the strong and competent. A legal order that is to find broad support and is to maintain an enduring equilibrium among rationally self-interested persons (or intelligent devils) must achieve a more equal distribution of incentives towards participation, must accommodate persons in rough proportion to the cost and value of their participation. If it is to govern rational persons concerned to maximize the security and extent of their own external freedom, such an order must assign larger domains of external freedom to the strong and competent. These thoughts lead to the objection that, even if the publicity argument does, without appeal to a (moral) universalizability principle, support a secondary preference for equality, this preference is for the wrong, un-Kantian sort of equality.

But is it really? Consider how Kant relates the egalitarian preference to the legally inferior status of women, which he repeatedly endorses (for example, GTP 8:292.4, 295.15; *RL* 6:314.29):

Thus, if the question is raised whether it conflicts with the equality of spouses that the law says about the man in relation to the woman: he shall be your master (he the commanding, she the obeying part), then [the answer is that] this cannot be viewed as conflicting with the natural equality of a human couple so long as this mastership is based only on the man's natural superiority in the capacity to further the common interest of the household.   (*RL* 6:279.16–25)

It would seem then that the egalitarian preference Kant himself (here at least) endorses is rather like the one that can be supported by the morality-free argument I have sketched—and, sadly, rather unlike the one we would expect to flow from Kant's morality. There is some reason then to keep faith in my interpretation of Kant as holding that the *Rechtslehre*, its secondary preferences included, can successfully be presented on its own.

Here it may be said once again that my reading is uncharitable by saddling Kant with a political doctrine that is morally odious by our current standards as well as by Kant's own, properly understood. My response is that, while there may be more charitable *mis*interpretations, mine is actually the most charitable interpretation available to us. Kant clearly did hold inegalitarian views with respect to women and members of the lower classes—these views occur too frequently and are too sharply expressed to be discounted as slips of the pen. On my reading, these views can be explained and, to some extent, excused by reference to his goal of developing a *freestanding* liberalism—a goal that he may well have thought morally important for much the same reasons Rawls deems it so. I find this reading the most charitable even though it leads me to conclude that Kant's attempt fails in the end to specify a liberalism that both Kantian moralists and intelligent devils can endorse.

Notes

A. It is worth correcting here three interrelated mistakes Kant tends to make in this context. The first is that he tends to associate the just explicated consequence of his definition of *Recht*, A, with the claim, B, that inner states *cannot* be made the object of external legislation. (He opens the *RL* proper by writing that it will have to do with 'the laws for which an external legislation is possible' (*RL* 6:229.5–6; see also *MS* 6:220.12–13).) Claim B goes beyond the definition of *Recht* and is actually false. For it is surely not impossible to promulgate laws that require or forbid certain inner states, for example, setting oneself a certain end (intention). And it is also not impossible to apply such laws accurately and effectively—indeed, most existing legal systems rely on findings of intent (*mens rea*) in defining crimes (for example, murder) and in dispensing punishments. What Kant should say about such external laws is not that they are impossible, but that they make no contribution to the maintenance of secure domains of external freedom and are thus not among the conditions under which each person's freedom can coexist with that of all others according to a universal law of freedom. Such laws—among which is of course the Categorical Imperative, which governs the agent's inner choice of maxims—fall outside *Recht* as Kant defines it. What is necessary for *Recht* is only persons' outward conformity to law—the legality of their conduct—and not inner conformity or morality.

The second mistake is that Kant conflates the definitional point about the *content* of legal restrictions necessary for *Recht* with a similar point about the *criteria* involved in such restrictions. The former point, A, is that the laws necessary for any particular instantiation of *Recht* will not constrain persons' inner states. This point is true. The latter point, C, is that such a body of law will constrain persons' external conduct by reference only to outer criteria. This claim is false, as can easily be seen through an example. Conflicts over the use of external objects can be avoided by a body of law that ensures that each object has at most one owner. But such conflicts can also be avoided by a body of law that incorporates familiar exceptions—exceptions that, for example, allow me to use your boat and forbid you to prevent me from using your boat, if we have certain inner states (for example, we both believe that someone else is drowning and that I need the boat to rescue her and intend to do so). These laws, which restrict your use of your boat in exceptional circumstances and my use of your boat otherwise, make just as necessary a contribution to one instantiation of *Recht* as the more straightforward law, which restricts only my use of your boat, makes to another. A body of law that makes *criterial* use of inner states does not thereby overstep the mandate of *Recht*, which is to maintain mutually secure domains of external freedom.

At times, Kant conflates the two points I have last distinguished, A and C, with yet a fourth point, D, according to which legal restrictions (and institutional mechanisms), in order to fall within the mandate of *Recht*, must be selected solely by reference to the purpose of maintaining mutually secure domains of external freedom. (We must not prefer one property regime over another on the grounds that the latter would engender hunger among the poor—unless such hunger would make them rebellious and thereby render persons' domains of external freedom less secure.) This claim, D, is distinct from the others and, like B and C, does not follow from the definition of *Recht*.

B. Here it might be said that Kant's argument is after all comprehensive by declaring irrelevant all the other interests that persons actually have or that might be attributed to them. In one sense this charge is trivially true. But it is also self-defeating by dissolving the distinction between political and comprehensive conceptions of social justice. *Any* argument seeking to justify social institutions by reference to the interests of persons affected by them—and how else are social institutions to be justified?—will attach relative weights to indefinitely many possible interests. The charge becomes more substantial if it accuses Kant of *idealizing* where he should have been *abstracting*. (For this distinction, see Onora O'Neill, *Constructions of Reason: Explorations of Kant's Practical Philosophy* (Cambridge: Cambridge University Press, 1989), ch. 11, and *Towards Justice and Virtue* (Cambridge: Cambridge University Press, 1996), ch. 2.) Instead of assuming that all other interests have zero weight, Kant ought to have made no assumptions about their relative weights at all. But it is unclear how an argument that leaves open whether persons' interest in salvation, say, is infinitely greater or infinitely smaller than their interest in external freedom (or somewhere in between) can support any substantive conclusions at all. And yet, as the next paragraph of text brings out, Kant does accommodate O'Neill to some extent by showing that his argument covers at least a certain range of interest attributions: thanks to a shared strong interest in their own external freedom, moral and selfish persons can, despite discrepancies among their other interests, converge upon the same set of social arrangements. This suggests how Kant might have tried to meet the accusation that, by focusing on persons' interest in external freedom, he is embracing an ideal of the 'unencumbered self' (Michael Sandel, *Liberalism and the Limits of Justice* (Cambridge: Cambridge University Press, 1982)). He could have argued that the interests of deeply social persons, just as those of rugged individualists, involve a basic interest in external freedom. Still, it remains possible to imagine persons for whom this interest is completely dominated by other (for example, religious) interests.

C. Kersting commits this conflation several times in different guises. One interesting further example comes in a long footnote (*WF* 41 n. 63), which presents an apparently devastating refutation of Ebbinghaus. Kersting first quotes Ebbinghaus's acknowledgement that '*Recht*, as the a priori law of the determination of external freedom, is required by the categorical imperative as the law of pure practical reason' (*PdF* 242; Kersting quotes this essay from another source). Kersting then quotes further that the 'attempt to conceive of *Recht* in its objective perfection as dependent on the legislation of inner freedom and hence of ethics is from Kant's point of view a wholly absurd conclusion . . . that has been drawn from an erroneous interpretation of the dependence of both legislations on the categorical imperative as the highest moral principle comprising both *Recht* and ethics' (*PdF* 243). Since Kersting conflates the claim that the Categorical Imperative requires *Recht* with the claim that *Recht* is dependent on the Categorical Imperative, he infers from these quotes that Ebbinghaus is forced to attribute to Kant the absurd view that the Categorical Imperative, too, is independent from Kant's teachings on freedom and autonomy. But there is a much more plausible way of reading Ebbinghaus. In the first passage, Ebbinghaus says that the Categorical Imperative requires *Recht*. In the second passage, Ebbinghaus *denies* that *Recht* is dependent on the Categorical Imperative. Ebbinghaus is not saying there, as Kersting has it, that the dependence of both legislations on the Categorical Imperative exists but has been misinterpreted. Rather, Ebbinghaus is rejecting as erroneous the interpretation that takes both legislations (rather than ethical legislation alone) to be dependent on the Categorical Imperative. Kersting cannot see this reading of Ebbinghaus, because he cannot see that Ebbinghaus, by saying that the Categorical Imperative requires (entails) *Recht*, has by no means conceded the dependence of *Recht* on the Categorical Imperative.

7

Whence Public Right? The Role of Theoretical and Practical Reasoning in Kant's *Doctrine of Right*

Bernd Ludwig

I

For every reader familiar with Kant's *Groundwork of the Metaphysics of Morals*, the second paragraph of the 'Universal Principle of Right' in Kant's *Metaphysical First Principles of the Doctrine of Right* is, I think, a surprising one when encountered for the first time: reason says . . . that my freedom *is* in its idea restricted to those conditions and may also forcefully [*thätlich*] be so restricted by others' (*MS*, §C, 6:230).

These words are not difficult to understand by themselves: the 'conditions' Kant refers to in this passage are stated by the *allgemeine Rechtsgesetz*, the 'Law of Right' as Mary Gregor calls it: 'Any action is *right* if it can coexist with everyone's freedom in accordance with a universal law, or if on its maxim the freedom of choice of each can coexist with everyone's freedom in accordance with a universal law' (*MS* 6:230).[1]

This 'general principle', obviously, stems in some way from the Categorical Imperative, the 'supreme principle of the doctrine of morals': 'Act on a maxim which can also hold as a universal law!' (*MS* 6:226). The lesson seems to be a simple one: the doctrine of Law is an integral part of Kant's moral philosophy and the Categorical Imperative is its main normative principle. But what does

I thank Ken Westphal and Allen Wood for inspiring exchanges on a previous draft of this chapter. Although our discussions could not settle all of our disagreements, we all know better now *where* we disagree—and the reader of the present volume will find it out easily as well.

[1] I used the following translations of Kant's works: *The Metaphysics of Morals*, ed. and trans. Mary Gregor (Cambridge: Cambridge University Press, 1996); *Groundwork of the Metaphysics of Morals*, trans. H. J. Paton (New York: Harper & Row, 1965); *Critique of Pure Reason*, trans. N. K. Smith (New York: Macmillan, 1929); *Prolegomena*, trans. J. Feiser Internet Encyclopedia (*P.*). Translations of quotations from the *Critique of Practical Reason* are my own.

it mean to say, as Kant does in the *Rechtslehre*, that 'my liberty' *is* restricted 'in its idea'—and how is *this* restriction related to the permission for others, to restrict my liberty forcefully or 'by deed' (*thätlich*)—that is, restrain my actions in time and space?

This is, no doubt, a very strong statement, and to many it will look more like an absurdity than a mere paradox. Liberty—to speak with Thomas Hobbes, for example—is the absence of external impediment; and a 'free man' is 'he, who is not hindered to doe what he has a will to' (*Leviathan*, ch. 21), but he is not at all—like Kant declares—one who is *restricted by others* in a certain way. What Kant tells us here is twofold. It is, on the one hand, the well-known fact that his 'Law of Right' does not *expect* or *demand* that we are motivated by the idea of duty when we restrict our actions to the conditions of possible coexistence with the freedom of everyone according to a universal law. This would turn the 'Law of Right' into an *ethical* law.[2] On the other hand, the 'Law of Right' *expects* or *demands* nonetheless that *everyone* in fact *does act* in the way described, and this has something to do with the purported fact that everyone's liberty *is* restricted 'in its idea'. This finally renders legitimate the use of force by others, if anyone acts 'against the law'.

Thomas Pogge has proposed to look at Kant's *Rechtslehre* (that is, the *Doctrine of Right*) as a theory describing a *Rechtslehre* game.[3] This is, in fact, a very helpful device for examining the main thoughts underlying Kant's Philosophy of Right, and I will hence make use of it in the following.

Like any other game (chess or soccer, for example), this *Rechtslehre* game is ruled by (as we at least hope) a coherent set of norms that themselves define the game. These norms instruct us about the possible and impossible moves in the

---

[2]   Even at the risk of suggesting misinterpretations, I will adopt here the convenient shorthand 'juridical law' as well as 'ethical law' for 'law in a juridical/ethical *lawgiving*'. Therefore some explanation might be helpful. The *law* that forbids stealing, for example, is, of course, *the same law* in both 'lawgivings' (*MS* 6:219): 'Don't steal!' When *considered* as 'backed by threats' it may be called 'juridical law', 'ethical law' otherwise. *Every* law can be considered as 'ethical', since it is always possible to comply just for the sake of behaving morally (hence the 'universal ethical command', 'act in conformity with duty from duty' (*MS* 6:391; cf. Vig. 27:584, line 36)). Those 'ethical laws' that prescribe wide duties of virtue (as, for example, the 'ethical law of perfection' (*MS* 6:450)) cannot be considered as 'juridical laws' (*MS* 6:239; cf. *MS* 6:383) as well; they are thus called 'direct ethical laws'. Although there are special '*juridical* duties' (as, for example, the non-interference with another's property or the performance of covenant), these are always 'ethical duties' as well. In *these* contexts the term 'juridical' indicates the *origin* of the laws, which is the '*juridical* lawgiving' (especially when the laws are *positive*—that is, given by a lawgiver who is authorized in some way by natural law (*MS* 6:224)); 'juridical' does *not* point to a special kind of 'juridical *obligation*' here (indeed, Kant himself never uses a term like this. In both lawgivings the *obligation* is just '*moral* obligation' (see §B). It stems from the 'supreme principle of the doctrine of Morals' (*MS* 6:226), which 'as such only [*überhaupt nur*] affirms what obligation is' (*MS* 6:225; cf. Vig. 27:525, line 26). See n. 10 and also Mark Timmons, this volume.

[3]   Thomas Pogge, 'Is Kant's *Rechtslehre* Comprehensive?', *Southern Journal of Philosophy*, 36 (1997), suppl., 161–88, repr. with revisions in this volume as 'Is Kant's *Rechtslehre* a "Comprehensive Liberalism"?'.

game at a given moment. When playing the game, we usually pay attention to these norms. This undoubtedly is an adequate description of what happens in the *Rechtslehre* game as well. Having contracted, for example, we normally perform our covenants according to the special laws pertaining to the given case. If we do not (whether through carelessness or voluntarily), a special set of rules will apply and we may be *coerced* to comply or perhaps even be put in prison by others according to the rules of a 'subgame' constituted by so-called Penal Law. But there is an interesting difference here between the *Rechtslehre* game and, for example, chess. The former includes an important and explicit set of rules that come into play only when other rules have been broken. Let me call them 'secondary rules'. This is indeed not special about *Recht*, but rather typical for those games where it is unreasonable to expect that all players are able to comply with all the ('primary') rules all the time, and where it is difficult—if not impossible—to go back to a previous stage of the game when those 'primary rules' have been transgressed. If we compare soccer to chess, for example, it is obvious that the former game would lose most of its appeal if the whole system of penalty rules were abolished and the game would always end immediately after the first foul play. On the other hand, we can reasonably expect that even a moderately skilled chess-player will strictly obey all the rules of the game, and if he, by inattentiveness, does not, we will perhaps generously give him the opportunity to try another move but there is no special rule, for example, that applies when the king has moved across more than one square.

But what happens if one player impertinently insists on moving his king right across the chessboard? No doubt the chess game is over then. The same applies if one soccer team refuses to allow a free kick after a foul play inside the opposite penalty area. When the game is over, the norms of the game do not apply anymore. Of course, you cannot win the game if you refuse to follow its norms, but in any case there is no further 'necessity' to act according to these norms anymore. Since it is thus obvious that we usually can get rid of all the norms of a given game by just risking, or even expressively declaring, the end of the game in question, we need an *external* reason for paying any attention to the norms—that is, for taking part in the game. The rules of chess or soccer do not tell us *that* we have to play chess or soccer, but only *how* we have to play it—as long as we actually *want* to play it. It is not difficult to find out why the professional soccer player usually is inclined to comply with the rules, even if he is facing defeat (we will look for an explanation of his behaviour only if he does *not*). The amateur obeys the rules of chess as long as he enjoys playing the game or just enjoys the company and esteem of his opponents.

It should be obvious by now that Kant's *Rechtslehre* game isn't a game 'just for fun and recreation' like pinball, chess, or soccer: we are not at all free to decide whether we want to take part in it. *'Exeundum est e statu naturali'* (*R.* 6:97) is a Categorical Imperative for human beings, and, if they do not act the way the 'Law of Right' *demands*, they may *nevertheless* be forced by others to do so—that is what the above quote from §C of the *Rechtslehre* teaches us (cf. *Ref.* 7735, 19:503 as well).

Maybe self-interest often gives selfish reasons for participating in the game and obeying its rules (just as self-interest usually is a sufficient reason to participate in a game—at least as long as you can reasonably expect to win). We may in fact take part in the *Rechtslehre* game just as in any other game, just because this is sometimes an easy way to pursue our interests. Throughout most of our lifetime this is the way our compliance with legal norms is in fact *motivated*: it is just a rule of prudence, for example, to use the correct lane on the motorway if we want to reach our destination unhurt. As long as we comply with the juridical rules in this matter, talking about *obligation* seems to be pointless. Playing the *Rechtslehre* game does not differ in principle from playing chess or soccer *then*. To use a phrase of Johann Christoph Lichtenberg, sometimes the necessitation by the law is just as painful as the pressure of the atmosphere: coercion is actually unnecessary then indeed. As we all know, Kant himself states in 'Perpetual Peace' that even (rational) devils would pay attention to the rules of the *Rechtslehre* game for the sake of their own preservation *if only* the state were instituted in a way that performance of the civic duties furthers private interest sufficiently. But obviously this 'motivating mechanism' will not work without some system of penalties, and this system of penalties again has to be justified beforehand, because it interferes with the liberty or freedom of the subjects. Consequently the 'devils' example', far from answering the question why anyone who actually does *not* want to conform to the norms of this special game may be *coerced* by others to do so, rather presupposes that coercion and penalties *are* justified or at least justifiable (and the example of the devils was, of course, not intended by Kant as an answer to *this* question[4]).

Hence the crucial question of Kant's *Rechtslehre* is *not* 'What [motivating[5]] reasons might human beings have to take part in the *Rechtslehre* game?' or 'For

---

[4] In this famous passage (EF 8:366), Kant talks about the problem that the 'Princes' refuse to institute republican constitutions. Their argument (as proclaimed 1794 by Rehberg in the *Berlinische Monatsschrift*) is: only a people of angels is fit for republican government. Kant disagrees. The problem would be solvable even *for* (not *by*) a people of (rational) devils, because it depends only on a right 'ordering' of the society, which is in fact in the reach of those 'Princes' ('im Vermögen der Menschen') who refuse to do just this. See Bernd Ludwig, 'Will die Natur unwiderstehlich die Republik? Einige Reflexionen anläßlich einer rätselhaften Textpassage in Kants Friedensschrift', *Kant-Studien*, 88 (1997), 218–28, and 'Bemerkungen zum Kommentar Brandts: Will die Natur unwiderstehlich die Republik?', *Kant-Studien*, 89 (1998), 80–3.

[5] The borderline between Kant's concepts of *jus* and *ethica* would be blurred if our *duty* to comply with the law would be founded on *those* reasons that would in fact *motivate* us *if we were* 'rationally' pursuing our

which typical (or even natural) human end is the *Rechtslehre* game the most adequate means?' If we want to give an appropriate interpretation of the above quote from §C, the question Kant's text demands us to answer is instead 'What [justifying] reasons do people have for the claim that they are allowed to force *others* to conform to the rules of, that is to take part in, the *Rechtslehre* game, even if the people coerced are in fact inclined *not* to do so?' Or, the other way around, 'Why can no human being complain about being coerced to conform with the "Law of Right"?' It may be tempting at first sight to identify the third or even this fourth question with the first or the second. But this is impossible on Kantian premises, since it would presuppose a principle (call it 'Chruschow's maxim') like the following: 'We may forcefully restrain people if we thereby further their *true* interests—whether they actually want it or not!' This is the route to paternalism—not to Kantian or even non-Kantian liberalism.

An adequate answer to the question 'Why can no human being complain about being coerced by others to conform with the "Law of Right"?' is not straightforward, since Kant does not bother his readers with any obvious argument during the five short sections of the Introduction to the *Doctrine of Right*. But, if we are applying the principle of interpretative charity, we will assume that he actually did not feel the need to be explicit here. Consequently the answer to our question has to be obvious from the preceding parts of the text and from those other writings upon which they depend.

In Sections II to V, I will try to expound the rudiments of Kant's theory of Right by focusing on the *players* of the *Rechtslehre* game: *Persons*. These sections link the Introduction to *The Metaphysics of Morals* and the Introduction to the *Doctrine of Right* (*MS* 6:214–42) to the metaphysical doctrines of Kant's first and second *Critiques*. The *Rechtslehre* game will show as the most fundamental and comprehensive game persons might play: it is the game whose norms are the norms human beings have to refer to whenever they justify their actions to others and whenever they expect others to do the same. In Sections VI to VIII, I then argue that the two main parts (*MS* 6:245–355) of the *Doctrine of Right*, 'Private Right' and 'Public Right', can best be understood as the Exposition of

---

happiness—that is, founded on our so-called *rational* interests. Consider the following: Suppose I were (morally) obliged to do that which I would be motivated to do if I were rational. If I then acted in conformity with the law *because I knew* that this furthers my interest best (that is, I acted intelligently *and* justly/rightly (*Legalität*, see *MS* 6:219)), this would be just *the same thing* as acting *from* duty (that is, acting well (*Moralität*, *MS* 6:219)). Were I asked, 'Why did you do it?', I would have to answer, 'Just because it furthers my interests best and it is not even unjust!' What *else* could I answer (or what *further/different* maxim could I adopt) if I wanted to act *from* duty? It does not even make sense then to support my claim that I acted morally by saying 'I would have acted the same way even if I had not been motivated by my (rational) interests' (since then my action would not have been performed *from* duty as well). Hence Kant's rational and knowledgeable *devils* would in fact be *angels* under these assumptions.

a fundamental set of Rules and Institutions that is required to play the *Rechts-lehre* game in a world where *Persons* do not only deal with each other, but with *Things* as well: the 'mine and yours' in external objects presupposes the concept of a *possessio noumenon*, and the application of this very concept presupposes voluntary agreement of persons—that is, *positive* laws given by a general unit-ed will. It is *not* my aim here to give any assessment or critical justification of Kant's arguments. I only intend to set out the aim and the separate steps as far as we can find them in his texts. Maybe there is a big gap separating what Kant actually said from what Kant should have said according to some standards that were not his own—but that is not my concern in the following pages.

II

The rules of the *Rechtslehre* game are (as Kant tells us in §B) addressed to *Per-sons*, just as—we might add—the rules of chess are addressed to chess-players. The chess-player's moves are 'in principle' (*in der Idee*) restricted to those moves that conform to the norms of chess. When the moves of the pieces on the chess-board do not comply with the rules of the game, they are not *moves in the game*—the pieces are mere 'matter in motion', nice to look at, at best.

A person's actions are—as already mentioned—'in the Idea' restricted to those that conform to the 'Law of Right'. If the chess-player tries to make a move that is not in conformity with the norms of the game, he may be prevent-ed from making it *as a move in the game*—or the game is over. But, if a person does not act in conformity with the 'Law of Right', the game is not over at all. The next round of the game will start and the person will be forcefully restrained by others and by means of the 'secondary rules' mentioned above. To be a chess-player *means* to be subject to the rules of chess—as long as the game continues. To be a person *means* to be subject to *those* norms that are essential for playing the *Rechtslehre* game—that is, essential for being a person. This is quite trivial and there is no reason to assume that Kant would have dissented from calling the *Rechtslehre* a 'game' in this way.

But what is it to be a *person*? Can we give up being persons just as we can give up being chess-players? Can we escape from the norms of the *Rechtslehre* game just by declaring the end of the game? Would others then lose their right of forceful restriction in accordance with the 'Law of Right', just as they lose their privilege to insist on our conformity with the norms of chess when we cease to be chess-players? Can we move our limbs without acting as persons—just as we can move the pieces on the chessboard without playing chess?

It is in fact *obvious* that others indeed would *not* lose their right of forceful restriction at all if we would decide (*per impossibile*, of course) to worm ourselves through time and space as *non*-persons, just as 'matter in motion'. On the contrary, *their* right to forceful restriction would expand infinitely since *im*personal beings—'things'—may *by right* be treated in any possible way. Their freedom—that is, the freedom of things—is so to speak 'in the Idea' restricted *absolutely*: a *thing* (according to Kant) is an object that 'lacks freedom' (*MS* 6:223).

If we compare chess, soccer, and the *Rechtslehre* game in this respect, the peculiarity of the latter appears in bright light. If the chess-player violates one of the chess rules, the game is over. All former 'chess duties' and 'chess rights' of the players become null. If the soccer player violates one of the soccer rules, another set of soccer rules comes into play (the soccer 'penal rules'), and if he does not want to obey even these rules, the game is over. All former 'soccer duties' and 'soccer rights' of the players become null. However, if a person violates one of the legal rules, another set of rules comes into play (the 'penal law'), and if he does not want to obey these rules, he will *by right* be forced to comply *nevertheless*. There seems to be no way out of *this* game. There is only something like a 'last exit' for it—and this ultimately proves to be nothing but a 'U-turn'. If we could stop playing the *Rechtslehre* game, *all* duties and *all* rights would vanish immediately (including the duty to conform to the rules of soccer if you contracted to be a soccer player), because the rules of this *special* game are nothing but the rules that govern our *general* practice of *justifying our free actions*. Where there is no possibility of justification, nothing can be either just or unjust. Leaving the *Rechtslehre* game *means* nothing less than giving up speaking of *unjustified* claims; it *means* giving up the possibility of even declaring it unjust to be forced to comply with the rules of the game. Once someone had claimed to have left the *Rechtslehre* game, there would be no way left to him to call it *unjust* if he was still treated as if he were still in it. Even worse, there would be no way for him to call unjust *any* treatment by others. That is exactly the situation Kant points to when he declares that being a mere 'thing', not a 'person', means 'lacking freedom', and thus lacking the 'Independence from being constrained by another's choice' (*MS* 6:237). Leaving the *Rechtslehre* game—if this were possible at all—would thus be nothing but giving up the *privilege* of being treated as a *person*.

III

Kant gives his definition of *person* in the *Philosophia practica universalis*, that subsection of the Introduction to *The Metaphysics of Morals* that explains those main concepts that are common—as Kant claims explicitly (*MS* 6:222)—to *both* parts of the book, to the *Doctrine of Right* as well as to the *Doctrine of Virtue*. 'A *person* is a subject whose actions can be *imputed* to him. *Moral* personality is therefore nothing other than the freedom of a rational being under moral laws' (*MS* 6:223). The concept of a person thus leads back immediately to the concept of *imputation*, which 'in the moral sense is the *judgment* by which someone is regarded as the author (*causa libera*) of an action, which is then called a *deed* (*factum*) and stands under laws' (*MS* 6:227). A *person*, therefore, is a being that can be regarded—and regards herself—as the *causa libera* of actions. But what does follow from this elementary insight? Kant at least thought that nearly everything required for the foundation of a theory of obligation (*Verbindlichkeit*) can be derived by *analysis* of the concept of a *causa libera* in the framework of Transcendental Idealism—together with man's consciousness of being such a *causa libera*. We can go even further. To find a solution for the problem of 'imputation' is obviously one of the main objects of Kant's philosophy as a whole. In a draft of the *Preisschrift über die Fortschritte der Metaphysik* he declares: 'Critical Philosophy has its origin in Moral philosophy with regard to the imputability of our actions' (Ak. 20:335).[6] It thus seems to be a promising strategy for the study of Kant's foundation of morals if we focus on the question: 'How does our picture of human action fit into the framework of a causally determined *nature*?' The question 'How should one live?' raises a paradox that is partially answered by the principles of Kant's *theoretical* philosophy. It is perhaps surprising that this question of *practical* reason is answered in a great part by *theoretical* reason already.

What is required for a 'free cause' to be a *cause* at all? Kant was not the first thinker to link the concept of a cause to the concept of law, but he was the first to make specific use of it in the theory of human agency. The most prominent formula expressing the conceptual connection of cause and law is the statement of the Second Analogy in the first edition of the *Critique of Pure Reason*: The 'Principle of the causal connection among appearances' (A202): 'Everything that happens, that is begins to be, presupposes something upon which it follows according to a rule' (A189). To be a cause and to produce something according to a rule are, for Kant, equivalent, and *theoretical* reason *alone*—as Kant insists —cannot solve the problem of human 'Freedom' just *because* it cannot discover the specific *causal law* underlying free agency. But it provides the conceptual framework for the solution. As Kant points out in the second *Critique* (*KpV* 5:48), the 'supposition that a freely acting cause might be a being in the world

[6] 'Ursprung der critischen Philosophie ist Moral, in Ansehung der Zurechnungsfähigkeit der Handlungen.'

of sense' can in fact be defended in the *Critique of Pure Reason*, since it can be shown to be free of contradiction.[7] But—as Kant adds immediately—we can only place the 'unconditioned' (*das Unbedingte*), that is, the ultimate cause, into the world of the 'Intelligible' without being able to realize the possibility of an appropriate *agent*. This is all that is in reach of theoretical reason: 'But where determination by laws of nature comes to an end, all *explanation* comes to an end as well. Nothing is left but defence—that is, to repel the objections of those who profess to have seen more deeply into the essence of things and on this ground audaciously declare freedom to be impossible' (*G.* 4:459).

The solution to the problem of the proper agent of human action is supplied indirectly by the second *Critique*: 'This vacant place is now filled by pure practical reason with a definite law of causality in an intelligible world (by freedom)—namely, the moral law' (*KpV* 5:49).[8] Agency or *causa libera* thus presupposes an *intelligible world* with its own 'causal' law that is independent of the causal laws of nature. This was already the central claim of the third section of the *Groundwork*, and Kant reaffirms this in the second *Critique*: 'it has been elsewhere proved that, if freedom is predicated of us, it transports us into an intelligible order of things' (*KpV* 5:42). To regard oneself as a free being is to understand oneself as a member of an intelligible order (or world). To be a member of such an intelligible world *means* to be a causal agent, which again is nothing else but 'acting on principle', being ruled by law. Only as far as man realizes himself as being capable of acting in accordance with a law, can he claim to act *himself*, being a *causa libera*.

IV

Being free and being the object of a '*law* of freedom' are one and the same thing—this is the message of Kant's *theoretical* philosophy up to this point. But

---

[7] Cf. e.g. *KrV* B28: 'But though I cannot *know*, I can yet *think* freedom . . . provided due account be taken of our critical distinction between the two modes of representation, the sensible and the intellectual, and of the resulting limitation of the pure concepts of understanding.'

[8] There is a pertinent passage in the *Prolegomena* as well: 'This faculty is called reason, and, so far as we consider a being (man) entirely according to this objectively determinable reason, he cannot be considered as a being of sense, but this property is that of a thing in itself, of which we cannot comprehend the possibility—I mean how the ought (which however has never yet taken place) should determine its activity, and can become the cause of actions, whose effect is an appearance in the sensible world. Yet the causality of reason would be freedom with regard to the effects in the sensuous world, so far as we can consider objective grounds, which are themselves ideas, as their determinants. For its action in that case would not depend upon subjective conditions, consequently not upon those of time, and of course not upon the law of nature, which serves to determine them, because grounds of reason give to actions the rule universally, according to principles, without the influence of the circumstances of either time or place' (*P.* 4:345).

what is *specific* about the law, or the laws, underlying human agency, intrinsically linked to the concept of an intelligible cause? The answer of the second *Critique* is well known. It is expressed in the 'Fundamental law of pure practical reason': 'Act so that the maxim of thy will can always at the same time hold good as a principle of universal legislation' (*KpV* 5:30).

This is not the place for deep investigation into Kant's argument for this formula. The underlying idea is familiar and is easily spelled out. A principle of determination that is *not* a causal principle of *nature*[9] has to be a *formal* one. The solution of 'Problem II' in the second *Critique* is: 'It is the legislative form, then, contained in the maxim, which can alone constitute a principle of determination of the [free] will' (*KpV* 5:29). The lesson of the first seven sections of the second *Critique* reads thus: a being—human or superhuman—who understands herself or expects to be recognized as a free agent, responsible for her actions because she has a will that is 'distinct from desires' (*G.* 4:461), has to understand herself necessarily as subject to the 'Fundamental law of pure practical reason'.

What Kant is interested in for his argument of the second *Critique* is, of course, the *converse* of this theorem. Only because we are conscious of the moral law *as an imperative* can we recognize ourselves as free agents: 'He judges, therefore, that he can do a certain thing because he is conscious that he ought, and he recognizes that he is free—a fact that but for the moral law he would never have known' (*KpV* 5:30; cf. the first paragraph of the Preface, *KpV* 5:3, and Vig. 27:505–7).

Now Kant's central claim in §E of the *Rechtslehre* should become transparent: 'Right in the narrow sense . . . is indeed based on everyone's consciousness of obligation in accordance with a law' (*MS* 6:232; cf. Vig. 27:520 ff.). It is only the *consciousness* of being obliged by the moral law that can prove our freedom. The '*moral* concept of Law', which 'refers to the concept of obligation' (§B), applies only to beings who are free, who are 'in the Idea' restrained to a sphere of outer freedom defined by the moral law—which in turn is nothing else than the principle of free agency. As we saw in the beginning, things—that is, *im*personal beings—are not subject to the moral law (but only to *natural* laws) and lack the capability of being *causae liberae* and, hence, are not the subject of imputation.

What seems to have confused some readers is the fact that Kant, immediately after the previous citation, states that *Recht* does *not* demand that free

---

[9] Man can be 'defined as regards his causality by means of a law that cannot be reduced to any physical law of the sensible world; and therefore our knowledge is extended beyond the limits of that world' (*KpV* 5:50).

agents determine *themselves by their consciousness of the law*.[10] This statement should be quite clear now when the concept of *Rechtslehre* is taken into account. It is a mere consequence of the *definition* of 'external Right' that the latter concerns 'only the external, and practical relation of persons' (§B). Although the *Rechtslehre* game applies only to *persons* and thus *demands* that these persons obey the rules of the game, it nevertheless does *not* demand that they follow the rules of the game only for the sake of giving evidence to themselves that they *are* indeed persons (as chess-players are not supposed to follow the rules of chess just for the sake of giving evidence that they are playing chess).

We can now revisit Kant's argument from a practical viewpoint in order to illustrate how it works in the *Rechtslehre*. Take anyone who claims the right to be free from a certain restraint by other human beings. She thus *presupposes* that she herself and a fortiori her fellow human beings are free agents, possible subjects of *imputation* and thus responsible for their actions. Otherwise it would be as *pointless* to claim any right of that kind, as it *is* pointless to claim any right against a lion or even to expect such a claim from a tree. This, according to Kant's analysis, *means* that she takes them and herself to be members of a world of free agents—that is, causes in a noumenal realm. This again, in the framework of Transcendental Idealism, *means* that she must recognize herself (as well as others) as acting according to a specific law—that is, according to the *moral* law. Acting according to the moral law again *means* that the external liberty is 'in the Idea' restricted to those actions that are in conformity with this specific law of the agent, since otherwise she cannot be recognized as an agent of this kind (that is, a person or a *causa libera*). To state it in analogy to

---

[10]   Observe the passage in §C where Kant insists that the 'Law of Right' 'is indeed a law that lays an obligation on me, but it does not at all expect, far less demand, that I *myself ought to* limit my freedom to those conditions just for the sake of this obligation' (*MS* 6:231). Maybe the arrangement of the translation given obscures the emphasis of Kant's text. Kant does *not* deny here that 'I myself ought to limit my freedom to those conditions' (that would render the passage nonsensical: it would talk about an obligation lacking any 'ought' addressed to the obliged person (cf. e.g. *MS* 6:225, last sentence)). Kant here denies only that the 'Law of Right' requires that I do this just 'for the sake of this obligation'. Although I am *obliged* to act justly (or rightly), juridical *lawgiving as such* does not require that I act just *from duty* (otherwise it would cease being merely *external* lawgiving). 'Juridical lawgiving' is nothing but 'Moral als Rechtslehre betrachtet' (*P.* 8:383) or 'Moral in der Bedeutung als Rechtslehre' (*P.* 8:386). The concept of 'obligation' (*Verbindlichkeit*, which is defined as 'moral necessitation' (*MS* 6:487) or as 'necessitation by the moral law' (Vig. 27:492))belongs to the (moral) *law* as such and not to a specific *lawgiving* (see *MS* 6:225 and §B). It will thus lead into deep confusion to talk *sensu stricto* about special *juridical obligations* or *ethical obligations* in Kant (whereas the term 'moral obligations' will do no harm because it is just a pleonasm: '*natural* laws' do not oblige—and *tertium non datur*). It is the concept of a 'ground for determining our choice' (*Bestimmungsgrund der Willkür*) alone that can be classified as a juridical *or* as an ethical (*Triebfeder*) (*MS* 6:218). See n. 2.

Hobbes's phrase cited above: 'A free man is he who is restricted only by universal laws to do what he has a will to.'[11]

What is thus *not* required is that the agent, in order to be treated within the limits of the rules of the *Rechtslehre* game, is *actually* 'acting on principle'. (Obviously you might treat any beast, incapable of this kind of action, within these limits as well without doing anything unjust.) In order to acquire the status of beings who enjoy the *privilege* of being treated as persons, human beings must 'admit' that they actually *are capable* of 'acting on principle', and that they *are obliged* to do so (just as the chess-player will admit that he is capable of following the rules and that he is required to do so as long as he expects to be recognized as a chess-player). If they do so (and, in fact, as *rational* beings they can *not* avoid to do so), their 'independence from being constrained by another's choice' (*MS* 6:237) reaches just as far as their actions *can be considered* as being actually governed by such a 'principle'.

If we extend this way of looking at Kant's Principle of Right to his Categorical Imperative in general, we might sum up in the following way: the 'Supreme principle of the doctrine of morals' (which applies to *both* parts of *The Metaphysics of Morals* (*MS* 6:226; cf. *MS* 6:222)) must be regarded as guiding our actions as long as we expect others to *justify* their actions and as long as we give *justifications* for ours. If we stop doing this, we treat ourselves as well as others like any other material body, determined by laws of nature alone: there will be much to be *explained* (or even to be *excused*)[12] then, but nothing to be *justified*.[13]

If the foregoing account of Kant's foundation of *Recht* is correct, we have to take seriously Kant's numerous claims that the *Rechtslehre* is an inseparable part of his *metaphysics* of morals, and cannot be detached from the latter's foundations—that is, from the framework of his Transcendental Idealism (it can, of course, be detached at the cost of losing its *foundation*). Let me just mention two major points already discussed above. We cannot take Kant's statements that a cause presupposes a law and that being a *causa libera* implies being restrained by this law 'in the Idea' for granted. They are—true or false—*metaphysical* claims and, as the history of philosophy shows, open to contro-

---

[11]   This more closely resembles John Locke's definition of liberty or freedom than Hobbes's: 'As freedom of nature is, to be under no other restraint but the law of nature' (*Second Treatise of Government*, §22).

[12]   It makes sense to *explain* why the dog bites the arriving guest ('It's just an unmanageable animal, and it escaped from the leash!'). Maybe we even want to *excuse* the dog for doing so ('Sorry, but it did expect the postman!'). But it would be rather strange to claim that the dog (or even a snake or a flea) was *justified* in biting somebody (although we might think that *we* were justified in not holding it back from biting).

[13]   For a related view, see e.g. T. M. Scanlon, 'Contractualism and Utilitarianism', in A. Sen and B. Williams (eds.), *Utilitarianism and Beyond* (Cambridge: Cambridge University Press, 1982), 103–28, esp. 116.

versy. Kant himself knew well why he delivered a new, relevant, and complex argument in the second *Critique*. Further, a defence of Kant's claim that the 'supposition that a freely acting cause might be a being in the world of sense' refers back to the *Critique of Pure Reason*, where the corresponding concept is shown to be free of contradiction by applying to it the phenomena/noumena distinction.[14]

V

If we look back to Kant's foundations of the 'Universal Principle of Right' given in the previous sections, we will note three important *negative* characteristics:

1. There is no reference to human desires, needs, or interests: an action's being just or unjust does not at all depend on its furthering the well-being of the actor or of any other member of the human race, either individually or collectively, either actually or 'in the long run', either in fact or hypothetically.

2. There is no reference to any rational pursuit of life or the constitution of a person as a source of individuality.

3. There is no reference to human nature in the sense of being prone to conflict or even to war. This should not be astonishing at all, since the main argument was centred around the problem of how 'free agency' can be conceived as compatible with the concept of a causally closed *nature*.

Hence there was no reference necessary to desires, life plans, or the problem of human interaction. While the first two points are worth noting in contrast to all kinds of utilitarian and, say, Fichtean Conceptions of Right, the third will be important for a correct understanding of Kant's conception of Public Right and the state in particular.

The famous connection of Right with an 'Authorization to use Coercion' (§D) and Kant's further claim that any strict Right might be *represented* as a possibility to use coercion (§E) prove to be *immediate* consequences from the definition of the concept of Right when considered in the light of the Principle of Right from section C. Let us note that the analytical[15] connection of Right, on

---

[14] See *KrV* B30.

[15] In the title of section X of the Introduction to the *Doctrine of Virtue*, Kant claims that 'the supreme Principle of the Doctrine of Right was analytic' (*MS* 6:396). It should be obvious from the context of §C to §E of the *Doctrine of Right* and from the subsequent text in section X of the *Doctrine of Virtue*, that Kant here

one hand, and the use of coercion, on the other, was already stated in that section (thus the 'proof' in section D is merely a kind of visual aid, which will lead us astray if we expect something new from it). If external freedom is 'in the Idea' limited to the conditions of conformity with the external freedom of others and thus may be actively limited by others, then any coercion that does not interfere with *this* (that is, limited) external freedom is *by definition* just, or right, since 'any action is *right* if it can coexist with anyone's freedom in accordance with a universal law' (*MS*, §C, 6:230). Whether we *describe* a strict right itself, on the one hand, or the coercion that is authorized by it, on the other, this does not make any difference, since juridical lawgiving ignores the motives or maxims[16] of the actors—as long as they act in accordance with external laws (§E). To make use of a simple analogy: whether we paint the various territories of a political world map with different colours on a blackboard or whether we draw only the national borders that separate the territories in question, both methods will give the same political map (and it is merely a matter of convenience that we usually draw the borders first and colour the territories afterwards). A *system* of strict rights is the same as a *system* of just coercion. The difference is only one that concerns the person we actually consider as the subject of obligation (*Verbindlichkeit*). We may speak of a person's duty (that is, the '*matter*' of her obligation (*MS* 6:222)) to act in conformity with her strict rights, or we may speak of the other people's duty to refrain from coercion as far as the former's rights require it. We may speak of a person's liberty to do what his strict right allows, or we may speak of another person's liberty to hinder the former in doing what he has no right to do.

But *who* is in fact authorized to use this coercion? Kant does not consider this question at the abstract level of analysis considered so far; answering it requires further and more specific argument.

---

refers back to the 'analytical' connection between Right and coercion in §D of the *Doctrine of Right*, but definitely *not* to the 'universal law of Right' in §C (as has been suggested sometimes). If we adopt the terminology from the *Groundwork*, the Universal Law of Right is, of course, a '*synthetisch*-praktischer Satz' (*G.* 4:420); this *must not* be translated as 'a practical statement which is a synthetic proposition', but as 'a statement which *is practical* due to a synthesis'—as far as I know Kant himself does *never* mistake imperatives for propositions, because the 'ought' it contains does not 'analytically' follow from the will of him who is addressed by that imperative (as it is the case with Kant's so-called hypothetical imperatives). Note that Kant abandons the terminology of *synthetisch-praktisch* and *analytisch-praktisch* after the *Groundwork* because it is in conflict with a different use of synthetical/analytical in the second *Critique*. For details, see Bernd Ludwig, 'Warum es keine, hypothetischen Imperative gibt, und warum Kants hypothetisch-gebietende Imperative keine analytischen Sätze sind', in H. Klemme, B. Ludwig *et. al.* (eds.), *Aufklärung und Interpretation* (Würzburg: Könighausen und Neumann, 1999), 105–24.

[16]   In Kant *recht* and *unrecht* are predicates only for (external) *actions*, while *gut* and *böse* are predicates for the *will* and its (internal) *maxims*.

Let us thus take a closer look at the *Rechtslehre* game. There are human beings who act as persons—that is, who act according to the Universal Principle of Law. This embraces the use of just coercion by others (collectively or individually) if one of them does not comply with the principle itself. If we assume—with Kant (see below)—that the paradigm case of freedom is being free from chains or other physical impediments to bodily motion set up by others, and if we assume further that our persons in question know what it means to make a promise concerning an action (that is, to promise to do or to forbear something in the future), then we can already put together a model of a primitive version of the *Rechtslehre* game. Just think of a small society of barbers (or hairdressers) and poets whose only needs are a daily shave (or hairdo) and some poems for recreation. It is easy to decide what is just (right) and what is unjust in their interaction. As long as they do not interfere physically and as long as the poets deliver the poems they promised as a 'payment' for the shave they receive from the barbers, everything is just (or right). Any use of coercion is unjust as long as it is not a hindrance of a hindrance of freedom. If one of the barbers refuses to shave a poet after receiving a poem, he will by right be coerced (in a suitable way). There is, of course, reason to doubt that this 'game' will be at all stable, at least if the 'malicious' nature of human beings is taken into account. We have only to consider questions like: Who will actually prevent unjust behaviour? Who will decide what is unjust in a given case (was *this* poem worth *that* shave)? Who will be authorized to introduce new rules for cases yet undecidable (how many rhymes are required for a poem, how many wounds will convert a shave into a massacre)? and so on. What is important here is to observe that Kant himself does *not* address questions of this kind at all in the context of the Introduction to the *Doctrine of Right*. He obviously is not interested in such small-scale *Rechtslehre* games here at all—and it is easy to see why.

The next step in his exposition of the concept of Right broadens the view and takes into consideration the rights to *external objects*. This is where all the questions just mentioned become more pressing than before—even without taking into account 'human nature'—and hence call for a solution that includes solutions for small-scale *Rechtslehre* games as well.

VI

When a rational being considers himself as a member of the noumenal realm, he regards his own will as the free cause of his actions; when he considers himself as a member of the phenomenal realm, he regards these actions as mere appearances of his will (*G.* 4:453). Since all human *actions* in the world of sense are at least in part bodily movements, 'independence from being constrained by another's choice' (*MS* 6:237) is in the first place freedom from (unauthorized) physical necessitation by others. Integrity of the body is hence the paradigm for enjoying the *innate* 'right of a person with regard to himself' (*MS* 6:250).[17] But what about external objects, what about *things* (which themselves—as mentioned above—lack freedom) persons can make use of? According to Kant's 'a priori proposition with regard to empirical possession' a further right is connected *analytically* with a person's right to be free from physical necessitation: the right to those external objects that are 'physically connected' with the person's body—for example, the apple in my hands or the land on which I have lain down (*MS* 6:247, 250). Whoever tries to grab the apple from my hand or to push me out of the place where I have lain down has to interfere with my *body* and thus with my 'right in regard to myself' (as long as I did not violate another's right earlier, of course).

But what about external objects that are *not* actually connected with the person's body? What about my coat I have left in the wardrobe and my house I have left for work?[18] What happens when 'any conditions of empirical possession in time and space' are put aside? What about *property* or *property rights*? Since the right to a thing *not* 'physically connected' with the person's body, obviously, is not contained *analytically* in the person's right with regard to himself, the 'proposition about the possibility of possessing a thing *external to myself* . . . *is synthetic*' (*MS*, §6, 6:250). This is not the place to dwell comprehensively on Kant's argument for this proposition,[19] but it is nevertheless possible to appreciate the role of Kant's concept of *Practical Reason* in this place. This will show

---

[17]   Kant applies the traditional distinction between *Ius naturale absolutum* and the *Ius naturale hypotheticum* as we find it, for example, in Achenwall's *Jus naturae* (repr. in Kant's Works, vol 19; for this distinction see Ak. 19:326). According to the principles of the first part, *soul, body* and *just actions* are everyone's *proprium*. Exterior objects are at issue in the second part.

[18]   In the following I will concentrate on external 'things' only, even though Kant has in mind *three* classes of external objects: things, another's choice to perform a specific deed, and another's status in relation to me (*MS*, §4, 6:247). It will become evident that even Kant himself focused on the first class in the first chapter of 'Private Right' (take, for example, the 'that is [d. i.]', which identifies the two different formulas of the Postulate (*MS* 6:246): this identity, of course, does *not* hold for 'another's choice'). In the first chapter Kant does not use the term 'property' (*Eigentum* (*dominium*)), which applies only to objects from the first class. He talks about mine and yours (*meum et tuum*) generally. Later (in chapter 2) he adds in passing that 'an external object that in terms of its substance belongs to someone is his property (*dominium*), in which all rights in this thing inhere'—and this 'can be only a corporeal thing' (*MS* 6:270). For a complete catalogue of what belongs to the concept of *dominium* compare for example Achenwall, *Elementa Iuris naturae* (Göttingen: Ioh. Wilhelm Schmidt, 1750), §306–31.

[19]   For a further discussion, see Bernd Ludwig, *Kants Rechtslehre* (Hamburg: Meiner, 1988), and 'Postulat, Deduktion und Abstraktion in Kants Lehre vom intelligibelen Besitz', *Archiv für Rechts- und Sozialphilosophie*, 82 (1996), 250–9.

once again the absence of any considerations concerning human desires or interests, rational life plans or even the problem of human interaction in the central passages of Kant's *Doctrine of Right*—but it will show as well to what degree his argument depends on doctrines from the first two *Critiques*.

Before looking at Kant's argument in detail, a general remark about the scope of theories of property is necessary: we always have to keep in mind that *any* action and, accordingly, any use of exterior objects is subject to the 'Law of Right' in the first place. Hence any property rights will *never* expand the owner's rights in his object beyond the limits determined by that law. A theory of property, therefore, does not primarily address the question *what* persons may rightfully do with things they own, but above all the question *who* has the right to use the things in question according to the 'Law of Right'. Any special privileges (the right to use, to sell, or to manage, the thing, the right to the capital value of it) result merely from the right to hold back *others* from a certain behaviour—that is, it results from the right to make a certain use *exclusively*.[20] If any use of an object is already unjust by itself, a property right in the object does not render that use rightful: whoever shoots an innocent human being is a murderer, no matter whether he is the rightful owner of the gun and the bullet. And to withhold the one and only lifebelt available from the one and only drowning passenger is unjust, whoever the rightful owner of that lifebelt might be.

Kant's main argument for exclusive property rights proceeds in two steps: an argument to support—or prove—an a priori principle of 'mine and yours', and then the deduction[21] of a concept of a *possessio noumenon* by help of this principle. When this concept of a *possessio noumenon* is once deduced (at the end of *MS*, §6, 6:252), further steps are required to put this concept to work (§§7–9).

The first part of the argument runs as follows (*MS* 6:246). (1) Suppose there were a practical law that prohibited making use of a certain object of choice, although this use 'could coexist with everyone's freedom in accordance with a universal law'. This practical law would, obviously, be self-contradictory, because it would prohibit something that is *by definition* (§C) right. (2) Now it is evident that exercising control over certain objects of choice by using them— like eating an apple or lying down on a vacant piece of land—and thus excluding others from them *is right* (as the 'a priori proposition with regard to

---

[20] For a recent account, see Jeremy Waldron, *The Right to Private Property* (Oxford: Oxford University Press, 1988), 31 ff.

[21] Although Kant's use of the term 'deduction' is not at all uniform (there are in fact 'deductions' of *Kategorien*, *Erkenntnisse*, *Grundsätze*, *Begriffe*, and even *Einteilungen*, to mention only a few), it is obvious that in *this* very context the object of the 'deduction' in question is a 'concept', *not* the 'Postulate' or any other 'principle' or 'theorem'.

empirical possession' shows). From (1) and (2) together, it follows immediately (3) that any law that forbids the use of objects of choice *generally* (*absolutes Verbot*) is self-contradictory. Next, consider the laws of pure practical reason. (4) They have to be 'formal laws' that abstract from the matter of choice and hence they will treat all objects of choice purely as such, regardless of any other of their properties (see *KpV* 5:28 for the 'formal' character of practical laws). If pure practical reason states a formal law concerning mine and yours, this can thus only be a law about objects of choice in general (otherwise it would depend on the *matter*, not on the *form* alone). (5) As a consequence, the only possible laws of pure practical reason concerning mine and yours are the following two: 'It is possible for me (or you) to have *any* external object of choice as mine (or yours)', and '*All* external objects of choice belong to no one (they are *res nullius*)'—*tertium non datur*. According to our previous conclusion (3), the second of these laws would lead to a 'contradiction of outer freedom with itself'. Hence the 'Postulate of Pure Practical Reason concerning mine and yours': 'It is possible for any external object of my choice to be reckoned as rightfully mine if I have control of it (and only insofar as I have control of it) without being in [physical] possession of it' (*MS* 6:252).

Although this principle was established by 'removing' or 'disregarding' something (that is, 'merely by *leaving out* empirical conditions, as it is justified in doing by the law of freedom' (*MS* 6:255)), it leads—paradoxically—to an 'extension' of the concept of possession—and of practical reason itself (*MS* 6:247). This will become evident at least when we turn to the second part of Kant's argument, to the '*Deduction* of the concept of merely rightful possession of an External Object (*possessio noumenon*)', which takes place in the concluding paragraph of §6.

But let us just pause briefly and look at what Kant has established up to this point. If we take part in the *Rechtslehre* game, we regard ourselves as persons. We thus have to consider ourselves as *causae liberae*, acting in accordance with a *formal* law. When we then apply this very principle of 'free agency' to our question about rightful use of exterior objects, we realize that 'a maxim, by which, if it were to become a law, an object of choice would *in itself* (objectively) have to *belong to no one* (*res nullius*) is contrary to right [*rechtswidrig*]' (*MS* 6:246, second formula of the Postulate). To act according to such a maxim would thus mean to refuse to act *as a person*—that is, to give up the privilege of being treated by others according to the general rule of Right (in that peculiar respect at least). It is an immediate consequence of this insight that denying bluntly the possibility of 'mine and yours' would be the same thing as leaving the *Rechtslehre* game altogether. And a further consequence is that whoever claims to have something as his own, has indeed *right* to do so and is thus authorized to use coercion to establish this *suum*—as long as it does conform with the general principle of Right, of course (see below).

The remaining *deduction* of the *concept* of a non-physical possession is very short and simple. If it is—as the postulate claims in its *third* formula given by Kant—'a duty of Right to act towards others so that what is external (usable) could also become someone's' (*MS* 6:252; for a *fourth* formula see *MS* 6:257), and if—as Kant had already proven in the *Exposition* (§6)—'the concept of an external object that belongs to someone . . . rests simply on that of non-physical possession' (*MS* 6:252), *then* the concept of non-physical 'possession' (that is, 'of a merely rightful possession'), must be *possible*. That means, this concept does *refer* to something (namely, to the 'Gegenstand des Begriffs', although we do not yet know what this something might 'look like').[22] Hence the *concept* of possession is indeed 'enlarged' extensionally by this deduction, from the merely empirical concept of physical possession to the pure rational concept of 'non-physical possession'.

But, as Kant points out, this deduction does not at all give us any 'extension of knowledge' concerning this very concept (whose roots obviously get lost in the intelligible realm). The only thing we have to take for granted ('for morally practical purposes' (*MS* 6:281)) is *that* it refers to[23] an object (just like the concept of freedom itself). Therefore, we have to enquire into the principles of its 'application' to things[24] in the world of sense independently from the arguments considered so far. Let us recall, that the object of the *empirical* concept of possession was 'holding' (*detentio*) (*MS* 6:246, 249). What is thus the object of the *pure rational* concept of possession? It is (§7), of course, nothing but 'an intellectual relation to an object, insofar as I have it *under my control* . . . and the object is *mine* because my will to use it as I please does not conflict with the law of outer freedom' (*MS* 6:253). If we ask now under what condition the alleged 'conflict' between *my will* and the *law of outer freedom* will not arise, the final answer is obvious (§8):

Now, a unilateral will cannot serve as a coercive law for everyone with regard to possession that is external and therefore contingent, since that would infringe upon freedom in accordance with universal laws. So it is only a will putting everyone under obligation,

[22] We have to take account of Kant's theory of concepts here. A concept is *possible* if and only if it refers to an object (*Gegenstand*). The 'possibility' of a concept is more than its being free from contradiction. For the Wolffian roots of this interpretation of 'possible concepts', see Manfred Kuehn, 'Der Objektbegriff bei Christian Wolff und Immanuel Kant', in Klemme, Ludwig, *et al.* (eds.), *Aufklärung und Interpretation*, 39–56.

[23] We might say more properly: 'that practical reason *requires* that it refers to an object.'

[24] I use the term 'thing' (not 'object') in this place to prevent mixing up the 'object' (*Gegenstand*) that is the reference of the concept of 'non-physical possession' with the exterior 'object' (the 'thing') that is mine thanks to this 'non-physical possession'.

hence only a collective general (*common*) and powerful will, that can provide everyone this assurance. (*MS* 6:256)

The *object* of the 'pure rational concept' of a *possessio noumenon* is the 'control over an exterior object of choice established by a general will'. Thus 'only in a civil condition can something be mine or yours' (*MS* 6:256). The first important concept that belongs to the sphere of Public Right has come into view: the General Will.

An important side effect of Kant's method should be mentioned here before examining the interrelation of private right and public right more closely. As we have seen, the 'possibility' of the concept of a 'non-physical possession' was established *independently*, without any reference to the special condition of its 'application', which was the lawgiving of a general will. Accordingly there is a 'prerogative of Right arising from empirical possession' (*MS*, §9, 6:257; cf. *MS* 6:264), which makes non-physical possession possible *even before* the general will is *in fact* established. He who is holding an external object is justified to prevent anyone 'who does not want to enter with him into a condition of public lawful freedom from usurping the use of that object, in order to put to his own use, in conformity with the postulate of reason, a thing that would otherwise be annihilated practically' (*MS* 6:257). It should have become obvious by now, that Kant's 'justification of property' has taken a highly idiosyncratic round-about route. (1) Property is just, *because* the proprietor's claim to *exclude others* is just (*not* the other way around!). And (2) this latter claim is just only *because* the *others* have *no rights* that are opposed to this very claim (*not* because the proprietor has—or must have—specific 'extra' rights *to* certain things!)—as long as it is in conformity with the Axiom of Right, of course.[25] To make a slightly paradoxical use of Hohfeld's famous terms: When I *claim* a *property right* to an object that actually belongs to no one, my *privilege* to use this object becomes a *claim right*, only *because* the other's *privileges* to make use of it fade away (as long as they are mere *privileges*, not yet claim rights themselves).[26] In short, property (if once introduced) is justified, *because* there is no general right to resist the *introduction* of property.[27] The rules of the *Rechtslehre* game apply to persons, and if

---

[25]　I cannot go into the problems of rightful *acquisition* here, which is the main topic of the second chapter of the *Rechtslehre* (*MS* 6:258–96).

[26]　This will lead to Kant's theory of *first* acquisition (§§11–17) in a quite natural way.

[27]　'Having a right to a thing' and 'being authorized to hinder others in the use of a thing' are (§§D and E) two sides of the same coin. It will thus be sufficient to give justifying reasons *either* for the left-hand *or* for the right-hand side of the 'equation' in question to justify both claims jointly. While a justification via the *left*-hand side will have to take into account specific properties of the things, their *matter* (as relation to basic human needs or something like that), Kant's justification via the *right*-hand side takes into account the *formality* of moral principles alone. This connects to Kant's 'paradox of method' (*KpV* 5:62): Trying to justify the left-hand side independently would thus be—from Kant's point of view—the 'Grund aller Verwirrungen der Philosophen' (*KpV* 5:64) with respect to property.

only *one* of these persons claims a right to property, there is no right for others to resist this very introduction of property.

It should be mentioned in passing that the duty to enter into a society of property-owners is in fact *conditional* for Kant. If there were enough places on the earth's surface that 'men could be so dispersed on it that they would not come into any community with one another . . . the community would not be a necessary result of their existence on the earth' (*MS* 6:262). Entering into a political society is a *categorical* imperative nevertheless.[28] Just as the performance of a covenant is a *particular duty* only if there is in fact a contract, entering into a society is a duty only if there is no possibility left to 'disperse' into *vacuos locos*. If someone claims some property right, there are, obviously, only three possible reactions left to others: the *first* is to insist that the object in question should remain a *res nullius*, the *second* is to avoid conflict by leaving the object in question to the first possessor and keep away from any further contact, and the *third* is to join a society with him under a united will to determine property in exterior objects. But, since Kant's Postulate of practical reason prohibits the first option *categorically*, and since the places in the world are limited, there is no way to escape Civil Society anymore: '*Exeundum est e statu naturali*.'[29]

Hence there is a 'provisionally rightful possession'—as Kant calls it—that holds 'comparatively as rightful possession' (§9). And this is the key to Kant's solution of the vexing problem that property introduced by *a* general will should be possible even before *the* general will of *all* women and *all* men in *all* countries and in *all* times is *in fact* established.[30] Thanks to the 'prerogative', it

---

[28] *Categorical* imperatives may state *conditional* duties. An imperative is 'hypothetical' only if the condition stated in the antecedent is that the obliged person has a certain *end*. For further details, see Ludwig, 'Warum es keine hypothetischen Imperative gibt'.

[29] As Kant points out later, the individual 'must unite itself with all others (*with which it cannot avoid interacting*), subject itself to a public lawful external coercion' (*MS* 6:312; emphasis added).

[30] Robert Filmer's famous critique of Hugo Grotius' contractual foundation of property pointed to this very problem more than 100 years earlier: a purely contractual foundation of property presupposes a mutual contract of all mankind. John Locke tried to answer the attack in chapter 5 of the *Second Treatise*. In one—central—respect his answer is quite similar to Kant's. According to Locke, labour 'puts a distinction' between the thing mixed with that labour and those things that are in *natural* (!) *common*. Hence labour 'removes' an object out of that *common state nature left it in* (as long as there is 'enough and as good' for others). Thus the *natural* (!) right of the others to use that object is cancelled, and the former *natural* right of the labourer becomes a *property* right thereby (because he may now exclude the others without violating any right). While Locke's 'opponents to appropriation' lose their *natural* rights in the things, owing to the '*denaturalizing*' labour of the appropriator, Kant's 'opponents to appropriation' never had such a right, because that would involve action on an unjust maxim (as the Postulate shows). Although Locke and Kant give quite different accounts of property rights, they *both* share the assumption that property rights in general are justified *because* the *opponents* do not have a *right* to oppose (*not* the other way around: that the owners have any *additional* right to the thing!), that is because privileges (in respect to 'objects lacking freedom') become claim rights when all opposing privileges vanish. For Locke's theory of property as a defence of Grotius' *con*-

is already sufficient indeed to act 'in conformity with the Idea of a possible unit-ed *will*' (*MS* 6:258). The legitimacy of 'stepping back' from the *real* unity of the wills (created by a *real* agreement or contract) to the *Idea* of a united will is, as we have seen, a consequence of Kant's method in sections 1–6 of 'Private Right'.

VII

We have already touched on Kant's public right when the concept of a general lawgiving will was mentioned as an essential part of the application (or realiza-tion) of the concept of a non-physical possession. This becomes even more evi-dent at the end of §8, immediately after the concept was introduced: 'But the condition of being under a general external (i.e. public) lawgiving accompanied with power is the civil condition' (*MS* 6:256). The immediately following sen-tence is Kant's first statement of the famous *exeundum est e statu naturali* in the form of a 'corollary': 'If it must be possible, in terms of rights, to have an exter-nal object as one's own, the subject must also be permitted to constrain every-one else with whom he comes into conflict about whether an external object is his or another's to enter along with him into a civil constitution' (*MS* 6:256).

As we can now see, the necessity of an external *lawgiving* ('Gesetz*gebung*'), not just as an enforcement-cadre for natural laws but as well as a *lawgiver* ('Gesetz*geber*') of *positive* laws (*MS* 6:224, 227; cf. Vig. 27:528–9), is derived from the necessity of applying the concept of 'Right' to the use of *external* objects of choice. There is no *natural* distribution of external objects intro-duced by *natural law* (as there is for the innate right, as, for example, to the limbs of one's own body), but *property* is an artefact of the human will. Although the underlying concept of a 'non-physical possession' can already be proven as 'possible' by pure practical reason alone, property—that is, mine and yours in external objects—has nonetheless to be *created* by the *positive law* of a general united will: otherwise it would be a violation of the other's freedom. But a 'general will' alone—as is familiar to any student of Law and Right—does not yet make up the entire concept of a civil constitution:

Every state contains three *authorities* within it, that is, the general united will consists of three persons (*trias politica*): the *sovereign authority* in the person of the legislator; the *executive authority* in the person of the ruler (in conformity to law); and the *judicial*

---

tractual theory against Filmer's *paternalistic* attack, see B. Ludwig, 'Arbeit, Geld, Gesetz. Eine Neubestim-mung von Aufgabe und Ziel der Eigentumstheorie John Lockes', in K. G. Ballestrem, V. Gerhardt, H. Ottmann, and M. P. Thompson (eds.), *Politisches Denken, Jahrbuch 2001* (Stuttgart: Metzler, 2001), 69–104.

authority (to award to each what is his in accordance with the law) in the person of the judge.   (*MS* 6:313)

These three authorities draw a parallel to the three propositions in a 'practical syllogism': Law, command, and verdict (*MS* 6:313). I can only mention in passing that the three 'chapters' (*Hauptstücke*) of Kant's 'Private Right Concerning what is Externally Mine and Yours in General' correspond just to these three propositions of the syllogism and hence to the three powers of the state—that is, to the fundamental structure of public right. The legislative authority belongs to the 'united will' of the people and thus corresponds to chapter 1 (as already considered). The executive authority prescribes the 'rules in accordance with which each [subject] can acquire something' (*MS* 6:316), those rules that are already the topic of chapter 2 ('How to acquire something in general' (*MS* 6:258)); and it is even more apparent that the 'Public Court of Justice', which is the main topic of chapter 3 (*MS* 6:296), anticipates the third power in the state.

When we collect these things together, it becomes obvious that Kant's concept of state, 'the form of a state as such, that is of *the state in Idea*, as it ought to be in accordance with pure Principles of Right' (*MS* 6:313), is nothing but the elaboration of the concept of a set of rules and institutions necessary for playing the *Rechtslehre* game in its most extensive version: a game of *persons* who share a world of *external objects of choice*. When we considered earlier the 'small-scale *Rechtslehre* game' of barbers and poets with fairly small needs, we saw that many problems in determining what is just and unjust action might already occur on a very simple level and that even this small-scale game would probably become unstable owing to human nastiness alone. What is remarkable with the 'large-scale game' considered now is the fact that 'human nature' did not play an important role in Kant's exposition. What about human needs and desires? What about human passions? What about 'maxims of violence' and 'tendencies to attack one another' (*MS* 6:312)? Kant mentions them only once near the end of Private Right (*MS* 6:307), and he adds a little later that they are of no prominent importance for his public right as well: 'However well disposed and law-abiding men might be, it still lies *a priori* in the rational Idea of such a condition [that is, a state of Nature] that . . . individual men, peoples and states can never be secure against violence from one another, since each has its own right to do *what seems right and good to it*' (*MS* 6:312).

Maybe there are human beings who know how to live without enforcement-cadres,[31] without a general will giving laws concerning mine and yours, without

---

[31]   Obviously the question whether enforcement of rightful behaviour of human beings is actually *necessary* is a question of *anthropology*. But we have to keep in mind that this question can *not* be answered in

rulers who specify the rules of acquisition, and even without courts that state what is right or wrong in a given case. But as long as *external objects* of choice are part of their game this could happen only by chance. These people can do only what '*seems* right and good to *each of* them' (and this might indeed work out peacefully for *some* time in *very* small communities of *very* peace-loving people who have a *huge* capacity to anticipate their fellow's desires and needs), but they have no obligatory common principle of justice, since the rightful regulation of the use of *external* objects can be determined only by *positive* law, by *positive* rules, and by verdicts that are to some extent *arbitrary*:

although each can acquire something external by taking control of it or by contract in accordance with its [own] *concepts of Right*, this acquisition is still only provisional as long as it does not yet have the sanction of public law, since it is not determined by public (distributive) justice and secured by an authority putting this right into effect. (*MS* 6:312)

VIII

This is not the place to enquire further into the details of Kant's public right. The question I wanted to resolve was 'Whence public right?' and the time has come to sum up.

We started by considering the *Rechtslehre* game as the most fundamental and comprehensive game *persons* might play. It is the game whose norms are the norms they have to refer to whenever they justify their actions to others and whenever they expect others to do the same. If anyone does not comply with the norms of this game, there is no base for him to complain in case he is coerced by his fellows. The fundamental norm of this game, the 'general principle of Right', was established by investigating the concept of a person, who is a being capable of *imputation* and who can thus be considered as a *causa libera*. Since this latter kind of cause cannot be recognized by theoretical reason alone, it can only be *inferred* from a given law, the law of freedom. Whoever claims to be a person (and *claiming* the opposite would be a pragmatic self-contradiction, of course), and thus to be 'independent from being constrained by another's choice', concedes to be object of this law—that is, a participant in the *Rechtslehre* game. As long as external objects are not taken

---

general: in many situations *some* people act lawfully without any enforcement while *others* do not. Kant *justifies* coercion (in §§C and D), and he *assumes* (in §§8 or 42, for example) as a matter of course that it is sometimes necessary.

into consideration, the institutional framework of the *Rechtslehre* game is not worth mentioning, since it is rather easy to discern what counts as a justified (or as an unjustified) action: any unauthorized coercion—that is, any unauthorized interference with another's body—is unjust. Interference with another's body is authorized only if it is a hindrance of unjust actions, or if it is allowed by virtue of a previous promise (or a contract).

The framework of the *Rechtslehre* game becomes more complex when external objects of choice, especially *things*, come into play. The 'mine and yours' in external objects presupposes the concept of a *possessio noumenon* then, and the application of this very concept presupposes voluntary agreement of persons—that is, *positive* laws given by a general united will, a set of *positive* rules for acquisition, and further *positive* principles of proper judgement. Thus the *Rechtslehre* game in its comprehensive form presumes public right—that is, a 'state' with three separate powers, and, if we look further, the 'Right of Nations' and 'Cosmopolitan Right' as well.

'Whence public right?' Kant's answer itself is quite simple (although its metaphysical presuppositions are not at all): because human beings then—and only then—can give account of what is just or unjust in their mutual communication *and* in their dealing with any of those objects in this world that they want to use for whatever basic needs—or for whatever silly purpose they might have in mind:

And the end which is a duty in itself in such external relationships, and which is indeed the highest formal condition of all other external duties, is the *right* of men *under coercive public laws* by which each other can be given what is due to him and secured against attack from any other. But the whole concept of external right is derived entirely from the concept of *freedom* in the mutual external relationships of human beings, and has nothing to do with the end which all men have by nature (i.e. the aim of achieving happiness) or with the recognised means of attaining this end.   (*G.* 8:289)

8

Kantian Desires: Freedom of Choice and Action in the *Rechtslehre*

Katrin Flikschuh

> In Deliberation, the last Appetite, or Aversion, immediately adhering to the action, or to the omission thereof, is what we call the Will; the Act, (not the faculty) of Willing. Will, therefore, is the last Appetite in Deliberating.
>
> Hobbes, Leviathan, pt. I, ch. 6

> The capacity for Desire is the capacity to be by means of one's representations the cause of the objects of these representations. The capacity of a being to act in accordance with its representations is called *life*.
>
> Kant, MS 6:211[1]

I. Introduction

Of the two citations above, the first is undoubtedly the more familiar: it is the one that most current discussions on the relation between desires, reason, and action in political and economic theory are heir to. To many readers the materialist metaphysics behind Hobbes's description of the will as an appetite may sound excessive in its apparent reduction to a simple physiological function of what may seem to them to be, at the very least, complex psychological processes. Of course, the dominant interpretation of Hobbesian willing as constituting merely the final link in a causal chain of internal physiological

My thanks to Diarmuid Costello, Gordon Finlayson, Tom Sorell, Mark Timmons, and Ken Westphal for comments on earlier versions of this paper.

[1] Citations from the *Rechtslehre* are based on Mary Gregor's translation of *The Metaphysics of Morals* (Cambridge: Cambridge University Press, 1991); those from Kant's historical and political essays use H. B. Nisbet's translation of *Kant's Political Writings*, ed. Hans Reiss (Cambridge: Cambridge University Press, 1971).

reactions to external stimulation may rest on a misunderstanding of his actual position.[2] Although the quoted passage refers to the *act* of willing, what really matters is the *faculty* of deliberation whose activities precede the act. Hobbes regards deliberation as a kind of judgement between competing desires and aversions, involving a weighing of passions and a reckoning of consequences. In so far as it includes intellectual exertions such as these, one rightly expects deliberation to amount to more than simply the greater physical force of the dominant desire over others. Yet precisely how the weighing is done or the reckoning accomplished Hobbes does not say. Thus it may be the ambiguity, not so much in his account of the role of deliberation in action, as in his conception of it as a particular faculty that has allowed the dominant interpretation to become pervasive. Any reference to deliberation as a distinct faculty has tended to drop out of the picture, so that an agent's eventual course of action has come to be seen as decided by the 'greater force' of the dominant desire over others. Such an account of willing in action may be reductive, but it does have the virtue of being straightforward. Given the emphasis in the human sciences on the parsimony of theoretical assumptions, it is not surprising that the Hobbesian model of action deliberation has proved to be attractive to many economists and political scientists alike.

By contrast, Kant's remark looks tortured and obscure. His characterization of desiring as a mental *capacity* suggests that he conceives of it as an activity over the exercise of which agents have at least some degree of rational control. This goes against the Hobbesian physiological understanding of desiring as constituting 'vital motion'. On the other hand, Kant too equates with *life* a (rational) being's capacity to act on its desires. I take this association of desiring with individual life or vitality, shared by Hobbes and Kant alike, to be distinctive of the modern view of desires as supplying a (legitimate) *subjective* dimension to agents' deliberation about action. Notwithstanding disagreements within this general outlook as to how precisely to conceive the relation between desire and reason in action deliberation, the modern view is committed to the view that it is the presence of an agent's desires in action deliberation that makes that deliberation the agent's *own*. In ceding, through the concept of desire, such large grounds to subjective authority within the deliberative process, the modern view distinguishes itself from the pre-modern classification of action types into virtues and vices, where the latter provide standards of

---

[2] A refreshing antidote to the dominant interpretation is provided by Tom Sorell in his discussion of Hobbesian 'right reasoning' in *Hobbes* (London: Routledge & Kegan Paul, 1986), ch. 3. For an earlier defence of Hobbes against the dominant interpretation, see also Howard Warrender, *The Political Philosophy of Thomas Hobbes* (Oxford: Clarendon Press, 1957).

objective evaluation with reference to which agents judge the appropriateness of their particular actions.[3]

Although the moral superiority of the pre-modern view over the modern conception of desires and action deliberation has been widely canvassed recently, it is at least doubtful whether Kant, for one, can be turned into a virtue ethicist about practical reasoning.[4] Whether he fits unambiguously into the modern perspective is perhaps no less doubtful. One influential interpretation refers to Kant as a psychological hedonist about individuals' desires, if only in order to account for his moral rigorism. On this view, Kant's moral rigorism is a consequence of his disdain for human desires and emotions, where this disdain is itself a consequence of his impoverished understanding of desires and their rightful place in human life.[5] More recent interpretations of his ethics have contested this picture, and have attributed to Kant a subtler, more differentiated, even a more sympathetic understanding of desire-based agency. Andrews Reath, for example, argues that heteronomous actions, though not freely determined, need not be hedonistic. They can be premissed on agents' capacity to form an idea of happiness, where this includes their long-term goals and projects as well as their concern for the well-being of others. According to Reath, then, Kant, far from being a psychological hedonist, acknowledges the legitimate, if limited, place of desires in human life and practical deliberation.[6] More radically and more contentiously, Henry Allison claims that Kantian desire-based actions *can be* thought of as freely determined, at least

---

[3] In political philosophy, the virtue-based approach to action deliberation has been given a forceful revival by recent communitarian writers. Unfortunately, their passionate rejection of modern liberalism often leads communitarians to pass over the tensions that result from advocating a virtue-based approach to practical reasoning in ethics whilst retaining a desire-based account in economics. Studies in the history of modern economic thought show that it is precisely the unsustainable degree of tension between traditional virtue ethics, on the one hand, and the 'growth of commerce', on the other, that brought about the eventual shift, in early modern Europe, from the pre-modern to the modern conception of action deliberation. See, especially, J. G. A. Pocock, *The Machiavellian Moment* (Princeton: Princeton University Press, 1977); Albert Hirschman, *The Passions and the Interests* (Princeton: Princeton University Press, 1977); Istvan Hont and Michael Ignatieff, 'Needs and Justice in the Wealth of Nations', in Hont and Ignatieff (eds.), *Wealth and Virtue* (Cambridge: Cambridge University Press, 1983), 1–44.

[4] The revival of virtue ethics can be seen, to some degree, as having developed out of the more general communitarian critique of liberalism especially during the 1980s. See e.g. Michael Sandel, *Liberalism and the Limits of Justice* (Cambridge: Cambridge University Press, 1982); also Alasdair MacIntyre, *After Virtue* (London: Duckworth, 1981). For Kant's relation to virtue ethics, see Roger Sullivan, 'The Positive Role of Prudence in the Virtuous Life', *Jahrbuch für Recht und Ethik*, 5 (1997), 461–70; see also the collection of essays in S. Engstrom and J. Whiting (eds.), *Aristotle, Kant, and the Stoics* (Cambridge: Cambridge University Press, 1996).

[5] See Allen Wood, 'Kant's Compatibilism', in A. Wood (ed.), *Self and Nature in Kant's Philosophy* (Ithaca, NY: Cornell University Press, 1984), 73–101.

[6] Andrews Reath, 'Hedonism, Heteronomy, and Kant's Principle of Happiness', *Pacific Philosophical Quarterly*, 70 (1989), 42–72.

if one accepts a non-moral interpretation of the Kantian idea of freedom.[7] According to Allison's well-known Incorporation Thesis, there can be no action for Kant without an appropriate reason for action, including desire-based actions. In so far as they are rational, agents adopt a candidate desire as a reason for action by incorporating it into their maxim of action. To this extent even desire-based actions are rationally determined rather than merely pathological forms of behaviour. More contentious is Allison's related claim that reasons for action need not be *moral* reasons in order for the act to qualify as freely determined. At least in the *Critique of Pure Reason*, according to Allison, Kant regards subjects' capacity for rational deliberation as a sufficient condition for the attribution to them of practical freedom. In so far as desire-based actions display at least a limited degree of the spontaneity of reason required by the Kantian idea of freedom, they can qualify as freely determined action even where they are not incorporated into explicitly moral reasons for action.[8]

Although these correctives to the attribution to Kant of a hedonistic conception of desire are broadly right, they also show that Kant remains within the modern view of desiring as contributing a distinctly subjective dimension to action deliberation.[9] His struggles with the modern view are evident nowhere so much as in his political writings, especially in some of his occasional essays. Here Kant appears at times to be almost obsessed with the question of how to conceive the relation between desires and reason in the context of modern political agency. On the one hand, his fascination with desires in their modern political context reveals the very large debt Kant owed to Hobbes in the formation of his own political thinking. At the same time his eventual resolution of this problem also shows up the distance that Kant travelled from Hobbes *within* this modern framework. It is Kant's attempted resolution of the conflict between desires and moral deliberation in the political context that this chapter is principally concerned with.

---

[7] Henry Allison, *Kant's Transcendental Idealism* (New Haven: Yale University Press, 1983), ch. 15, and *Kant's Theory of Freedom* (Cambridge: Cambridge University Press, 1991). For critical discussions of *Kant's Theory of Freedom* see the papers by S. Engstrom, A. Reath, and M. Baron in the symposium on Allison's book in *Inquiry*, 36 (1993), 405–41.

[8] While Allison's Incorporation Thesis has been adopted by many Kant interpreters, his views concerning the 'limited spontaneity' of non-moral reasons for action has met with more resistance. I set out my objections in chapter 2 of *Kant and Modern Political Philosophy* (Cambridge: Cambridge University Press, 2000). For similar objections, see also S. Engstrom, 'Kant on Rational Agency', *Inquiry*, 36 (1993), 405–18.

[9] This is not inconsistent with the demand that, when they act from duty and in accordance with the Categorical Imperative, agents must try, so far as is within their power, to *abstract* from their particular inclinations.

My reasons for focusing on Kant's political writings, especially on the *Rechts-lehre*, are threefold. First, despite recent revisions regarding the relation between desires, reason, and action in Kant's ethics, relatively little work has been done on the notion of desire-based actions in his political writings. This would not matter were it not the case that the role of the concept of desire in political thinking differs from its function in ethics. Speaking summarily, subjects' desires in ethics may be said to refer to their affective attitudes towards others as well as towards themselves: attitudes of sympathy and resentment, guilt, admiration, and so on. These affective attitudes describe a person's psychological responses to qualities, dispositions, and attitudes observed in others, which influence the person's own dispositions and attitudes towards those others.[10] Let us say that, in ethics, desires describe subject–subject relations. By contrast, desires in the context of political agency typically specify relations between subjects and objects—more properly, between subjects with regard to objects. Desires here have an economic function: they denote a relation of want between subject and material object, and a consequent relation of competition between subjects with regard to those objects. Since they are essentially object-oriented, desires in the political context often seem less intangible than their psychologically complex counterparts in ethics. But the political conception possesses a complexity that arises from its own dynamic. As Hobbes argued so convincingly, economic desiring is almost invariably conflictual, though it is so independently of the concept's affective functions: conflict stems from the relative scarcity of available objects of desire, and gives rise only derivatively to affective attitudes between subjects. At the same time, their objective basis is precisely what makes desires so hard to dismiss or ignore in the political context.

My second reason for focusing on the *Rechtslehre* is that, partly as a result of the neglected distinction just mentioned, the attribution to Kant of a broadly Hobbesian political outlook is still widespread.[11] This is often justified by invoking the contrast between the morality of good will in ethics and the prudence of self-interest in politics. On the one hand, this encourages a somewhat schizophrenic conception of practical reasoning according to which subjects are exhorted to act virtuously in the sphere of ethics, whilst being expected to

---

[10] See P. F. Strawson, 'Freedom and Resentment', in his *Freedom and Resentment and other Essays* (London: Methuen Publishers, 1974), 1–25; also R. Jay Wallace, *Responsibility and the Moral Sentiments* (Cambridge, MA: Harvard University Press, 1994), ch. 2.

[11] For a Hobbesian interpretation of the *Rechtslehre*, see Otfried Höffe, 'Kant's Principle of Justice as a Categorical Imperative of Law', in Y. Yovel (ed.), *Kant's Practical Philosophy Reconsidered* (Dordrecht: Kluwer Academic Publishers, 1989), 149–67. See also the exchange between Bernd Ludwig, 'Will die Natur unwiderstehlich die Republik?' and Reinhardt Brandt, 'Antwort auf Bernd Ludwig', *Kant-Studien*, 88 (1997), 218–36. Also, contrast Guyer, Holtman, and Wood, this volume.

reason merely prudentially in the sphere of politics. On the other hand, attempts to save the unity of Kant's account of practical reasoning by attributing an ethical vision to his political philosophy tend to do so at the expense of the specifically economic function of desiring in the political context.[12] The question is whether it is possible to identify an account of economic and political agency in the *Rechtslehre* that is non-prudential without subordinating political agency under ethical agency.

The third reason, finally, for focusing on desire formation and desire-based agency in the political context has to do with recent developments in contemporary economic and political thinking. Despite the dominance, traditionally, of the Hobbesian model, doubts have been raised about its adequacy under current economic and political conditions.[13] It is becoming evident that something is amiss in standard economic assumptions about agent rationality and agent motivation. Part of the wider concern of this chapter is to ask whether a Kantian approach to desire formation and desire-based agency in political thinking can furnish the background to a revised, though modern, account of economic desiring.

The rest of this chapter consists of three further sections. Section II offers an outline of how the problem of desire-based agency emerges in the *Rechtslehre* in connection with Kant's account of external freedom, or freedom of choice and action. If we do (as I think we must) treat the universal principle of Right as a version of the Categorical Imperative, the question is whether desire-based economic choices can plausibly be conceived as subject to the constraints of Kant's supreme principle of morality. Section III considers this question in some detail, drawing attention to noticeable differences between Kant's more pathologically inclined view of desires in his earlier political essays and his moves towards what one might call a more cognitive account of desire formation in the *Rechtslehre*. In elaborating on this difference, I argue for a position halfway between the views of Reath and Allison. While objectively valid reasons for action play a greater role in Kantian desire-based agency than the account given by Reath allows for, desire-based actions are not free, in Allison's sense of limited spontaneity, unless they are constrained by *moral* reasons for

---

[12]   See Christine Korsgaard, 'Taking the Law into our own Hands: Kant on the Right to Revolution', in A. Reath, B. Herman, and C. Korsgaard (eds.), *Reclaiming the History of Ethics: Essays for John Rawls* (Cambridge: Cambridge University Press, 1997), 297–328.

[13]   See Amartya Sen, 'Rational Fools', *Philosophy and Public Affairs*, 6 (1977), 317–44, and *Ethics and Economics* (Oxford: Basil Blackwell, 1987). See also James Griffin, 'Against the Taste Model', in J. Elster and J. Roemer (eds.), *Well-Being and Interpersonal Comparisons of Well-Being* (Cambridge: Cambridge University Press, 1991), 45–69; and Thomas Scanlon, *What We Owe to Each Other* (Cambridge, MA: Harvard University Press, 1998), esp. pt. 1, 17–145.

action. The concluding section considers some of the implications of the Kantian account of desire formation and desire-based agency for current political and economic thinking.

II. External Freedom, Prudence, and Virtue in the *Rechtslehre*

Any account of desire-based but freely (that is, morally) determined agency must offer a non-prudential reading of Kant's conception of external freedom in the *Rechtslehre*. However, the latter is frequently taken to support a Hobbesian interpretation of the text. This indicates certain ambiguities in Kant's exposition of external freedom. Prior to *The Metaphysics of Morals* Kant does not explicitly distinguish between internal freedom and external freedom. When he does, the definition of internal freedom, which pertains to the sphere of ethics, remains largely identical with the idea of a good will and the related conception of autonomous willing familiar from his ethical writings.[14] By contrast, the meaning of external freedom, which pertains to the sphere of law (or politics), has to be gleaned from his definition of the concept of Right in the *Rechtslehre*.

Kant derives the concept of external freedom from the 'innate right to freedom of each' (*MS* 6:238). This innate right comprises subjects' innate equality, their independence from the arbitrary will of another, and their right to free interaction with others on an equal footing. Independence from the will of another and the right to free interaction with others imply subjects' capacity for freedom of choice and action. This preliminary conception of external freedom is further substantiated by Kant's definition of the concept of Right, which regulates the form of external relations between agents with regard to their choices:

The concept of right . . . has to do, *first*, only with the external and indeed practical relation of one person to another, insofar as their actions, as facts, can have (direct or indirect) influence on each other. But, *second*, it does not signify the relation of one's choice to the mere wish of the other . . . but only a relation to the other's choice. *Third*, in this reciprocal relation of choice, no account is taken of the matter of choice, that is, of the end each has in mind with the object he wants.   (*MS* 6:230)

The concept of Right thus abstracts from the content of agents' choices and from the maxims of their actions: agents' action intentions are of no consequence in judging the rightfulness of their external relations with one another.[15]

---

[14]   For a detailed discussion of the concept of internal freedom, see Engstrom, this volume.
[15]   Kant characterizes maxims as subjective principles of action. I here follow the dominant interpretation of maxims as agents' (internal) action intentions.

The same emphasis on the form of external relations between agents recurs with the universal principle of Right: 'Any action is right if it can coexist with everyone's freedom in accordance with a universal law, or if on its maxim the freedom of choice of each can coexist with everyone's freedom in accordance with a universal law' (*MS* 6:231).

The reference to subjects' maxims should not mislead one into thinking that internal intentions matter after all. All the universal principle of Right requires is that the *execution in action* of an agent's maxim not violate the external conditions of choice of another. In a business transaction between two agents, for example, the intention of the one may well be to profit from the relative disadvantage of the other. Though such a maxim may be ethically unworthy, it is not contrary to Right so long as in acting on that maxim the agent does not violate the external conditions of choice of the other.

The *Rechtslehre* focuses on external property relations between subjects: the argument in Section I of the text concerns subjects' freedom of choice and action in relation to their (economic) capacity to claim as theirs external objects of their choice. An exposition of Kant's property argument is beyond the scope of this chapter.[16] Of principal interest here is the relation between economic desiring and political self-legislation. The mentioned ambiguities in the concept of external freedom arise from the tension between its two components: object-oriented (that is, desire-based) choice, on the one hand, and freedom as autonomous willing (that is, self-legislation), on the other. External freedom endorses subjects' determination of their power of choice by material objects. Yet materially determined choice conflicts with freedom as autonomous willing. So, at least, Kant's distinction between heteronomous willing and autonomous willing in the *Groundwork* leads one to believe, where autonomous willing is said to presuppose the will's independence from determination by sensuous impulses. Indeed, the *Groundwork* tends to equate autonomous willing with good willing and with moral worthiness: that agent acts autonomously who makes it his or her maxim to act from duty and in accordance with the Categorical Imperative, guided by the idea of an unconditionally good will. Since purity of will and maxim are defining characteristics of internal freedom, autonomous willing in the *Groundwork* is virtually identical with what Kant subsequently calls internal freedom.[17] As we have seen, purity of will and maxim are not required for actions' outward con-

[16] I offer a detailed analysis of Kant's property argument in 'Freedom and Constraint in Kant's *Metaphysical Elements of Justice*', *History of Political Thought*, 20 (1999), 250–71.

[17] The contrast between internal freedom and external freedom is sometimes explained with reference to Kant's *Wille/Willkür* distinction in *The Metaphysics of Morals*. Lewis White Beck has argued that, once we distinguish between *Willkür* as denoting 'capacity for choice' and *Wille* as referring to reason's legislative

formity with the universal principle of Right. Indeed, its indifference with respect to agents' maxims justifies the coercive character of the universal principle of Right. It is *because* outward conformity of action does not require inward conformity of the will that the principle is externally enforceable. The question is whether the universal principle of Right functions exclusively as an externally imposed constraint on action, or whether its normative grounds derive from Kant's general conception of the self-legislative character of practical freedom. Here scholarly assessment divides over conflicting textual evidence. Those committed to the view that juridical principles are externally imposed focus on Kant's remarks about the different motivational incentives underlying juridical and ethical actions respectively:

All lawgiving can be distinguished with respect to incentives. That lawgiving which makes an action a duty and also makes this duty an incentive is ethical. But that lawgiving which does not include the incentive of duty in the law and so admits of an incentive other than the idea of duty itself is juridical. It is clear that in the latter case this incentive that is something other than the Idea of duty must be drawn from sensibly dependent determining grounds of choice, inclinations and aversions, and among these from aversions, since it is a lawgiving which constrains, not an allurement, which invites. (*MS* 6:219)

Kant's claim that juridical action admits of an incentive other than duty, and that this must be a sensibly based incentive that appeals to an aversion, invites the conclusion that subjects' outward conformity with the universal principle of Right rests on enlightened self-interest—that is, on a disinclination to suffer the sanctions of an externally enforced, coercive law in the case of non-conformity of one's actions with it. Those who reject prudential interest as the only available or even most relevant motivational incentive appeal to Kant's insistence that law and ethics are equally subject to the moral law, conformity with which cannot be based on prudential reasons:

In contrast to the laws of nature, the laws of freedom are called moral laws. As directed merely to external actions in conformity to law, they are called juridical laws, but if they also require that the laws themselves be the determining grounds of actions, they are ethical laws, and then one says that conformity with juridical laws is the legality of an action and conformity with ethical laws is its morality. (*MS* 6:214)

authority, the apparent conflict disappears between Kant's 'two concepts of freedom'. See Beck, 'Kant's Conception of the Will in their Political Context', in his *Studies in the Philosophy of Kant* (Minneapolis: Bobbs Merrill, 1965), 215–29. However, Nelson Potter rightly cautions that Kant's formal distinction between *Wille* and *Willkür* sheds little light on its implications for his substantive conception of practical freedom. See Potter, 'Does Kant Have Two Concepts of Freedom?', in G. Funke and J. Kopper (eds.), *Akten des Vierten Internationalen Kant Kongresses* (Berlin: Walter de Gruyter, 1978), 590–6.

Here Kant subsumes law and ethics under the more general category of morality, assigning both distinct spheres of moral competence. Since *all* laws of freedom are laws of moral self-legislation, juridical laws *can* be self-legislated even though, in contrast to ethical laws, they are *also* externally enforceable. Hence the normative ground of juridical laws of freedom lies in subjects' capacity of self-legislation, not in an appeal to their prudential self-interest.

Those interested in Kant as a political thinker often favour a prudential interpretation.[18] By contrast, those who approach the *Rechtslehre* from the perspective of Kant's ethics frequently defend a non-prudential reading of external freedom. Political interpreters have an acute sense of the distinctness of political agency from ethics. This reflects their appreciation of the economic function of desiring and explains their resistance to reducing political to ethical agency. Such resistance is entirely justified. However, the conclusion need not follow that, if political agency is not ethical agency, then, since ethical agency is non-prudential, political agency must be prudential.

Ethicists sometimes express similar objections. There is something odd about attributing to Kant a non-prudential conception of agency in one branch of morality, and a prudential one in the other branch. Such motivational divisions would amount to a deep failure on Kant's part to provide a unified conception of moral agency. If one wants to avoid such moral schizophrenia, the two branches of morality must be shown to add up to a unified conception of agency. These considerations lead some to interpret juridical duties as 'indirect ethical duties'.[19] Even if the principle of Right is externally enforceable, what justifies it is agents' capacity to make it their maxim to act from the duties of justice. When they do, agents are not acting from prudential motives. Instead, they embrace an ethical conception of justice as a duty of virtue. But, while ethical interpretations succeed in preserving a notion of self-legislation relative to the principle of Right, they do so by making acting from justice a virtue of ethics. As a consequence, the economic function of desiring as a distinctive component of *political* agency falls by the wayside.

In sum, political interpretations of the *Rechtslehre* preserve Kant's distinction between politics (law) and ethics at the price of reducing the universal principle of Right to an externally imposed constraint on external freedom. By contrast, ethical readings preserve the self-legislative character of lawful external freedom by subordinating politics to ethics. While political interpreters commit themselves to a broadly Hobbesian view of desiring and desire-based

---

[18] Höffe, 'Kant's Principle of Justice', 156–8.
[19] Korsgaard, 'Kant on the Right to Revolution', 317.

agency, ethical readings tend to ignore the economic function of desiring alto-gether. The question is whether it is possible to account for economic desiring within the framework of Kant's general conception of freedom as the capacity for self-legislated agency.

III. From Nature to Reason: Desires in the Essays and in the *Rechtslehre*

The advantage of distinguishing between the affective role of desires in ethics and their object-oriented function in economics and in politics is that it helps one to focus on what is at stake in disputes between prudential and ethical interpretations of the *Rechtslehre*. Even if one rejects a prudential conception of political agency, one cannot simply ignore the economic dimension of indi-viduals' desires for material objects of their choice by talking about justice as a virtue instead. It is more appropriate to ask whether economic desiring can be conceived in a manner that does not equate political agency with the pursuit of prudential self-interest. Here it is instructive to consider, if only briefly, the historical context of Kant's approach to economic desiring.

In her perceptive comparison between Stoic and Kantian cosmopolitanism, Martha Nussbaum asks why, in contrast to the Stoics, Kant displayed little faith in the possibility of 'enlightening the passions'.[20] For the Stoics, 'passion-al enlightenment formed an integral part of their cosmopolitan ideal': trans-forming angry passions into pacific ones was a necessary first step from war towards the achievement of peace. By contrast, Kant's view of the passions in 'Perpetual Peace' 'must be defined in terms of the suppression of the evil forces in human beings rather than in terms of their education'.[21] Nussbaum finds it 'more than a little odd that Kant, familiar as he clearly was with Stoic ideas, including ideas about the passions, did not seriously consider their view as a candidate for truth in this area'.[22] But this ignores the fact that by Kant's time the passions had undergone—were still undergoing—a radical conceptual transformation largely dictated by new economic imperatives. Studies in the history of early economic thought paint a fascinating picture of this transfor-mation, which, beginning during the latter half of the seventeenth century and continuing well into the nineteenth century, revalued old moral vices as new

---

[20] Martha Nussbaum, 'Kant and Cosmopolitanism', in J. Bohman and M. Lutz-Bachmann (eds.), *Per-petual Peace: Essays on Kant's Cosmopolitan Ideal* (Cambridge, MA: MIT Press, 1997), 46.
[21] Ibid.
[22] Ibid. 46–7.

economic virtues.[23] A particularly relevant factor was the growth of overseas commerce and trade, which 'entered the language of politics at a very rapid pace towards the end of the seventeenth century',[24] rendering obsolete the traditional preoccupation of statecraft with internal security and external warfare. The market, it was recognized, 'had its own laws—laws which differed sharply from those of politics',[25] such that political thinking struggled hard to catch up with economic practice. As the traditional virtues of thriftiness and frugality that had sustained agricultural economies became an impediment to new economic development, encouraging the vice of individual acquisitiveness became an imperative for economic survival.

This gradual shift from a virtue-based to a desire-based account of individual agency was accomplished with greater hesitancy than critics of early capitalism often recognize. Despite the astounding economic productivity that accompanied the 'triumph of commerce', observers were alarmed by the manifest insatiability of individuals' desires with their 'twin outcomes of private property and social corruption'.[26] The question became paramount whether it was either possible or desirable to tame the passions, and if so, by what means and to what extent. Was the attempt to set up legal constraints on economic activities an exercise in futility, such that one did best to resign oneself to 'the unbridled pursuit of the passions' in the hope that the system might cull itself naturally? Or should one 'steer the passions' by means of carefully devised economic policies?[27] Ought one to transform the passions by enlightening their bearers as to their 'true interests'?[28] Or was there not ground for optimism in observing the natural give and take between the calm passions and the hot, where one passion countervailed another, maintaining a harmonious equilibrium between selfish drives and social impulses?

Little has been written on Kant's relation to economic thinking.[29] In many ways this neglect is not surprising. Kant's political writings show little explicit interest in the details of economic theory. The overwhelming concern of his political essays is with the *moral* improvement of humankind, leading to the

---

[23]   As mentioned in n. 3 above, an accessible history of this transformation can be found in Hirschman, *Passions and Interests*, and in Pocock, *Machiavellian Moment*. See also J. A. W. Gunn, 'Interest will not Lie', *Journal of the History of Ideas*, 29 (1968), 551–64; Istvan Hont, 'Free Trade and the Economic Limits to National Politics: Neo-Machiavellian Political Economy Reconsidered' in J. Dunn (ed.), *The Economic Limits to Modern Politics* (Cambridge: Cambridge University Press, 1992), 41–120.

[24]   Pocock, *Machiavellian Moment*, 425.

[25]   Hont, 'Free Trade', 43.

[26]   Ibid. 65.

[27]   Hirschman, *Passions and Interests*, 83.

[28]   Gunn, 'Interest will not Lie', 556.

[29]   A notable exception is Samuel Fleischacker, 'Values behind the Market: Kant's Response to the Wealth of Nations', *History of Political Thought*, 17 (1996), 379–407.

eventual abolition of war through a growing commitment to peace. At the same time Kant's political thinking was deeply affected by the phenomenon of trade. His cosmopolitanism constitutes a political response to the observed increase in commercial transactions. Indeed, Kant has often been criticized for his optimistic anticipations regarding the pacifying effects of commerce on trading nations. This apparent optimism obscures the fact that Kant's assessment of the motives behind individuals' actions in the political and economic sphere is often ambiguous, fluctuating between faith in humanity's eventual moral progress and deep pessimism over the depravity of mankind in its ineliminable propensity to evil. When alluding to individuals' inclinations and desires, the similarity is often striking between the language of Kant's economic contemporaries and his own choice of terms. Especially in his political essays Kant's ambivalence about individuals' desires resonates with the uncertainties of economic thinkers regarding the balance of fate between morality and economics. There is an equally striking *contrast* between the outlook of the earlier essays and the tone of the *Rechtslehre*. If the essays tend to align desires with the darker, pathological forces of human nature, the *Rechtslehre* draws a closer connection between desiring, understanding, and practical reasoning. A shift is thus discernible from a passionate conception of desiring in the essays, to a more reasoned account of them in the *Rechtslehre*.

(*a*) Desires and Nature in the Essays

The terminological overlap between Kant and his economic contemporaries is especially evident in his reflections on the design of nature in 'Perpetual Peace'. As Samuel Fleischacker notes, Kant's account of nature's provisional arrangements in dispersing human beings across the earth has an economic dimension resembling Adam Smith's theory of the four stages of human historical and economic development.[30] Of course, Kant is principally interested in the idea of *moral* progress: nature disperses individuals through war in order to compel them to peace. Economic incentives are one of the means adopted by nature to further this end: camels for the nomads, reindeer for the Ostiaks, driftwood for the Eskimos. These means of transport and trade that nature affords human beings ensure the irresistible rise of commerce. The theme is pursued with enthusiasm in 'Idea for a Universal History with a Cosmopolitan Purpose': 'thanks be to nature for fostering social incompatibility, enviously competitive vanity, and an insatiable desire for possession and even power' (I. 8:21). But

---

[30] Ibid. 385.

this Mandevellian picture of private vices yielding public benefits is not Kant's only view on the matter. While it is certain *that* nature will 'compel man to do that which he ought to do by the laws of freedom' (EF 8:365), it is less clear *how* it will accomplish this feat. 'Perpetual Peace' remains famously undecided on this question, offering prudential, ethical, and systemic explanations alike. A Hobbesian appeal to the rational self-interest of morally depraved reasoners is evident in Kant's notorious assertion that 'the problem of setting up the state can be solved even by a nation of devils, so long as they are rational' (EF 8:366). Yet only a few pages further on Kant repudiates the scheming of the 'political moralist', insisting that 'a true system of politics cannot take a single step without first paying tribute to morality' (EF 8:380). A steady focus on the concept of duty will ensure the moral transformation of political and economic motives: one must resist as self-fulfilling prophecies the predictions of those who doggedly insist on the incorrigible corruption of human passions. Elsewhere again, Kant expresses a position simultaneously less despairing and less ambitious in its admiration of the cunning of nature, which ensures the countervailing balance of human passions by ensuring that contact between peoples remains constant but limited. Cultural and linguistic barriers among peoples engaged in mutual trade will keep them apart even while economic interests bring them together.

This ambiguity about the political economy of desires is noticeable not only in 'Perpetual Peace'. Kant repeatedly plays off a first-person, motivational viewpoint against a third-person, historical perspective. In 'On the Common saying: That May Be Correct in Theory, but It Is of No Use in Practice', when considering whether humanity is progressing or regressing, Kant argues against Mendelssohn that, while observing the selfish actions of individuals will lead one to despair over the possibility of moral progress, the picture is more promising when looked at from an enlarged, historical perspective. From that perspective the seemingly disparate and self-regarding endeavours of individual actors add up to a justified hope in the possibility of progress, making it a duty to act in accordance with that hope (GTP 8:308–12). 'Universal History' makes a similar point from a different angle by drawing attention to 'annual [population] statistics in large countries'. From an individual's perspective human actions appear arbitrary and even futile. But, in general, human actions display a remarkably predictable pattern, making them seem 'just as subject to natural laws as are changes in the weather' (I. 8:2).

Prudential, moral, and systemic explanations are used interchangeably in passages like these, often without a clear sense of the possible tension between them. This echoes the ambivalence of contemporary economic thinkers regarding the systemic moral and political effects of individual desiring. Like

his contemporaries, Kant acknowledges the economic productivity of individuals' capacity for desire whilst remaining troubled by their moral implications.
Like them, he remains undecided about how to negotiate the opposing tendencies at play in economic desiring at the levels of individual action and social
consequence. As Nussbaum notes, on the whole Kant casts individuals' desires
in a negative light, even if he concedes that their historical effects may yet be
positive. Desires are potentially calamitous natural forces within the human
constitution, which require either the countervailing powers of a strong
Hobbesian state or a reasoned moral commitment to progress, or both. To be
sure, even in the essays a different view occasionally emerges. In 'Speculative
Beginnings of Human History', Kant describes desires as distinctly human
and as different from natural instinct: 'It is a peculiarity of reason that it is able,
with the help of the imagination, to invent desires which not only *lack* any corresponding natural impulse, but which are even *at variance* with the latter'
(MA 8:111). This astute distinction between desires and instinct offers
glimpses of a conception of desiring as dependent on cognitive capacities,
which is closer to the view developed in the *Rechtslehre*. Even so, the underlying picture is one in which pathological and rational tendencies within human
nature do battle with one another, with reason eventually gaining the upper
hand and establishing true moral freedom in its defeat of pathological desiring.

(*b*) Desires and Reason in the *Rechtslehre*

The approach of the *Rechtslehre* differs from that of the essays on at least two
counts. First, Kant barely mentions the idea of humanity's moral progress. The
focus is on individual *agency* and on individuals' *duties of action*. Secondly, the
scope of juridical duties is considerably narrower in the *Rechtslehre*. In the
essays the triad of 'freedom, equality, and independence' represents an ideal of
human emancipation to be achieved through the gradual process of moral historical enlightenment. By contrast, the *Rechtslehre* distinguishes, as we have
seen, between subjects' innate rights and their acquired rights. The former is
explicitly set aside.[31] The *Rechtslehre* focuses exclusively on the category of
acquired rights, which comprises property rights and derivative contractual
rights.

These shifts from a historical to an agent-centred perspective and from a
comprehensive emancipatory ideal to the specific delimitation of juridical
rights and duties have certain consequences. Kant's attitude towards economic
desires is less ambivalent because, considered strictly in relation to individuals'

[31] Cf. *MS* 6:238.

property claims, all reference to individuals' moral depravity is omitted. More-over, individuals' claims to property are acknowledged as legitimate *and* as entailing direct obligations of justice. This direct connection between individ-uals' capacity for economic desire and their capacity to acknowledge and to honour ensuing obligations of justice implies a view of desiring as susceptible to the constraints of practical reasoning. In so far as agents' acknowledgement of the obligations of justice entailed by their economic actions depends on their recognizing these obligations as theirs—that is, as resulting from their actions—it must be possible for agents to discharge these obligations of their own accord—that is, autonomously. Were agents not capable of taking politi-cal responsibility for their economic actions, their right to external choice and action could not be a right of *freedom*, at least not in Kant's sense of practical freedom as consisting in the capacity for self-legislation.

But agents can take political responsibility for their economic choices only in so far as it is within their capacity to desire consistently with the require-ments of justice. Therefore, agents must be capable of at least some degree of reasoned insight into the structure of desiring: they must be capable of reflec-tion on their standing as rational beings who have the capacity for desire. Moreover, as self-legislating rational beings, they must be able to give desires a moral form. My claim is that Kant's definition of the capacity for desire in *The Metaphysics of Morals* does possess the requisite first-personal reflexive struc-ture. Let us return to this definition: 'The capacity for desire is the capacity to be by means of one's representations the cause of the objects of these represen-tations. The capacity of a being to act on its representations is called *life*' (*MS* 6:231).

Kant does not think of agents as subject to the causality of their desires. The definition implies that agents are the causes of their desires as well as of desire satisfaction (attaining the object of desire). Causality appears to refer to two distinct causal processes here. To say that one is, or has the capacity to be, the cause of desire satisfaction may amount to no more than the claim that the causal efficacy of one's having a desire depends on one's identifying and pursu-ing the necessary means to the attainment of the desired object. One then causes the attainment of the object of one's desire by means of the capacity for instrumental reasoning combined with the capacity for object-directed motor action. This sense of causal efficacy remains at the level of desire attainment rather than desire formation. Yet, when Kant talks about the capacity for desire, he is alluding not primarily to desire attainment, but to desire forma-tion. The claim that it is 'by means of one's representations' that one is the cause of the objects of one's desires goes beyond the more familiar view of externally given objects as stimulating one's desire for them. Kant's contention is that subjects have the capacity to form a conception of a possible, though not as yet existent, object of desire. It is this capacity for creatively imagining possible objects of desire that the reference to 'representations' draws attention to.

Two points are therefore worth bearing in mind when elaborating the status of subjects' representational capacities in relation to desire formation. The first concerns the role of the understanding in the representation of an object in general, including objects of desire. The importance of representations in Kant's general theory of knowledge is well known. For Kant, knowledge is representational in the sense that our sensible experience of external objects is conceptually mediated. Objective knowledge does not result from a mere receptivity of the senses, but requires the activity of the understanding in the recognition of a sensible intuition *as* an object: objective knowledge consists in the representation of an intuition as an object under the concept of an object. This requires the application of general rules of cognition (that is, pure categories) to sensible intuition. It is only in virtue of their capacity to bring an intuition under the rules of the concept of an object that subjects can cognize an intuition as a determinate object. This general view of the cognitive structure of empirical experience must extend to objects of desire as well: the recognition of a sensibly given intuition as an object of desire requires the application of the rules of the understanding to that intuition. As is equally well known, however, Kant does not think of these operations of the understanding as more or less automatic processes. Experience of sensibly given objects is not only cognitive but also conscious: the 'I think', as the formal condition of conscious experience, 'must be able to accompany all my representations' (*KrV* B131). Again, this must include my representations of objects of desire. Given his general theory of knowledge, Kant must think of object-oriented desiring as requiring complex cognitive and reflexive capacities on the part of the desiring subject. (Of course, desiring requires more than a capacity for reflexively conscious conceptual representation. There must be something that distinguishes the cognition of objects of desire from the cognition of objects in general. The above remarks are not intended to exclude physiological and psychological criteria of desire formation; I simply focus on what subjects' representational capacities imply about Kant's conception of desire formation that more familiar accounts tend to omit.) The importance to Kant of the cognitive component of desire formation is emphasized in his distinction between 'concupiscence' and 'desire'. While 'concupiscence is always a sensible modification of the mind', which can stimulate to action, 'it has not yet become an act of the capacity for desire'. Only 'the capacity for desiring in accordance with concepts is called the capacity for doing or refraining from doing what one pleases' (*MS* 6:213). The implication is that whoever cannot form and act in accordance with a conception of the object of his or her desire does not choose and act on the basis of a (fully developed) capacity for desire.

The second point I want to make concerns the relation between desires and the productive imagination. Unusually, Kant's definition makes no reference to sensibly given intuitions. The capacity to represent to oneself possible objects of desire does not require the presence of a corresponding sensible intuition. Presumably, this does not mean that subjects do not also form representations of objects of desire on the basis of sensibly given intuitions. Nonetheless, the capacity for desire formation as such depends on cognitive and imaginative capacities rather than on being sensibly affected by (already given) objects of desire. We can form a conception of a possible object of desire even in the absence of sensibly given stimuli. This creative aspect of desire formation is strangely neglected by currently dominant views of desiring as a physiologically and/or psychologically responsive stimulus to action. Yet a large number of our desires are ones we end up *not* acting on: we can imagine desirable objects or states of affairs which we desire to obtain but the obtaining of which we judge to be impossible. Likewise, we are able to 'desire in the imagination'— that is, to desire without desiring the attainment of the imagined object of desire. Again, many of the desires we do act on consist in attempts to bring about the realization of not as yet existent ends on the basis of our mere conception of their desirability. Our ability to form a conception of their desirability by means of the imagination guides our attempts at their practical realization. Thus, although we are the causes of our desires in the sense of being causally efficacious in bringing about the attainment of their objects, the sense of causal efficacy is secondary to the principal meaning of 'being the cause of'. Principally, rational beings' cognitive and imaginative capacities enable them to form a conception of (not as yet existent) objects of desire, thus making them the 'rational causes' of the desires they come to have.

(c) Desires, Morality, and Freedom in the *Rechtslehre*

Even if desiring presupposes subjects' cognitive and imaginative capacities, this does not suffice for *non-prudential* desiring. Rational desiring is not moral desiring merely in virtue of being rational. One can be a rationally desiring subject in Kant's sense of the term without being someone who desires in accordance with the constraints of morality. Still, in so far as rational desiring requires awareness of oneself as a rationally desiring subject, such awareness implies an ability to reflect on and to evaluate one's desires. Rational desiring implies evaluative desiring. But evaluative desiring presupposes in turn commitment and appeal to some normative assumptions and principles. Although

Kant's remarks on evaluative desiring in *The Metaphysics of Morals* are sketchy and obscure, his distinction between 'interests of inclination' and 'interests of reason' sheds some light on the difference between self-interested and self-legislated economic desiring.

The Metaphysics of Morals distinguishes between aesthetic pleasure and practical pleasure. The creative aspect of desiring is most apparent in relation to aesthetic pleasure, which is itself distinct from desiring in the strict sense. Aesthetic pleasure 'is not connected with any desire for an object, but is already connected with a mere representation that one forms of an object (regardless of whether the object of representation exists or not)' (*MS* 6:212). Aesthetic pleasure constitutes a more abstract, contemplative kind of pleasure than that which accompanies our practically efficacious capacity for desire. The latter is practical pleasure, pleasure in relation to action. In the case of practical pleasure, the feeling of desire that accompanies the pleasure can either 'precede the determination of the will', or it can 'follow upon the determination of the will'. In the former case, Kant speaks of an 'interest of inclination', in the latter of an 'interest of reason' (*MS* 6:212). This evokes the contrast between hypothetical imperatives and the Categorical Imperative set out in the *Groundwork*. In the case of interests of inclination, where the feeling of pleasure precedes the determination of an agent's will, desire formation is pathologically affected. Experienced as a *sensible* modification of the mind, an antecedent feeling of pleasure stimulates desire formation. This does not mean that pleasurable sensation and desire formation are identical. The representation of a pleasurable sensation as a possible object of desire requires the application of the rules of the understanding in the cognition of such a (possible) object of desire. Even where practical desiring is pathologically affected in the sense of being stimulated by the senses, the transformation of a pleasurable sensation into the judgement of an object of desire requires cognitive capacities on the part of the desiring subject.

In addition to cognitive capacities, practical desiring also requires evaluative capacities: the subject must judge whether the conceived object of desire is practically attainable. With regard to interests of inclination, the relevant rules of such feasibility judgements are those associated with the hypothetical imperative. The subject evaluates the possible realization of the conceived object of desire in terms of the means necessary to its attainment. Crucially, instrumental desire evaluation makes no reference to the effects on others of one's pursuit and attainment of the object of one's desire.[32] Desire evaluation in

---

[32] Of course, such instrumental evaluation might take into account the usefulness of others as means to one's desired ends. I am grateful to Ken Westphal for pointing this out to me.

accordance with hypothetical imperatives is rational, but means–ends oriented. It lacks a moral dimension that would distinguish between the feasibility of pursuing a particular desire, and the moral legitimacy of so doing. As such it remains essentially self-regarding.

Where the feeling of pleasure 'follows upon an antecedent determination of the capacity for desire', Kant speaks of an 'interest of reason'. Here the feeling of pleasure does not consist of a sensible modification of the mind. It is a 'sense-free inclination', or 'intellectual pleasure' (*MS* 6:213). Kant appears to have in mind the pleasure or contentment that accompanies the resolve to act from duty and in accordance with the Categorical Imperative.[33] Sense-free pleasure arises from acknowledgement of one's moral duties, on which one acts without resentment. In the case of 'interests of reason', desire formation is restrained by something that gives rise to a feeling of pleasure in virtue of its influence on desire formation: desire formation is restrained by principles of pure practical reason. Kant's allusion to the Categorical Imperative indicates that this second mode of desire evaluation includes a moral dimension. Subjects' practical evaluation of their desires is not restricted to feasibility judgements but includes, additionally, judgements concerning their moral permissibility. In contrast to merely instrumental evaluation, this second mode presupposes subjects' capacity and willingness to form and pursue their desires in a manner that takes into consideration the possible effects on others of their desire-based actions, and to act accordingly. This does not mean that economic desire formation can ever be wholly sense free. Economic desiring is desiring in relation to material objects of one's choice; it cannot be either sense free or merely intellectual to the degree to which ethical contentment or aesthetic pleasure may be. However, economic desire evaluation can be sense free to the extent that, despite the fact that their desires are object oriented, rationally desiring subjects can acknowledge the presence of others as a morally constraining condition on their desire-based actions. In so far as they are the rational causes of their desires, subjects have the capacity to guide desire formation and desire pursuit in accordance with principles of practical reason.

IV. Desiring, Self-Legislation, and Economic Agency

The above account of Kantian desiring in the *Rechtslehre* is sketchy and incomplete. This is partly because, his remarks in the general introduction to *The*

---

[33] Cf. *KpV* 5:72–89.

Kantian Desires 205

Metaphysics of Morals aside, Kant does not thematize the concept of (economic) desires in the *Rechtslehre*. Any attempt to render explicit the connection between desire and external freedom requires an exposition of Kant's complex property argument: there is no space to do so here. In any case, my contention is not that Kant offers a fully worked-out account of reasoned desiring in the *Rechtslehre*. Nonetheless, even from the brief discussion of the distinction between internal and external freedom outlined above, it should be clear that Kant requires something like the conception of rationally constrained economic desiring sketched if political agency is to qualify as non-ethical but freely determined agency. Unless individuals can bring their economic choices and actions into accord with the universal principle of Right as a principle of political self-legislation, prudential interpretations of external freedom are difficult to avoid, where the sole motive to compliance with an externally enforced law is fear of sanctions. For the same reason, it makes sense to distinguish economic desires from the general concept of desire. As they stand, neither Reath's account of desire-based agency in Kant's ethics, nor Allison's non-moral theory of Kantian freedom capture what is required for political agency in the *Rechtslehre*. According to Reath, desire-based actions need not be hedonistic, but invariably are heteronomously determined and thus non-moral. For Allison, desire-based agency can qualify as free agency if we assume a non-moral conception of freedom that regards the capacity for rational deliberation as a sufficient presupposition of practical freedom. What Kant requires in the *Rechtslehre* is a conception of economic desiring and agency that can qualify as freely determined in so far as such desiring is morally constrained by the requirements of the universal principle of Right. This does not mean that economic desiring must be ethical. As a moral principle of external freedom, the universal principle of Right abstracts from the worthiness of agents' disposition towards others. It requires only that the free choices of each be in *outward* conformity with the equal right to freedom of everyone else. This is why I both emphasized and restricted myself to the importance of agents' taking into account the *effects* of their actions on others relative to economic desiring and action. In focusing on this particular moral constraint, it is possible to suggest against a view such as that offered by Reath that economic desiring *can* qualify as freely determined, while emphasizing against Allison that desire-based agency is freely determined only in so far as it accords with the constraints on action of Kant's supreme principle of morality.

More generally, a Kantian conception of economic desiring may prove helpful in current attempts to rethink modern economic agency. Despite the traditional predominance of the Hobbesian model, there is a growing recognition among economists of its inadequacies under contemporary economic conditions.[34] If individuals' acquisitive drives fuelled competitive economic growth during the early stages of free trade, the ecological limits of economic growth as well as deep and persistent global inequities call for a more cooperative model of economic agency. Yet economists often find it extremely difficult to give up their assumption of desiring individuals as self-interested pursuers of their own advantage, which to many represents a basic truth about human nature as evidenced by casual observation of actual individual behaviour.[35] Two aspects of the Hobbesian model of economic desiring contrast sharply with the Kantian account. The first is the essentially physiological analysis of Hobbesian desiring, and the consequent temptation to equate desiring with instinctual behaviour. The second is the view of economic desiring as intrinsically and necessarily amoral.

With respect to the physiological aspect, one might ask whether Kant's cognitive conception of desiring does not reflect actual economic behaviour at least as well as the Hobbesian model. Economic desiring *is* a life-sustaining activity. But, as Kant observes, in contrast to other animals, nature has equipped human beings so badly in the essentials of life, that they must produce everything for themselves. Economic agents must conceive of as yet non-existent economic projects; they must assess their feasibility; they must identify the necessary means to their realization; and they must outwit their competitors in the market. All this requires thought and foresight. Put like this, few would deny that economic desiring requires highly complex and sophisticated cognitive capacities, especially capacities of the imagination. These are rarely acknowledged explicitly in current theories of economic agency. Here an interpretation along Kantian lines might present a more accurate picture of actual economic behaviour than the Hobbesian, physiological view.

In Section III, I argued that, in so far as rational desiring is evaluative desiring, it implies, for Kant, a capacity for moral evaluation. Here again Kant's account differs sharply from the Hobbesian conception. The view is widespread that we cannot be held responsible for our desires. Indeed, if our desires are physiological processes—even if they are psychological responses to physiological processes—it is difficult to hold individuals to account for their economic desires and pursuits. At least at the level of economic agency, however, it is also

---

[34] See e.g. Albert Hirschman, 'Against Parsimony', *Economics and Philosophy*, 1 (1985), 7–21; Hamish Stewart, 'A Critique of Instrumental Reason in Economics', *Economics and Philosophy*, 11 (1995), 57–83; Daniel Hausman and Michael McPherson, 'Economics, Rationality, and Ethics', in D. Hausman (ed.), *The Philosophy of Economics* (Cambridge: Cambridge University Press, 1994), 252–77.

[35] This emerged in conversation with one of my colleagues from the economics department. Interestingly, it was the casualness of their observations that confirmed to my colleague the truth of economists' assumptions.

deeply counterintuitive to say that we are not or cannot be held responsible for our desires. Abnegation of responsibility may be more persuasive with respect to the affective desires in ethics. In the economic context, recognition of the deep injustices suffered by many as a consequence of the unconstrained economic actions of others is precisely to affirm responsibility for action. If the standard Hobbesian conception is unable to account for individual economic responsibility in the face of an acknowledgement of persistent economic injustices, there is something wrong about interpreting actual economic behaviour along those lines. The Hobbesian model underestimates actual economic agents' cognitive, imaginative, and moral capacities and in so doing relieves them of their duties of justice. Here Kant's account, which emphasizes these duties even whilst acknowledging the legitimacy of economic desiring, will repay further conceptual and practical exploration.

9

Revolution, Contradiction, and Kantian Citizenship

Sarah Williams Holtman

I. Introduction

To many critics, Immanuel Kant's *Rechtslehre* has value principally as an example of what a theory of justice should not be. To wit, Kantian justice requires slavish adherence to rigid rules that are backed by harsh penalties and insensitive to real-world complexities and imperfections. These characteristics, critics often note, are nowhere more apparent than in Kant's discussion of revolution. However unjust the legal system, however corrupt the public officials, revolution never is justified: 'a people has a duty to put up with even what is held to be an unbearable abuse of supreme authority . . . [and] its resistance to the highest legislation can never be regarded as other than contrary to law, and indeed as abolishing the entire legal constitution' (*MS* 6:320).[1] Friends of Kant's practical philosophy too find this position on revolution at best overstated and at worst untenable, though unlike critics they typically do not further conclude that this has insurmountable consequences for the theory of justice as a whole.

Here I use the term 'revolution' in the sense in which we typically intend it: the forcible replacement of one political authority with another.[2] That Kant's

Thanks to Katrin Flikschuh, Thomas E. Hill, Onora O'Neill, Kenneth Westphal, and Allen Wood for very valuable comments.

[1] Citations to *The Metaphysics of Morals* and 'On the Common Saying: That May Be Correct in Theory, But It Is of No Use in Practice' are from *Practical Philosophy*, ed. and trans. Mary Gregor (Cambridge Edition of the Works of Immanuel Kant; Cambridge: Cambridge University Press, 1996). Those to 'The Contest of Faculties' are from *Kant's Political Writings*, ed. Hans Reiss, trans. H. B. Nisbet (Cambridge: Cambridge University Press, 1970).

[2] While Kant does not clarify, this apparently is his primary concern in addressing revolution. Moreover, he takes challenges to legislative, executive, and judicial authority equally seriously. For a thorough discussion, see Peter Nicholson, 'Kant on the Duty Never to Resist the Sovereign', *Ethics*, 86 (1975), 214–30.

discussions of revolution, not only in the *Rechtslehre* but in the earlier essay 'On the Common Saying: That May Be Correct in Theory, but It Is of No Use in Practice', seem to display all the characteristics critics and friends cite is undeniable. There are abundant statements (like the one quoted above) that apparently encapsulate a dogmatic view and leave nothing of consequence to discuss. Bold phrasing, though, can often mask subtlety, both in a view itself and in the argument for it. In what follows, I explore some of the subtleties that fill the spaces between Kant's rigid proclamations on the subject of revolution. Noting that Kant's views on revolution seem almost Hobbesian, I detail telling differences between the Hobbesian and Kantian perspectives on revolution, differences no less real for being all too easy to miss. Turning in Section III to the problems that clearly remain in Kant's discussion, I argue that these arise not from any deep failing in his theory of justice, but from an error in seeing that theory through to its natural conclusion. I close with four suggestions about the role of revolution in the realm of Kantian justice.

II. Kant on Revolution

(*a*) Kant through a Hobbesian Lens

What immediately strikes many about Kant's discussion of revolution is that it shares several features with Hobbes's treatment of the same topic. Indeed, one way of poignantly capturing what troubles critics about Kant's views on revolution is to point out what seems amiss in Hobbes's case.[3] According to Hobbes, one is never justified in using force to remove political authorities, no matter how corrupt, incompetent, or unjust these might be and no matter what degree of honesty, effectiveness, and justice the proposed replacement seems to promise, at how low a cost, or with what degree of certainty. This is because human nature and the world are such that the likely result of destabilizing the political system in place, preferably one headed and firmly controlled by a single sovereign with absolute power, will be a diminution in the central power necessary to protect citizens from one another and make possible cooperation for mutual benefit. Even if civil society does not fall into anarchy, for Hobbes a war of all against all, the attendant risks are inevitably more weighty and more likely than any benefits for which we reasonably might

---

[3]   My account of Hobbes is stylized; it functions to highlight differences with Kant, not as sensitive textual interpretation. Though Hobbes's views surely are more nuanced than I suggest, I think my general characterization fair.

hope. Given that self-interest demands that we behave as though we have authorized all the state's acts as our own, exchanging promises to this effect with all other citizens, to engage in revolutionary activity is unjust. Given that each of us takes self-interest narrowly conceived as her most fundamental guiding principle, we also act contrary to our own commitments and are guilty of a kind of self-contradiction when we engage in such activity.[4]

We can capture what is so troubling about Hobbes's absolutist position on revolution if we consider his inability to distinguish between two people we typically deem very differently positioned; call them the foole and the reformer. The foole, to whom Hobbes explicitly responds, is ready to violate the sovereign's commands whenever the gains this promises outweigh the risks, punishment and others' distrust most significant among them. Guided only by a narrow self-interest that hardly extends beyond the most personal pleasures and pains, the foole claims, with Hobbes, that reason requires one to do what will probably be most conducive to self-interest so understood. Where justice demands absolute obedience to law, no matter what the costs and benefits involved, indeed that we treat the sovereign as though we have placed all our power entirely in his control, the foole claims it will sometimes be quite unreasonable to act justly.[5] Among the acts sometimes condoned by Hobbesian reason, but not by Hobbesian justice, the foole surely will include revolution.

The reformer, as I will characterize her, is not sceptical of justice, but embraces it. She too is ready to violate sovereign commands, under appropriate circumstances even a command prohibiting overthrow of the political system in place. Yet, her ground for engaging in these actions is not that they will probably serve self-interest. Rather, her illegal actions must, in her best estimation, be reasonably calculated, based on standards others can grasp and endorse, to serve the cause of justice. Further, they must do so in some substantial way by opposing laws (or a legal system) that significantly burden some or all citizens. Accepting an intimate connection between a system of laws, institutions, and authorized decision-makers and the realization of justice, our reformer also acknowledges that whole political systems, or components of them, may be so deeply unjust as to warrant coercive efforts in the name of a greater justice. She holds open the possibility of undertaking such action where injustice is sufficiently severe, alternative courses are unavailable

---

[1]   Thomas Hobbes, *Leviathan*, ed. Edwin Curley (Indianapolis: Hackett, 1994). A 'narrow' self-interest always prefers my well-being to that of others. When conflicts between self and others arise, Hobbesian persons pursue their own more immediate desires and aversions.

[5]   Hobbes, *Leviathan*, 90–1.

or ineffective, and success without morally significant costs is sufficiently likely.[6]

The trouble with Hobbes's view is that his responses to the foole and the reformer will be precisely the same.[7] It makes no difference to Hobbes whether one acts for personal gain or to combat injustice. Acts opposing a political system or seeking to remove the governing power weaken, or place at risk, the only reliable means we have of avoiding a chaos in which each opposes all others in a futile attempt to defend herself. Thus the loss one risks in any such action is almost always greater than any possible benefit.[8] Given the near impossibility of cooperating without a central political power in place, any act that weakens that power and encourages its demise is also likely to realize these dire consequences. If this were not enough, Hobbes reminds us that human beings tend, even at their best, to calculate the nature and likelihood of consequences poorly. When drawn by self-interest or passion (for justice or otherwise), their limited capacities are still less adequate to the task. In short, the probable result of disobedience to law, revolution most of all, is fiasco, and the fact that it seems otherwise to us is no reliable evidence to the contrary. This does not change with one's reason for disobedience; the cause of justice conveys no more legitimacy on such actions than does that of self-interest. One who breaks the law, or worse one who explicitly seeks to remove the structures and leaders that make possible a functioning political system, undermines justice and involves herself in contradiction.

When we compare it with Hobbes's view, the special vehemence with which critics respond to Kant's discussion of revolution becomes easy to understand. First, Kant too is unwilling to allow that even deep corruption, incompetence, or injustice might warrant revolution. Secondly, and worse, Kant grounds this rigid position not in self-interest, but in our commitment to respecting each as a free, equal, and independent citizen. We might expect one like Hobbes, who can recognize no higher moral calling than narrow self-interest, to be ready to ignore corruption and the like in favour of a reliable calm. But surely we should expect more from one who offers a rich account of moral duty that not only rises above, but seems often to reject outright, the call of self-interest.

More specifically, Kant's discussion of revolution seems to share three significant features with Hobbes's. First, Kant holds that only the state can remedy

---

[6] My aim is not to determine what would count as sufficient injustice or sufficient likelihood of success; it is to provide Kantian grounds for thinking that something could.

[7] Hobbes and the reformer understand 'justice' differently. Still, he will not merely explain that her commitment to a cause other than self-interest is nonsensical, but he will seek to prove that her actions jeopardize the self-interest that must be her end.

[8] Circumstances immediately imperilling life or jeopardizing all reasonable means of self-defence are Hobbes's sole exceptions.

certain defects that render justice otherwise unrealizable: 'before a public law-ful condition is established, individual human beings, peoples and states can never be secure against violence from one another . . . unless [a people] wants to renounce any concepts of right . . . it must leave the state of nature' (*MS* 6:312). Secondly, Kant too sees revolution as antithetical to the continuing possibility of a stable civil society: 'any resistance to the supreme legislative power, any incitement to have the subjects' dissatisfaction become active, any insurrection that breaks out in rebellion, is the highest and most punishable crime within a commonwealth, because it destroys its foundation' (GTP 8:299). Finally for Kant, one who undertakes or advocates revolutionary activ-ity not only threatens the existence of justice by destroying the foundation on which it must be built, but involves herself in absurdity or self-contradiction (*MS* 6:320–2).

As for Hobbes, it then seems, concern to maintain some stable government is paramount for Kant. It supersedes all other considerations, even those for the justice that the state is meant to secure. Where stability is at issue, the foole is one with the reformer, the cause of justice one with injustice, self-contradiction, and the blind pursuit of personal interest.

(*b*) Examining the Details

(*i*) *Kantian justice and the justification of the state*

While there is no gainsaying that Kant's views on revolution, presented in broad outline, share much with Hobbes's, the details of Kant's discussion pro-vide another picture.[9] Most basic among the similarities noted is the claim that the conditions necessary for justice to take root, and ultimately to flourish, exist only within the state:

Before the names of just and unjust can have place, there must be some coercive power to compel men equally to the performance of their covenants, by the terror of some punishment greater than the benefit they expect by the breach of their covenant . . . and such power there is none before the erection of a commonwealth.[10]

It is true that the state of nature need not, just because it is natural, be a state of *injus-tice* . . . of dealing with one another only in terms of the degree of force each has. But it would still be a state *devoid of justice* . . . in which when rights are *in dispute* . . . there would be no judge competent to render a verdict having rightful force.   (*MS* 6:312)

---

[9]   While others explore obvious connections with discussions in Kant's *Groundwork*, I rely primarily on his political writings. My approach follows the relevant texts, which do not appeal to the *Groundwork*.
[10]   Hobbes, *Leviathan*, 89.

When we examine these claims more closely, though, we can see that they in fact presuppose disparate conceptions of justice and distinct accounts of our obligation to act justly and of the relationship between justice and the state. For Hobbes, justice is the performance of valid covenants, mutual promises accompanied by a reasonable expectation of fulfilment on all sides.[11] It binds because strict conformity by all is the best way to serve the narrow self-interest of each over a lifetime. Justice cannot be had in the state of nature because human beings, its subjects, are virtually incapable of committing themselves to anything but the pursuit of a narrow self-interest and are extremely shortsighted in this pursuit.[12] Driven by the appetite of the moment, they cannot be trusted to fulfil their promises to others even though they grasp, in cooler hours, that the cooperation this would foster indeed would be the best way to serve self-interest over time.[13] The trust necessary for regular performance of covenants, and so for justice, cannot develop without some punishment sufficiently immediate, likely, and harsh that it outweighs the anticipated benefits of breach. Only the state can adequately effect this end by backing threats with regular and stiff punishments applied to those within a broad geographic area. So only within the state can justice and its violation become a reality.

That we must have pause before claiming any near connection between Hobbes and Kant on a justice-related issue should now be clear enough simply from comparing their conceptions of justice and especially their accounts of our obligation to follow its commands. Stated in its imperative form, Kant's first principle of justice commands: 'so act externally that the free use of your choice can coexist with the freedom of everyone in accordance with a universal law' (*MS* 6:231).

Not surprisingly, given Kant's larger moral theory, we are obligated to act in accord with this principle not because it serves individual self-interest, whether broadly or narrowly construed, nor even because it conduces to the happiness of a people (GTP 8:289). It rather binds as a dictate of reason that prescribes the appropriate treatment of each conceived as (or as capable of becoming) a free, equal, and independent citizen.[14] That its dictates run contrary to self-interest

---

[11] Ibid. 82–6, 89.

[12] As many commentators emphasize, Hobbes's psychological egoism is qualified. For our purposes it is enough that, the vast majority of the time, Hobbesian persons act from what they believe will serve self-interest.

[13] Hobbes, *Leviathan*, chs. 13–17.

[14] Two clarifications are required: (1) in explaining why justice binds I am not suggesting that, according to Kant, just acts must be done for reasons of justice. As I shortly explain, one need not act for reasons or on motivations of justice in order to act justly; (2) I am assuming, contra some interpretations, that Kant's principles of justice follow by argument from his larger moral theory. I will not argue the point here. I provide reasons for accepting this traditional understanding of the relationship between Kant's theories of morality

or community happiness is, by itself, no reason at all to challenge its obligating force. More substantively, Kantian justice requires: that in our interactions with others, we ensure that what we do is compatible with a significant freedom in each to pursue individual ends; that, as the subjects of coercive laws, we bear like burdens, imposing on others no limits we do not ourselves bear; and, finally, that our actions are compatible with acknowledging the capacity of each for self-government—for participating in just decision making within a community and for using freedom effectively (within the bounds of justice) to shape and secure an individual life (*MS* 6:314; GTP 8:290–6).[15]

These treatments of justice differ in two significant ways. While neither is a surprise, it will be important to keep them in mind, and it is worth making them explicit. First, our only reason to act justly on Hobbes's view is that this best will serve self-interest.[16] One should honour valid covenants because doing so sustains the atmosphere of trust necessary for the regular success of cooperative enterprises. The state in turn makes justice possible not by reminding us that mutual long-term commitment to promise keeping serves the self-interest of each, but by making it both likely and sufficiently apparent in each particular case that promise breaking will not pay.[17]

On Kant's account, by contrast, the obligation to act justly rests not on some overarching goal to be maximized, approximated, or attained. Rather, reason tells us that only just action is compatible with each living the life of a free, equal, and independent citizen (*MS* 6:236–43, 312–14).[18] So far from promoting individual self-interest, conforming my actions to justice satisfies duties both to assert my own worth in relation to that of others and to do no wrong to others even when meeting these duties runs contrary to self-interest both long and short term (*MS* 6:236–7). The Kantian state is necessary, then,

---

and justice in 'Kant, Ideal Theory and the Justice of Exclusionary Zoning', *Ethics*, 110 (1999), 32–58. For detailed discussion, pro and con, see chapters by Guyer, Wood, and Pogge, this volume.

[15] Kantian justice thus makes substantive, not merely procedural, demands. This applies even to Kant's civil equality, which some mistakenly deem satisfied whenever we scrupulously apply extant laws. Civil equality is tied to the demand for substantive freedom due 'every member of the society as a human *being*' (GTP 8:290). Just laws may not, for example, grant freedom to practise religion or pursue positions to some and not others on slim or arbitrary grounds. Nor may they permit anyone to contract away her rights entirely or allow anyone to be punished on grounds other than criminal guilt or to suffer a harsher penalty than others who commit the same crime. Thus, while we might attempt to ensure that we treat each as free, equal, and independent by instituting a set of procedures, these would serve more fundamental substantive requirements. Any procedure would be subject to criticism for failure to satisfy justice's more basic demands.

[16] Like Kant, Hobbes appeals to reason as the ultimate source of our obligation. But Hobbesian reason is merely instrumental. Kantian reason, as we will see, is far richer.

[17] Hobbes, *Leviathan*, 89.

[18] Fully worked out, Kant's argument to this effect parallels that accompanying his *Groundwork* discussion of the formula of humanity.

not to transform a chaos ruled by force and wiles into an order where appetites are coercively reigned in for mutual advantage. It is required to ensure that persons can treat others, and ensure that they themselves are treated, as free, equal, and independent citizens.[19]

Secondly, and relatedly, Hobbesian persons do not internalize commitments; they do not regularly act to further any ongoing end in the face of a more immediate and conflicting desire. To compensate for this, they require a state that will employ punishments (actual and threatened) in such a way that they behave as though they had such commitments. Kantian persons, however, need not deal 'with each other only in terms of the degree of force each has' (*MS* 6:312). They can, it appears, regularly cooperate and shape their actions to avoid interfering with others even when immediate self-interest might dictate otherwise.

When it comes to establishing and carrying out the requirements of justice in concrete circumstances, however, Kantian citizens also require assistance that only the state can supply, and it is this need that determines the central features of the Kantian state. Kant summarizes the difficulty that disables justice in the state of nature early in his discussion of public right:

It is . . . not some deed that makes coercion through public law necessary. On the contrary, however well disposed and law-abiding human beings might be, it still lies a priori in the rational idea of such a condition (one that is not rightful) that before a public lawful condition is established individual human beings, peoples and states can never be secure against violence from one another, since each has its own right to do *what seems right and good to it* and not to be dependent upon another's opinion about this. (*MS* 6:312)

The problem we face without the state is not that we will be driven by self-interest or malevolence without a force to keep us in check. It is that, even with the best will in the world and a deep commitment to adhering to the demands of justice, we will be unable satisfactorily to determine what justice requires and how to attain it. This may be because some or all persons will err in judging what highly general standards of justice require in complex real-world circumstances—not only what more specific laws these standards give rise to, but how to apply these appropriately in individual cases and how to execute them without unduly interfering with anyone's freedom, equality, or independence.

But these errors, so common among human beings (the subjects of Kantian justice), are ones at least some highly evolved persons might avoid. What we

---

[19] Kant does not discount the state's role in curbing self-interest and malevolence. He does make clear that, even where these are absent, we will require the state to secure justice.

cannot avoid is that, even when we all apply the principle of justice consistently and without any error in reasoning, we still may apply it differently. So general a standard cannot but be underdetermined in some cases. While any of several interpretations might serve justice if we regularly adhered to them, alternative interpretations, applied by different people at the same time (or over time), may result in what we all can see is unjust treatment for some.[20] Without some appointed authority charged with a final decision, though, we will have no satisfactory way of settling disputes about justice or of choosing among equally good interpretations. This is because all persons, in Kant's view, are to be treated as capable of recognizing, evaluating, and committing themselves to the requirements of justice; without some reasonable allocation of final responsibility for decisions, there will be no way of settling disputes or making choices that does not accept the decision of one over that of others on arbitrary, inadequate, or even malign grounds.

The solution to this problem, Kant tells us, is a state comprising three 'authorities': one legislative, one judicial, and one executive. We are to conceive of these authorities as together forming 'the general united will', a will in which each participates *qua* citizen and that is the only foundation for fully justifiable laws, laws that deprive us of complete freedom to determine our own course only to return that freedom to us in the form of restrictions that help us conform to the requirements of justice (*MS* 6:313). The solution, more concretely, is: first, to supply settled laws that establish what the most general tenets of justice require in more concrete circumstances; secondly, to provide a wise and indifferent judge who determines for all, and without bias, how such laws will apply to concrete cases; and, thirdly, to assure an authorized enforcer who not only possesses power but alone is charged with executing the judge's decree.

Various procedures might assist designated lawmakers, judges, and executives in better interpreting and applying standards of justice and the laws they recommend than would be likely for any individual citizen, and Kant apparently is committed to some such procedures as demands of justice.[21] Importantly, though, a greater capacity for identifying and implementing justice is

---

[20] Kant is not explicit about why justice is possible only within the state. He does say that this is due neither to our inevitable moral failings nor to errors in judgement, though he believes each typically plays a significant role. Since legislative, judicial, and executive functions serve to specify concrete requirements of justice, the problem of underdetermination apparently is the one Kant has in mind. This conclusion may appear to contradict Kant's emphasis on justice as determinate in a way that, for example, virtue is not. But to say that the most general requirements of justice are often underdetermined is not to say that they leave open the possibility for independent choice that virtue does. Moreover, Kant's very point in emphasizing that justice requires the state is that we will contravene its broad demands unless we make those more determinate through laws.

[21] One such procedure might be provision for political expression, discussed in the next section.

not what primarily necessitates the state on Kant's view. Most significantly, it addresses the difficulty that arises when each is equally not only an authority on, but possessed of authority to make and implement, judgements of justice. Nevertheless, as we will see more clearly in what follows, what justifies the state's legislative, judicial, and executive actions is not mere success in coordination. As Kant repeatedly makes clear, a state's actions fully serve the purposes that warrant its existence only when they are just. They must conform to the substantive standard that demands respect for the freedom, equality, and independence of each. Hobbes's state, we might say, is designed to secure a justice wedded to a larger goal of self-interest for persons lacking effective commitment even to the narrow end that is their sole motivation. Kant's state makes possible the realization of a substantive right that reigns in self-interest for persons each committed to, responsible for securing, but imperfectly capable of achieving justice in circumstances complex and mutable.[22]

(ii) Revolution as self-contradiction

To illuminate further Kant's argument and distinguish it from Hobbes's, consider now the several ways in which Kant believes revolution involves self-contradiction. Four sources of contradiction seem especially significant for drawing out Kant's view about the problem revolution presents.

Frequently when Kant appeals to self-contradiction to explain what is wrong with revolution, he suggests that the contradiction arises from wishing to be judge in one's own suit (see *MS* 6:320). There are various ways in which we might attempt to make sense of this claim. In particular we might appeal to another of his references to positions as 'diametrically opposed' or contradictory, this in a footnote distinguishing between assassination of the head of state and his formal execution.[23] The first, Kant tells us, while absolutely forbidden and deserving of harshest penalty, nevertheless is compatible with a commitment to the state as foundation for justice. We properly may conclude that self-preservation, the nearly inevitable response where one faces death if one does not inflict it, typically underlies this act. Not so formal execution, which 'rejects the authority of the law itself' (*MS* 6:321 n.).

---

[22]   Christine Korsgaard interprets Kant as instead committed to a 'deeply procedural' conception of the general will and thus of justice. Without procedures making it possible to act collectively, some simply impose private will on others. Adherence to procedure must be prior to justice's substantive concerns, not the other way round. See 'Taking the Law into our own Hands: Kant on the Right to Revolution', in A. Reath, B. Herman, and C. Korsgaard (eds.), *Reclaiming the History of Ethics: Essays for John Rawls* (New York: Cambridge University Press, 1997), 309–13. I believe Kant may (wrongly) have drawn this conclusion. In Section III, I challenge the claim that it is the most reasonable extension of basic Kantian commitments.

[23]   This footnote directly follows an early reference to the absurdity of seeking to be judge in one's own suit.

We can understand the special heinousness of formal execution, Kant says, if we consider two different maxims (or principles) on which an ordinary criminal might act. The typical criminal accepts legal institutions and the body of laws and judgements that flow from them as necessary to securing justice, the treatment of each as free, equal, and independent citizens. On reflection, he finds that he cannot but be committed to such treatment for himself and has no adequate grounds to distinguish himself from others. Nevertheless, accepting justice as universally obligating and the structure of legal institutions and decisions as necessary to its realization, he occasionally makes an exception to this rule for himself. We know from Kant's most famous writing on moral philosophy that this involves the criminal in a kind of contradiction. Although we will not explore details, the principle of exception, once universalized, will be incompatible with one of the laws to which the criminal's more general acceptance of justice commits him. Kant does not emphasize the contradiction, characterizing the typical criminal as one who 'only deviates' from or evades the law (*MS* 6:321 n.). Not so, however, the criminal who, rather than carving out an exception for himself, makes crime his rule. His maxim is not one that seeks, on what we can see are inadequate grounds, to make an exception to justice and the institutions on which it depends. Rather, he takes as his rule the violation of freedom, equality, and independence in others: 'His maxim is therefore opposed to the law not by way of *default* only but by *rejecting* it or, as we put it, his maxim is *diametrically* opposed to the law, as contrary to it (hostile to it so to speak)' (*MS* 6:321–2 n.).

One who assassinates state officials to effect a change in legal institutions, says Kant, is akin to the typical criminal. She does not reject justice or the state as necessary to its realization; she makes for herself an exception to principles of justice and respect for laws, likely in the face of real or perceived threats to life, or perhaps to serious threats to freedom, equality, or independence. One who participates in formal execution, however, does not make an exception from fear. She announces her own suitability to make judgements about justice without the assistance of settled laws, an unbiased judge, or an authorized enforcer. But this is to deny that no one has a purchase on justice, to claim that purchase for oneself, and in reality to elevate 'violence . . . above the most sacred rights brazenly and in accordance with principle' (*MS* 6:322 n.). If one has neither special purchase on justice nor authority from others to play a special role in its orderly determination and execution, then she holds her position by force or wiles only. This does not do justice but makes a mockery of it.

Now we can see, I think, that in fact there are two senses in which the revolutionary might seek to be judge in her own case and in so doing engage in self-contradiction. In the first, the revolutionary engages behind the scenes in assassination or other activities designed to topple the government in place. The aim is not, or not primarily, to put oneself or one's group in charge; it is to ward off anticipated bodily threats (to oneself or those one holds dear) or to prevent other serious injustice. Accepting the principle of justice, the necessity of the state for its realization, and the general prohibition on revolution, she makes an exception for herself on what she sees as legitimate grounds. She acts as judge in her own case by authorizing herself to determine whether the conditions for a legitimate exception have been met. She believes (or convinces herself) that she has grounds for acting that do not contravene more basic commitments and so may do what is usually prohibited. In fact, she is seduced by the special interest she has in her own case, the very special interest that the state itself, in all its aspects, is meant in part to counter. We may call this error, leading her into contradiction, one of bias.

The revolutionary who undertakes formal execution, however, seeks to judge her own case not by giving herself authority to identify legitimate exceptions to foundational commitments in circumstances where she is an interested party. Instead, she undertakes to make supreme her own judgement about the appropriate legislation, application, and execution of justice. She judges in her own case in the sense that she purports to interpret *for all* universally applicable standards. Her contradiction is that, in the name of a justice acknowledging the political authority of each, she takes that authority to herself by power only. The principle she follows is one of individual rule, not of a mutual agreement to abide by standards equally concerned with each and to which each commits herself. In the name of justice, she undertakes what is anathema to it.[24]

A third source of self-contradiction has been more discussed by interpreters and brings Hobbes most immediately to mind.[25] A moderate constitution, one that purports to make room for a *right* of revolution, Kant says, is an 'absurdity' (*MS* 6:320). Such a constitution designates which persons or bodies will hold legislative, judicial, and executive authority and at the same time permits their removal by force. But the very reason for conveying political authority is to create a situation in which we may establish, without force and wiles, the proper division of freedom among persons who may come into conflict.

---

[24] Kant's point is not that every assassination involves one kind of contradiction and every public execution the other. Indeed, for Kant no one *actually* makes crime or injustice her rule (*MS* 6:322 n.). Kant's aim is rather to distinguish between rejecting justice outright and doing, on occasion, what conflicts with it.

[25] See Korsgaard, 'Kant on the Right to Revolution'; Thomas E. Hill, Jr., 'A Kantian Perspective on Political Violence', *Journal of Ethics*, 1 (1997), 105–40.

Making that very force an acceptable means of removing political authority undoes what one purports to do and so involves a kind of contradiction. One might avoid this by establishing some further authority to determine when the people appropriately may remove leaders from power. But then this overseer would be the chief authority and again one who might (or might appear to) transgress justice, thus requiring a third authority, and so on. In short, the only way to solve the problem created by the equal authority of each on issues of justice is the designation of positions of authority and procedures for filling them without any reservation for revolution. Call the failure to recognize this fact an error of authority.

Before we can complete our exploration of self-contradiction and its place in Kant's critique of revolution, we must examine one last reference in 'Theory and Practice'. Here, in concluding his discussion of the place of freedom of political expression within the just commonwealth, Kant characterizes that commonwealth as possessing two essential features. The first of these is obedience to valid coercive laws within a tripartite constitution. The second is what he calls a 'spirit of freedom' (GTP 8:305). This is the sense that one is not merely free, but indeed required, to evaluate the legal system to determine whether the laws as expressed, applied, and executed in fact satisfy the demands of justice. This spirit must prevail within the just state, says Kant, so that one may avoid falling 'into contradiction with himself' (GTP 8:305). Kant's demand for such a spirit stems from his claim that citizens possess inalienable rights against the state that it does wrong not to honour (GTP 8:303). It fits well with his further advocacy of 'negative resistance', the lawmaking body's refusal to honour government requests that would contravene justice (*MS* 6:322). It also complements his caveat on a categorical imperative prohibiting revolution. While we may not seek to remove state authorities, we may, indeed should, refrain from performing any immoral acts the state may demand of us (*MS* 6:371).

This fourth contradiction is not that of one who seeks special treatment for herself on inadequate grounds, nor of one who seeks to replace the judgement of those who share political authority with that effected by strength alone. Moreover, it is not that of one who fails to see that the only way to decide disputes among equals is to establish an authority as supreme. Rather, it is the contradiction in which I involve myself by allowing my own life and lives of others to be ruled by standards that have not survived my reasoned evaluation. We are equal and fallible judges of what justice requires of us. In a complex and mutable world in which we often are moved by self-interest, we are especially prone to error. It does not follow, though, that we must never exercise judgement. Rather, we must find some mechanism that allows us to overcome inevitable divisions while preserving the best means we have of meeting justice's demands for each person on each occasion. This last requires the participation of each, in particular the educated, informed, committed participation. We contradict the fundamental standards of justice that we accept not only by making a special place for ourselves in their regard, or by refusing to accept the consequences of the equality of persons, but by foregoing our participation in their enunciation, adjudication, and application.

(iii) Two political ideals

Stability.   One way to capture the essence of what we can now see as telling differences between Kantian and Hobbesian approaches to revolution is to sketch the opposing conceptions of stability that emerge from our discussions. A virtue of political systems that has recently received special attention, stability is not, of course, the same thing to all people. Moreover, the sort of stability one person counts as a virtue of a political system another may reject as a more or less serious failing or an unrealizable (therefore dangerous) ideal.

We can think of a political system's stability, in general, as its ability to withstand forces that might tend to alter or abolish the features for which we value such a system in the first place. Although revolution often threatens stability so understood, their relationship depends in the end on whether changes undertaken support or undermine the aims such a system is to serve.

For Hobbes, revolution is a threat to stability because it risks undermining the peace that only the state can secure. Although some particular states may do a better job than others of fulfilling the ever-shifting desires of their citizens, we seek and are justified in establishing a state not based on its relative ability to satisfy such desires, but for its ability to establish a reliable, lasting peace in which citizens can undertake cooperative ventures. It is the difficulty of establishing such a peace that Hobbes sees as for each of us the main obstacle to satisfactory human existence. The state serves its purpose so long as it provides the means to attain and secure that peace.

For Kant, we now know, if a state is fully to serve its underlying purpose, it cannot aim merely at securing an atmosphere in which cooperation for mutual desire satisfaction can regularly occur. Rather, it must be designed at once to secure just treatment for each and to acknowledge that each must be able to commit herself to its laws as genuinely fulfilling this aim. Securing just treatment requires, in part, the establishment of political authorities who remove lawmaking, interpretation, and application from the hands of individual citizens. Nevertheless, citizens must continue to participate in these functions as evaluators and advisers, and in a sense as lawmakers—as capable of committing themselves to legal structures and standards as though they themselves had put them in place. The stability crucial to Kant maintains the state so understood. Whether *this* sense of stability is inevitably threatened by revolution in all its manifestations, we will explore in the next section. But where what we seek goes so far beyond peace and places such substantial demands on legal structures and institutions, it is hardly obvious that this is the case.

Consistency. A second useful measure of comparison as we close the first phase of our discussion is the notion of consistency. Both Hobbes and Kant claim that revolution involves participants in deep inconsistency, in contradiction. But again, the conceptions of consistency at work differ importantly.

For Hobbes, we might say, contradiction arises when one who, by her very nature, must pursue desire acts in a way more likely to thwart than serve it over the long term. If we think of each as committed in principle to satisfying desire over a life, then to commit oneself to a revolution that risks the peace most conducive to this end is to hold two contrary principles, to involve oneself in contradiction. We may understand Hobbes's references to contradiction in this way; still we must also see them as largely metaphorical. For Hobbes, effective human commitment to any principle at all is, at best, unusual. There is only the passage from the pursuit of one desire to another with little capacity for lasting and effective commitment that might regulate, guide, or serve as a standard by which to evaluate actions.[26] It is precisely because human beings cannot make such commitments that they must, in Hobbes's view, accept the rule of force as legitimate. It provides the only forum for cooperative pursuit to which they can aspire.

For Kant, consistency is not a metaphor, though at times it is an aspiration rather than a description. Human beings, in Kant's view, are capable of genuine commitment to principles of justice. We can apply these as standards to our own past, present, and future actions, interpret and augment them, and evaluate others' success in applying them to concrete circumstances. We can also appreciate that we sometimes run afoul of these commitments, either by manufacturing exceptions unwarranted by the circumstances or by proclaiming a continuing commitment while engaging in activities that fly in the face of the presuppositions that underlie it. For Hobbes, we might say, to accuse a citizen of inconsistency is just to remind her to submit to the judgement of another. For Kant it is to remind her to attend to her own judgement.

---

[26] For Hobbes, we can appreciate our reasons for adhering to the laws of nature, which indeed are principles of self-interest. Without external force, however, these laws do not effectively govern us.

III. The Foole and the Reformer

Unlike Hobbes, Kant can allow the reformer's commitment to justice, her appreciation of its relationship to the state, and her acceptance of civic responsibilities. In all this she is, for Kant, importantly distinct from the foole. Nevertheless, it remains clear that Kant does not distinguish the reformer from the foole in a more practical way. We may understand what motivates the reformer, even applaud her good intentions. Like the foole, though, she places the state, and so justice, at unwarranted risk as a result of faulty reasoning. For Kant, her error is one we must meet with harshest penalty.

In this final section, I critically examine Kant's practical conclusion and suggest considerations mitigating in favour of a more nuanced response.

(*a*) Evaluating Kant's Practical Conclusions

To evaluate Kant's conclusion that revolution can never be justified, I want to ask how it fits with the details of his views on justice, the state, and citizenship as they are now before us. More particularly, let us consider whether we should view the reformer as inevitably mired in contradiction. As we have described her, the reformer is not committed to substituting her own judgement for that of the whole, allying herself with force while proclaiming loyalty to justice. Her commitment to justice, and to the state as crucial for its realization, is genuine. So too is her acceptance of equality with all others and her recognition that nothing distinguishes her from them as a decision-maker.

For Kant, the reformer instead joins what we have called the errors of bias and authority. By making an exception of herself in a case where she is biased, she allows special proximity to colour her judgement about the relationship between honouring the equal authority of each and refraining from coercive response to unjust laws, leaders, and institutions. Misled by special interest, the reformer supposes that she honours the equality of each when in fact she grants a special and unwarranted authority to herself for this one occasion. As a consequence, we might even characterize her as, at once, acknowledging a political authority and making it subject to removal by force. The reformer thus forgets that our only way of solving the problem of the equal authority of each is formal designation of one final authority on matters of justice without reservation. But is the reformer's judgement necessarily tainted in every case? Does she involve herself inevitably in contradiction as Kant suggests? I think not, and for reasons Kant himself helps us to appreciate.[27]

---

[27] Kenneth Westphal argues that, properly read, Kant himself advocates a less rigid approach to revolution in the imperfect circumstances I will consider. See 'Kant on the State, Law, and Obedience to Author-

If I have understood Kant correctly, his claim that we require the state in order to honour moral equality rests, most fundamentally, on the view that the demands of justice are inevitably underdetermined. Since no argument will resolve many significant disputes, we need some designated authority to settle on one just option.

Justice may indeed be underdetermined for some, even many, circumstances. This does not mean, though, that it is underdetermined in all circumstances and for all questions. Certain laws and institutions will clearly contravene basic Kantian commitments. Claims to the contrary can readily be shown to rest on flawed reasoning or mistake of fact. This seems to be the case, for example, where what is at issue is the state's participation in genocide, slavery, or severe discrimination on cultural, religious, or racial grounds. To exterminate a group of people, or to deprive them entirely or substantially of freedom and independence on grounds that cannot meaningfully distinguish them from others, flies in the face of Kantian justice. While it is true that the most violent controversy often surrounds precisely such matters, it is also true that the foundational commitments of Kantian justice, most evidently commitment to the freedom and equality of persons, take a clear stand on one side of such issues. At least as to these questions, we might as individual citizens pronounce a law, policy, institution, or regime in conflict with justice without concern that we had made a mistake or that some equally just position was being advanced on the other side.[28]

Of course, some further considerations are in order. Otherwise, what I have said might seem both to oversimplify and partially to miss Kant's main concern. First, even if we agree that the answer to some questions is clear from the standpoint of Kantian justice, that does not mean that it is clear how best to address related concrete issues. It may be evidently unjust to deprive a person of a basic liberty of citizens (freedom of expression, say) on racial grounds, but unclear whether a law requiring a permit to parade in a public place in fact effects such injustice. Secondly, even where we think a law clearly does contra-

ity in the Alleged "Anti-Revolutionary" Writings', *Journal of Philosophical Research*, 17 (1992), 383–426. I agree that the less rigid approach squares with Kant's larger views, but I do not think Kant himself arrives at this conclusion.

[28] Kant certainly believed that women and members of some racial groups lack qualities suiting them for civic participation. But this does not mean that the state rightly may treat them as it will. Indeed, Kant classes women among passive citizens. While they have no vote, the law must scrupulously respect their interests in freedom and equality. As a result, even accepting Kant's errant conclusions, women are due protection from the kind of severe harms and deprivations I have in mind. Even those not protected by justice on Kant's view merit substantial, if inadequate, moral protections. Most important for present purposes, Kant's errors in assessing the capacities of women and members of some racial groups do not mean that his theory permits severe deprivations on the grounds of racial or gender bias but that he had a very poor grasp of the facts.

vene Kantian justice, issues still arise about how best to respond to it. Whether coercive response is warranted, especially in its most extreme forms, will surely be controversial, and it is most importantly this decision that the reformer makes contrary to the equality of persons. Thirdly, even if the demands of Kantian justice regarding the substance of a law are clear, Kantian justice is not the only conception going. To seek to impose one's own conception of justice coercively thus contravenes the equal authority of each.

In partial response to these concerns, we should keep in mind the following. First, injustice is sometimes clear even in concrete cases. There are some policies and institutions—for example, a package of laws that together deprive individuals completely or substantially of their civil liberties—whose injustice is uncontroversial as applied to that group. That many cases are more difficult potentially limits the range of my claim, but does not render it incorrect. Secondly, Kant's absolute prohibition on revolution seems, without warrant, to elevate one potential threat to the equality of persons over all other concerns of justice. True, by responding controversially to unjust laws and institutions, I may contravene equality by acting as though my method is a reasonable response to a clear injustice when some other would serve as well or better. However, where the injustice of laws and institutions is clear and deep, to forgo all coercive response sometimes may close off a highly effective, perhaps the only or most effective, route to justice. Thus it may perpetuate significant violations of freedom, independence, *and equality*. It is at least unclear, then, that Kant has grounds for taking the position he does, a point to which I will return shortly.   Thirdly, it is true that commitment to divergent conceptions of justice within a political society will make some issues all the more controversial. Kantian justice is, I think, sensitive to this fact. Nevertheless, the most basic commitments of Kantian justice, as we have said, take a clear stand on some actions. Slavery, genocide, and severe deprivations of liberty on arbitrary grounds fall outside the bounds of what is acceptable. That some will disagree may have consequences for our response to them, but not for a decision about the permissibility of these acts.

With substantial reason to doubt that concerns for equality warrant absolute prohibition on revolution, let us return to 'the spirit of freedom', the last source of contradiction to which Kant's discussion refers. We express this spirit, recall, not only by giving our opinion on political issues, but by refusing on occasion to honour or comply with the requests of the head of state. The spirit of freedom is thus not simply contemplative; to avoid contradiction, the Kantian citizen must act, not merely think.

And, if this is true, it becomes increasingly doubtful that Kant may forbid revolution absolutely consistent with his own commitments. For the Kantian state to fulfil all demands that justice places on it, it must address both issues of obedience to law and citizens' active evaluation of it. Concern to ensure the conditions necessary and conducive to active evaluation gives special reason to worry that by entirely prohibiting one response to unjust laws we will skew the mix in an unjustifiable way. In closing, I offer several more concrete reasons for thinking that Kant's rigid conclusion regarding revolution does just this. Since my claim depends in part on some features of moral psychology, I will appeal to an example to illustrate more effectively. I choose the case I do first because it surely involves the kind of deep and clear injustice that I think Kant's argument, as it stands, cannot satisfactorily address. Secondly, my reformers, who did not achieve their primary aim, may help us to recognize some of the more subtle influences and implications of revolution for a citizen's appreciation of and commitment to justice. Having raised substantial reasons to doubt that revolution inevitably violates moral equality, my aim here is to show that it may sometimes be essential to foster or preserve the central elements of Kantian citizenship, the spirit of freedom in particular. Revolutionary activity, in short, sometimes may be a means of avoiding contradiction.

(b) Coercive Action, Moral Psychology, and the Spirit of Freedom

(i) An example

In July 1944 a group of generals, assisted behind the scenes by a number of German citizens opposed to the Nazi regime, attempted unsuccessfully to assassinate Adolf Hitler. Although motivations were surely mixed, some even self-serving or venal, let us assume for present purposes what seems to have been the case. The attempt had as its main aims, first, a halt to the political executions and death camp exterminations daily accelerating during this period. It thus opposed the very sort of deep injustice that is unacceptable from a Kantian standpoint. Secondly, the conspirators sought not only a speedier end to the war that was destroying the country, but to replace the Nazi regime with leaders capable of rebuilding just political structures within Germany. They also hoped to win support from outside in order to rebuild the infrastructure required for these efforts.[29]

These aims reflect a deep concern for justice and a sense of responsibility for securing it. They also demonstrate a commitment to the state as the vehicle for attaining it. They seem to characterize reformers of the sort of interest to us. A

---

[29] I take my example from the memoirs of Christabel Bielenberg, wife of one of the 1944 conspirators. See *The Past is Myself* (London: Chatto & Windus, 1968).

halt to executions and exterminations of persons innocent of genuine wrongdoing evidently aims to serve justice, as do efforts towards a new political system. Moreover, the devastation wrought by Allied bombing and terms of
surrender that would leave Germany no voice in its own future could both reasonably be seen as likely and substantial obstacles to the restoration of just laws
and institutions. Materially and psychologically, their effects on aspirations for
justice could not but be damaging, possibly devastating.

None of our reformers' primary aims was realized. Hitler survived un-
scathed, and conspirators were imprisoned, most later hanged. Nevertheless,
the attempt clearly sought to serve significant aims of justice. In such a case,
must the concern to avoid controversial methods absolutely bar citizens committed to reform from a revolutionary course?

(ii) Four implications of revolution

Before we turn to implications of moral psychology, two points are in order.
The first concerns the significance of likelihood of success to justification for
revolution. The second concerns the relationship among Kantian justice,
Kantian principles, and consequences.

First, I have chosen an example where revolution was unsuccessful because
Kant observed that failure is frequent and rightly found this relevant to conclusions about justifiability. Yet, if we can justify unsuccessful revolution on
Kantian grounds (as I believe), this does not make probability of success irrelevant to justification. As Kant saw, revolutions can often thwart their own aims.
They can spawn extensive unrest, encourage more severe abuses of state power,
and alienate a population without whose support reforms cannot succeed.
Moreover, these effects may be long term. For these reasons and others, my
argument is only that revolution may sometimes be justified, not that we
should undertake it lightly or in any but dire conditions.

Secondly, the discussion that follows (even parts of what precedes) may raise
eyebrows. I sometimes appeal to the *consequences* of revolution, yet Kant's
argument rests on his theory's deep commitment to moral equality. Why
should appeal to consequences carry weight with him? The point I want to
press, though, is not that we properly determine the justifiability of revolution
by weighing good consequences against ill. It is that the basic commitments of
Kantian justice must be given voice in the concrete circumstances of our lives.
They must take into account, among others, the features of moral psychology
that encourage or thwart the realization of Kantian citizenship and of Kantian
justice more generally. Kant's deep theoretical reason for condemning acts like
those at hand is that these are based on controversial judgements of justice.
Where, as here, underdetermination poses no problem, there remain only

arguments based on what most likely will honour central aspects of citizenship under the circumstances.

Vision.   Consider first the function of the reformer as moral visionary. Many, perhaps even most, see that times are bad, people are suffering, injustices are occurring. But especially if they themselves are suffering physical hardships and psychological strains, most may have difficulty forming a comprehensive picture of the ills being done and of the steps necessary to move towards positive change.

Could the 1944 attempt provide any such picture? After all, its planning and execution were necessarily kept as secret as possible. Conspirators could not precede the attempt with public or even semi-public criticism of the Nazi regime. But it is in just such an atmosphere of repression that an act as extreme as assassination, indeed even its mere attempt, can make evident the scope and depth of injustice. That some would make such an attempt, aware of the likelihood of failure, imprisonment, and execution, and aware too that by biding their time they could survive to pursue less risky strategies, suggests genuine motivations of justice. It also encourages others to ask what perception of the present situation, and what hope for the future, could cause one to take such risks.

News of the act, even when reported as here as a traitorous failure, can be a catalyst for thought, preparing those now nearly incapacitated to grasp the wrongs done to them and in their name. I do not suggest that such attempts are the only way to achieve this end, or that they are usually the best or even acceptable. I do suggest that there are conditions, not typical but far too common in history, when precisely this sort of extreme action is highly conducive to awakening a citizenry to gross injustice. Fear and horror have a power to close our eyes to our evaluative role as citizens. If that role is a necessary component of the just state on the Kantian view, we cannot deem revolution inevitably counter to justice.

Sense of justice.   A second justice-related role for the reformer complements the first; it is that of awakening in those beleaguered by fear and suffering a passion for justice. The search for some way to explain a surprising act of bravery (or foolishness) can provoke intellectual acknowledgement of injustice that must be righted. But seeing deeply, perceptively, what must be done and being moved to do it typically demands more. It requires that the intellectual response be accompanied by an affective one, one we often call a sense of justice.[30] Great fear and hardship, loss of one's larger view—these work to deaden one's affective responses, including those to injustice. If one is surrounded by

---

[30] Among others, Martha Nussbaum, Barbara Herman, and Marcia Baron address this point.

political repression, cultural extermination, betrayal—if the most modest protest, even quiet criticism, could mean death—one may not merely fall silent, but actually cease to feel the pull of justice. In such circumstances, seeing that others have allowed their sense of justice to motivate action may not only open our eyes to injustice, but move us to action as well. Hume's analogy to the strings of a harp is apt. An act widely known and deeply courageous can do much to stir the tones of justice. And these, as many observe, can motivate and inform. If justice demands of citizens not only that they see, but that they act, it cannot in all circumstances deny this route to the cultivation of affective response.[31]

Orientation. A third feature of revolution with positive links to justice lies not in the active revolutionary, but in the possibility of revolution. If revolution is a moral impossibility, I must limit not only the range of acceptable responses to injustice, but also the depth and degree of injustice that I can grasp and my ability to compare one injustice with another. I become unable to see what is disrespectful of or damaging to freedom, equality, and independence, and why.

Suppose nothing ever can be bad enough to warrant forcible resistance, especially that political stability, now in a narrow sense, is always to be favoured over the richer one I earlier attributed to Kant. Now the standard by which I identify and assess wrongs, and by which I determine what justice requires in various circumstances, will be limited in serious ways. The same will be true if consistency is always to be measured in terms of the appropriateness of my actions to sustaining this narrow stability and not to the richer notion of participatory citizenship earlier found in Kant. This, we might think, is part of what happened in Germany in the 1930s and 1940s. Along with many other factors, the sense many had that obedience was supreme may have helped prevent citizens from acknowledging the depth of the wrongs being done around them. Again we must doubt that, consistent with his own commitments, Kant may deny that revolution and justice sometimes go hand in hand.

Self-conception. A last central relationship between revolution and a rich Kantian justice concerns the Kantian citizen's ability to maintain her identity as such. The Kantian citizen is not merely a child to be directed. She participates in judging and attempts to address errors in laws and institutions. More impor-

---

[31] Kant's practical philosophy is widely thought to reject affect as irrelevant to the questions it treats. Even those who acknowledge that his theory of virtue recognizes some role for affect doubt that the same is true of the theory of justice. Kant's own discussion of the French Revolution seems to belie this conclusion. While he condemned the revolutionaries as violators of justice, Kant cited its affective consequences as encouraging evidence of the moral disposition of the human race and of its moral progress. See 'The Contest of Faculties', 182.

tantly, she counts herself responsible for these. They are her own and their failings are her failings in an important sense. Injustice may be so thoroughgoing, mere expression of dissent so effectively silenced, that one cannot but conclude that to exist in the community is to ally oneself with injustice. At the least, it is to tolerate it in a way inconsistent with one's responsibilities as a citizen. In these circumstances, to deny active resistance, on occasion even resistance as extreme as assassination, may be effectively to deny the citizen a central way of maintaining her view of herself as such. The chief participants in the 1944 attempt were generals, officials and former officials with substantial international connections, captains of industry, and skilled lawyers. All maintained some political influence; all hoped to participate in Germany's rejuvenation as a just state in the aftermath. Many did what little they could to curb the effects of Nazism within Germany and to elicit aid from without. For such persons to stand by and do nothing when reasonable opportunity arose might understandably be seen, most importantly by themselves, as the equivalent of complicity. In some circumstances, to fail to act with force may be to cease to be able to see oneself as a citizen committed to, and accepting responsibility for, justice. Again an absolute prohibition on revolution may be inconsistent with the citizenship that is central to Kantian justice.

IV. Conclusion

I have argued that Kant's accounts of justice, citizenship, and the state are far richer than his response to revolution initially suggests. Indeed, we uncover that richness in part by exploring the details of Kant on revolution. Cases of deep and clear injustice, moreover, do not raise the concerns stemming from underdetermination that provide the main theoretic ground for strictly prohibiting revolution on Kant's view. Once we set this concern aside, features of moral psychology provide strong reason to think that, despite the hazards of revolution, we sometimes respect free, equal, and independent citizens best by attempting to remove the government in place. Although the method the revolutionary employs is controversial, its ability to awaken and inform the capacities of citizenship in others and to preserve them in ourselves will sometimes better honour citizenship than a decision never to act on a controversial judgement.

10

Punishment, Conscience, and Moral Worth

Thomas E. Hill, Jr.

In *The Metaphysics of Morals* Kant offers us pieces of a theory of *punishment*, a metaphorical description of *conscience*, and an elaboration of his earlier account of the *moral worth* of actions. My questions concern relations among these. How is conscience analogous to punishment in Kant's theory, and how is it different? What is the role of *fear* of punishment and *pangs* of conscience? Are these morally acceptable motives? Can an autonomy-based moral theory approve of institutions that rely on fear of judicial punishment or of individuals who need to be moved by the painful prodding of conscience? Can there be any moral worth in such motives?

I begin with a sketch of Kant's views about punishment and conscience. Since my main concern is with how punishment and conscience *motivate* us, my plan is simply to highlight some features of Kant's views that are relevant to my questions about motivation. In these background sections I draw from previous papers that discuss Kant's conceptions of punishment and conscience separately and in more detail.[1] Some points may be controversial, but my aim for now is simply to summarize my understanding of Kant's conceptions in order to facilitate the later discussion.

The background for what I say about punishment is an ongoing debate about the interpretation of Kant's provocative remarks about punishment, reinvigorated by new challenges to the formerly accepted view of Kant as a prime

I am grateful to the participants at the Spindel Conference at the University of Memphis, October 1997, and especially to Nelson Potter, for helpful comments and discussion.

[1] These papers include 'Four Conceptions of Conscience', *Nomos XL: Integrity and Conscience* (New York: New York University Press, 1998), 13–52; 'Kant on Punishment: A Coherent Mix of Deterrence and Retribution?', *Jahrbuch für Recht und Ethik*, 5 (1997), 291–314, repr. in Thomas E. Hill, Jr., *Respect, Pluralism, and Justice: Kantian Perspectives* (Oxford: Oxford University Press, 2000), 173–99; and 'Kant's Anti-Moralistic Strain' and 'Making Exceptions without Abandoning the Principle', in *Dignity and Practical Reason in Kant's Moral Theory* (Ithaca, NY: Cornell University Press, 1992), hereafter abbreviated as *DPR*.

example of a retributivist.[2] To preview briefly, what I suggest is the following: although Kant does endorse standards of punishment commonly associated with retributivism, his rationale for endorsing those standards is far from the familiar retributivist thought that evildoers inherently deserve to suffer. To the contrary, the retributive elements in Kant's theory are more firmly rooted in considerations of comparative justice and honesty in public expressions of moral judgement. On the other side, although Kant does hold that any legal system must use the fear of punishment to deter citizens from crime, punishment for Kant is far more than a deterrence system of social control—we do not punish 'simply to deter crime'.

The background for my later discussion of motives is this. Endless debates have raged over the interpretation and value of Kant's views about the 'non-moral' motives of sympathy and compassion, but surprisingly little attention has been given to the place and value of the other motives on which I want to focus: fear of punishment and the prompting of conscience. These incentives, like sympathy and reasonable self-love, have often been thought respectable, even worthy, motives for doing what is right; but they are not unproblematic from the perspectives of Kantian moral theory and reflective common sense. How are we to understand these motives? Can acting from such motives be morally worthy? Are they morally indifferent motives, perhaps necessary at times but of no credit to those who act on them? Or, worse, are they morally objectionable, unworthy of us as free and rational persons?

These are large questions, and my aim is only to raise the issues, offer some suggestions, and invite discussion. Although my initial questions are about Kant's moral theory, as expressed especially in *The Metaphysics of Morals*, my long-range interest extends beyond this. I want to consider whether, as I suspect, there are both important insights and serious flaws in Kant's ethical writings on these topics and, if so, what a reasonable Kantian ethics, suitably revised and supplemented, might say on the issues in question.[3] Ultimately, of course, as philosophers we want to assess this whole Kantian approach, compared to the best alternatives—but that is not the issue at present.

---

    [2] See e.g. Sharon Byrd, 'Kant's Theory of Punishment: Deterrence in its Threat, Retribution in its Execution', *Law and Philosophy*, 8 (1980), 151–220; Donald Scheid, 'Kant's Retributivism', *Ethics*, 93 (1983), 262–82; Jeffrie Murphy, *Kant: The Philosophy of Right* (London: Macmillan, 1970), 109–49, and Jeffrie Murphy, 'Kant's Theory of Criminal Punishment', in his *Retribution, Justice and Therapy: Essays in the Philosophy of Law* (Dordrecht, Holland: D. Reidel, 1979), 82–92; and Sarah Holtman, 'Toward Social Reform: Kant's Penal Theory Reinterpreted', *Utilitas*, 9 (1997), 3–21.
    [3] In this chapter, I am concerned more with interpreting and extending Kant's ethics than with criticizing it, but I hope it is clear that I do not mean to endorse all of the views of Kant's that I summarize and try to understand sympathetically.

I. Kant's Theory of Punishment: Some Main Points

Several ideas about Kant's theory of punishment will be especially relevant when we turn to punishment as a motive.

1. We have a moral duty to obey the law. There is an important exception, for we must not obey any order to commit acts that conflict with 'inner morality'.[4] That case aside, juridical duties are also indirect ethical duties (*MS* 6:220). That is, apart from the exception just mentioned, conformity to the law is a strict moral duty; and making it our principle to do so from duty is a requirement of virtue—even though legal authorities cannot demand this.

2. This qualified duty to conform to legal requirements is not a free-standing moral axiom but is derived from more fundamental moral premises together with assumptions about the human condition. The more basic ideas are the Categorical Imperative, the innate rights to freedom and equality, the universal principle of justice, and its corollary authorizing coercion to 'hinder hindrances to freedom' (*MS* 6:225–6, 229–32, 236–8). From these starting points Kant attempts to derive the duty to establish and maintain a Sovereign legal authority with the right to make laws and to punish lawbreakers.

3. Although not subject to legal constraint, the Sovereign authority in any legal system can be gravely wrong in its legislation. Errors of fact and judgement are common even when legislators are conscientiously trying to be guided by the moral law. And, of course, legislators are not always conscientious. Nonetheless, the errors and corruption of lawmakers are not in themselves a justification or excuse for disobeying the law (*MS* 6:318–23). Except when the law orders us to do something intrinsically immoral, legal offences are *ipso facto* moral offences.[5]

[4] See *MS* 6:322, 371–2 and *R.* 6:15 n. See also Hans Reiss, 'Postscript', in *Kant: Political Writings*, 2nd edn., ed. Hans Reiss, trans. H.B. Nisbet (Cambridge: Cambridge University Press, 1991).

    In this chapter, I have used the following translations of Kant's works: *The Metaphysics of Morals*, ed. and trans. Mary Gregor (Cambridge: Cambridge University Press, 1991); *Religion within the Boundaries of Mere Reason*, trans. George di Giovanni, in *Religion and Rational Theology*, ed. and trans. Allen W. Wood and George di Giovanni (Cambridge: Cambridge University Press, 1996); *Groundwork of the Metaphysics of Morals*, trans. H. J. Paton (New York: Harper & Row, 1964); and *Critique of Practical Reason*, trans. L. W. Beck (New York: Macmillan, 1965).

[5] This is not to say that the ideas of 'legal offence' and 'moral offence' are the same but merely that (apart from the exceptions noted) when one commits a legal offence this is also a moral offence (against the moral requirement to obey the law).

4. Lawmakers and judges should determine the manner, extent, and scope of punishment by rules commonly associated with 'retributivism'. That is, (*a*) all and only those who break the law are to be punished, (*b*) the severity of punishment should be proportionate to the gravity of the crime, and (*c*) the manner of punishment should be 'like for like' ('an eye for an eye') except when physically or morally impossible. Also, (*d*) punishment presupposes that the agent had the freedom necessary to conform to the law, and (*e*) punishments degrading to humanity are prohibited (*MS* 6:328–37). The law should be concerned only with intentional 'external acts' that violate enforceable public requirements (*MS* 6:230). Whether our motives are morally worthy is not the business of the courts. Moral unworthiness is not equivalent or proportionate to legal culpability, even though (with the exception noted) every criminal act is presumably based on a maxim that is morally unworthy to some degree.[6]

5. Punishment is a practice through which officials and the public express moral disapproval of criminal acts. In this respect punishment differs significantly from many other sorts of disincentives that serve to promote social order. It is not simply a useful public device to control behaviour. It expresses public condemnation of 'external' (but intentional) acts contrary to laws that should be obeyed. This expressive aspect of punishment, I think, is an inseparable part of the traditional and common understanding of what it is to *punish* someone, as opposed to merely venting anger, using negative conditioning, or frightening others into conformity. Also, if we suppose (as I do) that Kant took the expressive aspect of punishment for granted, then this helps to narrow the gap between Kant's basic moral premises and his particular rules regarding who should be punished, how much, and in what manner.[7] That is, once we see punishment as, in part, a *statement* of public disapproval, then we can invoke Kant's standards of honesty and fairness to see why, for example, punishments cannot be varied

---

[6] Kant implies that the degree cannot be determined with any assurance and that it is not the business of the courts to assess.

[7] These are points discussed in my earlier paper 'Kant on Punishment'. I do not claim that Kant explicitly notes the expressive function of punishment, but only that it would be a natural assumption and helps to make sense of his position. Even more, I do not claim that Kant held an expressive *theory* of punishment of the sort that Joel Feinberg describes in his justly famous paper, 'The Expressive Function of Punishment', in his *Doing and Deserving* (Princeton: Princeton University Press, 1971), 95–118. The expression of official and public disapproval is a constitutive feature of what we commonly understand as *punishment*, but it is a feature that may make the practice of punishment more problematic rather than a feature that explains why the practice is justified.

simply for pragmatic reasons and convicted criminals cannot be pardoned whenever it would be useful.[8]

To forestall misunderstanding, I should add that my suggestion is not that expressing public disapproval is the justifying aim of punishment. Rather, the expressive function is simply a feature of the practice that itself needs to be justified. We should not deprive people of liberty and make them suffer *in order to* express our moral disapproval, but the fact that punishment is a practice through which disapproval is expressed must be taken seriously when we think about how to impose punishment fairly and honestly and also when we consider whether the practice is justifiable at all.

6. The ultimate justification for having the practice of punishment is not retribution or deterrence, as these are commonly understood. The *lex talionis* is a policy of returning to wrongdoers an equivalent to losses they inflicted on another, but Kant justifies it as 'the only unwavering standard', not because wickedness inherently warrants the infliction of suffering (*MS* 6:332).[9] Despite some suggestions to the contrary, Kant's premiss is not that it is intrinsically good for criminals to be unhappy in proportion to their moral unworthiness; and he certainly did not think that it is the business of the state to try to bring about such proportionality.

For a long time Kant's theory of punishment was almost universally regarded as the paradigm of retributivism, but recent scholars have rightly called attention to the fact that the need to deter crime plays a crucial role in Kant's justification of the right and duty of the state to punish lawbreakers. But this recognition of the need for deterrence seems at odds with the many passages in *The Metaphysics of Morals* that initially led so many to label Kant's theory *retributivist*. Various commentaries have suggested ways in which deterrence and retribution might be mixed in Kant's theory of punishment. A common first step is

---

[8] For example, it is dishonest to express a severe moral judgement on one person and a mild judgement on another if the only difference has to do with external factors, unrelated to their offences. And it is not fair to profess public disapproval of some offenders on a certain basis but then refuse to make the same judgement on others. These considerations do not fully justify Kant's inflexible policy of proportionate punishment for all of the guilty, but they provide a strong presumption for proportionality.

[9] In a passage referring to the 'inner wickedness' of murderers at *MS* 6:333–4, Kant seems to take a different view, but I argue that even this uncharacteristic passage does not imply that it is the business of the state to mete out punishment in accord with inner wickedness. The passage seems to be an *ad hoc* response to a possible worry that, by not assessing the comparative inner moral worth of murderers, strict application of *lex talionis* would make idealistic revolutionaries suffer just as much as vicious ones. Kant argues that, at least in the case of Scottish rebels of 1745–6, execution would have been worse for the vicious revolutionaries. See *DPR* 186.

to distinguish the rules governing the practice (or institution) of punishment from the justification of having such practice. Given this distinction, it has been suggested that *deterrence* is the justifying aim of having the institution and *retributive policies* are constitutive features of the institution, features that either promote the justifying end or serve as side constraints.[10] Another proposal is that the *threat of punishment* is justified by the aim of deterring crime, but the *execution of punishment* is justified independently by considerations of justice and the requirement to treat persons as ends in themselves.[11]

These proposals are improvements on earlier one-sided interpretations, but I suspect that they do not yet fully capture the retributive side of Kant's thought. In any case, the suggestion that for Kant the aim of punishment is deterrence seems misleadingly oversimplified. Clearly, Kant did not want the operative aim of *judges* (and other enforcement officials) in administering the law to be to deter future crime, either by 'making an example' of convicted criminals or by making them realize the price they will pay for further wrongdoing. This point is rightly acknowledged by commentators who distinguish the working policies of the practice from its 'justifying aim'. Also, Kant makes plain that legislators, in deciding what sanctions to assign to various legal offences, should be guided by *lex talionis* and a prohibition of degrading punishments, not by a pragmatic policy of assigning whatever will most efficiently deter crime. But, even if these constraints on judges and legislators are considered part of the practice rather than its justification, it would still be misleading to say that for Kant the aim of the practice is to deter crime. That aim has an important role, but it is only part of a much more complex story.

The background of the story includes everyone's innate natural rights to freedom and equality, which in turn must be rooted in the basic moral law expressed in various forms of the Categorical Imperative.[12] A crucial premiss is the universal principle of justice (*Recht*), which says (roughly) that it is unjust to hinder the external liberty of another if that hindrance could not take place under a system of laws in which everyone is entitled to liberty equally. In a state of nature, acts against this principle would be violations of 'right' in a slightly attenuated, but still important, sense: they are acts that 'ought to be prohibited by law' and they may be coercively opposed even in a state of nature. The often-cited corollary of the principle of justice is supposed to express its implicit meaning more fully: violations of the principle can be coercively

---

[10]   Scheid, 'Kant's Retributivism', 262–5.

[11]   Byrd, 'Kant's Theory of Punishment', 157, 184–98.

[12]   This is well presented by Byrd, even though she occasionally writes of deterrence as the justifying aim of threats of punishment—a description, I think, that does not do justice to the fuller understanding of Kant's position that, in most respects, her article shows.

opposed as 'hindrance to hindrances to (legitimate) freedom' (*MS* 6:231). This points us towards a justification of punishment, but there are obviously more steps needed. For example, we have yet no specification of how much, in what ways, and by whom coercion may be exercised. Kant fills in some gaps by asserting a moral duty to establish and obey a Sovereign not subject to legal constraints (*MS* 6:311 ff.). This, he argues rather unconvincingly, is conceptually necessary for the possibility of justice. Then Kant moves rather quickly to a description of the authoritative powers of the Sovereign and the moral principles that *should* constrain legislation and enforcement even though no one has the right to force the hand of the Sovereign.

Gaps remain, but enough pieces of the story are in place to make clear that it is better to avoid simple descriptions like 'in Kant's theory the justifying aim of punishment is deterrence'. Of course, that waves a hand towards Kant's view, but the trouble is that it points indiscriminately to a whole variety of un-Kantian deterrence theories at the same time. We could as easily say that punishment is to make justice possible, to protect the legitimate liberties of citizens, or respect the Sovereign's moral and legal right to use coercion to maintain justice. Admittedly, any one of these descriptions would also over-simplify; brief slogans almost invariably do. Punishment for Kant would lose its rationale if threats of punishment never, or rarely, deterred offenders, but 'deterring crime' is not a self-sufficient moral goal, and principles specifying whom to punish, how much, and in what ways are far from being settled by seeing what means most efficiently achieve this end—or even the end of 'minimizing violations of justice'.

II. Conscience: The Inner Judge

Apart from a few brief references, Kant does not make much of the idea of *conscience* in the *Groundwork* or the second *Critique*. In *The Metaphysics of Morals* and later in *Religion* he explains, in metaphorical terms, how he views conscience.[13] His conception of conscience, I think, is distinctive in some respects, and perhaps initially surprising; but in the end it can be seen to fit well with his basic moral theory.

In some popular views, conscience replaces reason as a way of determining what is right. It is viewed as a God-given instinctual sense that tells us whether what we are doing, have done, or are proposing to do is wrong. On this view, although conscience itself may be infallible, its voice (like that of the ancient

---

[13] G. 4:422, 404; *KpV* 5:98; *MS* 6:233–5, 400–1, 438–42; *R.* 6:185–6.

oracles) can be misunderstood, misheard, or distorted through self-deception, distracting influences, and so on. A different conception of conscience was well described in the sermons of Bishop Butler.[14] Butler used 'conscience' as the name of a faculty of reason, able to discern 'in a calm hour' what is fitting for human beings to do in their particular situations. Reason, in Butler's view, relies on a natural teleology of human faculties. We have self-love, benevolence, and particular passions; and conscience is just reflective reason, determining what it is fitting for a person with such natural dispositions to do. In more recent times, cultural relativists treat conscience as nothing but the psychological manifestations of having internalized the social norms of our culture. Kant's view is interestingly different from all of these.

For Kant, *reason* determines the basic principles of right conduct, *judgement* is needed to apply them, and strength of *will* must be developed to follow our best judgements unfailingly. *Conscience*, in Kant's view, does not serve any of these functions. It does not tell us generally what is right: that is the job of reason. Conscience does not tell us what the principles of right imply for more specific situations: that is the job of judgement. And conscience is not the ready power to do what we judge right despite temptations: that is virtue, or strength of will, to do right. Our reason can be obscured by self-deception, but conscience seems to speak unavoidably even when we do not want to consult it. Our moral judgements can err, but (Kant says) conscience cannot. Our strength of will can be deficient, but conscience makes us suffer even so. How are we to understand all this?

Kant discusses conscience in metaphorical terms. A person with a conscience has a sort of internal judicial system. It is as if we were called into court to account for our conduct. We accuse ourselves, try to defend ourselves, and then the inner judge of conscience reaches a verdict—guilty or not guilty—and passes sentence. Not a legislator who makes the laws and not a legal expert who simply informs us of their implications, conscience is the inner judge that either acquits us or condemns us to suffer for our failures. The relevant charge in this court, significantly, is not violation of what is objectively, and correctly, judged to be a moral requirement. Rather, the relevant charges, in effect, are of two kinds: (1) that we have failed *to act in accord with our own general moral judgements* (for example, the judgements we make about right and wrong when not specifically focused on our own situation) and (2) that we have failed in our *duty of due care* by not being sufficiently serious and careful in determining in particular what our duties are.[15]

   [14] Joseph Butler, *Five Sermons*, ed. Stephen L. Darwall (Indianapolis: Hackett, 1983).
   [15] Here I put together ideas from Kant's *The Metaphysics of Morals* and his *Religion within the Boundaries of Mere Reason*. The duty of due care is from *R.* 6:185–6.

When we judge what is right in general we are supposed to be guided by the moral law; but making such judgements is not the job of conscience. Rather, conscience holds up our *acts-as-we-perceive-them* for comparison with the *general-moral-judgements-that-we-accept* (for example, regarding others) in order to see whether we have acted well by our own lights. And conscience also has the second task: to pass judgement on whether we have been careful and diligent in our initial moral judgements about what generally human beings may do in various situations. In this second capacity, Kant remarks, paradoxically, that conscience is 'judgment passing judgment upon itself' (*R.* 6:186).

Conscience, so conceived, cannot err, Kant says (*MS* 6:401). His view is understandable, even if exaggerated. The idea is that, although we can make mistakes in our particular judgements about what morality objectively requires in various situations, we are not liable to the same sorts of mistakes when we compare 'inner' thoughts (that is, what we *intend* to be doing in the situation as we perceive it and what we *think* that human beings may do in such a situation). Errors of fact, for example, can lead to misjudgements about whether our actual acts were permissible, but those errors do not prevent us from seeing (when it is so) that our acts-as-we-perceive-them are at odds with our moral judgements-as-we-accept-them. No doubt, contrary to Kant, we can make errors even in comparing these 'inner' thoughts. If so, Kant's denial that there can be an 'erring conscience' is an exaggeration, not strictly true. But a significant contrast remains between judgements of conscience and judgements of objective duty, as Kant conceives these. That is, the latter are vulnerable to many sources of error that the former are not. Misunderstanding the material facts about the situation that we are in, for example, commonly leads to mistakes about what it is objectively right to do in that context, but that sort of error does not affect the judgement of conscience.[16]

Conscience, then, is like judicial punishment in several ways. Both condemn, or acquit, us by judging fallible conceptions of our acts by normative standards that may not be objectively justifiable. *At best* both the laws of the judicial system and the moral judgements at work in conscience are made with respect and proper understanding of the moral law: the public legislator's in the first case and the individual moral agent's in the second. But public law-

---

[16] 'Objectively right' here raises questions. Unlike many consequentialists, Kant is not primarily concerned with what is 'right' independently of the knowledge and understanding of the agent. The universal law formulas, for example, test agents' subjective principles (maxims) and so the results always depend, in a way, on how they conceive the situation they are in. But Kant also has, I think, a notion of objective right as what reason would prescribe *given a correct assessment of the facts, a clear understanding of the basic moral law, and no distorting influences on judgement.* Kant apparently thought that the well-intentioned Scottish rebels mentioned at *MS* 6:333–4 did what was objectively wrong in this sense, even though they mistakenly judged what they did to be morally justified (and so, as some say, they were 'subjectively right').

makers in determining the judicial standards can be foolish and corrupt, and, despite Kant's greater faith in them, individual agents are obviously not immune to ignorance and vice when they apply their basic understanding of the moral law to specific situations. Kant thought that, though imperfect, both the laws of the state and the demands of conscience must be followed. Kant admits these may conflict when the laws of the state require a person to do something in conflict with inner morality; but in all other cases an informed conscience is supposed to demand conformity to public laws, no matter how bad the laws are. Thus, apart from a (rarely mentioned) exception, the imperatives to follow law and conscience are both strict.

There are differences, of course. The range of public law is narrower than that of conscience, for it is restricted to external acts that may be coerced. Conformity to conscience is supposed to be sufficient for a *morally blameless* life, but conformity to public law, obviously, is not. But even here there is a parallel: conformity to public law is supposed to be sufficient for a *legally blameless* life (that is, for immunity from judicial punishment and condemnation).

Let us focus now on how punishment and conscience function as motives. Both have a dark side and a bright side; or, better, each of them, I suggest, can be interpreted as an unworthy motive or as a worthy motive. Conscience is usually regarded as an admirable motive, but it may not be. Fear of punishment is usually regarded as an unworthy motive, but it need not be.

III. A Problem: Fear of Punishment as an Apparently Unworthy Motive

Kant's ethics is famous for its insistence that moral agents have autonomy of the will. They recognize moral requirements, then, as what they must do, irrespective of anticipated rewards and punishments. Only acts from duty have moral worth; even if acting from other motives is quite natural and unobjectionable in many situations, when the duty is clear, evident, and salient, to conform to duty from motives that are utterly unrelated to a will to do right seems at least morally suspect. It falls short of a Kantian ideal, and perhaps it displays insufficient attention to the (imperfect) duty to strive for moral perfection. Even common opinion, for example, would think it 'unworthy' of a human being (and not just failure to achieve a special moral praiseworthiness) to rescue a drowning rich man with mind and heart focused on potential reward money—even if one would have managed to do it 'from duty' had the man been poor. Does Kant's theory of punishment, as sometimes thought, represent a retreat from these bold moral ideas? Is it, perhaps, a sign of Kant's willingness to compromise with hard realities of human nature?

Why might we suspect this? One line of thought might run as follows: despite Kant's eloquence in favour of fulfilment of duty from respect for moral law, when he turns to the problem of how to establish and maintain a just social order under laws, he advocates a legal system that does not require a moral motivation and would suffice even to keep order among fiends. The law, he says, is to be concerned only with 'external' acts and so disregards the moral worth of the agent's motives, enforcing the same strict requirements whether the offender's motives were high-minded or base. Now this might seem to reflect a weakening of Kant's professed faith in the capacity of every moral agent to do his or her duty from respect for the moral law alone. Why, we might wonder, should we utterly disregard this capacity when concerned with matters of law and justice, resting our trust entirely in citizens' fear of punishment rather than their will to do what is right?

This worry rests partly on misunderstanding. Kant never denies that moral agents *can* be just from respect for the moral law. In fact, since all juridical duties are 'indirectly ethical duties', Kant implies that we have an (imperfect) ethical duty to conform to them from respect for the moral law that grounds them. And that we ought implies that we can, at least often and increasingly so, if we strive for moral perfection. We must presume, then, that we can be law-abiding citizens because we acknowledge our duty, under justice, to follow the law. Perhaps most people do, at least under good social conditions. Kant's claim that a legal system should be designed to be effective, even among egoists with no moral sense, does not imply that most citizens will follow it with that attitude or that they would resort to crime without such tough-minded law enforcement. Coercion (for example, through punishment) is needed, Kant thought, to make a just social order possible, but this implies only that we cannot do without coercion at least as a 'fall-back' motivation provided to the weak and corrupt. It does not imply that each and every citizen needs to be moved by fear of punishment, nor even that the weak and corrupt always need this.

There is, however, another possible source of the suspicion of Kant's reliance on threats of punishment. This is the thought that, by advocating a system thoroughly reliant on non-moral incentives, such as the fear of punishment, Kant endorses a motivation that is, from a Kantian point of view, unworthy of morally mature human beings, a rather ugly motive needed only by the weak and corrupt. To be fair, the critic will not say that Kant *recommends* the motive of fear of punishment, but does he not rest content with it as a crucial pillar of human society, as a motivational attitude that, though unworthy in itself, is acceptable to exploit and use for good ends? Even if necessary in extreme cases, one might think, a social system that by design relies exclusively on threats expresses contempt for our better natures.

This worry is more interesting than the last and it is not entirely rooted in misunderstanding of Kant's views. However, I suggest that, with suitable supplement, Kant's main points about the morality of punishment allow for a more appealing way of thinking about the problem. The practice of punishment, even as Kant interprets it, can and should tap into finer motives than the mere amoral fear of legally inflicted pain and deprivation. To be sure, the practice does serve to provide protection to the liberties of law-abiding citizens by means of threatening unwanted consequences to would-be offenders who refuse to be moved in any other way; but, despite the impression that Kant may at times give, that is far from the entire picture about how the practice of punishment draws upon our motivational resources. In order to lay the background for this suggestion, I turn next to an analogous motive: the prompting and pangs of conscience.

IV. An Analogous Problem: Conscience as an Apparently Unworthy Motive

A bad conscience 'hurts', and, as we have seen, Kant treats this pain as analogous to the suffering imposed on lawbreakers by the system of criminal justice. If fear of punishment is an unworthy motive for doing what duty requires, then it would seem that it is equally unworthy to do one's duty from fear of a bad conscience. And, if the system of criminal justice systematically relies on threats that exploit our unworthy fear of punishment, and so expresses contempt for our better natures, the same would seem to be true of conscience. It prods, pricks, nags, and even torments moral offenders, pressuring them (it seems) to change their ways. It helps to prevent us from sliding into immoral practices, it seems, because we are aware that our conscience, that inner judge, will exact a heavy price if we do. It does not simply inform us of what is right but warns us, threatens us, and reminds us of the sanctions it will impose for disobedience.

Obviously, we need a distinction here. There are different ways that we can respond to conscience. In the worst case, of course, a person may be moved solely by a desire to avoid the discomforts of a bad conscience. We sometimes say, for example, 'I couldn't sleep if I did *that*', suggesting that all that holds us back from doing something awful is a desire to avoid insomnia. Actually, this is often said with false modesty: it is not 'cool' to display one's moral commitments. If it is really the pangs of *conscience* (in Kant's sense) that the agent fears, then the agent must believe that the act expected to bring on the pain is wrong and contrary to his or her own moral judgement. On Kantian and other internalist moral theories, no one could be indifferent to violating his or her own moral judgements. So, on these theories, it is not even possible to care only about the pain incurred when one transgresses conscience; moral agents necessarily have some regard for doing what they believe right. Nonetheless, it is possible to be exclusively focused on the discomforts that violating conscience will bring, and thus also possible to be moved on particular occasions just by a desire to avoid those discomforts. The ugliness of this worst-case motivation is highlighted when we realize that, if that is all that deters the agent, then he or she might violate conscience and then take a pill to block the discomfort if that were possible. If all that keeps me from betraying a friend is that it would cause me to lose sleep, then I must be quite ready to do it if I have an adequate supply of (non-addictive) sleeping pills.

The worst case just described may not be the only possibility, but the alternative is not yet clear. Given that we often speak with respect of deeds motivated by conscience, it would be very odd to suppose that these were simply a matter of someone's choosing to avoid pain. If conscience were viewed simply as a faculty that 'informs' us what we ought to do, then we might praise these 'conscientious' acts as nothing more than acts guided by our moral beliefs or, in other words, instances of 'acting from duty'. But that idea is not available to Kant, for, as mentioned, he held that we determine what we ought to do through reason and judgement, not conscience. Kantian conscience speaks, after self-accusation and self-defence, as a judge who enforces the law, passes sentence, and so makes us suffer for our misdeeds. Or, in advance, it threatens, or warns, of the sentence and consequent suffering that we can expect if we do not scrupulously try to avoid wrongdoing. So, it seems, being motivated by conscience (as Kant conceives it) must be like being motivated by fear of punishment in that anticipation of *pain inflicted for wrongdoing* plays a significant role.

It is not obvious, then, that it is morally worthy to be motivated by conscience. Whether it is so depends on how, more specifically, we understand that motive in particular cases.

V. Anticipation of Grief and Concern to do Morally Worthy Acts

Let us consider some other cases in which an apparently simple motive can be understood in different ways.

(*a*) Anticipation of Grief

Suppose, to explain our giving life-preserving aid or advice, we said, 'We would grieve terribly if you died.' We might be expressing the attitude that we want to prevent the untimely death of the other person in order to satisfy our desire to avoid pain for ourselves. But that is not the only possibility. In many cases the remark would be more plausibly understood as an expression of love, a deep attachment manifested in our disposition to experience pain when those we love suffer or meet an untimely death. The experience of grief, so understood, is painful, but what 'hurts' is the recognition of their loss and our inability to continue a cherished relationship with them. If we hope that others will grieve for us when we die, at least for a short while, this is not because we want them to suffer but because we hope that they will remember us with love and respect and we know that, at least for most human beings, such memories are inevitably painful for a while after the death of a loved one.

Sometimes we cannot, in fact, have the good we want in a situation without some necessary pain, but we can readily imagine what it would be like to do so and wish that this were possible. For example, at present doctors may sometimes need to manipulate injured limbs and then to rely on the patient's reports of pain in order to identify the injured parts; but we can imagine and wish that they could get the information otherwise. Again, we may in fact be unable to work our hardest to accomplish challenging projects without suffering anxiety in the process and being liable to painful disappointment if we fail, but we can imagine this and wish it were possible. With grief it seems different: it is hard to imagine loving someone deeply and yet experiencing no pain when first facing and remembering the good we have both lost. Even if we can imagine that drugs or Stoic training could enable us to love, face the loss, and yet feel no pain, it is far from obvious that transforming ourselves in these ways would be worth what we would lose in doing so.

How, then, might the thought that we would grieve for someone lead to our doing something? As the idea 'crosses our mind', as we say, we are imaginatively entertaining 'how it would be' if the loved one died, and this typically is an unpleasant, even painful, thought. But why? It is not quite like imagining ourselves having a headache, which is unpleasant to anticipate simply because we dislike being in pain. We shudder, and recoil, at the thought of the untimely death of loved ones because we value them, not just because we hate to be in pain. The thought moves us (for example, to act protectively), not like a painful itch that drives us to scratch, but like a jarring 'wake-up call' that focuses our attention on something we value for its own sake.

(*b*) Concern to Do Morally Worthy Acts

Some Kantians may look with suspicion at an analogy between the motives of love and conscience, and so let us also look at another complex motive—one that seems to have a Kantian moral dimension. Acting from duty is supposed to be morally worthy; acts from other motives, apart from this, are supposed to lack moral worth. But suppose that someone is strongly *motivated to do acts that are morally worthy*? Is this a morally worthy motive, the sort of motive that makes acts deserving of moral esteem?

It all depends on how, more specifically, we understand the motive. There are several possibilities, some morally admirable, some ugly. What would be morally admirable? This, for Kant, is acting out of respect for the moral law, nothing less. But, given Kant's theory, the description 'acts that have moral worth' picks out just those acts that fulfil duty and are motivated by respect for moral law. So, on one possible reading, 'a concern to do acts that have moral worth' can be a stand-in (for Kantians) for *doing one's duty from duty*, even though strictly 'having moral worth' is not the same idea as 'fulfilling duty from duty'. Consider an analogy.[17] Suppose papers deserve A's only if they are academically excellent by the usual standards of clarity, cogency, understanding of issues, originality, and so on. Genuinely good students will be primarily concerned with academic excellence rather than getting A grades *per se*. But, assuming fair and proper grading, they will take for granted that A papers are academically excellent. They may even express this concern when they say that they are working for A's (that is, trying to do all A work). Referring to the desired papers as 'A papers' serves (approximately) to *pick out* the intended set of papers, but not by describing the essential features for which they are valued. Similarly, a good person whom we may describe as 'trying to act in a morally worthy way' may be ultimately concerned, not so much with deserving moral esteem, but with doing what is right because it is right.

But there is also a less sympathetic way to understand the concern to do acts of moral worth. Assuming for now that 'morally worthy acts' are 'acts deserving of moral esteem', the agents' focus of attention could be exclusively on their

---

[17] Here is an alternative analogy. When sorting apples, I am asked why. I reply, 'I want to select all the really bright red ones'. The enquirer might wonder, a bit perversely, why I am so 'hung up' on colour. But suppose I am assuming that the bright red ones are tastier, more nourishing, and so on, and my main concern, after all, was to select the tastier, more nourishing apples. When I explained why I was sorting the apples as I was, I referred to a visible identifying mark rather than the object of my ultimate concern, as we often do, unless someone explicitly presses us to explain our more basic or ground-level motivation. By analogy, to say 'I want to do acts of moral worth' (or, more naturally, 'I want to act in a morally worthy way') may express a basic respect for the moral law even though that is not mentioned explicitly.

own moral records and how others should view them.[18] There are much worse motives, no doubt. At least the concern in question is to *deserve* esteem for one's deeds, not merely to *receive* it. But, still, the motive may not reflect a morally worthy respect for moral law. Admittedly, what we might call 'wanting to deserve their esteem' can be a complex motive that *includes* respect for the standard that must be met to deserve esteem; but we can imagine the less admirable case in which we have no direct respect for the standards themselves but only want to be in a position where others *should* be prepared to praise, approve, and esteem us. The more common case, no doubt, is wanting others *actually* to praise, esteem, and approve of what we do, but we may entertain (and even 'act out') *fantasies of deserved but unrecognized esteem* for doing morally heroic deeds. Here it would be, in a sense, our having 'moral worth', rather than following the moral law, that we valued. And, if we understand the motive in this way, there is no moral worth in acting from concern for moral worth.

The bottom line, again, is that simply described motives often need a fuller explanation before we can think clearly about how to assess them. Having seen how this is so with regard to anticipation of grief and concern to do what is morally worthy, let us return to consider *conscience* as a motive.

VI. Motivation by Conscience: Worthy and Unworthy Versions

It is clear that being motivated directly and exclusively by aversion to the discomfort, insomnia, and even torments that conscience may cause us is not a morally admirable motive for doing what we know is the right thing to do. But conscience, as Kant sees it, does not move us to do our duty simply by holding up an inspiring ideal that draws us joyfully to realize our nature as rational autonomous persons. It warns, threatens, accuses, and generally disturbs our peace of mind. Since mere aversion to pain is not a morally worthy motive, especially when our duty is definite, how can anticipation of a tormented conscience play a motivational role in the life of a good person? Is it merely a regrettable but necessary 'back-up' motive, not in itself an expression of our higher nature but merely a natural device that serves a purpose when better motives fail?

---

[18]   A promising alternative idea of moral worth, developed by Robert Johnson in a manuscript not yet published, understands 'morally worthy acts' from the deliberative stance as those morally worthy of choice—that is, those whose maxim is such that (compared with other maxims for the situation) it is worthy of choice by a good will, when choosing as such. This makes the idea that 'only acts from duty have moral worth' not so much a lesson about how to allocate praise and esteem, as often thought, but more a lesson about the reasons that should be primary for us when we know, and are deliberately considering, that we have a duty in a situation.

The analogies with grief and concern to do morally worthy acts suggest a way of approaching these questions. Although we can be concerned in an unworthy way about the pain that a bad conscience brings, sometimes what seems to be merely 'wanting to avoid the pain' may in fact be a deeper, and better, motive. The pain may be a natural human reflection of our recognition that we have failed to show full respect for the moral standards that we recognize as authoritative. A bad conscience hurts because, sometimes in spite of ourselves, we care about whether we make our moral judgements with due care and live by them. Conscience often warns, prods, and jars us to reform, but not by a simple stimulus-response reflex mechanism. Nor does it move us merely by prompting us to act under a freely chosen maxim of pain avoidance. Rather, the hurting conscience—the painful awareness that the inner judge has passed sentence—alerts us and makes us more vividly aware of our respect for the moral law and its requirements, as far as we can judge, on the particular occasion. Its phenomenology, no doubt, has a basis in natural human psychology, but it is morally significant because it expresses our recognition and acceptance of the authority of moral reasons. Pangs of conscience, we might say, are a particular form of the dark side of 'respect for moral law' that Kant describes in the *Critique of Practical Reason*: they are instances of the general fact that our recognition of the legitimate claims of others strikes down our self-conceit. They turn our mind, painfully, not to the discomfort of violating our moral standards, but to those standards themselves. Our respect for the moral law shows itself, in a natural human way, by the fact that we cannot hold our acts up to the law and see that we fall far short without experiencing the glaring difference with discomfort. The metaphors regarding conscience may be overworked, but the central point remains: being motivated by conscience may be (and one hopes often is) fundamentally a matter of being motivated by respect for morality, and so ultimately by respect for the legitimate claims of others and our own better nature.

Our analogies also suggest that even what we describe in suspect ways may actually be instances of acting from respect for the moral law. This is because, as before, our description may simply pick out the intended acts by an identifying feature that is not the essential object of our concern. For example, given Kant's assumptions, 'avoiding what would cause me the discomforts of a bad conscience' identifies the same set of acts as 'avoiding what would be a failure to live by my best moral judgements'. If our governing intention is to avoid the acts described in the second way, then we are moved by respect for the moral law. Even if we pick out the set of acts we mean to avoid by the first description, our basic motive may still be respect for the moral law—though we did not explicitly mention the essential feature that makes these acts morally worthy.

So, in several ways, what we think of as 'being moved by conscience' may be more, and better, than 'being moved by aversion to pain'.

VII. Fear of Punishment as a Motive: Worthy and Unworthy Versions

Socrates, as described in Plato's *Crito*, looks down on the fear of punishment as an unworthy motive, but paradoxically he later seems to include as a reason for not escaping prison his belief that then he would be *rightly* condemned and punished as one who would destroy the laws. Perhaps he disapproved of the *fear* of punishment because he saw it as a raw, unexamined emotion, whereas, by contrast, his aversion to being subject to *justified* punishment and condemnation was a motive that he could rationally approve on due reflection. Kant's view, I suspect, was similar, or ought to have been.

Recall our background assumptions. Certain special cases aside, the judicial punishment should be carried out without interference—even in an imperfectly just system.[19] Lawbreakers are presumed to be not only in violation of a legal requirement but also in violation of their indirectly ethical duty to conform to all moral requirements from duty. Even if the law unjustly forbids what would not be wrong to do apart from the legal prohibition, the act that violates the prohibition is presumed to be wrong because it disobeys legitimate state authority. The presumption, then, is that those convicted of crimes have intentionally and freely done acts of a kind for which they can be rightly condemned and punished. They have also shown a failure to act on respect for the moral law when they needed to. So, although the law is not (in Kant's view) in the business of full moral assessment of the character, motives, and moral worth of citizens, we can suppose, at least for practical purposes, that criminals in normal cases have acted wrongly and from less than worthy moral motives.[20] Moreover, punishments express public condemnation, and, if justly imposed, they convey their message honestly and equally for citizens who commit the same crime.

What about the motive of fear of punishment, then? We have seen how it can be understood as something unworthy, second best, or at least short of the Kantian ideal. But how could it be something better?

---

[19] The special cases, as mentioned earlier, are where the law demands of the citizen that he or she commit an act in conflict with inner morality. Such acts for Kant no doubt included rape, sodomy, murder, and so on.

[20] There is a gap, I think, between Kant's idealized assumptions (especially regarding criminals' freedom and moral knowledge) and the realities of our world, but I am setting aside for now doubts about Kant's background assumptions.

Suppose, first, that we understand 'fear', not as a raw terror in anticipation of future pain or loss, but more broadly as a strong aversion to an outcome that is felt *and judged* to be a bad thing. Fear of this sort could be, in part, an attitude stemming from values endorsed in rational reflection. Like Kantian respect, it could be essentially a motivating recognition of authority that is also experienced as a feeling. Those who speak approvingly of 'fear of God', I suspect, sometimes have something like this in mind.

Whether we call the motive 'fear' or not, the sort of aversion to punishment that has the best claim to moral significance is not a knee-jerk reaction, but a commitment to a policy (or maxim) to avoid incurring the *justified* moral disapproval of fellow citizens expressed in judicial punishment (when properly applied). Even if a crime is not immoral apart from its being authoritatively prohibited, Kant's presumption is that we would be wrong (barring certain exceptional cases) to violate the legal prohibition. So, whether or not the laws are good, avoiding the justified disapproval of others expressed through punishment can be a principled policy rather than a mechanical response to impulse. We can understand it as a maxim freely adopted by a moral agent.

Moreover, the maxim need not fall under a more basic maxim of self-love. That is, our reason for affirming it is not necessarily that it serves as a means to a personal non-moral end—such as avoiding embarrassment and financial loss. The essential and sufficient ground may be a commitment to doing what is right with respect to the laws of the land. Although discomfort at the thought of being justly punished may be the first sign that we are in danger of violating our moral commitment, the analogy with pangs of conscience suggests that what the discomfort reveals need not be an aversion to pain but rather an unwillingness to betray our moral standards. We may 'pick out' what we want to avoid by the description 'avoiding (justified) punishment', but the essential feature of our concern may be something deeper—namely, avoidance of wrongdoing. If so, the ultimate ground is respect for the moral law, which is, for Kantians at least, a morally worthy motive.

Some may object that all efforts to defend a morally significant 'fear of punishment' are trivial, for the following reason. The motive under consideration, it might seem, is simply a hybrid, a combination of disparate elements—a moral concern to avoid wrongdoing *per se* plus a non-moral aversion to incurring the negative responses of others. We all know that Kant holds that the first is morally worthy, the second is not, and whether an act is morally worthy depends on which motive is actually operative in the case. So, after all, the suggestion that there might be morally worthy fear of punishment is nothing but a new spin on old doctrines.

A new spin may, in fact, help to correct old misunderstandings, but what I am suggesting is more than this. A principled (and felt) aversion to incurring the justified disapproval of our fellow citizens for our intentional acts is not simply a conjunction of a concern to do right and a desire to maintain a good reputation. In the best case, the pain we want to avoid is inseparable from the recognition that we have done wrong. Moreover, for us as human beings, the inseparability is deep. Even if it would be godlike to care only to do right without any regard for the approval of others, this is not an option for us—nor should we wish it to be. In fact, a proper regard for the opinion of others is an expression of respect for them as fellow legislators of moral law. It also respects their capacity, as moral equals, to judge in particular cases what is right and what is wrong. To suppose that our respect for moral law is utterly independent of any concern for what others think, so that we have only pragmatic and self-interested grounds to avoid their reasonable moral disapproval, is a kind of moral arrogance incompatible with recognition of the humanity of each person as an end in itself. Respect for moral law is, in an important way, like respect for law (that is, legal authority) in a just democratic community. Respect for law in a just democracy is ultimately respect for our fellow citizens, and respect for moral law in Kant's basic theory, as I understand it, is ultimately respect for humanity in each person. If so, what we call 'fear of punishment' can, at its best, be a specific form of respect for moral law and so a worthy motive. In so far as its source is autonomous recognition of 'the moral law within', it is—like response to conscience at its best—a form of *self-respect* as well.

Why does all this matter?[21] Presumably, as moral philosophers we are trying to achieve a better understanding of our moral concepts, and recognizing the strengths and weaknesses of classic moral theories, such as Kant's, may well be useful for this purpose. But, more specifically, how we view punishment as a motive is a significant part of how we understand our moral relations with others. Moralists often seem to believe that only they, and perhaps a few others, obey the law from admirable motives whereas the vast majority who obey the law do so only because they want to avoid the pain and deprivations that the law threatens. This belief encourages a self-righteous attitude that is deeply contemptuous of others: because 'they' lack moral motivation, 'we' must determine what is right and keep 'them' in line by threats. I doubt that the underlying belief can be sustained empirically, and I suspect that it stems from a confusion. It is observed, no doubt correctly, that the prospect of punishment is a significant aspect of the motivation of most law-abiding citizens, but

---

[21]   I am grateful to Andrews Reath for having encouraged me to address this question, for readers may well have doubts about it. I regret that my response here must be so brief and merely suggestive.

it is not noticed that the thought of punishment can motivate in quite different ways. What we call 'fear of punishment' is in fact complex and ambiguous. Understood in one way, it is a morally unworthy motive but probably not the sole or primary explanation of why most citizens are law abiding. Understood in another way, fear of punishment is probably a motivating factor for most citizens but not a motive that altogether lacks moral worth. If my conjecture here is correct, we who conscientiously obey the law do not stand to most fellow citizens as the high-minded to the contemptible. Rather, we all relate to each other as imperfect moral agents who, despite lapses, generally show their respect for each other by maintaining a reasonable moral aversion to incurring the justified disapproval of their peers, as would be expressed in just punishment. Although Kant does not say all this, it is compatible, I believe, with the main features of his moral and political theory.

11

Motive and Rightness in Kant's Ethical System

Mark Timmons

One deeply entrenched assumption of ethical theorizing is that the rightness of an act does not depend on one's motive in performing the act. Considerations of motive are generally understood to affect the moral quality of one's character and hence the moral worth of one's actions. But, on the assumption under consideration, the rightness of an act is to be sharply distinguished from whatever moral worth it may possess; moral worth depends on motive, rightness does not.

The assumption, which I dub the Independence Thesis, is shared by advocates of different types of normative moral theory—virtue ethics, consequentialism, and deontological ethics. One finds the thesis being attributed to Aristotle,[1] although Mill explicitly embraced it,[2] as have other utilitarians and consequentialists generally, including G. E. Moore.[3] Perhaps its most ardent defender, W. D. Ross,[4] held a deontological moral theory, and it was accepted by Henry Sidgwick, who attempted to combine common-sense morality with utilitarianism.[5] This thesis is also reflected in Anglo-American law in the orthodox doctrine that motive is irrelevant to criminal liability.[6] The fact that the thesis is common ground among major types of moral theory and is found

I would like to thank the audiences at Brown University, Universität Erlangen, and the University of Mississippi for discussion of an earlier version of this paper. For their comments on an earlier version of this paper, I would like to thank Robert Audi, Marcia Baron, Josh Glasgow, Michael Gorr, Onora O'Neill, Tom Nenon, Thomas Pogge, David Shoemaker, and Allen Wood.

[1] Aristotle, *Nicomachean Ethics* 1105b, trans. T. Irwin (Indianapolis: Hackett Publishing Co., 1985), 40.

[2] See J. S. Mill, *Utilitarianism* (1861; Indianapolis: Hackett Publishing Co., 1979), 18, where Mill writes: 'utilitarian moralists have gone beyond almost all others in affirming that the motive has nothing to do with the morality of the action, though much with the worth of the agent.'

[3] G. E. Moore, *Ethics* (New York: Oxford University Press, 1912), 77–80.

[4] W. D. Ross, *The Right and the Good* (Oxford: Oxford University Press, 1930), 4–6, and *The Foundations of Ethics* (Oxford: Oxford University Press, 1939), ch. 6.

[5] Henry Sidgwick, *The Methods of Ethics*, 7th edn. (New York: Dover Publications, Inc., 1907), 201–4.

[6] See e.g. J. Hall, *General Principles of Criminal Law*, 2nd edn. (Indianapolis: Bobbs-Merrill, 1960), 88, and Glanville Williams, *Criminal Law: The General Part*, 2nd edn. (London: Stevens, 1961), 48–50. For a

in the law is not surprising when one considers that it is rooted in pre-theoretical, common-sense moral thinking. We are used to distinguishing *what* a person did from *why* she did it, sometimes issuing separate moral judgements about the act and its motive. Thus, we have occasion to say, for example, that so and so did the wrong thing (committed perjury), but her motive was good (to save a life).

Kant is also taken to have embraced the Independence Thesis, and those who attribute the thesis to Kant typically take the examples in the first chapter of the *Groundwork* (G. 4:397–9) as evidence of Kant's commitment to it. Ross, for example, writes:

Again, the doctrine is stated very explicitly by Kant, when near the beginning of the *Grundlegung* he distinguishes between doing what is your duty and acting from duty (i.e. from a sense of duty). He clearly implies that you can do the former even when your motive is a purely selfish one; and I believe that he consistently describes action from a sense of duty not as the only action that is right, but as the only action that has moral worth, thus making the motive (or, as he prefers to call it, the principle or maxim of action) the ground of moral goodness, but the nature of the action apart from its motive the ground of its rightness.[7]

Although Ross is mistaken in claiming that Kant explicitly embraces the Independence Thesis (he simply does not expressly say that one's motives are always irrelevant to every kind of duty), Kant does strongly suggest by his examples that the rightness of an act is independent of one's motives. (Think of the shopkeeper giving correct change and hence doing the right act, but from self-interested motives.)

My principal aim in this chapter is to examine the issue of how, if at all, motives bear on the rightness of acts in Kant's ethical system, with particular attention given to the various duties of virtue elaborated in the second part of *The Metaphysics of Morals*. There are two main reasons for engaging in this study, one having to do with our understanding of Kant's normative moral theory, the other having to do with moral theory generally.

First, there is some reason to think that, even if Kant's *Groundwork* treatment of motive and rightness commits him to the Independence Thesis, it is not so clear that his treatment of duties of virtue is consistent with this thesis. In order to fulfil a duty of virtue, one must, so it seems, have the right end, and

---

recent defence of this doctrine in the law, see Antony Duff, 'Principle and Contradiction in Criminal Law: Motives and Criminal Liability', in A. Duff (ed.), *Philosophy and the Criminal Law* (Cambridge: Cambridge University Press, 1998), 156–204.

  [7] Ross, *Foundations*, 139.

if having the right end requires being appropriately motivated, then we are led to agree with Marcia Baron in her contribution to this volume: 'In the *Groundwork*, conformity of the action with duty does not depend on the agent's motive or . . . on the agent's end. In *The Metaphysics of Morals*, this is true of juridical duties but not of ethical duties . . .'.[8]

But even in the *Groundwork* one finds some reason for doubting that Kant is committed in that work to the Independence Thesis. For instance, in Kant's suicide example in chapter 2, the maxim to be tested by the Categorical Imperative is: 'from self-love, I make it my principle to shorten my life when its longer duration threatens more troubles than it promises agreeableness' (*G.* 4:422).[9] Talk of acting *from self-love* seems to refer to one's motive in committing suicide, and this motive is crucially relevant in Kant's argument for the claim that the suicide maxim cannot be conceived of as a law of nature and hence that the action in question is morally wrong. In this example, the wrongness of the act is made to depend on one's motives.

The other main reason for examining this issue of the bearing of motive on rightness in Kant's ethical system is that the Independence Thesis has recently come under attack by philosophers who want to argue that motive does sometimes bear on an act's rightness.[10] If such attacks are cogent, then it is of some interest in judging the overall plausibility of Kant's ethics to get clear about Kant's considered position on this matter. And, of course, getting clear about this matter in Kant's ethics should have some bearing on the debate in contemporary ethics over the plausibility of the Independence Thesis.

In what follows, I will begin in Section I by clarifying the notions of rightness and motive featured in the Independence Thesis. Then, in Section II, I consider challenges to the idea that Kant's ethics respects the Independence Thesis based on the claim that fulfilling certain duties of virtue require that one's dutiful actions be motivated by the thought of duty. I argue against this claim by showing why the various considerations one might marshal in its favour are unpersuasive. In Section III, I go on to reinforce this result by

---

[8] Marcia Baron, this volume, 402.

[9] I have used the translation of Kant included in the Cambridge Edition of the Works of Immanuel Kant: *Groundwork of the Metaphysics of Morals*, ed. and trans. Mary Gregor (Cambridge: Cambridge University Press, 1997); *Critique of Practical Reason*, ed. and trans. Mary Gregor (Cambridge: Cambridge University Press, 1997); *The Metaphysics of Morals*, ed. and trans. Mary Gregor (Cambridge: Cambridge University Press, 1996).

[10] See e.g. Michael Stocker, 'Intentions and Act Evaluations', *Journal of Philosophy*, 67 (1970), 589–602; Steven Sverdlik, 'Motive and Rightness', *Ethics*, 106 (1996), 327–49; and Michael Gorr, 'Motives and Rightness', *Philosophia*, 27 (1999), 581–98. In Anglo-American law, the entrenched doctrine that motive is irrelevant to criminal liability has recently been challenged by Christine Sistare, 'Agent Motives and Criminal Law', *Social Theory and Practice*, 13 (1987), 303–26, and Douglas Husak, 'Motive and Criminal Liability', *Criminal Justice Ethics*, 8 (1989), 3–14.

appealing to various doctrinal and textual considerations. However, in Section IV, I argue that, although Kantian duties do not (with one possible exception) require that one act from the motive of duty, a case can be made for claiming that motives can be and are relevant to the rightness of actions. In the end, we get a mixed verdict regarding the Independence Thesis and Kant's ethical system: on the one hand, Ross is correct (and some recent interpreters of Kant are wrong) in thinking that in Kant's system the content of one's duties does not include a motive component; on the other hand, motive (including non-moral motives) can affect the rightness of one's actions, and so, strictly speaking, the Independence Thesis (as I interpret it) does not hold in relation to Kant's ethical system. Finally, in Section V, I ground matters regarding the relevance of motive to rightness in Kant's ethics in a general Kantian theory of moral relevance.

I. The Independence Thesis

So far, I have characterized the Independence Thesis (IT for short) as the claim that rightness is independent of motive; motive is irrelevant vis-à-vis the rightness of an act. However, this admittedly rough characterization needs clarification. For one thing, we need some understanding of both motive and rightness as these figure in the IT, and, for another, the thesis, as it is intended by its advocates, makes only a qualified claim about the bearing of motive on rightness. In this section, I first want to clarify talk of rightness and then work towards a proper formulation of the IT. The concept of motive involves various complications that I will deal with in the following section.

(*a*) Rightness and Deontic Evaluation Generally

In clarifying the notion of rightness operative in the IT, I shall restrict myself to two remarks. First, talk of rightness is shorthand for talk about the deontic status of actions. An action is either morally wrong (forbidden) or not, in which case it is morally right (permitted).[11] Within the category of morally right actions, we distinguish between actions that are morally obligatory and those that are not, the latter being morally optional (merely permitted). Thus, there are three basic deontic categories—the forbidden, the obligatory, and the optional—and we can consider the bearing of motive on an act falling into any

---

[11] Here, we are concerned with the all-things-considered deontic status of actions.

one of these categories. For instance, one possibility is that some instance of a morally wrong act is such that its wrongness depends partly on the agent's motive in performing it. Another possibility is that in some cases we are morally obliged to act from some particular motive, so that lacking a proper motive means that the act will fail to fulfil the obligation. Although Ross, in defending the IT, is mainly concerned to argue that our various obligations do not require that we act from some particular motive, we should understand the IT to be claiming that, whatever deontic status an action has, it has that status independently of the agent's motive.

The second remark about rightness (and the deontic categories generally) is that there are various notions of right (and wrong) action and we need to specify which of these are featured (or may be featured) in the IT. There are two sets of distinctions concerning right action that we need to consider: *formal rightness/material rightness* and *objective rightness/subjective rightness*. Let us take these up in order.

An act is formally right (in the sense of being obligatory) when, given the agent's (morally relevant) non-moral beliefs about the situation, the act is the right thing to do—the act in question is the right act to perform in situations that are such as the agent believes them to be. An act is materially right when it is formally right and the agent's non-moral beliefs about the situation are correct.[12] These two notions represent two perspectives one can take in evaluating the deontic status of actions. The notion of formal rightness represents a first-person point of view: what is relevant in judging the formal rightness of an act is the agent's intentions, which reflect her beliefs about what she is doing or plans to do. The notion of material rightness represents a third-person point of view from which the agent's intentions are not solely relevant. If you are in my care and it is my duty to give you a certain medicine, then, if I give you what I think is the prescribed medicine but through no fault of my own the substance in question is a lethal poison, I do what is formally right: I intend to give you your medicine. Despite my intentions, however, I poisoned you (accidentally, of course), and so my act, although formally right, was materially wrong.

The importance of this distinction in relation to Kant's ethics should be fairly obvious. The decision procedure associated with Kant's Universal Law Formula of the Categorical Imperative involves formulating one's maxim to test the rightness of one's action. But, as Kant points out, maxims may involve various sorts of mistakes in the agent's conception of what she is doing: 'A *maxim* is the subjective principle of acting . . . [and] contains the practical rule

---

[12] I take these distinctions from C. D. Broad, *Broad's Critical Essays in Moral Philosophy* (London: George Allen & Unwin Ltd., 1971), 76–8, 234–8.

determined by reason conformably with the conditions of the subject (often his ignorance or also his inclinations) . . .' (*G.* 4:422). Thus, as a decision procedure to guide one's choices, the universalization test can reliably lead to conclusions about the formal rightness of actions (though, of course, one is aiming to come to conclusions about the material rightness of the act). One might therefore conclude that Kant's ethical theory can only deliver judgements about the formal rightness and wrongness of actions, but I believe this would be a mistake. I have argued elsewhere[13] that Kant's theory does have the resources to generate conclusions about the material rightness of an act, a claim that I will simply take for granted. Thus, in examining the IT in relation to Kant's ethical views, we can consider the bearing of motive on both the formal and material rightness of actions. However, because nothing crucial relating to the topic at hand rests on whether we are viewing Kant's theory as yielding an account of formal rightness, material rightness, or both, I will continue to talk simply about the rightness and wrongness of actions in relation to Kant's ethical system.

In addition to the formal/material conceptions of rightness, philosophers often distinguish between objective and subjective rightness. The former notion is roughly equivalent to the notion of material rightness, but the latter notion is quite different from the notion of formal rightness. An act is *objectively right* if it really is right, independently of what the agent or anyone else might believe about its rightness; whereas an action is (in one sense) *subjectively right* (for a person to perform on some occasion) if the agent believes that the action is objectively right.[14] Formal rightness allows for mistakes in the agent's morally relevant non-moral beliefs; subjective rightness allows for mistakes in moral belief as well. Clearly, the IT is not concerned with the notion of subjective rightness since there are cases where it is obvious that one's motive affects the subjective rightness of an act: acting from the motive of duty requires that one believe that the act in question is objectively right, and so motive, at least in this sort of case, does affect the subjective rightness of the act.[15]

[13] See Mark Timmons, 'Decision Procedures, Moral Criteria, and the Problem of Relevant Descriptions in Kant's Ethics', *Jahrbuch für Recht und Ethik*, 5 (1997), 389–417.

[14] Here, I am borrowing from my 'Objective Rightness', in *The Cambridge Dictionary of Philosophy*, 2nd edn., ed. Robert Audi (Cambridge: Cambridge University Press, 1990), 624–5.

[15] This point is made by Sverdlik, 'Motive and Rightness', 334. Here is an appropriate place to acknowledge my indebtedness to this article in my thinking about the IT in relation to Kant's ethics.

(*b*) The Independence Thesis Formulated

I mentioned at the outset that the IT makes a qualified claim about the bearing of motive on rightness, and before proceeding it will be useful to explain the qualifications.

First, some duties may have as their content the adoption (in the sense of coming to have), development, or maintenance of some particular motive. It is plausible that one has duties of self-perfection, including a general duty to develop or strengthen some motivating characteristics such as kindliness, compassion, and so forth, and to rid oneself of, or at least control, other motives like revenge. Certainly we find such duties in Kant, both duties to others and duties to oneself. The duty of beneficence, for instance, involves developing a disposition to act in certain beneficial ways towards others that presumably involves coming to be motivated by a direct concern for their welfare. Again, one's duty of moral self-perfection according to Kant involves striving to make considerations of duty the sole and sufficient motive in fulfilling one's obligations (see *MS* 6:446–7). One might, therefore, restrict the IT so that it applies only to actions other than those having to do with motives. But the fact that some duties have motives as their content is not a challenge to the IT. Let me explain.

The main point to be made is that we can distinguish external and internal duties. External duties are duties that involve external acts like returning a borrowed object, while internal duties are duties to engage in some mental activity like developing certain attitudes or striving to develop certain motives.[16] The act of engaging in the fulfilment of both types of duty is (normally) something done for a reason—a reason that explains one's action in terms of some objective or goal that one is attempting to bring about through the action. Such reasons are motives (see below). Just as external acts can be performed from some motive, an internal act can also be performed from some motive. I may, for instance, succeed in developing a disposition of gratitude owing perhaps to my belief that being this way will be socially beneficial to me. Calculated self-interest motivates my endeavour to develop this particular trait. If we interpret the IT, as I think we should, as applying to both external and internal acts, then the claim is that what makes some act right (or wrong) does not depend on one's motive in performing that act.

However, there is one important aspect of the IT worth making explicit. The thesis does not make the sweeping claim that considerations of motive are never relevant to the deontic status of one's actions; rather, it claims that the

---

[16] The distinction is clearly made by Kant when, in distinguishing juridical from ethical duties, he writes that 'In all lawgiving (whether it prescribes internal or external actions . . .' (*MS* 6:218). See also *MS* 6:393.

deontic status of one's actions does not depend on *one's* motive in performing the act. It is plausible to claim that my having a duty of gratitude towards someone depends in part on facts about my benefactor's own motives in benefiting me. If my benefactor's motive is really calculated self-interest or even a deep hatred for me, then I have (in fact) no duty of gratitude towards that person (even if I do not know this and think I ought to show gratitude).[17] In this case, another person's motive is part of the external circumstances that are morally relevant in determining the deontic status of my action.

With these observations in mind, we can formulate the IT as follows:

> IT The deontic status of an act (whether internal or external) is independent of the agent's motive (or relevant motive set) in performing that act.[18]

So in thinking about the plausibility of the IT in general and also in relation to Kant's ethics, our main question is nicely stated by Steven Sverdlik: 'does the motive of an action ever suffice to move an action out of one of the three deontic categories and into another? Could a motive make an otherwise wrong act merely permissible? Could a motive make an act that is merely permissible into an obligatory one?'[19]

(c) Maxims, Intentions, and Motives

On Kant's moral theory, the morality of an action is determined by considering whether or not the maxim corresponding to the action is universalizable.[20] Maxims are mental states that arguably are, or involve, an agent's intention(s) with regard to the action under consideration. Expressions of maxims that we find in Kant's works vary in terms of what sort of information is included. Focusing for a moment on maxims of action, expressions of what we might call simple maxims have the form,

> I will ———, if/whenever ———,

where the blanks are to be filled with the agent's characterization of the action and circumstances respectively.

---

[17] This claim is defended by Fred Berger, 'Gratitude', *Ethics*, 85 (1975), 298–309.

[18] Two comments are in order here. First, the parenthetical remark about a relevant motive set is meant to recognize the fact that often one's actions are the product of a complicated set of motives. Secondly, we might also ask whether motive makes any difference to the so-called degree of deontic status, that is, whether motive affects the stringency of one's obligations or the degree of wrongness of an action, but I will ignore such possibilities here.

[19] Sverdlik, 'Motive and Rightness', 333.

[20] Much of this section is based on section 1 of my 'Evil and Imputation in Kant's Ethics', *Jahrbuch für Recht und Ethik*, 2 (1994), 113–41.

In *The Metaphysics of Morals*, Kant speaks of maxims of ends as distinct from maxims of actions (*MS* 6:395), and he claims that 'An *end* is an object of the choice (of a rational being), through the representation of which choice is determined to an action to bring this object about' (*MS* 6:381). Since, according to Kant, every action has an end (*MS* 6:385), we can express what we might call complex maxims this way,

I will ____, if/whenever ____, in order to ____,

where the first two blanks are filled as before and the third blank is a specification of an end, adopted or embraced by an agent and which she thinks is promoted by the action described in the maxim.[21] Complex maxims can be understood as resulting from compressed bits of practical reasoning on the agent's part, where the agent either explicitly or implicitly reasons from certain general aims or intentions to more specific intentions that she believes will help her carry out the more general ones. Looked at in this way, complex maxims of the above form can be usefully understood as a fusion of two maxims: a simple maxim of action plus a maxim of ends.

Since maxims are, or involve, an agent's intentions, and since one's intentions at least partly determine the identity of the action itself, they are relevant for evaluating the deontic status of actions. But this fact about Kant's view is not unique among competing moral theories; it has been generally thought, by advocates of competing types of moral theory, that deontic status depends on one's intentions. Intentions are thus commonly distinguished from motives and advocates of the IT accept the verdict we find in Sidgwick, where, after a brief discussion of the deontic relevance of intentions and motives, he remarks: 'our judgments of *right* and *wrong* strictly speaking relate to intentions, as distinguished from motives.'[22]

Things get messy, however, when we ask what motives are and how they are related to intentions. As a number of philosophers have pointed out, terms such as 'motive', 'intention', and 'purpose' are often used interchangeably in ordinary English. Even within the law, where there has been some attempt to define motive in relation to intention, one finds a variety of conflicting con-

---

[21] Unfortunately, this simple schema is misleading in suggesting that considerations of circumstance, act, and end can be neatly distinguished in all contexts of action. However, matters are far more complex. For instance, certain terms denoting one's action entail what D'Arcy calls 'constitutive circumstances'. To describe an action as theft entails, among other things, that the person did not own the item she took and that the owner had not given her permission to take or use it. See Eric D'Arcy, *Human Acts* (Oxford: Oxford University Press, 1963), chs. 1, 2. In general, as D'Arcy argues, the distinctions between act and circumstance and act and consequence are flexible and context sensitive.

[22] Sidgwick, *Methods*, 204. See also, Broad, *Critical Essays*, 78–81, and Mill, *Utilitarianism*, ch. 2 n. 2.

ceptions of motive.[23] Here is not the place to sort out the mess; rather I plan to make a few brief remarks about motives, particularly as they relate to Kantian maxims.

Motives are plausibly understood as psychological states (sometimes occurrent, sometimes not) that typically can serve as explanatory *sources* of action—serving to explain, in some deep or ultimate way, an agent's choices and action. They do so, in part, by revealing some goal or end that the agent finds attractive or desirable for its own sake and in terms of which the agent's interest in or attraction to some course of action can be explained.[24] For instance, if Andy is taking a logic course because he aims to get an undergraduate degree in philosophy (for which such a course is a requirement), one relatively immediate end of his action is the goal of earning a degree in philosophy. Suppose Andy's main reason for having this end is to please his parents and that he wants to please his parents to ensure that they leave him their fortune (even though he is already quite wealthy), and suppose further that his getting that money is something to which Andy has a direct, non-derivative attraction. Here, we have a (non-pejorative) rationalizing explanation (an explanation of the agent's action in terms of relevant aspects of his overall psychological set), involving a series of ends and terminating with an end that underlies the entire course of action and represents the agent's motive.[25]

In the case just described, Andy's basic motive is greed. We have a battery of common terms that are typically used to denote motives: ambition, gratitude,

[23] For an overview of differing conceptions of motive in the law, see Sistare, 'Agent Motives', 303–7, who distinguishes two main views: the intentions-as-affective-states view and the motives-as-intentions view. Although philosophers differ on whether or not motives are mental states, those who think they are typically advocate one of the two views just mentioned. Sverdlik, 'Motive and Rightness', 334–9, for instance, takes motives to be basic desires; M. Beardsley, 'Intention and Motive', in M. Bradie and M. Brand (eds.), *Action and Responsibility* (Bowling Green, OH: Applied Philosophy Program, 1980), 71–9, on the other hand, takes them to be ultimate intentions. (Of course, if one takes an intention to be a desire, as some have, then these two views collapse.) Note that, even if one accepts the motives-as-ultimate-intentions view, one has not thereby compromised the IT; the defender of that thesis will claim that certain intentions—those ultimate intentions that are one's motives—are not deontically relevant.

[24] Two comments are in order here. First, given the flexibility of motive talk in ordinary parlance, it is possible to distinguish between basic and non-basic motives where the latter do not directly involve intrinsic desires (though may be traceable to such desires). But, in distinguishing motives from intentions (as is commonly done in ethics and law), I am restricting the term in the way indicated. (I thank Robert Audi for pressing me on this point). Secondly, I am ignoring Anscombe's distinction between forward-looking motives that concern a further end of action on the agent's part and backward-looking motives that, strictly speaking, do not. But nothing important for our purposes turns on such differences. See Elizabeth Anscombe, *Intention*, 2nd edn. (Ithaca, NY: Cornell University Press, 1963), sect. 13.

[25] Note that motive explanations do not always serve as justifying reasons or even as considerations that the agent takes to justify some course of action. Lust may be the sole motive behind some adulterous act and hence helps explain what the person found attractive about some course of action and hence why he did it, even if he does not think that he is justified in what he has done.

lust, love, hatred, jealousy, and compassion, just to list a few. Such terms, when used to denote motives, indicate some end (for example, money or valuable goods) to which an individual has an attachment and which explains in some deep way the agent's behaviour.

We can understand how motives figure in Kant's theory of action if we understand both how they relate to maxims in patterns of rationalizing explanation and what sources they have.

The relation between motives and maxims is simply this: if motives are psychological states that represent ultimate ends of action for which one acts, and if, for Kant, having an end is a matter of adopting a maxim of ends (thus setting oneself to bring about some state of affairs that is the end), then, since maxims are intentions, it follows that motives are, for Kant, ultimate intentions.

Moreover, according to Kant's theory of action, such intentions have two main sources: desire and reason. Some motives (maxims expressing one's ultimate ends) are based on desire. The desire for one's own happiness is the basis for many ultimate ends one adopts. Here I think it is helpful to think of desires as prompting an agent to make certain choices—adopt certain maxims—rather than thinking of them as motives.[26] Whether some desire does in fact lead one to adopt some maxim depends upon whether the agent allows the desire to have such influence on choice.[27] In Kantian terminology, desires as such are (or perhaps reflect) incentives (*Triebfedern*) to action without necessarily being motives to action. By contrast, a rational or reason-based motive has its source, for Kant, in respect for the moral law that provides a rational incentive to action. In cases involving both desire-based motivation and reason-based motivation, then, a motive can be understood in Kant's system as a maxim of ends that serves as a terminus in a rationalizing explanation of an agent's choices and actions.

A motive as an end of action may thus be mentioned in the expression of an agent's maxim and will necessarily be mentioned when one is interested in giving a full and illuminating rationalizing explanation. One might express such a complex maxim, mentioning certain immediate ends as well as one's ultimate end as having the form,

I will ____, if/whenever ____, in order to ____, out of ____,

where the final blank mentions the agent's motive(s).

---

[26]   Defence of this claim would require developing it in the context of a full account of Kant's theory of action.

[27]   Here I have in mind the so-called incorporation thesis (as labelled by Allison): 'An incentive [empirical impulses including desires and aversions] can determine the will to an action *only insofar as the individual has taken it up into his maxim*' (R. 6:24).

We can now return to the IT and express it in Kantian terms:

KIT   In Kant's ethics, the deontic status of an act (whether internal or external) is independent of the agent's motive(s), that is, the agent's ultimate maxim(s) of ends.

The fact that a complex maxim revealing an agent's plan of action may include reference to an agent's motive does not automatically show that KIT is false; it depends on the question of whether reference to an agent's motive is deontically relevant, to which we now turn.

II. Obligatory Ends and the Motive Content Thesis

One way in which motive might be relevant to the deontic status of an act would be if certain duties involved performing actions from certain motives; if, that is, motive, together with some act, was part of the duty's content. Let us call this the Motive Content Thesis (MCT for short). In defending the IT, Ross was mainly concerned to argue against the MCT, and it is on this latter thesis that those who think that Kant is not committed to the IT tend to focus. Specifically, some interpreters argue that the IT fails to hold in connection with Kant's doctrine of obligatory ends as elaborated in the *Tugendlehre*, because fulfilling such obligations requires that one's motive be the motive of duty. In this section, I explore the plausibility of this claim, arguing that it should be rejected.

According to Kant's doctrine of obligatory ends, there are two fundamental obligatory ends: one's own perfection and the happiness of others. In connection with both of these general ends, Kant elaborates various subsidiary duties—some of them duties of commission (whose justification depends on the fact that these more specific requirements involve activities that are crucial in promoting and maintaining these most general ends) and some of them duties of omission (whose justification depends on the fact that certain actions, if performed, would destroy or hinder the promotion or maintenance of these ends). Some philosophers have claimed that adoption of the two most general obligatory ends, as well as the adoption of various more specific ends (that partly constitute the adoption of the most general ones), are cases where fulfilling the duty requires acting from duty and thus motive is relevant to deontic status in such cases.

One important implication of accepting the MCT in relation to Kant's ethics is that, given Kant's account of moral worth, the fulfilment of any such duty (that is, a duty to perform some action from the motive of duty) necessarily results in the relevant action's having moral worth.[28] That is, if there are some duties whose performance requires that we act from duty, then necessarily actions that have what Kant calls 'legality' (they fulfil one's duty) also possess 'morality' (they have moral worth).[29] Let us call this the Strong Thesis about moral worth. The MCT (together with Kant's account of moral worth) and the Strong Thesis about moral worth imply each other.

Certain ethical duties, then, are supposedly duties whose fulfilment requires that one act from duty; a moral motive is part of their very content and so necessarily actions that fulfil such duties have moral worth. This is what, in the quote above, Baron was suggesting, and we find it being explicitly advocated by O'Neill and Herman.[30] Let us consider this view in some detail.

(*a*) A Presumptive Case Against the Moral Content Thesis in Relation to Obligatory Ends

It will be useful to begin with a challenge to those who maintain that the MCT holds in connection with duties of virtue towards others. Since the duty of beneficence is often cited as an example in Kant where the thesis in question holds (and seems to be as plausible a candidate in relation to this thesis as any other duty in Kant's system), I will simply focus on it.

According to Kant, the general duty to make the happiness of others one's own end is explained as the requirement to adopt a maxim of beneficence—that is, 'making the well-being and happiness of others my *end*' (*MS* 6:452). According to the motive content interpretation of the duty of beneficence, fulfilling this duty involves: (1) adopting the end in question from the motive of duty and (2) on occasion performing specific acts of beneficence guided by one's commitment to the end. However, one can, it seems, adopt a maxim of beneficence for non-moral reasons: one might believe that one's own well-being is more likely to be promoted by adopting such ends, or one might be the kind

---

[28] Clearly, for Kant, the only motive that is a candidate for inclusion as part of the content of some duty is the motive of duty. For one thing, all other motives are desire based and on Kant's view we do not always possess the sort of control over our desires that would be required for them to be part of one's duty as the MCT requires. Additionally, were Kant to require that we fulfil this or that duty from some non-moral motive, then, in connection with that duty, it would not be possible to perform it in a morally worthy manner. But Kant holds that every dutiful action is capable of having moral worth. Thus, in considering the MCT in relation to Kant's ethics, we need address only the question of whether, in addition to performing some internal or external action, we must also act from the sole motive of duty.

[29] Here, I am appealing to the legality/morality distinction, as Kant draws it at *KpV* 5:81. See n. 32 for more on this distinction.

[30] Onora O'Neill (formerly Nell), *Acting on Principle* (New York: Columbia University Press, 1975), chs. 4–6, and Barbara Herman, *The Practice of Moral Judgment* (Cambridge, MA: Harvard University Press), 15, 34, 186.

of person Kant describes as a philanthropist, 'Someone who finds satisfaction in the well-being (*salus*) of human beings considered simply as human beings, for whom it is well when things go *well* for every other' (*MS* 6:450). If so, then the MCT fails to hold in connection with the duty of beneficence: one can fulfil the obligation to adopt the well-being of others as an end, yet one's motive need not be the motive of duty. This conclusion is reinforced by what Kant says about the ethical duty of commission one has to oneself to develop one's natural talents, 'And it is not merely that technically practical reason *counsels* him to do this as a means to his further purposes (or art); morally practical reason *commands* it absolutely and makes this end his duty' (*MS* 6:387). Here, Kant is apparently allowing that one might adopt this end of self-perfection for prudential reasons rather than moral ones, and so (by implication) he is allowing that one can distinguish between cases in which the duty is fulfilled (and one's adoption of the relevant end fulfils a duty), and cases where the end is adopted from duty, in which case one's action has moral worth.

There is one ethical duty that may be an exception. Moral perfection, according to Kant, 'consists subjectively in the *purity* (*puritas moralis*) of one's disposition to duty, namely, in the law being by itself alone the incentive, even without admixture of aims derived from sensibility, and in actions being done not only in conformity with duty but also *from duty*' (*MS* 6:446). Kant goes on to explain that our duty here is to strive to make the moral law one's sole and sufficient motive (in contexts of duty). But whether the duty is to act successfully from the motive of duty or only to strive to do so, we have here an apparent case in which the motive of duty is part of the content of a duty of perfection to oneself. We can grant this, however, since the interesting cases, about which there is some dispute, are all the other ethical duties featured in Kant's *Tugendlehre*.[31]

In general, then, the case for denying the MCT in relation to ethical duties is simply that such duties, although they require that we adopt general ends of action, can be fulfilled by adopting them from non-moral motives; moral rightness and moral worth thus do not collapse in connection with such duties. The burden is therefore on anyone who would deny this claim.

(*b*) Attempts to Rebut the Presumption

There are two main types of reasons to which one might appeal in an attempt to rebut the presumption against the motive content interpretation of the duty

---

[31] Michael Gorr and Thomas Pogge have suggested to me that perhaps we should not interpret Kant's duty of moral self-perfection as having the motive of duty as part of its content. After all, the duty to perfect myself morally is the duty to bring it about in the future that I act from the sole motive of duty (or at least make it the case that I strive to do so) when duty calls, and I might best promote this end by, say, reading various novels, though, of course, I need not read them from the sole motive of duty.

of beneficence and other Kantian *Tugendlehre* duties: doctrinal reasons and conceptual reasons. Reasons of the former type appeal to various doctrines in Kant's moral philosophy; reasons of the latter type proceed from narrowly conceptual considerations having to do with the virtue concepts that figure in the *Tugendlehre* system of duties. Let us proceed to consider various specific arguments in defence of the MCT (and hence against the IT) falling under these two broad headings.

(i) Doctrinal reasons

There are at least three specific doctrinal considerations that one might be tempted to use in an effort to argue that the MCT holds in connection with certain duties of virtue: (1) Kant's way of distinguishing between juridical duties and ethical duties that make up respectively the *Rechtslehre* and the *Tugendlehre*; (2) Kant's claim that actions that fulfil duties of virtue are meritorious; and (3) the fact that the *Tugendlehre*, as the very title indicates, concerns duties of virtue. Let us consider these in order.

(1)   In the general introduction to *The Metaphysics of Morals*, Kant explains the division between juridical and ethical duties in terms of two types of lawgiving: external and internal. All lawgiving involves, according to Kant, both a law, which specifies the action that is obligatory (the duty), and an incentive, which, he writes, 'connects a ground for determining choice to this action *subjectively* with the representation of the law' (*MS* 6:218). Kant summarizes the differences between these two types of lawgiving as follows:

All lawgiving can therefore be distinguished with respect to the incentive (even if it agrees with another kind with respect to the action that makes it a duty, e.g., these actions might in all cases be external). That lawgiving which makes an action a duty and also makes this duty the incentive is *ethical*. But that lawgiving which does not include the incentive of duty in the law and so admits an incentive other than the idea of duty itself is *juridical*.   (*MS* 6:218–19)

Passages like this in which Kant either implies (as in this passage) or mentions the incentive of duty being 'included' in the law might be read as claiming that ethical duties have as part of their content (part of what is required) that one perform some action (external or internal) from the sole motive of duty.[32]

But I think there is another, more plausible reading of Kant's views about juridical versus ethical lawgiving that has no such implication. Briefly put, I read Kant's remarks about two types of lawgiving as having to do first of all

---

[32]   In chapter 17, this volume, Baron claims that there is good evidence that ethical duties require that one fulfil them from duty and cites passages at *MS* 6:214, 216, and 220–1 as passages supporting this contention.

with a certain precondition on some action's being a duty at all (moral obligation requires some incentive to perform the required act) and second of all
with two types of incentives that provide the basis for distinguishing two main
types of duties. But such views about the nature and types of obligation do not
entail anything in particular about the content of ethical as compared to juridical duties and so do not entail the idea that to fulfil certain ethical duties
requires (as part of the duty) that one must act from the sole motive of duty.
Let me explain.

We can usefully distinguish between (1) questions about the preconditions
for moral obligation, (2) questions about the particular grounds of various specific obligations, and (3) questions about the content of one's obligations.
Questions of the second sort concern the considerations that determine one's
duties—considerations that, according to the IT, exclude one's motives—while
questions of the third variety concern the very content of one's obligations—
content that, according to the MCT, sometimes includes motives.

However, questions of the first sort include questions about what must be
true of agents in general if they are the type of creature susceptible to moral
obligation at all. Though I cannot argue the case here, Kant is plausibly interpreted as embracing some form of ethical internalism—the metaethical thesis
according to which (roughly), for an individual to be morally obligated, it
must be true of her that she has sufficient reason for acting accordingly.[33] To
relate this to Kant's views, the idea is that all moral obligation necessarily
involves the agent having some sufficient reason (some sufficient incentive
(*Triebfeder*)) for performing the act in question, where talk of reasons here
involves both normative reasons for action and motivating reasons for action.
The basic idea is that in order for an individual to be morally required to perform some action, it must be true of the agent that (1) there is an all-things-
considered good normative reason for her to perform the action in question,
which (2) is motivationally available to her. In the case of all duties then—both
juridical and ethical—there must be some sufficient reason available to the
agent in relation to the duty in question, and, since duties are not based on
pathological incentives (desires and aversions), the thought of duty must be
available as an incentive. Thus, Kant remarks in relation to juridical duties
(which, unlike ethical duties, are not expounded in terms of the incentive of
duty): 'All that ethics teaches is that if the incentive which juridical lawgiving
connects with that duty, namely external constraint, were absent, the idea of
duty itself would be sufficient as an incentive' (*MS* 6:220).

---

[33] Internalist readings of Kant can be found in Thomas Nagel, *The Possibility of Altruism* (Oxford:
Oxford University Press, 1970), ch. 2, and Mark Timmons, 'Kant and the Possibility of Moral Motivation',
Southern Journal of Philosophy, 23 (1985), 377–98.

What is potentially misleading in the passage quoted above is Kant's talk of a kind of lawgiving that 'makes duty the incentive'. I do not think we should read this as saying that acting from duty is part of the content of ethical duties. To explain why not, let us consider Kant's characterization of lawgiving in general, keeping in mind my remarks about Kant's internalism.

At the beginning of the general introduction to *The Metaphysics of Morals*, entitled 'On the Division of a Metaphysics of Morals', Kant gives us his generic characterization of lawgiving:

> In all lawgiving (whether it prescribes internal or external actions, and whether it prescribes them *a priori* by reason alone or by the choice of another) there are two elements: **first**, a law, which represents an action that is to be done as *objectively* necessary, that is, which makes the action a duty; and **second**, an incentive, which connects a ground for determining choice to this action *subjectively* with the representation of law. Hence the second element is this: that the law makes duty the incentive.   (*MS* 6:218)

Notice two things here. In the parenthetical remark, talk about lawgiving prescribing actions either a priori or by the choice of another (which is the basis of the distinction between ethical and juridical lawgiving respectively) has to do with the basis of the law—whether it sets forth the act as rationally required or as required at the bidding of some external authority. It does not have to do with the content of what is required. Note also the manner in which Kant generically describes the incentive element in all lawgiving: law making duty the incentive. Law makes duty the incentive, not by making the motive of duty part of the content of the duty, but by connecting an action with a kind of (available) sufficient reason for action.

Now, although all duties must be appropriately related to the incentive of duty in the manner just explained, certain duties can also be represented in relation to what Kant calls external incentives—incentives for compliance that involve the threat of legal punishment and that therefore appeal to one's aversions. This class of duties composes the category of juridical duties that are elaborated in the *Rechtslehre*. Other duties, however—those featured in the *Tugendlehre*—cannot by their very nature be so represented; for them, the incentive that provides the relevant connection between the action or omission required and the agent's choice is the moral law itself. The latter is the kind of lawgiving that, in Kant's words, 'makes an action a duty and also makes this duty the incentive'.

So I maintain that we should read these passages as addressing an important question about the precondition of obligation in which Kant is committing himself to some form of ethical internalism. Notice further that the metaethical thesis of internalism is logically independent of the issue of motive and rightness with which we are concerned. Internalism makes a claim about the conditions of moral obligation and does not entail anything either about the specific sorts of considerations that determine one's obligations (type 2 questions) or about the contents of one's obligations (type 3 questions). Thus, even if it is true, on Kant's view, that all ethical lawgiving (obligation) necessarily involves having a reason sufficient to motivate the agent, and even if the incentive in question must be the thought of duty, it does not follow that the contents of one's duties (what one is required to do) is to act from duty. I conclude that Kant's remarks in 'On the Division of a Metaphysics of Morals' do not support the MCT in relation to ethical duties.

There is another passage in the general introduction to *The Metaphysics of Morals* that might be thought to support the MCT in relation to Kant's ethical duties. Kant writes:

As directed merely to external actions and their conformity to law [moral laws] are called *juridical* laws; but if they also require that they (the laws) themselves be the determining grounds of actions, they are *ethical* laws, and then one says that conformity with juridical laws is the *legality* of an action and conformity with ethical laws is its *morality*. (*MS* 6:214)

Now in the *Critique of Practical Reason* at *KpV* 5:81, Kant distinguishes between the legality and the morality of actions in terms of moral motivation: an act has legality just in case it conforms to the moral law; it has morality if it not only conforms to the moral law but is done from the motive of duty. The passage just quoted from *MS* 6:214 thus seems to be saying that ethical duties involve as part of their content the motive of duty, since only if they do have such content does it follow that conformity with them involves not just legality but morality as well. However, it is not clear that Kant uses the legal/moral distinction univocally throughout his works. As Marcus Willaschek has pointed out, in *The Metaphysics of Morals*, Kant seems to draw the legal/moral distinction not in terms of one's motive but simply in terms of the type of law to which one's action conforms.[34] So perhaps the passage does not so clearly support the MCT in relation to Kant's ethical duties after all. In any case, I think passages like the one in question here (if taken to support the MCT) ought to be balanced against the kinds of considerations I bring forth against the MCT.

---

[34]   Marcus Willaschek, 'Why the *Doctrine of Right* does not belong in the *Metaphysics of Morals*', *Jahrbuch für Recht und Ethik*, 5 (1997), 209–10. (See *MS* 6:225 for a passage where it seems especially clear that the legality/morality distinction is not being drawn in terms of motive.)

(2) Kant claims that actions that fulfil duties of virtue are meritorious (*MS* 6:390).[35] If we assume that the concepts of moral merit and moral worth are, for Kant, identical, or at least that an act's being meritorious entails its having moral worth, then it follows that actions that fulfil duties of virtue have moral worth. Since moral worth is a matter of acting from the sense of duty, we are led to embrace the Strong Thesis about moral worth: fulfilling duties of virtue necessarily involves acting from duty. And, if we accept this thesis, we are (as noted above) committed to the view that the MCT holds in relation to them and consequently that the IT does not.[36]

I think this argument can be disposed of in fairly short order. Robert Johnson[37] has convincingly argued that Kant's notions of moral merit and moral worth are not identical, and that actions can be meritorious without having moral worth. Here, for brevity's sake, I will simply summarize some of the main results Johnson reaches about moral merit, referring the interested reader to his article.

Kant's characterization of a meritorious action has two parts, the first concerning an action's possessing merit, the second concerning degrees of merit: (1) 'If someone does *more* in the way of duty than he can be constrained by law to do, what he does is *meritorious* (*meritum*)' (*MS* 6:228); (2) 'The greater the natural obstacles (of sensibility) and the less the moral obstacle (of duty), so much the more merit' (*MS* 6:228). Regarding the possession of merit, then, the crucial idea is that meritorious actions cannot be coerced by law—in relation to them coercion is not possible. Johnson points out that ethical duties that require the adoption of some end qualify as meritorious since it is not *physically possible* for someone to be coerced into adopting an end, while ethical duties whose fulfilment involve specific actions or omissions qualify as meritorious (when they reflect the pursuit of an obligatory end), since coercion is not *morally possible* (that is, permitted) in regard to them. As Johnson remarks: 'the rationale for judgments of merit is grounded in the reasonable idea that the merit of such actions should be attributed to the agent's own initiative (rather, than, say the prospect of punishment).'[38] In this way, then, the various ethical duties featured in the *Tugendlehre* differ from the juridical duties featured in the *Rechtslehre*; fulfilling duties of the former sort are necessarily meritorious.

---

[35]   In his *Lectures on Ethics*, Kant writes, 'in the observance of ethical laws, every action is a *meritum* . . .' (Col. 27:290; see also Vig. 27:561).

[36]   O'Neill (Nell), *Acting on Principle*, 50, n. 23, makes the assumption in question.

[37]   Robert Johnson, 'Kant's Conception of Merit', *Pacific Philosophical Quarterly*, 77 (1996), 310–34.

[38]   Ibid. 318.

Note that this characterization of merit in terms of objects of possible coercion does not entail anything in particular about one's motivation in performing such meritorious actions. So, it would seem that actions fulfilling ethical duties can possess merit even if they are not done from the motive of duty. Moreover, this conclusion is supported by the fact that ascriptions of merit and of worth relate to distinct evaluative purposes—ascriptions of the former sort serve the purpose of assigning praise and blame to agents, ascriptions of the latter sort serve the purpose of judging one's own level of moral perfection. If we follow Johnson on this matter, appealing to the Kantian doctrine that fulfilling ethical duties is necessarily meritorious does not provide straightforward support for the MCT and hence against the IT, as some have thought.

(3) The duties featured in the second half of *The Metaphysics of Morals* are called duties of virtue, hence the title of the section, *Metaphysische Anfangsgründe der Tugendlehre*. Moral virtue, for Kant, is 'the moral strength of a *human being's* will in fulfilling his *duty . . .*' (*MS* 6:405). The moral strength in question is just the thought of one's duty being a sole and sufficient motive in fulfilling one's duties, and so one might conclude that fulfilling the various duties of virtue requires that one act from duty.

The immediate problem with this argument is that one can, reminiscent of Aristotle, distinguish between acting virtuously and virtuous action. Actions of the former sort are actions that spring from whatever motives confer moral worth on an agent and her action, and are definitive of having a morally virtuous character. However, actions of the latter sort involve only, in the words of Sidgwick, 'a settled resolve to will a certain kind of external effects',[39] where questions about any motives underlying such a resolve or disposition are not directly relevant. Unless we find in Kant some reason to suppose that he does not or cannot allow this distinction, then we should not suppose that fulfilling duties of virtue requires acting from the motive of duty.[40]

However, this is not the end of the matter. It may be that, if we examine some of the various specific duties of virtue (particularly the main duties of commission such as beneficence and gratitude falling under the obligatory end of others' happiness), we may find that Kant's concepts of beneficence, gratitude, and perhaps other duties as well require that actions fulfilling them spring ultimately from the motive of duty. This thought brings us to what I am calling conceptual reasons for thinking that the MCT holds in connection

---

[39] Sidgwick, *Methods*, 224.

[40] Kant warns against the 'practice of virtue' becoming a mere habit instead of being guided by principles (*MS* 6:409). This suggests that there is room in Kant to distinguish an act of virtue from a virtuous act.

with certain *Tugendlehre* duties and that consequently the IT does not hold for Kant. Let us examine this matter.

(ii) Conceptual reasons

The suggestion under consideration is that, owing to the very concept of the duty in question, certain ethical duties cannot be fulfilled unless one acts from duty. Not all Kantian ethical duties are plausible candidates in support of this suggestion. The concepts that refer to Kant's duties to oneself—both duties of omission (suicide, sexual defilement, intemperance) and duties of commission (duties to develop one's various powers and capacities[41])—do not entail anything in particular about one's motive in fulfilling them. One can and often does conform to, and thus fulfil, these various duties for purely prudential reasons. It is in connection with duties to others that the suggestion in question might be thought to hold.

Kant divides duties to others into duties of love and duties of respect. In connection with duties of respect, Kant lists three main negative duties: duties to refrain from being arrogant, from engaging in defamation, and from being malicious. Whether we focus on these duties as they relate to one's character or as they relate to specific actions, I see no reason to suppose that refraining from such vices and the activities to which they lead require that one be motivated by the thought of duty. One might simply be averse to such actions and the associated vices or one might avoid such things out of calculated self-interest.

In connection with duties of love, Kant specifies three main duties of commission: duties of beneficence, gratitude, and sympathetic joy. We can think of these duties as requiring that we become beneficent, grateful, and sympathetic people—that is, that we develop certain traits of character—and that we act out of these traits by performing acts of beneficence, gratitude, and sympathy in appropriate circumstances on at least some occasions. But what, for example, is involved in having a truly beneficent disposition and, consequently, what is it to perform a truly beneficent act? Consider how Barbara Herman characterizes a truly beneficent act:

There are also certain kinds of action that cannot be done at all unless done from the motive of duty (as a primary motive). For example, not every act of bringing aid is a beneficent act. It is beneficent only if the agent conceives of what he is doing as an instance of what *any* moral agent is required to do when he can help another, and acts to help for that reason. For Kant, only the motive of duty could prompt someone to act

---

[41]   Excluding, of course, the duty of moral perfection mentioned above.

on a maxim with such content—for no other motive responds to a conception of action that regards the agent himself as impersonally or is impartial in its application.[42]

Hence, on this reading, at least in connection with one of the primary duties of love, the MCT holds and hence the Kantian ethical system is incompatible with the IT.

Here is an initial response. One can agree that not every helping act counts as an act of beneficence. If I offer you my assistance, but my immediate aim is to help you along so that I can set you up for a terrible fate, my underlying motive of malice rules out my helping action as one of beneficence. The idea here is that beneficence involves both an external aspect (helping actions) and an internal aspect (one's state of mind). However, granting this, it is a further step to claim that genuine acts of beneficence require the specific motive of acting from duty. In the *Groundwork* (*G.* 4:398–9), Kant describes the naturally sympathetic person who takes immediate delight in the well-being of others— he calls the actions of this sort of person acts of beneficence. Moreover, an individual might reason to the conclusion that beneficence pays (at least in the long run) and adopt the end of beneficence for self-interested reasons. In both cases, so it seems, we have individuals who adopt the well-being of others as their end and act accordingly. In the light of such cases, then, the MCT does not hold in connection with the duty of beneficence and Herman's characterization of this duty in Kant is mistaken.

However, this reply is too quick because it fails to consider two important elements in Kant's duty of beneficence. First, there are passages where Kant seems to require that genuine beneficence be non-selfish in the sense that to be a person who is disposed to help others out of calculated self-interest does not satisfy the relevant duty. 'To be beneficent, that is, to promote according to one's means the happiness of others in need, *without hoping for something in return*, is everyone's duty' (*MS* 6:453; emphasis added). This emphasized restriction apparently rules out our calculating egoist. Moreover, Kant describes our obligation of beneficence as the duty to promote the *morally legitimate* ends of others. 'The duty of love for one's neighbor can, accordingly, also be expressed as the duty to make others' *ends* my own (provided only that these are not immoral)' (*MS* 6:450). The qualification is important. It is *morally constrained* beneficence that it is our obligation to adopt as an end. This feature of the duty of beneficence seems to rule out the naturally kind-hearted person whose helping acts are non-selfish but who simply responds directly and unrestrictedly to the plight of others. So, the duty of beneficence we find

---

[42]   Herman, *Practice*, 15. See also p. 34.

in Kant's writings is the duty non-selfishly to adopt the well-being of others constrained by moral considerations. Perhaps, then, Herman is correct and we ought to conclude that the MCT does apply to some of Kant's duties.

Still, I resist this conclusion. It seems to me that even in the case of Kantian beneficence (with the two qualifications just described) one can distinguish the dutifulness of adopting beneficence as an end (and performing beneficent acts) from doing so in a way that has moral worth. If so, then we are not committed to the MCT in relation to this duty.

Consider Mr Hidebound Altruist. Like the man of natural sympathy Kant describes, he has the well-being of others as an end, not from calculated self-interest, but from a natural liking for others. He is also very selective in how he promotes the well-being of others. He believes that one is more likely to promote the well-being of others if one operates within the bounds of duty. It is not that he is committed to duty and for that reason restricts his benevolence accordingly; rather his controlling motive is others' well-being. Mr H.A. performs genuine acts of beneficence, flowing as they do from having beneficence as an end, but he is not acting from duty. Relating this example to Herman's remarks: she characterizes the truly beneficent person as someone who (1) must conceive of her helping acts as an instance of what anyone should do, and (2) acts to help for that reason.[43] What my example challenges is the second of her claims. Mr H.A. acts in recognition of the fact that what he is doing is what duty calls for, but he does not act from duty. Since my example seems to capture Kant's concept of beneficence, I conclude that this concept does not entail acting from the motive of duty. Further, since none of the other concepts associated with the *Tugendlehre* duties seems to entail acting from duty (with the one exception already noted), these duties, too, should not be interpreted according to the MCT.[44]

Let me conclude this section by raising an issue about moral worth that I have been putting off. The issue concerns the fact that there are two ways in which moral considerations might play a motivational role in the overall psychological economy of an agent, and do so in a way that confers moral worth. As a *primary motive*, the thought of duty (of some action's being morally

[43] It is interesting to consider O'Neill's (Nell's) characterization of fulfilling the duties of beneficence and perfecting oneself. On p. 106 of *Acting on Principle*, she raises the question of 'why should acts done to treat other rational natures as ends, to perfect ourselves, or to make others happy, be considered morally worthy' (and thus done from the motive of duty). Her response (as I understand it) is that 'Morally worthy acts need only strive for objective ends in the knowledge that they are such ends' (p. 111). But this characterization simply incorporates the first of Herman's requirements, which is arguably too weak as an account of Kantian moral worth, as my example shows.

[44] Obviously I cannot stop here to defend this claim in detail; I offer it as a challenge to anyone who would suppose otherwise.

required) motivates one to act accordingly. However, Herman and Baron have
noted the importance of moral considerations playing a limiting, regulative
function.[45] As an effective *limiting* motive, the motive of duty has as its object
that the agent act only in morally permissible ways. Roughly, it operates like
this. In cases where the agent takes what she is doing to be permissible, whatever original motive is behind the act serves as the primary motive. In cases
where the agent believes that the action is impermissible, the moral motive
interferes with the performance of the act in question. Now, to this point I
have not explicitly distinguished between these two models of moral motivation, and one might wonder whether fulfilling the duty of beneficence (and
possibly other Kantian duties) might be such that necessarily the motive of
duty functions in a limiting role and thus, after all, that, in fulfilling the duty
in question, one is necessarily motivated by the thought of duty.[46]

The short answer to this query (which is enough for our purposes) is negative—fulfilling the duty of beneficence does not require that the thought of
duty play a limiting role. This can be seen if we go back to the case of Mr Hidebound Altruist. I described the case as one in which there is a lack of the kind
of moral commitment that must be present if the thought of duty is to play the
sort of limiting role that is needed for an action's having moral worth. Mr H.A.
is not committed to duty for the sake of duty and so is not committed in the
right way for it to be the case that his brand of constrained benevolence counts
as being done from duty. It is beyond the scope of this chapter to sort out the
difference between cases in which one's commitment to staying within the
bounds of duty expresses genuine moral commitment of the sort needed for
moral worth, and cases in which this is not so.[47] However, it is reasonably clear
from my example that beneficence does not require having the motive of duty
as a limiting motive in the right way to confer moral worth.

I conclude that the presumption against interpreting Kant's system of ethical duties as involving the motive content thesis has not been overturned by
any of the doctrinal or conceptual considerations we have been examining.

---

[45] See Barbara Herman, 'On the Value of Acting From the Motive of Duty', reprinted in her *Practice*;
and also her 'Motives', in *Encyclopedia of Ethics*, 2nd edn. vol. ii, L. Becker and C. B. Becker (eds.) (New York
and London: Routledge, 2001), 1185–8; and Marcia W. Baron, *Kantian Ethics Almost without Apology*
(Ithaca, NY: Cornell University Press, 1995), chs. 4–5.

[46] This is not how Herman is thinking of moral motivation in connection with beneficence; she is
explicit in the quoted passage about the duty motive operating as primary motive.

[47] I believe this point about the kind of commitment comes out in Baron, *Kantian Ethics*, 140–1 n. 22,
where she explains that the kind of moral commitment implicated in moral worth involves a complex set of
manifestations that signify a genuine commitment to morality, and not just (as in my example) a commitment contingent on certain beliefs about the value of acting dutifully vis-à-vis some other end.

III. Bolstering the Presumptive Case

In arguing that we should reject the MCT, I have been swimming against a certain current of recent Kant interpretation. Let me now reinforce what I have been saying by offering a few additional reasons for rejecting that thesis.

First, if we accept the MCT, Kant's ethical theory is impoverished. We expect a plausible ethical theory to be able to make sense of various kinds of moral evaluations that reflect our various purposes. As mentioned at the outset, common-sense moral thinking does distinguish between the deontic status of what one does and the morality of the agent. In connection with the duty of beneficence, we can and do distinguish between what a person does in helping someone and her motives for doing so, and think that such actions (unless done from some evil motive) are dutiful or at least morally right. The same goes for the other duties featured in Kant's ethical system. Kant's moral theory loses its capacity to make such moral judgements if we tie the duty of beneficence to the motive of duty and then claim that one fulfils the duty only if done from that motive. Moreover, even were it true that the texts bear out this restricted reading, I see no reason why Kant's ethical theory lacks the resources for distinguishing between the rightness of an ethical duty and its moral worth.

Secondly, Kant formulates the fundamental moral principle of the *Tugendlehre* as follows: 'act in accordance with a maxim of *ends* that it can be a universal law for everyone to have' (*MS* 6:395), and he uses the universalization test associated with this version of the Categorical Imperative to derive the duty of beneficence. Kant formulates the maxim of ends to be tested as 'to make others' *ends* my own (provided only that these are not immoral)' (*MS* 6:450). Notice that there is no mention of one's motive in this maxim. Moreover, from the argument for the claim that adopting such a maxim is a duty that we find in the *Tugendlehre* at *MS* 6:393 and *MS* 6:451, it does not appear that the conclusion he derives specifies acting from duty as part of the duty of beneficence. Furthermore, when one examines Kant's arguments for the various other duties that compose the *Tugendlehre* system (where he consistently appeals to the Humanity formulation of the Categorical Imperative), we do not find him drawing moral conclusions that involve acting from duty as a component.[48] The argument he uses, for instance, to conclude that suicide is wrong is that it amounts to 'debasing humanity in one's person' (*MS* 6:423), while he argues that respectful treatment of others is a duty because failure to

---

[48] With, of course, one notable but (as explained in n. 31) apparent exception: the duty to make the motive of duty one's sole and sufficient motive.

do so violates a 'dignity (*dignitas*) in other human beings' (*MS* 6:462). These arguments make perfect sense as arguments for omitting or performing such actions, even if one's ultimate intention is other than acting from duty. This strikes me as good reason for being suspicious of the MCT in connection with Kant's system of duties.

Thirdly, throughout the *Tugendlehre*, Kant has two related projects going: he is concerned not only with setting out a system of duties that cannot be externally coerced, but he is also concerned with moral character and its proper development. Because he is interested in moral character and its development, Kant remarks in the Preface that, in teaching ethics, 'the kind of incentive by which, as means, one is led to a good purpose (that of fulfilling every duty) is not a matter of indifference' (*MS* 6:377). So, throughout the *Tugendlehre* we find some emphasis given to the proper incentive that is to play a large part in the teaching and inculcating of the virtues. Now, for the ideally virtuous person, the sorts of duties featured in Kant's system are complied with out of the sort of motivation characteristic of genuine virtue—the motive of duty. Moral education ought to aim at cultivating this motive. Of course, among the various duties to oneself is the duty to strive to make the moral law one's sole and sufficient motive (in contexts where duty calls). In one place, Kant refers to what he calls the universal ethical duty as the requirement to 'act in conformity with duty *from* duty' (*MS* 6:391). But the fact that the virtuous person would act in this way, and that the rest of us ought to strive toward this kind of ideal, does not mean that fulfilling duties of virtue requires that one act from duty. Another way to put the point is this. From Kant's universal ethical duty, we ought to strive to be the sort of person who fulfils her or his duties from the motive of duty. Thus, we ought to be beneficent from duty, we ought to be grateful from duty, and so on with respect to all of the various ethical duties. Proper moral development depends crucially on coming to recognize the rational authority of considerations of duty and striving to make duty one's sole and sufficient motive (in contexts of duty).

But, important as this is for proper moral education and development, what Kant has to say about such matters does not entail that, in order to fulfil say, the duty of beneficence, we must have acted from duty: we need to distinguish fulfilling the duty in question *qua the duty of beneficence* and fulfilling the more general duty of acting from duty. We can fulfil the former without fulfilling the latter.

If we are mindful of the fact that in the *Tugendlehre* Kant is simultaneously setting forth a system of duties as well as addressing issues of character and development, and if we are also mindful of how these projects are related in this work, we will be less likely to read various of Kant's remarks as supporting the MCT.

Finally, having considered some of the alleged textual evidence in favour of the MCT, let me now offer one bit of textual support for the denial of this thesis. As we have noted, if Kant did hold the MCT, then he would be committed to the Strong Thesis about moral worth and consequently would not be able to draw the legality/morality distinction between actions the performance of which merely fulfil a duty and those which, in addition, are done from the sole motive of duty and hence indicate moral worth. However, in the Introduction to the *Tugendlehre* (*MS* 6:398), Kant presents a chart that he calls a 'schema' of duties of virtue viewed in accordance with the principles he has been setting forth. One major division represented in the chart is between 'What is Material in Duties of Virtue' and 'What is Formal in Duties of Virtue'. He mentions one's own perfection and the happiness of others as what is material in duties of virtue (that is, what is required). What is especially interesting for our concerns is that, with regard to what is formal in duties of virtue (that is, concerning possible reasons for action), Kant mentions both 'the law which is also the incentive on which the *morality* of every free determination of the will is based' and 'the *end* which is also the incentive on which the *legality* of every free determination of the will is based' (*MS* 6:398). Unfortunately, Kant does not comment on the chart and its distinctions. However, the distinction within the formal aspect of duties of virtue between legality and morality make perfect sense on my interpretation of fulfilling such duties, but it does not make sense if one interprets these duties according to the MCT.

I conclude that, on balance, we should interpret the duties of virtue so that the legality/morality distinction can be made, which, of course, means that we should reject the MCT.

IV. The Relevance of Motive to Rightness in Kant's Ethical System

Even if we reject the MCT, we have not thereby completely vindicated the IT in relation to Kant's ethical system. In fact, I want to show that Kant's moral theory is committed to the denial of the IT, indicating in this section *how* motives can be relevant to the deontic status of an action in Kant's ethical system. In the following section, I explain *why* they can have such relevance.

But, before proceeding, it may help the reader digest the interpretation of Kant I am defending if we pause for a moment and consider how my view is situated vis-à-vis its competitors that I have been criticizing. The main theses involved are the MCT and the IT (as they relate to Kant's ethics). Since the two theses are apparently incompatible,[49] there remain three possible stances one might embrace regarding them. Fig. 11.1 is a visual aid summarizing the three stances. Ross, as we have seen, claims that Kant accepts the IT, which would mean that Kant must deny the MCT. Recent Kantians such as Herman and Baron hold that Kant does accept the MCT, which means that on their reading Kant must deny the IT. I deny both theses, agreeing with Ross that for Kant the motive of duty is not part of the content of one's duties, while agreeing with Herman and Baron that the IT is false: motive is relevant for fulfilling certain Kantian duties (but relevant in ways other than such duties having as part of their content the motive of duty).

Main Theses	Ross	Recent Kantians	Me
MCT?	No	Yes	No
IT?	Yes	No	No

Fig. 11.1. Three views on the relevance of motive to rightness in Kant's ethics

Although a full exploration of the ways in which motive can be deontically relevant in Kant's ethics is well beyond the scope of this chapter, I shall proceed briefly to indicate three main ways in which motive can be deontically relevant for Kant. First, there are cases in which certain actions fail to fulfil a duty if the action is performed from a certain motive. Secondly, there are cases where otherwise forbidden actions may, owing to motive, be morally permitted. Thirdly, there are cases in which an otherwise optional action is made wrong by one's motive. I take these up in order.

(1) In my discussion of the general duty of beneficence (at least as Kant understands it), I have already noted that not any old helping action done on purpose can fulfil this duty. J. Llewellyn Davies objected to Mill's acceptance

---

[49] In correspondence, Thomas Pogge suggested to me that one might be able to embrace the MCT (and hold that fulfilling certain duties requires that one act on the basis of some motive—the motive of duty for Kant) and still accept the IT by claiming that, if one performs the action that is part of one's duty to perform but fails to perform it from the motive of duty, one might be said to have done the right act even if one does not *fully* satisfy the duty. This position would apparently require that we distinguish between doing a right act in the sense of performing an action that is required (and not just permitted), yet failing to fulfil (fully) one's duty. This kind of position would complicate matters and I will not pursue it here. However, let me point out that I see no basis for attributing the MCT to Kant, and any attraction attaching to the idea that one can partly fulfil a duty without fully fulfilling it is already accommodated in Kant's system by the fact that for Kant we have a duty to perform our various duties from the motive of duty. If we fulfil our duty of beneficence and yet fail to do so from the sole motive of duty, there is still a duty of moral perfection that we have not fulfilled.

of the IT by describing a case where, he thought, motive was deontically relevant. 'Suppose that a tyrant, when his enemy jumped into the sea to escape from him, saved him from drowning simply in order that he might inflict upon him more exquisite tortures . . .'.[50] Davies thinks that, owing to the tyrant's motive, the helping action in such a case is morally wrong.[51] Likewise, we have seen that the fulfilment of the Kantian duty of beneficence is not compatible with certain motives such as malice and (on the interpretation I offered) calculated self-interest. So, in connection with this duty (and others), it is clear that fulfilment of certain duties by performance of external actions rules out acting from certain motives. Hence, in general, actions that might otherwise fulfil certain duties in Kant's system might not do so if they flow from certain motives: otherwise duty-fulfilling actions become either merely optional (as in the case of beneficence from self-interest) or positively wrong when performed by certain motives (as in the case of 'helping' from malice).

(2) I mentioned at the outset that, in the *Grundlegung*, Kant's suicide example invokes the motive of self-love, which suggests that there may be room in Kant for claiming that certain acts of killing oneself are not wrong. In one place, Kant does characterize willfully killing oneself as murder, from which it follows that it is morally wrong (*MS* 6:422). However, in considering various matters of casuistry in relation to suicide, he asks: 'Is it murdering oneself to hurl oneself to certain death (like Curtius) in order to save one's country?—or is deliberate martyrdom, sacrificing oneself for the good of humanity, also to be considered an act of heroism?' (*MS* 6:423). This passage continues with Kant asking about three further cases: about a 'great king' who carried poison that he intended to take in case of capture so that he could not be coerced into acts that would harm his country; about someone who took his own life for fear of unintentionally harming others as a result of an incurable disease he contracted; and about the morality of being vaccinated against smallpox, which, although it puts a man's life in danger, is done '*in order to preserve his life*' (*MS* 6:424). In each of these examples, a question about the person's motive is pivotal in the determination of the deontic status of specific acts of killing oneself. Though Kant does not answer his own questions, leaving them for his readers to ponder, one might plausibly argue that, from within the Kantian moral system, some of the actions in question are not morally wrong owing to the person's motive.

---

[50] The passage is quoted in Mill, *Utilitarianism*, ch. 2 n. 2.

[51] In reply to Davies's analysis of this case, one might insist we must distinguish between the tyrant's act, his motive, and his further acts, and claim that the motive was surely a bad one, his further acts of torturing his victim were wrong, but that we need not conclude that the original act in question was wrong. (Michael Gorr in correspondence urged this rendering of the example.) But, aside from the details of this particular case, the point is that for Kant (as for Davies) motive is relevant to an action's deontic status.

There are two, related ways in which motive might be relevant here. First, if one defines suicide as murder (and hence as necessarily morally wrong), questions about one's motives in killing oneself are relevant for determining whether one's action is correctly described as a case of suicide. Secondly, if suicide is defined merely as intentionally bringing about one's own death, then various motives might be relevant for determining the justifications one might have for engaging in an act that is otherwise wrong. Considered in this manner, we would say that, in certain contexts, owing primarily to one's motive, an otherwise wrongful act (killing oneself) is permissible.[52]

(3) Another broad category of action where motive is crucial is the category of malicious actions.[53] Kant includes malice as one of the three main vices of hatred opposed to our duty of love towards others. He also describes some of the vices opposed to respect for others as at bottom motivated by malice. Since a malicious act is by definition an act having a certain motive, it seems rather obvious that motive can be deontically relevant for Kant. However, in order to make clear that it is the motive in question that can be deontically relevant, I want to consider some examples. Whereas in the case of killing oneself we had examples of otherwise wrongful actions made right by one's motive, here we have examples of otherwise permissible actions made wrong by one's motive.

For example, Kant treats the desire for revenge as 'the sweetest form of malice' and describes the vengeful person as one who makes 'it one's end to harm others without any advantage to oneself' (*MS* 6:460). In discussing avenging wrongs out of the motive of revenge, he argues that 'It is, therefore, a duty of virtue . . . to refrain from repaying another's enmity with hatred *out of mere revenge . . .*' (*MS* 6:460; emphasis added). These remarks suggest that one's motive can be deontically relevant as revealed by comparing similar cases involving punishment. If, for example, a certain form of punishment would be morally right to inflict on someone as a response to culpable wrongdoing, then Kant's remark here suggests that inflicting this kind of harm is itself wrongful if done from the malicious motive of revenge.

The motive of malice is also an apparently wrong-making feature of certain acts of defamation and ridicule that Kant presents as vices that are contrary to duties of respect towards others. Kant defines defamation as 'the immediate inclination, with no particular aim in view, to bring into the open something

---

[52] For a discussion of how motives are both part of the very definition of certain legal offences and how they can figure relevantly in justifications and excuses in the law, see Sistare, 'Agent Motives', and Husak, 'Motive and Criminal Liability'.

[53] We have already touched on malice in connection with helping others (where it makes an otherwise dutiful action either permissible or wrong); here the concern is with cases in which motive makes an otherwise permissible action wrong.

prejudicial to respect for others' (*MS* 6:466). The fact that this sort of inclination prompts action with no other particular aim means that Kant is thinking of defamation as an underlying motive that prompts certain negatively prejudicial acts. At bottom, this motive is a kind of malice (involving as Kant says, a malicious pleasure (*MS* 6:466)). A malicious motive also explains why certain acts of ridicule are wrong. Kant characterizes ridicule as the holding-up of a 'person's real faults, or supposed faults as if they were real, *in order to deprive him of the respect he deserves* . . .' (*MS* 6:467; emphasis added). Ridicule, as Kant defines it, differs from defamation in that acts of the former sort are aimed at exposing others to laughter while the latter are aimed at exposing others to criticism. In the case of both vices, there are arguably examples in which an otherwise permissible act becomes wrong if done out of malice. For instance, Kant distinguishes friendly banter involving exposing another's faults (which is morally innocent) from cases in which such remarks are delivered in order to deprive the person of respect. Here, again, otherwise permissible actions are wrong when performed from a certain motive.

I have touched but on a few examples of duties from Kant's ethical system whose deontic status is arguably affected by motive.[54] Kant's discussion of the vices of envy and ingratitude suggest many more. However, I have done enough to make a presumptive case for the claim that motives are taken by Kant to be deontically relevant. I now want to strengthen my case by looking to Kant's normative moral theory as a way of grounding the deontic relevance of motives.

V. Grounding the Relevance of Motive in Kant's Moral Theory

Whatever stand one takes on the relevance of motive to rightness in Kant's ethics, it ought to be anchored in a general account of moral relevance. Elsewhere[55] I have argued that (1) a normative moral theory—a theory that purports to reveal what features of an action at bottom make the act right or wrong—is just a theory of moral relevance and that (2) the Humanity formu-

---

[54] Although we are concerned with the question of whether one's motive can affect which of the three basic deontic categories some act belongs to, motive can also affect which type of act (from among those falling within one of the basic categories) the action belongs to. For instance, Kant distinguishes between acts of greed and acts of avarice according to motive: 'The *maxim of greedy* avarice (prodigality) is to get and maintain all the means to good living *with the intention of enjoyment.*—The maxim of *miserly* avarice, on the other hand, is to acquire as well as maintain all the means to good living, but *with no intention of enjoyment*, (i.e., in such a way that one's end is only possession, not enjoyment)' (*MS* 6:432).

[55] Timmons, 'Decision Procedures'.

lation of the Categorical Imperative serves this role in Kant's ethics. Thus, (3) it is facts about the bearings of one's actions on the maintenance and flourishing of humanity (as Kant understands this notion) that are the morally relevant facts determining the (objective) deontic status of an action. I suggest then, that (4) the *Tugendlehre* system of duties be viewed as a specification, in fairly broad outline, of the various types of actions and omissions that bear most directly on the maintenance and flourishing of humanity.

To make this a bit more concrete, humanity (personality), as Kant characterizes it, concerns our rational natures and, in particular, our capacities as end-setting creatures. According to Kant, not only are we able to set ends in response to the promptings of desire and inclination; we are capable of a kind of autonomy that, he says, 'is that property the will has of being a law to itself (independently of every property belonging to objects of volition)' (*G.* 4:440). Thus, it is our natures as autonomous agents that provide the objective basis for right and wrong action. Actions that destroy or degrade humanity are prima facie wrong; actions that promote humanity are prima facie right. Thus, for example, maintenance of one's own autonomy requires that we omit actions that destroy or degrade autonomy, and so such actions as suicide, drunkenness, and gluttony are wrong (or tend to be wrong). Similar remarks apply to the other duties featured in the *Tugendlehre*, the basic idea being that the various types of action and disposition that are forbidden or required are types of action and disposition that bear on the maintenance and flourishing of humanity.

Given this framework, we can readily understand why various motives can be deontically relevant for Kant. Motives such as loyalty to others that motivates the martyr and self-preservation that motivates the individual to undergo a risky vaccination are motives that are necessarily aimed at the maintenance of 'humanity in the person'. Granted, in the martyrdom case one is intentionally bringing about one's own death and so this fact about the act counts against doing it, but the fact that one's ultimate aim is the preservation of the lives of others is also a relevant fact about the act and therefore should be considered in determining the all-things-considered deontic status of the action in question. Whether one's aim does justify the act of killing oneself is a difficult question, perhaps depending on other morally relevant features of the situation. However, the important point here is that motive is relevant and we have an explanation, from within the Kantian framework, of why it is relevant.

Malice involves a direct hatred for humanity, disposing the person infected with this vice to 'rejoice immediately' (*MS* 6:460) in the misfortune of others. This kind of motive is thus necessarily contrary to respecting humanity, and consequently is a morally relevant fact in determining the deontic status of actions so motivated.

It is interesting to note in connection with malice that Kant's overall account of moral relevance allows for two main ways in which facts about one's motives can be deontically relevant. First, and most obviously, actions whose performance would in fact negatively affect the humanity in oneself or others (where there are no considerations that would justify such performance) are wrong. If someone's malicious gossip affects you negatively by, for instance, setting others against you thereby interfering with your pursuit of legitimate interests, the act is wrong. Here, the idea is that acts of malice are by their very nature oriented towards degrading humanity in the person and, thus, often have this very effect. But Kant's moral theory, though obviously at odds with various forms of consequentialist theory in rejecting hedonistic and eudaimonistic conceptions of the good as well as rejecting maximizing conceptions of moral action, also differs in allowing for and making sense of the deontic evaluation of actions that are causally inefficacious. The fact that an action, because of its mental component and in particular its motive, can express certain deontically relevant attitudes means that the act can be right or wrong apart from its actual effects on humanity in the person. Acts of malice, for instance, simply because they express an attitude that is hostile towards humanity in the person, are (presumptively) wrong.

One might consider various generalizations about motive and rightness— for example, that a 'good' motive usually justifies an otherwise wrongful act while a 'bad' motive can make wrong an otherwise permissible act—but I doubt any such claims would correctly characterize Kant's considered views on the matter. Recall, for instance, his infamous essay in which he denies that a benevolent motive makes a difference to the deontic status of a lie. In order to sort out the bearing of motive on rightness in Kant's ethics will require, I suggest, nothing less than an extensive examination of the various Kantian duties and matters of casuistry associated with each.

In any case, not only do we have some textual evidence that motives can be deontically relevant for Kant, we also have an explanation of why they can be relevant. In fact, when one considers that, for Kant, the motives behind an action are high-level intentions and that, in general, one's intentions are deontically relevant if only because they help determine the identity of one's actions, the presumption, it seems to me, should be that, unless there is good reason to suppose otherwise, one's motives can be deontically relevant. Indeed, if one were to suppose they were irrelevant, how might this fact be explained within the Kantian framework? Contrast standard act utilitarianism. An act utilitarian has a principled explanation of why motive is deontically irrelevant: according to the utilitarian theory, it is only the values of the consequences of actions that bear on the deontic status of an action; motives are on the wrong end of the temporal sequence to matter deontically.[56] I suggest that, for Kant, there is no principled reason for excluding motives from considerations of deontic status; there is thus good reason to reject the IT in relation to Kant's system of duties.

VI. Conclusion

I have argued for the following conclusions. (1) The Motive Content Thesis (MCT) applied to Kant's ethics—the claim that at least some Kantian duties have as part of their content the requirement that one act from duty—is mistaken. In supporting this claim, I have examined various doctrinal and conceptual claims that might be used to support the thesis and found them unpersuasive. Here, I take sides with Ross and against some recent Kant interpreters. However, (2) the Independence Thesis (IT) does not hold for Kant: motives can be included among the set of considerations that determine the deontic status of an action. Here, I disagree with Ross's more general claims about Kant's theory and find myself in agreement with interpreters like Herman over the general relevance of motive to rightness in Kant's ethical system (though, of course, for reasons other than appeal to the MCT in relation to Kant's ethics). In supporting this claim I considered various bits of textual evidence as well as the general philosophical case that can be made in support of the claim. Finally, I briefly indicated why motives are relevant to rightness in Kant's moral philosophy by appealing to Kant's general account of moral relevance.

I have not been able to explore questions about how my results affect the overall plausibility of Kant's moral theory, but in the light of recent (and, I think, plausible) challenges to the old doctrine that rightness is independent of one's motives, I hope my efforts will be viewed as bolstering the plausibility of both Kant's ethics and Kantian ethics generally.

---

[56] Here, I am reporting what utilitarians say about the matter, though matters are rather delicate since utilitarians like Mill do allow that intention is deontically relevant and so owe us some story about how intentions differ from motives in this way.

12

The Inner Freedom of Virtue

Stephen Engstrom

Kant holds that virtue is a kind of strength. Virtue, he says, is 'a moral strength of the will' (*MS* 6:405), 'the strength of a human being's maxim in the observance of his duty', a strength that is known only through the hindrances it is able to overcome, which lie in opposing natural inclinations (*MS* 6:394).[1] In presenting this view of virtue, Kant does not fancy himself to be an innovator, but rather supposes that strength is what the ancient authors generally had in mind when they praised the virtue of the sage. Moreover, when he introduces the idea of virtue in *The Metaphysics of Morals*, he seems clearly to be taking for granted that his readers understand that it goes without saying, as a matter of the very meanings of the terms, that *virtus* is *fortitudo moralis*, and that *fortitudo* is 'the capacity and considered resolve to oppose a strong but unjust opponent' (*MS* 6:380).[2]

Many of Kant's readers today, however, find his conception of virtue to differ substantially from, and to fall short of, the classical ideal presented in the ethical systems of the ancients. In particular, Kant's account is likely to remind

I am grateful to Mark Timmons and Allen Wood for their helpful comments.

[1] Translations of passages from Kant's writings are my own, though I have consulted the commonly used English translations.

[2] Kant recognizes, of course, that *virtus* refers specifically to a certain ideal of manliness. In one of his lecture courses on ethics, he is reported to have said, 'The very Latin word *virtus* originally signifies nothing else but courage, strength, and constancy, and the symbol for it indicates the same: a Hercules, with lionskin and club, striking down the hydra, which is the symbol of all vice' (Vig. 27:492). The German term *Tugend* also conveys some suggestion of masculine virtue, though less prominently. But the notion of strength (*Stärke*) that figures in Kant's conception of virtue as a moral strength is a more general concept, one whose generality is liable to be obscured if it is linked directly to the specific images of lionskin and club. We will do better if we view this strength in the light of the fact that Kant's treatment of virtue is informed by the idea, pervasive among ancient Greek ethicists, that virtue is a kind of health of the soul, and vice an illness, where, as with their analogues in the body, health is understood to lie in a certain order among the parts, illness in their disorder (*MS* 6:384, 409; cf. *A.* 7:251). The strength in which virtue is said to consist can thus be regarded as *robustness*, the strength of health (see *MS* 6:397, where *robur* is provided as a gloss for *Stärke*). Kant's description of virtue as a type of fortitude (*MS* 6:380), or constant condition of courage (*A.* 7:256), can be understood along similar lines.

us of the condition of character that Aristotle identifies under the heading of continence. Describing continence as a kind of strength of resolve present in one who, recognizing and choosing to do what is right, manages to act on that choice, to abide by it in conduct, despite the presence of 'strong and bad appetites' that stand in opposition to it, Aristotle contrasts this condition with genuine virtue, where the soul is not hampered by such appetites and hence not divided in inner struggle.[3] Kant, on the other hand, arguing that the very concept of duty contains a notion of constraint that in turn implies the presence of resisting inclinations and hence a certain degree of reluctance to do what duty requires (cf. e.g. *MS* 6:379), sees virtue as a capacity for self-constraint or self-compulsion (*MS* 6:394) and even characterizes it as 'moral disposition in battle' (*KpV* 5:84). And the impression is of course reinforced by the fact that these remarks about virtue recall the conflict between the motive of duty and inclination so prominent in the examples Kant presents in his discussion of moral worth in the *Groundwork of the Metaphysics of Morals* (*G.* 4:397–9).[4]

The question whether, or to what extent, virtue as Kant conceives of it involves motivational harmony has received considerable attention in recent years, and there seems to be general agreement that significantly more harmony is involved than some of his remarks may seem to suggest.[5] This chapter, however, is concerned with a different, though not altogether unrelated, set of questions that can be raised concerning Kant's account of virtue as strength. These questions, which have received considerably less attention, relate to his theory of practical freedom and arise from the fact that Kant suggests in various places that the strength he says virtue consists in is a certain type of freedom.[6] The chief aim of this chapter is to explore his account of this freedom, which he elaborates in the Introduction to the *Doctrine of Virtue* in *The Meta-*

---

[3] Aristotle, *Nicomachean Ethics* VII.1–2, 9; esp. 1146a9–16.

[4] Indeed, though it includes no mention of virtue, the *Groundwork*'s discussion of moral worth has itself often been taken to betray a failure on Kant's part to mark Aristotle's distinction between virtue and continence. Rosalind Hursthouse, for example, in commenting on Kant's attribution of moral worth to the character of the person who helps others from the motive of duty despite being cold by temperament, concludes that Kant displays here 'a total lack of recognition' of this distinction's existence ('Virtue Ethics and the Emotions', in Daniel Statman (ed.), *Virtue Ethics* (Edinburgh: Edinburgh University Press, 1997), 107).

[5] For some recent discussion, see Barbara Herman, 'On the Value of Acting from the Motive of Duty' and 'Integrity and Impartiality', both in *The Practice of Moral Judgment* (Cambridge, MA: Harvard University Press, 1993); Paul Guyer, 'Duty and Inclination', in *Kant and the Experience of Freedom* (Cambridge: Cambridge University Press, 1993); Marcia W. Baron, *Kantian Ethics Almost without Apology* (Ithaca, NY: Cornell University Press, 1995), chs. 5–6; Christine M. Korsgaard, 'From Duty and for the Sake of the Noble: Aristotle and Kant on Morally Good Action', in S. Engstrom and J. Whiting (eds.), *Aristotle, Kant, and the Stoics: Rethinking Happiness and Duty* (Cambridge: Cambridge University Press, 1996); and Nancy Sherman, *Making a Necessity of Virtue* (Cambridge: Cambridge University Press, 1997), ch. 4.

[6] Some of these questions are touched on in Christine M. Korsgaard, 'Morality as Freedom', in *Creating the Kingdom of Ends* (Cambridge: Cambridge University Press, 1996); see esp. 176 ff.

physics of Morals. To the extent that this freedom turns out to be incompatible with the conflicts among motives found in the continent person, however, our examination of it will have a bearing on the question about motivational harmony as well.

I. Habit and Freedom

One of the points at which this conception of freedom surfaces in Kant's texts is a passage in which he criticizes traditional attempts to define virtue in terms of habit or custom. As we shall see, Kant thinks it is possible to define virtue as a kind of habit, but he rejects certain standard attempts to do so, especially those that characterize virtue in terms of custom.

1. Before turning to the remarks in which Kant brings up freedom, we may begin with a brief examination of his initial criticism of definitions of virtue in terms of habit, which occurs near the beginning of the Introduction to the *Doctrine of Virtue*:

> But virtue is not to be defined and esteemed merely as *habit* [*Fertigkeit*] and (as the prize essay of court-chaplain Cochius puts it) as a long-standing *custom* [*Gewohnheit*], acquired through practice, of morally good actions.[7] For if this [that is, habit] is not an effect of considered, firm, and ever more purified principles, then, like any other mechanism arising from technically practical reason, it is neither equipped for all situations nor adequately secured against the alteration that new temptations can bring about.   (*MS* 6:383–4)

Two reasons are presented here for rejecting the stated definition. The first appears to be essentially the same as the one given in the *Groundwork* for denying that inclinations, or habitual sensible desires, can be the source of an action's moral worth—namely, that by themselves they fail to ensure that actions springing from them are in conformity with duty. The second reason seems to be that habits, even habits that, in normal circumstances at least, yield 'morally good actions', may depend on certain conditions unconnected with

---

[7]   For understandable reasons, recent English translations of the *Doctrine of Virtue* render *Gewohnheit* as 'habit' and *Fertigkeit* as 'aptitude' (Gregor) or 'skill' (Ellington). In this chapter, however, I follow Abbott's practice of translating the former as 'custom' and the latter as 'habit' (though for the latter I also sometimes use 'readiness'). Kant's Latin gloss for *Fertigkeit* is *habitus* (*MS* 6:407; cf. *A.* 7:147), and when he uses *Gewohnheit* and *Angewohnheit* he has in mind *consuetudo* and *assuetudo* respectively (cf. e.g. *MS* 6:407; *A.* 7:148–9), which have an etymological connection with our 'custom' but not with 'habit'. Since Kant defines virtue as a kind of *Fertigkeit*, we can more easily see his conception of virtue as continuous with traditional conceptions of it as a kind of *habitus* or *hexis* if we bear his Latin gloss in mind.

the consciousness of duty and hence give way if those conditions cease to hold. Imagine, for instance, that the shopkeeper Kant describes in his well-known example (*G.* 4:397) is assisted by a young clerk. The clerk is instructed by the shopkeeper to charge the same price for every customer, and he develops a habit of doing so, but simply from doing what he is told, without any real understanding of the action as in conformity with duty, and without even sharing in the shopkeeper's understanding of it as good business practice. Then he goes off and sets up a shop of his own, but soon his business falters, and the temptation arises to charge unfair prices to inexperienced customers. He has no firm comprehension of obligation, but only a habit he has long practised. What is to prevent him from departing from it? Or, again, suppose that another clerk, finding employment in a business where charging a reasonable price is the common practice, follows the example of her peers, perhaps without even noticing that she is doing so. Later she obtains a similar position in another firm, in which many of the clerks charge prices unfairly. The very predisposition that initially led to the habit of charging a reasonable price will now tend to undermine that habit and support another.[8]

These problems are at least largely traceable to the fact that the habits in question are either altogether 'blind' in that they are regularities of conduct that do not depend for their possibility on the subject's being conscious of the rule that constitutes them, or else at least 'morally blind' in the sense that, even where such consciousness is involved in their establishment (for example, in the case of the clerk who is given instructions based on the shopkeeper's exercise of technically practical reason), they do not depend on the subject's recognition that the rule is in agreement with duty, the recognition on which all morally worthy action is based. These sorts of blindness seem to constitute at least an important part of what Kant has in mind in suggesting that the problems he points out stem from the fact that the habits in question are 'mechanism[s] arising from technically practical reason'. For later, when discussing how virtue is to be acquired, he portrays custom as 'a permanent inclination without any maxim' and as 'a mechanism of the way of sensing rather than a principle of the way of thinking' (*MS* 6:479). It would appear, then,

---

[8] The sort of contingency these two cases illustrate can also be seen in another of Kant's well-known examples from the *Groundwork*, that of the 'sympathetically attuned' philanthropist whose habitual sympathy (but not his ability to help) is extinguished by his own cares and concerns (*G.* 4:398). Because this philanthropist's generous inclination to help others expresses, and hence is contingent on, his sense of his own capacity to provide assistance and so ultimately his sense of his own prosperity, it depends on conditions unconnected with the consciousness of duty. As will emerge below (Section IV.3), the generosity involved in virtue springs from consciousness of freedom (true magnanimity), not from consciousness of personal prosperity, and therefore is not contingent in this way. (The example of the philanthropist will be considered further in n. 30.)

that, if there can be habits that unlike custom are not mechanical and blind, then it may be possible to define virtue in terms of habit while avoiding the problems Kant describes, provided that the conception of habit involved is suitably qualified. Kant himself seems to acknowledge this when, in his criticism of Cochius' definition quoted above, he implicitly suggests that habit could be acceptable if it arises in the right way, namely, from 'considered, firm, and ever more purified principles'; and eventually, as we shall see, he employs such a qualified conception of habit in one of his own definitions of virtue.

2. Some pages later, however, Kant offers rather more puzzling grounds for thinking that virtue cannot be understood in terms of custom: 'unlike technical maxims, moral maxims cannot be grounded on custom (for this belongs to the physical constitution of the determination of the will); on the contrary, even if the exercise [*Ausübung*] of them were to become custom, the subject would therewith lose *freedom* in adopting his maxims, which [freedom] however is the character of an action done from duty' (*MS* 6:409). At first sight, Kant's point here might seem to be this: when we adopt a maxim on the basis of custom, we do so because we have fallen into a kind of rut, which makes it at least difficult for us to choose otherwise; but freedom in adopting our maxims implies the possibility of choosing otherwise, so, to the extent that custom is the basis of our choice, our freedom in adopting our maxims is eroded. But this reading does not fit with other things Kant says about freedom. In particular, he rejects the idea that freedom entails the possibility of choosing otherwise, as the following passage illustrates: 'The less a human being can be compelled physically [that is, coerced], and the more he can be compelled morally (through the mere representation of duty), the freer he is' (*MS* 6:382 n.; cf. *MS* 6:226–7). Someone who is to the greatest extent subject to moral compulsion would be no more capable of choosing otherwise than in accordance with duty than someone whose choice is based in custom, but, far from taking this lack of 'capacity'—which properly speaking is not a lack of any genuine capacity, but rather the absence of an *in*capacity (*MS* 6:227)—to imply any undermining of freedom, Kant suggests in this passage that it is not only compatible with the greatest freedom, but even intimately connected with it. If we take seriously this suggestion that the greatest capacity to be morally compelled is the height of freedom, then it seems we must suppose that in claiming that custom deprives us of freedom Kant is making the point that the choice of maxims on the basis of custom involves a loss of freedom in adopting maxims precisely because such a basis limits the extent to which one can be compelled morally, in so far as such compulsion involves quite a different basis for choice—namely, the mere representation of duty.

Now the suggestion that one is free to the extent that one can be compelled by the mere representation of duty bears a very close resemblance to Kant's famous doctrine that freedom is autonomy, the self-legislation that he claims lies at the basis of morality and is expressed in action done from duty. And, because of this resemblance, it will likely call to mind a familiar criticism that has been often raised against that doctrine—namely, that it has the unacceptable implication that those who lack autonomy will also lack freedom and therefore will not be morally accountable for their actions.

While this criticism has often been made, many of Kant's interpreters have argued convincingly that it rests on misunderstanding.[9] In many of the passages in which Kant speaks of freedom or autonomy, a careful reading reveals that he is thinking of these as belonging not just to the character of action done from duty, but to that of imputable action in general, whether it be in accordance with duty or opposed to it. Noteworthy cases in point are his definitions of freedom, which, because of their importance for the discussion to follow, deserve a brief examination.

II. Practical Freedom in General

Kant presents two definitions of freedom, one 'negative', the other 'positive'. We may begin with a few comments on how they are related.

1. These definitions express, not different types of freedom, but different ways of defining the same freedom—what he calls 'practical freedom', freedom of the power of choice (*Willkür*)—one by indicating what it is *not*, the other by stating what it essentially *is*.[10] According to the negative definition, freedom of

---

[9] In its usual form, the criticism is that Kant overlooks, or at least fails clearly to mark, the difference between freedom as autonomy and the familiar sort of freedom that coincides with moral accountability. This complaint has a long history. It was raised by Sidgwick a century ago, and another century before that the problem was discussed by Kant's contemporaries, including Reinhold and Fichte. (Kant attempts to clear up one of the misconceptions underlying the criticism at *MS* 6:226–7.) For some recent discussion, see Nelson Potter, Jr., 'Does Kant have Two Concepts of Freedom?' in G. Funke and J. Kopper (eds.), *Akten des 4. Internationalen Kant-Kongresses* (Berlin: de Gruyter, 1974); Allen W. Wood, 'Kant's Compatibilism', in Allen W. Wood (ed.), *Self and Nature in Kant's Philosophy* (Ithaca, NY: Cornell University Press, 1984), 78–82; Thomas E. Hill, Jr., *Dignity and Practical Reason* (Ithaca, NY: Cornell University Press, 1992), 81–2, 105–6; Christine M. Korsgaard, *Creating the Kingdom of Ends* (Cambridge: Cambridge University Press, 1996), 160–76; Henry Allison, *Kant's Theory of Freedom* (Cambridge: Cambridge University Press, 1990), 94–9, 133–6; and Frederick Neuhouser, *Fichte's Theory of Subjectivity* (Cambridge: Cambridge University Press, 1990), 144–8.

[10] As an articulation of the essence of freedom (*G.* 4:446), the positive definition is a real definition. (Real and negative definitions are briefly contrasted in the Jäsche *Logic*: §106 n. 2, 9:144.) The most general idea of freedom that Kant articulates—'the transcendental idea of freedom' (*KrV* A533/B561)—is that of an unconditioned cause. Such a cause is not determinable by anything outside of itself, but instead deter-

the power of choice is the independence of that power from determination by sensible impulses; according to the positive definition, freedom is that same power's dependence on—that is, its determinability by—the moral law, and hence its determinability by pure practical reason, or the pure will, the faculty that legislates that law (*MS* 6:213; cf. *G.* 4:446; *KpV* 5:33, 93–4).

Kant says the positive definition 'flows' from the negative, on the grounds that, because the power of choice, as a type of causality, must be determinable by some cause in accordance with a law, and because for a power of choice to be determined by sensible impulses is just what it is for it to be determined by 'alien causes', or in accordance with laws that are foreign in the sense that they can be known only through their effects (that is, empirically), a power of choice not determinable by sensible impulses must be determinable in accordance with a law of its own—that is, a law that can have effects only through being known—and hence must be determinable by the faculty of cognizing laws a priori—that is, by pure reason.[11] But it is equally true that the negative definition can be inferred from the positive. For the very idea of determination, because it involves the thought of a necessity based in the sufficiency of the ground (or cause) to produce the consequence (or effect) in the thing or power it determines, implies that a single power cannot be determinable by each of two opposing grounds. That is to say, if two grounds are opposed, one must cancel in whole or in part the effect of the other (cf. *KrV* A265/B320 1, A273/B329), and therefore it cannot be that each itself is sufficient to produce the effect it would produce in the absence of the other; so the possibility of a power's being determined by one such ground excludes the possibility of its being determined by the other. Thus given that the consciousness of obligation involves feelings of constraint and reluctance (cf. Section III.2 below), which reveal pure reason and sensibility to be opposing grounds in relation to the power of choice, it follows that, if the power of choice can be determined by pure reason, through the representation of the moral law, then it cannot be

---

mines itself to act and so is absolutely spontaneous in its action. The transcendental idea of freedom thus involves both the concept of cause and that of spontaneity. Accordingly, freedom in general is definable (positively) as the capacity of a cause to determine itself to action and (negatively) as the independence of that cause from determination by alien causes. The positive and negative definitions that we shall be considering, however, are not definitions of freedom in this most general, transcendental sense, but definitions of practical freedom, the freedom of human beings—that is, freedom as a property of the power of choice that is first revealed through consciousness of the moral law (*KrV* A533–4/B561–2).

[11] I have sketched here what I take to be the essentials of the line of thinking Kant follows at the beginning of chapter III of the *Groundwork*. In doing so, however, I have made use of his distinction between the power of choice (*Willkür*), or the faculty exercised in the choice of maxims and actions, and the will (*Wille*), or practical reason itself; this distinction is not explicitly drawn in the *Groundwork*, but it does figure in the similar definitions of freedom given in *The Metaphysics of Morals* (*MS* 6:213–14).

determined by sensibility, through the latter's impulses. The positive definition therefore implies the negative.

2. Kant formulates the positive definition of freedom in a number of different ways. Since the determinability of the subject's power of choice by the moral law is just the possibility of that power's exercise according to the law, that is, the capacity of the subject to choose to act according to it, or out of respect for it (just as the power's *determination* by the law is just its *actual* exercise according to the law), Kant's positive definition amounts to a definition of freedom as the capacity to choose to act according to the moral law (see *MS* 6:226–7; *KpV* 5:30). Again, since the determinability of the subject's power of choice by the moral law is just the *legislation* of that law by the subject's *own will* (for this legislation lies in the subject's own consciousness of obligation, through which alone the will can determine the power of choice to conform to its law), freedom can also be positively defined as the self-legislation, or autonomy, of the will, or of practical reason (see *G.* 4:446–7; *KpV* 5:33). And, since the determinability of the power of choice by the moral law is also just the capacity of *pure* reason to determine that power (a capacity revealed through the unconditionality of the Categorical Imperative), freedom can also be positively defined as the practicality (or causality) of pure reason (*MS* 6:213–14, 221). We have then a variety of ways of expressing what freedom essentially is: viewed as it were from below, it can be characterized as the determinability of the power of choice by the moral law, or as the capacity to choose to act according to it; viewed from above, it can be characterized as the autonomy of the will, or as the practicality of pure reason.

Consideration of these definitions reveals that in stating them Kant is not thinking of freedom as characteristic only of action done from duty, for none of them excludes the possibility of an exercise of the capacity to choose to act according to the moral law in which an action is chosen that is not in accordance with that law. That the power of choice is determinable by the moral law implies that it is not determinable by sensible impulses, but it does not imply that an exercise of this power can never be a choice of action not in accordance with that law. For though sensible impulses are not causes that are by themselves sufficient to determine this power, it might still be possible for them, under certain conditions, to have an influence upon its exercise (cf. Section III.1 below). So the choice of action contrary to the moral law does not by itself imply that in that choice the subject lacks the capacity to choose to act according to the law, nor therefore that the subject is not free and accountable for the action. Autonomy of the will is self-legislation, but legislation is not (in the case of human beings at least) the same as compliance.

3. But this response to the familiar criticism obviously leaves unexplained the passages that have suggested to many readers that Kant sees freedom as in some way distinctively characteristic of morally worthy action, action done from duty. The remark we took note of earlier may again serve as an example: 'The less a human being can be compelled physically, and the more he can be compelled morally (through the mere representation of duty), the freer he is' (*MS* 6:382 n.). And, more emphatically still, Kant says of the moral strength in which virtue consists that 'only in its possession is [the human being] free' (*MS* 6:405). Nor does this response remove the puzzlement occasioned by Kant's suggestion in the passage quoted earlier that custom deprives us of freedom. If freedom is indeed the capacity to choose to act according to the moral law, and if as such it is a necessary condition of accountability, then it is hard to see why custom must be opposed to freedom. We do not generally take the fact that an action is customary or habitual to imply that the agent is beyond the pale of accountability. In fact, as those who regard virtue as a kind of habit often point out, if we think the action is habitual we may praise or blame the agent all the more; and Kant himself recognizes this point.[12] If the presence of custom does not eliminate the capacity to choose to act according to the moral law, and if freedom consists in this capacity, then customary action must still be free.

It seems clear, therefore, that in order to make sense of Kant's suggestion that custom deprives us of freedom we must suppose, as many of his readers have, that he is operating with two different conceptions of freedom,[13] and that

---

[12] Or so his students' lecture notes suggest (Col. 27:292–3; Vig. 27:569–70), and so one might in any case surmise from his remarks regarding the estimation of merit and culpability (*MS* 6:228; *A.* 7:148). Kant seems to hold that custom increases the degree of an action's imputability, except where it has arisen from influences upon the individual in childhood, in which case it may (like a quality of temperament) reduce the level of imputability. In general, the role a habit may play in determining the degree of an action's imputability is determined by whether and if so to what extent the habit is itself imputable.

[13] Sidgwick, for example, argues that, 'in different parts of Kant's exposition of his doctrine, two essentially different conceptions are expressed by the same word freedom; while yet Kant does not appear to be conscious of any variation in the meaning of the term' (*The Methods of Ethics*, 7th edn. (London: Macmillan, 1907), 511). Citing Kant's assertion in the *Groundwork* that 'a free will and a will under moral laws are one and the same' (*G.* 4:447), Sidgwick observes with some justice that the description of a will as 'under' or 'subject to' moral laws has an uncertain meaning: 'A will subject to its own moral laws *may* mean a will that, so far as free, conforms to these laws; but it also *may* be conceived as capable of freely disobeying these laws' (*Methods*, 514–15). It is very unlikely, however, that there is any unclarity in Kant's mind as to the intended sense; for elsewhere, when using the phrase 'under moral laws', he emphasizes that he employs this expression rather than '*in accordance with* moral laws' precisely because he means to signify a relation to those laws that does not imply conformity (*KU* 5:448–9 n.). Sidgwick assumes that the second of the two sorts of freedom he distinguishes is properly defined as the capacity to choose to act either in accordance with or against the moral law (see *Methods*, 58, 511), rather than simply as the capacity to choose to act according to it. Because of this assumption, Sidgwick does not see that the two sorts of freedom he says Kant confuses are, though not indeed identical, in fact intimately related (as will emerge in Section III.4).

the freedom he regards as incompatible with custom is different from practical freedom in general, the freedom expressed in the positive and negative definitions considered above. And upon closer examination it does appear that, in the passage we considered (*MS* 6:409), Kant signals that he has another sort of freedom in view, for he speaks not of the freedom characteristic of action under, or subject to, the law of duty (even if not in accordance with it), but rather of the freedom that is 'the character of action done from duty'. We have a prospect of making sense of Kant's suggestion, then, if we suppose that, in speaking of the freedom that is the character of action done from duty, he has in mind, not practical freedom in general, or independence from determination by sensible impulses, but rather a freedom peculiar to action done from duty, a freedom the lack of which would imply a lack of virtue, but not a lack of autonomy and accountability.

III. Inner Freedom and Freedom as Strength

As it happens, Kant does explicitly identify a type of freedom to which he seems to think virtue bears an especially close relation. He calls it 'inner freedom' and describes it as the condition of all duties of virtue (*MS* 6:406) and as the basis of virtue itself (*MS* 6:408). Determining what inner freedom is, and how it differs from practical freedom in general, however, is not an altogether straightforward matter.

1. Although most of what Kant says on this topic is to be found in *The Metaphysics of Morals*, it will be useful to begin by turning to the *Critique of Practical Reason*, where a brief discussion of inner freedom is to be found. There inner freedom is characterized as a 'capacity [*Vermögen*] . . . to release oneself from the impetuous importunity of the inclinations to such an extent that none of them, not even the dearest, has influence on a resolution for which we are now to make use of our reason' (*KpV* 5:161). Since the resolution mentioned here is evidently an exercise of the power of choice, this characterization of inner freedom may at first appear to be not significantly different from the negative definition of practical freedom noted earlier, according to which freedom is the independence of the power of choice from determination by sensible impulses. A closer examination does reveal some differences, however, one of which in particular might be regarded as especially significant. This difference becomes apparent once we recognize that in speaking of influence here Kant has in mind something other than determination.

To describe how the human power of choice is related to sensible impulses, Kant employs the notions of determination and affection. 'The human power of choice', he says, 'is one that is indeed *affected*, but not *determined* by [sensible] impulses' (*MS* 6:213; cf. *KpV* 5:32, 117). Kant means here to be expressing the general character of the human power of choice as sensible yet free: for a power of choice to be affected by sensible impulses is just what it is for it to be sensible, and for it not to be determined by them is just what it is for it to be nevertheless free (*KrV* A534/B562). The notion of *influence*, however, does not figure in Kant's descriptions of this general relation of the human power of choice to sensible impulses, and its absence seems not to be a coincidence. For in the above passage from the second *Critique*, Kant implicitly suggests that influence by inclinations is something to which one may or may not be subject; and at an earlier point he remarks, similarly, that, while human freedom does not imply 'complete independence from inclinations and needs', it is still possible 'to hold the determination of one's will free of their influence' (*KpV* 5:118). It thus appears that to be affected by sensible impulses or inclinations is not necessarily to be influenced by them, and that not being influenced by such impulses involves more than not being determined by them. In its mention of influence rather than determination, then, the above characterization of inner freedom appears to go beyond what is stated in the negative definition of practical freedom.

Admittedly, it may at first be unclear what this distinction between determination and influence amounts to. On reflection, however, it seems possible to find a real basis for it in the difference between an acting cause that contains the *sufficient* ground of the actuality of the effect it produces in a thing or a power, and an acting cause that does not. In the former case, the production would be determination; in the latter, mere influence. Accordingly, where the acting cause influences but does not determine, the production of the effect in the thing or power influenced must depend also on something other than the acting cause. Thus, whenever the power of choice is influenced by some sensible impulse that affects it, its exercise (or the part of its exercise that depends on the influence) always depends not only on the impulse, but in addition on a further condition, namely, the presence of a weakness in the subject's will (practical reason) sufficient to leave the power of choice liable to be influenced by the sensible impulse;[14] but when, on the other hand, the power of choice is determined by the moral law, everything requisite for the effect is already contained in the will and its representation of that law.

To say, then, that the human power of choice is not determined by the impulses affecting it and is therefore free is not to say that such impulses cannot influence it. Indeed, it is only by assuming the occurrence of such influ-

---

[14]   This weakness is not, of course, to be identified with weakness of will in the usual sense.

ence that we can conceive how an exercise of the free power of choice, as the capacity to choose to act according to the moral law, can be the choice of action contrary to that law; in the absence of such influence, there would be no possibility that a power of choice determinable by the moral law might choose to act contrary to it (cf. *R.* 6:36). In his characterization of inner freedom, Kant thus appears to go beyond what is implied in the definition of practical freedom in general: whereas practical freedom (according to the negative definition) is the independence of the power of choice from *determination* by sensible impulses or alien causes (*MS* 6:213; *G.* 4:446), inner freedom is characterized in terms that make reference to an independence not only from determination but even from *influence* by sensible impulses.

2. But noticing this difference does not advance us as far as might at first be supposed. For in the passage we are considering, Kant describes inner freedom as a *capacity* (*Vermögen*) to release oneself from the inclinations' importunity to the extent of achieving independence from their influence, and it is not at all obvious that this capacity is more closely tied to virtue than is practical freedom in general. If it is possible to have the capacity to choose to act according to the moral law even if one does not so choose, then it seems also possible to have the capacity to achieve independence from influence by sensible impulses even if one does not actually achieve it.

Moreover, it is difficult on reflection to see how the capacity here identified as inner freedom could be anything beyond the very capacity picked out by the positive and negative definitions of practical freedom in general. On Kant's account of the consciousness of obligation, there are two moments or aspects that must be distinguished: an intellectual representation of reason (the representation of law), and a feeling based in the receptivity of the power of choice. Thus, on the one hand, the consciousness of obligation depends on practical reason's bringing to bear on one's own case its idea of the moral law, an idea that in this relation involves not only the thought of oneself as acting in accordance with that law, but further—precisely because the idea in question is that of a law, which involves necessity—the thought of oneself as *necessarily* acting in accordance with it, so that the possibility (though not of course the bare conceivability) of one's acting otherwise is excluded. Yet, on the other hand, the consciousness of *being bound* by this law—which is expressed in the 'ought' of the Categorical Imperative—is a feeling of being *necessitated* by the law, and this necessitation implies constraint, or compulsion, and thereby reveals the presence in oneself not only of opposing inclination, but ultimately of a sensible nature that is independent of the moral law and from which can arise inclinations owing to whose presence any actual conformity of the power of choice to the moral law involves, or at least may involve, some measure of reluctance.

And the awareness of this constraint and reluctance is equivalent to the aware-ness of affection by sensible impulses (though not to the awareness of determi-nation by them) and hence to an awareness that the possibility that one might allow oneself to be influenced by sensible impulses to act contrary to the moral law is not something that one is in a position to regard as already actually excluded. There is accordingly a discrepancy present in the consciousness of obligation itself between what is included in the practical thought of the law on which that consciousness depends—namely, the thought of oneself as nec-essarily acting in accordance with the law, and hence the thought of the exclu-sion of the possibility of one's acting otherwise—and what the feelings of constraint and reluctance reveal—namely, that this possibility is one that one is not in a position to deem already actually excluded.

But what is of particular importance here for our purposes is the modality involved in practical reason's representation: the thought that necessitates in the consciousness of obligation is itself a practical representation of oneself as *neces-sarily* acting in conformity with the moral law.[15] For since this modality is inter-nal to the thought that necessitates in the consciousness of obligation, and since the original idea of practical freedom (the positive concept of it, through which, in the consciousness of obligation, freedom is first revealed) is just the idea of the capacity to realize what pure practical reason represents in its necessitating thought, that original idea contains from the start the idea of the capacity to exercise the power of choice in such a way that through this exercise one *neces-sarily* acts in conformity with the moral law. And, since bringing the power of choice into this relation to the moral law is possible only by exercising it in a way that secures its independence from influence by sensible impulses (the very independence the lack of which is manifested in the feelings of constraint and reluctance involved in the consciousness of obligation), the original idea of free-dom is from the start the idea of a capacity to release oneself from the importu-nity of the inclinations to such an extent that none of them has influence on the exercise of the power of choice. Thus, Kant says, the 'consciousness of the *capac-ity* to become master of one's inclinations that rebel against the law' is, 'though not immediately perceived, nevertheless correctly inferred from the moral Cat-egorical Imperative' (*MS* 6:383).[16] Though independence from determination by sensible impulses does not imply independence from influence by them, it does imply the *capacity* to be independent from such influence. So it does

---

[15] 'For humans and all created rational beings moral necessity is necessitation' (*KpV* 5:81; cf. *G.* 4:434; *MS* 6:223).

[16] It is presumably on these grounds that Kant later suggests that inner freedom is intimately related to, or even the same as, the *innate* dignity of the human being (as a moral being) (*MS* 6:420).

appear that the capacity Kant characterizes as inner freedom in the passage we have been considering is a capacity one already has simply in virtue of having practical freedom in general, and therefore possession of the former no more implies the actual presence of virtue than does possession of the latter.

It is clear, nevertheless, that in so far as this characterization of inner freedom involves the notion of independence from influence as well as from determination by sensible impulses, it also involves a conception of a sort of freedom specifically characteristic of virtue. So, although Kant's characterization of inner freedom does not itself specifically pick out this other sort of freedom, it does strongly suggest that the distinction and the relation between these two sorts of freedom have not escaped his notice.

3. To make further headway, however, we need to turn to the more detailed treatment of inner freedom presented in *The Metaphysics of Morals*. In this work, Kant makes clear that (as one would expect) in speaking of this freedom as *inner* he intends to contrast it with what he calls outer freedom. Indeed, he says that the division of *The Metaphysics of Morals* into its two branches, the *Doctrine of Virtue* and the *Doctrine of Right*, is founded on a division of the concept of freedom, which both branches share in common, into the concepts of inner and outer freedom (*MS* 6:406; cf. *MS* 6:218 n.).[17] So a brief consideration of these two concepts should throw some further light on inner freedom and its relation to virtue.

The distinction between inner and outer freedom, negatively conceived, is based on a distinction drawn among the sources from which a power of choice might be determined. Inner freedom is independence of the power of choice from inner sources; outer freedom is independence from outer sources. This contrast between inner and outer is clearly different from the one that is already implicit in the definitions of practical freedom in general. In the negative concept of practical freedom the power of choice is represented as independent from determination by 'alien causes' (*G.* 4:446), while in the positive concept, the concept of freedom as autonomy, it is represented as determinable by the subject's own practical reason, or will (*MS* 6:213–14, 221)—what Kant calls one's 'true self' (*G.* 4:458, 461). In these definitions, all sensible impulses are regarded as outer, for they all lie outside the power of choice, whereas the will, as the inner determining ground of this power, lies within it. Inner freedom, however, is obviously not the independence of the power of choice from

---

[17]   This division (which is not introduced in the *Groundwork* or the second *Critique*) belongs to the application undertaken in *The Metaphysics of Morals* of 'universal moral principles' to 'the special *nature* of the human being, which is known only through experience' (*MS* 6:217). It parallels the division within theoretical philosophy of the metaphysics of nature into the sciences of psychology and physics, which concern the objects of inner and outer sense, respectively (see *MAN* 4:469–70; *KrV* A846/B874).

determination by the will. On the contrary, the inner/outer distinction that figures in the distinction between inner and outer freedom is drawn among sources all of which count as alien causes according to the original concept of freedom. From among those alien causes, sensible impulses are now all to be regarded as inner. For inner freedom is independence from sources that are inner in the sense that they are present in oneself (though not oneself considered merely as will or as intelligence, but as a human being, endowed with a sensible nature)—in particular, it is independence from feelings and sensible desires (*KpV* 5:161; *MS* 6:407). Outer freedom, in contrast, is 'independence from the necessitating power of choice of another' (*MS* 6:237).

Some uncertainty as to how Kant draws the distinction between inner and outer freedom may be occasioned by the fact that, in addition to distinguishing between inner and outer sources from which a power of choice might be determined, he also distinguishes between the inner and the outer employment of that power—that is, between its employment in the determination of ends and its employment in the choice of actions (*MS* 6:214). These distinctions are not altogether unrelated, for Kant points out that, while others may be able to compel one to perform a certain action, it is utterly impossible for them to compel one to make something one's end (*MS* 6:381). It is clear, however, that the two distinctions do not coincide, for, as will become apparent below when we consider Kant's discussion of the affects and passions (Section IV.2), he takes inner freedom to lie in an independence from inner sources in the outer as well as the inner exercise of the power of choice. We may, therefore, take the distinction between inner and outer freedom to be based on the distinction between sources of determination, while recognizing that the way in which this latter distinction is related to that between inner and outer employment implies that, whereas inner freedom pertains to the entire employment of the power of choice, outer freedom pertains only to its outer employment.

4. The foregoing characterization of inner freedom as an independence from determination from an inner source is merely negative, of course. But Kant also offers the following positive characterization, which identifies the capacity in which it consists: inner freedom is 'the capacity [*Vermögen*] for self-constraint not by means of other inclinations, but by pure practical reason' (*MS* 6:396). Presumably we are to understand this capacity to be the same as the capacity to release oneself from the influence of the inclinations, the capacity in which inner freedom was said to consist in the second *Critique*. One releases oneself from the influence of the inclinations by constraining oneself by pure practical reason. So, here again, the characterization of inner freedom does not itself pick out a type of freedom distinctive of virtue. Just as having the capacity to release oneself from the influence of the inclinations does not imply

that one has released oneself, so having the capacity for self-constraint does not imply that one has constrained oneself.

But Kant goes on to draw the following important distinction: 'One may also indeed say that the human being is obliged *to acquire* virtue (as a moral strength). For while the capacity [*Vermögen*] (*facultas*) to overcome all sensibly opposing impulses can and must be absolutely *presupposed* on account of his freedom, yet this capacity as *strength* (*robur*) is something that must be acquired' (*MS* 6:397). From this passage we can see how Kant's characterization of inner freedom as the *capacity* for self-constraint by pure practical reason (as well as his characterization of it in the second *Critique* as the *capacity* to release oneself from the influence of the inclinations) is linked to his definition of virtue as a moral *strength*. For it is clear from our preceding discussion of inner freedom that the capacity, or faculty, that Kant here says must be absolutely presupposed on account of freedom—the capacity to overcome all sensibly opposing impulses—is in fact just inner freedom itself.

But what is particularly of interest in this passage is that the intimate connection it asserts between capacity and strength yields two different but closely related senses of 'inner freedom'. Kant is claiming that there is no inconsistency in saying, on the one hand, that the capacity to overcome all sensibly opposing impulses is presupposed, and hence to that extent something we take ourselves already to have, while also saying, on the other hand, that it is something that must be acquired, provided that, in saying the latter, we are speaking of that same capacity as strength. If this strength is nothing but that capacity itself (as strength), then it must be just the strength to overcome all sensibly opposing impulses, and so it is evidently through the exercise of such strength that one manages—in so far as one manages at all—to release oneself from the importunity of the inclinations to the extent of being independent from their influence. Presumably, then, Kant is prepared to speak of inner freedom in two different but closely related senses. On the one hand, 'inner freedom' can signify the very capacity identified in the positive and negative characterizations of it considered above; on the other hand, it can signify that same capacity in so far as it is also strength, where this strength constitutes the independence of the power of choice not only from determination but even from influence by sensible impulses. The two senses differ in that only the latter implies virtue; but they are at the same time intimately related in that inner freedom in the latter sense *is* inner freedom in the former sense, but inner freedom in so far as it is in a developed condition or state—in so far, that is, as it has been strengthened.[18]

---

[18] In a full discussion of Kant's conception of inner freedom, this distinction between the presupposed capacity and the capacity to be acquired (strength) would merit further elaboration. Because the con-

It is worth emphasizing that this duality of sense does not reflect an equivocation of the sort that Kant has sometimes been accused of. For given the way the two notions are related, it is perfectly correct to speak of the strength as the same as the capacity—even though to have the capacity is not necessarily to have the strength—and hence perfectly legitimate to use the same term to refer to both. In so far as it is the capacity itself that develops, becomes strength, the capacity *is* the strength. As we have seen, the capacity of freedom, the capacity to choose to act according to the moral law, is also the capacity to bring the exercise of the power of choice into *necessary* conformity with that law, and, as this necessary conformity is possible only in so far as the capacity is strength, the capacity of freedom is the capacity to develop itself into such strength. So this strength is just the realization of the capacity. In Aristotelian terms, it is the first actuality of the capacity of inner freedom.[19]

In sum, then, the distinction between inner freedom as capacity and inner freedom as strength enables us to take Kant's definition of virtue as a moral strength to be in effect a characterization of virtue as freedom itself in its developed, or realized, form. And this enables us to understand how, though in one sense freedom implies only accountability, not virtue, Kant can also legitimately say, as we noted earlier, that only in the possession of virtue is a human being free.

---

sciousness of obligation is *based* in the practical representation of oneself as necessarily acting in conformity with the moral law, so that the consciousness of being bound, or necessitated, by this law is dependent on that practical representation and thus posterior to it, the *original* conception of the capacity to overcome all sensibly opposed inclinations is a conception of that capacity as *realized* in action that necessarily conforms with the moral law. This means that the consciousness of obligation ultimately involves an understanding of inner freedom according to which (1) it is originally in our possession, not merely as a capacity, but as actualized; (2) this actuality of inner freedom (though not the capacity) has nevertheless been lost, as the feelings of constraint and reluctance in the consciousness of obligation reveal; and therefore (3) the acquisition of this actuality (that is, the acquisition of the capacity as strength) is a *re*-acquisition. Thus Kant suggests at one point that inner freedom is innate, yet something of which one can deprive oneself (*MS* 6:420), and elsewhere he speaks of virtue's mastery over natural impulses as 'reacquired freedom' (*MS* 6:485).

[19] I take this way of understanding such strength to be compatible with Kant's insistence that virtue is always in progress, always in struggle, 'moral disposition in *battle*' (*KpV* 5:84). In the ideal of virtue, this strength is represented as of a degree sufficient to yield the necessary conformity of the exercise of the power of choice to the moral law represented in the consciousness of obligation (the strength *is* the necessity), but since the sort of strength a human being can achieve is always an acquired strength and hence a matter of disposition rather than nature, the human being is never in a position to suppose that whatever degree of strength may have been acquired at a given point in time is the equivalent of that represented in the ideal (cf. *KpV* 5:33). Drawing on his students' lecture notes, we might speculate that Kant regards strength (*Stärke*) as a kind of 'force' (*Kraft*). He reportedly contrasts force with capacity (*Vermögen*) by saying that capacity is the ground of the *possibility* of action, whereas force is the ground of its *actuality*. Ground of actuality could be understood as more than ground of possibility if its presence tends to make action *necessary*. See Ak. 29:823–4. At Ak. 28:565, Kant is reported to have said: 'With a capacity we imagine only the possibility of force. Between capacity and force lies the concept of *conatus*.' Virtue in so far as it can be judged to be present in a human being could thus be viewed as *conatus*, and virtue in the ideal as 'force'.

IV. Inner Freedom as Strength

We are now prepared to take a closer look at Kant's view of inner freedom as a strength that must be acquired, and in particular to consider how it enters into the account of virtue offered in the Introduction to the *Doctrine of Virtue*.

1. We saw earlier that Kant rejects certain standard attempts to define virtue in terms of habit or custom, but, in his discussion of inner freedom and its relation to virtue (*MS* 6:407), he returns to a consideration of habit (*habitus*), or what he calls 'readiness' (*Fertigkeit*), and, after giving a general characterization of it as 'a promptness to act [*Leichtigkeit zu handeln*] and a subjective perfection of the *power of choice*',[20] acknowledges that virtue can after all be defined as a habit of a certain *type*, one that he contrasts with custom and describes as '*free* readiness (*habitus libertatis*)'. The difference between these two types of habit is that, whereas custom is a 'uniformity of action that has become a *necessity* through its frequent repetition', free habit 'proceeds from freedom'. Here Kant appears to be opposing the necessity he says is involved in custom to the freedom involved in free habit, and it is presumably on account of this opposition that he says, in the passage we considered earlier (Section I.2), that where maxims are grounded on custom the subject suffers a loss of freedom.

Although Kant does not explicitly offer further clarification of his characterization of free habit as proceeding from freedom, it now seems clear, given the distinction we have seen him draw between capacity and strength, that the freedom he has in mind is just freedom as capacity, and accordingly that in speaking of a habit, or readiness, that 'proceeds from freedom' he means a habit that stands to capacity in the way that capacity as strength stands to capacity. Thus free habit, habit that proceeds from freedom, would be the capacity of freedom developed into a readiness, or a promptitude that makes for facility in its exercise. This understanding of free habit seems to be confirmed by the definition of virtue that Kant immediately goes on to provide. Echoing his earlier criticism of Cochius, he first denies that virtue can be defined simply as 'readiness in free lawful actions', but he then states that a satisfactory definition can be reached if we add to this phrase a specification that places the readiness

---

[20] Gregor renders *Leichtigkeit zu handeln* as 'facility in action'. I depart from this translation partly because elsewhere Kant gives *promptitudo* as a gloss of *Leichtigkeit* (A. 7:147) and partly in order to preserve the infinitival construction that the latter term governs (*zu handeln*), which shows that he is speaking of a quality that belongs to a capacity rather than to its exercise (as we should in any case expect, given that he is characterizing habit and immediately goes on to describe it as a perfection of the power of choice). Otherwise, 'facility' would obviously be the correct term to use; indeed, Kant's choice of *Leichtigkeit* makes it clear that he is thinking that to the extent that there is promptness-to-act in the capacity, there is also facility-in-action in its exercise.

and promptitude not in the actions themselves or in the power of choice, but rather in the capacity of freedom itself as conceived in the positive definition: 'readiness in free lawful actions to determine oneself through the representation of law in action' (*MS* 6:407). Thus virtue is freedom ready to exercise itself; it is the *capacity* to determine oneself through the representation of law in action in so far as it has developed into *readiness* so to determine oneself. And so the 'moral strength of the will' in which virtue was initially said to consist turns out to be describable as a readiness of freedom, which makes for facility in its exercise.

The foregoing considerations put us in a position to see that Kant's insistence that virtue be defined in terms of freedom rather than custom runs parallel to his insistence in the *Groundwork* that the moral worth of an action lies in its being done from duty rather than inclination (*G.* 4:397–9). The point he makes in the *Groundwork* is (in effect) that a particular action has *moral worth* only if what moves the person to choose it is nothing other than the recognition that the action is unconditionally necessary, which is just the exercise, in a given instance, of freedom, the capacity to determine oneself through the representation of law in action. The point we have just seen him make about the definition of virtue implies that an action is *virtuous* only if what moves the person to choose it is nothing other than the same recognition that the action is unconditionally necessary, which again is just the exercise, in a given instance, of freedom, except that in this case this capacity of freedom is developed or cultivated to the point of being habit, or readiness to determine oneself through the representation of law in action.

But at the same time the foregoing considerations also reveal that Kant recognizes a distinction that parallels Aristotle's distinction between continence and virtue. Kant has room for a notion of mere continence in so far as he recognizes the possibility of actions that are morally worthy but not virtuous. Like the troubled philanthropist Kant describes in the *Groundwork*, who, despite the fact that his mind is 'overclouded by his own grief, which extinguishes all sympathy with the fate of others', 'tears himself out of this deadly insensibility' to perform a helping action (*G.* 4:398), the merely continent person may also, despite having to struggle against strong opposing inclinations, perform actions that have genuine moral worth. But, though a degree of strength is manifested in this performance, it is not the strength of virtue. Kant's account of virtue as a readiness to act that yields facility in action implies that, to the extent that an action is not only morally worthy but also virtuous, the state of mind it involves will be characterized neither by struggle to tear oneself out of insensibility in the event that sympathy has lapsed or other cooperating inclinations are absent, nor by the sort of struggle against opposing inclinations in which the merely continent person is engaged: 'The true strength of virtue is *the mind at rest*, with a considered and firm resolution to bring virtue's law into practice' (*MS* 6:409). Alluding to the Stoic doctrine of *apathia*, Kant calls this state of mind based in the strength of virtue 'moral apathy'.[21]

2. Now as we have noted, Kant takes virtue to be a development of the capacity of freedom conceived as *inner* freedom: virtue is a moral strength in relation to sources of influence that lie *within* the human being (*MS* 6:380). Thus, as he goes on to indicate, the readiness in which virtue consists is conceived in relation to sources of influence on the power of choice that lie within the human soul, sources he arranges under the headings of affect (*Affekt*) (for example, anger, fear) and passion (*Leidenschaft*) (for example, hatred, avarice). Kant's discussion of the affects and passions in the *Doctrine of Virtue* is sketchy, but, if we draw on the more detailed treatment provided in his *Anthropology from a Pragmatic Point of View* (part I, book iii), we can briefly outline his account along the following lines.

Affects are practical feelings, feelings that lie in a comparison of one's actual circumstances, including what belongs to one's state, or condition, with the object of some desire (and thus depend on the presence of that desire), and as such they always arise in particular circumstances and are in general short lived; practical feelings become affects in so far as they reach a level of intensity or agitation at which they can interfere with one's exercise of understanding and judgement in the choice of particular actions, and this happens owing to a deficiency in practical reflection, on account of which the feeling or circumstance in question is not seen in its proper relation to the totality of one's state of feeling or the totality of one's circumstances. Passions, on the other hand, are inclinations and as such are habitual in character, and their object is always a relation between oneself and others; inclinations with such objects become passions in so far as they become strong enough to interfere with one's exercise of reason in setting ends for oneself. Affects and passions can also be contrasted by saying that passions interfere with reason in its determination of the practical principle, or maxim, that specifies one's end and serves as the major premiss in practical reasoning, whereas affects interfere with the exercise of judgement in finding the minor premiss whereby the principle brings itself into relation to one's actual circumstances in the determination of action. Since practical feelings depend on inclinations (or in

---

[21] For a discussion of some respects in which Kant's accounts of apathy, the affects, and the passions resemble Stoic doctrines, see Michael Seidler, 'Kant and the Stoics on the Emotional Life', *Philosophy Research Archives*, 7 (1981), 1–56.

some cases on instinct) in the way that the exercise of judgement in the minor premiss depends on the exercise of reason in the major, with the result that their intensity tends to be greater where the inclination is stronger, and since it is from inclinations that passions arise, many affects depend on passions (for example, anger occasioned by the actions of a hated rival, or a miser's rage over a lost penny). Some affects, however, are natural, having a basis in instinct (for example, fear in the face of an unexpected and immediate threat to life and limb). Passions, on the other hand, because they are inclinations, are always and essentially self-inflicted and hence sufferings for which one has only oneself to blame.[22] For while many inclinations have their basis in instinct, and as such can be called 'natural inclinations' and are to that extent, considered in themselves, good (cf. *R.* 6:58; *A.* 7:267), inclinations are nevertheless always habitual and presuppose acquaintance with their object (*MS* 6:212; *R.* 6:28–9 n.) and therefore, unlike instincts, are within our power to regulate in so far as their presence and strength depend on the extent to which, through our attention, our choices, and our actions, we allow them to develop. Thus whenever inclinations—even natural inclinations—are allowed to become strong enough to hinder, or render difficult, the moral intention or resolve (pure reason's determination of the power of choice), 'it is the human being himself who puts these hindrances in the way of his maxims' (*MS* 6:394). Moreover, where such hindering inclinations are also passions, they have as their object a relation between oneself and others that stands in direct (essential) conflict with the moral end, and therefore, because this object involves persons (free, accountable beings) and so can be represented only through the exercise of reason, passions are never simply blind in the way that bare custom is, but always involve a maxim and are thus, as true vices, morally culpable (cf. *A.* 7:266; *MS* 6:408).[23] The fact that their objects can be represented only through rational concepts also means that passions

---

[22] Kant seems to take the German term for passion—*Leidenschaft*—to express what he regards as a distinctive essential feature of a passion, namely, that it is not a bare suffering, but rather a suffering that one *makes*, a *self-inflicted* suffering; for he contrasts inclinations that have a merely instinctual basis with passions proper by calling them 'mere passivities' (*Bloß-Leidendes*) (see *A.* 7:269), and he also characterizes passion as self-enslavement and abandonment of inner freedom (*A.* 7:267; cf. *A.* 7:253; *KU* 5:272 n.). This feature of passions is tied to the fact that passions directly interfere with our choice of ends, rather than of actions. Affects, which directly interfere with our choice of actions rather than of ends, do not share this character of being essentially self-inflicted. Thus one person can arouse affects in another (for example, fear or sympathy) as a means of influencing the latter's power of choice in its outer employment, but no one can ever produce a passion in another, just as no one can ever compel another to make something an end (*MS* 6:381) (though Kant often points out that, if we suffer from a passion, others are likely to exploit it to their advantage).

[23] Because the object of a passion is originally represented through reason rather than sensibility, it is possible for a passion to brood on its object continually, and accordingly passions characteristically tend to do so (*MS* 6:408). It is through this obsessive contemplation of its object that a passion (for example,

can never arise from the natural inclinations, which belong to mere self-love; they are always modes of self-conceit (cf. *KpV* 5:73–4).

To achieve inner freedom, then, is to achieve independence from these affects and passions (that is, independence from influence by the feelings and inclinations in which they respectively consist). But Kant stresses that this independence, and hence also the condition of 'moral apathy', which is included within it,[24] must be founded on strength, and in particular on two requisite components of inner freedom—namely, self-mastery and self-governance. Moral apathy is consequent upon these in something like the way in which, in the realm of outer action, civic peace is consequent upon the strength of civil authority under law.[25] Self-mastery is a mastery over inclinations that prevents the growth of passions. Self-governance is com-posure, the control over one's thoughts through which one's feelings are tamed and influence from affects is thereby precluded. Although Kant does not elaborate, these two requisites are quite different in character. The difference corresponds to a distinction he elsewhere draws between discipline and culture (cf. *KrV* A709–10/B737–8), which in turn corresponds to his further distinction between positive vice and mere defect (*MS* 6:390, 407–8). The function of self-mastery is negative and correcting, whereas that of self-governance is positive and habilitating. Self-mastery is a self-discipline that not only limits inclinations generally but extirpates those whose objects stand in direct conflict with the end of pure reason, thereby preventing them from growing into passions; self-governance is a cultivation of one's capacities of understanding, reflection, and judgement to a condition where their exercise is not subject to influence by feeling.

3. The presence of these two requisite components in inner freedom is reflected in Kant's view of how inner freedom as strength is to be acquired.

---

vengeance), unlike inclinations that arise directly from sensibility, can strengthen and sustain itself even in the absence of regular opportunities to satisfy itself. (By artificial means, however, a similar strengthening is possible in the case of certain natural inclinations (see *A*. 7:266; *MA* 8:112–13).)

[24] Kant seems to take apathy to *consist* in the absence of affects, for he defines moral apathy as a species of 'affectlessness' (namely, one that springs from the strength of the feeling of respect for the moral law); but he also identifies 'the proscription not to let oneself be mastered by one's feelings and inclinations' as 'the duty of apathy', so he evidently takes apathy to *depend* on the absence of passions, since to let oneself be mastered by an inclination is just to have a passion (*MS* 6:408).

[25] Although there is not space to explore it here, this broadly Platonic political analogy figures promi-nently in Kant's account of virtue. At one point Kant says that the moral strength in which virtue consists is 'a moral *necessitation* through [a human being's] own legislating reason in so far as the latter constitutes itself into an authority *executing* the law' (*MS* 6:405). Here we also see again the same idea of capacity as strength: legislating reason's constituting itself into an executive authority is just a capacity's developing itself into strength. In a virtuous subject, the autonomy of practical reason is 'at the same time an *autocracy* of the same' (*MS* 6:383; cf. *MS* 6:338–9).

After drawing his distinction between bare capacity and capacity as strength in the passage we considered earlier, Kant mentions two things that must be done:

One may also indeed say that the human being is obliged *to acquire* virtue (as a moral strength). For while the capacity (*facultas*) to overcome all sensibly opposing impulses can and must be absolutely *presupposed* on account of his freedom, yet this capacity as *strength* (*robur*) is something that must be acquired, through the elevation of the moral *motive* [*Triebfeder*] (the representation of the law) through contemplation (*contemplatio*) of the dignity of the pure rational law in us, and at the same time also through practice (*exercitio*).   (*MS* 6:397)

We can take these two elements, contemplation and practice, to be the activities in which the exercise of virtue itself consists and through which, respectively, the inclinations and feelings are brought under the governance of reason.[26] The contemplation of the dignity (necessity) of the pure rational law in us exercises and thereby strengthens the will itself (that is, pure reason's capacity to determine the power of choice) and hence also the feeling of respect for the moral law present in ourselves and in others, and it thereby works against the development of passions, which, by misrepresenting the fundamental relation in which human persons, merely as such, stand to one another and to themselves under this law, always involve a violation of respect for persons as ends in themselves. Practice lies in the exercise of pure practical reason *in action* and hence is a cultivation, not only of pure practical reason, but also of the powers of understanding and judgement through which is achieved the self-composure wherein they are not liable to interference from feelings.

It would be wrong to suppose that the contemplation Kant mentions is to be thought of as a mental gazing at an inner object or form. Since he takes morality to be based in practical reason, he must be thinking of something other than the theoretical cognition under examination in the first *Critique* (*MS* 6:217), and it is equally clear that he does not have in mind intellectual intuition (cf. *KpV* 5:31). Rather, the contemplation in question is a kind of reflection (cf. *KU* 5:204), and consideration of what Kant says elsewhere about how attending to the pure rational law in us elevates the moral motive suggests that this contemplation is really nothing other than 'the self-consciousness of a pure practical reason' (cf. *KpV* 5:29). Moreover, since Kant denies that prac-

---

[26] It is worth noting that Cochius' definition of virtue (Section I.1) mentions one of these elements—namely, practice—but overlooks the other. It is this omission that leaves his definition unable to exclude habits that are morally blind (for example, that of the sympathetic philanthropist described in the *Groundwork*), and this is accordingly what Kant has in view when he stresses, in criticizing the definition, that habit, or readiness, cannot be virtue unless it is 'an effect of considered, firm, and ever more purified principles'.

tical philosophy is needed in order to achieve virtue, we should not suppose that this contemplation or self-consciousness must take the abstract form that it does in philosophical reflection (cf. *G.* 4:403–4). When he stresses the motivational effects of considering the moral law or virtue in its purity, as he often does (see *G.* 4:411 n.; *KpV* 5:151 ff.; *MS* 6:376; *R.* 6:49–50), Kant is thinking in the first instance of the effect that witnessing the efficacy of this law working by itself alone in action (that is, without assistance from other motives) has on our capacity of moral feeling (*MS* 6:399–400), and he has in mind especially the use of certain *examples*, not as models of conduct, but rather as proofs of the practicability (*Tunlichkeit*) of free self-determination: such proofs inspire the freedom that is in us by making manifest its exercise in another. One of Kant's favourite examples in this connection is that of a subject who steadfastly maintains his resolution to be truthful even though his ruler threatens him with death unless he bears false witness against an innocent person.[27] From Kant's discussion of how this sort of example functions (*KpV* 5:155–6, 160–1), it emerges that he takes the acquisition of inner freedom as strength fundamentally to involve what might be described as freedom's attainment of self-consciousness. For he suggests that this inner freedom, or independence even from *influence* by inclinations, is achieved through the consciousness of our freedom (as independence from *determination* by inclinations): when inspired or encouraged by another's example, this awareness becomes an enlivened consciousness of our own capacity likewise to achieve an independence even from influence by inclinations; since, however, this latter consciousness includes 'a lively wish' to achieve such independence (*KpV* 5:156; cf. *A.* 7:253–4)[28] and so is itself a strengthening of the idea of the law of duty, it can become efficacious in our *own* conduct, in our *own* observance of this law, and when it does it comes to include a positive feeling of self-

---

[27] In order to be proofs of practicability, such examples must be *actual*, not merely the products of an author's imagination; they must exhibit conduct such as might be found in biographies or histories, rather than that of 'mere heroes of romance' (*KpV* 5:154–5). Thus, in one particularly detailed discussion of this type of example in the second *Critique*, Kant indicates that he has an actual historical instance in mind, that of 'an honest man whom someone wants to induce to join the calumniators of an innocent but otherwise powerless person (say, Anne Boleyn, accused by Henry VIII of England)' (*KpV* 5:156). Possibly the case is that of Henry Norris, groom of the stole, who was among those fraudulently accused of consorting with the queen. In his *History of England*, Hume gives a brief but moving account: 'Norris had been much in the king's favour; and an offer of life was made him, if he would confess his crime, and accuse the queen: But he generously rejected the proposal; and said, that in his conscience he believed her entirely guiltless: But, for his part, he could accuse her of nothing, and he would rather die a thousand deaths than calumniate an innocent person' ((Indianapolis: Liberty Classics, 1983), iii. 236).

[28] It is to this wish that Kant is referring in his often misunderstood remark in the *Groundwork* that to be 'completely free' of the inclinations must be 'the universal wish of every rational being' (*G.* 4:428); the freedom of which he is speaking here is inner freedom as strength (see *G.* 4:454; *KpV* 5:160–1).

respect—'*respect for ourselves* in the consciousness of our freedom' (*KpV* 5:161)²⁹—through which the law has yet greater facility in determining the power of choice. Thus inner freedom as strength can be characterized as freedom become self-conscious: this *practical* (efficacious) self-consciousness that lies in the *feeling* of respect for ourselves as free brings the capacity of freedom to *strength*, and this strength, itself inwardly manifested in the strength of that feeling, is just inner freedom itself. Because it lies in freedom's self-consciousness, this strength amounts to magnanimity (cf. *KpV* 5:152; *A.* 7:293), or the 'elevation of soul' in which the virtuous motive itself consists (*KpV* 5:71–2; *MS* 6:437, 465), and as such underlies the constant vigour and cheer that Kant sees as characteristic of the virtuous frame of mind (*MS* 6:484–5; *R.* 6:23–4 n.; cf. *KU* 5:272).

It would also be wrong to infer from Kant's account of moral apathy that he supposes the influence pure reason's determination of the power of choice has upon the faculty of desire to be merely negative—that is, to lie merely in the extirpating of inclinations directly opposed to the end of pure reason, in the preventing of their development, and in the limiting of all the others so that, in circumstances where they might otherwise prompt us to action contrary to duty, they have no hindering influence on reason's determination of the power of choice. For Kant holds that practice, in addition to the positive effect it has upon the powers of understanding and judgement (namely, the self-composure it yields through the exercise of these powers in the observance of duty), also has positive effects in the faculty of desire itself in that through it there arise inclinations (broadly understood, as habitual, but not necessarily sensible, desires) and thereby indirectly the dispositions of feeling that belong to them. Thus, speaking at one point of the duty of beneficence, he says, 'One who often practises this and succeeds in his beneficent purpose eventually comes actually to love his beneficiary'; such beneficence, he adds, produces in us the love of humanity 'as readiness [*Fertigkeit*] of inclination to beneficence in general' (*MS* 6:402; cf. Col. 27:419).³⁰ And in a similarly in-

---

²⁹ This self-respect in the consciousness of one's freedom might be described as moral self-esteem. As Kant's interpreters have often rightly pointed out, respect as esteem (whether for oneself or for another) should be distinguished from respect for persons in general, which Kant identifies with respect for the moral law itself (*G.* 4:401 n.). Yet if, as Kant suggests, respect for the moral law is the consciousness (feeling) of pure reason's practicality, this practicality being freedom positively conceived (*KpV* 5:29; *MS* 6:213–14), then respect for the moral law and for persons generally is equally respect for freedom, and accordingly the object of esteem is nothing but this same freedom *as strength* in an individual person. These two senses of 'respect' are thus related in a way that parallels the intimate linkage we have found between Kant's two senses of 'inner freedom'. For some discussion of the two sorts of respect, see Stephen L. Darwall, 'Two Kinds of Respect', *Ethics*, 88 (1977), 36–49.

³⁰ Kant is here drawing on a general fact about the practice of beneficence, one that figures also in the case of the 'sympathetically attuned' (*teilnehmend gestimmt*) philanthropist he describes in the *Groundwork* (*G.*

direct way, this same practice will bring with it the free development of the capacity to share in others' feelings, which is integral to this inclination to beneficence (see *MS* 6:456–7). Since this sort of inclination, like everything else that belongs to virtue, ultimately proceeds from freedom, or the practicality of pure reason, it is an example of what Kant calls a 'sense-free inclination (*propensio intellectualis*)', that is, 'a habitual desire from a pure interest of reason' (*MS* 6:213). In addition, because all inclinations are habitual, even natural inclinations depend on the exercise of choice in respect of both their strength and their specific objects and therefore can reflect in a positive way the influence of pure reason upon the faculty of desire.

Although, as was stated earlier, Kant takes our mere consciousness of being *bound* by the moral law to reveal that we have a sensible nature from which can arise natural inclinations that may in certain circumstances come into conflict with that law (for example, when a ruler threatens us with death), and hence further that we can never rule out the possibility of our acting contrary to it, so that human virtue is to that extent always 'moral disposition in *battle*', we can now see how nevertheless Kant's account of virtue as a moral strength describes a condition of peace within the soul (moral apathy), which, at least where conditions are not unfavourable, can be sustained and developed. And, although in describing moral strength as something whose degree is known only through the magnitude of the hindrances it is able to overcome (*MS* 6:394, 405) Kant may give the impression that virtue as he understands it is in fact Aristotelian continence, this impression dissolves when we recognize that the 'strong and bad appetites' against which the continent person struggles—that

---

4:398). (A deeper basis of this fact is suggested by Kant's remarks at *KpV* 5:159–60; cf. also *Nicomachean Ethics* IX.7, esp. 1168a3–10.) The difference between the sympathetic philanthropist's 'readiness of inclination' and the similar readiness of inclination belonging to virtue lies in the different grounds that serve as the bases of the determination of the power of choice to the practice from which these inclinations, as habits, derive: in the one case it is inner freedom as strength, in the other it is consciousness of one's own productive capacity (in general as well as in relation to others' well-being), a capacity unconnected with duty (see n. 8).

It is often supposed that this philanthropist's sympathy is natural rather than acquired. But while Kant does seem to suggest that this man has a 'good-natured temperament' and is one whom nature has 'fashioned for philanthropy' (see *G.* 4:398), he never suggests that this man's sympathy springs *immediately* from nature, or temperament. On the contrary, his careful (yet often misunderstood) specification that this man delights in the satisfaction of others 'so far as it is [his] own work' indicates that his inclination to help (which as an inclination presupposes prior acquaintance with its object and hence in this case prior helping action) has arisen from *practice* in accordance with the general fact about the practice of beneficence noted above. Moreover, Kant expressly indicates that the philanthropist's sympathy is *teilnehmend* rather than *mitteilend* (that is, free and based in his active powers, not unfree and passive, as it would be if it sprang directly from nature, or temperament (see *MS* 6:456–7)); indeed, if the sympathy were *mitteilend*, the philanthropist's inclination to help would not be immediate, as Kant says it is, for the helping action would then be desired only as a means to something further—namely, others' satisfaction and the agreeable *Mitteilung* it would produce.

is, the passions, which, together with their attendant affects, can influence the power of choice—will not be present to the extent that virtue is established, and further that this moral strength, even though it can be *measured* only through the opposing hindrances it can overcome, nevertheless constitutes itself in part through its production of sense-free inclinations through which it furthers its necessary end, and in addition moderates and positively influences the natural inclinations themselves.

13

Happiness as a Natural End

Robert N. Johnson

To have any end of action whatsoever is an act of *freedom* on the part of the acting subject, not an effect of *nature*.

MS 6:385

It is unavoidable for human nature to wish for and seek happiness.

MS 6:388

These two claims from the *Doctrine of Virtue* seem inconsistent, if we assume that we do not freely do what we unavoidably do and that to wish for and to seek something is to have it as an end of action.[1] The inconsistency, if genuine, is not harmless. The first claim (hereafter, 'E') and equivalent statements elsewhere express the extent of Kant's belief in free will, as well as feature in his arguments that there are ends that are duties and that such duties cannot be constrained by others but only *self*-constrained.[2] The second claim (hereafter, 'H') and equivalent statements elsewhere feature in Kant's arguments that we can have no direct duty to pursue our own happiness, that prudential rationality is distinct from mere skillfulness, and that, unlike the Categorical Imperative (CI), the problem of the 'possibility' of a hypothetical imperative needs no solution.[3] This is, in other words, an inconsistency between basic premisses of Kant's moral philosophy.

Thanks to Jack Kultgen, Andrew Melnyk, Alex von Schönborn, Mark Timmons, and Allen Wood for valuable criticisms and suggestions.

[1] The apparent inconsistency is featured in contemporary debates among Kantians; see e.g. Hannah Ginsborg, 'Korsgaard on Choosing Non-Moral Ends', *Ethics*, 109.1 (1998), 5–21, and Christine Korsgaard, 'Motivation, Metaphysics, and the Value of the Self: A Reply to Ginsborg, Guyer, and Schneewind', *Ethics*, 109.1 (1998), 49–66.

[2] e.g. *MS* 6:380. Translations of passages out of *The Metaphysics of Morals*, the *Groundwork of the Metaphysics of Morals*, and the *Critique of Practical Reason* are all from Immanuel Kant, *Practical Philosophy*, ed. and trans. Mary J. Gregor (Cambridge: Cambridge University Press, 1996). Translations of passages out of *Religion within the Boundaries of Mere Reason* are all from *Religion and Rational Theology*, ed. and trans. Allen W. Wood and George di Giovanni (Cambridge: Cambridge University Press, 1996).

[3] e.g. *MS* 6:386, 387–8; *G.* 4:417; *KpV* 5:25; *R.* 6:6 n.

I am not confident that there *is* any way of squaring E and H, given the uses to which Kant puts them. I *am* confident that the most plausible ways that Kantians have tried to put them together fail, and in what follows I show why. I argue that no interpretation of E and H renders them consistent without making one or the other claim useless to Kant. Although this makes my project a negative one, my justification is that, as will become apparent, I do not think Kant's readers have appreciated the gravity of the problem, and progress on it cannot be made until the issue is faced squarely. The first step to recovery, after all, is admitting that you have a problem.

Some, of course, may already think that E and H are *obviously* inconsistent, and that I am merely banging my head against a wall by seriously considering ways of rendering them consistent. But I do not, nor do those who find plausible the interpretations I will discuss, assume simple-mindedly that, merely because of his intellectual stature, Kant could not have held inconsistent views. That is clearly ridiculous. Anyone who sets out to develop a systematic and complete philosophy runs the risk of coming to conclusions in one area that are inconsistent with positions espoused in others, if for no other reasons than having too little time and too many details to work out. Indeed, I am happy to admit that Kant may have held inconsistent views in some *single* area of enquiry. What I find unacceptable, however, is the idea that Kant should have, without openly acknowledging it, *repeatedly* put forth propositions in a *single* area of enquiry that he himself could see were utterly inconsistent. With regard to E and H, the idea is all but incredible. The claims are found a page apart in the *Doctrine of Virtue*, and Kant adhered to both over many years of thinking about these issues, years during which his views were subjected to scrutiny by numerous and capable minds. So it seems safe to assume that Kant himself did not believe E and H, more or less literally construed, were inconsistent. Hence, I do not regard the charitable attempts to extricate him from inconsistency in what follows to be, from the outset, futile or misguided. Naturally, none of this implies that, at the end of the day, they will not turn out to be genuinely inconsistent. It only implies that, if they do (as I fear) turn out to be inconsistent, it will not be obvious why. As for the thought that Kant could give up either proposition and still maintain many distinctive elements of his moral view, it will become clear in what follows that I do not believe that he can.

There are some otherwise important issues that I will set aside or deal with only briefly for present purposes. First, as is well known, Kant changed his views several times concerning the role and importance of happiness in human life and, more specifically, in morality.[4] I am not, however, locating the follow-

---

⁴ See e.g. Reinhard Brandt, 'The Deductions in the *Critique of Judgment*: Comments on Hampshire and

ing discussion within those changes, though I discuss views that are clearly present in and central to not only the *Doctrine of Virtue*, but also the *Groundwork*, the second *Critique*, and *Religion*. Secondly, in some places Kant gives judgement a central role in practical reasoning.[5] But since I focus on ethical texts in which judgement is not emphasized, and since its role is not strictly relevant to the issue here, I do not discuss it.[6] Thirdly, commentators have long pointed out that Kant had at least two conceptions of happiness at work both within and across several texts: a maximum amount of pleasure, and a systematic integration of ends over one's entire life.[7] Fortunately, though I favour emphasizing the latter, my project does not require me to take sides on which is primary, nor to consider the relationship between them. Fourthly, it is nonetheless worth pointing out that here I assume the standard view that for Kant happiness is a subjective state of satisfaction rather than the achievement of some objective ideal. For the most part, what happiness is, in the final analysis, is for each to decide for herself.

Several more brief comments. When Kant claims that happiness is our natural end, I take him to mean that it is our *final* end in the traditional sense of that term (that is, happiness is something pursued for its own sake, rather than for the sake of something else). That, of course, makes the position that we freely adopt happiness as our end distinctive, not only in the sense that it is our own *happiness* that is freely adopted, but also in the sense that it is as a *final* end that we freely adopt it.[8] Further, I take it that final ends can nevertheless be *conditional* ends, or ends that *are* ends only on the condition that something else is an end. Hence, Kant's claim that the only unconditioned good is a good will does not entail that a good will is the only final end.[9] Happiness can be rationally pursued for its own sake and yet be so pursued only on the condition that we preserve and respect our own good will in pursuing it. Finally, even if we

---

Horstmann', in E. Förster, *Kant's Transcendental Deductions* (Stanford, CA: Stanford University Press, 1989), 177–90.

    [5] e.g. *KU*, 'First Introduction to the *Critique of Judgment*', 20:200–1, and 200 n.

    [6] See e.g. Ginsborg, 'Korsgaard on Choosing Non-Moral Ends', for an interpreter who claims that the role of judgement is crucial in prudential reasoning. Her reading does not, however, try to square the inconsistency between E and H.

    [7] Cf. *KpV* 5:22, 73; *G.* 4:405, 418; *R.* 6:5, 36–7. For example, the two conceptions are discussed by H. J. Paton in his analysis of the argument in his translation of the *Groundwork of the Metaphysics of Morals* (New York: Harper & Row, 1964), 29, and, more fully, in his *The Categorical Imperative: A Study in Kant's Moral Philosophy* (New York: Harper & Row, 1967), 85–7, 92, 105–7, 126–7; and Mary Gregor, *The Laws of Freedom* (New York: Barnes & Noble, Inc., 1963), 78, 177.

    [8] A possible exception is his view that ensuring our happiness is a means to protecting our moral integrity.

    [9] Cf. Korsgaard, 'Two Distinctions in Goodness', in her *Creating the Kingdom of Ends* (New York: Cambridge University Press, 1996), 249–74.

take H and like statements to be about ends in a purely descriptive sense—as what we *do* as opposed to *should* adopt as an end—E should be taken to cover both descriptive and normative ends. For E does not mean that any end we *ought* to have we ought freely to will to have, still less that any end we *do* have we ought freely to will to have. It is clear enough that, in E, Kant's position is that any end we do have we have only because we freely willed to have it, whether it is an end we *ought* to have, and whether we *ought* to have willed to have it.

I

Initially it may not seem that H has anything to do with our ends. It may instead seem to concern only what we desire. And, because it need not follow from the fact that we desire something that it is our end, accepting E might not seem to force us to the problematic conclusion that we must have freely adopted happiness as our end. Making something one's end requires binding oneself to it as one's aim or purpose; desiring something is being bound, not by oneself, but by the thing desired. Given this, H may appear only to concern a natural desire for happiness and so may not appear to be inconsistent with E.

Clearly, Kant often *does* talk about a natural 'impulse'(*ein Antrieb der Natur*) (e.g. at *MS* 6:380) towards happiness, and says, roughly, that this impulse is a constant and inescapable source of temptation rooted in human psychology. This impulse even explains in part why we adopt happiness as our end by providing, as it were, the target at which the will aims. So Kant's claim that ends are *objects of free choice* should be taken to mean that they are *that at which one freely aims one's choice*. Having an end is, after all, not like having an apple, and adopting ends is not like collecting apples in a basket. Just as the fact that I am pointing my finger at you does not entail that I exercise any control over you, the *object* of my pointing, so the fact that my choosing aims at something does not entail that I exercise control over the object of my choosing (*R*. 6:6 n.). One's freedom is exercised over one's finger, not necessarily over the things at which it aims, and in this sense to *aim* one's finger at anything 'is an act of freedom on the part of the [aiming] subject'. Ends, in the sense of *that at which we aim our choices*, are presented by natural impulses (or, in the case of the moral law, by reason), and so we need not be able to exercise freedom over them for ends to be the objects of our freely determined choices.

Even so, Kant repeatedly goes further than this to insist (1) that happiness naturally is our end, not merely something that *could* be our end, or is merely presented by human nature as a possible target for our choices, and even (2) that we naturally *will* happiness as our end.[10] This is why I think H and like claims really do mean more than just that we naturally *desire* happiness. Indeed, they must mean more. Consider, for instance, the use he makes of H in his discussion of imperatives of prudence in the *Groundwork*:

There is, however, *one* end that can be presupposed as actual in the case of all rational beings (insofar as imperatives apply to them, namely as dependent beings), and therefore one purpose that they not merely *could* have but that we can safely presuppose they all actually *do have* by a natural necessity, and that purpose is *happiness*. The hypothetical imperative . . . may be set forth not merely as necessary to some uncertain, merely possible purpose but to a purpose that can be presupposed surely and a priori in the case of every human being, because it belongs to his essence.   (G. 4:415–16)

This passage makes it clear that nature does more than merely present happiness as a *potential* target of the human will. The human will actually aims at happiness, actually has it as its end by a natural necessity (*Naturnotwendigkeit*) because this 'belongs to his essence' (*zu seinem Wesen gehört*).[11] Of course, E implies that this *could not* be so, that it could not belong to a human being's essence to have happiness as an end, since any end he has he must have freely adopted himself.

The further point (2), that it belongs to our essence not merely to have but to *will* happiness as an end, follows from the context. For this passage comes from Kant's discussion of how imperatives of various sorts are possible. The possibility of a hypothetical imperative, unlike that of the CI, needs no 'solution' (*Auflösung*) for two reasons (G. 4:419). First, it is analytic that 'who wills the end also wills (necessarily in conformity with reason) the sole means to it that are within his control' (G. 4:417). Call this principle 'HI'. Notice that the HI is *not* the principle that 'who *desires* the end also wills the means', a principle that, given our many varied and conflicting desires, would make rational action impossible. The HI asserts instead that it is irrational to *will* an end and yet refuse to will the necessary means to realize it, where 'willing' involves setting oneself actually to pursue the end.[12] The HI thus explicitly derives the binding power of a particular imperative from the prior *willing of an end* by the agent, not from his merely *desiring* it.

[10] *MS* 6:382; notice it is not merely the 'interiority' of having ends that puts them beyond coercion, but it is something about ends in particular—their essential tie to voluntariness—that underlies Kant's claim here. Also, see the *Groundwork*, where he speaks of 'the ends that a rational being proposes *at his discretion* as effects of his actions (material ends)' (G. 4:428).

[11] Although Kant uses different words, *Absicht* and *Zweck*, in this and other passages, it is abundantly clear that, in these contexts, he is using them as synonyms.

[12] Here I draw on Thomas E. Hill, Jr., 'The Hypothetical Imperative', in his *Dignity and Practical Reason* (Ithaca, NY: Cornell University Press, 1992), 17–37.

Secondly, since where no end is willed, no hypothetical rational requirement applies, the possibility of a hypothetical imperative requires that we assume that some end is willed. In the case of imperatives of skill, we assume a possible willed end. In the case of prudence, however, we (supposedly) know that we all actually do will the end in question—namely, our happiness. Indeed, as H and like claims state, it is by natural necessity—again, because it belongs to our essence—that we will our own happiness as our end. Thus, suppose prudential imperatives (or 'counsels') carry the force of rational recommendations. Given the HI, which requires that we *will* our own happiness as an end (and not merely that we *desire* it), the possibility of prudential imperatives, then, is in no need of solution *only if we know that we actually will this end.* Hence, Kant's position regarding the possibility of a hypothetical imperative clearly and unequivocally entails that we will our own happiness by a natural necessity, rather than, as E and like claims imply, by an act of freedom on our part. Notice that, by contrast, *nothing at all* would follow about the rationality of willing the means to happiness from the claim that nature implants in us a mere desire, impulse, or craving for it.

II

When Kant speaks of 'necessity' in his practical philosophy, he is often referring to the rational necessitation of the will, or the 'ought' of rationality. For this reason, H and like claims that happiness is a 'necessary end' might be taken to mean that we rationally *ought* to make happiness our end, where 'happiness' is some normative ideal such as a coherent life plan, and making it our end involves developing such a plan and then willing it.[13] After all, there are cases in which we go willy-nilly for the present pleasure (for example, a cigarette), instead of pursuing what we know deep down is our 'real' happiness (for example, long-term health). In such cases, we seem to be irrational, and our irrationality may seem to be in our not willing an end we rationally ought to be willing (that is, some coherent conception of our own happiness), rather than in simply failing to will a means to an end that we have willed. Kant's claim that we adopt the end by natural necessity, then, would not be interpreted as following from the fact that it belongs to our *sensible* natures to will happiness. Rather, it would be the claim that it belongs to our *rational* essence, to the nature of rationality itself, to will happiness (as a coherent ideal), in much the

---

[13] The following, I believe, is part of what Allen Wood has in mind in *Kant's Ethical Thought* (Cambridge, MA: Cambridge University Press, 1999), 65 ff.

way that it is supposed to belong to the nature of rationality to conform to the CI. Since any fully rational agent necessarily follows the CI, we imperfectly rational agents *ought* to follow it. Just so, since any fully rational agent necessarily adopts her own happiness as an end, as *imperfectly* rational agents we *ought* to do so. This imperative would clearly be distinct from the HI, which requires only that we will the necessary *means* to our (willed) ends. One does not violate the HI when one fails to will the end connected to a means one fails to will in a given case. Here, by contrast, we are talking of the rational necessity of willing an end.

Happiness as a *rationally* necessary end also offers as an alternative to my interpretation its own 'solution' to the possibility of a hypothetical imperative. In my interpretation of this, it is by natural necessity that we will our own happiness. In the current interpretation, by contrast, it would be by rational necessity that we do so. Hence, it would interpret Kant as holding that the possibility of a hypothetical imperative requires no solution because we can assume that we *rationally ought* to will our own happiness.

To be sure, this alters the meaning of the HI, which now will read: who *rationally ought* to will the end *rationally ought* to will the necessary means to it. That would leave us no way of rationally criticizing the refusal to will necessary means to ends that you will *independently* of whether you ought to will those ends. But this is a relatively minor issue. What is much more worrisome is that the assumption that we already rationally ought to will our own happiness does not solve *any* problem about the possibility of the hypothetical imperative that Kant might be interested in. In fact, it raises a far more serious problem about the possibility of a rational imperative to pursue happiness. For while it is surely plausible to hold that the possibility of hypothetical imperatives needs no solution because the HI as standardly understood is analytic, the claim that we rationally ought to pursue some coherent conception of happiness makes the possibility of hypothetical imperatives suddenly quite controversial. This is one strike against the rational necessity interpretation.

Admittedly, we do seem irrational in failing to pursue happiness when we go for a present pleasure that endangers it. But there is no irrationality beyond violating the HI (or CI). Where we are not being merely stupid or immoral (for example, in not developing our natural potential), we are simply failing to take necessary means to our own happiness, where the means require refusing a present pleasure. Or so I believe. Let me explain.

Suppose someone merely goes for whatever presently seems most pleasing to him. Such a person, let us say, holds that his happiness consists simply in the pursuit of the present pleasure, one after another. This seems to be a limiting case of having a conception of happiness. Without knowing anything else, one might think this is an irrational conception, on its face. But it is hard to see how one could continue to claim this once one adds that he pursues this policy in conformity to the CI and the HI—that is, takes means necessary to achieve the present pleasure and doesn't act immorally. For the CI requires us to develop our talents and insulate ourselves against future temptations. Hence, even if his only conception of happiness is the pursuit of the present pleasure, still, on moral grounds, he cannot forsake his future happiness altogether, and, again on moral grounds, he cannot ignore the development of his talents and abilities. Once we add the moral contours that restrict any permissible conception of happiness, once we determine that he does not fail to take the means to his ends, and really has no ends other than pursuing present pleasures, where is the irrationality?

By contrast, if he constructs some long-term conception of his own happiness spread over his entire life, and really *wills* it, but goes for some fleeting pleasure instead, he is indeed being irrational. But this is a clear-cut case of failing to take means that are necessary to make his long-term plan succeed. It just so happens in this case that the necessary means involve refusing a present pleasure. There is no need to suppose that, in going for the present pleasure, he has thrown over a *rationally acceptable* conception of happiness for a *rationally unacceptable* conception.

The pursuit of fleeting present pleasures, even if in conformity with the HI, and even if within moral bounds (including duties of self-development, and so on), may still seem to many not to constitute a rational life-plan at all. They will insist that rational persons have, not merely *some* conception of their happiness, but a conception of a certain shape. Failing to have that shape, and to will it, would be *making a mistake* of some sort, failing to see that this is what our *real* happiness consists of. But I do not see how this judgement can be defended on Kantian grounds. I can see how a person might have as ends, say, 'smoking whenever and however much I want' and 'being healthy throughout my life', thinking that there is no real incompatibility between these, and refusing to give up either. This is surely a rational failing; you can achieve one, but not both, of these ends. Failing to render one's ends consistent with one another, however, is for the most part just failing to conform to the HI: you cannot achieve long-term health (or the present pleasure of smoking) unless you give up the present pleasure of smoking (or long-term health). Where this is not a failure to conform to the HI, it is merely a failure of our theoretical reasoning capacities to work out the causal and other natural connections between the elements we count as parts of our happiness (that is, mere stupidity or obtuseness). Moreover, often, rather than willing inconsistent ends, one is not really willing one of the ends at all: if I can see that smoking and long-term health are utterly incompatible, and yet continue to smoke with impunity, not because of physical addiction or a weak will, then it might be that I really do not will long-term health at all. None of these failures resolve themselves into forms of practical irrationality that go beyond violating the HI.

If we cannot accept some person's conception of happiness, even though it conforms to the HI and is not in any way immoral, it seems to me that this is nothing more than a difference in taste, which, though important in many ways, is not grounds of objective rational assessment. Distaste for such a life plan instead of a long-term ideal of some sort (given it is within moral bounds) is compatible with regarding it as within rational bounds, and, I think, respecting such a life plan is precisely what Kant believes is required if we are to respect others as persons.[14] What makes another's permissible ends valuable is simply that they chose them. To refuse to acknowledge any value in a person's permissible chosen ends, even if they are not to our liking, is to refuse to acknowledge their choices as rational agents, and hence to fail fully to respect them as ends.

Thus, that there is no irrationality beyond violating the HI or CI in pursuing irrational ends I take to be a second strike against the rational necessity interpretation. But I will not rest my case on either of the above two points. For even if there were not these difficulties with a rational requirement to pursue happiness, the very idea of such a requirement is inconsistent with Kant's account of why there can be no direct duty to pursue it.[15] There can be none, not because there can be no *moral* 'ought' to pursue one's own happiness, but rather because there can be no 'ought' of any kind to do so. 'Ought' implies constraint, and that in turn requires some basis for voluntary *reluctance*.[16] In Kant's view, there is no basis for reluctance in the case of our pursuit of happiness, because nature has already determined that we shall will happiness as our end. Kant's entire line of argument here would make no sense on the supposition that H and like claims concern the *rational necessity* of pursuing happiness.

I suspect that many will object that 'ought' implies *involuntary* resistance from *non-rational* and *unwilled* sensible impulses, rather than resistance from our will. And it follows from this that there *could* be a source of reluctance to willing happiness that is not itself grounded in our naturally willing happiness. And, indeed, Kant sometimes claims that our natural impulses hinder the force of practical reason. This is not Kant's fundamental message concerning

---

[14] See Thomas E. Hill Jr., 'Happiness and Human Flourishing in Kant's Ethics', *Social Philosophy and Policy*, 16.1 (Winter 1999), 143–75.

[15] *MS* 6:388, There is, of course, an *indirect* duty to ensure our happiness, but in this case, Kant claims, our happiness is a mere means to fulfilling our duty to preserve our own 'morality' or 'moral integrity'.

[16] See e.g. *MS* 6:386, 'eine Nötigung zu einem ungern genommenen Zweck'.

the concept of an 'ought', however. Consider two examples of areas in which our natural resistance to the moral law is clearly made out to be voluntary.

First, Kant claims that a 'holy will' is *not* under any rational imperatives, yet *is* nevertheless under the moral law. The law is simply not an 'ought' for such a will. And the reason it is not, he argues, is that such a will 'would not be capable of any maxim conflicting with the moral law' (*KpV* 5:32). It is thus the capacity of *voluntary* action against the moral law, the capacity *to adopt maxims* that conflict with it, that a holy will lacks and hence that serves as the basis of the reluctance that in turn makes the moral law into a constraint. It is not merely that a holy will lacks non-voluntary sensible impulses that makes its reluctance to the moral law impossible.

Secondly, Kant's interpretation of the religious doctrine of the 'radical evil in human nature' requires that our reluctance to the moral law be voluntary. The possible positions one might hold regarding our natural goodness or iniquity are, according to Kant, that man is by nature good, by nature evil, both or neither. He rules out all intermediate positions, arguing that

If the moral law in us were not an incentive of the power of choice, the morally good (the agreement of the power of choice with the law) would be = a [the good], and the not-good, = 0 [the mere lack of a ground of the good]; the latter, however, would be just the consequence of the lack of a moral incentive, = a × 0. In us, however, the law is incentive, = a. Hence, the lack of the agreement of the power of choice with it (= 0) is possible *only as the consequence of a real and opposite determination of the power of choice, i.e., of a resistance on its part,* = –a [*nur als Folge von einer realiter entgegengesetzten Bestimmung der Willkür, d.i. einer Widerstrebung derselben*]. (*R.* 6:23 n.; emphasis added; see also *R.* 6:24)

The 'on its part' here means 'on the part of the power of choice'. Hence, any resistance to the moral law is a 'real and opposite determination of the power of choice', and must be if the law is to be an 'incentive' for us. It is indeed an incentive for us, so the resistance to the moral law that makes it into an 'ought' is a 'real and opposite determination of the power of choice' as well. Therefore, it is *not* the existence of involuntary non-rational tugs towards pleasure that explains the rational 'ought'. It is our voluntary willing of the end of happiness. But, if there is already present in us a voluntary willing of our happiness, then there can be no rational 'ought' to will it.

This is strike three against the rational necessity interpretation of H. The natural necessity of willing happiness cannot in any way be made out to be some rational imperative to will happiness.

III

I have been putting a lot of emphasis on the point that the rational 'counsels' of prudence are normative for us only if we *will* our own happiness as an end. One might think this leaves open the possibility that merely *having* happiness as an end, and not necessarily willing it as an end, is what nature implants in us.[17] But it does not. E, as do statements elsewhere of the same ilk, concerns the *having* of ends, not their adoption, making it clear that any having of an end must be the result of its free adoption by the agent.[18] Hence, even if we only 'have' happiness as our end, it still follows, according to E, that we must therefore have freely willed it as our end. H, of course, is inconsistent with this: *we* have not made happiness our end; *nature* has.

Moreover, and more importantly, the weaker position that we *have* happiness as our end only by a natural necessity again leaves the possibility of prudential imperatives without solution. For nothing follows from conjoining the principle that whoever wills an end wills the means with the claim that we necessarily *have* happiness as an end. Nothing follows because, *ex hypothesi*, having happiness as an end does not entail willing it as an end. We are left, then, with no explanation of why the counsels of prudence have rational weight with us. Of course, if they do, it could only be because we go on to will our own happiness, given that we have it as an end by nature. But then we need to explain the gap between *having* and *willing* happiness as an end in order to solve the 'problem' of the possibility of prudential imperatives. Their rational grip on us—*pace* Kant—would create a problem in need of a solution after all, indeed no less a problem than the possibility of the CI.

Notice that the gap cannot be filled by a rational imperative that we ought to will any natural ends we have, since that would just raise the problem of the possibility of this further imperative. What, after all, is irrational about refusing to will an end one has but need not will by nature? On the other hand, one might claim that, in this case, nature gives us the end of happiness as a means to self-preservation. Hence, if we *have* an end by nature, and we assume that any natural end is a means to self-preservation, then perhaps we rationally *should* will those means. But this obviously just appeals to the HI again, raising a further problem about why the HI should hold in this case independently of whether we will our own self-preservation. And the last-ditch move of claiming that we just *naturally* will self-preservation merely reintroduces the original problematic idea that we will *anything* by nature.

[17] This is Hill's position in 'The Hypothetical Imperative', 25 n. 3.
[18] Notice this in e.g. *R.* 6:6 n.

We might as well admit the mysterious idea that we will our own happiness at the outset. Hence, it must be not merely that we *have* happiness as an end by nature, but that we *will* it as our end, by nature.

IV

But does Kant really need a claim as strong as E? Would not the weaker position that we freely adopt all of our *ethical* ends be sufficient? That would allow that, by contrast, nature determines that we shall will the end of happiness. And, after all, E features in the *Doctrine of Virtue* almost entirely in an argument meant to exclude the possibility of coercing ends that are duties. And, while Kant may contend that *ethical* ends are non-coercible on the grounds that they must be freely adopted, perhaps he is assuming that the end of *happiness* is obviously non-coercible on different grounds—namely, that we cannot avoid adopting it, by nature, in the first place.[19]

Unfortunately, Kant really does need the stronger claim—the claim that having *any* end is an act of freedom—in order to argue that *ethical* ends in particular cannot be coerced. For he argues that ethical ends in particular cannot be coerced on the grounds that *the very concept of an end* precludes it:

An *end* is an object of the choice (of a rational being), through the representation of which choice is determined to an action to bring this object about.—Now, I can indeed be constrained by others to perform *actions* that are directed as means to an end, but I can never be constrained by others *to have an end*: only I myself can *make* something my end.—But if I am under obligation to make my end something that lies in concepts of practical reason . . . this would be the concept of an *end that is in itself a duty*. . . . That ethics contains duties that one cannot be constrained by others (through natural means) to fulfill follows merely from its being a doctrine of *ends*, since *coercion* to ends (to have them) is self-contradictory.   (*MS* 6:381)

Kant not only intends to hold E as a conceptual truth, but thinks he needs it to argue for the central claim of the *Doctrine of Virtue*, that there are ends that are duties. Notice, in particular, that it is only *after* his claim about ends in general, that 'I can indeed be constrained by others', that he goes on to establish his point about the case of constraint to a particular kind of end—namely, a moral end. And also it is *merely* from the fact that it is a doctrine of ends that it follows that ethics contains duties that cannot be constrained by others. This makes it clear that E is and must be a claim that covers *all* ends, not merely ethical ends.

---

[19]   In support, one could avert to Kant's claim, at *R.* 6:6 n. that, because nature determines this end, it is 'therefore otiose to say of that end that one *ought* to have it'.

V

Still, the fact that 'happiness' is an 'indeterminate' concept of imagination might seem to lessen the conflict between E and H (*G*. 4:415–18). Indeed, the concept is empty (it is the 'general name' for subjective determining grounds), and, because of the subjective variability of what brings pleasure or fulfilment, it is not a source of practical laws (*KpV* 5:25). Further, the constituents of happiness cannot be extrapolated from experience of what has brought us or others fulfilment in the past. This means, among other things, that we cannot determine which set of *particular* ends, once achieved, will constitute happiness for us.[20] Will riches do it? Kant asks. Health? It is unclear, since these bring their own risks to happiness, such as envy and excess. The most that can be said is that 'happiness' is the *formal* or *second-order* end of fulfilling some or other of the agent's particular non-moral ends in some or other coherent manner.[21] One might thus think Kant can hold (consonant with E) that, although the adoption of the *particular* ends that will constitute an agent's conception of happiness, as well as the way those ends are arranged over an entire life, is always an act of freedom, *that* the agent has such a second-order end to so realize is not (again, consonant with H). As we make decisions guided by the counsels of prudence, we freely pursue particular aims that, when ordered appropriately, constitute our own conceptions of happiness.

Strictly speaking, of course, Kant's position in E is that having *any* end and so even a formal or second-order end is an act of freedom. So the particular inconsistency in maintaining E together with H, where 'happiness' is understood only as a second-order end, would remain. That is a picky problem. A problem that is not picky concerns the use Kant must make of H. For assume that the particular ends that constitute a person's (indeterminate) conception of happiness are not given by nature but are adopted freely. Then Kant's argument that we cannot have our own happiness as an obligatory end would establish a claim that is so hollow and uninteresting as to make it hard to see why he thought it important. Although it would then be true that we cannot be obligated to adopt the second-order end of having some end or other, it would be false that we could not be obligated to pursue the *particular* ends that realize our formal end of happiness, since we do *not*, so far as H is concerned, already will

---

[20] By 'constitute' here I mean something like J. L. Ackrill's idea of a constitutive end, in 'Aristotle on *Eudaimonia*', in A. O. Rorty (ed.), *Essays on Aristotle's Ethics* (Berkeley and Los Angeles: University of California Press, 1980), 15–34.

[21] This needs some refining, since Kant includes the *moral* happiness of having done one's duty from duty in his account of happiness.

those ends by nature. H would thus become the trivial claim that it is naturally unavoidable for us to have the end of having some end or other.

Although I think there is more to Kant's position than merely that the end of happiness in this mere formal or second-order sense is naturally necessary, I do not think that, therefore, his view is that the *particular* constitutive ends we desire *themselves* are necessary either. His main idea seems to be just that, given that we are not 'gods', we have needs that cannot be met by pure thought alone, with no effort or intention on our parts. Kant says that

satisfaction with one's whole existence is not, as it were, an original possession and a beatitude, which would presuppose a consciousness of one's independent self-sufficiency, but is instead a problem imposed upon him by his finite nature itself, because he is needy and this need is directed to the matter of his faculty of desire, that is, something related to a subjective feeling of pleasure or displeasure underlying it by which is determined what he needs in order to be satisfied with his condition.   (*KpV* 5:25)

We are naturally designed in such a way that we must use our wills to meet our needs. But the conception guiding our will of what will meet those (real) needs must be based on our own subjective relationship to those needs, through pleasures and pains. Thus happiness is 'a problem imposed' on us by our 'finite nature'. So H is not an uninteresting claim about a 'formal' sense of happiness, nor an interesting but far more controversial claim that we have 'by nature' all of our particular constitutive ends, but the interesting yet not overly controversial position that, given we are limited beings with rational wills and physical needs, we are designed in such a way that we *must* meet our needs through our own rational agency, and that requires a connection between those needs and our own agency represented in a conception, however indeterminate, of our own happiness. This is, one could say, a deeper explanation of why we must, because of our natures, have our own happiness as an end. It does not render H consistent with E, however.

VI

I am not ready to say that I have decisively refuted all of the above ways of rendering E and H consistent. But I do take myself to have shown that there are sufficient difficulties with them to show that the problem has not been solved.

14

Instituting Principles:
Between Duty and Action

Onora O'Neill

Much discussion of the practicality—or conversely of the formalism—of Kant's ethics has concentrated on the capacity of the Categorical Imperative to discriminate principles of duty from other practical principles. Yet, even supposing that principles of duty can be identified, they will still not fully answer the question 'What ought I to do?' Any principle can be enacted or embodied or instituted in many different ways, among which agents have to decide.

Kant makes this point emphatically in *The Metaphysics of Morals*[1] for the case of duties of virtue. A typical claim in the *Doctrine of Virtue* runs as follows: 'if the law can prescribe only the maxim of actions, not actions themselves, this is a sign that it leaves a playroom (*latitudo*) for free choice in following (complying with) the law, that is, that the law cannot specify precisely in what way one is to act and how much one is to do by the action for an end that is also a duty' (*MS* 6:390).[2]

Seemingly the situation is easier in the case of duties of right, for the immediately preceding section is explicitly titled in capitals: ETHICS DOES NOT GIVE LAWS FOR ACTIONS (*IUS* DOES THAT), BUT ONLY FOR MAXIMS OF ACTIONS (*MS* 6:388). So we apparently have two cases: in *ius* the law prescribes actions; in

---

[1] Quotations from Kant use the following translations from the Cambridge Edition of the Works of Immanuel Kant: *The Metaphysics of Morals* and *Critique of Practical Reason* included in *Practical Philosophy*, ed. and trans. Mary Gregor (Cambridge: Cambridge University Press, 1996); *Critique of Pure Reason*, ed. and trans. Paul Guyer and Allen W. Wood (Cambridge: Cambridge University Press, 1998); *Critique of the Power of Judgment*, ed. Paul Guyer, trans. Paul Guyer and Eric Matthews (Cambridge: Cambridge University Press, 2000), and *Lectures on Ethics*, ed. Peter Heath and J. B. Schneewind, trans. Peter Heath (Cambridge: Cambridge University Press, 1997).

[2] There are numerous more specific versions of the same claim: 'there is no law of reason [for cultivating one's own perfection] for action but only a law for maxims of actions' (*MS* 6:392); 'The law [of beneficence] holds only for maxims, not for determinate actions' (*MS* 6:393); 'ethical obligation to ends . . . involves only a law for *maxims* of actions' (*MS* 6:395).

ethics the law prescribes maxims of ends, which can be expressed by various sorts of action.[3]

However, the similarity between the two cases is more significant than this difference. In each case the law prescribes only a type or pattern of action, in short a principle, law, or rule (which can be incorporated into an agent's maxims), and principles of all sorts are indeterminate. However, conformity to or neglect of principles of duty is ultimately a matter of doing or refraining from particular, determinate acts, and in the case of duties of virtue particular patterns of action. The difference between the cases lies in the type of principle at stake: principles of right prescribe *types of act*; principles of virtue prescribe *types of end*. Neither sort of principle can be used to pick out an act-token or a particular way of realizing an end.

The conventional response to this gap is to point out that Kant holds that it must always be a matter for judgement by particular agents just how they will conform to a particular principle, or just how they will pursue a particular end. An account of principles of duty is not *supposed* to tell one which particular act to do or just how to pursue an end. It is meant simply to show what type of actions should be done, what type of ends should be pursued. One must look to accounts of judgement for a view of the way in which the gap between principle and particular act, or pattern of action, is to be bridged.

Surprisingly, many contemporary discussions of ethical judgement are wholly unhelpful in showing how the gap between principle and act is to be bridged; in fact they say nothing at all about practical judgement. Many broadly anti-Kantian writers, including Peter Winch, John McDowell, David Wiggins, and at times Bernard Williams, depict judgement as the crux of the moral life, yet focus not on practical judgement but on judgement of the context or situation in which action is undertaken. They see ethical judgement as a matter of *appreciating* or *appraising* or *attending to* what is *salient* about situations and cases of ethical significance. This focus is often linked to certain types of Wittgensteinian and Aristotelian views, and emphasizes the ethical importance of perception and sensitivity to particular situations. A typical formulation is offered by McDowell, writing quite recently, when he characterizes judgement or deliberation as 'a capacity to read the details of situations' or a 'capacity to read the details of situations in the light of a way of valuing actions', or a 'capacity to read predicaments correctly'.[4]

---

[3] Kant comments on the changed meaning of the term *ethics*. In antiquity it covered both right or justice and duties that are not a matter of right; modern usage contrasts *ius* and *ethica*, duties of right and duties of virtue (*MS* 6:379).

[4] See John McDowell, 'Deliberation and Moral Development' in S. Engstrom and J. Whiting (eds.), *Aristotle, Kant, and the Stoics* (Cambridge: Cambridge University Press, 1996), 19–35, at 23, 26. See also

Accounts of judgement as sensitivity to circumstances or cases are accounts of a type of *theoretical* judgement. This can be seen in two ways. First, such judgements are essentially third personal: appraisals or readings of a situation are as open to spectators as they are to agents. It is a common literary device to ascribe good judgement of situations not to protagonists but to bystanders—the chorus, the confidant, the faithful friend. The onlooker may even be the first to realize that what is going on in the playground is not play but serious bullying, or that what is going on at a party is not idle chatter but flirtation that is turning to infidelity or gossip that is turning into slander.

Secondly, this type of judgement focuses on a *particular situation that is already present to be judged.* By contrast, practical judgement is agents' judgement deployed in producing or shaping a particular act or pattern of action. Practical judgement cannot presuppose that the particular is there to be judged.[5]

The appraisal of situations, and of their details, is of course of great ethical importance—if we do not notice the bullying, we cannot consider whether to desist (or, if spectators, to intervene); if we do not notice that flirtation is turning to infidelity, or gossip to slander, we can hardly consider whether to desist (or, if spectators, to deflect the conversation, to turn away, or to encourage it). But noticing and appraising a situation is not practical judgement; having noticed the bullying we still need to decide whether to desist or to intervene, and if so to judge which approach will be most likely to work rather than to worsen the victims' lot; having noticed the incipient infidelity or slander, there is still the practical question whether to try to check it.[6]

I. Indeterminacy in Theoretical and Practical Judgement

These considerations show, I believe, that an awareness of indeterminacy and a gesture towards the ethical significance of judgement cannot by themselves

---

David Wiggins, 'Deliberation and Practical Reason', in his *Needs, Values, Truth: Essays in the Philosophy of Value* (Oxford: Blackwell, 1987), 215–37; and Bernard Williams, 'Persons, Character and Morality', in his *Moral Luck* (Cambridge: Cambridge University Press, 1981), 1–19. This emphasis on judgement of ethically significant situations is not unique to writers who are opposed to principles and to theory. For example, Barbara Herman insists, in her powerful papers on Kant's ethics, that 'the rules of moral salience constitute the structure of moral sensitivity' and that they 'guide the normal moral agent to the perception and description of the morally relevant features of his circumstances' (Barbara Herman, 'The Practice of Moral Judgment', in her *The Practice of Moral Judgment* (Cambridge, MA: Harvard University Press, 1993), 73–93, esp. 78; see also her 'Making Room for Character', in *Aristotle, Kant and the Stoics*, 36–60).

[5] Could not this sort of judgement be applied to merely envisaged or imagined possibilities or options? The difficulty is that what we conceive or imagine cannot be fully determinate: a response to or reading of an abstract possibility cannot fully guide action.

[6] Onora O'Neill, 'The Power of Example', in her *Constructions of Reason: Explorations of Kant's Practical Philosophy* (Cambridge: Cambridge University Press, 1989), 165–86, esp. 185.

tell us much, or at any rate not enough, about practical judgement. The problem is not simply that the moral law and maxims of duty, and especially those of duties of virtue, are 'too indeterminate'. Kant notes the indeterminacy of concepts and of principles in many contexts, and classically in the Schematism of the first *Critique*, where he points out that general logic can contain no complete rules for judgement 'because if it sought to give general instructions how we are to subsume under these rules that could only be by means of another rule. This in turn for the very reason that it is a rule, again demands guidance from judgement' (*KrV* A133/B172).

But this general point about indeterminacy is common to all judgement. In practical as in theoretical judgement, agents deal with concepts and principles that are inevitably incomplete. (This is not to say that they will be *empty*, as certain commentators have thought in their more enthusiastically antitheoretical moments: concepts, descriptions, rules, maxims, and principles are simply and unavoidably *indeterminate*.)

To get beyond this general point we need to take account of the fact that indeterminacy raises quite different problems for theoretical and for practical judgement. In theoretical judgement the particular is given, and *the principle or rule may or may not be given*. Kant divides theoretical judgements into *determining* (*determinant*) and *reflecting* (*reflective*) judgements: 'If the universal (the rule, the principle, the law) is given, then the power of judgment, which subsumes the particular, is **determining**. If, however, only the particular is given for which the universal is to be found, then the power of judgment is merely **reflecting**' (*KU* 5:179).

Theoretical judgement *of both sorts* begins with some particular situation or action, and asks either whether a certain description or principle applies (the case of determinant judgement) or which of many possible descriptions, and indirectly which of many possible principles, is appropriate (the case of reflective judgement). This direction of thought—from particular to description or principle—is assumed in the accounts of ethically significant judgement favoured by McDowell and Wiggins and many others. Their concern is with what Kant calls reflective judging, where the appropriate description or principle is not given antecedently, so has to be sought. Their focus on the difficulties of reflective judging underpins their scepticism about the relevance of moral principles, and supports their scepticism about obligations. Reflective judging is no doubt important if we are to think and act discerningly, but it is not the same as practical judgement.

In practical judgement the problems created by the indeterminacy of principles are quite different, and in some ways deeper, because *the particular that is to exemplify the principle, description, rule (or maxim) does not (yet) exist* (and may never exist). The problem that Kant raises in the sentence quoted at the start of this chapter, and in many other passages, is that of an agent who has some maxim(s), whose content is some principle(s) with component act description(s), and who aims to act—not that of someone who has an act, so to speak, and strives to find whether a given description applies, or to find the 'right' or appropriate description and so the appropriate principle that should be adopted as a maxim. The agent's stance is practical, or prescriptive.[7] The practical problem for such an agent is not that of finding (one of many) descriptions or principles that apply (to what?) and incorporating them into a maxim, but that of moving from (one or more) principles that have been incorporated into some maxim(s) towards action.[8] Acts have to be produced, instituted, or enacted by the agent. Here it does not even make sense to speak of the task of judgement as that of 'subsumption under principles' or 'application of principles', or even as that of finding the relevant (salient) description or principle; all of these notions presuppose that a particular is given. The practical task is different: it is to satisfy or contribute to satisfying a maxim and so the principles that maxim incorporates.

The distinctive task of practical judgement is not confined to ethically significant practical judgements. I may have decided to do something that I take to be merely and obviously permissible, and do not think of as raising any significant ethical questions—to buy the groceries on Tuesday, not Wednesday; to make a cake; to find out about politics in Morocco—but each decision leaves open many different possible actions and patterns of action. The most mundane decisions, like the most morally significant maxims, are adopted before an act is done or adhered to in acting: in either case they underdetermine action, in that they specify act-types or end-types; but what is done will be an act-token, or a pattern of act-tokens. If an act or pattern of action is to achieve what I set myself to do, I must select act-tokens that satisfy the principle or decision. Yet seemingly a principle can offer no guidance about choosing one rather than another act-token or pattern of action by which it might be satisfied. Neither highly abstract nor relatively specific principles can 'specify precisely in what way one is to act and how much one is to do' (*MS* 6:390). Neither determinant nor reflective judgement can help here, for both of these are forms of theoretical judgement, usable only where particulars are available to be judged.

---

[7]   For an account of Kant's maxims as *prescriptions* rather than as objects of *introspection* or of *ascription*, see Onora O'Neill, 'Kant's Virtues', in R. Crisp (ed.), *How Should One Live?* (Oxford: Clarendon Press, 1996), 77–97, esp. 92–7.

[8]   We do not 'have' a particular act, an act-token, until the deed is done or not done—and then the practical problem is over. Kant sometimes speaks of the particular past act as a deed (*Tat*), at other times as that which has been done (*factum*) (*MS* 6:227, 230 n. k, 371 n. u); his term for an act-type is *Handlung*.

How, one may ask, has so much writing on ethics come to concentrate on a form of theoretical judgement rather than on practical judgement? Is it due to a problematic view of ethics as a spectator sport, or more elegantly a matter of moral connoisseurship? Or does it perhaps derive from the false assumption that all ethical judgement is retrospective judgement of deeds already done? The theoretical focus can seem appropriate if one imagines that all ethical judgement aims to assess what has already been done (one's own acts or another's), for then the particular is already given, and the need may be to pass retrospective judgement on it. Kant does not overlook the role of retrospective, theoretical judging of acts already done. One sort of retrospective judgement that he often discusses is that of a judge giving judgement on a case; another is that of agents retrospectively passing judgement on their own deeds and misdeeds: the activity of conscience.

Kant discusses this retrospective conception of conscience in many passages in his writings on ethics, often using judicial metaphors to emphasize the parallel. In the *Lectures on Ethics* he is reported as speaking of conscience as 'a faculty of judging ourselves according to moral laws' (Col. 27:351); in the *Critique of Practical Reason* he speaks of 'the judicial sentences of that wonderful capacity in us which we call conscience' (*KpV* 5:98); in *The Metaphysics of Morals* the juridical metaphors, and with them the retrospective perspective of the agent accused and beset by a guilty conscience, are once again predominant.[9]

Even this retrospective use of theoretical judgement to assess deeds already done (that is, where the particular is given) is demanding. Kant uses examples of retrospective, determinant judgement (the simple case!) in the Schematism passage, where he points out that it is not enough to have good (practical) principles. He notes that

A physician, a judge or a ruler may have at command many excellent pathological, legal or political rules, even to the degree that he may become a profound teacher of them, and yet, none the less, may easily stumble in their application. For, although admirable in understanding, he may be wanting in natural power of judgement. He may comprehend the universal *in abstracto* and yet not be able to distinguish whether a case *in concreto* comes under it.   (*KrV* A134/B173)

The problem here is evidently not that the task of judgement is practical in the sense of guiding action: Kant is imagining that both rule and particular are

---

[9]   This conception of conscience as retrospective is predominant but not invariable in Kant's writings. At some points Kant speaks of conscience as active where nothing has yet been done. For example, 'the human being thinks of conscience as *warning* him (*praemonens*) before he makes his decision' (*MS* 6:440). Cf. Hill, this volume.

given, and that the task is that of determinant judgement.[10] He thinks of the judge not merely as having certain 'excellent rules' but as having a case to judge, of the physician as having both excellent rules and a patient (it is less clear what the ruler is judging). In these examples the task of judgement is clearly theoretical, although it may be followed by a task that needs practical judgement.[11] Once the judge has reached a guilty verdict, sentencing may follow; once the physician has a diagnosis, treatment may be prescribed. The quandary attributed to the inadequate judge or physician, for whom the retrospective and theoretical task of determinant judgement of cases proves defeating, is due to their lack of that 'peculiar talent which can be practiced only, and cannot be taught . . . [whose] . . . lack no school can make good' (*KrV* A133/B172). But the Schematism has *nothing* to say about the quite different task of practical judgement.

II. Does Kant Need an Account of Practical Judgement?

Let us return to practical judgement. One quite appealing thought about practical judgement might be that we do not need any account of it because it does not matter which of the many actions that exemplify a maxim of duty is done. Suppose that we have a duty not to deceive: will not any non-deceiving action fulfil the requirement? Or suppose that we think that it is a duty not to be indifferent to others: will not any way of living that adequately expresses a maxim of rejecting indifference fulfil the requirement? Seen in this way, the *latitudo* of maxims of virtue is just that they leave things open: any act or pattern of action that satisfies the maxim is as good as any other. Equally the indeterminacy of maxims of right is simply a lesser form of latitude, which is indifferent as between any act-tokens of the required type. There are countless ways of satisfying any maxim adopted, and we should not get bothered about the lack of an account of how to judge between ways of living virtuously or acting rightly. However, this does not seem to be quite what Kant has in mind.

Immediately after his characterization of the latitude of wide duties Kant remarks that this should not be understood as 'permission to make an excep-

---

[10] This use of determinant judgement can make ethical judgements about what has been done, but because it is not apt for practical judgement it cannot be used to shape action ethically. See, for example, 'We have a faculty of judging whether a thing is right or wrong, and this applies no less to our actions than to those of others. This faculty resides in the understanding' (Col. 27:297).

[11] Kant's picture of the theoretical aspect of judicial and medical judgement may, of course, be oversimplified.

tion, but only as permission to limit one maxim of duty by another (e.g. love of one's neighbour in general by love of one's parents), by which in fact the field for the practice of duty is widened' (*MS* 6:390).

It is clear enough that the issue is not one of making exceptions, yet the idea of limiting one maxim of duty by another does not look likely to help clarify the activity of practical judgement. How can the fact that we adopt and are bound by a plurality of maxims of duty help, as opposed to complicate, practical judgement? The thought that conflicts of obligations constitute a *reductio ad absurdum* of any ethic of rights or obligation, of the very notion of moral requirement, has been widely advocated in recent writing on ethics (often by the very writers who assimilate ethical judgement to reflective judging).[12] More pointedly, are not close relatives of the two maxims of duty that Kant cites, those of civic and of familial duty, a canonical instance of a moral dilemma that has been discussed by countless writers from Cicero to Sartre? How can such examples be expected to help us understand how we are to limit one maxim by another? More ominously, is not the problem of moral dilemmas or conflicts between duties one of the notorious quagmires in Kant interpretation?[13]

It seems to me that, on the contrary, the remark about 'limiting one maxim by another' may shed useful light on Kant's conception of practical judgement. On Kant's account the Categorical Imperative identifies a number of principles of duty, *each* of which is relevant in *all* contexts. A plurality of principles of obligation is and a plurality of maxims (or a single complex maxim) should be the *invariable* context of dutiful action. Practical judgement is *always* a matter of finding a way of achieving a range of aims and objectives while conforming to a plurality of principles of duty, and of doing so while taking account of the varied realities and vulnerabilities of human life.

III. Practical Judgement and Moral Conflict

So if an adequate account of practical judgement is to be found, it is important to consider how acting under multiple requirements, with the possibility that

---

[12] See Bernard Williams, *Ethics and the Limits of Philosophy* (London: Fontana, 1985).

[13] And does not Kant immediately make the problem worse by reminding us that 'a human being cannot see into the depths of his own heart' (*MS* 6:392), so suggesting that a requirement to enact a plurality of maxims may be stymied not only by the indeterminacy of the maxims, but by agents' uncertainty about their own maxims? For discussion of the implications of Kant's insistence on our lack of self-knowledge (and hence of knowledge of our own maxims), and of his account of virtue, see Onora O'Neill, 'Kant's Virtues', 89–91.

they will lead to ethical conflict, can be approached. The short passage in *The Metaphysics of Morals* in which Kant writes about moral conflict has been much discussed recently, and I apologize for returning to it. I have divided it into two parts so as to consider its two claims in turn.

Both in the German and in the liberally interpolated Latin in this paragraph Kant introduces distinctions that are not easy to grasp. The passage begins:

A *conflict of duties* (*collisio officiorum s. obligationum*) would be a relation between them in which one of them would cancel the other (wholly or in part). But since duty and obligations are concepts that express the objective practical *necessity* of certain actions and two rules opposed to each other cannot be necessary at the same time, if it is a duty to act in accordance with one rule, to act in accordance with the opposite rules is not a duty but even contrary to duty; so a *collision of duties* and obligations is inconceivable (*obligationes non colliduntur*).   (*MS* 6:224)

This part of the passage, up to the claim that a collision of duties is inconceivable, is not, I think, hard to interpret. It does not say that there can be no moral conflict. It makes a modal claim about principles: 'two rules opposed to each other cannot be necessary at the same time.' There cannot, for example, be pairs of rules requiring that people be open in all dealings and wholly secretive in all dealings, or rules commanding both honesty and deceitfulness, both beneficence and indifference. The first part of the passage simply proposes a *consistency constraint on principles of obligation* (that is, on *rationes obligationum* or *rationes obligantes*); it insists that there cannot be incompatible principles (*rationes*) of obligation—that is, principles of obligation that could not hold 'at the same time', so could never be jointly satisfied. This point has been widely accepted in recent writing on duty and obligation[14] as a welcome constraint on any theory of ethical (or other) requirements. However, the first section of the passage does not assert that there cannot be moral conflicts or dilemmas, or that aspects of an agent's maxim cannot be incompatible; it says nothing about maxims.

In some, indeed in many, cases Kant's fundamental principles of obligation can clearly be jointly instantiated 'at the same time'. So they are at least com-

---

[14]   Ruth Barcan Marcus, 'Moral Dilemmas and Consistency', *Journal of Philosophy*, 77 (1980), 121–36; Barbara Herman, 'Obligation and Performance', in her *The Practice of Moral Judgment*, 159–83; Thomas E. Hill, Jr., 'Moral Dilemmas, Gaps and Residues: A Kantian Perspective', in H.E. Mason (ed.), *Moral Dilemmas and Moral Theory* (Oxford: Oxford University Press, 1996), 167–98; Onora O'Neill, 'Duty and Virtues', in A. Phillips Griffiths (ed.), *Ethics* (RIP supplementary volume 35) (Cambridge: Cambridge University Press, 1993), 107–20, esp. 115–18, 'Principles, Institutions and Judgement', in J. Tasioulass (ed.), *Law, Value and Social Practices* (Aldershot: Dartmouth, 1997), 59–73, *Towards Justice and Virtue: A Constructive Account of Practical Reasoning* (Cambridge: Cambridge University Press, 1996).

patible in this rather weak sense; they are not *intrinsically incompatible*. His view may not be simply that these principles are compatible—that is, jointly satisfiable in *some* circumstances—but more strongly that they are *intrinsically compatible*, in that there are no circumstances in which they are not jointly satisfiable. The basic principle of all duties of right is simply 'so act externally that the free use of your choice can coexist with the freedom of everyone else according to a universal law' (*MS* 6:231). Arguably the universal law demanding respect for external freedom is that of non-interference, and dutiful non-interferers will find that their multiple conformities to the fundamental principle of right cannot conflict in *any* circumstances. The fundamental principle of negative perfect duties, such as those of refraining from suicide and refraining from promising falsely, also cannot come into conflict. Conflict can arise only when one or more duty demands positive action.

The underlying principles of duties of virtue, by contrast, often require positive action, but since they are principles of *imperfect* duty, they do not have to be fulfilled on every occasion. If there is difficulty or impossibility in being beneficent on one occasion, action may legitimately be postponed until opportunity arises. The principles of virtue will therefore be both *intrinsically consistent* with one another and *intrinsically consistent* with the non-interference required by the fundamental principle of right.

However, problems can arise if we have a particularly urgent case of imperfect duty requiring present action that would breach some perfect duty: this case troubles Kant and is the theme of *On a Supposed Right to Lie from Philanthropy*; at some points he suggests that a simple priority rule such as 'observance of perfect duty always trumps observance of imperfect duty' is needed.[15] Such a rule would achieve intrinsic consistency among all fundamental principles of obligation, at least for a very wide range. Even without it, Kant's principles of duty are not intrinsically inconsistent, in that they are jointly satisfiable in some (indeed many) situations.

By contrast, multiple principles of *perfect* obligation that require *positive action* might not only be contingently incompatible (incapable of joint satisfaction in some situations), but intrinsically incompatible (incapable of joint satisfaction in any situation), or in constant tension (incapable of joint satisfaction in most situations). However, Kant's principles of right and of virtue look as if they should be not merely compatible, but intrinsically compatible.

All this, however, tells one little enough. Even if Kant's fundamental universal principles of obligation cannot conflict, this does not show that we will not experience moral conflict. Many human duties are special duties arising

[15] See e.g. *Lectures on Ethics* (Vig. 27:537).

from the specific circumstances and institutions with which we live, the particular roles and responsibilities we have assumed, the attachments and relationships we have nurtured. We are always faced not only by the abstract principles of universal duty, but by webs of special duties that should (but may not) be aligned with, even derivable from, these fundamental principles, and that link us in complex ways to others. *The Metaphysics of Morals* develops systems of requirement from the fundamental principles of duty, but it offers no guarantee that all the component duties of a system of right or of a doctrine of virtue will be compatible in all situations. Our special duties may include obligations to obey the law, obligations to keep promises and contracts made, obligations to support dependents. There is little doubt that these special obligations can turn out not to be jointly satisfiable 'at the same time'. Moreover, since some special duties *require* performance 'at the same time', the imperfection that rendered fundamental principles of virtue consistent with one another and with principles of right cannot guarantee that we have consistent duties. Our maxims will constantly incorporate reference to such special duties, which can be in conflict. This brings us back to the second part of Kant's comments on moral conflict.

> However, a subject may have in a rule which he prescribes to himself, two *grounds* of obligation (*rationes obligandi*) one or other of which is not sufficient to put him under obligations (*rationes obligandi non obligantes*), so that one of them is not a duty. When two such grounds of obligations conflict with each other, practical philosophy says not that the stronger takes precedence (*fortior obligatio vincit*) but that the stronger *ground of obligation prevails* (*fortior obligandi ratio vincit*). (*MS* 6:224)[16]

The difficult part of this passage lies in the obscure phrase *rationes obligandi*. This phrase is standardly translated as 'ground of obligation', following, but I think losing, the sense of the German word *Verpflichtungsgrund*. This standard rendering makes the *rationes obligandi* appear even grander and more abstract than the *rationes obligantes*. However, I do not think it is a convincing translation for several reasons. First, it simply loses the linguistic parallels Kant offers between differing *rationes* (reasons, principles; or, in the passage from

---

[16] There are also brief but useful discussions of moral conflict in the *Lectures on Ethics* (Vig. 27:508–9, 537) and in the *Doctrine of Method* of the *Critique of Practical Reason*. The latter runs 'The method [of moral instruction] takes the following course. At first it is only a question of making appraisal of actions by moral laws a natural occupation and, as it were, a habit accompanying all our free actions as well as our observation of those of others, and of sharpening it by asking first whether the action objectively *conforms with the moral law*, and with which law; by this, attention to such law as provides a *ground of obligation* is distinguished from that which is in fact obligatory (*leges obligandi a legibus obligantibus*)' (followed by an illustration of surpassing obscurity) (*KpV* 5:159).

the *Critique of Practical Reason*, 5:159, between differing *leges*). Secondly, the reading loses sight of the fact that the *rationes obligandi* are described as features not of laws or principles of obligation in the abstract, but of 'the rule a subject prescribes for himself'—that is, of a maxim. Since the *rationes obligandi* are elements of maxims, they are particular to situations and occasions. But what are they?

Let me at least offer a translation that I think is truer to the text. I would render *rationes obligandi* as 'obligating reasons', which preserves the linguistic parallels of the text, takes on board the point that the gerundive is often used for a more specific modal demand ('obligating reasons' can be those of some particular agent in a particular context; *principles of obligation* cannot), and so brings out the agent-related character of these reasons. All of this fits with Kant's insistence that these reasons are internal to 'a rule which he [a subject] prescribes to himself'—that is, internal to maxims.

But what makes *rationes obligandi* reasons? It is simply, I think, that these are the various aspects of a maxim that refer either to *rationes obligationum*—that is, to fundamental reasons or principles of obligation—or to special duties that have been acquired by an agent. Kant does not deny that agents can find themselves seeking to meet ethical demands that may (contingently) conflict. His claim in the disputed passage is only that this is due not to any intrinsic conflict between fundamental principles of duty, but to contingent conflict in a particular case between the many *rationes obligandi* an agent incorporates or has reason to incorporate into a maxim.[17]

Let us now return to the idea that practical judgement involves 'limiting one maxim by another'. How can this task make sense if maxims can incorporate multiple *rationes obligandi*? And let us begin with the easy case, without difficult conflict. Here, I believe that the task of practical judgement can be helped rather than stymied by this plurality of demands. For practical judgement is the task of finding some particular act or pattern of action that meets the requirements. This task is more clearly specified if it is a matter of finding some way of acting that meets a plurality of requirements. So, in asking what I should do, my task is to find a way of avoiding injury that does not involve lying, a way of living beneficently that does not involve self-abasement, a way of avoiding theft that does not require indifference to others, and so on. In most cases *guidance is provided by the task of limiting one maxim by another*: we

---

[17] I am therefore unpersuaded by Barbara Herman's suggestion that the *rationes obligandi* are 'facts of a certain sort [that] have moral significance because they are defining features of our (human) rational natures that limit what we can rationally will', although I agree with her conclusion that moral conflict is '*in the agent*, in her maxim of action' ('Obligation and Performance', 169).

identify acceptable forms of beneficence by ruling out beneficence that relies on theft, or on deception, or on violence to others, and so on; we identify acceptable ways of avoiding deception if we rule out as beneath consideration those that injure, are cruel, involve self-abasement, and so on. With good fortune we can manage much of our lives pursuing quite varied plans and goals, without injuring, perjuring, lying, or stealing and also without indifference, self-stultification, or self-abasement. In each context of action, duty—as well as self-interest—makes multiple demands, *but this is generally useful rather than damaging in working out how to shape actions and lives.*

Two analogies may be helpful here. The first is mathematical. Just as certain equations can be solved only because we know a sufficient number of constraints, so certain questions about how we ought to act are more readily and better resolvable if we take account of the constraints of multiple principles of obligation. But a more helpful analogy may be that of the equally practical judgement of the designer, craftsman, or poet, who has to discover or find *some* way of making that meets *multiple* demands. Imagine that you have to design a wheelbarrow. It has to roll smoothly, to be light enough even for feeble gardeners, to be durable enough for rough use, and to be made of available and affordable materials. A clay wheelbarrow will not do; nor will one made of lead. The multiplicity of demands is not a demonstration that there can be no satisfactory wheelbarrows but it constrains and thereby shapes the activities of those who make wheelbarrows. So with the ethical constraints that action faces, the task of practical judgement about what we ought to do is to find some act that satisfies multiple *rationes obligandi*.

IV. Conflict and Casuistry

Of course, not every equation has a solution, and not every design problem can be solved. Equally, practical judging cannot always find a way of meeting all moral demands. Agents will sometimes find no act or pattern of action can fully satisfy all the *rationes obligandi* that they accept and seek to incorporate into their maxim. (Nor, of course, can we always find ways of attaining, or even pursuing, all our projects or desires.)

It is reasonably clear that Kant accepts this point. The most prominent evidence lies, I think, in his multiple discussions of 'casuistical questions' in *The Metaphysics of Morals* and throughout the *Lectures on Ethics*. There is also suggestive evidence in his numerous allusions to the problem of right action in the face of tyranny that are scattered in many different texts.

Kant often comments on casuistry with conventional hostility, labelling it both jesuitical and hair-splitting.[18] However, many of his examples of casuistical questions are by no means hair-splitting or trivial. They are examples of important moral dilemmas that can arise in particular cases. They include the following. Is killing oneself to save one's country or to help mankind suicide or heroism (*MS* 6:424)? Is conventional politeness a form of lying (*MS* 6:431)? Is miserliness mistaken thrift or slavish subjection of oneself to material goods (*MS* 6:434)? Can self-respect and proper pride become arrogance (*MS* 6:437)? Is paternalism by the powerful beneficence, or violation of others' freedom (*MS* 6:454)? How much of our resources should we use 'in practicing beneficence' (*MS* 6:454)? Might the world be better with full compliance with the requirements of justice but no social virtues (*MS* 6:458)? Questions like these, with appropriate switches in vocabulary, have raised burning issues generation after generation.[19]

What does Kant think that we should do when we cannot find a way of satisfying multiple *rationes obligandi* such as those invoked in the casuistical questions? If he has no answer, will not his account of dutiful action fail us where we most need help, in the hard cases? Kant certainly does not provide any step-by-step or algorithmic method for answering the casuistical questions (presumably his hostility to 'jesuitical' casuistry is because he thinks it aspires to such methods). He comments in the *Doctrine of Method* of *The Metaphysics of Morals* that taken properly casuistry is not a *doctrine* but a *practice*: 'casuistry is not so much a doctrine about how *to find* something as rather a practice in how *to seek* truth. So it is *woven into ethics* in a *fragmentary* way . . . and is added to ethics only by way of a scholia to the system' (*MS* 6:411).

Clearly we should not expect to be offered an algorithm or even a recipe for practical judgement that could resolve moral conflict.[20] However, as with mathematics and design, the lack of a comprehensive method for resolving all

---

[18]   In the *Lectures on Ethics* see the following passages: Col. 27:356, which depicts casuistry as dealing with small scruples, concern about trivialities; Mro. 29:615, which depicts casuistry as a micrology, as done by Jesuits and remarks that 'It is so called because it has to do with specific and particular cases'; Vig. 27:557, which once again depicts casuistry as dealing with trifles but notes that sometimes small failings lead to large ones: a child with a habit of hitting may become a murderer. Nevertheless, Kant sometimes hankers for a complete system of casuistry (e.g. at Vig. 27:619) and always regards it as educationally useful (e.g. the *Doctrine of Method* of *The Metaphysics of Morals* and Vig. 27:702).

[19]   Some of the lists of casuistical questions trail off into trivia—and sometimes Kant comments wryly on the point; but all the lists begin with significant conflicts.

[20]   The aspiration to algorithms is strictly speaking inappropriate outside formal systems: the indeterminacy of concepts and principles precludes true practical algorithms. Indeed, we should probably not expect to find even 'quasi-algorithms', except for very minor aspects of action such as doing multiplication or putting the right postage stamps on letters.

problems does not cast doubt on the entire field of endeavour. And, as with mathematics and design, progress may be possible: if we can identify some of the sources of contingent incompatibility between principles, we may be able to reduce them.

If I have only Stone Age technology to hand, I will fail to produce a wheelbarrow. If I have only nineteenth-century technology, I will fail in my attempt to design a television. Equally, if the institutions that are to hand are unjust in deep ways, or there has been prior wrongdoing, whether another's or my own, then I may find that the *rationes obligandi* that I accept or believe that I ought to accept cannot all be satisfied in some cases. Unjust institutions and prior wrongdoing can make moral conflict common and recalcitrant.

At this stage of a chapter that is growing too long, a very few illustrations must suffice. One that surfaces again and again in Kant's writing is the conflict between the (special) duty to obey rulers (*MS* 6:320) and the terrible deeds they may demand. A less political version of the problem arises when powerful wrongdoers demand that one join them. We are asked to consider the predicament of 'an honest man whom somebody wants to induce to join the calumniators of an innocent but otherwise powerless person (say, Anne Boleyn, accused by Henry VIII of England)' (*KpV* 5:155; cf. *KpV* 5:158–9), or of someone of whom a would-be murderer demands information about his intended victim's whereabouts (VRM 8:425–30). We are also often asked to consider the implications of promising falsely and thereby entering into special duties that may prove incompatible.

Such examples are not distant from the most discussed examples of moral conflict in our own time, which are often depicted as arising out of unjust institutions. Sartre's student cannot combine filial and patriotic duty because of the Nazi occupation; Sophie's cruel choice is imposed by the same murderous tyrants; Vaclav Havel's depiction of daily collaboration in falsehood presupposes a regime that demands that collaboration.[21] In such cases we can see quite readily what it would take to eliminate the conflict, even if we are powerless to do so.

In cases of conflict, there is then often little to be done, as it were, on the spot. Both Barbara Herman and Thomas Hill have argued that a Kantian approach to obligation is fully compatible with, indeed requires, serious attention to the aftermath of failure to meet all requirements when there is conflict and that in such circumstances remorse, regret, restitution, or other remainders and

---

[21] Vaclav Havel, 'The Power of the Powerless', in *Living in the Truth*, trans. J. Vladislav (London: Faber & Faber, 1986), 36–122, esp. sect. III.

residues may be owed.[22] Unmet *rationes obligandi* are not simply wiped off the map, as (on some, even if not on the most plausible, readings) unmeetable prima facie duties are wiped away: they maintain their claims on us. In the *Lectures on Ethics*, Kant makes this point more explicitly than he does in the passages Herman discusses when he writes: 'Now we can never say here that it is absolutely impossible to fulfil both duties, and the duties remain even though they are not fulfilled; for, as we have said, laws and rules can never contradict one another; there is, rather, a contrary action of the ground of one duty against those of another, and this brings it about that the two cannot coexist' (Vig. 27:537).

The demands of unmet, contingently unmeetable *rationes obligandi* are often seen as requiring emotional and attitudinal responses: we pay the price of unmet demands in residues and remainders such as regret, agent regret, and remorse. But where the sources of conflict lie in unjust institutions, the most appropriate responses may have to be more active. They might take the form of efforts to bring about institutional changes that put an end to or reduce the sources of conflict. Agents who face a conflict among their obligating reasons can seek to eliminate the sources of (recurrent) conflict. They can seek to establish a well-ordered society, a system of right expressed in the institutions of a republican state, and a cosmopolitan world order, whose special duties are not so prone to conflict. Yet, even in a well-ordered society within a cosmopolitan world order, special duties taken on without wrongdoing and with all due care and attention may, in the event, turn out to conflict or not to be compatible with other obligations. Political, economic, and social institutions can never eliminate all possibility of conflicts among obligating reasons.

A parallel set of long-term responses to moral conflict may be relevant in the domain of virtue. Since prior wrongdoing is one of the sources of moral conflict, its reduction would also help reduce (recurrent) conflict between obligating reasons. In this case the task is also partly one of constructing better social institutions but mainly (in Kant's view) one of forming or reforming characters. It begins with the tasks of moral education, of self-knowledge, and of self-improvement. On each, Kant has a great deal to say. He emphasizes the ways in which children may be brought to awareness of their duties, to hatred of ill doing, to distinguish advantage from morality. He emphasizes the importance of seeking self-knowledge and self-discipline throughout our lives, and the dangers of being beguiled by excessive, enthusiastic conceptions of total virtue,

---

[22] This conclusion rejects the thought that obligations are merely prima facie up to the point at which they are shown to be actual, and that they have no continuing claim if they cannot be made actual. See also Herman, 'Obligation and Performance'.

as if ordinary virtue were not hard enough. He emphasizes the importance of securing the regulative virtue of courage and the importance of 'ethical ascetics'[23] and the need to construct a social order in which virtue is supported—the ethical commonwealth of *Religion within the Boundaries of Mere Reason.* Above all he emphasizes that progress towards virtue is a task that does not come to an end:

Virtue is always *in progress* and yet always starts *from the beginning.* It is always in progress because, considered *objectively*, it is an ideal and unattainable, while yet constant approximation to it is a duty. That it always starts from the beginning has a *subjective* basis in human nature which is always affected by inclinations because of which virtue can never settle down in peace and quiet with its maxims adopted once and for all but, if it is not rising, is unavoidably sinking.   (*MS* 6:409)

The construction of just institutions and the construction of good characters are both unending tasks; such success as we may have will never eliminate moral conflict entirely. But in seeking both we make active and constructive as well as amending responses to duties that would otherwise go under where obligating reasons conflict.

---

[23] 'Ascetics is that part of the doctrine of method in which is taught not only the concept of virtue but also how to put it into practice and cultivate the *capacity for* as well as the will to virtue' (*MS* 6:412).

15

Self-Legislation and Duties to Oneself

Andrews Reath

I. Introduction

In this chapter, I focus on some of Kant's 'foundational' remarks about duties to oneself and on some of the problems that they raise. I mean what the syntax of this sentence implies in that the problems that interest me lie more in what Kant says to clarify the basis of duties to oneself than in the idea of such duties themselves. I will not be questioning the general coherence of duties to oneself. Instead I will be concerned for the most part with what such duties, as well as what Kant says about them, tell us about his general understanding of certain features of duty and obligation.

I see no special problems in understanding how one can have duties to oneself, especially in the context of a Kantian theory in which respecting humanity as an end in itself plays a defining role. For there to be duties to oneself, we must have non-prudentially based reasons for adopting certain attitudes towards (certain aspects of) ourselves—for example, for valuing certain of our powers and capacities, interests, our moral standing, and so on. The absolute value of humanity provides a perfectly general basis for respecting such capacities and interests in any human being. That we as agents are in a special position either to support or, on the other hand, to neglect or undermine the relevant capacities and interests in ourselves, and that we can and do act in ways that evidence failure to accord proper value to these capacities and interests, give us occasion to apply to ourselves the general reasons stemming from the absolute value of humanity. Of course, despite their common basis, we should not expect any precise correspondence between self-regarding and other-regarding duties, since the failures of self-respect to which we are liable do not always parallel the characteristic failures to respect others that occasion our duties to them. That aside, the

Thanks to Stephen Engstrom for his comments.

general point is that merely having a share in the dignity due to persons in virtue of their humanity does not guarantee that one will respect its instantiation in one's own case.

The problems on which I focus emerge from Kant's attempt to dispel an apparent conceptual difficulty that he thinks attends the concept of duties to oneself. Essentially, I think that he takes a fairly straightforward concept and, rather than shedding light on it, puts it under a cloud. But obfuscation makes sport for commentators. In the game that I favour, you get points by extracting something of interest from Kant's fleeting remarks (perhaps more interest than he intended), and that is what I will try to do. I begin with a brief commentary on the introductory sections of Kant's treatment of duties to oneself. I then focus on the general model of duty that appears to be operative in these passages. Here I will be concerned both with how we should understand this general model of duty if we are to accommodate duties to oneself (as I think we should), and with how duties to oneself fit into a general model of duty that can be supported on independent grounds. As the chapter proceeds, I also examine the connection, if any, between duties to oneself and Kant's notion of self-legislation—his thesis that the agents who are subject to moral requirements must be regarded as their legislators. Finally, at the end of this chapter, I ask how duties to oneself fit into the social conception of morality and practical reason that I think we may attribute to Kant, and some variant of which is widely accepted among contemporary theorists who draw inspiration from Kant (constructivists, contractualists, and so on).

II. An Antinomy in the Concept of Duties to Oneself?

In §§1–3 of the Doctrine of the Elements of Ethics (*MS* 6:417–20)[1] Kant raises a foundational question about the concept of duties to oneself that takes the form of an antinomy: the concept of a duty to oneself at first seems contradictory (§1). But there are duties to oneself, since, if there were not, there would be no duties whatsoever (§2). Like his other antinomies, this one is resolved by appeal to some distinction between noumena and phenomena, in this case a distinction between human beings viewed as natural beings with reason—*homo phenomenon*—and human beings 'thought in terms of their *personality* . . . as

---

[1]   References to *The Metaphysics of Morals* are to the translation by Mary Gregor (Cambridge: Cambridge University Press, 1996). References to the *Grounding for the Metaphysics of Morals* are to the translation by James W. Ellington, 3rd edn. (Indianapolis: Hackett, 1993). Though I use Ellington's translation, I prefer Paton's title.

beings endowed with *inner freedom*'—*homo noumenon* (§3). This distinction is to dispel the initial appearance of contradiction, thus securing the possibility of duties to oneself, presumably by giving us two different senses in which to understand the agent in such duties. Going through these arguments in more detail will enable me to raise some of the questions and problems that I wish to address.

The contradiction that Kant sees arises when

> the I *that imposes obligation* [*das Verpflichtende Ich*] is taken in the same sense as the I *that is put under obligation* [*dem Verpflichteten*]. For the concept of duty contains the concept of being passively constrained [*einer passiven Nötigung*] (I am bound [*verbunden*]). But if the duty is a duty to myself, I think of myself as *binding* and so as actively constraining (I, the same subject, am imposing obligation [*Ich bin . . . der Verbindende*]). And the proposition that asserts a duty to myself (I *ought* to bind myself) would involve being bound to bind myself . . . and hence a contradiction.   (*MS* 6:417)

A noteworthy feature of this passage is Kant's adoption of an apparently voluntaristic and social model of duty within which obligations are generated by some kind of interaction between agents. This passage implies that in any duty there is an agent who is passively constrained and an agent who actively constrains the first through an act of volition. The passively constrained agent is the subject of obligation (*subiectum obligationis*)—the agent bound to act in a certain way. The active agent imposes the obligation on the subject through his will and (as indicated by a later remark at *MS* 6:442) is the agent *to whom* the duty is owed. Duties to oneself require that a single agent occupy both roles, but that appears to involve a contradiction when that agent is 'taken in the same sense'. The problem is not simply an inconsistency in the idea of a single agent both constraining and being constrained. Rather, the idea of constraint becomes meaningless or incoherent when a single agent occupies both of these roles, and that leads to a contradiction. Kant continues: 'One can also bring this contradiction to light by pointing out that the one imposing obligation (*auctor obligationis*) could always release the one put under obligation (*subiectum obligationis*) from the obligation (*terminus obligationis*), so that . . . he would not be bound at all to a duty he lays upon himself [*der er sich auferlegt*]. This involves a contradiction' (*MS* 6:417). When I occupy both roles, I (the active agent who imposes the obligation) am free to release myself when I (the passively constrained agent) am disinclined to fulfil the obligation, and that makes the idea of constraint meaningless. But a duty that one is not bound to fulfil (or where disinclination to fulfil the duty is a reason to be released from it) is self-contradictory.

The second prong of the antinomy, however, asserts that, were there no duties to oneself, 'there would be no duties whatsoever, and so no external duties either' (*MS* 6:417). Since there clearly are some such duties, it follows that there are duties to oneself. There may be some temptation to read Kant as saying that duties to oneself are in some sense the foundation of all duty—for example, because a failure to live up to one's obligations to others shows an insufficient regard for one's own capacity for principled conduct (that is, for one's personality), and therefore a failure of self-respect. (In literal Kant-speak, in violating your duty you would act in a way that is beneath your dignity as a moral agent and bring dishonour on your personality, thus displaying improper regard for that part of yourself.) For duties to oneself to be the foundation of all duty, one would have to hold that respect for one's own moral capacities is the fundamental reason for complying with any duty—so that, for example, the duty to respect the dignity of one's own personality provides the basic reason to fulfil one's other duties, or is in some way the reason why they are duties. However, such a view seems untenable: the reason to treat others according to moral standards is that they make claims on us in virtue of their humanity, and such considerations should be sufficient to motivate our conduct.[2]

Moreover, while Kant's theory may allow for the view that respect for one's own personality provides supporting reasons for conscientiousness in one's duties to others, that is not the issue here. His argument (for the claim that, if there were no duties to oneself, there would be no duties whatsoever) reads as follows: 'For I can recognize that I am under obligation to others only insofar as I at the same time put myself under obligation, since the law by virtue of which I regard myself as being under obligation proceeds in every case from my own practical reason; and in being constrained by my own reason, I am also the one constraining myself' (*MS* 6:417–18). Kant's point here is that the kind of self-constraint involved in laying down obligations on yourself is the foundation of all duty, so that any difficulty in the idea of constraining or binding

---

[2] Even so, one might still hold that duties to oneself play an important subsidiary role in much moral conduct. For example, one might hold that certain duties to oneself are morally central because they are duties to develop those rational capacities and sensibilities that enable one to fulfil one's duties generally. Or one might argue that self-respect provides a subsidiary reason, indeed a basic reason with the strength of duty, to fulfil one's duties to others, because you dishonour yourself by failing to do so. (For suggestions of this sort, see Nelson Potter, this volume.) However, there still must be reasons independent of one's attitude towards oneself that make these actions duties. You only dishonour yourself by acting in certain ways, for example, if there is an independent basis for regarding the action as wrong. (Here consider Hume on why regard for the virtue of an action cannot be the primary motive to virtuous conduct, *Treatise*, bk. III, pt. II, sect. 1.)

oneself that vitiated the concept of duties to oneself would also undermine duty generally.[3]

In the *Groundwork*, Kant argues that all duties are in some sense self-imposed or self-legislated in that agents bound to moral requirements are bound in such a way that they must be regarded as legislating for themselves.[4] Kant's thesis that rational agents legislate moral requirements for themselves needs to be stated with care. The basic idea (I would argue) is that moral requirements are rooted in principles that are generated by a deliberative procedure—the CI procedure[5]—that is grounded in or constitutive of the nature of rational volition, and that all moral agents are equally authorized to employ. Moral principles 'proceed in every case from my own practical reason' (*MS* 6:417) in that the deliberative process by which they are generated—the procedure whose employment gives a principle the status of law—is constitutive of rational volition, and is a process in which I have an equal share. My capacity to guide my own willing by this deliberative process (that is, by the CI) invests me with agency in the fullest sense by enabling me to act as an autonomous sovereign agent (an agent with the capacity to give law through my will), and, when my willing does have the form of law, I maintain and express my sovereign status. As an agent with this capacity, I have equal authority to employ the deliberative process that determines whether a principle has the status of practical law. A further dimension of this thesis is that a principle is morally binding only if it can be given this kind of justification—that is, only if (my) employment of the CI procedure shows that the principle has the form of law and is thus a principle that I can legislate as universal law.

No matter how one interprets Kant's claims about moral agents giving law for themselves, it should be clear that legislating the moral law is not the special

---

[3] As a point of clarification, we should note that all choice, prudential as well as moral, can involve the kind of self-constraint involved in controlling one's choices, setting aside motives that distract one from one's goals, and so on. The kind of self-constraint that appears problematic is not that kind of self-control, but that of imposing obligating on yourself through your own will.

[4] The key claim is: 'The will is thus not merely subject to the law, but subject to the law in such a way that it must also be regarded as legislating for itself, and only on this account as being subject to the law (of which it can regard itself as author)' (*G*. 4:431). Arguments for the claim follow in the ensuing three paragraphs, and thereafter Kant refers to the moral agent as autonomous legislator, bound only to laws that he gives to himself. I discuss these claims in 'Legislating the Moral Law', *Nous*, 28.4 (1994), 435–64, and 'Autonomy of the Will as the Foundation of Morality', manuscript.

[5] The 'CI procedure' normally refers to the deliberative procedure associated with the Formula of Universal Law. However, I will use it very broadly to refer to some interpretation of the Categorical Imperative—that is, a deliberative procedure based in any of the formulas—which can be used to generate substantive moral principles. It is unclear how the Formula of Universal Law bears on duties to oneself, and it is generally agreed that Kant bases such duties on the Formula of Humanity. So for the purposes of this chapter, it may be best to think of the 'CI Procedure' as a procedure of deliberation associated with the Formula of Humanity.

province of any one individual. Since moral principles are universal in scope, one legislates for moral agents generally, and not just for oneself. Moreover, the agents for whom one gives law have the same rational capacities and legislative status as oneself. From this it should follow that one can only will as moral laws principles that (it is reasonable to think) could command agreement among rational agents generally and that such principles are arrived at through a process of deliberation in which all agents have a share. It is for such reasons that the fundamental principle underlying this deliberative procedure may be understood as the higher-order principle of willing principles that can gain the agreement of all members of a community of ends.[6]

Though it is less widely recognized, it is still the case that it is a conceptual truth that moral requirements are self-legislated (principles that we impose on ourselves): this thesis is a node in the analytical argument in the second section of the *Groundwork*, which unpacks what is contained in the ordinary concept of duty as involving unconditional requirements on action. The fact that it follows from the concept of an unconditional requirement that they are legislated by those agents subject to them permits Kant to deny that there is any general incoherence in the idea of constraining or binding oneself through self-imposed principles. But if there is no general incoherence in the idea of being bound to self-given principles, then there should be nothing incoherent in the self-constraint at issue in the limited case of duties to oneself. Conversely, if an incoherence in the idea of binding oneself (imposing obligations on oneself) undermined the idea of duties to oneself, it would undermine all duties. Since there is no reason to think the latter, we can dismiss the prospect of the former.

The argument of §2, if successful, indicates that the apparent inconsistency in the concept of duties to oneself should be resolvable, though without showing how. The 'Solution' in §3 is supposed to fill this gap, suggesting that the contradiction dissolves when we understand the agent in duties to oneself in two different senses. Kant writes that, when we are conscious of being subject to duty, we think of ourselves 'under two different attributes', as sensible beings and as intelligible beings with 'the incomprehensible property of freedom' (transcendental freedom). This dual view of ourselves is evidently the basis of the distinction in the next paragraph between *homo phenomenon* and *homo noumenon*—between man as a natural being with reason who 'can be determined by his reason, as a cause, to actions in the sensible world' and 'the same

---

⁶ Here, obviously, I have in mind Kant's remarks about acting as a legislating member of a kingdom of ends (*G*. 4:433–6). I consider the implications of the fact that moral agents give law for equal co-legislators at some length in 'Legislating for a Realm of Ends: The Social Dimension of Autonomy', in A. Reath, B. Herman, and C. M. Korsgaard, *Reclaiming the History of Ethics: Essays for John Rawls* (Cambridge: Cambridge University Press, 1997).

man thought in terms of his personality . . . as a being endowed with inner free-dom' (*MS* 6:418). However, a problem now arises because Kant seems baldly to assert rather than to argue that there is no contradiction in the idea that a being with personality or inner freedom can have obligations to himself: 'But thought in terms of his personality . . . the same man is regarded as a being that is capa-ble of obligation [*ein Verpflichtung fähiges Wesen*] and, indeed, [of obligation] to himself (to the humanity in his own person)' (*MS* 6:418). In other words, Kant seems simply to claim that one who is capable of obligation has obligations to oneself.[7]

In fact, there is an argument that we can read into this passage that supports this response and shows that it is not vacuous. Agents who are subject to duties must view themselves 'under two attributes' because they are moved by differ-ent kinds of incentives. Agents who experience moral principles as duties are moved by sensible incentives that can conflict with reason. But they also have an interest in acting from moral principles, and thus assume a capacity to act from reasons that make no reference to empirically given desire-based interests; in other words, they ascribe transcendental freedom (personality) to them-selves. Moreover, drawing on the argument in the second section of the *Ground-work*, just cited, agents subject to unconditional requirements are bound in such a way that they must regard themselves as their legislators. That is, not only do they ascribe transcendental freedom to themselves, they may also ascribe to themselves a special legislative capacity, a capacity to give supreme law through their willing. Furthermore, rational agents are committed to according supreme value to this capacity, and it confers a special status on them (that of sovereign legislator) in virtue of which they possess dignity and are entitled to respect. Now agents with this legislative capacity can act in ways that do not acknowledge its proper value—for example, by failing to preserve or develop this legislative capacity, by acting as though they did not possess it or were not entitled to the special moral standing that it confers, by exercising it in a way that is unworthy of someone in whom it is vested, and so on. Accordingly there is occasion for this legislative capacity in oneself (call it one's 'personality' or 'humanity') to make claims on one's own attitudes and choices.

---

[7] I am grateful to Bernd Ludwig for pointing out a problem with Mary Gregor's translation, which I have altered in accordance with his suggestion. The claim that I want to suggest can be read into this passage, and that I argue can be defended, is the claim that one who has obligations has obligations to oneself. However, what Kant says here is that the human being regarded as possessing personality is 'capable of obligation [*ein Verpflichtung fähiges Wesen*], and indeed to himself . . .'. *Verpflichtung* does not specify whether the agent is *der Verpflichtende* or *der Verpflichtete* (the agent who obligates or the agent who is obligated), and presumably includes both. The assumption of beings who are 'capable of obligation' (*ein Verpflichtung fähiges Wesen*) is in fact sufficient for the argument, since all such beings presumably have obligations.

In this way Kant can in fact argue that those who have obligations have obligations to themselves. Briefly, those who are subject to obligations must also possess certain deliberative capacities of supreme value, and these capacities make claims on their choices and attitudes towards themselves. However, this reading of the passage introduces two further problems. First, it is unclear how appeal to the two aspects plays any role in dispelling the apparent contradiction. We expect the distinction between phenomena and noumena to rescue the idea of constraining or binding oneself from becoming meaningless by enabling us to think of the agent in two different senses. But in fact it is the agent as noumena who occupies both roles of binding and bound (*der Verbindende* and *der Verbunden*). Only the self regarded as transcendentally free can be subject to obligation; Kant is explicit that in thinking of man as a natural being (as phenomenon) 'so far the concept of obligation does not come into consideration' (*MS* 6:418). And the capacities that make special claims on our choices are those attributed to the self as noumenon. Crudely put, it is the legislative capacities of the noumenal self—our humanity or personality—that impose demands on the noumenal self's choices and attitudes towards itself. Intuitively it seems correct that duties to oneself require that we think of a single agent in two different senses, but the distinction between phenomenon and noumenon has not provided a way to do this. Secondly, if the basis of duties to oneself are the claims that one's own humanity makes on one's actions and attitudes, then the apparent contradiction in the concept of duties to oneself is removed, not by viewing the subject under two different aspects, but, it would seem, by moving away from the voluntaristic and social model of duty that seems to have created the problem in the first place. Quite simply, if duties to oneself come from the fact that I am vested with certain capacities whose value I ought to acknowledge, it is unclear both how I bind myself to such duties through an act of volition and how I could release myself from any such obligations. The basis of duties to myself would be the perfectly general value of my humanity (or the capacity for humanity in me), in conjunction with my being specially positioned either to care for or to neglect it in my own case, and there is nothing that I could do that would release myself from any duties that it imposes.

In the balance of this chapter, I address a number of issues raised by these arguments. First, I will examine the suppositions about duty that lead to the apparent contradiction in the idea of duties to oneself—what I have been calling the 'voluntaristic and social model of duty' according to which obligations are imposed by one agent actively constraining another agent through his or her will. I think that it is fairly clear that this model does not represent Kant's considered view about duty in the simple form in which it appears to be employed in this passage. Still I think that Kant is a kind of voluntarist about duty: one dimension of his view that moral requirements are self-legislated is that they are, in some sense, created through rational volition, indeed by the willing of those agents subject to duty. I also think that Kant's understanding of morality is essentially social in certain respects, in that the volitional process that gives rise to duties should ultimately be viewed as a deliberative process in which all rational agents have an equal share, the aim of which is to arrive at principles that all agents can endorse. So it is important to see what modifications may be needed in the model of duty that is operative in these passages. Here I want to draw on these remarks about duties to oneself to get clear about the general model of duty, specifically to get a model of duty that can accommodate duties to oneself; but also to see how duties to oneself fit into a general model of duty that can be supported on independent grounds.

I then want to assess the alleged kinship between the notion of constraining oneself at issue in duties to oneself and in self-legislation. If one were worried that the concept of a duty to oneself presupposed an untenable notion of binding or constraining oneself, then a gesture towards the idea of self-legislation (binding oneself through self-given laws) would seem appropriate. The same problems that Kant raises here for duties to oneself have been raised by others in regard to the idea of self-legislation. G. E. M. Anscombe, for example, dismisses Kant's notion of self-legislation as patently absurd—though, it must be said, her objection is not based on a very nuanced understanding of what Kant meant by self-legislation.[8] So, if one had shown that the idea of giving laws for oneself was not only coherent, but essential to an accurate understanding of moral requirement, it would be proper to allay these concerns about duties to oneself by noting their parallels with self-legislation. However, I will argue that duties to oneself and self-legislation have less in common than Kant supposes in that they involve different senses of constraining or binding oneself.

III. The Model of Duty

Let me begin with two extended observations about the model of duty with which Kant operates in these and related passages in the *Doctrine of Virtue*. After exploring this model, I will suggest some modifications.

First, the opening of §1 suggests the view that duties are standardly generated by a kind of volitional activity or interaction between rational agents,

---

[8] See 'Modern Moral Philosophy', in G. E. M. Anscombe, *Collected Philosophical Papers*, iii, *Ethics, Religion and Politics* (Minneapolis: University of Minnesota Press, 1981).

which, looking ahead (as well as back to the *Groundwork* (*G.* 4:433–4)), I will characterize as the reciprocal interaction and mutual influence of rational wills who coexist as (equal legislating) members of a community of ends. As we have seen, in this passage (§1) Kant states that the concept of duty involves the idea of being passively constrained, but he also implies that in any instance of duty there is standardly an agent who actively constrains the subject through his or her will, to whom the subject has the duty—hence the idea that duties are generated by some kind of volitional activity or interaction.[9]

This reading is reinforced by the assertion in §16 that 'duty to any subject is moral constraint by that subject's will' (*MS* 6:442). The context of this remark is to note that what we might call the 'beneficiary' of the duty—the person (or thing) for whom the subject of duty is directed to care, that would benefit from the performance of the duty—is not always the person to whom one has the duty. Kant claims that the 'constraining subject' to whom one has a duty is always a person, indeed one 'given as an object of experience, since man is to strive for the end of this person's will and this can happen only in a relation to each other of two beings that exist' (*MS* 6:442). We can have duties not to destroy inanimate beauty, duties not to be cruel to animals, and a duty to regard all our duties as divine commands. But while these are, respectively, 'duties with regard to' (*in Ansehung*) animals, inanimate beauty, and 'what lies entirely beyond the limits of our experience', they are not *duties to* these beings and entities. We can have duties only to beings with whom we can enter a certain kind of (reciprocal) relationship. In the case of animals and inanimate objects, this is precluded by their lacking wills; with transcendent entities (God and angels), the problem seems to be that we cannot interact or have relationships with them (at least not in ways that we know of). In each of the above cases, the duties are 'with regard to' these entities, but 'to ourselves'.[10]

What does Kant mean by 'moral constraint by a subject's will'? The 'moral constraint' readily connects to the familiar idea that limits on permissible conduct towards an individual are established by what that agent wills or can

---

[9]   Here note Kant's references to *das Verpflichtende Ich, der Verbindende, einer aktiven Nötigung, das nötigende (verpflichtende) Subjekt*, etc., at *MS* 6:417, 442.

[10]   It is easy to provide examples in which the beneficiary of a duty is not the person to whom it is owed. You promise a dying friend that you will help his children get through college; or you agree to the organizer of a conference to get your paper to your commentator by a specified date. It would seem that the first duty created by the promise is to your friend/to the organizer, but that the beneficiary is the friend's children/the commentator (though one may have further duties to the beneficiary in each of these cases).

Since Kant treats the distinction between duties to oneself and duties to others as exhaustive, we may assume his view to be that in every case there is an agent to whom a duty is owed, thus an agent who actively imposes the duty through an exercise of will. The presence of an agent who actively binds the subject of duty would accordingly be a general feature of duty within this model.

reasonably endorse. At the most general level, our duty in relation to others is to act only from principles that they can at the same time will, or to act towards others in ways that we can justify to them as agents with autonomy by appeal to jointly willed principles. If an agent affected by your conduct cannot reasonably endorse your conduct (or cannot will the general principle that would warrant it), then it is impermissible. How one is obligated to act in specific circumstances is thus a function of the particular principles that an agent can will or reasonably endorse.

There are different ways of understanding how another's will might be the source of these constraints, and these lead to different pictures of the form of activity by which agents might be thought to constrain or impose obligations on each other. Assuming that these constraints take the form of principles, one option is that they are principles that the agents with whom we interact explicitly voice or accept. A second option is that they are principles that it is reasonable for others to endorse, or that they are committed to accepting as rational agents with autonomy. A third option envisioning minimal activity on the part of the constraining agent is suggested by a reading of the absolute value of humanity or the capacity for rational volition. Moral constraint by a subject's will could be construed as the limits on conduct that are set by the absolute value of an agent's humanity—that, in virtue of its absolute value, an agent's capacity for rational volition is a source of reasons that make claims on rational conduct. Of these options, the third is best folded into the second, since humanity has its absolute value in virtue of attitudes that rational agents have towards their humanity that are implicit in the nature of rational choosing. And I will simply suggest without argument that, of the remaining two, it is preferable to opt for the second, according to which the standard of what an agent wills is ideal rather than actual acceptance of some set of principles. However, I would add this proviso: the only reliable way that we have of ascertaining which principles agents with autonomy would find it reasonable to endorse in the ideal is through some kind of actual deliberative interaction with the kinds of agents we encounter under normal circumstances.

Moral constraint by a subject's will would accordingly be constraint by a principle or set of principles that the subject can reasonably will or endorse (or that the agent is committed to accepting as a rational agent with autonomy), which gives that agent a claim of some kind in the situation in question. But it should also be clear that (according to Kant), if the principle is reasonably endorsed by the agent to whom one has the duty, it is reasonably endorsed by any agent, including the passively constrained subject of duty. The principles by which we are bound in particular circumstances are not idiosyncratically willed by the agent advancing the claim, but are general principles that any agent can reasonably endorse. For that reason, these constraints should be understood as mutual and reciprocal limits and claims that agents jointly impose on each other through their willing.

The second general observation is that the interaction through which agents are thought to impose duties on each other has a kind of formal structure that is a function of the various *positions* or *roles* that agents can occupy within such interaction. If we succeed in articulating the various positions that make up this structure, we will have the model of duty that Kant employs. The two principal positions encountered so far are those of the passively bound agent, whom we may call the *subject* of duty (*subiectum obligationis*), and the active constraining agent, to whom the subject has the duty. Kant at one point refers to the latter as the *author* (*auctor obligationis*), but, for reasons that will become clear, I will refer to the (agent in the) *source* position (the agent who is the source of the duty, to whom one has the duty). A third position is that of the *beneficiary* of a duty (the agent who would be the object of the subject's attention if the duty is fulfilled). As we will see, such positions represent roles that individuals can play in a complex normative structure, and are defined by specific deliberative questions and procedures for seeking resolution of them. They also represent different aspects of our relationship to moral principles. One potential advantage of developing this model is that it should provide a simple way to assess the coherence of the concept of a duty to oneself and to make plain the kind of self-constraint that it presupposes. Duties to oneself simply rest on the possibility of a single agent occupying both the subject and source positions (the 'to' position). However, to see what this amounts to, we need to develop the model further, and in particular to see what the source position entails.

The idea of positions within a form of interaction should not strike us as strange given Kant's talk in the *Groundwork* (and elsewhere) of agents who legislate universal law through their maxims. Duties obviously have subjects—agents who are bound to act in certain ways under certain circumstances. Kant continues one line of the law tradition in ethics in thinking that duties are (in some sense) created by a process of volition and thus may also be understood to have a legislator. The language of moral legislation is appropriate, owing to Kant's belief that moral principles are generated and given authority by the application of a deliberative procedure that is acknowledged to be law creating, much as positive civil laws are enacted by a sovereign carrying out a recognized legislative procedure. In addition, Kant's revolutionary insight that agents who are subject to duties must be regarded as their legislators is just the claim that the subject and legislative positions must be occupied by the same agents—in particular, that one who can occupy the subject position must also be able to occupy the legislative position.

Since Kant says that the agent to whom a subject has a duty actively imposes obligation on that subject through his will, one may be tempted to identify the source position suggested by these texts from the *Doctrine of Virtue* with the more familiar legislative position of the *Groundwork*. That is, one might think that the agent actively imposing obligation (*der Verbindende* or *der Verpflichtende*) is its 'legislator', and that the duty is owed to the agent in the legislative position. A legislator, after all, is an agent who actively imposes obligations on some set of subjects through the exercise of his or her will, and Kant appears to hold that a duty is to a particular agent in virtue of that agent's active role in imposing obligation or binding the subject. However, identifying the source position with the legislative position would be a mistake, since that would lead to an anomaly in the agent to whom the subject has the duty. Kant holds that the agent subject to a duty is also its legislator, 'since the law by virtue of which I regard myself as being under obligation proceeds in every case from my own practical reason' (*MS* 6:417–18). But, if the agent in the legislative position is also the person to whom one has the duty, it would follow that all of one's duties are to oneself. That seems clearly wrong. Alternatively, we might make better sense of self-legislation by understanding moral principles as willed through a deliberative process in which all rational agents have an equal share. Again, if the person to whom one has a duty is the legislator, would it then follow that all duties are to all agents? That is equally unacceptable. If, as one might want to hold, the self that legislates is the impersonal self who could be any agent, and if the will of this impersonal self is the shared will of rational agents generally, to be constructed through a deliberative process in which all agents have an equal share, then these two options are not really distinct. Both make the idea that duties are standardly 'to' some distinct agent or set of agents quite idle in roughly the same way.

The general point is that, if the agent who is the source of the duty is its 'legislator', then no particular agent is singled out as the person to whom the subject has the duty. If we agree that there is standardly some particular agent to whom the subject in any given situation has the duty, who is the source of the obligation (say, the source of the claim on the subject's conduct), then the source position must be kept distinct from the legislative position. Each may be a position from which agents can constrain or bind others in some sense, but if so the kinds of constraint exercised will differ. The reason for this is that the agent to whom one has a duty is some specific individual—for example, an individual who has some kind of claim on one's conduct. But no discrete individual is singled out as the legislator of a moral principle. While any moral agent must be able to identify with and to participate in the 'legislative process', it is not owned by any particular individual.

So far I have been treating the idea that there is an agent active in imposing obligation to whom the subject has the duty (the source position) as basically unproblematic. But perhaps we need to rethink the source position. Is the idea that a duty is standardly to some specific agent or set of agents really a well-defined notion that we want to retain?[11] I think that we can define the source position through the idea that duties standardly are to some specific individual (for example, to the person who is the source of the claim on the subject's conduct). I also think that we should retain this idea, though circumspection is called for in characterizing this agent as active in imposing obligation. It may clarify things to note that there are different senses in which an agent might be the source of an obligation that Kant appears to conflate in the passages from the *Doctrine of Virtue*. A legislator is the source of binding norms by carrying out a legislative procedure. In a different sense, the agents with whom one interacts are a source of reasons for action, or claims on one's actions, in accordance with jointly willed principles. The second of these is what the source position amounts to. The distinction that Kant evidently fails to draw is that simply as occupant of the source position one is not the source of these general principles in the way that a legislator's will is the source of law.

Very generally, the individual to whom one has a duty in a given situation is the individual whose condition, interests, circumstances, or relationship or past dealings with oneself, and so on, give one reasons for action that make a special claim on one's conduct. That is to say that it is the person who, under the circumstances, is the source of reasons for one to act, or the source of some claim on one, in accordance with jointly willed principles. Put another way, the person to whom one has the duty is the person towards whom one is required to direct a certain kind of regard by some moral principle or set of moral considerations. That duties are standardly to specific individuals is a basic feature of Kant's moral theory because Kantian principles in effect tell us to direct certain forms of moral regard towards the individuals with whom we interact. The directionality and sense of the 'to' is given by the fact that the fundamental moral requirement (expressed in one way) is to adopt certain attitudes towards those with whom we interact. We have a general duty to show proper regard that is specified by substantive principles that pick out certain facts about a person's condition, needs, interests, circumstances, and so on, as the source of reasons for one to treat or view those individuals in certain ways.

---

[11] For another discussion of the idea that duties are to someone, see Thomas E. Hill, Jr., 'Servility and Self-Respect', in his collection *Autonomy and Self-Respect* (Cambridge: Cambridge University Press, 1991), 16–18.

We may safely maintain that duties are standardly to specific individuals as long as we recognize both that the way in which one can come to have a duty and what follows from one's having a duty to some individual (or group of individuals) vary widely from one kind of duty to another. Perfect duties of justice give one clear understanding of what it is for a duty to be to another, and it is in this context that the phrase 'duty owed to an individual' is most fitting. But we can hold that duties are standardly to specific agents without maintaining that they are owed to individuals in the way that duties of justice are owed.[12] Principles of respect for rights, of non-deception or non-manipulation, of promise and contractual obligations, of mutual aid, of beneficence, of gratitude, of loyalty, of respect, and so on, generate duties towards individuals in different ways. They single out different features of a person's condition or circumstances as giving rise to reasons for action, and what they give reasons to do (whether it is to perform or refrain from some specific action, to adopt certain attitudes, and so on) will depend upon the principle—and often on the circumstances of action as well. Similarly, whether performance of a duty can be demanded or enforced, what forms of complaint or censure may be voiced, and by whom, when a duty is not fulfilled will differ widely between duties of justice and duties of virtue, between perfect and imperfect duties, and so on (as specified by further jointly willed principles). It is unlikely that the 'to' (in the phrase 'duty to X') indicates any unique relationship beyond that sketched above, in that there is no unitary account of how individuals come to have claims on others (are sources of reasons for action), or of what follows from the existence of such claims.

The agent who is the source of a duty, to whom the subject has the duty, is, then, a claim-holder of some kind whose humanity constrains permissible conduct in ways specified by jointly willed principles. That agent is the source of reasons for action according to jointly willed principles, but is not, as such, the source of those principles. What, then, remains of the idea that an agent who is the source of a duty actively binds the subject of duty, or exercises 'moral constraint through his or her will'? What Kant says about this topic requires some modification. I have suggested that we interpret Kant's claim that duty presupposes an agent who actively constrains or binds the subject as the claim that duties are generated by the reciprocal interaction and mutual influence of equal legislating members of a community of ends. Both what Kant says and my reading of it fit the activity of 'moral legislation' better than they fit any

---

[12] For this reason I have tried to use the phrase 'agent to whom one has the duty' rather than 'agent to whom the duty is owed' wherever stylistic considerations permit. Where I have used the latter I intend it in a broad sense.

activity of the agent who is the source of a duty. Is there indeed any interesting sense in which the agent who is the source of a duty is 'active' in binding the subject of duty through his or her will? Simply as the source of a duty an agent is not active at the 'legislative level' of willing or laying down principles that are generally binding, but there is room for activity and interaction between agents who are concerned to resolve normative issues by appeal to shared (that is, co-legislated) principles—interaction at what we might call the 'level of agency'. For example, substantive principles that determine what the general demand for proper regard requires in specific circumstances enable individuals to advance certain kinds of claims and mutual demands. Settling what an individual may legitimately demand, or what constraints apply to some agent's conduct, by appeal to shared principles (determining the proper application of such principles) standardly involves some kinds of dialogue and interchange between agents. There are various ways in which jointly willed moral principles structure and mediate a kind of interaction between agents by putting individuals in a position (the source position) to express and to advance legitimate claims and to demand certain concrete forms of respect.

The conclusion that I want to draw in this section is that these pages of the *Doctrine of Virtue* employ a certain model of duty, but one which needs to be expanded by adding a legislative position that is distinct from the positions of subject, source, and beneficiary. These positions are associated with different deliberative concerns and represent different roles that individuals may play in moral reasoning and deliberation. The concern of agents in the legislative position is to arrive at general authoritative principles that all can endorse, and they do so by use of the Categorical Imperative. The resulting principles require them, as agents, to direct certain forms of regard towards those with whom they interact, or who are potentially affected by their choices, and they determine individuals' duties in specific situations. In that way these principles specify situations in which agents are subject to duty and create various subject positions. Conversely they pick out certain facts about the condition and circumstances of agents as sources of reasons that make claims on permissible conduct. In so doing, they put individuals in a position to express and advance certain kinds of claims, thereby specifying various 'source positions' that agents can occupy in their interaction with others (or with themselves). Agents in the subject and source positions are concerned respectively with the duties by which one is bound and with the demands that one may legitimately place on the attitudes and conduct of agents generally. These questions are resolved by principles arrived at by the Categorical Imperative.

Finally, we should note that within this model there are different levels (or perhaps just different deliberative tasks) in which agents can interact and exert reciprocal influence on each other. At the legislative level there is deliberation guided by the Categorical Imperative, the aim of which is to settle on principles that any agent can endorse. At the level of agency there is a kind of give-and-take between individuals as subjects and sources of duties which is mediated by jointly willed principles. Here the concerns are to determine the bearing and proper application of jointly willed principles and to settle on the legitimate claims that they support and what they give individuals reason to do in specific situations.

IV. Implications

So far I have developed this model of duty primarily with duties to others in mind. Let me now return to duties to oneself and to some of the questions raised by Kant's so-called antinomy, and consider some of the implications of this model for duties to oneself. There are three specific points that I want to make. First, I want to comment on how this model supports the overall coherence of duties to oneself. Secondly, contrary to what Kant implies in the second prong of his antinomy, this model makes it clear that there is no special link between duties to oneself and self-legislation in that different senses of constraining or binding oneself are at issue in each. Finally, it shows how duties to oneself fit into an essentially social picture of morality.

(*a*) The Coherence of Duties to Oneself

The model of duty outlined here makes it clear that a duty to oneself is one in which a single agent occupies both the subject and source positions—is both the subject of duty and the source of the claim on the subject's choices. (As an aside, the same individual may, but need not be the 'beneficiary' of such duties. If we accept Kant's claim that lying violates a duty to oneself, we would have a case where other agents are the beneficiaries of a self-regarding duty. Here respect for one's own personality and for the natural purpose of one's capacity to communicate one's inner thoughts would give one reasons to be honest with others.) I see no particular bar to filling out the schema in this way (same individual as subject and source). It may not be easy to ascertain what these duties are, how we should react to those who, in our judgement, fail to fulfil them, and so on. But as long as there are reasonable principles that pick out certain facts about ourselves and our capacities for rational choice as the source of (non-prudential) reasons for us to regard or treat ourselves in certain ways, there can be duties to oneself.

In §3 (the 'Solution to this Apparent Antinomy'), Kant appears to suggest that the idea of a duty to oneself is sustainable only if, in thinking of a single agent as both the subject of duty and its source, we are taking that agent in two different senses. Earlier we saw that Kant's attempt to provide these different senses through the distinction between phenomena and noumena is misleading, since it is the agent as noumenon who is both the subject and the source of the duty (*der Verbunden* and *der Verbindende*). However, the model of duty does give us different ways of viewing a single agent by setting out different positions that an agent can occupy within a complex structure or form of interaction that is sustained by the reasoning of a plurality of agents. It is an added benefit that the different senses of the agent are provided not by a distinction with distinctly metaphysical overtones but, roughly, by a distinction between different roles that an agent can occupy within a kind of social structure or form of social interaction.

(*b*) Self-Legislation and Duties to Oneself

Put in terms of this model of duty, Kant's claim that moral principles are legislated by those subject to them is the claim that the agents who occupy the subject position also occupy the legislative position. I noted earlier that the way in which agents bind themselves through their own legislation needs to be stated with care. The legislative position is not uniquely occupied by any single agent, but is shared equally with others. Moreover, the activity of giving law through one's willing is not carried out by individuals in isolation, but occurs in the context of and is made possible by a deliberative procedure that is social in nature— a procedure that all agents have equal authority to employ, the aim of which is to generate authoritative principles that all members of a community of ends (equal co-legislators) can endorse, whose successful employment by any individual requires confirmation by concurring judgements of others, and so on.[13] Thus the claim that one is bound by one's own legislation refers to the active and shared role that any agent has in the deliberative procedure that generates the constraints on one's conduct.

A view commonly attributed to Kant is that one is bound to moral requirements *because* one legislates them (for oneself?),[14] as though one imposes obli-

---

[13] For further discussion of these points, see 'Legislating for a Realm of Ends: The Social Dimension of Autonomy'.

[14] A reason for attributing this view to Kant is that he says as much at *G.* 4:431: the will is 'subject to the law in such a way that it must be regarded also as legislating for itself *and only on that account as being subject to the law*...' (emphasis added). For further discussion of the ways in which the italicized phrase needs qualification see 'Legislating the Moral Law', 456–9.

gation on oneself by simply exerting one's will in the form of a universal principle intended to guide one's own conduct. While it is strictly speaking correct that one is bound to moral requirements because of one's legislative role, this idea can be understood in a way that is misleading. Agents are not bound to moral principles simply by the fact of their share in the legislative process. Rather they are bound to moral requirements by what makes them valid moral principles, which is that they result from an authoritative deliberative process (that is, the CI). What gives authority to this process is that it is the deliberative procedure that is constitutive of (autonomous) agency. As such it confers on any individual the power of (autonomous) agency—which is to say, confers the status of sovereign legislator on that agent—and gives any agent an equal share in the willing of universal law. To the extent that I am committed to my own agency, I am committed to guiding my will by this deliberative procedure (the CI), and my share in its employment allows me to accept the resulting principles through my understanding of the reasoning that stands behind them (from the inside, as it were). In a word, I am bound to moral principles by the fact that they result from an authoritative deliberative procedure, and what gives the procedure authority for me is the legislative role that it confers on me.

By now it should be evident that self-legislation and duties to oneself involve different notions of constraining oneself, which correspond to the senses of constraining or imposing obligation associated respectively with the legislative level and the level of agency. In self-legislation 'I am the one constraining myself' in that I am through my legislative role the source (with others) of the principles by which I am bound. I have argued that my binding or imposing obligation on myself should here be understood as my active role as a co-legislator in willing principles that apply to agents generally. In a duty to oneself, 'I am the one constraining myself' in that I am, in virtue of my humanity, a source of reasons or claims applying to my own actions in accordance with jointly willed principles. The constraints are claims that my own humanity makes on my conduct stemming from jointly willed principles concerned with how individuals should regard or treat themselves. In certain respects, the relationship that I have to myself in a duty to self is more individualized. In self-legislation one wills for agents generally, and this capacity to will principles that others can recognize as authoritative is what makes one an agent. In a duty to yourself, *your* humanity makes claims on you as an agent—though these claims are generated by a legislative process and the resulting principles that mediate between you as subject and you as the source of reasons for yourself.

(c) Duties to Oneself and a Social Conception of Morality

It is often thought that a purely social conception of morality leaves no room
for duties to oneself. Proponents of such conceptions of morality take that
thought to argue against the existence of duties to oneself, and proponents of
duties to oneself take it to argue against purely social conceptions of morality.
However, I have (I believe) been assuming a conception of morality as social. I
attribute to Kant (as well as endorse) the idea that duties are generated by a
kind of volitional activity between agents, which I have characterized as the
reciprocal interaction and mutual influence of rational wills who coexist as
members of a community of ends. So far, I see no reason to think that this conception of morality excludes the possibility of duties to oneself. Furthermore,
I take it that this general conception of morality is accepted in some form by
many contemporary Kantian theorists, many of whom are favourably disposed towards duties to oneself. So I will conclude with a brief suggestion as to
how duties to oneself are consistent with and fit into an essentially social conception of morality.

What makes a conception of morality 'social' is a large issue, but what starts
one in that direction might be the belief that moral principles in some way
arise out of relations between individuals and presuppose some kind of interaction between individuals.[15] From here one can get different conceptions of
morality as social in nature depending on whether the interaction that one has
in mind occurs at the 'legislative level' or at the 'level of agency'. Characterizations of morality as social commonly focus on the latter. They think that such
a conception takes moral principles (or the need for them) to be generated by
a kind of interaction between individuals at the level of agency—for instance,
by demands that individuals make on each other as agents advancing their own
interests in a social setting. According to such a view, the need for morality is
created by the conflicting interests of largely self-concerned agents, and its
purpose is to regulate interaction between agents in some impartial manner
(for example, to establish limits on individual conduct, to set out legitimate
demands that individuals may advance against each other, and so on). Such a
conception of morality would appear to leave no room for duties to oneself,
but only by begging an important question, since it defines morality in such a
way as to exclude duties to oneself. It is fair to ask why we should accept such a
definition of morality.

However, a conception of morality that takes moral principles to be generated by a deliberative process in which all agents have a share is equally a social

---

[15] See Kurt Baier, *The Moral Point of View*, 215, 234. Baier is cited by Lara Denis in 'Kantian Ethics and
Duties to Oneself', *Pacific Philosophical Quarterly*, 78.4 (1997), 321–48.

conception of morality. I have suggested that we attribute to Kant the view that the legislative capacities that we possess as individuals are to be exercised with and among others, guided by the regulative aim of arriving at general principles that all members of a community of ends can endorse. This is a social conception of morality that takes moral principles to be generated by interaction between agents at the legislative level. If this legislative process generates principles concerning how individuals should treat themselves, then there is room for duties to oneself within a social conception of morality.

This suggestion raises an immediate question: what role does deliberation addressed to a plurality of agents play in generating duties to oneself, and why is this sort of mutual and reciprocal influence needed to generate such duties? One reason to assume a plurality of legislators in arriving at interpersonal principles is to ensure that the principles realize certain self-standing moral ideals such as equal consideration for the interests of all or equal respect for each individual considered as an agent with autonomy. A process of deliberation in which all members of some moral community have an equal share (among other things) considers the impact of potential principles on individuals from the perspective of each individual. In this context, that the resulting principles can be endorsed by all, or can be justified to each person (from his or her own perspective), reflects the fact that they give adequate weight to the interests of, or show equal respect for each person. Equal respect and justifiability to each person (and so on) are central moral ideals that principles governing interpersonal conduct and attitudes should express. But they do not seem to be at issue in duties to oneself.

However, in a Kantian context, that a principle is endorsable by any rational agent does more than indicate that it satisfies certain purely moral ideals. It shows in addition that the principle carries the authority of reason, and that points to a role for a plurality of legislators in generating principles of self-regarding duty.[16] The normative force of principles that are willed through a process of deliberation in which all individuals have a share will not depend on assumptions or values that not all agents must accept. A deliberative process whose regulative aim is general agreement among a plurality of agents will eliminate proposed principles of self-regarding duty that are purely personal in nature, or that have only partial authority that depends on values that are reasonably rejected. We might also want to say that it will uncover any considerations that are pertinent to the adoption of

---

[16] For further discussion of Kant's views about the authority of reason, see Onora O'Neill, *Constructions of Reason: Explorations of Kant's Practical Philosophy* (Cambridge: Cambridge University Press, 1989), chs. 1–3 and *Towards Justice and Virtue* (Cambridge: Cambridge University Press, 1996), ch. 2.

any proposed principle. All of this is to say that such principles bear the authority of reason. So a partial answer to this question is that it is through a deliberative process in which all agents have a share that a principle comes to have the authority of reason, and that any principles that ground genuine duties must have this imprimatur.

16

Duties to Oneself, Motivational Internalism, and Self-Deception in Kant's Ethics

Nelson Potter

In both his works on moral philosophy that deal with applications of the Categorical Imperative, Kant makes it clear that he believes there are duties to oneself (DOS). In the earlier of these two works, the *Groundwork*, we learn very little about the underlying rationale for such duties, though they are referred to; but, so far as the *Groundwork* is concerned, it might seem that Kant had simply taken over a traditional classification of duties without much of a rationale for doing so. In contrast, in Kant's *Metaphysics of Morals*, in the second part, the *Tugendlehre*, there is a much fuller discussion of duties to oneself, and the account given of them has been made part of a larger theory of inner, specifically *ethical* duties. The present chapter will be devoted primarily to achieving better understanding of the Kantian doctrine of DOS from this later work. After we consider the general doctrine of DOS (Section I), we will discuss the related Kantian themes of motivational internalism (Section II), and the idea of self-deception (Section III), both of which are deeper-lying but important doctrines connected to Kant's views on DOS.

I

Kant has been criticized for his view on DOS. Henry Sidgwick in *Methods of Ethics* repeatedly says that he thinks this aspect of Kant's views is quite mistaken, and in the 1960s there was a debate in the journals involving Marcus Singer, Warner Wick, and others, on whether this aspect of Kant's views was

An earlier version of Section I of this chapter was presented at the Central Division American Philosophical Association meetings in 1996; I am indebted to my commentator on that occasion, Robert Louden, and to those in the audience who raised questions. An earlier version of Sections II and III of this chapter was presented to the Central States Philosophy Conference in October 1993; I am indebted to my commentator on that occasion, Richard Eggerman, and to those who raised questions from the audience.

defensible.[1] One of the main issues in both cases was the criticism that, if we had a duty to ourselves, we could always release ourselves from it. But a duty from which one can release oneself at any time is not a duty at all. Therefore there are no DOS.[2]

Another major line of criticism had to do with conceptions of morality. It has often been claimed that morality is essentially social and interpersonal in character. If this is correct, then an 'intrapersonal' moral duty, a DOS, would not be possible. And it is often added that what are called 'DOS' are really matters of mere prudence ('I ought to invest my savings wisely'; 'I ought to exercise regularly') rather than specifically moral concerns. With respect to this second criticism, it can be said at once that Kant would not accept an account of morality that made it solely interpersonal. This disagreement about the character of morality is deep and complex, and I will not try further to resolve it here.[3] For the present I am most interested in Kant's conception of DOS; by getting clear about this we can better understand both the structure of Kant's moral philosophy, and the underlying issues about DOS.[4]

Early in *The Metaphysics of Morals*, in the general introduction, where he is discussing both law and ethics together, Kant writes:

In all lawgiving (whether it prescribes internal or external actions, and whether it prescribes them a priori by reason alone or by the choice of another) there are two elements: **first**, a *law*, which represents an action that is to be done as *objectively* necessary, that is, which makes the action a duty, and **second**, an incentive, which connects a

---

[1] See Marcus G. Singer, *Generalization in Ethics* (New York: Alfred A. Knopf, 1961), 311–18. 'Duties and Duties to Oneself', *Ethics*, 73 (1963), 133–42, responding to Daniel Kading, 'Are There Really No Duties to Oneself?' *Ethics*, 70 (1960), 155–7, and Warner A. Wick, 'More about Duties to Oneself', *Ethics*, 70 (1960), 158–63, and 'Still More about Duties to Oneself', *Ethics*, 71 (1961), 213–17.

[2] Interestingly, Kant himself presents this argument and replies to it in *MS* 6:417. Hence he was aware of one of the main lines of criticism.

[3] For further discussion of this issue, see William Frankena, 'The Concept of Morality', *Journal of Philosophy*, 63 (1966), 688–96. As I comment further below, Kant's moral philosophy as spelled out in *The Metaphysics of Morals* has two parts: the juridical (outer) and the ethical (inner). Juridical morality in Kant deals only with interpersonal duties, and thus corresponds more closely to the views of those more recent authors who insist that morality is limited to the interpersonal.

[4] In discussing this issue, I will entirely omit such discussion of DOS as it occurs in Kant's *Groundwork*—mainly in the two traversals of Kant's famous four examples, the first immediately after the introduction of the 'universal law' versions of the CI (*G.* 4:421–3) and the second after the introduction of the 'respect for persons' version (*G.* 4:429–30). In my view the first presentation of the arguments for DOS is quite unsatisfactory: the arguments are not successful in showing that there are duties to oneself of the sorts claimed. The second version of the arguments in *Groundwork* is not so bad as the first, but to understand this sketchy second traversal well, it must be filled out from the fuller account of DOS in the *Tugendlehre* (the second half of *The Metaphysics of Morals*, which deals with 'ethics' in Kant's sense). For more on this see my 'What Is Wrong with Kant's Four Examples', *Philosophy Research Archives*, 18 (1993), 213–29.

ground for determining choice to this action *subjectively* with the representation of the law.   (*MS* 6:218)⁵

Next Kant distinguishes law and ethics from each other based on this two-part character of legislation or lawgiving (*Gesetzgebung*):

That lawgiving which makes an action a duty and also makes this duty the incentive is *ethical*. But that lawgiving which does not include the incentive of duty in the law and so admits an incentive other than the idea of duty itself is *juridical*. . . . Conformity [of action with law] in which the idea of duty arising from the law is also the incentive to the action is called its *morality*. . . . Just because ethical lawgiving includes within its law the internal incentive to action (the idea of duty), and this feature must not be present in external lawgiving, ethical lawgiving cannot be external.   (*MS* 6:219)

For Kant, then, the contrast between law and ethics is mainly a contrast between kinds of incentives to each.⁶ The incentives for law are 'external' rather than intrinsic: keep your speed below the speed limit on the interstate, or you risk having to pay a fine. The incentives in ethics are 'internal' in a double sense: they arise from the practical reason of the agent, and they track the rationale for the moral precept itself. The *reason* one should not make a lying promise is because anyone who does is taking unto himself a special privilege that it would not be possible for everyone to have, or, more intuitively, because those who make lying promises are acting parasitically, relying on others to tell the truth and gain the trust of others, thereby making the liar's deception successful, or because making a lying promise would wrongly exclude from consideration the interests, intentions, and rights of another.⁷ In the previous sentence, for an ethical person, whose motives are as ethics requires, 'reason' would refer both to the reasons that *justify* the precept, and to the reasons that *motivate* the agent to act in accord with what the precept requires. There is, in

---

⁵ Quotations from Kant's *Metaphysics of Morals*, *Groundwork of the Metaphysics of Morals*, and the *Critique of Practical Reason* are included in *Practical Philosophy*, ed. and trans. Mary Gregor (Cambridge: Cambridge University Press, 1996). Quotations from Kant's *Religion within the Boundaries of Mere Reason* are from the translation by George di Giovanni that is included in *Religion and Rational Theology*, ed. and trans. Allen W. Wood and George di Giovanni (Cambridge: Cambridge University Press, 1996).

⁶ However, as a consequence of this difference in incentives, there are also differences in the scope of actions required. Duties of *Recht* deal only with duties to others. DOS cannot be required of one externally (e.g. enforced as a legal requirement), but only through the inner motivational self-constraint of duty. The same is true of imperfect duties to others.

⁷ These rationales against making a lying promise of course echo Kant's arguments in the *Groundwork* passages referred to above, Kant's second example in both cases. I take it that a lying promise, as Kant calls it, is a promise one never intends to keep. Qua promise its not being kept is a violation of duty to the promisee, and hence is classified as a violation of a perfect duty to another. In contrast, as we shall see below, when Kant discusses *lying* in *The Metaphysics of Morals*, he discusses it as a violation of a duty to *oneself*.

other words, in the ethical ideal, an *identity* of justifying and motivating reasons. Ethical lawgiving, since it is essentially concerned with the motives on which the agent acts, must be internal legislation, not external; it must have reference to the agent's moral motives, which are internal and are intrinsically related to the rationale that justifies the precept, rather than to externally coercive motives the law makes use of. We shall return to this theme of motivational internalism after exploring further the rationale for Kantian duties to oneself.

Duties to oneself are and can only be a part of *ethical* theory in Kant's specific sense of that term (that is, the motivation for performing them must be internal and intrinsic). They relate in an essential way to the moral self, the agent who performs the actions. They cannot be externally imposed nor enforced. All ethical duties (to others or to oneself) involve what Kant refers to as 'self-constraint' (*Selbstzwang*): the moral agent imposes the duty on herself (see *MS* 6:381). Such self-constraint must, however, be self-constraint according to a principle of inner freedom, rather than being merely one heteronomous desire constraining another (*MS* 6:394). Since ethics includes as within its reach concern with the motives of the agent, this idea of self-imposed duties will be central: as an ethical person I not only avoid dishonesty, but I avoid it because I am internally, intrinsically committed to avoiding such actions because they are wrong.

This, having been said, must be qualified. The second element of lawgiving in the earlier quote from *MS* 6:218 must be *available* for there to be a proper duty. For example, the fear of punishment would not be available for one who lived in a state of nature, and the pure ethical motive would not be available for an individual who somehow failed to possess Kantian moral freedom, and hence in such cases we would not have (respectively) legal or ethical lawgiving (*Gesetzgebung*). Nevertheless, legal or moral duties may be fulfilled by an agent acting out of different motives. For example, a person living in civil society may refrain from assault on another out of purely moral motives, without reference to any fear of punishment; and one may perform a charitable act of benevolence merely because he knows people are watching whose admiration he desires. Such acts would fulfil the respective legal or ethical duties in question, even though the agent was moved to fulfilment of them out of alternative motives. The story is complicated a bit in the case of ethical duties, because we *also* have a duty to perform such duties from the motive of duty. To say that certain motives, legal or ethical, are *available* is to say that, failing any other motives for fulfilling a given duty, this (reliable) motive will suffice to motivate the performance of the duty. Legal and ethical motives are reliable, not in the sense that individuals always follow their lead, and hence never act contrary to the duty in question, but in the sense that, if they did pay attention to such motives and choose to incorporate them into their maxims, such motives would be adequate for the performance of the required action.

Once we introduce this idea of moral 'self-constraint', we have a partial response to the Sidgwick/Singer argument against duties to oneself. Any duty that is self-imposed is one that in some sense I can release myself from at will. I can release myself at will from my self-imposed determination to do nothing dishonest, for instance. Of course, if and when I do this, I will probably then be undertaking actions that are contrary to morality (that is, dishonest actions). Hence, if I 'release' myself in this way, I am not succeeding in releasing myself from a duty I have, for, if I go on to perform a dishonest action, I have still violated my duty not to so act. Hence there are self-imposed duties from which I cannot release myself at will.[8] I describe this as only a 'partial' response to Sidgwick/Singer, because it relies on the intuition that we cannot at will free ourselves from obligations to refrain from dishonest actions by such a self-release. But then perhaps the duty to refrain from dishonest actions is never merely self-imposed. Even so, unless we reject the intuition, the argument shows the limits of the possibility of releasing ourselves from duties.

This Kantian conception of the ethical, related as it is to the concept of 'dutiful self-constraint', lies at the basis of the Kantian conception of duties to oneself. The ethical in Kant is inner, and has to do with the moral agent's motives and ends: his long-term moral commitments. That is also the focus of DOS. All duties to oneself have to do with the self as a moral agent, and as a self having the ability to impose duties on itself (that is, with maintaining and developing the self's specifically moral capacities).

This ability to engage in moral self-constraint lies at the basis of all morality, as Kant himself argues, in arguing that there must be duties to oneself:

For suppose there were no such duties: then there would be no duties whatsoever, and so no external duties either. For I can recognize that I am under obligation to others only insofar as I at the same time put myself under obligation, since the law by virtue of which I regard myself as being under obligation proceeds in every case from my own practical reason; and in being constrained by my own reason, I am also the one constraining myself.   (*MS* 6:417–18)

Duties to oneself are duties that relate to this moral self that is the source of self-constraint. Our duty is to preserve and to improve, so far as possible, this

---

[8] Kant's own reply to this line of objection, that such duties are owed by the phenomenal self to the noumenal self (*MS* 6:418), is irrelevant, and not a helpful reply, so far as I can tell.

moral capacity within us. More specifically, the end that is at the same time a
duty that is the principle of all duties to oneself is the goal of self-perfection.
Many other moral theories never get to mentioning self-constraint or the
moral self, and hence never get to a conception of duties to oneself, nor would
such theories move beyond the social realm of personal interaction in order to
visit the interior of the self. In fact some views would altogether reject such
conceptions, saying that they are no part of moral theory.

The duties to oneself that Kant actually discusses in the *Tugendlehre* preserve or promote, or forbid acting against such powers in ourselves; this is the
unifying principle of such seemingly disparate duties. Suicide is obviously the
self-destruction of such powers. Other acts allegedly temporarily interfere
with such powers, most plausibly drunkenness, but also gross overeating, and
masturbation, according to Kant. Kant regards lying as a violation in the first
instance of a duty to oneself; his discussion of lying tends to identify the deception of others with the deeper and more serious action of *self*-deception.
Understandably, self-deception poisons the well of inner awareness (for example, awareness of our own motives of action) and thus undermines in a fundamental way our ability to be accurately aware of our inner self, its motives, and
actions (see *MS* 6:429–32, and further discussion below). Vices such as avarice
and servility underestimate or altogether deny our inner moral powers, and
their value. Other actions promote it indirectly, such as acquiring skills to earn
a living, and keeping oneself physically fit. The perfection that is the goal of
DOS is the achievement of the inner state of great motivational power in pursuing all one's duties from the motive of duty. We humans will never achieve
perfection here, and our progress will finally be cut off by natural death.[9]

If a moral theory were entirely social, with no merely personal, or what we
might call intrapersonal, inner duties, then there could be no DOS. Interestingly, Kant's realm of *Recht*—right or law—has just this character, and so if it
were the whole of Kant's practical philosophy, there would be no DOS in that
philosophy.

Could we perhaps dispense with DOS as a part of the duties of *virtue*? Kant
says we could not, because all duties require an exercise of self-constraint. In a
sense all duties are partially DOS because the agent must use the powers of self-
constraint that are presupposed by any duty to recognize and undertake any
duty at all (*MS* 6:417–18). In ordinary parlance we may call a person lacking

---

[9] Unless we were imperfect beings, constantly under temptation, and hence at risk of turning away
from our inner moral powers, we would not have such duties to maintain, preserve, protect, and promote
and develop these powers—i.e. those duties that are called 'duties of virtue'. Hence Kant says that 'For finite
holy beings (who could never be tempted to violate duty) there would be no doctrine of virtue, but only a
doctrine of morals . . .' (*MS* 6:383). This passage is further discussed below.

in self-respect when we mean he has too few moral scruples; according to this way of speaking, the willingness to engage in fraudulent behaviour is a violation both of duties to others, and also of duties to oneself, with both violations flowing from the same lack of the self-constraint that is mandated by duty.

I have argued elsewhere that for Kant the basic form of moral proposition is one in which the subject refers to the agent, and the predicate places an action requirement upon the agent, as in 'Persons must not tell lies'.[10] Perhaps there are other moral theories in which such basic propositions make no reference to agents; in such theories complete moral statements may, for example, simply attribute moral predicates to states of affairs, with no direct reference to the agents whose duties are thought to be an implication of such statements. Perhaps utilitarianism in some versions is such a theory. In such a theory the question of whether there are agents who may have moral duties is entirely distinct from the truth of the moral propositions with which the theory makes its start, for these statements merely attach moral or value predicates to states of affairs, and tell us nothing directly about moral agents.

But for Kant basic moral statements already include an explicit reference to a competent moral agent—namely, the subject who makes the moral judgement—and, since the basic competence in question is the inner power of moral self-constraint, for Kant morality *must* include an account of duties to oneself. Without such an account, there is no account of the basic moral capacity, which is simply moral freedom. To put the point differently, since moral freedom is an inner power of the self, morality cannot dispense with an account of it, and of the duties relating to its preservation and perfection in fragile, finite moral persons such as ourselves. We can begin to understand Kant's claim that there can be no moral duties at all unless there are first duties to oneself.

The Kantian doctrine of duties to oneself is not, it now appears, a mere thoughtless taking-over of a traditional classification of duties, that has no deeper meaning. The idea that there are duties to oneself is basic to the structure of Kant's ethical thought, including his well-known emphasis on the importance of moral freedom. What might seem to be a disparate collection that Kant brings together and describes as duties to oneself, it now turns out, has a common characteristic: a significant relation to the goal of preserving, maintaining, developing, and perfecting the very centre of our being as human

---

[10]   See my 'The Synthetic A Priori Proposition of Kant's Ethical Philosophy', in *Jahrbuch für Recht und Ethik*, 5 (1997), 438–59. I believe that Kant often operates in his philosophy with a conception of what is a 'basic proposition' for the subject matter. For example, his famous statement in the *Critique of Pure Reason* to the effect that 'Thoughts without content are empty, intuitions without concepts are blind' (*KrV* A51/B75) can be regarded as saying that the basic theoretical proposition on which all others are built is one that would bring an intuition under a concept.

beings, our moral self. Duties to oneself are closely related to one another with a common rationale, and this is a rationale that cannot possibly be shared by the other part of the duties of virtue, imperfect duties to others. We will need an entirely distinct account of how we can happen to have duties of virtue to others, and this is reflected in the fact that the duties of virtue to others are built around a distinct end that is at the same time a duty.

In the present account of the rationale for DOS, one thing might seem to be missing—namely, the Categorical Imperative (CI). Does the rationale for DOS make essential use of the CI, or is the CI being forgotten about in this late work? It is hard to see much use of the familiar 'universal-law' formula, except in an indirect sort of way, as follows: the universal law principle is first introduced as the only purely formal principle, where being formal is understood as an absence of connection to merely personal ends, such as thirst or sexual desire (see *G.* 4:400 ff., 420–1). The purely moral incentive, which is central to the power of moral self-constraint, is formal in this same sense. The chief DOS is to preserve and develop our powers of acting from such a purely formal motivation, and that power is the essence of the agent's moral freedom.

The relation of DOS to the second formulation of the CI is more direct. The doctrine of DOS is a spelling-out of the nature of the moral self, which gives us a deeper and fuller understanding of the idea of respect for persons as mentioned in the second formulation of the CI. The list of duties to oneself can be read simply as a list of ways one ought to act so as to respect one's own moral person. Hence the Kantian doctrine of DOS can be taken to be a direct application of the idea of respect for persons, where the person to be respected is the agent's own.

Some sort of motivationally externalist moral theory could be developed that made no reference to such refined inner capacities, and indeed it seems that Kant's realm of *Recht* is such a theory. Humans in such a theory have external incentives for refraining from wrongful acts, which are punishments for violations of law, and, even when they may not be free in the fullest moral sense, they may still be able to take account of the risks of punishment in deciding how to act. They can be said to be free at least according to some soft determinist conceptions of freedom.

But, Kant would add, unless the agent has the full inner capability of self-constraint under moral law for intrinsic reasons, including moral reasons, he is neither free nor would he have any duties to himself. DOS and moral freedom thus come together.

But could not an agent have such moral freedom and not have DOS? One way this could happen is if the agent had a kind of moral *perfection*, and there were *no* possibility that she might ever give in to temptation. But, given the human facts of life that (1) such capabilities are an accomplishment, and that (2) current temptation may cause us to neglect and deny these capabilities— we humans it seems never escape temptation—we do have duties in this respect, and the entire account of DOS in the *Tugendlehre* consists of duties that follow from exactly this conception: that we human beings are fallible, constantly subject to temptation, subject to the possible turning away from our better natures, and that the positive aspects of our moral self must be cultivated, improved, and strengthened over time. What we thus (fallibly) possess is the basic capability for moral freedom, and therefore for having any moral duties at all—namely, the power of moral self-constraint. This is an inner, psychological capability, and it is also a condition of morality existing in us as agents. A complete account of morality must include this inner aspect of what Kant calls ethics, and hence there are and must be DOS.

Let me come at this last point in a different way: the end that is at the same time a duty that relates to DOS is one's own moral perfection. To speak of ends is to be reminded of human finiteness, because of the sorts of gaps that are endemic to human ends. Some of our ends or goals are never accomplished, because they are beyond our power, or because we weakly falter in trying to accomplish them; even when we do achieve a goal, doing so takes effort and time, and of neither of these do we have an unlimited supply. If we were morally perfect finite beings, we would have no DOS, because we would not fall short of the end of our own moral perfection. Strengthening our moral muscle of self-constraint not only helps us fulfil our duties to others; it is also the taking of steps towards our own moral self-perfection.

As Thomas Hill's article 'Servility and Self-Respect'[11] brought out so well, the object of at least some of these DOS is certain of the inner moral capabilities of the human agent, in virtue of which the agent has dignity and is also the bearer of certain rights, quite apart from any accomplishments. Hence all human beings, even those who have committed terrible deeds or who fail to have even very moderate life accomplishments, are possessed of human dignity and therefore rights. Such modest or faulty agents must act towards themselves with proper self-respect, and the rest of us must respect such agents as well. Such treatment recognizes their dignity and their rights. Hence, the other side of the DOS we owe to our own valuable moral nature is the respect that all others owe this same nature, as well as the respect that we owe such natures in all others.

---

[11] 'Servility and Self-Respect' first appeared in the *Monist*, 57.1 (1973), 87–104, but it has often been reprinted.

I have shown how the idea of DOS is deeply embedded in Kant's ethical theory, and how it relates to his conceptions of the moral agent, and of moral freedom. There are other conceptions of ethics according to which there would be no DOS, or where the fact of DOS or of no DOS would be peripheral and uninteresting. But within a Kantian theory, with its emphasis on moral freedom, on the inner power of moral self-constraint, independent of desire, and on the permanent fallibility and the possibility of improvement for human agents, duties to oneself are indispensable.

II

In addition to the features of Kant's theory just mentioned, which together make the conception of DOS central to it, is another that we mentioned above, and now need to discuss more fully: the internal relation of duty and motivation in ethics. Perhaps there are other conceptions of duties to oneself, but in its Kantian version the doctrine of DOS requires an internal relation between obligation and motivation. This is because of the Kantian doctrines surrounding a central idea that we have already alluded to: in the case of morally good action, there is an identity of obligating and motivating reasons, or, to put it another way, the (motivating) reasons the agent has for performing the morally required action are the same as the (justifying) reasons why that action is morally required. Any other relation between obligation and motivation, as when the agent performs a morally required benevolent action because she likes the person who will be benefited, will be a merely accidental relation, which as such cannot assure the performance of morally required actions. The primary inner moral capability of self-restraint that is essential to inner moral freedom is the power to do what is required for the reasons that it is required. The capability of acting from this inner motivation is the motivational element that backs up all ethical obligations (see the Kantian passages quoted from near the beginning of this paper from *MS* 6:218, 219), and is in this sense part of their 'lawgiving' (*Gesetzgebung*); the goal of cultivating and developing this same internalist motivation is the primary goal of Kantian duties to oneself.

Yet, as we shall also see, the main problem with DOS is the possibility of erring in judging of our own motives. And this is a deep and perhaps incurable moral sickness because human moral agents fall into such errors by engaging in self-deception about their own motives.

Kant has been thought by some to be a 'motivational internalist' in the sense just discussed, probably beginning with the inventor of this terminology, W. D. Falk. Internalism has a variety of different versions, some outlined by William

Frankena and some developed by Thomas Nagel and Stephen Darwall,[12] but it is roughly the view that one's having a moral obligation to do something entails that one has some motivation to do that same thing.

Kant's internalist view is that, if an agent has a moral duty to perform a certain action, then she must have an adequate moral motivation to perform that same action. This belief or assumption has the character of a transcendental presupposition of the Kantian moral philosophy. I have argued at length elsewhere that, when Kant insists that the Categorical Imperative is a synthetic a priori proposition, he is making a claim about the *motivational power* of the moral imperative as a source or cause of action.[13] The motive to act must be a moral motive, because for any other kind of motivation the connection between the requiredness of the action and the motivation for performing it would be contingent, and hence could not meet the requirement for a necessary presupposition. In the absence of such an assumption's being true, we could not be certain that the individual had the capability of performing or avoiding the action in question, and hence was accountable. The very term Categorical Imperative describes a kind of *motivation* that is unconditional, and hence incompatible with the always conditional nature of occurrences in the phenomenal world, within which the belief–desire model reigns. That is, phenomenal actions are based on the Kantian model of the hypothetical imperative, where the combination of a desire and a belief about how the desire may be satisfied move us to action. Once we notice that the character of moral demands is motivationally unconditional, we understand that the story that must be told about our capability of engaging in (motivationally) moral action requires us to move beyond the phenomenal world. As we say this sort of thing, we are starting to descend into the complexities of Kant's metaphysical theory of human moral freedom; in the present essay we shall not carry out such a descent, but will instead dwell on the implications of the Kantian doctrine of freedom for his views on duties to oneself.

In my earlier paper just alluded to, I tried to show that the core ethical synthetic a priori proposition that is presupposed by the formulations of the Categorical Imperative is the following:

[12] See W. D. Falk, *Ought, Reasons, and Morality* (Ithaca, NY: Cornell University Press, 1986); William Frankena, 'Obligation and Motivation in Recent Moral Philosophy', in A. I. Melden (ed.), *Essays in Moral Philosophy* (Seattle: University of Washington Press, 1958); Thomas Nagel, *The Possibility of Altruism* (Oxford: Oxford University Press, 1970); and Stephen Darwall, *Impartial Reason* (Ithaca, NY: Cornell University Press, 1983). For a more recent discussion of the same issues, see chapter 3 of David O. Brink, *Moral Realism and the Foundations of Ethics* (Cambridge: Cambridge University Press, 1989).

[13] See my 'The Synthetic A Priori Proposition of Kant's Ethical Philosophy', *Jahrbuch für Recht und Ethik*, 5 (1997), 437–59.

(1) A rational being is a being with a moral nature.

One of the clearest textual confirmations that Kant wished to affirm just such a principle as (1) comes from Kant's *Religion within the Boundaries of Mere Reason,* where he writes about the 'Original Predisposition to Good in Human Nature' as follows:

We may justifiably bring this predisposition, with reference to its end, under three headings, as elements of the determination of the human being:

(1) The predisposition to the *animality* of the human being, as a *living being*;

(2) To the *humanity* in him, as a living and at the same time *rational* being;

(3) To his *personality*, as a rational and at the same time a *responsible* being.
      (*R.* 6:26)

In a significant footnote to the end of this passage Kant explains,

We cannot consider this [the third predisposition] as already included in the concept of the preceding one, but must necessarily treat it as a special predisposition. For from the fact that a being has reason [it] does not at all follow that, simply by virtue of representing its maxims as suited to universal legislation, this reason contains a faculty of determining the power of choice [*Willkür*] unconditionally, and hence to be 'practical' on its own; at least, not so far as we can see.   (*R.* 6:26 n.)

We can now see that (1), like the CI itself, is synthetic, because these quotations say that there is no contradiction in imagining an otherwise rational being lacking the power to determine choice independently of heteronomous incentives.[14]

Let us now turn to examine some of the evidence that our 'moral nature' includes motivation. Throughout the *Groundwork* Kant is concerned with moral motivation when he is discussing the Categorical Imperative. For example, at the beginning of chapter 2, when he is considering the question of

---

[14] Why should (1) also be regarded as a priori? We can give a rather general kind of answer to this question: the concepts of rational being and moral nature are likely to be regarded by Kant as a priori concepts, and the synthetic connection between them seems unlikely to be based on experience alone. But, as we have already suggested above, and will further suggest below in a discussion of Kant's 'moral nature', there is another more specific reason for thinking such a proposition a priori. It states a causal relation of a special sort, because our moral will is or can be a cause of action; in action from duty the CI is the principle that motivationally determines the action. Because this sort of causation is a causation of freedom, it lies beyond the scope of possible experience; any statement expressing such a causal relation would not be empirical but a priori.

whether morality may not be a 'phantom of a human imagination' (*G.* 4:407), the question he considers is whether a morally *motivated* action has ever been performed. And when he raises the question of whether the CI is 'possible', he seems to be asking, once again, a question about the possibility of moral motivation (*G.* 4:417–20). Again, his discussion of autonomy is largely in terms of *motivation*: heteronomy is said to be the will's being determined by something outside itself, whereas autonomy is the will's self-determination (*G.* 4:431, 433). Also, in the second *Critique*, the central question is said to be: can pure reason be practical? And if pure reason can be practical, this means, Kant tells us, that 'of itself, independently of anything empirical, [pure reason can] determine the will' (*KpV* 5:42). So, again and again, the issue concerns 'determination of the will'. The Categorical Imperative is a principle, not just in the sense of being a basic *Satz* or precept (*Vorschrift*), and thus a *Grundsatz*, but also in the sense of being a causal principle of explanation, analogous to the way that gravity or the law of gravitation might be said to be a physical principle to be invoked to explain physical phenomena.[15]

Quoted near the beginning of this chapter was a passage from *The Metaphysics of Morals*, general introduction (*MS* 6:218), where Kant stated that all legislation had two elements: a first that states what action is required, and a second that provides an incentive to perform such an action. In this passage Kant then distinguishes between ethical legislation, where duty is also the motive, and juridical legislation, where a motive other than the idea of duty is permitted. This again makes clear that a quasi-theoretical statement, which we might call a *Satz* or a *Vorschrift*, is by itself incomplete, unless an incentive is added.[16]

When we are talking about inner, ethical motivation, there will be an identity of justifying and motivating reasons, which is action from duty. To have the power to act from such motives is to be free. The reasons that justify performing an action, committing oneself to an end, or even committing oneself

---

[15]   Henry Allison discusses this in *Kant's Theory of Freedom* (Cambridge: Cambridge University Press, 1991), 230, 241, 244, 248, but he does not connect this discussion with Kant's claim that the Categorical Imperative is synthetic a priori.

[16]   Confirmation for the claim that for Kant laws (ethical or juridical) must include an adequate incentive comes from an unlikely place in the *Rechtslehre*. In a little section on Equivocal Rights, Kant mentions a troubling sort of case that he finds problematic (*MS* 6:235–6; cf. GTP 8:300 n.). Following a shipwreck a man floating in the water finds another clinging to a large piece of wood. He knocks him away, taking possession of the piece of wood for himself; this causes the other man to drown and saves the life of the first. The first has murdered the second, and yet in this instance the result of his not murdering him in this way would have been his own death by drowning. Since the penalty for murder is also death, the law in such a case is unable to provide a superior incentive for obeying the law, since there is no more severe penalty than death. In such a case the law is subjectively not a law at all because it fails to be able to provide an adequate incentive for what it requires. Kant for this reason accedes to the proposition that a person who exercises this 'right of necessity' not be punished.

to giving priority to morality over self-interest in one's entire life, would also be the motivating reasons in action from duty.[17]

I do not wish to suggest that what is required within Kant's theory is that the moral motive be the strongest, though Kant himself does sometimes use strength language in this connection. The Kantian model, after all, involves the incentives being chosen or taken up into the faculty of choice (*Willkür*) and incorporated into a maxim. Only in this way will an incentive, regardless of strength, be the basis for an agent's action. If it is not by being the stronger incentive, how is it then that moral motivation is 'adequate'? This is a difficult question I do not undertake to answer here. Another difficult question: how can there be a motive from duty adequate to produce the performance of the morally required action, and yet the agent chooses to perform a different action, a wrongful action? We might say that the moral motivational strength we have been talking about is merely potentially or dispositionally present, requiring for its actualization an act of the faculty of choice (*Willkür*) of the agent. The Latin equivalent for Kant's term *Willkür* is *arbitrium*, which is the root of the English word 'arbitrary'. The suggestion is that choice in this sense is a basic act or surd that admits of no further explanation; I am not aware of anything in Kant's account of *Willkür* that contradicts such an understanding. But we do want to look further at the fact that we humans make certain kinds of choices, in particular, choices that implicate us in wrongdoing, even if they admit of no further account or explanation.

III

Kant himself takes us into the depths of human sinfulness in a variety of ways. In *Religion*, he tells us that all of us have incorporated evil into our maxims, and are thus guilty of original sin. This original sin, far from being a singular mis-step committed long ago and far away, perhaps even by an ancestor rather than by ourselves, is, according to Kant's account, I believe, offered as a general description of the source and character of human moral evil, whenever and wherever it occurs.

---

[17] When Kant introduces his famous principle (in *Religion*) that 'ought' implies 'can', he does not use it, as almost all recent discussions of the principle do, in the contrapositive. He uses it as stated, to mean that the fact that I am aware of being under an obligation implies that I have the ability to undertake to fulfil the obligation. Thus the CI is a synthetic a priori principle in the sense of a (free) causal principle; it is a statement about a causal power that we human beings have as free rational beings. It is the power to initiate original, autonomous, free causes of action in a way that is not the same as, is in fact incompatible with, the model of phenomenal, physical causal explanation as described in the Analytic of the *Critique of Pure Reason*.

In an important passage in *Religion* he describes the three distinct degrees of evil:

> *First*, the frailty (*fragilitas*) of human nature . . . I incorporate the good (the law) into the maxim of my power of choice (*Willkür*); but this good, which is an irresistible incentive objectively or ideally (*in thesi*), is subjectively (*in hypothesi*), the weaker (in comparison with inclination) whenever the maxim is to be followed.
>
> *Second*, the impurity (*impuritas, improbitas*) of the human heart consists in this, that although the maxim is good with respect to its object (the intended compliance with the law) and perhaps even powerful enough in practice . . . it has not, as it should be [the case], adopted the law *alone* as its *sufficient* incentive but on the contrary, often (and perhaps always) needs still other incentives besides it in order to determine the power of choice for what duty requires; in other words, actions conforming to duty are not done purely from duty.
>
> *Third*, the depravity (*vitiositas, pravitas*) or, if one prefers, the *corruption* (*corruptio*) of the human heart is the propensity of the power of choice (*Willkür*) to maxims that subordinate the incentives of the moral law to others (not moral ones).   (*R.* 6:29–30)

The first two levels of evil have to do with the corruption of human motives, in ways that leave open the possibility of acting contrary to duty; at the third level of evil the agent gives preference to personal desires over moral motives. It is Kant's doctrine in *Religion* that all human beings have fallen into corruption, and incorporated evil into their maxims, through a timeless noumenal choice. This is Kant's version of the Christian theological doctrine of original sin. The very concept of virtue, around which the second half of Kant's *Metaphysics of Morals* is built, is a concept that presupposes this sort of corruption, as the following passage introducing the concept in the introduction to the *Tugendlehre* makes clear:

> For finite *holy* beings (who could never be tempted to violate duty) there would be no doctrine of virtue but only a doctrine of morals, since the latter is autonomy of practical reason whereas the former is also *autocracy* of practical reason, that is, it involves consciousness of the *capacity* to master one's inclinations when they rebel against the law, a capacity which, though not directly perceived, is yet rightly inferred from the moral categorical imperative. Thus human morality in its highest stage can still be nothing more than virtue . . . (*MS* 6:383)

In the second division of *Religion*, Kant has already given us a description of such a 'finite holy will': it is the purely rational, and hence ahistorical account of a finite being without sin, which occupies the place in Kant's moral rational theology that Christology takes up in the Christian theological tradition. A finite holy being would be a creature like Christians believe Jesus Christ to have been, a being who never incorporated evil into his maxims, but who, as finite, would still have innocent desires and needs. For example, Jesus is thirsty, and there is an opportunity for drinking water, and he does so. In contrast, the virtue-related concept of autocracy is a strength concept. Our strength of will as more or less virtuous beings is a match for some personal desires, but perhaps not for others. Although Kant insists (*MS* 6:383–4), against Cochius and the Aristotelian tradition, that virtue is a matter of the inner principle of the will rather than of habit, yet there is now in Kant's account an element of something like habit in the development and strengthening of principles. In *Religion*, Kant describes virtue as a commitment to a continuous progress back to original innocence, where this original state is at best approached only asymptotically, in an infinite (temporal) progress. Hence, within time, we never completely over-come or erase our earlier venturing into sin, the original sin that each of us is guilty of. And, it seems to me, as I will try to indicate further below, in spite of what Kant says in criticism of the Aristotelian tradition of virtue, the Kantian continuous progress back towards original innocence suggests habit-building, encouragement, development, strengthening, and training.[18]

The concept of virtue, then, though a positive concept of praise when attri-buted to individual humans, presupposes an original sin, an incorporation of evil into the agent's maxims; since we are all guilty of this original sin, virtue is the highest moral state achievable in human life. But what can we say about this evil? Whence comes it, and what is its nature? So far as I am aware, it has hardly been noticed that Kant has some significant suggestions in answer to such questions: the major, perhaps the sole source of evil is *self-deception*, the inner lie, by which we defeat morality in us, and thereby defeat ourselves.

The centrality and overwhelming significance of self-deception is some-thing of a subterranean theme in Kant's moral philosophy.[19] It comes to the surface in Kant's discussion of DOS, and in the discussion contained therein of *lying*. In the *Tugendlehre* lying is classified as a violation of 'The Human Being's Duty to Himself Merely as a Moral Being'. In fact, it is the greatest such violation (*MS* 6:429). This classification has had a certain amount of attention from scholars, since more commonly, and perhaps more intuitively, lying is considered a violation of duty to the person lied to. Interestingly, in Kant's dis-cussion of lying, its origin is in lying that takes place inside the single moral agent, which then spreads outward to others, so that the original lie is inner. Hence, although there are external lies, which in certain instances may consti-

---

[18]   For further discussion of this difficult topic in Kant's ethics, see the chapter by Engstrom, this volume.

[19]   Allison, *Kant's Theory of Freedom*, 158, 159, 161, and elsewhere, emphasizes the importance of self-deception in Kant's account of evil. See *R.* 4:42 n., 37 n., and *MS* 6:429–31, 441.

tute violations of perfect duties to others, Kant in these passages concentrates his attention mainly on *inner* lies. By an internal lie a person 'makes himself contemptible in his own eyes, and violates the dignity of humanity in his own person' (*MS* 6:429). These are already strong statements that give lying a significance and centrality in one's account of sin that make it unusual. But there is more.

A bit later, Kant discusses the 'First Command of All Duties to Oneself' (*MS* 6:441–2), which is '*know* (scrutinize, fathom) *yourself*. . . in terms of your moral perfection in relation to your duty. That is, know your heart.' Kant gives additional emphasis to these ideas as he continues:

Moral cognition of one's self, which seeks to penetrate into the depths (the abyss) of one's heart which are quite difficult to fathom, is the beginning of all human wisdom. For in the case of a human being, the ultimate wisdom, which consists in the harmony of a being's will with its final end, requires him first to remove the obstacle within (an evil will actually present in him) and then to develop the original predisposition to a good will within him, which can never be lost. (Only the descent into the hell of self-cognition can pave the way to godliness.) (*MS* 6:441)

There seem to be two main patterns of this evil of self-deception. The first has to do with the agent's judgement of the strength of the inner motivation of duty and of personal desire. It is a transcendentally valid presupposition that the strength of the moral motive is always adequate to the morally required action. But we deny this strength to ourselves; we, as it were, weaken the moral motive, at least in our own estimation of it, and in the same way strengthen the personal incentives that tempt us, until we move lower and lower through the three stages of moral evil: frailty, impurity, and wickedness.

The second pattern of self-deception emerges clearly in Kant's discussion a little later in the *Tugendlehre*, 'On a Human Being's Duty to Himself to Increase His Moral Perfection, That Is for a Moral Purpose Only' (*MS* 6:446). Kant there explains why this duty to pursue moral perfection is an imperfect duty only:

The depths of the human heart are unfathomable. Who knows himself well enough to say, when he feels the incentive to fulfill his duty, whether it proceeds entirely from the representation of the law or whether there are not many other sensible impulses contributing to it that look to one's advantage (or to avoiding what is detrimental) and that, in other circumstances, could just as well serve vice? (*MS* 6:447)

His conclusion is that the reason such a duty of moral self-improvement is only an imperfect duty is because we are unable ever clearly to discern whether we have achieved our goal. Our failure is a failure of self-knowledge.[20] And that failure is because of our defeating ourselves through self-deception.

Thus Kant connects the specific wrong of lying with human evil in general. Self-deception is the primary way in which we violate our duties to ourselves. And, as we mentioned earlier, Kant considers duties to oneself as underlying all duties, because DOS have to do with the basic inner capacity for freedom that is exercised in any fulfilment of any duty.

This connection of the specific wrong of lying with human evil in general helps explain Kant's seeming fanaticism about lying (for example, in the late paper 'On a Supposed Right to Lie from Philanthropy'). Lying, whether inner or outer, poisons the well, making moral progress impossible. It is a very basic, all-pervasive, and not fully reversible evil, more significant than any other.

In sum, the first main sort of self-deception is deception about the strength of moral versus personal motives, leading through frailty and impurity to wickedness, in spite of the always adequate strength of the moral incentive within us. The second main sort is the self-deception by which we tell ourselves that we are acting for high and purely moral motives, when our real motives relate to self-love. Kant appears to believe that both sorts of self-deception are not fully reversible once we have fallen into them.

In recent years there have been a number of close discussions of certain texts in *The Metaphysics of Morals*, because Kant's views seem to be in tension with themselves, or, perhaps worse, actually contradictory (I am thinking of work by Nancy Sherman and Marcia Baron).[21] On the one hand, Kant insists that only purely moral motivation gives our actions moral worth. Other possible cooperating motives are condemned as valueless in themselves, and as leading to moral evil in the forms of frailty and impurity. This is a counsel of perfection, which, however, we are capable of accomplishing, because of the transcendentally valid presupposition of adequate moral motivation. And yet in the discussion of imperfect duties to others in the *Tugendlehre* Kant writes:

it is a duty to sympathize actively in [the fate of others]; and to this end it is therefore an indirect duty to cultivate the compassionate natural (aesthetic [*ästhetische*]) feelings in us, and to make use of them as so many means to sympathy based on moral

---

[20] This theme of scepticism about the possibility of self-knowledge is found elsewhere, as early as the *Groundwork*, where at the beginning of chapter 2 (*G.* 4:407–8), he doubts whether a morally perfect action has ever been performed. Another *Groundwork* passage (*G.* 4:424) is on the psychology of the transgressions of duty and also involves a sort of self-deception.

[21] See Nancy Sherman, 'The Place of Emotions in Kantian Morality', in Owen Flanagan and Amelie Oksenberg Rorty (eds.), *Identity, Character, and Morality: Essays in Moral Psychology* (Cambridge, MA: MIT Press, 1990), 149–70, and Marcia Baron, *Kantian Ethics Almost without Apology* (Ithaca, NY: Cornell University Press, 1995), ch. 6.

principles and the feeling appropriate to them. . . . For this is still one of the impulses that nature has implanted in us to do what the representation of duty alone might not accomplish [*nicht ausrichten würde*]. (*MS* 6:457)

This passage urges us to cultivate non-moral motives as an adjunct to purely moral motivation. Much has been said by other scholars about how we might mitigate these seemingly contradictory doctrines. I propose that the following can be added to these other discussions: the demand that we do our duty solely from the motive of duty is a command of moral perfection, like the biblical injunction Kant sometimes quotes: 'Be ye holy.' The indirect and conditional duty to promote active feelings of sympathy to motivate ourselves to help others is one consequential upon our having been guilty of original sin; we have thereby partially destroyed and undermined the moral incentive within us. Because of this not fully reversible destruction through self-deception, our moral nature now requires assistance from cooperating non-moral motives. However, we remain responsible for the self-deception and its results, including this descent into moral impurity.

I have tried to show first how central to Kant's *Tugendlehre* is his doctrine of duties to oneself. I think that, once we understand this doctrine, the traditional objections to this doctrine fall. This doctrine of duties to oneself presupposes a kind of motivational internalism that is again a central part of the Kantian moral philosophy. And in Kant's view, as I have tried to show, the chief enemy of moral perfection or virtue takes a very specific form, self-deception, as the central and chief form of moral evil, a form of moral evil from which we can never (at least from within a temporal perspective) fully recover.

17

Love and Respect in the
Doctrine of Virtue

Marcia W. Baron

I

In a memorable passage of the *Doctrine of Virtue* Kant writes:

In speaking of laws of duty (not laws of nature) and, among these, of laws for human beings' external relations with one another, we consider ourselves in a moral (intelligible) world where, by analogy with the physical world, *attraction* and *repulsion* bind together rational beings (on earth). The principle of **mutual love** admonishes them constantly to *come closer* to one another; that of the **respect** they owe one another, to keep themselves *at a distance* from one another; and should one of these great moral forces fail, 'then nothingness (immorality), with gaping throat, would drink up the whole kingdom of (moral) beings like a drop of water' (if I may use Haller's words, but in a different connection).   (*MS* 6:449)[1]

This is a passage I have always liked and cited approvingly. But I also find it perplexing. That love and respect are both vital moral forces certainly seems right. But do they pull us in opposing directions? I do not think so. Love would seem to be opposed to hate and also to indifference, but not to respect. The attraction/repulsion metaphor, intriguing though it is, does not seem apt. It surfaces again in Kant's discussion of friendship and indeed dominates that discussion; so we cannot write it off as an anomaly. It is by no means just one

I am very grateful to discussants at the 1997 Spindel Conference for stimulating and constructive discussion of an earlier draft of this paper, and in particular to Robert Johnson, both for the comments he presented at the conference and for discussion prior to the conference. I would also like to thank Onora O'Neill, Nelson Potter, Christine Swanton, Mark Timmons, David Velleman, and Allen Wood for their comments.
    [1] I am using the following translations: *The Metaphysics of Morals*, ed. and trans. Mary Gregor (Cambridge: Cambridge University Press, 1996); *Perpetual Peace and Other Essays*, trans. Ted Humphrey (Indianapolis: Hackett, 1983); and *Groundwork of the Metaphysics of Morals*, trans. H. J. Paton (New York: Harper & Row, 1964).

isolated passage that depicts love as bidding us to approach one another, respect as admonishing us to keep a distance.

What seems peculiar is not (not primarily, anyway) Kant's deployment of metaphors from Newtonian physics. That is familiar enough. Particularly in *Anthropology* and in his 'historical' writings, tension between conflicting forces characterizes social relations: tension between the need to confide in another and the need to guard one's secrets, and, more generally, between the desire to merge with others and the desire to feel separate and independent. Indeed, the driving force behind human progress is 'unsocial sociability' (that is, the 'tendency to enter into society, combined, however, with a thoroughgoing resistance that constantly threatens to sunder this society'). He elaborates:

This capacity for social existence is clearly embedded in human nature. Man has a propensity for *living in society*, for in that state he feels himself to be more than man, i.e., feels himself to be more than the development of his natural capacities. He also has, however, a great tendency to isolate himself, for he finds in himself the unsociable characteristic of wanting everything to go according to his own desires, and he therefore anticipates resistance everywhere, just as he knows about himself that for his part he tends to resist others. Now this resistance awakens all of man's powers. . . . In this way, the first true steps from barbarism to culture . . . now occur.   (I. 8:20–1)[2]

What I am drawing attention to is not the phenomenon of unsocial sociability, nor the claim that it is the source of human progress (curious though that claim is), but rather the particular claims about love and respect. Specifically, what is peculiar is the idea that love and respect are opposed, and that respect bids us to hold back from others.[3] It is intuitively odd;[4] moreover, the notion that respect bids us to hold back from others does not square with some of the specific duties of respect. Respect requires, for example, that we not be contemptuous, yet *that* would not fit under the heading of keeping one's distance. Related to this, duties of love and duties of respect are presented as differing from one another more than makes sense to me.

---

[2] See Allen Wood, 'Unsociable Sociability: The Anthropological Basis of Kantian Ethics', *Philosophical Topics*, 19 (1991), 325–51.

[3] That love bids us to approach others is less peculiar, but, as I shall explain shortly, it is peculiar if love is understood as a maxim rather than as a feeling.

[4] Let me explain what I find intuitively odd. If I think about what might lead one to maintain a distance when one loves another, respect is not high on the list. Of course this will depend on the nature of the love, and the nature of the person one loves; one could be in such awe of him or her that respect is indeed what leads one to keep some distance. (And, if so, the respect is respect not simply for the other as a person, but respect for the other as someone one looks up to.) But more likely, I should think, would be first, fear of rejection, and secondarily, fear of being overwhelmed and losing one's equilibrium. It would be more apt to say self-protectiveness and perhaps self-respect bid us to hold back than to say that respect does.

However, perhaps respect does bid one to hold back even when one is not in awe of the other. Imagine that A realizes that her attempt to draw B closer to her, to intensify their relationship, to make B a larger part

II

I turn now to the relation between duties of love and duties of respect. The distinction between duties of love and duties of respect is a distinction within duties of virtue to others. We do not find this division in the other duties of virtue—duties to self. They divide into perfect duties to self and imperfect duties to self, with no suggestion that the latter are duties of love. (No surprise there; self-love, unlike love of others, is not morally enjoined.[5]) Likewise, there is no suggestion in Kant's discussion of duties to self of a tension, and of a vital balance, between love and respect. So, it is within duties of virtue to others that we have this tension, and it is here that we find the distinction between duties of love and duties of respect. The key distinguishing feature, as Kant presents it, is this: duties of love obligate the person on the receiving end, whereas duties of respect do not. Duties of love are those 'duties to others by the performance of which you also put others under obligation' and duties of respect are those duties 'the observance of which does not result in obligation on the part of others' (*MS* 6:448).

This key distinction emerges from what is to most of us a more familiar difference between duties of respect and duties of love (a difference that likewise divides perfect duties from imperfect duties): duties of respect allow less latitude than do duties of love, just as perfect duties allow less latitude than do imperfect

of her life, and to put herself at the centre of B's life is (because of complicating circumstances) unfair to B. She realizes that a deeper relationship is probably not good for B, and has the sense that B has similar misgivings. She recognizes that, if she loves B, she should stop trying to intertwine their lives more fully. Is this a case of *respect* for B leading A to hold back? I see no reason for thinking that it is respect for B rather than love for B that leads A to hold back, i.e. leads her to shift the focus from her intense need to be with B more and to hear clearer expressions of B's love, to thoughts of what is best for B, and to the possibility that, given the circumstances, she is harming B by fostering a more intense, more committed, and more intimate relationship. Love, and not only respect, leads her to (try to) discard the idea that she cannot live without B or without having B at the centre of her life.

There is (at least) one type of love for which it makes some sense to say that love and respect operate as opposing forces: a parent's love for a child (particularly a child older than about three and not yet an adult). It is somewhat plausible to claim that, were it not for the 'opposing' force of respect, a loving parent would be apt to give the child 'too little space', to try to make all her choices for her—what to eat, how to spend her free time, what other children to associate with, what hobbies to have. Arguably it is respect for her child as an agent that checks this. This has some plausibility; still, love for one's child should itself involve a recognition that, as this loved one *is* a person, her future well-being (if not also her current well-being) mandate that the loving parent be less meddlesome and less ready to advise or cajole.

[5]   I here take issue with Joachim Hruschka, who speaks of Kant's 'duties of self-love' (Hruschka, 'Co-Subjectivity, the Right to Freedom and Perpetual Peace', *Proceedings of the Eighth International Kant Congress*, 1 (1995), 215–27, esp. 217–18). The textual evidence he cites in support of the assertion that Kant recognizes such a category of duties is *MS* 6:410, where Kant uses the phrase 'Pflichten der Selbstliebe und Nächstenliebe'. However, Kant uses the phrase not to endorse the categories but to say (after 'man is under obligation to regard himself, as well as every other man, as his end'), 'These are usually called duties of self-love and of love for one's neighbor; but then these words are used inappropriately'.

duties. We are not morally required always to come to others' aid; we are morally required always to treat others with respect. The latitude afforded by the duty to respect others does not include latitude as to when, or how often, one treats others with respect, but only to how one does this. Given the difference in latitude, it makes sense that beneficent acts obligate the recipient while acts of respect do not (*MS* 6:448). You are obligated to aid others, but not all others. So, if you choose to aid me, it is not an instance of rendering something that you owe me. Because of this, I should be grateful to you; I owe a debt of gratitude. By contrast, you owe *everyone* respect. So in respecting me you only render to me what you owe me, and thus your respect does not obligate me.

Another difference between duties of love and duties of respect—a difference that, unlike the last, I find problematic—is that while failure to fulfil duties of respect is a vice, failure to fulfil duties of love is mere lack of virtue. This is not to deny, of course, that there are vices associated with duties of love. But it is noteworthy that Kant calls them 'Vices of Hatred for Men', thereby indicating an asymmetry between them and the vices associated with duties of respect. Since the vices associated with duties of respect are called 'Vices that Violate the Duties of Respect for Other Men', one might have expected the vices associated with duties of love to be called 'Vices that Violate the Duties of Love'. Instead, they are called 'Vices of Hatred for Men', forming a subset of the violations of duties of love. This highlights the fact that the relation between the duties and the vices is somewhat different in each case: if I fail to fulfil a duty of love for another, I might simply be indifferent, and indifference is *not* among the vices associated with the duties of love. It is a mere lack of virtue, not a vice; the vices are vices of hatred, not mere indifference. But *any* violation of a duty of respect for others would be or reflect a vice; it would in no instance be a mere lack of virtue. It takes a greater failing to constitute a vice with respect to love, in other words, than it does to constitute a vice vis-à-vis respect.

The contrast between vices corresponding to love and vices corresponding to respect seems to me to be overdrawn (assuming that it is not just the occasional omission to help, but a maxim of indifference, that Kant is saying reflects a mere lack of virtue rather than vice).[6] And related to this, it is odd that

---

[6] I include the parenthetical qualifier thanks to prompting by Onora O'Neill. Something along the lines of the contrast Kant draws is inevitable, given the latitude accorded (and, I think, quite properly accorded) the duty to promote others' happiness. It is not morally incumbent on me to help others at every opportunity, whereas it is morally incumbent on me always to treat others with respect. So, omitting to help someone on an occasion when I could help would not necessarily be indicative of a vice. This I grant, but I take it that Kant is saying more than this. After all, omitting to help someone would not, I should think, necessarily be indicative of a lack of virtue. It would depend on why I omitted to help. Likewise, whether omitting to help reflects an underlying vice would also depend on why I omitted to help. For this reason, I understand his position to be that a maxim of indifference reflects merely a lack of virtue, rather than presence of a vice.

indifference is not a vice at all, not, presumably, even if it takes the form of utter indifference for all other persons. One reason why this does not seem right is that such indifference is not consistent with respect for humanity. How could one recognize the dignity of persons, recognize that as rational beings they have unconditional worth, and yet be indifferent to their fates? Its inconsistency with respect for humanity should be enough to render indifference to others a vice. Of course, utter indifference is also inconsistent with our duties of love, and Kant would, I assume, acknowledge that; but it would not cut any ice, since his position is that failure to fulfil duties of love is mere lack of virtue and constitutes vice only if it is (or involves) malice, ingratitude, or envy. My point is that even if we were to accept that position, the conflict between gross indifference and respect for others would itself dictate considering indifference a vice. (And a second point, which will be an undercurrent throughout my chapter, is that I do not see love and respect to be all that different in what they call for—not, anyway, when we are talking about practical love.[7])

Just as the contrast between vices corresponding to love and those corresponding to respect seems exaggerated, so does the contrast between love and respect in the opening quote. It does not seem correct to say of love and respect that one directs me to keep a distance from others, while the other directs me constantly to approach others. Now, if Kant is speaking of love and respect as feelings, the contrast is reasonably plausible. (More plausible for love than for respect, I think; it makes more sense to say that love as a feeling bids us to approach one another than to say that respect bids us to keep a distance.) So is he, when he contrasts love to respect, speaking of them as feelings? At one point he says he is. Shortly before the quote with which I opened, he says that love and respect 'are the feelings that accompany the carrying out of these duties' (*MS* 6:448). Each can exist without the other, he claims, but usually they are 'united by the law into one duty, only in such a way that now one duty and now the other is the subject's principle, with the other joined to it as accessory' (*MS* 6:448). It is hard to believe that Kant really means that as *feelings* love and respect are 'united by the law into one duty'. So, although he says he is speaking of them as feelings at this point, I am not convinced that he is.

---

[7] For an intriguing discussion that suggests that love and respect may differ even less than I suggest, see David Velleman, 'Love as a Moral Emotion', *Ethics*, 109 (1999), 338–74. For a rejoinder to my claims, see Robert Johnson, 'Love in Vain', *Southern Journal of Philosophy*, 36 (1997), suppl., 45–50. Johnson argues that 'a person who is genuinely committed to helping others and actively sharing in their fates may conceivably fail to show them respect, even to the point of mockery, arrogance, and ridicule (indeed, some missionaries may have unfortunately given actual examples of this)' (47–8). I would contend, however, that such missionaries, and anyone else who 'helps' arrogantly and mockingly, manifestly lack the obligatory end required by the duties of love. Their help is not genuine beneficence.

Two paragraphs later he signals that he is now speaking of love and respect as maxims. Just after the quote about love and respect as opposing forces, he says that 'in this context . . . love is not to be understood as *feeling*' but 'must rather be thought of as the maxim of **benevolence**' and that 'the same holds true of the **respect** to be shown to others' (*MS* 6:449). This is perplexing, for although the remarks at 6:448 make more sense if we understand them to be about love and respect as *maxims*, when he speaks of love and respect as opposing forces it makes more sense to suppose that he means love and respect as feelings. Do love and respect as maxims pull us in opposite directions? Surely the maxim of benevolence does not ask us 'constantly to *come closer* to one another' (*MS* 6:449). Benevolence is not genuine benevolence—genuine Kantian benevolence—if I do not respect boundaries (that is, if I treat the other not as an agent, but simply as a creature to be helped).[8] Benevolence requires that I promote (or seek) to promote her ends, not try to get her to have an end that I think she should have, or act as if something really were her end when it is not. In this way love—practical love—requires that I keep my distance, that I respect her as an agent, and do not try to remake her. Understood as a maxim, then, love seems to include respect, rather than to be an opposing force.

Most of the time, Kant seems to realize this. Indeed, at times he emphasizes it. So my point is not that he is missing some important truth, but rather that he veers away from his sensible claims and exaggerates the contrast, and the opposition, between love and respect. That he realizes that benevolence requires respect is apparent not only from his general discussion of how the maxim of promoting others' happiness is to be understood, but also from his remarks about helping the needy: since our aid to the poor man humbles him, 'it is our duty to behave as if our help is either merely what is due him or but a slight service of love, and to spare him humiliation and maintain his respect for himself' (*MS* 6:449; see also *MS* 6:453). (It is worth noting that part of what respect for others entails, Kant's discussion suggests, is a concern not to damage their self-respect.)

More generally, Kant makes it clear that, although love and respect can (he says) operate separately, usually they work together in 'such a way that now one duty and now the other is the subject's principle, with the other joined to it as accessory' (*MS* 6:448). I think this is the correct way to think of love and

---

[8] What Kant calls 'benevolence' (*Wohlwollen*) in this passage he later calls 'beneficence' (*Wohltun*). At *MS* 6:452 he introduces a distinction between benevolence and beneficence: 'Benevolence [*Wohlwollen*] is satisfaction in the happiness (well-being) of others; but beneficence [*Wohltun*] is the maxim of making others' happiness one's end, and the duty to it consists in the object's being constrained by his reason to adopt this maxim as a universal law.'

respect, although there is a different asymmetry that Kant does not note (and perhaps would deny). Whereas love, understood as a maxim, requires respect, respect does not require love. There can be (and often is) genuine respect without love. It is true, as Kant says, that a world with only respect and no love would indeed be a flawed world, but I take that to be a separate point, not a basis for claiming that respect needs love. Or, if one wants to allow that respect could reasonably be said to need love because a world with only respect would be deficient, at least it would have to be granted that respect does not need love the way love needs respect. Respect either does not need love at all or needs it in the highly attenuated sense just indicated. Not that this is the best that one could do by way of groping for support for the claim that respect needs love. It might be argued (though I will not attempt such an argument) that, if we were incapable of love, we would be incapable of respect. But even if we were to grant this dependence, love's dependence on respect would be much greater than (and different from) respect's dependence on love. Kant speaks, however, as if their dependence on each other is symmetric. Both, he says, can exist separately from each other and both can, and typically do, function together.[9]

To summarize, I have highlighted three puzzles. First (altering the order of presentation), it is hard to see why love and respect would (as maxims) pull us in opposing directions. Second, although Kant speaks of love and respect as if they are symmetrically dependent on each other, their dependence seems to be asymmetric. Respect does not need love as love needs respect. Love (understood as a maxim) requires respect; the reverse is not true. Third, it is puzzling that, whereas any violation of duties of respect for others is or reflects a vice, only some violations of duties of love are vices (specifically, vices of hatred). This last point is closely connected to what I will next explore: Kant's claim that duties of respect are strictly negative.

Before I do, let me mention a complicating factor that might bear on my discussion. Kant uses the word 'respect' (*Achtung*) in more than one sense. What is surely standard is respect based on the dignity of humanity, on something that we all have, and that does not vary in degree or in excellence from one person to the next. We are all equals; we are all equally deserving of respect. But he also suggests that some people deserve more respect than do others. Respect, thus understood, is based on something that differentiates some people from others. In the following quote he uses 'respect' first in the latter way and then in the way

---

[9]   Kant's illustration of how they can exist separately from one another is a little surprising, and does not do a lot to convince us of his claim. 'One can *love* one's neighbor though he might deserve but little *respect*, and one can show him the respect necessary for every man regardless of the fact that he would hardly be judged worthy of love' (*MS* 6:448). Does not everyone deserve respect, and does not Kant think so? Is he using 'respect' in a different sense in this passage? I address this below.

I take to be standard for him. 'One can *love* one's neighbor though he might deserve but little *respect*, and one can show him the respect necessary for every man regardless of the fact that he would hardly be judged worthy of love' (*MS* 6:448). This suggests that there are two types of respect or, if not two types of respect, two grounds for it. Each of us is entitled either to a base amount or to one type of respect, and some of us are entitled to more than that. There is respect that is necessary for everyone; then there is respect that is earned (or in some other way a case of special merit). The standard sense of 'respect' pertains when Kant says that one 'can show him the respect necessary for every man'; yet he also speaks of someone deserving little respect, and here respect is tied not to equality, but to a belief that people are unequal in their respect-worthiness. Respect, it seems, is due to those who excel in some pertinent way (or, if not excel, at least meet a threshold criterion). 'One can love one's neighbor though he might deserve but little respect.' Some pages later Kant says 'I cannot deny all respect to even a vicious man as a human being; I cannot withdraw at least the respect that belongs to him in his quality as a human being, even though by his deeds he makes himself unworthy of it' (*MS* 6:463). We can glean from his 'at least' that, in addition to respect that belongs to people in virtue of being people, there is also respect that is based on something else.[10] (It also is evident from the quote that someone may be unworthy of respect because of his evil deeds, and yet we are still morally obligated to respect him.[11])

I mention this ambiguity regarding 'respect' because it might shed light on some of what seems puzzling in Kant's contrast between respect and love. It would, at any rate, force an alteration in some claims that I have made. First, if respect enjoins me to look up to those whose excellence makes them worthy of great respect, that might bid me to keep a respectful distance, and thus oppose love (in so far as love bids us approach the other). The opposition between love and respect is more plausible if respect involves looking up to another. Second, I said that love requires respect, but I had in mind respect only in the standard sense. It is not evident to me that love requires that one regard the other as deserving of special respect because of some excellence. Having mentioned

[10]   Though not identical to it, the distinction between the two senses of 'respect' corresponds to the contemporary distinction, first drawn by Stephen Darwall in 'Two Kinds of Respect', *Ethics*, 88 (1977), 36–49, between recognition respect and appraisal respect. One difference between the two distinctions is that recognition is broader than its counterpart in Kant's ethics: recognition respect can be due someone in virtue of his or her societal or familial or other institutional role, e.g. as judge, school principal, or grandmother. I take it that, in the standard sense of 'respect' in Kant, respect is based on each person's inherent dignity and never on one's particular role or office.

[11]   Punishment even of the worst criminal must, Kant emphasizes, be constrained accordingly: 'quartering a man, having him torn by dogs, [and] cutting off his nose and ears' (*MS* 6:463) are impermissible. Why these considerations do not render capital punishment impermissible is a puzzle that I will not address.

this ambiguity, I will proceed as if it were not there, not knowing quite what to make of it.[12] (If I were to make something of it, I would try to account for as many anomalies as possible by claiming that Kant got confused about what he meant by 'respect'. But this would be a cheap and uncharitable way of dealing with what I find puzzling.)

III

I turn now to the question of why duties of respect would be, according to Kant, strictly negative. His claim that they are negative supports his picture of respect and love as opposing forces, where one functions to keep us at a distance and the other functions to bring us closer to one another. But it seems not to fit the rich, detailed discussion of the duties of respect and the vices associated with them. Many of the specific duties Kant enumerates as duties arising from the respect owed to others are, to be sure, duties to refrain from something (defamation, backbiting, wanton faultfinding, ridicule, mockery, arrogance). But there are positive duties as well. Explaining that to be contemptuous of others—to deny them the respect owed to others in general—is contrary to duty, Kant says: 'On this is based a duty to respect a human being even in the logical use of his reason, a duty not to censure his errors by calling them absurdities, poor judgment and so forth, but rather to suppose that his judgment must yet contain some truth and to seek this out' (*MS* 6:463). This duty is not merely negative, since we are to suppose that his judgement must yet contain some truth and seek it out. Kant goes on to say, in the same sentence, that we should try to uncover 'the deceptive illusion (the subjective ground that determined his judgment which, by an oversight, he took for objective), and so, by explaining to him the possibility of his having erred, to preserve his respect for his own understanding' (*MS* 6:463). Again, this is more than just refraining from certain actions; we are to try to preserve the person's respect for his own understanding, doing so by taking positive action (explaining, if we can, how he fell into the error, so that he does not simply blame it on his own stupidity).

---

[12]   One possibility is that despite developing a firmly egalitarian notion of respect, Kant was still influenced by the decidedly non-egalitarian view of a rather similar notion: honour. Honour theorists distinguish 'acquired' honour from 'natural' honour. Acquired honour, unlike natural honour, has to be earned. Perhaps, while insisting that respect is owed to everyone, Kant nonetheless thinks of respect as something one deserves only as long as one does not, by one's deeds, make oneself unworthy of it. I am relying, in my remarks about honour, on Jeremy Horder's intriguing discussion in his *Provocation and Responsibility* (Oxford: Clarendon Press, 1992), ch. 2.

Now it might be argued that, although occasionally duties arising from the respect owed to others call upon us to do something (rather than simply to refrain from something), nonetheless the core idea of duties of respect is to observe limits. After all, respect is 'to be understood as the *maxim* of limiting our self-esteem by the dignity of humanity in another person' (*MS* 6:449). Yet, the duties of respect presumably ask us to *recognize others' humanity*. How, then, can they be strictly negative? It might be argued that they require only that we act *as if* we recognized others' humanity, and recognized its moral significance. This is difficult to square with Kant's claim that we are 'under obligation to acknowledge, in a practical way, the dignity of humanity in every other man', but it might be argued that 'acknowledging' could be understood in a 'merely practical' way, as something that can be done simply by acting in a certain way, rather than as entailing certain attitudes and beliefs. That this is implausible is evident both from common sense—how can I treat you with respect if I think of you as a tool, not as someone worthy of respect, not as someone whose dignity makes a moral claim on me?—and from the fact that duties of respect are duties of virtue. Duties of virtue require that we have certain ends, not just (or primarily) that we perform certain (sorts of) acts.

It seems to me quite clear that duties of respect for others are not strictly negative. The problem, though, is that Kant is unequivocal in his claim that they are. The 'respect we are bound to show others . . . is only a *negative* duty' (*MS* 6:467). (More fully, 'It will be noticed that under the above heading [Ridicule] virtues were not so much commended as rather the vices opposed to them censured. But this is already implicit in the concept of the respect we are bound to show other human beings, which is only a *negative* duty.') And he writes some pages earlier, just after saying that respect is 'to be understood as the *maxim* of limiting our self-esteem by the dignity of humanity in another person': 'Moreover, a duty of free respect toward others is, strictly speaking, only a negative one (of not exalting oneself above others) and is thus analogous to the duty of Right not to encroach upon what belongs to anyone' (*MS* 6:449–50).[13]

So I face a problem. How can I make sense of Kant's claim, or, if I want to be bold and arrogant, somehow explain it away as a 'mistake' on Kant's part?[14]

---

[13] He continues: 'Hence, although it is a mere duty of virtue, it is regarded as *narrow* in comparison with a duty of love, and it is the latter that is considered a *wide* duty' (*MS* 6:450).

[14] Onora O'Neill has pointed out to me that it might be the case that the principle—the basic duty—is negative while the specific duties based on it are in some instances positive (i.e. not duties of omission). Thus, the duty of not exalting oneself above others is negative, even though some of the duties it entails— e.g. to suppose that a person's judgement must contain some truth and to seek it out—are positive. I find it difficult, though, to understand the basis for the claim that duties of respect are negative while duties of love are positive (and, along with that claim, the metaphor of attraction and repulsion) if the negative duties

IV

I will try as a point of entry some remarks from a paper by Allen Wood.[15] Wood suggests that one can treat another with respect even if one feels no respect for the other. 'In dealing honestly with you,' he writes, 'I treat you with respect in that dealing even if I do so only from self-interested motives and will cease treating you with respect as soon as it ceases to serve my self-interest. The actions commanded by FH [the Formula of Humanity as end in itself] are those which express respect for humanity, whatever the subject's feelings toward humanity may be'.[16] Wood's remarks suggest the following position (though in correspondence Wood has indicated to me that he does not endorse this view[17]): actions can fulfil duties of respect even if the agent has no respect for humanity, or fails to see the person in question as worthy of respect (as an end in herself). The actions lack moral worth, but nonetheless are in accordance with duty and thus fulfil duties of respect. If they fulfil duties of respect, then it is easier to make sense of Kant's claim that duties of respect are negative. It still does not explain how they can be negative, given that they require that we take positive action in some instances (for example, that, in addition to refraining from censuring another person's errors by calling them absurdities, poor judgement, and so forth, we suppose that his judgement must yet contain some truth and seek it out). But it does address my other argument—namely, that duties of respect require that we recognize others' humanity, that we acknowledge—really see— them as ends in themselves, as beings who deserve to be respected.

Wood is mainly discussing the *Groundwork*, where Kant's position is less clear, since he does not distinguish there between juridical duties and ethical duties. But in the *Doctrine of Virtue* it is evident that any duty of virtue— indeed any ethical duty—involves more than just performing actions that externally accord with duty. They have an internal side. I do not fulfil a duty of respect unless I have the proper end.

It might be helpful to digress slightly and consider how the relation between internal and external 'correctness' becomes more complex in *The Metaphysics of*

---

entail taking positive action, and if they are based on the idea that we are to recognize others' humanity. It is hard to see how thus classifying duties of respect as negative marks a significant contrast between duties of respect and duties of love.

[15] Allen Wood, 'Humanity as End in Itself', *Proceedings of the Eighth International Kant Congress*, 1.1, ed. Hoke Robinson (Milwaukee, WI: Marquette University Press, 1995), 301–19.

[16] Ibid. 305.

[17] Wood has explained by e-mail: 'The point I meant to make . . . was just that showing respect doesn't mean feeling something and then exhibiting that feeling in any way at all. It means conducting myself in certain ways (sc. constraining my ends by a recognition of someone's worth), and if I do that, it doesn't matter what feelings accompany it. But my conduct involves ends, and has an inner side.'

Morals than it is in the *Groundwork*.[18] In the *Groundwork* the view is pretty straightforward: an action can accord with duty even if it is done from self-interest—or, presumably, even if done from malice. The conformity of the action with duty is not dependent on the agent's motive.[19] Moreover, it is not dependent on the agent having the correct end (unless we are talking about immediate ends, ends that need to be stated before we can even make sense of the act as an intentional act[20]). If I help another in order to promote my own interest (by impressing onlookers, perhaps), my action of helping nonetheless accords with duty. It simply lacks moral worth (as it does if I help from a direct inclination to help—even though there I have the correct end). The distinction between the juridical and the ethical in *The Metaphysics of Morals* complicates the story.

Juridical duties are such that fulfilling them is in no way contingent on having a motive that is good, or even just decent (or even, for that matter, just not utterly heinous). One fulfils a juridical duty by acting externally correctly. One's attitude, one's motives, and one's end (again excluding ends that need to be stated before we can make sense of the act as an intentional act) do not bear on the action's rightness or on whether one indeed fulfilled the duty. Fulfilling a juridical duty is not dependent on having the right end. But this is not the case with duties of virtue. To fulfil a duty of virtue, I have to have the right end.

Here, then, is one difference between the relation between internal and external correctness in *The Metaphysics of Morals* and the same relation in the *Groundwork*. In the *Groundwork*, conformity of the action with duty does not depend on the agent's motive or (with the qualification noted above) on the agent's end. In *The Metaphysics of Morals*, this is true of juridical duties but not of ethical duties (not, anyway, of 'directly ethical duties', and it will be apparent in a moment that it is not true of indirectly ethical duties, either).[21]

---

[18] I do so not because I have this figured out, but in the hope that it will spur others to work on a topic that deserves more attention than it has received.

[19] In saying this I am taking issue with Onora O'Neill's discussion in *Constructions of Reason: Explorations of Kant's Practical Philosophy* (Cambridge: Cambridge University Press, 1989), 86–7.

[20] Thanks to Allen Wood for pointing out the need for the qualification.

[21] Indirectly ethical duties should not be confused with indirect duties. Directly ethical duties are duties of virtue (duties to have certain ends). Indirectly ethical duties are duties whose content is the same as juridical duties except that the kind of obligation is different: it is ethical (internal). One is to do what is also a duty of Right, but do it because it is a duty. See *MS* 6:220–1. By contrast, an indirect duty is a duty, e.g. to promote one's own happiness, that one has only because promoting that duty is a means to something else—specifically, to facilitate, typically by removing a barrier to, fulfilling one's 'real' duties. See *G.* 4:399: 'To assure one's own happiness is a duty (at least indirectly); for discontent with one's state, in a press of cares and amidst unsatisfied wants, might easily become a great *temptation to the transgression of duty*.' For discussion of indirect duties, see Henry E. Allison, *Idealism and Freedom: Essays on Kant's Theoretical and Practical Philosophy* (Cambridge: Cambridge University Press, 1996), 121–3.

Moreover, there is good reason to think that ethical duties require that one fulfil them from duty.[22] This need not be as peculiar as it sounds. It makes most sense if we understand it to mean that the agent must have adopted the obligatory end from duty for it to be the case that her act of helping another fulfils an ethical duty. It need not mean that what prompts the agent at the time of action is the thought of duty. Duty can operate as a secondary motive rather than a primary motive.[23] Whether Kant does hold that ethical duties require that one fulfil them from duty is not entirely clear to me. He could, arguably, allow that one may fulfil a duty of virtue by acting as one should, with the required end (for example, helping another with the end of promoting her happiness), even if one has not adopted the end from duty. I do not think this is Kant's position, but if it is, it leaves room for the distinction between acting from duty and acting in accordance with duty: one acts in accordance with ethical duty if one acts as one should, with the obligatory end; and one acts from duty only if in addition one adopted the end from duty. (The distinction would thus apply to duties of virtue, but only very clumsily, and with a major modification from the way it was presented in the *Groundwork*, since duties of virtue are duties to have certain ends.) If, however, Kant's view is that all ethical duties are such that they are fulfilled only if done from duty, then there is no distinction to be drawn, with respect to ethical duty, between acting from duty and acting in accordance with duty.

Thus, what in the *Groundwork* was a straightforward distinction between acting in accordance with duty and acting from duty is so much more elaborate in *The Metaphysics of Morals* that it only maps on awkwardly. We cannot act in conformity with directly ethical duty without having the right end, and it appears that we cannot do so without acting from duty. We cannot act merely in conformity with indirectly ethical duties at all; to act in conformity with them we must at the same time be acting from duty. We can, of course, act in accordance with juridical duty without acting from duty (and also without having the right end). Further challenges arise when we try to specify exactly how 'acting from duty' is to be understood in each instance. I have suggested that, in connection with duties of virtue, 'acting from duty' means not that the act that corresponds to—'fulfils'—a duty of virtue is prompted by duty as a primary motive, but that the agent adopted the obligatory end from duty. Clearly, more work is needed to sort this out.

---

[22] See *MS* 6:214, 219 and 220–1, and Thomas E. Hill, Jr., *Dignity and Practical Reason in Kant's Moral Theory* (Ithaca, NY: Cornell University Press, 1992), ch. 8.

[23] For an explanation of the primary/secondary distinction, see my *Kantian Ethics Almost without Apology* (Ithaca, NY: Cornell University Press, 1995), chs. 4–5.

I return now to my claim that one cannot fulfil duties of respect unless one has the relevant end. It seems to me quite evident that duties of respect, as duties of virtue, are not fulfilled merely by performing actions that externally accord with duty. But to this two replies could be tendered. First, it will be pointed out, duties of respect should perhaps not be seen as pure cases of duties of virtue. Qua duties of virtue they are not fulfilled by actions that externally accord with duty; but, although officially they are duties of virtue, their status as duties of virtue is, arguably, rather tenuous. They resemble juridical duties and are perhaps best thought of as only marginally duties of virtue. Of course, they are not juridical duties; unlike juridical duties, they do not entail rights to compel compliance. Nonetheless, their partial resemblance to juridical duties might well account for some of what I find puzzling about them. More about this in a moment.

Second, in so far as duties of respect do have an internal side, that internal side might itself be 'negative'. So, although this would not undercut my claim that duties of respect are not fulfilled merely by performing actions that externally accord with duty, it suggests another way to make sense of the idea that they are negative duties. For what they ask of us by way of attitude can be expressed negatively as the duty 'of not exalting oneself above others' (*MS* 6:449). Kant also explains respect as the maxim 'of limiting our self-esteem by the dignity of humanity in another person' (*MS* 6:449) and says that 'the duty of respect for my neighbour is contained in the maxim not to degrade any other to a mere means to my ends' (*MS* 6:450).

I am less impressed by the second point than by the first. That these explanations are all negative is of some significance, but, for reasons I gave earlier, not a great deal; for does not respect entail treating others always as ends, never as mere means, and does it not entail recognizing their inherent dignity? When we look at the vices Kant enumerates—vices that violate the duties of respect for others—it is clear that many of these are not merely failures to refrain from something, but failures to recognize others as deserving respect. I am not convinced, in short, that the 'internal' side to respecting others is distinctively negative. It is true that duties of respect are somewhat more naturally explicated in negative terms than are duties of love, but the difference seems to be pretty slight.

More promising is the suggestion that duties to respect others have a marginal status as duties of virtue. I think the more accurate way to make the point is to say that just as ethical duties differ in their latitude, in other respects, too, some are closer to juridical duties than are others. Kant's classification of duties is not exactly crisp; we should expect to see some scalar differences. Just as duties of self-respect are closer to juridical duties than are other ethical duties, duties of respect (though 'wider' than duties of self-respect) are closer to juridical duties than are duties of love.[24] Kant brings this out when he explains that a duty of respect towards others is, 'strictly speaking, only a negative one (of not exalting oneself above others) and is thus analogous to the duty of right not to encroach upon what belongs to anyone' (*MS* 6:449). He goes on to say that although it is a duty of virtue, it is narrow in comparison with a duty of love.

V

What this suggests is that the set of puzzles I have raised is best understood as pointing to the marginal status of duties of respect for others as duties of virtue. Still, the suggestion does not explain much; we can still ask why Kant chooses to contrast respect to love, and duties of respect to duties of love, as sharply as he does. Some suggestions from Robert Johnson provide a promising response. Johnson points out that all duties are derived from respect for humanity, and so in one sense duties of love and duties of respect are of a piece: they are all duties of respect in a wider, looser, and non-technical sense of 'duties of respect'. Once we distinguish the wider from the more technical sense of 'duties of respect', we can see that, understood in the wide way, duties of virtue are all duties of respect and are all positive, since they involve recognizing humanity as an end in itself. Understood in the narrow and technical way, duties of respect are a special type of (what in a wider sense can be thought of as) duties of respect. Perhaps—though I am not sure if this is a conjecture that Johnson would endorse—the reason why duties of love and duties of respect seem to me to be more alike than Kant claims and less like opposing forces than his metaphor suggests is that I am not distinguishing duties of respect in the technical sense from duties of respect in the wider sense (or at least not taking the distinction to heart). The similarity between duties of love and duties of respect stems from the fact that all are derived from respect for humanity. But when we take care to distinguish the technical from the wide way in which duties are duties of respect, it is easier to see why Kant says that duties of respect (understood in the technical way) are negative, and, in this way, stand in contrast to duties of love.

How far does this go towards addressing my puzzles? It does not solve them all, but it does go some distance, particularly on the question of why Kant so sharply contrasts duties of respect to duties of love, and why he treats duties of

---

[24] See Mary J. Gregor, *Laws of Freedom: A Study of Kant's Method of Applying the Categorical Imperative in the* Metaphysik der Sitten (Oxford: Basil Blackwell, 1963), ch. 12.

respect as negative duties. It is still a little hard to understand why respect would bid us to keep our distance from others, but if we suppose that Kant is speaking of respect in a more restrictive sense, corresponding to the duties of respect (understood in the technical way), it begins to make some sense. (I am not sure that it is wise to suppose this, but let me try out the idea anyway.)

Respect (understood the usual way) asks us to do two things: to take care not to butt into people's lives, but also to share their fates, to view ourselves as fellow humans, as 'rational beings with needs, united by nature in one dwelling place so that [we] can help one another' (*MS* 6:453). Respect for others requires us to balance two sometimes competing views: we view persons as agents whose freedom and self-direction are to be honoured, and also view them as needy and vulnerable and decidedly not self-sufficient. (It is the former view that is captured by respect in the narrow sense, and for which the metaphor of keeping one's distance makes at least some sense.) These two views are by no means always in tension, but sometimes they are. Kant exaggerates the extent to which they are in tension, and a good bit of what I find jarring in his discussion of love and respect as opposing forces stems, I think, from that exaggeration. In particular, he overestimates the degree to which keeping a distance from others is needed in order to respect others' freedom and self-direction, and to preserve self-respect. This is evident both from his discussion of friendship (*MS* 6:470–1) and from the fact that self-respect, in his view, requires not accepting favours that one can do without (*MS* 6:436). Not only is dependence in tension with agency; on Kant's view even interdependence is problematic unless the parties are dependent on each other to the same degree.[25]

Kant takes a good point too far. It is true that we should take care not to aid others in a way that makes them feel beholden to us, or inferior to us. Still, favour doing, whether within friendship or outside it, is not the threat to the recipient's self-respect—or to the friendship—that he suggests it is.[26] ('The relation of friendship is a relation of equality. A friend who bears my losses becomes my benefactor and puts me in his debt. I feel shy in his presence and

[25] And even if they are, there may be worrisome imbalance if one person aided the other before being aided by the other: 'one cannot, by any repayment of a kindness received, *rid* oneself of the obligation for it, since the recipient can never win away from the benefactor his *priority* of merit, namely having been the first in benevolence' (*MS* 6:455).

[26] And a good thing, too. Beneficence itself would be dubious if receiving favours were as problematic as Kant suggests. See Jean P. Rumsey, 'Re-Visions of Agency in Kant's Moral Theory', in Robin Schott (ed.), *Feminist Interpretations of Immanuel Kant* (University Park, PA: Pennsylvania State University Press, 1997), esp. 134–8. She points out that the Kantian virtuous agent is happy to aid others but reluctant to accept others' aid. Aristotle can get away with this—magnanimity is available only to an elite few—but it does not sit well with Kant's egalitarianism.

cannot look him boldly in the face. The true relationship is cancelled and friendship ceases.'[27]) Similarly, love arguably does need respect,[28] lest love be paternalistic or otherwise invasive, and respect may need love to check its tendency to aloofness; but love and respect are less different and less opposed than Kant suggests.

---

[27]   *Lectures on Ethics*, Louis Infield, trans. (Indianapolis: Hackett, 1981), 204–5.

[28]   I qualify my claim by inserting 'arguably' because, as I indicate in n. 4, I am not convinced that love normally needs to be tempered in this way. It is not, it seems to me, inherently possessive or invasive; unless it is deformed or (in the non-Kantian sense) pathological, it contains within it a concern for the loved one's well-being.

BIBLIOGRAPHY

Joshua Glasgow

This select bibliography includes literature in English and German published for the most part from 1970 to 2000. It is divided into three main sections: a General section on *The Metaphysics of Morals*, a section on the *Rechtslehre*, and a section on the *Tugendlehre*. The latter two sections are further divided into subtopics.

GENERAL

ALLISON, HENRY E. (1990), 'Wille, Willkür, and Gesinnung', in Allison, *Kant's Theory of Freedom* (Cambridge: Cambridge University Press), ch. 7.

ATWELL, JOHN E. (1986), *Ends and Principles in Kant's Moral Thought* (Dordrecht: Martinus Nijhoff).

AUNE, BRUCE (1979), *Kant's Theory of Morals* (Princeton: Princeton University Press), chs. 5–6.

BECK, LEWIS WHITE (1993), 'Kant's Two Conceptions of the Will in Their Political Context', repr. in Ronald Beiner and William James Booth (eds.), *Kant and Political Philosophy* (New Haven: Yale University Press), 38–49.

BRANDT, REINHARD (1993), 'Gerechtigkeit bei Kant', *Jahrbuch für Recht und Ethik*, 1:25–44.

DEGGAU, HANS-GEORG (1985), 'Die Architektonik der praktischen Philosophie Kants: Moral-Religion-Recht-Geschichte', *Archiv für Rechts- und Sozialphilosophie*, 71:319–42.

DONAGAN, ALAN (1985), 'The Structure of Kant's Metaphysics of Morals', *Topoi*, 4:61–72.

DREIER, RALF (1979), 'Zur Einheit der praktischen Philosophie Kants: Kants Rechtsphilosophie im Kontext seiner Moralphilosophie', *Perspektiven der Philosophie*, 5:5–37.

EBBINGHAUS, JULIUS (1968), *Gesammelte Aufsätze, Vorträge und Reden* (Darmstadt: Wissenschaftliche Buchgesellschaft).

Thanks to Sharon Byrd, H. F. Fulda, Thomas E. Hill, Jr., Bernd Ludwig, Onora O'Neill, Hoke Robinson, Kenneth R. Westphal, and Allen Wood for their help in compiling this bibliography.

EBBINGHAUS, JULIUS (1986), *Gesammelte Schriften*, 4 vols. (Bonn: Bouvier Verlag).

GALSTON, WILLIAM A. (1993), 'What Is Living and What Is Dead in Kant's Practical Philosophy?', in Ronald Beiner and William James Booth (eds.), *Kant and Political Philosophy* (New Haven: Yale University Press), 207–23.

GREGOR, MARY J. (1963), *Laws of Freedom: A Study of Kant's Method of Applying the Categorical Imperative in the Metaphysik der Sitten* (New York: Barnes & Noble).

—— (1993), 'Kant on Obligation, Rights and Virtue', *Jahrbuch für Recht und Ethik*, 1:69–102.

HEYD, DAVID (1997), 'Moral and Legal Luck: Kant's Reconciliation with Practical Contingency', *Jahrbuch für Recht und Ethik*, 5:27–42.

HILL, THOMAS E., JR. (2001), *Respect, Pluralism, and Justice: Kantian Perspectives* (Oxford: Oxford University Press).

HRUSCHKA, JOACHIM (1995), 'Co-Subjectivity, the Right to Freedom and Perpetual Peace', in Hoke Robinson (ed.), *Proceedings of the Eighth International Kant Congress* (Milwaukee, WI: Marquette University Press), vol. I. pt.1, 215–27.

HUDSON, HUD (1991), 'Wille, Willkür, and the Imputability of Immoral Actions', *Kant-Studien*, 82:179–96.

KORSGAARD, CHRISTINE M. (1996), 'An Introduction to the Ethical, Political, and Religious Thought of Kant', repr. in Korsgaard, *Creating the Kingdom of Ends* (Cambridge: Cambridge University Press), ch. 1.

LOUDEN, ROBERT (1999), *Kant's Impure Ethics* (Oxford: Oxford University Press).

MAUTNER, THOMAS (1981), 'Kant's Metaphysics of Morals: A Note on the Text', *Kant-Studien*, 72:356–9.

MULHOLLAND, LESLIE A. (1990), *Kant's System of Rights* (New York: Columbia University Press).

O'NEILL, ONORA (1989), *Constructions of Reason: Explorations of Kant's Practical Philosophy* (Cambridge: Cambridge University Press).

—— (1997), 'Kant on Reason and Religion: Reasoned Hope and Reason and Interpretation', in Grethe B. Peterson (ed.), *The Tanner Lectures on Human Values*, 18 (Salt Lake City: University of Utah Press), 267–308.

POTTER, NELSON (1994), 'Kant on Obligation and Motivation in Law and Ethics', *Jahrbuch für Recht und Ethik*, 2:95–112.

POTTER, NELSON, and TIMMONS, MARK (1997), '*Kant's* Metaphysics of Morals', *Southern Journal of Philosophy*, 36, Suppl.

SCHALLER, WALTER E. (1995), 'From the Groundwork to the Metaphysics of Morals: What Happened to Morality in Kant's Theory of Justice?', *History of Philosophy Quarterly*, 12:333–45.

—— (2000), 'Kant on Right and Moral Right', *Southern Journal of Philosophy*, 38:321–42.

STELKER-WEITHOFER, PRIMIN (1990), 'Wille und Willkür bei Kant', *Kant-Studien*, 81:304–20.

SULLIVAN, ROGER J. (1989), *Kant's Moral Theory* (Cambridge: Cambridge University Press).

WILLASCHEK, MARCUS (1997), 'Why the *Doctrine of Right* does not Belong in the *Metaphysics of Morals*: On Some Basic Distinctions in Kant's Moral Philosophy', *Jahrbuch für Recht und Ethik*, 5:205–27.

WOOD, ALLEN W. (1984), 'Kant's Compatibilism', in Wood (ed.), *Self and Nature in Kant's Philosophy* (Ithaca, NY: Cornell University Press), 73–101.

—— (1991), 'Unsocial Sociability: The Anthropological Basis of Kantian Ethics', *Philosophical Topics*, 19:325–51.

—— (1998), 'Kant's Historical Materialism', in Jane Kneller and Sidney Axinn (eds.), *Autonomy and Community: Readings in Contemporary Kantian Social Philosophy* (Albany, NY: State University of New York Press), 15–38.

—— (2000), 'Kant's Practical Philosophy', in Karl Ameriks (ed.), *The Cambridge Companion to German Idealism* (New York: Cambridge University Press), 57–75.

RECHTSLEHRE

GENERAL

ARENDT, HANNAH (1982), *Lectures on Kant's Political Philosophy*, ed. Ronald Beiner (Chicago: University of Chicago Press).

BALASUBRAMANIAN, RAJANGAM (1975), 'Some Reflections on Kant's Political Philosophy', in Herbert Herring (ed.), *Immanuel Kant: Proceedings of the Seminars at Calcutta and Madras* (Madras: Max Mueller Bhavan), 92–114.

BARTUSCHAT, WOLFGANG (1987), 'Praktische Philosophie und Rechtsphilosophie bei Kant', *Philosophisches Jahrbuch der Görresgesellschaft*, 94:24–41.

—— (1987), 'Apriorität und Empirie in Kants Rechtsphilosophie', *Philosophische Rundschau*, 34:31–49.

BATSCHA, ZWI (1976) (ed.), *Materialien zu Kants Rechtsphilosophie* (Frankfurt a.M.: Suhrkamp Verlag).

BECKER, DON (1993), 'Kant's Moral and Political Philosophy', in *Routledge History of Philosophy, Vol. 6: The Age of German Idealism* (London: Routledge), 68–102.

BEINER, RONALD (1997), 'Rereading Hannah Arendt's Kant Lectures', *Philosophy and Social Criticism*, 23:21–32.

BEINER, RONALD, and BOOTH, WILLIAM JAMES (1993) (eds.), *Kant and Political Philosophy: The Contemporary Legacy* (New Haven: Yale University Press).

BENSON, PETER (1987), 'External Freedom According to Kant', *Columbia Law Review*, 87:559–79.

BIELEFELDT, HEINER (1997), 'Autonomy and Republicanism: Immanuel Kant's Philosophy of Freedom', *Political Theory*, 25:524–58.

BOOTH, WILLIAM JAMES (1986), *Interpreting the World: Kant's Philosophy of History and His Politics* (Toronto: University of Toronto Press).

—— (1992) (ed.), *Essays on Kant's Political Philosophy* (Chicago: Chicago University Press).

BOWIE, NORMAN E. (1971), 'Aspects of Kant's Philosophy of Law', *The Philosophical Forum*, 2:469–78.

BRANDT, REINHARD (1982), 'Das Erlaubnisgesetz, oder: Vernunft und Geschichte in Kants Rechtslehre', in Brandt (ed.), *Rechtsphilosophie der Aufklärung* (Berlin: de Gruyter), 233–85.

—— (1982) (ed.), *Rechtsphilosophie der Auflklärung/Symposium Wolfenbüttel 1981* (Berlin: de Gruyter).

—— (1995), 'Zu Kants politischer Philosophie', in Hoke Robinson (ed.), *Proceedings of the Eighth International Kant Congress* (Milwaukee, WI: Marquette University Press), vol. I. pt. 1, 323–41.

—— (1997), *Zu Kants politischer Philosophie*, Sitzungsberichte der Wissenschaftlichen Gesellschaft der J. W. Goethe-Universität Frankfurt am Main (Stuttgart: Franz Steiner-Verlag).

BUHR, MANFRED (1974), 'Kant und das Grundproblem der klassischen bürgerlichen Philosophie', *Deutsche Zeitschrift für Philosophie*, 22:261–8.

CAVALLAR, GEORG (1992), 'Neuere nordamerikanische Arbeiten über Kants Rechts- und politische Philosophie', *Zeitschrift für philosophische Forschung*, 46:266–77.

CHAMPAGNE, ROLAND-A. (1998), 'At the Intersection of Political Theory and Philosophy: Hannah Arendt's Projection of Kant's Voice into the Political Arena', *Idealistic Studies*, 28:123–35.

DAHLSTROM, DANIEL O. (1997), 'Ethik, Recht und Billigkeit', *Jahrbuch für Recht und Ethik*, 5:55–72.

DEGGAU, HANS-GEORG (1983), *Die Aporien der Rechtslehre Kants* (Stuttgart: Frommann-Holzboog).

DIETZE, GOTTFRIED (1982), *Kant und der Rechtsstaat* (Tübingen: J. C. B. Mohr).

DREIER, RALF (1986), *Rechtsbegriff und Rechtsidee: Kants Rechtsbegriff und seine Bedeutung für die gegenwärtige Diskussion* (Frankfurt a.M: Metzner Verlag).

EBBINGHAUS, JULIUS (1988), 'Das Kantische System der Rechte des Menschen und des Bürgers in seiner geschichtlichen und aktuellen Bedeutung', in G. Geismann and H. Oberer (eds.), *J. Ebbinghaus, Gesammelte Schriften* 2 (Bonn: Bouvier Verlag), 249–82.

—— (1988), 'Kants Rechtslehre und die Rechtsphilosophie des Neukantianismus', in G. Geismann and H. Oberer (eds.), *J. Ebbinghaus, Gesammelte Schriften* 2 (Bonn: Bouvier Verlag), 231–48.

FLETCHER, GEORGE P. (1987), 'Law and Morality: A Kantian Perspective', *Columbia Law Review*, 87:533–8.

FLIKSCHUH, KATRIN (1997), 'On Kant's "Rechtslehre" ', *European Journal of Philosophy*, 5:50–73.

—— (1999), 'Freedom and Constraint in Kant's *Metaphysical Elements of Justice*', *History of Political Thought*, 20:250–71.

—— (2000), *Kant and Modern Political Philosophy* (Cambridge: Cambridge University Press).

FULDA, HANS FRIEDRICH (1997), 'Kants Postulat des öffentlichen Rechts (RL §42)', *Jahrbuch für Recht und Ethik*, 5:267–90.

—— (1998), 'Zur Systematik des Privatrechts in Kants *Metaphysik der Sitten*', in Dieter Hüning and Burkhard Tuschling (eds.), *Recht, Staat und Völkerrecht* (Berlin: Duncker & Humblot), 141–56.

—— (1999), 'Erkenntnis der Art, etwas Aeusseres als das Seine zu haben,' in O. Höffe (ed.), *Immanuel Kant. Metaphysische Anfangsgruende der Rechtslehre* (Berlin), 87–115.

GALLIE, WALTER B. (1979), 'Kant's View of Reason in Politics', *Philosophy*, 54:19–33.

GERHARDT, VOLKER (1981), 'Recht und Herrschaft: Zur gesellschaftlichen Funktion des Rechts in der Philosophie Kants', *Rechtstheorie*, 12:53–94.

—— (1991), 'Vernunft und Urteilskraft. Politische Philosophie und Anthropologie im Anschluß und Immanuel Kant und Hannah Arendt', in Martyn P. Thompson (ed), *John Locke und Immanuel Kant: historische Rezeption und gegenwärtige Relevanz* (Berlin: Duncker & Humblot), 316–33.

—— (1995), 'Der Thronverzicht der Philosophie. Über das moderne Verhältnis von Philosophie und Politik bei Kant', in Otfried Höffe (ed.), *Immanuel Kant, Zum ewigen Frieden* (Berlin: Akademie Verlag), 171–93.

—— (1996), 'Ausübende Rechtslehre: Kants Begriff der Politik', in G. Schöhrich and Y. Kato (eds.), *Kant in der Diskussion der Moderne* (Frankfurt a.M: Suhrkamp), 464–88.

GERRESHEIM, EDUARD (1974) (ed.), *Immanuel Kant 1724/1974: Kant als politischer Denker* (Bonn: Inter Nationes).

GREGOR, MARY (1991), ' "Natural Rights" in Kant's *Doctrine of Right*', in T. O'Hagan (ed.), *Revolution and Enlightenment in Europe* (Aberdeen: Aberdeen University Press), 23–9.

—— (1993), 'Kant on "Natural Rights"', in Ronald Beiner and William James Booth (eds.), *Kant and Political Philosophy* (New Haven: Yale University Press), 50–75.

—— (1994), 'Leslie Mulholland on Kant's Rechtslehre', *Dialogue*, 33:693–700.

GREY, THOMAS C. (1987), 'Serpents and Doves: A Note on Kantian Legal Theory', *Columbia Law Review*, 87:580–91.

GUTSCHKER, THOMAS (1999), 'Ästhetik und Politik: Annäherungen an Kants politische Philosophie', in Theo Stammen (ed.), *Kant als politischer Schriftsteller* (Würzburg: Ergon Verlag), 43–56.

HELLER, AGNES (1990), 'Freedom and Happiness in Kant's Political Philosophy', *Graduate Faculty Philosophy Journal*, 13:115–31.

HÖFFE, OTFRIED (1987), 'Der kategorische Imperativ als Grundbegriff einer normativen Rechts- und Staatsphilosophie', in Reinhard Löw (ed.), *OIKEIΩΣIΣ: Festschrift für Robert Spaemann* (Weinheim: Acta Humaniora, VCH), 87–100.

—— (1989), 'Kant's Principle of Justice as Categorical Imperative of Law', in Yirimahu Yovel (ed.), *Kant's Practical Philosophy Reconsidered* (Dordrecht: Kluwer Academic), 149–67.

—— (1992), '"Even a Nation of Devils Needs the State:" The Dilemma of Natural Justice', in Howard Williams (ed.), *Essays on Kant's Political Philosophy* (Chicago: University of Chicago Press), 120–42.

—— (1995) (ed.), *Immanuel Kant, Zum ewigen Frieden* (Berlin: Akademie Verlag).

—— (1999) (ed.), *Kants Rechtslehre* (Berlin: Akademie Verlag).

HOPTON, TERRY (1982), 'Kant's Two Theories of Law', *History of Political Thought*, 3:51–76.

HOWARD, DICK (1980), 'Kant's Political Theory: The Virtue of His Vices', *Review of Metaphysics*, 34:325–50.

HRUSCHKA, JOACHIM (1993), 'Rechtsstaat, Freiheitsrecht, und das "Recht auf Achtung von seinem Nebenmenschen"', *Jahrbuch für Recht und Ethik*, 1:193–206.

HÜNING, DIETER, and TUSCHLING, BURKHARD (1998) (eds), *Recht, Staat und Völkerrecht bei Immanuel Kant: Marburger Tagung zu Kants 'Metaphysischen Anfangsgründe der Rechtslehre'* (Berlin: Duncker & Humblot).

HUTCHINGS, KIMBERLY (1996), *Kant, Critique and Politics* (London: Routledge).

ILTING, KARL-HEINZ (1981), 'Gibt es eine kritische Ethik und Rechtsphilosophie Kants?', *Archiv für Geschichte der Philosophie*, 63:325–45.

KAEHLER, KLAUS E. (1993), 'Die Asymmetrie von apriorischer Rechtslehre und positivem Recht bei Kant', *Jahrbuch für Recht und Ethik*, 1:103–12.

KAUFMANN, MATTHIAS (1997), 'The Relation between Right and Coercion: Analytic or Synthetic?', *Jahrbuch für Recht und Ethik*, 5:73–84.

KAULBACH, FRIEDRICH (1973), 'Der Begriff der Freiheit in Kants Rechtsphilosophie', *Philosophische Perspectiven*, 5:78–91.

—— (1982), *Studien zur späten Rechtsphilosophie Kants und ihrer transzendentalen Methode* (Würzburg: Königsheusen & Neumann).

KERSTING, WOLFGANG (1983), 'Neuere Interpretationen der Kantischen Rechtsphilosophie', *Zeitschrift für philosophische Forschung*, 37:282–98.

KERSTING, WOLFGANG (1986), 'Ist Kants Rechtsphilosophie aporetisch? Zu Hans-Georg Deggaus Darstellung der Rechtslehre Kants', *Kant-Studien*, 77:241–51.

—— (1992), 'Politics, Freedom, and Order: Kant's Political Philosophy', in Paul Guyer (ed.), *The Cambridge Companion to Kant* (Cambridge: Cambridge University Press), 342–66.

—— (1993), *Wohlgeordnete Freiheit: Immanuel Kants Rechts- und Sozialphilosophie*, 2nd edn. (Frankfurt: Suhrkamp).

KERSZBERG, PIERRE (1996), 'Feeling and Coercion: Kant and the Deduction of Right', *Protosoz*, 8/9:223–36.

KIEHL, BETTY (1997), 'The One Innate Right', *Jahrbuch für Recht und Ethik*, 5: 195–204.

KNELLER, JANE, and AXINN, SIDNEY (1998) (eds.), *Autonomy and Community: Readings in Contemporary Kantian Social Philosophy* (Albany, NY: SUNY Press).

KÖNIG, PETER (1994), *Autonomie und Autokratie: Über Kants Metaphysik der Sitten* (Berlin: de Gruyter).

KÜSTERS, GERD-WALTER (1988), *Kants Rechtsphilosophie* (Darmstadt: Wissenschaftliche Buchgesellschaft).

LUDWIG, BERND (1988), *Kants Rechtslehre* (Hamburg: F. Meiner).

—— (1996), 'Postulat, Deduktion und Abstraktion in Kants Lehre vom intelligibelen Besitz', *Archiv für Rechts- und Sozialphilosophie*, 82:250–9.

—— (1999), 'Kommentar zum Staatsrecht (II) §§ 51–2; Allgemeine Anmerkung A; Anhang, Beschluß', in Otfried Höffe (ed.), *Klassiker auslegen: Immanuel Kants Metaphysische Anfangsgründe der Rechtslehre* (Berlin: Akademie Verlag), 173–94.

LUF, GERHARD (1978), *Freiheit und Gleichheit: Die Aktualität im politischen Denken Kants* (Wien: Springer).

MÜLLER, GABRIELE (1981), 'Kants politische Philosophie', *Liberal*, 23:64–72.

MURPHY, JEFFRIE G. (1994), *Kant: The Philosophy of Right* (Macon, GA: Mercer University Press).

O'FARRELL, FRANCIS (1978), 'Kant's Philosophy of Law', *Gregorianum*, 59:233–88.

O'NEILL, ONORA (1989), 'The Public Use of Reason', repr. in O'Neill, *Constructions of Reason: Explorations of Kant's Practical Philosophy* (Cambridge: Cambridge University Press), ch. 2.

PIPPIN, ROBERT B. (1985), 'On the Moral Foundations of Kant's Rechtslehre', in Richard Kennington (ed.), *The Philosophy of Immanuel Kant* (Washington, DC: CUA Press, 107–42).

POGGE, THOMAS W. (1988), 'Kant's Theory of Justice', *Kant-Studien*, 79:407–33.

REISS, HANS (1977), *Kants politisches Denken*, trans. Gisela Shaw (Bern: Lang).

—— (1999), 'Kant's Politics and the Enlightenment: Reflections on Some Recent Studies', *Political Theory*, 27:236–73.

RICKMAN, HANS PETER (1979), 'Kant's Political Philosophy', *Philosophy*, 54:548–51.

RILEY, PATRICK (1983), *Kant's Political Philosophy* (Totowa, NJ: Rowman Littlefield).

—— (1983), 'On De Lue's Review of Arendt's Lectures on Kant's Political Philosophy', *Political Theory*, 12:435–9.

—— (1986), 'Kantian Politics: The "Elements" of Kant's Practical Philosophy', *Political Theory*, 14:552–83.

—— (1989), 'The "Place" of Politics in Kant's Practical Philosophy', in Gerhard Funke and Thomas M. Seebohm (eds.), *Proceedings of the Sixth International Kant-Congress* (Washington, DC: University Press of America), vol. II. pt. 2, 267–78.

—— (1992), 'Hannah Arendt on Kant, Truth and Politics', repr. in Howard Williams (ed.), *Essays on Kant's Political Philosophy* (Chicago: University of Chicago Press), 305–23.

RITTER, CHRISTIAN (1974), 'Politik des Rechts', in Eduard Gerresheim (ed.), *Kant als politischer Denker* (Bonn: Inter Nationes), 44–58.

ROSEN, ALLEN D. (1993), *Kant's Theory of Justice* (Ithaca, NY: Cornell University Press).

SAITO, YUMI (1996), 'Die Debatte weitet sich aus', *Archiv für Rechts- und Sozialphilosophie*, 82.2:259–65.

—— (1996), 'War die Umstellung von §2 der Kantischen "Rechtslehre" zwingend?', *Archiv für Rechts- und Sozialphilosophie*, 83.2:238–50.

SHELL, SUSAN MELD (1980), *The Rights of Reason: A Study of Kant's Philosophy and Politics* (Toronto: University of Toronto Press).

STERN, DAVID S. (1991), 'Autonomy and Political Obligation in Kant', *Southern Journal of Philosophy*, 29:127–48.

STRANGAS, JOHANNES (1987), *Kritik der Kantischen Rechtsphilosophie: Ein Beitrag zur Herstellung der Einheit der praktischen Philosophie* (Cologne: Böhlau).

STRUCK, PETER (1987), 'Ist Kants Rechtspostulat der praktischen Vernunft aporetisch? Ein Beitrag zur neuerlich ausgebrochenen Kontroverse um Kants Rechtsphilosophie', *Kant-Studien*, 78:471–6.

TAYLOR, CHARLES (1984), 'Kant's Theory of Freedom', in J. N. Gray and Z. Pelczynski (eds.), *Conceptions of Liberty in Political Philosophy* (New York: St. Martin's), 100–21.

TERADA, TOSHIRO (1995), ' "The Universal Principle of Right" as the Supreme Principle of Kant's Practical Philosophy', in Hoke Robinson (ed.), *Proceedings of the Eighth International Kant Congress* (Milwaukee, WI: Marquette University Press), vol. II. pt. 2, 541–47.

TUSCHLING, BURKHARD (1988), 'Das "rechtliche Postulat der praktischen Vernunft:" seine Stellung und Bedeutung in Kants "Rechtslehre" ', in Hariolf Oberer and Gerhard Seel (eds.), *Kant: Analysen-Probleme-Kritik* (Würzburg: Königshausen und Neumann), 273–92.

UNRUH, PETER (1993), *Die Herrschaft der Vernunft. Zur Staatsphilosophie Immanuel Kants* (Baden-Baden: Nomos).

WEIDENFELD, WERNER (1973), 'Frieden im Spannungsfeld: Überlegungen zu Kants Theorie der Politik', *Beiträge zur Konfliktforschung*, 3:57–69.

WEINRIB, ERNEST J. (1992), 'Law as Idea of Reason', repr. in Howard Williams (ed.), *Essays on Kant's Political Philosophy* (Chicago: University of Chicago Press), 15–49.

WENTURIS, NIKOLAUS (1991), 'Reflexionen zu Kants politischer Theorie', in Martyn P. Thompson (ed.), *John Locke und Immanuel Kant: historische Rezeption und gegenwärtige Relevanz* (Berlin: Duncker & Humblot), 337–47.

WENZEL, UWE JUSTUS (1990), 'Recht und Moral der Vernunft. Kants Rechtslehre: Neue Literatur und neue Editionen', *Archiv für Rechts- und Sozialphilosophie*, 76:227–43.

WILLIAMS, HOWARD (1983), *Kant's Political Philosophy* (New York: St. Martin's).

—— (1992) (ed.), *Essays on Kant's Political Philosophy* (Chicago: University of Chicago Press).

WOOD, ALLEN W. (1999), 'Kant's Doctrine of Right: Introduction', in O. Höffe (ed.) *Kants Rechtslehre* (Berlin: Akademie Verlag), 19–39.

ORIGINS AND HISTORICAL CONNECTIONS

BÄRTHLEIN, KARL (1988), 'Die Vorbereitung der Kantischen Rechts- und Staatsphilosophie in der Schulphilosophie', in H. Oberer and G. Seel (eds.), *Kant: Analysen-Probleme-Kritik* (Würzburg: Könighausen & Neumann), 221–71.

BURG, PETER (1981), 'Die Verwirklichung von Grund- und Freiheitsrechten in den Preußischen Reformen und Kants Rechtslehre', in Gunter Birch (ed.), *Grund- und Freiheitsrechte im Wandel von Gesellschaft und Geschichte: Beiträge zur Geschichte der Grund- und Freiheitsrechte vom Ausgang des Mittelalters bis zur Revolution von 1848* (Göttingen: Vandenhoeck & Ruprecht), 287–309.

BUSCH, WERNER (1979), *Die Entstehung der kritischen Rechtsphilosophie Kants* (Berlin: Walter de Gruyter).

MANDT, HELLA (1976), 'Historisch-politische Traditionselemente im politischen Denken Kants', in Zwi Batscha (ed.), *Materialien zu Kants Rechtsphilosophie* (Frankfurt a.M.: Suhrkamp), 292–330.

OBERER, HARIOLF (1973), 'Zur Frühgeschichte der Kantischen Rechtslehre', *Kant-Studien*, 64:88–102.

—— (1983), 'Ist Kants Rechtslehre kritische Philosophie? Zu Werner Buschs Untersuchung der Kantischen Rechtsphilosophie', *Kant-Studien*, 74:217–24.

SANER, HANS (1973), *Kant's Political Thought: Its Origins and Development* (Chicago: University of Chicago Press).

SCHMIDT, JAMES (1999), 'Liberalism and Enlightenment in Eighteenth-Century Germany', *Critical Review*, 13:31–53.

SHELL, SUSAN (1993), 'Commerce and Community in Kant's Early Thought', in Ronald Beiner and William James Booth (eds.), *Kant and Political Philosophy* (New Haven: Yale University Press), 117–54.

KANT, LIBERALISM, AND OTHER POLITICAL THINKERS AND THEORIES

ALTMANN, ALEXANDER (1981), *Prinzipien politischer Theorie bei Mendelssohn und Kant* (Trier: NCO-Verlag).

APEL, KARL-OTTO (1983), 'Kant, Hegel und das aktuelle Problem der normativen Grundlagen von Moral und Recht', in Dieter Henrich (ed.), *Kant oder Hegel? Über Formen der Begründung in der Philosophie* (Stuttgart: Klett-Cotta), 597–624.

ASBACH, OLAF (1998), 'Internationaler Naturzustand und ewiger Friede: Die Begründung einer rechtlichen Ordnung zwischen Staaten bei Rousseau und Kant', in Dieter Hüning and Burkhard Tuschling (eds.), *Recht, Staat und Völkerrecht* (Berlin: Duncker & Humblot), 203–32.

AXINN, SIDNEY (1981), 'Rousseau versus Kant on the Concept of Man', *Philosophical Forum*, 12:348–55.

BARKER, MARTIN (1978), 'Kant as a Problem for Marxism', *Radical Philosophy*, 19: 24–9.

BOCKOW, JÖRG (1984), *Erziehung zur Sittlichkeit: Zum Verhältnis von praktischer Philosophie und Pädagogik bei Jean Jacques Rousseau und Immanuel Kant* (Frankfurt a.M.: P. Lang).

BOOTH, WILLIAM JAMES (1993), 'The Limit of Autonomy: Karl Marx's Kant Critique', in Ronald Beiner and William James Booth (eds.), *Kant and Political Philosophy* (New Haven: Yale University Press), 245–75.

BRANDT, REINHARD (1974), *Eigentumstheorien von Grotius bis Kant* (Stuttgart: Frommann-Holzboog).

—— (1991), 'Locke und Kant', in Martyn P. Thompson (ed.), *John Locke und Immanuel Kant: historische Rezeption und gegenwärtige Relevanz* (Berlin: Duncker & Humblot), 87–108.

—— (1999), 'Person und Sache: Hobbes' "jus omnium in omnia et omnes" und Kants Theorie des Besitzes der Willkür einer anderen Person im Vertrag', *Deutsche Zeitschrift für Philosophie*, 47:887–910.

BREHMER, KARL (1980), *Rawls' 'Original Position' oder Kants 'Ursprünglicher Kontrakt:' Die Bedingungen der Möglichkeit eines wohlgeordneten Zusammenlebens* (Königstein Ts.: Forum Academicum).

CATTANEO, MARIO A. (1988), 'Schopenhauers Kritik der Kantischen Rechtslehre', *Schopenhauer-Jahrbuch*, 69:399–407.

CHARRON, WILLIAM C. (1996), 'Public Reason, Mediation, and Markets: Kant against Rawls', in J. Ralph Lindgren (ed.), *Horizons of Justice* (New York: Lang), 21–49.

DALLMAYR, FRED (1991), 'Kant and Critical Theory', in Martyn P. Thompson (ed.), *John Locke und Immanuel Kant: historische Rezeption und gegenwärtige Relevanz* (Berlin: Duncker & Humblot), 288–312.

DARWALL, STEPHEN (1980), 'Is There a Kantian Interpretation of Rawlsian Justice?', in H. G. Blocker and E. Smith (eds.), *John Rawls' Theory of Social Justice* (Athens, OH: Ohio University Press), 311–45.

DAVIDSON, ARNOLD (1985), 'Is Rawls a Kantian?', *Pacific Philosophical Quarterly*, 66:48–77.

DE LUE, STEVEN M. (1980), 'Aristotle, Kant, and Rawls on Moral Motivation in a Just Society', *American Political Science Review*, 74:385–93.

DENNERT, JÜRGEN (1970), *Die ontologisch-aristotelische Politikwissenschaft und der Rationalismus. Eine Untersuchung des politischen Denkens Aristoteles', Descartes', Hobbes', Rousseaus und Kants* (Berlin: Duncker & Humblot).

DIESSELHORST, MALTE (1988), *Naturzustand und Sozialvertrag bei Hobbes und Kant* (Göttingen: O. Schwarz).

DOPPELT, GERALD (1988), 'Rawls's Kantian Ideal and the Viability of Modern Liberalism', *Inquiry*, 31:413–49.

DOYLE, MICHAEL W. (1983), 'Kant, Liberal Legacies, and Foreign Affairs, Part 1', *Philosophy and Public Affairs*, 12:205–35.

—— (1983), 'Kant, Liberal Legacies, and Foreign Affairs, Part 2', *Philosophy and Public Affairs*, 12:323–53.

DREIER, HORST (1988), 'Demokratische Repräsentation und vernünftiger Allgemeinwille: Die Theorie der amerikanischen Federalists im Vergleich mit der Staatsphilosophie Kants', *Archiv des öffentlichen Rechts*, 112:450–83.

ERDMANN, KARL DIETRICH (1986), *Kant und Schiller als Zeitgenossen der französischen Revolution* (London: Institute of Germanic Studies, University of London).

FETSCHER, I. (1991), 'Kommentar zu Kerstings "Eigentum, Vertrag und Staat bei Kant und Locke"', in Martyn P. Thompson (ed.), *John Locke und Immanuel Kant: historische Rezeption und gegenwärtige Relevanz* (Berlin: Duncker & Humblot), 135–43.

FIGAL, GÜNTER (1987), 'Recht und Moral bei Kant, Cohen und Benjamin', in Hans-Ludwig Ollig (ed.), *Materialien zur Neukantianismus-Diskussion* (Darmstadt: Wissenschaftliche Buchgesellschaft), 163–83.

FINNIS, JOHN M. (1987), 'Legal Enforcement of "Duties to Oneself": Kant vs. Neo-Kantians', *Columbia Law Review*, 87:433–56.

FOLKERS, HORST (1985), 'Einheit in geschichtlichen Rechtsbegriffen? Zum Begriff des Rechts bei Kant, Hegel, und Benjamin', *Archiv für Rechts- und Sozialphilosophie*, 71:246–61.

GALLIE, WALTER B. (1978), *Philosophers of Peace and War: Kant, Clausewitz, Marx, Engels, and Tolstoy* (Cambridge: Cambridge University Press).

GEISMANN, GEORG (1982), 'Kant als Vollender von Hobbes und Rousseau', *Der Staat*, 21.2:161–89.

GEORGE, ROLF (1988), 'The Liberal Tradition, Kant and the Pox', *Dialogue*, 27: 195–206.

GILROY, JOHN MARTIN (2000), 'Making Public Choices: Kant's "Justice From Autonomy" As an Alternative to Rawls' "Justice As Fairness"', *Kant-Studien*, 91:44–72.

GINSBERG, ROBERT (1974), 'Kant and Hobbes on the Social Contract', *Southwestern Journal of Philosophy*, 5:115–19.

GRCIC, JOSEPH M. (1983), 'Kant and Rawls: Contrasting Conceptions of Moral Theory', *Journal of Value Inquiry*, 17:235–40.

GREEN, LESLIE (1988), 'Kant's Liberalism: A Reply to Rolf George', *Dialogue*, 27: 207–10.

GREGOR, MARY (1988), 'Kant's Approach to Constitutionalism', in Alan S. Rosenbaum (ed.), *Constitutionalism* (New York: Greenwood Press), 69–87.

GUYER, PAUL (1997), 'Kantian Foundations for Liberalism', *Jahrbuch für Recht und Ethik*, 5:121–40.

—— (1998), 'Life, Liberty, and Property: Rawls and the Reconstruction of Kant's Political Philosophy', in Dieter Hüning and Burkhard Tuschling (eds.), *Recht, Staat und Völkerrecht* (Berlin: Duncker & Humblot), 273–92.

HAMON, LÉO (1982), 'Kants Bedeutung für das sozialistische Denken—einige Gedanken über die Rolle der Ideologie', *Die neue Gesellschaft*, 4: 371–77.

HARRIS, C. E., JR. (1979), 'Kant, Nozick, and the Minimal State', *Southwestern Journal of Philosophy*, 10:179–87.

HERB, KARLFRIEDRICH, and LUDWIG, BERND (1993), 'Naturzustand, Eigentum und Staat: Immanuel Kants Relativierung des "ideal des Hobbes"', *Kant-Studien*, 84:283–316.

HÖFFE, OTFRIED (1979), 'Zur vertragstheoretischen Begründung politischer Gerechtigkeit: Hobbes, Kant und Rawls im Vergleich', in Höffe, *Ethik und Politik: Grundmodelle und –probleme der praktischen Philosophie* (Frankfurt a.M.: Suhrkamp), 195–226.

—— (1984), 'Ist Rawls' Theorie der Gerechtigkeit eine kantische Theorie?', *Ratio*, 26:88–104.

HOWARD, DICK (1981), 'The Politics of Modernity: From Marx to Kant', *Philosophy of the Social Sciences*, 8:361–86.

—— (1991–2), 'Kant, Goldmann, and Democracy', *Philosophical Forum*, 23:84–102.

HÜBNER, KURT (1989), 'Die politische Philosophie Kants und Hegels—zwei Repliken auf die Französische Revolution', *Geschichte in Wissenschaft und Unterricht*, 40:404–19.

HÜNING, DIETER (1998), 'Von der Tugend der Gerechtigkeit zum Begriff der Rechtsordnung: Zur rechtsphilosophischen Bedeutung des suum cuique tribuere bei

Hobbes und Kant', in Dieter Hüning and Burkhard Tuschling (eds.), *Recht, Staat und Völkerrecht* (Berlin: Duncker & Humblot), 53–84.

HUNTER, GRAEME (1988), 'Liberalism, Kant, Pox: A Reply to Rolf George', *Dialogue*, 27:211–14.

IVISON, DUNCAN (1994), 'Human Nature and Political Order: Kant and Hume', in K. Haakonsson and U. Thiel (eds.), *History of Philosophy Yearbook*, 2:64–84.

KERSTING, WOLFGANG (1982), 'Sittengesetz und Rechtsgesetz—Die Begründung des Rechts bei Kant und den frühen Kantianern', in Reinhard Brandt (ed.), *Rechtsphilosophie der Aufklärung* (Berlin: de Gruyter), 148–77.

—— (1991), 'Eigentum, Vertrag und Staat bei Kant und Locke', in Martyn P. Thompson (ed.), *John Locke und Immanuel Kant: historische Rezeption und gegenwärtige Relevanz* (Berlin: Duncker & Humblot), 109–34.

—— (1999), 'Die doppelte Negation des Rechts: Kant und die Rechtsphilosophie des Marburger Neukantianismus', in Heiner F. Klemme *et al.* (eds.), *Aufklärung und Interpretation: Studien zu Kants Philosophie und ihrem Umkreis* (Würzburg: Königshausen & Neumann), 13–28.

KÖNIG, HELMUT (1981), *Geist und Revolution. Studien zu Kant, Hegel und Marx* (Stuttgart: Klett-Cotta).

KÖNIG, SIEGFRIED (1994), *Zur Begründung der Menschenrechte: Hobbes-Locke-Kant* (Freiburg: Verlag Karl Alber).

KRAUTKRAMER, URSULA (1979), *Staat und Erziehung: Begründung öffentlicher Erziehung bei Humboldt, Kant, Fichte, Hegel und Schleiermacher* (Munich: J. Berchmans).

LEHNING, PERCY (1991), 'Fairness to "Justice as Fairness?" Response to Nida-Rümelin', in Martyn P. Thompson (ed.), *John Locke und Immanuel Kant: historische Rezeption und gegenwärtige Relevanz* (Berlin: Duncker & Humblot), 360–77.

LLOYD THOMAS, DAVID A. (1980), 'Kantian and Utilitarian Democracy', *Canadian Journal of Philosophy*, 10:395–413.

LUCAS, HANS-CHRISTIAN (1998), ' ". . . eine Aufgabe, die nach und nach aufgelöst, ihrem Ziele beständig näher kommt" Geschichte, Krieg, und Frieden bei Kant und Hegel', in Dieter Hüning and Burkhard Tuschling (eds.), *Recht, Staat und Völkerrecht* (Berlin: Duncker & Humblot), 247–72.

LUDWIG, BERND (1993), 'Kants Verabschiedung der Vertragstheorie—Konsequenzen für eine Theorie sozialer Gerechtigkeit', *Jahrbuch für Recht und Ethik*, 1:221–54.

MARINOFF, LOUIS (1994), 'Hobbes, Spinoza, Kant, Highway Robbery and Game Theory', *Australian Journal of Philosophy*, 72:445–62.

MAY, TODD G. (1990), 'Kant the Liberal, Kant the Anarchist: Rawls and Lyotard on Kantian Justice', *Southern Journal of Philosophy*, 28:525–38.

MEYER, MICHEL (1987), 'Kant's Concept of Dignity and Modern Political Thought', *History of European Ideas*, 8:319–32.

MINOGUE, KENNETH (1991), 'Locke, Kant, and the Foundations of Liberalism', in Martyn P. Thompson (ed.), *John Locke und Immanuel Kant: historische Rezeption und gegenwärtige Relevanz* (Berlin: Duncker & Humblot), 269–83.

MULHOLLAND, LESLIE A. (1993), 'The Difference between Private and Public Law', *Jahrbuch für Recht und Ethik*, 1:113–58.

MÜLLER-SCHMID, PETER-PAUL (1986), 'Kants Autonomie der Ethik und Rechtslehre und das tomasische Naturrechtsdenken', *Jahrbücher für christliche Sozialwissenschaften*, 27:35–60.

MURPHY, JEFFRIE G. (1978), 'Hume and Kant on the Social Contract', *Philosophical Studies*, 33:65–79.

NAIDU, M. V. (1982), 'Kant, Clausewitz, Marxism, and Tolstoy on War and Peace', *Annual of the Canadian Peace Research and Education Association*, 14:33–5.

NEAL, PATRICK (1987), 'In the Shadow of the General Will: Rawls, Kant, and Rousseau on the Problem of Political Right', *Review of Politics*, 49:389–409.

NUSSER, KARL-HEINZ (1981), 'Das Kriterium der Moralität und die sittliche Allgemeinheit. Zur Bestimmung von Moralität und Rechtsbegründung bei Kant und Hegel', *Zeitschrift für philosophische Forschung*, 35: 552–63.

—— (1997), 'Kant, Rawls und die "Revolution des Friedens": Kants Nähe zur realistischen Interpretation der internationalen Beziehungen', *Zeitschrift für Politik*, 44:351–66.

O'HAGAN, TIMOTHY (1987), 'On Hegel's Critique of Kant's Moral and Political Philosophy', in Stephen Priest (ed.), *Hegel's Critique of Kant* (Oxford: Oxford University Press), 135–59.

O'NEILL, ONORA (1998), 'Political Liberalism and Public Reason: A Critical Notice of John Rawls, Political Liberalism', *Philosophical Review*, 106:411–28.

—— (2000), 'Kant's Justice and Kantian Justice', in O'Neill, *Bounds of Justice* (Cambridge: Cambridge University Press).

—— (Forthcoming), 'Constructivism in Rawls and Kant', in Sam Freeman (ed.), *The Cambridge Companion to Rawls* (Cambridge: Cambridge University Press).

PAGELS, KURT (1992), *Kant gegen Marx, Engels, Lenin* (Meppen: Ewert).

POGGE, THOMAS W. (1981), 'The Kantian Interpretation of Justice as Fairness', *Zeitschrift für philosophische Forschung*, 35:47–65.

POPOV, S. I. (1976), 'Der Humanismus Kants und die sozialdemokratische Konzeption des "ethischen Sozialismus"', in Teodor I. Oizerman and Manfred Buhr (eds.), *Revolution der Denkart oder Denkart der Revolution: Beiträge zur Philosophie Immanuel Kants* (Berlin: Akademie Verlag), 359–72.

RICHARDS, DAVID A. J. (1987), 'Kantian Ethics and the Harm Principle: A Reply to John Finnis', *Columbia Law Review*, 87:457–71.

RICHTER, FRIEDRICH, and WRONA, VERA (1974), 'Neukantianismus und Sozialreformismus', *Deutsche Zeitschrift für Philosophische Forschung*, 22:269–88.

RILEY, PATRICK (1982), *Will and Political Legitimacy: A Critical Exposition of Social Contract Theory in Hobbes, Locke, Rousseau, Kant, and Hegel* (Cambridge, MA: Harvard University Press).

RUNDELL, JOHN F. (1987), *Origins of Modernity: The Origins of Modern Social Theory From Kant to Hegel to Marx* (Madison, WI: University of Wisconsin Press).

SAMPLES, JOHN (1987), 'Kant, Toennies and the Liberal Idea of Community in Early German Sociology', *History of Political Thought*, 8:245–62.

SCHNEPF, ROBERT (1999), 'Rechtstaat und Staatenlose—Eine rechtsphilosophische Untersuchung in Auseinandersetzung mit Walzer, Rawls und Kant', *Archiv für Rechts- und Sozialphilosophie*, 85:200–21.

SEIDLER, VICTOR (1986), *Kant, Respect, and Injustice: The Limits of Liberal Moral Theory* (London: Routledge & Kegan Paul).

SHELL, SUSAN MELD (1985), 'What Kant and Fichte Can Teach Us About Human Rights', in Richard Kennington (ed.), *The Philosophy of Immanuel Kant* (Washington, DC: CUA Press), 143–60.

SIEBERS, TOBIN (1991), 'Kant and the Origins of Totalitarianism', *Philosophy and Literature*, 15:19–39.

SIEP, LUDWIG (1989), 'Person and Law in Kant and Hegel', in Reiner Schürmann (ed.), *The Public Realm: Essays on Discursive Types in Political Philosophy* (Albany, NY: SUNY Press), 82–104.

—— (1995), 'Kant and Hegel on Peace and International Law', in Hoke Robinson (ed.), *Proceedings of the Eighth International Kant Congress* (Milwaukee, WI: Marquette University Press), vol. I. pt. 1, 259–72.

STAHL, JÜRGEN, and FRANZ, DIETRICH-E. (1983), " 'Der ewige Friede ist keine leere Idee, sondern eine Aufgabe": Bemerkungen zu den Friedenskonzeptionene Kants und Fichtes', *Deutsche Zeitschrift für Philosophie*, 31:18–30.

STEINVORTH, ULRICH (1981), *Stationen der politischen Theorie. Hobbes, Locke, Rousseau, Kant, Hegel, Marx, Weber* (Stuttgart: P. Reclam).

THOMPSON, MARTYN P. (1991) (ed.), *John Locke und Immanuel Kant: historische Rezeption und gegenwärtige Relevanz* (Berlin: Duncker & Humblot).

TUSCHLING, BURKHARD (1998), 'Die Idee des Rechts: Hobbes und Kant', Dieter Hüning and Burkhard Tuschling (eds.), *Recht, Staat und Völkerrecht* (Berlin: Duncker & Humblot), 85–120.

VAN DER LINDEN, HARRY (1988), *Kantian Ethics and Socialism* (Indianapolis: Hackett).

VAN ERP, HERMAN (1994), 'Das Problem der politischen repräsentation bei Kant, Hegel, und Marx', *Philosophisches Jahrbuch der Görres Gesellschaft*, 101:165–76.

WARD, IAN (1994), 'The Sorcerer and His Apprentices: Kant and the Critical Legal Project', *Archiv für Recht und Sozialphilosophie*, 80:508–33.

WESTPHAL, KENNETH R. (1991), 'How "Full" is Kant's Categorical Imperative?', *Jahrbuch für Recht und Ethik*, 3:465–509.

WESTPHAL, KENNETH R. (1991), 'Hegel's Critique of Kant's Moral World View', *Philosophical Topics*, 19.2:133–76.

WILLIAMS, HOWARD (1987), 'Politics and Philosophy in Kant and Hegel', in Stephen Priest (ed.), *Hegel's Critique of Kant* (Oxford: Oxford University Press), 193–203.

WOLF, FRIEDRICH O. (1972), 'Kant and Hobbes Concerning the Foundations of Political Philosophy', in Lewis White Beck (ed.), *Proceedings of the Third International Kant Congress* (Dordrecht: Reidel), 607–13.

YACK, BERNARD (1993), 'The Problem with Kantian Liberalism', in Ronald Beiner and William James Booth (eds.), *Kant and Political Philosophy* (New Haven: Yale University Press), 224–44.

KANT'S COSMOPOLITANISM: INTERNATIONAL LAW, PERPETUAL PEACE, AND HUMAN RIGHTS*

ANDERSON-GOLD, SHARON (1988), 'War and Resistance: Kant's Implicit Doctrine of Human Rights', *Journal of Social Philosophy*, 19:37–50.

BIELEFELDT, HEINER (1997), 'Towards a Cosmopolitan Framework of Freedom: The Contribution of Kantian Universalism to Cross-Cultural Debates on Human Rights', *Jahrbuch für Recht und Ethik*, 5:349–62.

BOHMAN, JAMES, and LUTZ-BACHMANN, MATTHIAS (1996) (eds.), *Frieden durch Recht: Kants Friedensidee und das Problem einer euen Weltordnung* (Frankfurt a.M.: Suhrkamp). (A selection of the essays from this work for an English audience are anthologized in Bohman and Lutz-Bachman (eds.), *Perpetual Peace: Essays on Kant's Cosmopolitan Ideal* (Cambridge, MA: MIT Press, 1996).)

BYRD, B. SHARON (1995), 'The State as "Moral Person"', in Hoke Robinson (ed.), *Proceedings of the Eighth International Kant Congress* (Milwaukee, WI: Marquette University Press), vol. I. pt. 1, 171–89.

DOYLE, MICHAEL W. (1993), 'Liberalism and International Relations', in Ronald Beiner and William James Booth (eds.), *Kant and Political Philosophy* (New Haven: Yale University Press), 173–203.

GEISMANN, GEORG (1983), 'Kants Rechtslehre vom Weltfrieden', *Zeitschrift für philosophische Forschung*, 37: 363–88.

GERHARDT, VOLKER (1995), *Immanuel Kants Entwurf, 'Zum ewigen Frieden'. Eine Theorie der Politik* (Darmstadt: Wissenschaftliche Buchgesellschaft).

HABERMAS, JÜRGEN (1997), 'Kant's Idea of Perpetual Peace, with the Benefit of Two Hundred Years' Hindsight', in Bohman and Lutz-Bachmann (eds.), *Perpetual Peace* (Cambridge, MA: MIT Press), 113–53.

*There is, of course, much published on Kant's thought on these concepts. This bibliography is limited to works that directly address *The Metaphysics of Morals*.

JOERDEN, JAN (1995), 'From Anarchy to Republic: Kant's History of State Constitutions', in Hoke Robinson (ed.), *Proceedings of the Eighth International Kant Congress* (Milwaukee, WI: Marquette University Press), vol. I. pt. 1, 139–56.

KLEINGELD, PAULINE (1997), 'Kants politischer Kosmopolitismus', *Jahrbuch für Recht und Ethik*, 5:333–48.

MUTHU, SANKAR (2000), 'Justice and Foreigners: Kant's Cosmopolitan Right', *Constellations*, 7:23–45.

OREND, BRIAN (1999), 'Kant's Just War Theory', *Journal of the History of Philosophy*, 37:323–53.

RILEY, PATRICK (1995), 'Politics' Homage to Morality: Kant's Toward Eternal Peace after 200 Years', in Hoke Robinson (ed.), *Proceedings of the Eighth International Kant Congress* (Milwaukee, WI: Marquette University Press), vol. I. pt. 1, 231–42.

ROBINSON, HOKE (1995) (ed.), *Proceedings of the Eighth International Kant Congress* (Milwaukee, WI: Marquette University Press).

VUILLEMIN, JULES (1995), 'On Perpetual Peace, and on Hope as a Duty', in Hoke Robinson (ed.), *Proceedings of the Eighth International Kant Congress* (Milwaukee, WI: Marquette University Press), vol. I. pt. 1, 19–32.

WILLIAMS, HOWARD (1992), 'Kant's Optimism in his Social and Political Theory', in Williams, *Essays on Kant's Political Philosophy* (Chicago: University of Chicago Press), 1–14.

WOOD, ALLEN W. (1998), 'Kant's Project for Perpetual Peace', in P. Cheah and B. Robbins (eds.), *Cosmopolitics: Thinking and Feeling Beyond the Nation* (Minneapolis: University of Minnesota Press), 59–76.

THE STATE: SOCIAL CONTRACT, PROPERTY, PUBLICITY, JUSTICE, AND RIGHTS

ANSBRO, JOHN J. (1973), 'Kant's Limitations on Individual Freedom', *The New Scholasticism*, 4:88–99.

BAUMANN, P. (1994), 'Zwei Seiten der Begründung von Eigentum und Staat', *Kant-Studien*, 85:147–59.

BAYNES, KENNETH (1989), 'Kant on Property Rights and the Social Contract', *The Monist*, 72:433–53.

BRAKEMEIER, HEINZ (1985), *Die sittliche Aufhebung des Staates in Kants Philosophie* (Frankfurt a.M).

BROCKER, MANFRED (1987), *Kants Besitzlehre: Zur Problematik einer transzendental-philosophischen Eigentumslehre* (Würzburg: Königshausen & Neumann).

BUCK, WAYNE F. (1987), 'Kant's Justification of Private Property', in Bernard den Ouden and Marcia Moen (eds.), *New Essays on Kant* (New York), 227–44.

BYRD, B. SHARON (1993), 'Two Models of Justice', *Jahrbuch für Recht und Ethik*, 1:45–68.

CHADWICK, RUTH R. (1989), 'The Market for Bodily Parts: Kant and Duties to Oneself', *Journal of Applied Philosophy*, 15:129–39.

DAHLSTROM, DANIEL O. (1985), 'The Natural Right of Equal Opportunity in Kant's Civil Union', *Southern Journal of Philosophy*, 23:295–303.

DAVIS, KEVIN R. (1991), 'Kantian "Publicity and Political Justice"', *History of Philosophy Quarterly*, 8:409–22.

—— (1991), 'The Publicity Condition of Justice', in Gerhard Funke (ed.), *Akten des Siebenten Internationalen Kant-Kongresses* (Bonn: Bouvier Verlag), vol. II. pt. 2, 317–24.

—— (1992), 'Kant's Different "Public" and the Justice of Publicity', *Kant-Studien*, 83:170–84.

DODSON, KEVIN (1995), 'Kant's Idea of the Social Contract', in Hoke Robinson (ed.), *Proceedings of the Eighth International Kant Congress* (Milwaukee, WI: Marquette University Press), vol. II. pt. 2, 753–60.

EDWARDS, JEFFREY (1998), 'Disjunktiv-und kollektiv-allgemeiner Besitz: Überlegungen zu Kants Theorie der ursprünglichen Erwerbung', in Dieter Hüning and Burkhard Tuschling (eds.), *Recht, Staat und Völkerrecht* (Berlin: Duncker & Humblot), 113–34.

FALCIONI, DANIELA (1999), 'Fragen der Gerechtigkeit bei Kant: Was ist an sich recht? Was ist Rechtens?', in Heiner F. Klemme *et al.* (eds.), *Aufklärung und Interpretation: Studien zu Kants Philosophie und ihrem Umkreis* (Würzburg: Königshausen & Neumann), 59–86.

FULDA, HANS FRIEDRICH (1996), 'Der Übergang vom Privatrecht zum oeffentlichen Recht in Kants *Metaphysic der Sitten*', in U. Immenga, W. Moeschel, and D. Reuter (eds.) *Festschrift für Ernst-Jochen Mestmaecker* (Baden-Baden).

—— (1997), 'Kants Begriff eines intelligiblen Besitzes und seine Deduktion', *Jahrbuch für Recht und Ethik*, 5:103–19.

GERRAND, NICOLE (1999), 'The Misuse of Kant in the Debate about a Market for Human Body Parts', *Journal of Applied Philosophy*, 16:59–67.

GOERNER, E. A. (1975), 'On Patrick Riley's "On Kant As the Most Adequate of the Social Contract Theorists"', *Political Theory*, 3:467–8.

GREGOR, MARY J. (1985), 'Kant on Welfare Legislation', *Logos*, 6:49–59.

—— (1988), 'Kant's Theory of Property', *Review of Metaphysics*, 41:757–87.

HARTMANN, ANJA VICTORINE (1994), 'Der Platz des Rechtlichen Postulats in der Besitzlehre', in R. Brandt and W. Stark (eds.), *Autographen, Documente und Berichte zu Editionen, Amtsgeschäften und Werk Immanuel Kants* (Hamburg: F. Meiner), 109–20.

HERB, KARLFRIEDRICH, and LUDWIG, BERND (1994), 'Kants kritisches Staatsrecht', *Jahrbuch für Recht und Ethik*, 2:431–77.

HESPE, FRANZ (1995), 'Recht, rechtliche Verbindlichkeit und ursprünglicher Kontrakt bei Kant', in Hoke Robinson (ed.), *Proceedings of the Eighth International Kant Congress* (Milwaukee, WI: Marquette University Press), vol. II. pt. 2, 773–84.

—— (1998), 'Der Gesellschaftsvertrag: rechtliches Gebot oder rationale Wahl', in Dieter Hüning and Burkhard Tuschling (eds.), *Recht, Staat und Völkerrecht* (Berlin: Duncker & Humblot), 293–320.

HILL, THOMAS E., JR. (2001), 'Hypothetical Consent in Kantian Constructivism', *Social Philosophy and Policy*, 18.2:300–29.

HOLTMAN, SARAH WILLIAMS (1997), 'A Kantian Approach to Prison Reform', *Jahrbuch für Recht und Ethik*, 5:315–31.

—— (1999), 'Kant, Ideal Theory, and the Justice of Exclusionary Zoning', *Ethics*, 110: 32–58.

JOERDEN, JAN C. (1993), 'Das Prinzip der Gewaltenteilung als Bedingung der Möglichkeit eines freiheitlichen Staatswesens', *Jahrbuch für Recht und Ethik*, 1: 207–20.

KERSTING, WOLFGANG (1983), 'Kant und der staatsphilosophische Kontraktualismus', *Allgemeine Zeitschrift für Philosophie*, 8:1–27.

—— (1988), 'Kants vernunftrechtliche Staatskonzeption', *Prima Philosophia*, 1:107–30.

—— (1989), 'Gesellschaft als Postulat: Kant und das Problem der Gesellschaftsbegründung', *Prima Philosophia*, 2:325–38.

—— (1992), 'Kant's Concept of the State', in Howard Williams (ed.), *Essays on Kant's Political Philosophy* (Chicago: University of Chicago Press), 143–65.

—— (1995), 'Die bürgerliche Verfassung in jedem Staate soll republikanisch sein', in Otfried Höffe (ed.), *Immanuel Kant, Zum ewigen Frieden* (Berlin: Akademie Verlag), 87–108.

KÜHL, KRISTIAN (1984), *Eigentumsordnung als Freiheitsordnung: Zur Aktualität der Kantischen Rechts- und Eigentumslehre* (Freiburg: Alber).

LAURSEN, JOHN CHRISTIAN (1986), 'Kantian Politics: The Subversive Kant', *Political Theory*, 14:584–603.

LEBAR, MARK (1999), 'Kant on Welfare', *Canadian Journal of Philosophy*, 29: 225–50.

LÜBBE-WOLFF, GERTRUDE (1982), 'Begründungsmethoden in Kants Rechtslehre, untersucht am Beispiel des Vertragsrechts', in Reinhard Brandt (ed.), *Rechtsphilosophie der Aufklärung* (Berlin: de Gruyter), 286–310.

LUDWIG, BERND (1990), 'The Right of State in Immanuel Kant's Doctrine of Right', *Journal of the History of Philosophy*, 28:403–15.

—— (1993), 'Kants Verabschiedung der Vertragstheorie—Konsequenzen für eine Theorie sozialer Gerechtigkeit', *Jahrbuch für Recht und Ethik*, 1:221–54.

LUDWIG, BERND (2000), 'Politik als "ausübende Rechtslehre." Zur Staatstheorie Immanuel Kants', in H. Lietzmann and P. Nitschke (eds.), *Klassische Politik. Politikverständnisse von der Antike bis ins 19. Jahrhundert* (Leverkusen: Leske & Budrich), 175–220.

MERLE, JEAN CHRISTOPHE (2000), 'A Kantian Argument for a Duty to Donate One's Own Organs: A Reply to Nicole Gerrand', *Journal of Applied Philosophy*, 17: 93–101.

MUNZER, STEPHEN R. (1993), 'Kant and Property Rights in Body Parts', *Canadian Journal of Law and Jurisprudence*, 6:319–41.

O'NEILL, ONORA (2000), 'Kant and the Social Contract Tradition', in François Duchesneau, Guy Lafrance, and Claude Piché (eds.), *Kant Actuel: Hommage à Pierre Laberge* (Montréal: Bellarmin), 185–200.

RIEDEL, MANFRED (1970), 'Die Aporie von Herrschaft und Vereinbarung in Kants Idee des Sozialvertrags', *Philosophische Perspektiven*, 2:209–24.

—— (1981), 'Transcendental Politics? Political Legitimacy and the Concept of Civil Society in Kant', *Social Research*, 48:588–613.

SAAGE, RICHARD (1973), *Eigentum, Staat, und Gesellschaft bei Immanuel Kant* (Stuttgart: Kohlhammer).

SCHEFFEL, DIETER (1982), 'Thesen zu Kants transzendentaler Deduktion des Begriffs der Erwerbung durch Vertrag', in Reinhard Brandt (ed.), *Rechtsphilosophie der Aufklärung* (Berlin: de Gruyter), 311–20.

SCRUTON, ROGER (1992), 'Contract, Consent and Exploitation: Kantian Themes', in Howard Williams (ed.), *Essays on Kant's Political Philosophy* (Chicago: University of Chicago Press), 213–27.

ULEMAN, JENNIFER (1995), 'Kant on the Right to Property and the Value of External Freedom', in Hoke Robinson (ed.), *Proceedings of the Eighth International Kant Congress* (Milwaukee, WI: Marquette University Press), vol. II. pt. 2, 549–55.

—— (2000), 'On Kant, Infanticide, and Finding Oneself in a State of Nature', *Zeitschrift für philosophische Forschung*, 54:173–95.

VERWEYEN, HANJÜRGEN (1996), 'Social Contract among Devils', *Idealistic Studies*, 26:189–202.

VUILLEMIN, JULES (1991), 'Ist Kants Begründung des Besitzrechts vollständig?', in Gerhard Funke (ed.), *Akten des Siebenten Internationalen Kant-Kongresses* (Bonn/Berlin: Bouvier Verlag), vol. I., 31–47.

WEINRIB, ERNEST J. (1995), 'Publicness and Private Law', in Hoke Robinson (ed.), *Proceedings of the Eighth International Kant Congress* (Milwaukee, WI: Marquette University Press), vol. I. pt. 1, 191–201.

WEINSTOCK, DANIEL M. (1996), 'Natural Law and Public Reason in Kant's Political Philosophy', *Canadian Journal of Philosophy*, 26:389–411.

WESTPHAL, KENNETH R. (1997), 'Do Kant's Principles Justify Property or Usufruct?', *Jahrbuch für Recht und Ethik*, 5:141–94.

PUNISHMENT

AUXTER, THOMAS (1991), 'Kant's Theory of Retribution', in Gerhard Funke (ed.), *Akten des Siebenten Internationalen Kant-Kongresses* II, 2 (Bonn/Berlin: Bouvier Verlag), 307–16.

—— (1998), 'The World of Retribution', in J. Kneller and S. Axinn (eds.), *Autonomy and Community* (Albany, NY: SUNY Press), 191–211.

BRANDT, REINHARD (1996), 'Gerechtigkeit und Strafgerechtigkeit bei Kant', in G. Schönrich and Y. Kato (eds.), *Kant in der Diskussion der Moderne* (Frankfurt a.M: Suhrkamp), 425–63.

BYRD, B. SHARON (1989), 'Kant's Theory of Punishment: Deterrence in its Threat, Retribution in its Execution', *Law and Philosophy*, 8:151–200.

—— (1990), 'Strafgerechtigkeit bei Kant', in Wilfried Bottke and Anton Rauscher (eds.), *Gerechtigkeit als Aufgabe: Festgabe für Heinz Lampert* (St. Ottilien: EOS), 137–58.

CORLETT, J. ANGELO (1993), 'Foundations of a Kantian Theory of Punishment', *Southern Journal of Philosophy*, 31:263–84.

FLEISCHACKER, SAMUEL (1988), 'Kant's Theory of Punishment', *Kant-Studien*, 79: 434–49.

GILLESPIE, NORMAN (1997), 'Wrongful Risks and Unintended Consequences', *Jahrbuch für Recht und Ethik*, 5:85–101.

HILL, THOMAS E., JR. (1992), 'Kant's Anti-Moralistic Strain', repr. in Hill, *Dignity and Practical Reason in Kant's Moral Theory* (Ithaca, NY: Cornell University Press), ch. 9.

—— (1997), 'Kant on Punishment: A Coherent Mix of Deterrence and Retribution?', *Jahrbuch für Recht und Ethik*, 5:291–314.

—— (1999), 'Kant on Wrong-Doing, Desert, and Punishment', *Law and Philosophy*, 18.1:407–41.

HÖFFE, OTFRIED (1982), 'Kants Begründung des Rechtszwanges und der Kriminalstrafe', in Reinhard Brandt (ed.), *Rechtsphilosophie der Aufklärung* (Berlin: de Gruyter), 335–75.

—— (1989), 'Retaliatory Punishment as a Categorical Imperative', *Rivista Internazionale Filosofio del Diritto*, 66:633–58.

HOLTMAN, SARAH WILLIAMS (1997), 'Toward Social Reform: Kant's Penal Theory Reinterpreted', *Utilitas*, 9:3–21.

LIND, DOUGLAS (1994), 'Kant on Capital Punishment', *Journal of Philosophical Research*, 19:61–74.

MURPHY, JEFFRIE G. (1972), 'Kant's Theory of Criminal Punishment', in Lewis White Beck (ed.), *Proceedings of the Third International Kant Congress* (Dordrecht: D. Reidel), 434–41.

—— (1987), 'Does Kant Have a Theory of Punishment?', *Columbia Law Review*, 87:509.

OBERER, HARIOLF (1982), 'Über einige Begründungsaspekte der kantischen Strafrechtslehre)', in Reinhard Brandt (ed.), *Rechtsphilosophie der Aufklärung* (Berlin: de Gruyter), 399–423.

POTTER, NELSON (1998), 'The Principle of Punishment is a Categorical Imperative', in Jane Kneller and Sidney Axinn (eds.), *Autonomy and Community* (Albany, NY: SUNY Press), 169–90.

SCHEID, DON E. (1983), 'Kant's Retributivism', *Ethics*, 93:262–82.

—— (1986), 'Kant's Retributivism Again', *Archiv für Rechts- und Sozialphilosophie*, 72:224–30.

SCHWARZSCHILD, STEVEN S. (1985), 'Kantianism on the Death Penalty (and Related Social Problems)', *Archiv für Rechts- und Sozialphilosophie*, 71:343–72.

SHELL, SUSAN MELD (1997), 'Kant on Punishment', *Kantian Review*, 1:115–35.

TUNICK, MARK (1996), 'Is Kant a Retributivist?', *History of Political Thought*, 17:60–78.

AUTHORITY AND REVOLUTION*

ARNTZEN, SVEN (1995), 'Kant's Denial of Absolute Sovereignty', *Pacific Philosophical Quarterly*, 76:1–16.

—— (1996), 'Kant on Duty to Oneself and Resistance to Political Authority', *Journal of the History of Philosophy*, 34:409–24.

ATWELL, JOHN E. (1971), 'A Brief Commentary' (to Axinn 1971), *Journal of the History of Ideas*, 32:433–6.

AXINN, SIDNEY (1970), 'Kant on Authority', *Southern Journal of Philosophy*, 8:157–64.

—— (1971), 'Kant, Authority, and French Revolution', *Journal of the History of Ideas*, 32:423–32.

BECK, LEWIS WHITE (1971), 'Kant and the Right of Revolution', *Journal of the History of Ideas*, 32:414–22.

CARR, CRAIG L. (1989), 'Kant's Theory of Political Authority', *History of Political Thought*, 10:719–31.

CARTER, STEPHEN L. (1995), 'Religious Resistance to the Kantian Sovereign', *Nomos*, 37:288–308.

*There is substantial amount of literature devoted to Kant's impression of the French Revolution that is not included here.

DODSON, KEVIN E. (1997), 'Autonomy and Authority in Kant's "Rechtslehre"', *Political Theory*, 25:93–111.

DYKE, CHARLES (1971), 'Comments' (to Axinn 1971 and Beck 1971), *Journal of the History of Ideas*, 32:437–40.

GRCIC, JOSEPH M. (1986), 'Kant on Revolution and Economic Inequality', *Kant-Studien*, 77:447–57.

HANCOCK, ROGER (1975), 'Kant and Civil Disobedience', *Idealistic Studies*, 5: 164–76.

HANSSON, SVEN ODE (1994), 'Kant and the Revolutionary Slogan "Liberté, Egalité, Fraternité"', *Archiv für Geschichte der Philosophie*, 76:333–39.

HENRICH, DIETER (1976), 'Kant über Revolution', in Zwi Batscha (ed.), *Materialien zu Kants Rechtsphilosophie* (Frankfurt a.M.: Suhrkamp), 359–65.

—— (1993), 'On the Meaning of Rational Action in the State', repr. and trans. in Ronald Beiner and William James Booth (eds.), *Kant and Political Philosophy* (New Haven: Yale University Press), 97–117.

HILL, THOMAS E., JR. (1997), 'A Kantian Perspective on Political Violence', *Journal of Ethics*, 1:105–40.

—— (Forthcoming), 'Questions about Kant's Opposition to Revolution', *Journal of Value Inquiry*.

KORSGAARD, CHRISTINE (1997), 'Taking the Law into Our Own Hands: Kant on the Right to Revolution', in Andrews Reath, Barbara Herman, and Christine Korsgaard (eds.), *Reclaiming the History of Ethics: Essays for John Rawls* (Cambridge: Cambridge University Press), 297–328.

LOSURDO, DOMENICO (1987), *Immanuel Kant—Freiheit, Recht und Revolution*, trans. Erdmute Brielmayer (Cologne).

NICHOLSON, PETER (1976), 'Kant on the Duty Never to Resist the Sovereign', *Ethics*, 86:214–30.

—— (1992), 'Kant, Revolutions and History', in Howard Williams (ed.), *Essays on Kant's Political Philosophy* (Chicago: University of Chicago Press), 249–68.

SEEBOHM, THOMAS M. (1981), 'Kant's Theory of Revolution', *Social Research*, 48:557–87.

SPAEMANN, ROBERT (1976), 'Kants Kritik des Widerstandrechts', in Zwi Batscha (ed.), *Materialien zu Kants Rechtsphilosophie* (Frankfurt a.M.: Suhrkamp), 347–58.

WESTPHAL, KENNETH R. (1991), 'Kant's Qualified Principle of Obedience to Authority in the Metaphysical Elements of Justice', in Gerhard Funke (ed.), *Akten des siebenten Internationalen Kant-Kongresses* II. 2 (Bonn: Bouvier Verlag), 353–66.

—— (1991/92), 'Kant on the State, Law, and Obedience to Authority in the Alleged "Anti-Revolutionary" Writings', *Journal of Philosophical Research*, 17:377–420.

—— (1993), 'Republicanism, Despotism, and Obedience to the State: The Inadequacy of Kant's Division of Powers', *Jahrbuch für Recht und Ethik*, 1:263–81.

Wit, Ernst Jan C. (1999), 'Kant and the Limits of Civil Obedience', *Kant-Studien*, 90:285–305.

TUGENDLEHRE

General

Jones, Hardy E. (1971), *Kant's Principle of Personality* (Madison: University of Wisconsin Press).

O'Neill, Onora (1975), *Acting on Principle: An Essay on Kant's Ethics* (New York: Columbia University Press). (Published under the surname 'Nell').

Rawls, John (2000), 'Kant', *Lectures on the History of Moral Philosophy*, ed. Barbara Herman (Cambridge, MA: Harvard University Press).

Timmons, Mark (1997), 'Decision Procedures, Moral Criteria, and the Problem of Relevant Descriptions in Kant's Ethics', *Jahrbuch für Recht und Ethik*, 5:389–417.

Wood, Allen W. (1999), *Kant's Ethical Thought* (Cambridge: Cambridge University Press).

Virtue, Character, Emotions, Motives, and Friendship

Allison, Henry (1990), 'Virtue and Holiness', in Allison, *Kant's Theory of Freedom* (Cambridge: Cambridge University Press), 162–79.

Baron, Marcia W. (1988), 'Remorse and Agent Regret', *Midwest Studies in Philosophy* 13 (Notre Dame: University of Notre Dame Press), 259–81.

—— (1995), 'Sympathy and Coldness: Kant on the Stoic and the Sage', in Hoke Robinson (ed.), *Proceedings of the Eighth International Kant Congress* (Milwaukee, WI: Marquette University Press), vol. I. pt. 2, 691–703.

—— (1995), *Kantian Ethics Almost without Apology* (Ithaca, NY: Cornell University Press), pt. 2.

Cartwright, David (1987), 'Kant's View of the Moral Significance of Kindhearted Emotions and the Moral Insignificance of Kant's View', *Journal of Value Inquiry*, 21:291–304.

Denis, Lara (2000), 'Kant's Cold Sage and the Sublimity of Apathy', *Kantian Review*, 4:48–73.

Dotto, Gianni (1974), ' "Moralische Freundschaft" und "Reich der Zwecke"', in Gerhard Funke (ed.), *Akten des 4. Internationalen Kant-Kongresses Mainz* (Berlin: de Gruyter), 568–75.

Engstrom, Stephen (1996), 'Happiness and the Highest Good in Aristotle and Kant', in Stephen Engstrom and Jennifer Whiting (eds.), *Aristotle, Kant, and the Stoics: Rethinking Happiness and Duty* (Cambridge: Cambridge University Press), 102–38.

FAIRBANKS, SANDRA (2000), *Kantian Moral Theory and the Destruction of the Self* (Boulder: Westview Press).

FASCHING, MARIA (1990), *Zum Begriff der Freundschaft bei Aristoteles und Kant* (Würzburg: Königshausen & Neumann).

FISCHER, NORBERT (1983), 'Tugend und Glückseligkeit. Zu ihrem Verhältnis bei Aristoteles und Kant', *Kant-Studien*, 74:1–21.

GUYER, PAUL (2000), 'Moral Worth, Virtue, and Merit', in Guyer, *Kant on Freedom, Law, and Happiness* (Cambridge: Cambridge University Press), ch. 9.

HENSON, RICHARD G. (1979), 'What Kant Might Have Said: Moral Worth and the Overdetermination of Dutiful Action', *Philosophical Review*, 88:39–54.

HERMAN, BARBARA (1993), *The Practice of Moral Judgment* (Cambridge, MA: Harvard University Press).

HURSTHOUSE, ROSALIND (1999), *On Virtue Ethics* (Oxford: Oxford University Press), chs. 4–6.

JAMES, DAVID (1995), 'Kant on Ideal Friendship in the *Doctrine of Virtue*', in Hoke Robinson (ed.), *Proceedings of the Eighth International Kant Congress* (Milwaukee, WI: Marquette University Press), vol. II. pt. 2, 557–65.

JOHNSON, ROBERT (1996), 'Kant's Conception of Merit', *Pacific Philosophical Quarterly*, 77:310–34.

—— (1997), 'Kant's Conception of Virtue', *Jahrbuch für Recht und Ethik*, 5: 365–87.

KORSGAARD, CHRISTINE M. (1996), 'Creating the Kingdom of Ends: Reciprocity and Responsibility in Personal Relations', repr. in Korsgaard, *Creating the Kingdom of Ends* (Cambridge: Cambridge University Press), ch. 7.

—— (1996), 'From Duty and for the Sake of the Noble: Kant and Aristotle on Morally Good Action', in Stephen Engstrom and Jennifer Whiting (eds.), *Aristotle, Kant, and the Stoics: Rethinking Happiness and Duty* (Cambridge: Cambridge University Press), 203–36.

LOUDEN, ROBERT B. (1986), 'Kant's Virtue Ethics', *Philosophy*, 61:473–89.

LUCAS, GEORGE R., JR. (1988), 'Agency After Virtue', *International Philosophical Quarterly*, 28:293–311.

MARCUCCI, SILVESTRO (1999), ' "Moral Friendship" in Kant', *Kant-Studien*, 90: 434–41.

MARTIN, CONOR (1980), 'Emotion in Kant's Moral Philosophy', *Philosophical Studies* (Ireland), 27:16–28.

MICHALSON, GORDON E., JR. (1989), 'Moral Regeneration and Virtue in Kant', *Religious Studies*, 25:259–70.

MUNZEL, G. FELICITAS (1999), *Kant's Conception of Moral Character* (Chicago: University of Chicago Press).

NUYEN, A. T. (1995), 'The Heart of the Kantian Moral Agent', *American Catholic Philosophical Quarterly*, 69:51–62.

O'NEILL, ONORA (1989), 'Kant After Virtue', in O'Neill, *Constructions of Reason: Explorations of Kant's Practical Philosophy* (Cambridge: Cambridge University Press), ch. 8.

—— (1996), 'Kant's Virtues', in Roger Crisp (ed.), *How Should One Live? Essays on the Virtues* (Oxford: Oxford University Press), 77–97.

RUMSEY, JEAN P. (1989), 'The Development of Character in Kantian Moral Theory', *Journal of the History of Philosophy*, 27:247–65.

—— (1990), 'Agency, Human Nature, and Character in Kantian Theory', *Journal of Value Inquiry*, 24:109–21.

SCHALLER, WALTER E. (1987), 'Kant on Virtue and Moral Worth', *Southern Journal of Philosophy*, 25:559–73.

—— (1993), 'Should Kantians Worry about Moral Worth?', *Dialogue*, 32:25–40.

SHERMAN, NANCY (1990), 'The Place of Emotions in Kantian Morality', in O. Flanagan and A. O. Rorty (eds.), *Identity, Character, and Morality* (Cambridge, MA: MIT Press), 149–70.

—— (1995), 'Kant on Sentimentalism and Stoic Apathy: Comments on Marcia Baron', in Hoke Robinson (ed.), *Proceedings of the Eighth International Kant Congress* (Milwaukee, WI: Marquette University Press), vol. I. pt. 2, 705–11.

—— (1995), 'Reasons and Feelings in Kantian Morality', *Philosophy and Phenomenological Research*, 55:369–77.

—— (1997), 'Kantian Virtue: Priggish or Passional?', in Reath, Herman, and Korsgaard (eds.), *Reclaiming the History of Ethics: Essays for John Rawls* (Cambridge: Cambridge University Press), 270–96.

—— (1997), *Making a Necessity of Virtue: Aristotle and Kant on Virtue* (Cambridge: Cambridge University Press).

—— (1998), 'Concrete Kantian Respect', *Social Philosophy and Policy*, 15.1:119–48.

SULLIVAN, ROGER J. (1997), 'The Positive Role of Prudence in the Virtuous Life', *Jahrbuch für Recht und Ethik*, 5:461–70.

TRIANOSKI, GREGORY (1989), 'Natural Affection and Responsibility for Character: A Critique of Kantian Views of the Virtues', in O. Flanagan and A. O. Rorty, eds., *Identity, Character, and Morality* (Cambridge, MA: MIT Press), 93–109.

WOOD, ALLEN W. (2001), 'Kant vs. Eudaimonism', in Predrag Cicovacki (ed.), *Kant's Legacy: Essays Dedicated to Lewis White Beck* (Rochester: University of Rochester Press).

ENDS, DUTIES, RIGHTS, AND KANTIAN CASUISTRY

ALLISON, HENRY E. (1993), 'Kant's Doctrine of Obligatory Ends', *Jahrbuch für Recht und Ethik*, 1: 7–23.

ATKINSON, R. F. (1992), 'Kant's Moral and Political Rigorism', repr. in Howard Williams (ed.), *Essays on Kant's Political Philosophy* (Chicago: University of Chicago Press), 228–48.

ATWELL, JOHN E. (1974), 'Objective Ends in Kant's Ethics', *Archiv für Geschichte der Philosophie*, 56:156–71.

—— (1995), 'Kant and the Duty to Promote Others' Happiness', in Hoke Robinson (ed.), *Proceedings of the Eighth International Kant Congress* (Milwaukee, WI: Marquette University Press), vol. I. pt. 2, 727–33.

AUXTER, THOMAS (1982), 'Essential Ends', in Auxter, *Kant's Moral Teleology* (Macon, GA: Mercer University Press), ch. 7.

BARON, MARCIA W. (1995), *Kantian Ethics Almost without Apology* (Ithaca, NY: Cornell University Press), pt. 1.

BAUM, MANFRED (1998), 'Probleme der Begrünung Kantischer Tugendpflichten', *Jahrbuch für Recht und Ethik*, 5:41–56.

BROADIE, ALEXANDER, and PYBUS, ELIZABETH (1974), 'Kant's Treatment of Animals', *Philosophy*, 49:375–83.

—— (1981), 'Kant and Direct Duties', *Dialogue*, 20:60–7.

CHOLBI, MICHAEL J. (2000), 'Kant and the Irrationality of Suicide', *History of Philosophy Quarterly*, 17:159–76.

CUMMISKEY, DAVID (1996), *Kantian Consequentialism* (New York: Oxford University Press).

DENIS, LARA (1999), 'Kant on the Wrongness of "Unnatural" Sex', *History of Philosophy Quarterly*, 16:225–48.

—— (1999), 'Kant on the Perfection of Others', *Southern Journal of Philosophy*, 37:21–41.

—— (2000), 'Kant's Conception of Duties Regarding Animals: Reconstruction and Reconsideration', *History of Philosophy Quarterly*, 17:405–23.

—— (2001), *Moral Self-Regard: Duties to Oneself in Kant's Moral Theory* (New York: Garland).

DONAGAN, ALAN (1977), *The Theory of Morality* (Chicago: Chicago University Press).

EGGERMAN, RICHARD W. (1990), 'Kantian Strict Duties of Benevolence', *Southwest Philosophy Review*, 6:81–8.

EISENBERG, PAUL D. (1972), 'Kant on Duties to and Duties Regarding, Oneself or Others', in Lewis White Beck (ed.), *Proceedings of the Third International Kant Congress* (Dordrecht: D. Reidel), 275–80.

ENGSTROM, STEPHEN (1995), 'Happiness and Beneficence', in Hoke Robinson (ed.), *Proceedings of the Eighth International Kant Congress* (Milwaukee, WI: Marquette University Press), vol. I. pt. 2, 735–40.

GREGOR, MARY J. (1990), 'Kants System der Pflichten in der Metaphysik der Sitten', in Bernd Ludwig (ed.), *Immanuel Kant: Metaphysical Anfangsgründe der Tugendlehre* (Hamburg: Meiner), pp. XXIX–LXVI.

GUEVARA, DANIEL (1999), 'The Impossibility of Supererogation in Kant's Moral Theory', *Philosophy and Phenomenological Research*, 59:593–624.

HILL, THOMAS E., JR. (1991), 'Servility and Self-Respect', repr. in Hill, *Autonomy and Self-Respect* (Cambridge: Cambridge University Press), ch. 1.

—— (1991), 'Self-Respect Reconsidered', repr. in Hill, *Autonomy and Self-Respect* (Cambridge: Cambridge University Press), ch. 2.

—— (1991), 'Self-regarding Suicide: A Modified Kantian View', repr. in Hill, *Autonomy and Self-Respect* (Cambridge: Cambridge University Press), ch. 7.

—— (1992), 'Humanity as an End in Itself', repr. in Hill, *Dignity and Practical Reason* (Ithaca, NY: Cornell University Press), ch. 2.

—— (1992), 'Kant on Imperfect Duty and Supererogation', repr. in Hill, *Dignity and Practical Reason* (Ithaca, NY: Cornell University Press), ch. 8.

—— (1992), 'Making Exceptions without Abandoning the Principle: or How a Kantian Might Think about Terrorism', repr. in Hill, *Dignity and Practical Reason* (Ithaca, NY: Cornell University Press), ch. 10.

—— (1993), 'Beneficence and Self-Love: A Kantian Perspective', *Social Philosophy and Policy*, 10:1–23.

—— (1996), 'Moral Dilemmas, Gaps, and Residues: A Kantian Perspective', in H. E. Mason (ed.), *Moral Dilemmas and Moral Theory* (New York: Oxford University Press), 167–98.

—— (1999), 'Happiness and Human Flourishing in Kant's Ethics', *Social Philosophy and Policy*, 16:143–75.

—— (2000), 'Kant on Responsibility for Consequences', in Hill, *Respect, Pluralism, and Justice*, 155–72.

JAMES, DAVID N. (1999), 'Suicide and Stoic Ethics in the *Doctrine of Virtue*', *Kant-Studien*, 90:40–58.

JENSEN, HENNING (1989), 'Kant and Moral Integrity', *Philosophical Studies*, 57: 193–205.

JESKE, DIANE (1996), 'Perfection, Happiness, and Duties to Self', *American Philosophical Quarterly*, 33:263–76.

JOERDEN, JAN C. (1997), 'Der Widerstreit zweier Gründe der Verbindlichkeit: Konsequenzen einer These Kants für die strafrechtliche Lehre von der "Pflichtenkollision"', *Jahrbuch für Recht und Ethik*, 5:43–52.

MASSEY, STEPHEN J. (1983), 'Kant on Self-Respect', *Journal of the History of Philosophy*, 21:57–74.

McCarty, Richard (1989), 'The Limits of Kantian Duty, and Beyond', *American Philosophical Quarterly*, 26:43–52.

—— (1991), 'Moral Conflicts in Kantian Ethics', *History of Philosophy Quarterly*, 8:65–81.

O'Neill, Onora (1989), 'Between Consenting Adults', repr. in O'Neill, *Constructions of Reason: Explorations of Kant's Practical Philosophy* (Cambridge: Cambridge University Press), ch. 6.

—— (1998), 'Necessary Anthropocentrism and Contingent Speciesism', *Aristotelian Society Suppl.*, 72:211–28.

Potter, Nelson (1985), 'Kant on Ends that are at the Same Time Duties', *Pacific Philosophical Quarterly*, 66:78–92.

—— (1993), 'Reply to Allison', *Jahrbuch für Recht und Ethik*, 1:391–400.

—— (1993), 'What is Wrong With Kant's Four Examples', *Journal of Philosophical Research*, 18:213–29.

Reath, Andrews (1994), 'Kant's Principles for the Imputation of Consequences', *Jahrbuch für Recht und Ethik*, 2: 159–76.

Regan, Tom (1976), 'Broadie and Pybus on Kant', *Philosophy*, 51:471–72.

Schaller, Walter E. (1987), 'Kant's Architectonic of Duties', *Philosophy and Phenomenological Research*, 48:299–314.

Stark, Cynthia A. (1997), 'The Rationality of Valuing Oneself: A Critique of Kant on Self-Respect', *Journal of the History of Philosophy*, 35:65–82.

Stubb, Anne C. (1980), 'Morality and Our Treatment of Animals', *Philosophical Studies*, 27:29–39.

Wood, Allen W. (1998), 'Kant on Duties Regarding Non-Rational Nature I', *The Aristotelian Society*, Suppl., 72:189–210.

Feminism and Kant's Ethics and Politics

Baier, Annette C. (1997), 'How Can Individuals Share Responsibility?', in Robin May Schott (ed.), *Feminist Interpretations of Immanuel Kant* (University Park, PA: Pennsylvania University Press), 297–318.

Baron, Marcia (1997), 'Kantian Ethics and Claims of Detachment', in Robin May Schott (ed.), *Feminist Interpretations of Immanuel Kant* (University Park, PA: Pennsylvania University Press), 145–70.

De Laurentiis, Allegra (2000), 'Kant's Shameful Proposition: A Hegel-Inspired Criticism of Kant's Theory of Domestic Right', *International Philosophical Quarterly*, 40:297–312.

Elshtain, Jean B. (1986), 'Kant and Rational Politics: Woman as a Suspect Category', in Elshtain, *Meditations on Modern Political Thought: Masculine/Feminine Themes from Luther to Arendt. Women and Politics* (New York), 21–35.

HERMAN, BARBARA (1993), 'Could It Be Worth Thinking About Kant on Sex and Marriage?', in Louise M. Antony and Charlotte Witt (eds.), *A Mind of One's Own: Feminist Essays on Reason and Objectivity* (Boulder: Westview), 49–67.

JAUCH, URSULA PIA (1990), '"Die Tugend des Frauenzimmers ist eine schöne Tugend": Oder Kant als Kohlberg im 18. Jahrhundert? Zur Geschlechterdifferenz in der Ethik Kants', *Il Cannocchiale*, 2:61–74.

KOFMAN, SARAH (1982), 'The Economy of Respect: Kant and Respect for Women', trans. Nicola Fisher, *Social Research*, 49:383–434.

MENDUS, SUSAN (1992), 'Kant: "An Honest but Narrow-Minded Bourgeois"?', repr. in Howard Williams (ed.), *Essays on Kant's Political Philosophy* (Chicago: University of Chicago Press), 166–90.

MOSSER, KURT (1999), 'Kant and Feminism', *Kant-Studien*, 90: 322–53.

RUMSEY, JEAN P. (1997), 'Re-Visions of Agency in Kant's Moral Theory', in Robin May Schott (ed.), *Feminist Interpretations of Immanuel Kant* (University Park, PA: Pennsylvania University Press), 125–44.

SCHRÖDER, HANNELORE (1997), 'Kant's Patriarchal Order', in Robin May Schott (ed.), *Feminist Interpretations of Immanuel Kant* (University Park, PA: Pennsylvania University Press), 275–96.

SEDGWICK, SALLY (1990), 'Can Kant's Ethics Survive the Feminist Critique?', *Pacific Philosophical Quarterly*, 71:60–79.

TUANA, NANCY (1992), Woman and the History of Philosophy (New York: Paragon House), ch. 4.

INDEX

Achenwall, Gottfried 117 n., 119 n.,
    122 n., 125, 125 n., 174 n., 174 n.
Ackrill, J. L. 329 n.
acquired right 44–6
    postulate of 54–64
acquisition, rights of 121
    see also principle of external
    acquisition
affect 308–11
agency 166–7
    and constraint 351–6
    desire based vs. virtue based 195–6
    economic conception of 204–7
Allison, Henry 30 n., 31 nn. 12 & 13,
    187–8, 190, 205, 265 n., 294 n.,
    383 n., 386 n., 402 n
analyticity
    of judgments 7–8, 26–32
    Kant's conception of 27–32
    of principles of right 61–6
Anscombe, Elizabeth 264 n., 357
apathy (moral) 308, 310
Aristotle 255, 274, 290, 307, 386, 406 n.
Audi, Robert 264 n.
autonomy 294–6

Baier, Kurt 368 n.
Baron, Marcia W. 5 n., 188 n., 229 n.,
    257, 267, 269 n., 278, 282, 290 n.,
    388
Baumgarten, Alexander Gottlieb 76 n.,
    77 n.
Beardsley, Monroe 264 n.
Beck, L. W. 1 n., 28 n., 31 n., 32 n., 192 n.
beneficence 15, 18–19, 275–8, 314, 396 n.
    duty of 4–5, 18–19, 261, 267–8,
    282–3

benevolence 396
Berger, Fred 262 n.
Berlin, Isaiah 134, 148 n.
Bielenberg, Christabel 227 n.
Bittner, Rüdiger 136
Boleyn, Anne 312 n., 345
Brandt, Reinhard 108 n., 189 n., 318 n.
Brink, David O. 381 n.
Broad, C. D. 259 n.12, 263 n.
Buckle, Stephen 106 n.
Butler, Joseph (Bishop) 240
Byrd, Sharon 234 n., 238 nn. 11 & 12

Cairns, Huntington 112 n.
casuistry 343–7
Categorical Imperative (principles of)
    humanity formulation 6, 12 13,
    286–7
    universal law formulation 6, 12
causa libera 166–9
choice (Willkür) 137, 238–40, 243–8,
    384
    see also freedom
Cicero 338
Cochius, Leonhard 293, 307, 311 n., 386
coercion:
    and authorization 47–54, 76–7
    concept of 76
    pathological vs. practical 77–8
    and universal principle of right
    46–54
conscience 239–41, 336
    feeling of 17
    and juridical punishment 241–2
    as a motive 224–5, 248
consequentialism (and deontology in
    Kant's ethics) 14–15

Printed in the United States
27795LVS00001B/87-106

9 780198 250104